P9-CDN-085

Gertrude de Nile, 1901 -

Saint College.

THE ENGLISH POETS

T. H. WARD.

VOL. IV.

THE NINETEENTH CENTURY:

WORDSWORTH TO TENNYSON.

THE
ENGLISH POETS

SELECTIONS

WITH CRITICAL INTRODUCTIONS

BY VARIOUS WRITERS

AND A GENERAL INTRODUCTION BY

MATTHEW ARNOLD

EDITED BY

THOMAS HUMPHRY WARD, M.A.

Late Fellow of Brasenose College, Oxford

VOL. IV

WORDSWORTH TO TENNYSON

NEW EDITION, WITH ADDITIONS

New York
THE MACMILLAN COMPANY.
and London
1897

[*All rights reserved*]

AM MADISON RANDALL LIBRARY UNC AT WILMINGTON

Copyright, 1894, by

THE MACMILLAN CO.

Press of J. J. Little & Co.
Astor Place, New York

PR1173
.W3
1903
v.4

The Editor wishes to express his thanks to Hallam, Lord Tennyson ; to Messrs. Smith, Elder & Co. ; and to Mrs. Matthew Arnold, for the permission which they have kindly given him to print extracts from the poems of Lord Tennyson, Robert Browning, and Matthew Arnold.

89914

The Editor wishes to express his thanks to
Matthew Lord Tennyson; to Messrs. Smith, Elder
& Co.; and to Miss Matthew Arnold for the
permission which they have kindly given him to
print extracts from the poems of Lord Tennyson,
Robert Browning, and Matthew Arnold.

CONTENTS.

'Not Chaos, not
The darkest pit of lowest Erebus,
Nor aught of blinder vacancy, scooped out
By help of dreams—can breed such fear and awe
As fall upon us often when we look
Into our minds, into the mind of man—
My haunt, and the main region of my song.
—Beauty—a living presence of the earth,
Surpassing the most fair ideal forms
Which craft of delicate spirits hath composed
From earth's materials—waits upon my steps;
Pitches her tents before me as I move,
An hourly neighbour. Paradise, and groves
Elysian, Fortunate Fields—like those of old
Sought in the Atlantic main—*why should they be*
A history only of departed things,
Or a mere fiction of what never was?
For the discerning intellect of man,
When wedded to this goodly universe
In love and holy passion, shall find these
A simple produce of the common day.
—I, long before the blissful hour arrives,
Would chant, in lonely peace, the spousal verse
Of this great consummation:—*and, by words*
Which speak of nothing more than what we are,
Would I arouse the sensual from their sleep
Of Death, and win the vacant and the vain
To noble raptures; while my voice proclaims
How exquisitely the individual mind
(And the progressive powers perhaps no less
Of the whole species) to the external world
Is fitted:—and how exquisitely, too—
Theme this but little heard of among men—
The external world is fitted to the mind;
And the creation (by no lower name
Can it be called) which they with blended might
Accomplish:—this is our high argument.'

Wordsworth's poetry and his idea of the office of poetry must be traced, like many other remarkable things, to the French Revolution. He very early, even in his boyhood, became aware of that sympathy with external nature, and of that power of discriminating insight into the characteristic varieties of its beauty and awfulness, which afterwards so strongly marked his writings. 'I recollect distinctly,' he says of a description in one of his early poems, 'the very spot where this struck me. The moment was important in my poetical history: for I date from it my consciousness of the infinite variety of natural appearances which have been unnoticed by the poets of any age or country, and I made a resolution to supply in some measure the deficiency.' We have abundant evidence how he kept his purpose.

While Wordsworth was at Cambridge, the French Revolution was beginning. The contagion of the great ideas which it proclaimed caught him as it also laid hold on so many among the nobler spirits of the young generation. To him at that time, as he tells us himself,

> 'The whole earth
> The beauty wore of promise ; that which sets
> The budding rose above the rose full blown.'

The wonder, the sympathy, the enthusiasm which swept him and them away like a torrent, though in his case the torrent's course was but a short one, left ineffaceable marks on his character and his writings. He was not at first so easily shocked as others were at the excesses of the revolution. His stern North-country nature could bear and approve much terrible retribution for the old wrongs of the poor and the weak at the hands of nob'es and kings. In his *Apology for the French Revolution*, 1793, he sneered at Bishop Watson for the importance which the Bishop attached to 'the personal sufferings of the late royal martyr,' and for joining in the 'idle cry of modish lamentation which has resounded from the court to the cottage': and he boldly accepted the doctrine that in a time of revolution, which cannot be a time of liberty, 'political virtues are developed at the expense of moral ones.' — But though the guillotine and the revolutionary tribunal had not daunted him, he recoiled from the military despotism and the fever of conquest in which they ended. The changes in his fundamental principles, in his thoughts of man and his duties, were not great : the change in his application of them and in his judgment of the men, the parties, the institutions, the measures, by which they were to be guarded and carried out, was great indeed. The hopes and affections which revolutionary France had so deeply disappointed were transferred to what was most ancient, most historic, most strongly rooted by custom and usage, in traditional and unreformed England. With characteristic courage he never cared to apologise for a political change which was as complete and striking as a change to a new religion. He scarcely attempted directly to explain it. He left it to tell its own story in his poetical creations, and in the elaborate pictures of character, his own and others', inserted into his longer works, *The Prelude* and *The Excursion.* But he was not a man to change with half a heart. He left behind him for ever all the beliefs and antici-pations and illusions which, like spells, had bound him to Jacobin France. He turned away from it in permanent and strong disgust, and settled down into the sturdy English Tory patriot of the begin-ning of the century.

But this unreserved and absorbing interest in the wonderful ideas and events of the French Revolution, transient as it was, had the effect upon him which great interruptions of the common course of things and life have on powerful natures. They were a call and a strain on his intellect and will, first in taking them in, then in judging, sifting, accepting or refusing them, which drew forth to the full all that he had of strength and individual character. But for that, he might have been, and doubtless would have been, the poet of nature, a follower, but with richer gifts, of Thomson, Aken-side, perhaps Cowper. But it was the trial and the struggle which he went through, amid the hopes and overthrows of the French Revo-lution, which annealed his mind to its highest temper, which gave largeness to his sympathies and reality and power to his ideas.

Every one knows that Wordsworth's early poetry was received with a shout of derision, such as, except in the case of Keats, has never attended the first appearance of a great poet. Every one knows, too, that in a quarter of a century it was succeeded by a growth of profound and enthusiastic admiration, which, though it has been limited by the rise of new forms of deep and powerful poetry, is still far from being spent or even reduced, though it is expressed with more discrimination than of old, in all who have a right to judge of English poetry.

This was the inevitable result of the characteristic qualities of Wordsworth's genius, though for a time the quarrel between the poet and his critics was aggravated by accidental and temporary circumstances. Wordsworth is destined, if any poet is, to be im-mortal; but immortality does not necessarily mean popularity. That in Wordsworth which made one class of readers find in him beauty, grandeur, and truth, which they had never found before, will certainly tell on the same class in future years :—

> ' What he has loved,
> Others will love, and he will teach them how.'

But mankind is deeply divided in its sympathies and tastes; and for a large portion of it, not merely of those who read, but of those who create and govern opinion, that which Wordsworth loved and aimed at and sought to represent will always be the object, not only of indifference but of genuine dislike. Add to this that Wordsworth's genius, though great, and noble, and lofty, was in a marked way limited, and that in his own exposition and defence of his view of poetry he was curiously and unfortunately one-sided and inadequate, and provokingly stiff and dogmatic. This, of course, only affected an extinct controversy. But the controversy marked at once the power and the bold novelty of Wordsworth's attempt to purify and exalt English poetry. Wordsworth was, and felt himself to be, a discoverer, and like other great discoverers, his victory was in seeing by faith things which were not yet seen, but which were obvious, or soon became so, when once shown. He opened a new world of thought and enjoyment to Englishmen; his work formed an epoch in the intellectual and moral history of the race. But for that very reason he had, as Coleridge said, like all great artists, to create the taste by which he was to be relished, to teach the art by which he was to be seen and judged. And people were so little prepared for the thorough and systematic way in which he searched out what is deepest or highest or subtlest in human feeling under the homeliest realities, that not being able to understand him they laughed at him. Nor was he altogether without fault in the misconceptions which occasioned so much ridicule and scorn.

How did he win this deep and lasting admiration? What was it in him which exposed him not merely to the mocks of the scorner but to the dislike of the really able men who condemned him?

That Wordsworth possessed poetical power of the very highest order could be doubted by no one who had read the poem which concluded the first volume of the fiercely attacked *Lyrical Ballads*, the *Lines written above Tintern Abbey.* That which places a man high among poets, force and originality of thought, vividness and richness of imagination, command over the instrument of language, in its purity, its beauty, and its majesty, could not be, and was never, denied. But this alone does not explain what is distinctive and characteristic in what called forth so much enthusiasm, and such an outcry of disapprobation.

What was special in Wordsworth was the penetrating power of his perceptions of poetical elements, and his fearless reliance on the simple forces of expression, in contrast to the more ornate ones. He had an eye to see these elements, where—I will not say no one had seen or felt them, but where no one appears to have recognised that they had seen or felt them. He saw that the familiar scene of human life,—nature, as affecting human life and feeling, and man, as the fellow creature of nature, but also separate and beyond it in faculties and destiny—had not yet rendered up even to the mightiest of former poets all that they had in them to touch the human heart. And he accepted it as his mission to open the eyes and widen the thoughts of his countrymen, and to teach them to discern in the humblest and most unexpected forms the presence of what was kindred to what they had long recognised as the highest and greatest.

Wordsworth's poetry was not only a powerful but a conscious and systematic appeal to that craving for deep truth and reality which had been gathering way ever since the French Revolution so terribly tore asunder the old veils of conventionality and custom. Truth is a necessary element in all good poetry, and there had been good poetry in the century before Wordsworth. But in Wordsworth the moral judgement and purpose of the man were joined to the poet's instinct and art ; and he did, as the most sacred and natural of duties, what he would anyhow have done from taste and for his pleasure. When that inflexible loyalty to truth which was the prime condition of all his writings—not mere literal truth, but the truth which could only be reached by thought and imagination,— when this had been taken in, it was soon seen what an amazing view it opened of the new riches and wonders of the world, a scene of discovery which Wordsworth was far from exhausting. It was a contrast, startling all and baffling many, to the way in which, since Shakespeare and Milton, poetry had been content to skim the surface of the vast awful tracts of life and nature, dealing with their certainties and riddles, with their beauty and their terror, under the guidance of sentiments put on for the most part like a stage dress, and in language which seemed not to belong to the world which we know. Thomson, Gray, and Burns, Wordsworth's immediate predecessors, had discovered, but only partially, the extent and significance of the faith which Wordsworth accepted and proclaimed in its length and breadth and height and depth, that Truth, in its infinite but ever self-consistent forms, is the first law of poetry. From his time, the eyes of readers, and the eyes of writers, have been opened ; and whatever judgement they may pass on his own poetry or his theories, they have followed both as critics and as composers, in the path which he opened.

Hence his selection of subjects. He began with nature, as in the *Evening Walk*, and the *Descriptive Sketches.* He had early and well learned his lesson of nature—learned to watch and note in her that to which other eyes were blind of expression and novelty in common sights. A habit was formed of indefatigable observation, like that which was the basis of Turner's power. And to a mind thus trained the scenes through which he passed, and among which his life was spent, furnished never-cloying food. His continental journeys left deep impressions upon him ; these impressions were answered by those of his home. The 'power of hills was on him '; the music of waters was in his ears ; light and darkness wove their spells for him. Looking to the same end as Turner, and working in the same spirit, he, with Turner, was a discoverer in the open face of nature : working apart from one another, these two mighty 'Lords of the eye,' seized and grasped what had always been visible yet never seen, and gave their countrymen capacities of perception and delight hardly yet granted to others. But as his mind grew, Nature, great as was her power, 'fell back into a second place,' and became important to him chiefly as the stage of man's action, and allied with his ideas, his passions and affections. And Man was interesting to him only in his essential nature, only *as man.* History had little value for him, except as it revealed character : and character had no interest unless, besides power or splendour, it had in it what appealed to human sympathies or human indulgence. For a Napoleon, with all his magnificence, he had nothing but loathing. Where he found truth, noble and affecting,—not bare literal fact, but reality informed and aglow with the ideas and forms of the imagination, and so raised by it to the power of an object of our spiritual nature,—he recognised no differences of high and low. In the same way as he saw greatness in the ideal histories of Venice and Switzerland, and in the legends of Rome, even if they were fictions, so he saw greatness, the greatness of human affections and of the primary elements of human character, in the fortunes and the sufferings of *Michael* and the *Leech gatherer.* He was very bold for his time, and took all consequences, which were severe enough, when he insisted that the whole range of the beautiful, the pathetic, the tragic, the heroic, were to be found in common lowly life, as truly as in the epic and the drama.

or in the grand legends of national history ; when he proclaimed that

> 'Verse may build a princely throne
> On humble truth.'

He claimed for *Lucy Gray*, for the 'miserable mother by the *Thorn*,' for the desolate maniac nursing her infant, the same pity which we give to Lear and Cordelia or to 'the dark sorrows of the line of Thebes.' Not in play but in deepest earnest he dwelt on the awfulness, the wonder, the sacredness of childhood : it furnished in his hands the subject, not only of touching ballads, but of one of the most magnificent lyrical poems—the ode on *Immortality*. He was convinced that if people would but think and be fair with themselves, they would not merely be moved by humble tragedies, like *Michael* and the *Brothers*, but would feel that there was as much worthy of a poet's serious art in the agonies of the mother of the *Idiot Boy*, and the terrors of *Peter Bell*, as in the 'majestic pains' of *Laodamia* and *Dion*. He has summed up his poetical doctrine with all his earnest solemnity in the thirteenth book of the *Prelude* :—

> 'Here might I pause, and bend in reverence
> To Nature, and the power of human minds,
> *To men as they are men within themselves.*
> How oft high service is performed within,
> When all the external man is rude in show,—
> Not like a temple rich with pomp and gold,
> But a mere mountain chapel, that protects
> Its simple worshippers from sun and shower.
> Of these, said I, shall be my song ; of these,
> If future years mature me for the task,
> Will I record the praises, making verse
> Deal boldly with substantial things; in truth
> And sanctity of passion speak of these,
> That justice may be done, obeisance paid
> Where it is due : thus haply shall I teach,
> Inspire, through unadulterated ears
> Pour rapture, tenderness, and hope—my theme
> No other than the very heart of man,
> As found among the best of those who live,
> Not unexalted by religious faith,
> Nor uninformed by books, good books, though few,
> In Nature's presence : *thence may I select*
> *Sorrow that is not sorrow, but delight;*

And miserable love, that is not pain
To hear of, for the glory that redounds
Therefrom to human kind, and what we are.

    *   *   *   *   *

Nature for all conditions wants not power
To consecrate, if we have eyes to see,
The outside of her creatures, and to breathe
Grandeur upon the very humblest face
Of human life. I felt that the array
Of act and circumstance, and visible form,
Is mainly to the pleasure of the mind
What passion makes them ; that meanwhile the forms
Of Nature have a passion in themselves,
That intermingles with those works of man
To which she summons him ; although the works
Be mean, have nothing lofty of their own ;
And that the genius of the Poet hence
May boldly take his way among mankind
Wherever Nature leads ; that he hath stood
By Nature's side among the men of old,
And so shall stand for ever.'

All this doctrine was strange to his age ; it has ceased to be so to ours. In various ways and with varying merit, Thackeray and Dickens and George Eliot, and a crowd of writers, poets and novelists, have searched out the *motifs* of the highest poetry in the humblest lives, and have taught the lesson that the real greatness and littleness of human life are not to be measured by the standards of fashion and pride. What made Wordsworth different from other popular poets, and made him great, was a puzzle and a paradox at first in his own time ; it is but a commonplace in ours. ' It was the union of deep feeling with profound thought : the fine balance of truth in observing, with the imaginative faculty in modifying the objects observed ; and, above all, the original gift of spreading the tone, the atmosphere, and with it the depth and height of the ideal world, around forms, incidents, and situations, of which, for the common view, custom had bedimmed all the lustre, had dried up the sparkle and the dewdrops. To find no contradiction in the union of old and new ; to contemplate the Ancient of Days and all His works with feelings as fresh as if all had then sprung forth at the first creative fiat ; characterises the mind that feels the riddle of the world, and may help to unravel it. To carry on the feelings of childhood into the powers of manhood : to combine the child's sense of wonder and novelty with the appearances which every day for perhaps forty years have made familiar :—

> " With sun and moon and stars throughout the year,
> And man and woman "—

this is the character and privilege of genius.' (Coleridge, *Biographia Literaria*, c. iv.).

Thus his range of materials was very large ; his extensive scale of interests gave him great variety : like his own skylark, he soars to the heavens, and drops into a lowly nest ; and as the wing sometimes flags, and the eye is wearied, he was unequal, and there was sometimes want of proportion in his subject and his treatment of it. But his principles of treatment, though he was not altogether happy in his exposition of them, were in accordance with his general idea of poetry. 'I have at all times,' he says, ' endeavoured to look steadily at my subject.' Where he succeeded—and no man can always in thought and imagination see what he wants to see—there was the fire and energy and life of truth, stamping all his words, governing his music and his movement, his flow or his rush. There is always the aim, the scrupulous, fastidious aim, at direct expression—at beautiful, suggestive, forcible, original expression : but first of all at direct expression. This he called, somewhat oddly, restricting himself to the language of common life, in opposition to so-styled 'poetic diction.' Happily he was inconsistent with his own theory. He showed with Burns how far deep down the pathetic and the tender go in common life, and how its language can be made by cunning artists to minister to their expression : but there are regions in poetry of glory and nobleness and splendour where Burns never came, and there Wordsworth showed that he was master of a richer and subtler wealth of words than common life supplies. But in his most fiery moments of inspiration and enthusiasm he never allowed himself to relax his hold on reality and truth : as he would scorn to express in poetry any word or feeling which was not genuine and natural, any sentiment or impulse short of or beyond the actual impression which caused them, so with the most jealous strictness he measured his words. He gave them their full swing if they answered to force and passion ; but he watched them all the same, with tender but manly severity. Hence with his power and richness of imagination, and his full command over all the resources of voice and ear, an austere purity and plainness and nobleness marked all that he wrote, and formed a combination as distinct as it was uncommon.

To purity, purity of feeling, pure truthfulness of expression, he is never untrue. In the wild excitement, or the lawless exaggeration, as in the self-indulgence and foulness of passion, he will recognise no subject of true poetic art. Keenly alive to beauty, and deeply reverencing it, he puts purity and the severity of truth above beauty. With his eager instincts of joy, it is only the joy of the pure-hearted that he acknowledges.

Wordsworth's great poetical design was carried out, first in collections of short pieces, such as those of his earlier volumes, the *Lyrical Ballads*, and the *Poems* of 1807 ; then in a great mass of Sonnets, varying from some of the grandest in the language to some very commonplace ; but as a whole, considering their number,—there are between four and five hundred of them,—a collection of great nobleness and wonderful finish : and finally in the long poem of *The Excursion*, itself a fragment of a greater projected whole, *The Recluse. The Excursion* was published in 1814, and it gave the key to all his poetical work. From that time to 1845 he published repeatedly new things and old : sonnets on all kinds of subjects, such as those on the *River Duddon*, the *Ecclesiastical Sonnets*, and those on the *Punishment of Death* ;—*Memorials* of his Tours in Scotland and on the Continent ; classical compositions like *Laodamia* and *Dion* ; tales in the romantic fashion, like *The White Doe of Rylstone*, or in the manner of the *Lyrical Ballads*, like *Peter Bell*, written in his earliest time, but not published till 1819. The reception of *Peter Bell* marks the change that had come over public opinion. ' It was,' says the biographer, 'more in request than any of the author's previous publications': it was published in April, and a new edition was wanted in May. Wordsworth had waited, and the world had begun to come round to him. Ridicule and dislike had not ceased. But in minds which loved nature, which loved nobleness, which loved reality, which loved purity and truth, he had awakened a response of deep and serious sympathy, which placed him, in the judgment of increasing numbers, far above the great poetical rivals round him. It was in vain that *The Edinburgh Review* received *The Excursion* with its insolent ' *This will never do* ' ;— it only showed that the Review had mistaken the set of the tide, and had failed to measure the thoughts and demands of the coming time. Wordsworth's reception at Oxford in 1839 was an outwark mark of the change, and of the way in which he had spoken to the hearts of men, and had been at length understood. The enthusiasm which gathered round him was most genuine, and

It was wholesome and elevating; it was one of the best influences of our time. But it became undiscriminating. It, not unnaturally, blinded men to defects, and even made them proud of defying the criticism which defects produced.

And there were defects. In his earlier days, at the high tide of his genius and strength, amid works matchless for their power and simplicity and noble beauty, Wordsworth's composition was sometimes fairly open to the criticism,—whether meant for him I know not,—conveyed in the following lines by one who fully measured his greatness :—

> ''Tis a speech
> That by a language of familiar lowness
> Enhances what of more heroic vein
> Is next to follow. But one fault it hath;
> It fits too close to life's realities.
> In truth to Nature missing truth to Art;
> For Art commends not counterparts and copies,
> But from our life a nobler life would shape,
> Bodies celestial from terrestrial raise,
> And teach us not jejunely what we are,
> But what we may be, when the Parian block
> Yields to the hand of Phidias.'
>
> (*A Sicilian Summer*, by Henry Taylor).

As life went on, he wrote a great deal, and with unequal power and felicity. It may be doubted whether he had the singularly rare capacity for undertaking, what was the chief aim of his life, a long poem—especially a philosophical poem. Strong as he was, he wanted that astonishing strength which carried Milton without flagging through his tremendous task. Wordsworth's power was in bursts ; and he wanted to go against the grain of his real aptitudes, and prolong into a continuous strain inspiration which was meant for occasions. In *The Excursion* and *The Prelude* there are passages as magnificent as perhaps poet ever wrote ; but they are not specimens of the context in which they are embedded, and which in spite of them, does not carry along with it the reader's honest enjoyment. We read on because we must. In his more ambitious works, such as *The Excursion*, Wordsworth seldom wants strength, finish, depth, insight. He not seldom wants the spring, the vividness, of his earlier works. There is always dignity, and often majesty ; but there is sometimes pompousness. His solid weight and massiveness of thought interest us when we are in the humour for serious work ; but it is too easy to find them oppressive, and to com-

plain of him as heavy and wearisome : nay, what is in him less
excusable, obscure. And so with his various series of sonnets
like those — full of beauty as they are — on the River Duddon :
he took in too much in his scheme of the series, and there was
not always material enough in comparison of the usually fine and
careful workmanship. Further, Wordsworth, like other men, had
his limitations. That large tracts of human experience and
feeling were unvisited by him and were beyond his horizon, is
not to be complained of : he deliberately and with high purpose
chose to forego all that under the fascination of art might mis-
lead or tempt. But of all poets who ever wrote, Wordsworth
made himself most avowedly the subject of his own thinking. In
one way this gives special interest and value to his work. But
the habit of perpetual self-study, though it may conduce to wisdom,
does not always conduce to life or freedom of movement. It
spreads a tone of individuality and apparent egotism, which though
very subtle and undefinable, is yet felt, even in some of his most
beautiful compositions. We miss the spirit of '*aloofness*' and
self-forgetfulness which, whether spontaneous or the result of the
highest art, marks the highest types of poetry. Perhaps it is from
this that he so rarely abandoned himself to that spirit of p'ayfulness
of which he has given us an example in the *Kitten and falling
leaves.* The ideal man with Wordsworth is the hard-headed, frugal,
unambitious dalesman of his own hills, with his strong affections,
his simple tastes, and his quiet and beautiful home : and this
dalesman, built up by communion with nature and by meditation
into the poet-philosopher, with his serious faith and his never-
failing spring of enjoyment, is himself. But nature has many sides,
and lies under many lights ; and its measure reaches beyond the
measure even of the great seer, with his true and piercing eye, his
mighty imagination, and his large and noble heart.

Wordsworth had not, though he thought he had, the power of
interpreting his own principles of poetic composition. This had
to be done for him by a more philosophical critic, his friend
Coleridge. Wordsworth, in his onslaught on the falsehood and
unreality of what passed for poetic diction, overstated and mistook.
He overstated the poetic possibilities of the speech of common life
and of the poor. He mistook the fripperies of poetic diction for
poetic diction itself. Some effects of these exaggerations and mistakes are visible in his composition itself, though they offend less
when the lines which tempt to severe criticism are read in their

own place and context ; but he would have done more wisely to have left them to find their own apology than to have given reasons which seemed paradoxes. In the hot controversy which followed, both disputants made false moves : the Edinburgh reviewers were false in their thrusts, Wordsworth was false in his parry. He was right in protesting against the doctrine that a thing is not poetical because it is not expressed in a certain conventional mintage : he was wrong in denying that there is a mintage of words fit for poetry and unsuitable for ordinary prose. They were utterly wrong in thinking that he was not a most careful and fastidious artist in language ; but they had some reason for their objections, and some excuse for their ridicule, when it was laid down without distinguishing or qualifying that there was no difference between the language of prose and poetry, and that the language of poetry was false and bad unless it was what might be spoken in the intercourse of common life. Wordsworth, confident of his side of truth, and stung by the flippancy and ignorant narrowness of his censors, was not the person to clear up the dispute. Coleridge, understanding and sympathising with what he really meant, never undertook a worthier task than when he brought his singular powers of criticism to bear on it, and helped men to take a more serious and just measure of his friend's greatness. He pointed out firmly and clearly what was untenable in Wordsworth's positions, his ambiguities, his overstatements. He put into more reasonable and comprehensive terms what he knew to be Wordsworth's meaning. He did not shrink from admitting defects, 'characteristic defects,' in his poetry ;—inequality of style, over-care for minute painting of details ; disproportion and incongruity between language and feeling, between matter and decoration ; 'thoughts and images too great for the subject.' But then he showed at what a height, in spite of all, he really stood :—his austere purity and perfection of language, the wideness of his range, the freshness of his thought, the unfailing certainty of his eye ; his unswerving truth, and, above all, his magnificent gift of imagination, 'nearest of all modern writers to Shakespeare and Milton, yet in a kind perfectly unborrowed and his own.' No more discriminating and no more elevated judgment of Wordsworth's genius is to be found than that which Coleridge inserted in the volume which he called his *Biographia Literaria.*

R. W. CHURCH.

The Reverie of Poor Susan.

At the corner of Wood Street, when daylight appears,
Hangs a Thrush that sings loud, it has sung for three years:
Poor Susan has passed by the spot, and has heard
In the silence of morning the song of the Bird.

'Tis a note of enchantment ; what ails her? She sees
A mountain ascending, a vision of trees ;
Bright volumes of vapour through Lothbury glide,
And a river flows on through the vale of Cheapside.

Green pastures she views in the midst of the dale,
Down which she so often has tripped with her pail ;
And a single small cottage, a nest like a dove's,
The one only dwelling on earth that she loves.

She looks, and her heart is in heaven : but they fade,
The mist and the river, the hill and the shade :
The stream will not flow, and the hill will not rise,
And the colours have all passed away from her eyes.

(1797)

Expostulation and Reply.

'Why, William, on that old grey stone,
Thus for the length of half a day,
Why, William, sit you thus alone,
And dream your time away?

Where are your books ?—that light bequeathed
To Beings else forlorn and blind !
Up ! up ! and drink the spirit breathed
From dead men to their kind.

You look round on your Mother Earth,
As if she for no purpose bore you ;
As if you were her first-born birth,
And none had lived before you !'

And hark! how blithe the throstle sings!
He, too, is no mean preacher:
Come forth into the light of things,
Let Nature be your teacher.

She has a world of ready wealth,
Our minds and hearts to bless—
Spontaneous wisdom breathed by health,
Truth breathed by cheerfulness.

One impulse from a vernal wood
May teach you more of man,
Of moral evil and of good,
Than all the sages can.

Sweet is the lore which Nature brings;
Our meddling intellect
Mis-shapes the beauteous forms of things :—
We murder to dissect.

Enough of Science and of Art;
Close up those barren leaves ;
Come forth, and bring with you a heart
That watches and receives.

(1798.)

LINES, COMPOSED A FEW MILES ABOVE TINTERN ABBEY, ON
REVISITING THE BANKS OF THE WYE DURING A TOUR.
JULY 13, 1798.

Five years have past; five summers, with the length
Of five long winters! and again I hear
These waters, rolling from their mountain-springs
With a soft inland murmur.—Once again
Do I behold these steep and lofty cliffs,
That on a wild secluded scene impress
Thoughts of more deep seclusion; and connect
The landscape with the quiet of the sky.
The day is come when I again repose
Here, under this dark sycamore, and view
These plots of cottage-ground, these orchard-tufts,

One morning thus, by Esthwaite lake,
When life was sweet, I knew not why,
To me my good friend Matthew spake,
And thus I made reply.

'The eye—it cannot choose but see:
We cannot bid the ear be still;
Our bodies feel, where'er they be,
Against or with our will.

Nor less I deem that there are Powers
Which of themselves our minds impress;
That we can feed this mind of ours
In a wise passiveness.

Think you, 'mid all this mighty sum
Of things for ever speaking,
That nothing of itself will come,
But we must still be seeking!

—Then ask not wherefore, here, alone,
Conversing as I may,
I sit upon this old grey stone,
And dream my time away.'

(1798.)

THE TABLES TURNED.

(An Evening Scene on the same Subject.)

Up! up! my Friend, and quit your books;
Or surely you'll grow double:
Up! up! my Friend, and clear your looks;
Why all this toil and trouble?

The sun, above the mountain's head,
A freshening lustre mellow
Through all the long green fields has spread,
His first sweet evening yellow.

Books! 'tis a dull and endless strife:
Come, hear the woodland linnet,
How sweet his music! on my life,
There's more of wisdom in it.

Which at this season, with their unripe fruits,
Are clad in one green hue, and lose themselves
'Mid groves and copses. Once again I see
These hedge-rows, hardly hedge-rows, little lines
Of sportive wood run wild : these pastoral farms,
Green to the very door ; and wreaths of smoke
Sent up, in silence, from among the trees !
With some uncertain notice, as might seem
Of vagrant dwellers in the houseless woods,
Or of some Hermit's cave, where by his fire
The Hermit sits alone.

            These beauteous forms,
Through a long absence, have not been to me
As is a landscape to a blind man's eye :
But oft, in lonely rooms, and 'mid the din
Of towns and cities, I have owed to them,
In hours of weariness, sensations sweet,
Felt in the blood, and felt along the heart :
And passing even into my purer mind
With tranquil restoration :—feelin
Of unremembered pleasure : s
As have no slight or trivial i
On that best portion of a goo
His little, nameless, unremem
Of kindness and of love. No
To them I may have owed an
Of aspect more sublime ; tha   ood,
In which the burthen of the
In which the heavy and the weary weight
Of all this unintelligible world,
Is lightened :—that serene and blessed mood,
In which the affections gently lead us on,—
Until, the breath of this corporeal frame
And even the motion of our human blood
Almost suspended, we are laid asleep
In body, and become a living soul :
While with an eye made quiet by the power
Of harmony, and the deep power of joy,
We see into the life of things.

                              If this
Be but a vain belief, yet, oh! how oft—
In darkness and amid the many shapes
Of joyless daylight; when the fretful stir
Unprofitable, and the fever of the world,
Have hung upon the beatings of my heart—
How oft, in spirit, have I turned to thee,
O sylvan Wye! thou wanderer thro' the woods,
How often has my spirit turned to thee!

    And now, with gleams of half-extinguished thought,
With many recognitions dim and faint,
And somewhat of a sad perplexity,
The picture of the mind revives again:
While here I stand, not only with the sense
Of present pleasure, but with pleasing thoughts
That in this moment there is life and food
For future years. And so I dare to hope,
Though changed, no doubt, from what I was when first
I came among these hills; when like a roe
I bounded o'er the mountains, by the sides
Of the deep rivers, and the lonely streams,
Wherever nature led: more like a man
Flying from something that he dreads, than one
Who sought the thing he loved. For nature then
(The coarser pleasures of my boyish days,
And their glad animal movements all gone by)
To me was all in all.—I cannot paint
What then I was. The sounding cataract
Haunted me like a passion: the tall rock,
The mountain, and the deep and gloomy wood,
Their colours and their forms, were then to me
An appetite; a feeling and a love,
That had no need of a remoter charm,
By thought supplied, nor any interest
Unborrowed from the eye.—That time is past,
And all its aching joys are now no more,
And all its dizzy raptures. Not for this
Faint I, nor mourn nor murmur; other gifts
Have followed; for such loss, I would believe,

Abundant recompense. For I have learned
To look on nature, not as in the hour
Of thoughtless youth ; but hearing oftentimes
The still, sad music of humanity,
Nor harsh nor grating, though of ample power
To chasten and subdue. And I have felt
A presence that disturbs me with the joy
Of elevated thoughts ; a sense sublime
Of something far more deeply interfused,
Whose dwelling is the light of setting suns,
And the round ocean and the living air,
And the blue sky, and in the mind of man :
A motion and a spirit, that impels
All thinking things, all objects of all thought,
And rolls through all things. Therefore am I still
A lover of the meadows and the woods,
And mountains ; and of all that we behold
From this green earth ; of all the mighty world
Of eye, and ear,—both what they half create,
And what perceive ; well pleased to recognise
In nature and the language of the sense,
The anchor of my purest thoughts, the nurse,
The guide, the guardian of my heart, and soul
Of all my moral being.
                              Nor perchance,
If I were not thus taught, should I the more
Suffer my genial spirits to decay :
For thou art with me here upon the banks
Of this fair river ; thou my dearest Friend,
My dear dear Friend ; and in thy voice I catch
The language of my former heart, and read
My former pleasures in the shooting lights
Of thy wild eyes. Oh ! yet a little while
May I behold in thee what I was once,
My dear dear Sister ! and this prayer I make
Knowing that Nature never did betray
The heart that loved her ; 'tis her privilege
Through all the years of this our life, to lead
From joy to joy : for she can so inform

The mind that is within us, so impress
With quietness and beauty, and so feed
With lofty thoughts, that neither evil tongues,
Rash judgments, nor the sneers of selfish men,
Nor greetings where no kindness is, nor all
The dreary intercourse of daily life,
Shall e'er prevail against us, or disturb
Our cheerful faith that all which we behold
Is full of blessings.   Therefore let the moon
Shine on thee in thy solitary walk ;
And let the misty mountain-winds be free
To blow against thee : and, in after years,
When these wild ecstasies shall be matured
Into a sober pleasure ; when thy mind
Shall be a mansion for all lovely forms,
Thy memory be as a dwelling-place
For all sweet sounds and harmonies ; oh ! then,
If solitude, or fear, or pain, or grief,
Should be thy portion, with what healing thoughts
Of tender joy wilt thou remember me,
And these my exhortations ! Nor, perchance—
If I should be where I no more can hear
Thy voice, nor catch from thy wild eyes these gleams
Of past existence—wilt thou then forget
That on the banks of this delightful stream
We stood together ; and that I, so long
A worshipper of Nature, hither came
Unwearied in that service : rather say
With warmer love—oh ! with far deeper zeal
Of holier love. Nor wilt thou then forget,
That after many wanderings, many years
Of absence, these steep woods and lofty cliffs,
And this green pastoral landscape, were to me
More dear, both for themselves and for thy sake ?

LINES WRITTEN IN EARLY SPRING.

I heard a thousand blended notes,
While in a grove I sat reclined,
In that sweet mood when pleasant thoughts
Bring sad thoughts to the mind.

To her fair works did Nature link
The human soul that through me ran;
And much it grieved my heart to think
What man has made of man.

Through primrose tufts, in that sweet bower,
The periwinkle trailed its wreaths;
And 'tis my faith that every flower
Enjoys the air it breathes.

The birds around me hopped and played,
Their thoughts I cannot measure:—
But the least motion which they made,
It seemed a thrill of pleasure.

The budding twigs spread out their fan,
To catch the breezy air;
And I must think, do all I can,
That there was pleasure there.

If this belief from heaven be sent,
If such be Nature's holy plan,
Have I not reason to lament
What man has made of man?

(1798.)

A POET'S EPITAPH.

Art thou a Statist in the van
Of public conflicts trained and bred?
—First learn to love one living man;
Then may'st thou think upon the dead.

A Lawyer art thou?—draw not nigh!
Go, carry to some fitter place
The keenness of that practised eye,
The hardness of that sallow face.

Art thou a Man of purple cheer?
A rosy Man, right plump to see?
Approach; yet, Doctor, not too near,
This grave no cushion is for thee.

Or art thou one of gallant pride,
A Soldier and no man of chaff?
Welcome!—but lay thy sword aside,
And lean upon a peasant's staff.

Physician art thou? one all eyes,
Philosopher! a fingering slave,
One that would peep and botanize
Upon his mother's grave?

Wrapt closely in thy sensual fleece,
O turn aside,—and take, I pray,
That he below may rest in peace,
Thy ever-dwindling soul, away!

A Moralist perchance appears;
Led, Heaven knows how! to this poor **sod**:
And he has neither eyes nor ears;
Himself his world, and his own God;

One to whose smooth-rubbed soul can cling
Nor form, nor feeling, great or small;
A reasoning, self-sufficing thing,
An intellectual All-in-all!

Shut close the door; press down the latch;
Sleep in thy intellectual crust;
Nor lose ten tickings of thy watch
Near this unprofitable dust.

But who is He, with modest looks,
And clad in homely russet brown?
He murmurs near the running brooks
A music sweeter than their own.

He is retired as noontide dew,
Or fountain in a noon-day grove;
And you must love him, ere to you
He will seem worthy of your love.

The outward shows of sky and earth,
Of hill and valley, he has viewed;
And impulses of deeper birth
Have come to him in solitude.

In common things that round us lie
Some random truths he can impart,—
The harvest of a quiet eye
That broods and sleeps on his own heart.

But he is weak; both Man and Boy,
Hath been an idler in the land;
Contented if he might enjoy
The things which others understand.

—Come hither in thy hour of strength;
Come, weak as is a breaking wave!
Here stretch thy body at full length;
Or build thy house upon this grave.

(1799.)

LUCY GRAY; OR, SOLITUDE.

Oft I had heard of Lucy Gray:
And, when I crossed the wild,
I chanced to see at break of day
The solitary child.

No mate, no comrade Lucy knew;
She dwelt on a wide moor,
—The sweetest thing that ever grew
Beside a human door!

You yet may spy the fawn at play,
The hare upon the green;
But the sweet face of Lucy Gray
Will never more be seen.

'To-night will be a stormy night—
You to the town must go;
And take a lantern, Child, to light
Your mother through the snow.'

'That, Father! will I gladly do:
'Tis scarcely afternoon—
The minster-clock has just struck two,
And yonder is the moon!'

At this the Father raised his hook,
And snapped a faggot-band;
He plied his work;—and Lucy took
The lantern in her hand.

Not blither is the mountain roe:
With many a wanton stroke
Her feet disperse the powdery snow,
That rises up like smoke.

The storm came on before its time:
She wandered up and down;
And many a hill did Lucy climb,
But never reached the town.

The wretched parents all that night
Went shouting far and wide ;
But there was neither sound nor sight
To serve them for a guide.

At day-break on a hill they stood
That overlooked the moor ;
And thence they saw the bridge of wood,
A furlong from their door.

They wept—and, turning homeward, cried,
'In heaven we all shall meet !'
—When in the snow the mother spied
The print of Lucy's feet.

Then downwards from the steep hill's edge
They tracked the footmarks small ;
And through the broken hawthorn hedge,
And by the long stone-wall :

And then an open field they crossed ;
The marks were still the same ;
They tracked them on, nor ever lost ;
And to the bridge they came.

They followed from the snowy bank
Those footmarks, one by one,
Into the middle of the plank ;
And further there were none !

—Yet some maintain that to this day
She is a living child ;
That you may see sweet Lucy Gray
Upon the lonesome wild.

O'er rough and smooth she trips along,
And never looks behind ;
And sings a solitary song
That whistles in the wind.

(1799.)

LUCY.

1.

She dwelt among the untrodden **ways**
  Beside the springs of Dove,
A Maid whom there were none to **praise**
  And very few to love:

A violet by a mossy stone
  Half hidden from the eye!
—Fair as a star, when only one
  Is shining in the sky.

She lived unknown, and few could **know**
  When Lucy ceased to be;
But she is in her grave, and, oh,
  The difference to me!

             (1799.)

2.

Three years she grew in sun and show**er,**
Then Nature said, 'A lovelier flower
On earth was never sown;
This Child I to myself will take,
She shall be mine, and I will make
A Lady of my own.

Myself will to my darling be
Both law and impulse: and with me
The Girl, in rock and plain,
In earth and heaven, in glade and bow**er,**
Shall feel an overseeing power
To kindle or restrain.

She shall be sportive as the fawn
That wild with glee across the **lawn**
Or up the mountain springs;
And hers shall be the breathing bal**m,**
And hers the silence and the calm
Of mute insensate things.

The floating clouds their state shall lend
To her ; for her the willow bend ;
Nor shall she fail to see
Even in the motions of the Storm
Grace that shall mould the Maiden's form
By silent sympathy.

The stars of midnight shall be dear
To her ; and she shall lean her ear
In many a secret place
Where rivulets dance their wayward round,
And beauty born of murmuring sound
Shall pass into her face.

And vital feelings of delight
Shall rear her form to stately height,
Her virgin bosom swell ;
Such thoughts to Lucy I will give
While she and I together live
Here in this happy dell.'

Thus Nature spake—The work was done—
How soon my Lucy's race was run !
She died, and left to me
This heath, this calm, and quiet scene ;
The memory of what has been,
And never more will be.

(1799.)

3.

A slumber did my spirit seal ;
  I had no human fears :
She seemed a thing that could not feel
  The touch of earthly years.

No motion has she now, no force ;
  She neither hears nor sees ;
Rolled round in earth's diurnal course,
  With rocks, and stones, and trees.

(1799.)

The Two April Mornings.

We walked along, while bright and red
Uprose the morning sun ;
And Matthew stopped, he looked, and said,
‘ The will of God be done ! ’

A village schoolmaster was he,
With hair of glittering grey;
As blithe a man as you could see
On a spring holiday.

And on that morning, through the grass,
And by the steaming rills,
We travelled merrily, to pass
A day among the hills.

‘ Our work,’ said I, ‘ was well begun :
Then, from thy breast what thought,
Beneath so beautiful a sun,
So sad a sigh has brought ? ’

A second time did Matthew stop,
And fixing still his eye
Upon the eastern mountain-top,
To me he made reply :

‘ Yon cloud with that long purple cleft
Brings fresh into my mind
A day like this which I have left
Full thirty years behind.

And just above yon slope of corn
Such colours, and no other,
Were in the sky, that April morn,
Of this the very brother.

With rod and line I sued the sport
Which that sweet season gave,
And, to the church-yard come, stopped short
Beside my daughter's grave.

Nine summers had she scarcely seen,
The pride of all the vale :
And then she sang ;—she would have been
A very nightingale.

Six feet in earth my Emma lay ;
And yet I loved her more,
For so it seemed, than till that day
I e'er had loved before.

And, turning from her grave, I met,
Beside the churchyard yew,
A blooming Girl, whose hair was wet
With points of morning dew.

A basket on her head she bare ;
Her brow was smooth and white :
To see a child so very fair,
It was a pure delight !

No fountain from its rocky cave
E'er tripped with foot so free ;
She seemed as happy as a wave
That dances on the sea.

There came from me a sigh of pain
Which I could ill confine ;
I looked at her, and looked again :
And did not wish her mine !'

Matthew is in his grave, yet now,
Methinks, I see him stand,
As at that moment, with a bough
Of wilding in his hand.

(1799.)

THE FOUNTAIN. A CONVERSATION.

We talked with open heart, and tongue
Affectionate and true,
A pair of friends, though I was young,
And Matthew seventy-two.

We lay beneath a spreading oak,
Beside a mossy seat ;
And from the turf a fountain broke,
And gurgled at our feet.

'Now, Matthew!' said I, 'let us match
This water's pleasant tune
With some old border-song, or catch
That suits a summer's noon ;

Or of the church-clock and the chimes
Sing here beneath the shade,
That half-mad thing of witty rhymes
Which you last April made !'

In silence Matthew lay, and eyed
The spring beneath the tree ;
And thus the dear old Man replied,
The grey-haired man of glee :

'No check, no stay, this Streamlet fears;
How merrily it goes !
'Twill murmur on a thousand years,
And flow as now it flows.

And here, on this delightful day,
I cannot choose but think
How oft, a vigorous man, I lay
Beside this fountain's brink.

My eyes are dim with childish tears,
My heart is idly stirred,
For the same sound is in my ears
Which in those days I heard.

Thus fares it still in our decay:
And yet the wiser mind
Mourns less for what age takes away
Than what it leaves behind.

The blackbird amid leafy trees,
The lark above the hill,
Let loose their carols when they please,
Are quiet when they will.

With Nature never do *they* wage
A foolish strife ; they see
A happy youth, and their old age
Is beautiful and free :

But we are pressed by heavy laws ;
And often, glad no more,
We wear a face of joy, because
We have been glad of yore.

If there be one who need bemoan
His kindred laid in earth,
The household hearts that were his own,
It is the man of mirth.

My days, my Friend, are almost gone,
My life has been approved,
And many love me ; but by none
Am I enough beloved.'

' Now both himself and me he wrongs,
The man who thus complains !
I live and sing my idle songs
Upon these happy plains ;

And, Matthew, for thy children dead
I 'll be a son to thee !'
At this he grasped my hand, and said,
' Alas ! that cannot be.'

We rose up from the fountain-side ;
And down the smooth descent
Of the green sheep-track did we glide ;
And through the wood we went ;

> And, ere we came to Leonard's rock,
> He sang those witty rhymes
> About the crazy old church-clock,
> And the bewildered chimes.

(1799.)

THERE WAS A BOY.

There was a Boy; ye knew him well, ye cliffs
And islands of Winander!—many a time,
At evening, when the earliest stars began
To move along the edges of the hills,
Rising or setting, would he stand alone,
Beneath the trees, or by the glimmering lake;
And there, with fingers interwoven, both hands
Pressed closely palm to palm and to his mouth
Uplifted, he, as through an instrument,
Blew mimic hootings to the silent owls,
That they might answer him.—And they would shout
Across the watery vale, and shout again,
Responsive to his call,—with quivering peals,
And long halloos, and screams, and echoes loud
Redoubled and redoubled; concourse wild
Of jocund din! And, when there came a pause
Of silence such as baffled his best skill:
Then, sometimes, in that silence, while he hung
Listening, a gentle shock of mild surprise
Has carried far into his heart the voice
Of mountain-torrents; or the visible scene
Would enter unawares into his mind
With all its solemn imagery, its rocks,
Its woods, and that uncertain heaven received
Into the bosom of the steady lake.

This boy was taken from his mates, and died
In childhood, ere he was full twelve years old.
Pre-eminent in beauty is the vale
Where he was born and bred: the church·yard hangs
Upon a slope above the village-school;

And, through that church-yard when my way has led
On summer-evenings, I believe, that there
A long half-hour together I have stood
Mute—looking at the grave in which he lies!

(1799.)

INFLUENCE OF NATURAL OBJECTS IN CALLING FORTH AND
STRENGTHENING THE IMAGINATION IN BOYHOOD AND
EARLY YOUTH.

[Prelude I.]

Wisdom and Spirit of the universe !
Thou Soul that art the eternity of thought,
And givest to forms and images a breath
And everlasting motion, not in vain
By day or star-light thus from my first dawn
Of childhood didst thou intertwine for me
The passions that build up our human soul ;
Not with the mean and vulgar works of man,
But with high objects, with enduring things—
With life and nature—purifying thus
The elements of feeling and of thought,
And sanctifying, by such discipline,
Both pain and fear, until we recognise
A grandeur in the beatings of the heart.
Nor was this fellowship vouchsafed to me
With stinted kindness. In November days,
When vapours rolling down the valley made
A lonely scene more lonesome, among woods,
At noon, and 'mid the calm of summer nights,
When, by the margin of the trembling lake,
Beneath the gloomy hills I homeward went
In solitude, such intercourse was mine :
Mine was it in the fields both day and night,
And by the waters, all the summer long.

And in the frosty season, when the sun
Was set, and visible for many a mile
The cottage windows blazed through twilight gloom,

D 2

I heeded not their summons : happy time
It was indeed for all of us—for me
It was a time of rapture ! Clear and loud
The village clock tolled six,—I wheeled about,
Proud and exulting like an untired horse
That cares not for his home. All shod with steel,
We hissed along the polished ice in games
Confederate, imitative of the chase
And woodland pleasures,—the resounding horn,
The pack loud chiming, and the hunted hare.
So through the darkness and the cold we flew,
And not a voice was idle ; with the din
Smitten, the precipices rang aloud ;
The leafless trees and every icy crag
Tinkled like iron ; while far distant hills
Into the tumult sent an alien sound
Of melancholy not unnoticed, while the stars
Eastward were sparkling clear, and in the west
The orange sky of evening died away.
Not seldom from the uproar I retired
Into a silent bay, or sportively
Glanced sideway, leaving the tumultuous throng,
To cut across the reflex of a star
That fled, and, flying still before me, gleamed
Upon the glassy plain ; and oftentimes,
When we had given our bodies to the wind,
And all the shadowy banks on either side
Came sweeping through the darkness, spinning still
The rapid line of motion, then at once
Have I, reclining back upon my heels
Stopped short ; yet still the solitary cliffs
Wheeled by me—even as if the earth had rolled
With visible motion her diurnal round !
Behind me did they stretch in solemn train,
Feebler and feebler, and I stood and watched
Till all was tranquil as a dreamless sleep.

(1799.)

THE GREEN LINNET.

Beneath these fruit-tree boughs that shed
Their snow-white blossoms on my head,
With brightest sunshine round me spread
 Of spring's unclouded weather,
In this sequestered nook how sweet
To sit upon my orchard-seat !
And birds and flowers once more to greet,
 My last year's friends together.

One have I marked, the happiest guest
In all this covert of the blest :
Hail to Thee, far above the rest
 In joy of voice and pinion !
Thou, Linnet ! in thy green array,
Presiding Spirit here to-day,
Dost lead the revels of the May,
 And this is thy dominion.

While birds, and butterflies, and flowers,
Make all one band of paramours,
Thou, ranging up and down the bowers,
 Art sole in thy employment ;
A Life, a Presence like the Air,
Scattering thy gladness without care,
Too blest with any one to pair ;
 Thyself thy own enjoyment.

Amid yon tuft of hazel trees,
That twinkle in the gusty breeze,
Behold him perched in ecstasies,
 Yet seeming still to hover ;
There ! where the flutter of his wings
Upon his back and body flings
Shadows and sunny glimmerings,
 That cover him all over.

My dazzled sight he oft deceives,
A Brother of the dancing leaves ;
Then flits, and from the cottage-eaves
          Pours forth his song in gushes ;
As if by that exulting strain
He mocked and treated with disdain
The voiceless Form he chose to feign,
          While fluttering in the bushes.

                                        (1803.)

YEW TREES.

There is a Yew-tree, pride of Lorton Vale,
Which to this day stands single, in the midst
Of its own darkness, as it stood of yore :
Not loth to furnish weapons for the bands
Of Umfraville or Percy ere they marched
To Scotland's heaths ; or those that crossed the sea
And drew their sounding bows at Azincour,
Perhaps at earlier Crecy, or Poictiers.
Of vast circumference and gloom profound
This solitary Tree ! a living thing
Produced too slowly ever to decay ;
Of form and aspect too magnificent
To be destroyed. But worthier still of note
Are those fraternal Four of Borrowdale,
Joined in one solemn and capacious grove ;
Huge trunks ! and each particular trunk a growth
Of intertwisted fibres serpentine
Up-coiling, and inveterately convolved ;
Nor uninformed with Phantasy, and looks
That threaten the profane ;—a pillared shade,
Upon whose grassless floor of red-brown hue,
By sheddings from the pining umbrage tinged
Perennially—beneath whose sable roof
Of boughs, as if for festal purpose, decked
With unrejoicing berries —ghostly Shapes
May meet at noontide ; Fear and trembling Hope,
Silence and Foresight ; Death the Skeleton

And Time the Shadow ;—there to celebrate,
As in a natural temple scattered o'er
With altars undisturbed of mossy stone,
United worship ; or in mute repose
To lie, and listen to the mountain flood
Murmuring from Glaramara's inmost caves.

(1803.)

TO A HIGHLAND GIRL.

(At Inversneyde, upon Loch Lomond.)

Sweet Highland Girl, a very shower
Of beauty is thy earthly dower!
Twice seven consenting years have shed
Their utmost bounty on thy head:
And these grey rocks ; that household lawn ;
Those trees, a veil just half withdrawn ;
This fall of water that doth make
A murmur near the silent lake ;
This little bay ; a quiet road
That holds in shelter thy Abode—
In truth together do ye seem
Like something fashioned in a dream ;
Such Forms as from their covert peep
When earthly cares are laid asleep !
But, O fair Creature ! in the light
Of common day, so heavenly bright,
I bless Thee, Vision as thou art,
I bless thee with a human heart;
God shield thee to thy latest years !
Thee, neither know I, nor thy peers ;
And yet thy eyes are fill'd with tears.

With earnest feeling I shall pray
For thee when I am far away:
For never saw I mien, or face,
In which more plainly I could trace

Benignity and home-bred sense
Ripening in perfect innocence.
Here scattered, like a random seed,
Remote from men, thou dost not need
The embarrassed look of shy distress,
And maidenly shamefacedness :
Thou wear'st upon thy forehead clear
The freedom of a Mountaineer :
A face with gladness overspread !
Soft smiles, by human kindness bred !
And seemliness complete, that sways
Thy courtesies, about thee plays ;
With no restraint, but such as springs
From quick and eager visitings
Of thoughts that lie beyond the reach
Of thy few words of English speech :
A bondage sweetly brooked, a strife
That gives thy gestures grace and life !
So have I, not unmoved in mind,
Seen birds of tempest-loving kind—
Thus beating up against the wind.

What hand but would a garland cull
For thee who art so beautiful ?
O happy pleasure ! here to dwell
Beside thee in some heathy dell ;
Adopt your homely ways and dress,
A Shepherd, thou a Shepherdess !
But I could frame a wish for thee
More like a grave reality :
Thou art to me but as a wave
Of the wild sea ; and I would have
Some claim upon thee, if I could,
Though but of common neighbourhood.
What joy to hear thee, and to see !
Thy elder Brother I would be,
Thy Father—anything to thee !
Now thanks to Heaven ! that of its grace
Hath led me to this lonely place.

Joy have I had ; and going hence
I bear away my recompence.
In spots like these it is we prize
Our Memory, feel that she hath eyes ;
Then, why should I be loth to stir ?
I feel this place was made for her ;
To give new pleasure like the past,
Continued long as life shall last.
Nor am I loth, though pleased at heart,
Sweet Highland Girl ! from thee to part ;
For I, methinks, till I grow old,
As fair before me shall behold,
As I do now, the cabin small,
The lake, the bay, the waterfall ;
And Thee, the Spirit of them all !

(1803.)

THE SOLITARY REAPER.

Behold her, single in the field,
Yon solitary Highland Lass !
Reaping and singing by herself ;
Stop here, or gently pass !
Alone she cuts and binds the grain,
And sings a melancholy strain ;
O listen ! for the Vale profound
Is overflowing with the sound.

No Nightingale did ever chaunt
More welcome notes to weary bands
Of travellers in some shady haunt
Among Arabian sands :
A voice so thrilling ne'er was heard
In spring-time from a Cuckoo-bird,
Breaking the silence of the seas
Among the farthest Hebrides.

Will no one tell me what she sings?—
Perhaps the plaintive numbers flow
For old, unhappy, far-off things,
And battles long ago :
Or is it some more humble lay,
Familiar matter of to-day?
Some natural sorrow, loss, or pain,
That has been, and may be again?

Whate'er the theme, the Maiden sang
As if her song could have no ending ;
I saw her singing at her work,
And o'er the sickle bending ;—
I listened, motionless and still ;
And, as I mounted up the hill,
The music in my heart I bore,
Long after it was heard no more.

(1803.)

YARROW UNVISITED. 1803.

[See the various poems the scene of which is laid upon the banks of the
Yarrow ; in particular, the exquisite ballad of Hamilton, beginning—

'Busk ye, busk ye, my bonny, bonny Bride,
Busk ye, busk ye, my winsome Marrow !']

From Stirling's castle we had seen
The mazy Forth unravelled ;
Had trod the banks of Clyde, and Tay,
And with the Tweed had travelled ;
And when we came to Clovenford,
Then said my ' *winsome Marrow,*'
'Whate'er betide, we'll turn aside,
And see the Braes of Yarrow.'

' Let Yarrow folk, *frae* Selkirk town,
Who have been buying, selling,
Go back to Yarrow, 'tis their own ;
Each maiden to her dwelling !

On Yarrow's banks let herons feed,
Hares couch, and rabbits burrow!
But we will downwards with the Tweed,
Nor turn aside to Yarrow.

'There's Galla Water, Leader Haughs,
Both lying right before us;
And Dryborough, where with chiming Tweed
The lintwhites sing in chorus;
There's pleasant Tiviot-dale, a land
Made blithe with plough and harrow:
Why throw away a needful day
To go in search of Yarrow?

'What's Yarrow but a river bare,
That glides the dark hills under?
There are a thousand such elsewhere
As worthy of your wonder.'
—Strange words they seemed of slight and scorn;
My True-love sighed for sorrow;
And looked me in the face, to think
I thus could speak of Yarrow!

'Oh! green,' said I, 'are Yarrow's holms,
And sweet is Yarrow flowing!
Fair hangs the apple frae the rock[1],
But we will leave it growing.
O'er hilly path, and open strath,
We'll wander Scotland thorough;
But, though so near, we will not turn
Into the dale of Yarrow.

'Let beeves and home-bred kine partake
The sweets of Burn-mill meadow;
The swan on still Saint Mary's Lake
Float double, swan and shadow!
We will not see them; will not go
To-day, nor yet to-morrow;
Enough if in our hearts we know
There's such a place as Yarrow.

[1] See Hamilton's ballad, as above.

'Be Yarrow stream unseen, unknown!
It must, or we shall rue it;
We have a vision of our own;
Ah! why should we undo it?
The treasured dreams of times long past,
We ll keep them, winsome Marrow!
For when we're there, although 'tis fair,
'Twill be another Yarrow!

'If Care with freezing years should come,
And wandering seem but folly,—
Should we be loath to stir from home,
And yet be melancholy;
Should life be dull, and spirits low,
'Twill soothe us in our sorrow,
That earth has something yet to show,
The bonny holms of Yarrow.'

TO THE CUCKOO.

O blithe New-comer! I have heard,
I hear thee and rejoice.
O Cuckoo! shall I call thee Bird,
Or but a wandering Voice?

While I am lying on the grass
Thy twofold shout I hear,
From hill to hill it seems to pass,
At once far off, and near.

Though babbling only to the Vale,
Of sunshine and of flowers,
Thou bringest unto me a tale
Of visionary hours.

Thrice welcome, darling of the Spring!
Even yet thou art to me
No bird, but an invisible thing,
A voice, a mystery;

The same whom in my school-boy days
I listened to; that Cry
Which made me look a thousand ways
In bush, and tree, and sky.

To seek thee did I often rove
Through woods and on the green;
And thou wert still a hope, a love;
Still longed for, never seen.

And I can listen to thee yet;
Can lie upon the plain
And listen, till I do beget
That golden time again.

O blessed Bird! the earth we pace
Again appears to be
An unsubstantial, faery place:
That is fit home for Thee!

(1804.)

AT THE GRAVE OF BURNS. 1803.

(Seven Years after his Death.)

I shiver, Spirit fierce and bold,
At thought of what I now behold:
As vapours breathed from dungeons cold
      Strike pleasure dead,
So sadness comes from out the mould
      Where Burns is laid.

And have I then thy bones so near,
And thou forbidden to appear?
As if it were thyself that's here
      I shrink with pain;
And both my wishes and my ear
      Alike are vain.

Off weight—nor press on weight !—away
Dark thoughts !—they came, but not to stay ;
With chastened feelings would I pay
    The tribute due
To him, and aught that hides his clay
    From mortal view.

Fresh as the flower, whose modest worth
He sang, his genius 'glinted' forth,
Rose like a star that touching earth,
    For so it seems,
Doth glorify its humble birth
    With matchless beams.

The piercing eye, the thoughtful brow,
The struggling heart, where be they now?—
Full soon the Aspirant of the plough,
    The prompt, the brave,
Slept, with the obscurest, in the low
    And silent grave.

I mourned with thousands, but as one
More deeply grieved, for He was gone
Whose light I hailed when first it shone,
    And showed my youth
How Verse may build a princely throne
    On humble truth.

Alas ! where'er the current tends,
Regret pursues and with it blends,—
Huge Criffel's hoary top ascends
    By Skiddaw seen,—
Neighbours we were, and loving friends
    We might have been :

True friends though diversely inclined ;
But heart with heart and mind with mind,
Where the main fibres are entwined,
    Through Nature's skill,
May even by contraries be joined
    More closely still.

The tear will start, and let it flow;
Thou 'poor Inhabitant below,'
At this dread moment—even so—
    Might we together
Have sate and talked where gowans blow,
    Or on wild heather.

What treasures would have then been placed
Within my reach ; of knowledge graced
By fancy what a rich repast !
    But why go on ?—
Oh ! spare to sweep, thou mournful blast,
    His grave grass-grown.

There, too, a Son, his joy and pride,
(Not three weeks past the Stripling died,)
Lies gathered to his Father's side,
    Soul-moving sight !
Yet one to which is not denied
    Some sad delight.

For *he* is safe, a quiet bed
Hath early found among the dead,
Harboured where none can be misled,
    Wronged, or distrest ;
And surely here it may be said
    That such are blest.

And oh for Thee, by pitying grace
Checked oft-times in a devious race,
May He who halloweth the place
    Where Man is laid
Receive thy Spirit in the embrace
    For which it prayed !

Sighing I turned away; but ere
Night fell I heard, or seemed to hear,
Music that sorrow comes not near,
    A ritual hymn,
Chaunted in love that casts out fear
    By Seraphim.

THOUGHTS SUGGESTED THE DAY FOLLOWING, ON THE BANKS OF NITH, NEAR THE POET'S RESIDENCE.

Too frail to keep the lofty vow
That must have followed when his brow
Was wreathed—'The Vision' tells us how—
 With holly spray,
He faltered, drifted to and fro,
 And passed away.

Well might such thoughts, dear Sister, throng
Our minds when, lingering all too long,
Over the grave of Burns we hung
 In social grief—
Indulged as if it were a wrong
 To seek relief.

But, leaving each unquiet theme
Where gentlest judgments may misdeem,
And prompt to welcome every gleam
 Of good and fair,
Let us beside this limpid Stream
 Breathe hopeful air.

Enough of sorrow, wreck, and blight;
Think rather of those moments bright
When to the consciousness of right
 His course was true,
When Wisdom prospered in his sight
 And virtue grew.

Yes, freely let our hearts expand,
Freely as in youth's season bland,
When side by side, his Book in hand,
 We wont to stray,
Our pleasure varying at command
 Of each sweet Lay.

How oft inspired must he have trode
These pathways, yon far-stretching road!
There lurks his home; in that Abode,
    With mirth elate,
Or in his nobly-pensive mood,
    The Rustic sate.

Proud thoughts that Image overawes,
Before it humbly let us pause,
And ask of Nature, from what cause
    And by what rules
She trained her Burns to win applause
    That shames the Schools.

Through busiest street and loneliest glen
Are felt the flashes of his pen:
He rules mid winter snows, and when
    Bees fill their hives:
Deep in the general heart of men
    His power survives.

What need of fields in some far clime
Where Heroes, Sages, Bards sublime,
And all that fetched the flowing rhyme
    From genuine springs,
Shall dwell together till old Time
    Folds up his wings?

Sweet Mercy! to the gates of Heaven
This Minstrel lead, his sins forgiven;
The rueful conflict, the heart riven
    With vain endeavour,
And memory of Earth's bitter leaven
    Effaced for ever.

But why to Him confine the prayer,
When kindred thoughts and yearnings bear
On the frail heart the purest share
    With all that live?—
The best of what we do and are,
    Just God, forgive!

'SHE WAS A PHANTOM.'

She was a Phantom of delight
When first she gleamed upon my sight;
A lovely Apparition, sent
To be a moment's ornament;
Her eyes as stars of Twilight fair,
Like Twilight's, too, her dusky hair;
But all things else about her drawn
From May-time and the cheerful Dawn,
A dancing Shape, an Image gay,
To haunt, to startle, and way-lay.

I saw her upon nearer view,
A Spirit, yet a Woman too!
Her household motions light and free,
And steps of virgin-liberty;
A countenance in which did meet
Sweet records, promises as sweet;
A Creature not too bright or good
For human nature's daily food;
For transient sorrows, simple wiles,
Praise, blame, love, kisses, tears, and smiles.

And now I see with eye serene
The very pulse of the machine;
A Being breathing thoughtful breath,
A traveller between life and death;
The reason firm, the temperate will,
Endurance, foresight, strength, and skill;
A perfect Woman, nobly planned,
To warn, to comfort, and command;
And yet a Spirit still, and bright
With something of angelic light.

(1804.)

'I WANDERED LONELY.'

I wandered lonely as a cloud
That floats on high o'er vales and hills,
When all at once I saw a crowd,
A host, of golden daffodils;
Beside the lake, beneath the trees,
Fluttering and dancing in the breeze.

Continuous as the stars that shine
And twinkle on the milky way,
They stretched in never-ending line
Along the margin of a bay:
Ten thousand saw I at a glance,
Tossing their heads in sprightly dance.

The waves beside them danced; but they
Out-did the sparkling waves in glee:
A poet could not but be gay,
In such a jocund company:
I gazed—and gazed—but little thought
What wealth the show to me had brought:

For oft, when on my couch I lie
In vacant or in pensive mood,
They flash upon that inward eye
Which is the bliss of solitude;
And then my heart with pleasure fills,
And dances with the daffodils.

(1804.)

ODE TO DUTY.

Stern Daughter of the Voice of God!
O Duty! if that name thou love
Who art a light to guide, a rod
To check the erring, and reprove;
Thou, who art victory and law
When empty terrors overawe;
From vain temptations dost set free;
And calm'st the weary strife of frail humanity!

There are who ask not if thine eye
Be on them; who, in love and truth,
Where no misgiving is, rely
Upon the genial sense of youth:
Glad Hearts! without reproach or blot;
Who do thy work, and know it not:
Oh! if through confidence misplaced
They fail, thy saving arms, dread Power! **around**
    them cast.

Serene will be our days and bright,
And happy will our nature be,
When love is an unerring light,
And joy its own security.
And they a blissful course may hold
Even now, who, not unwisely bold,
Live in the spirit of this creed;
Yet seek thy firm support, according to **their need.**

I, loving freedom, and untried;
No sport of every random gust,
Yet being to myself a guide,
Too blindly have reposed my trust:
And oft, when in my heart was heard
Thy timely mandate, I deferred
The task, in smoother walks to stray;
But thee I now would serve more strictly if I may.

Through no disturbance of my soul,
Or strong compunction in me wrought,
I supplicate for thy control ;
But in the quietness of thought :
Me this unchartered freedom tires ;
I feel the weight of chance-desires :
My hopes no more must change their name,
I long for a repose that ever is the same.

Stern Lawgiver ! yet thou dost wear
The Godhead's most benignant grace ;
Nor know we any thing so fair
As is the smile upon thy face :
Flowers laugh before thee on their beds
And fragrance in thy footing treads ;
Thou dost preserve the stars from wrong ;
And the most ancient heavens, through Thee, are fresh
    and strong.

To humbler functions, awful Power !
I call thee : I myself commend
Unto thy guidance from this hour ;
Oh, let my weakness have an end !
Give unto me, made lowly wise,
The spirit of self-sacrifice ;
The confidence of reason give ;
And in the light of truth thy Bondman let me live !

(1805.)

THE NIGHTINGALE.

O Nightingale ! thou surely art
A creature of a ' fiery heart ' :—
These notes of thine—they pierce and pierce ;
Tumultuous harmony and fierce !
Thou sing'st as if the God of wine
Had helped thee to a Valentine ;
A song in mockery and despite
Of shades, and dews, and silent night ;
And steady bliss, and all the loves
Now sleeping in these peaceful groves.

I heard a Stock-dove sing or say
His homely tale, this very day;
His voice was buried among trees,
Yet to be come-at by the breeze:
He did not cease; but cooed—and cooed;
And somewhat pensively he wooed:
He sang of love, with quiet blending,
Slow to begin, and never ending;
Of serious faith, and inward glee;
That was the song—the song for me!

(1806.)

THE MOUNTAIN ECHO.

Yes, it was the mountain Echo,
Solitary, clear, profound,
Answering to the shouting Cuckoo,
Giving to her sound for sound!

Unsolicited reply
To a babbling wanderer sent;
Like her ordinary cry,
Like—but oh, how different!

Hears not also mortal Life?
Hear not we, unthinking Creatures!
Slaves of folly, love, or strife—
Voices of two different natures?

Have not *we* too?—yes, we have
Answers, and we know not whence;
Echoes from beyond the grave,
Recognised intelligence!

Such rebounds our inward ear
Catches sometimes from afar—
Listen, ponder, hold them dear;
For of God,—of God they are.

(1806.)

ODE.

INTIMATIONS OF IMMORTALITY FROM RECOLLECTIONS OF EARLY CHILDHOOD.

> The Child is father of the Man;
> And I could wish my days to be
> Bound each to each by natural piety.

I.

There was a time when meadow, grove, and stream,
The earth, and every common sight,
    To me did seem
    Apparelled in celestial light,
The glory and the freshness of a dream.
It is not now as it hath been of yore ;—
    Turn wheresoe'er I may,
    By night or day,
The things which I have seen I now can see no more.

2.

    The Rainbow comes and goes,
    And lovely is the Rose,
    The Moon doth with delight
Look round her when the heavens are bare,
    Waters on a starry night
    Are beautiful and fair ;
    The sunshine is a glorious birth ;
    But yet I know, where'er I go,
That there hath past away a glory from the earth.

3.

Now, while the birds thus sing a joyous song,
    And while the young lambs bound
    As to the tabor's sound,
To me alone there came a thought of grief:
A timely utterance gave that thought relief,
    And I again am strong:

The cataracts blow their trumpets from the steep ;
No more shall grief of mine the season wrong ;
I hear the Echoes through the mountains throng,
The Winds come to me from the fields of sleep,
  And all the earth is gay ;
   Land and Sea
  Give themselves up to jollity,
   And with the heart of May
  Doth every Beast keep holiday ;—
   Thou Child of Joy,
Shout round me, let me hear thy shouts, thou **happy**
   Shepherd-boy !

4

Ye blessed Creatures, I have heard the **call**
  Ye to each other make ; I see
The heavens laugh with you in your jubilee ;
  My heart is at your festival,
  My head hath its coronal,
The fulness of your bliss, I feel—I feel it **all.**
   Oh evil day ! if I were sullen
   While Earth herself is adorning,
    This sweet May-morning,
   And the Children are culling
    On every side,
   In a thousand valleys far and wide,
   Fresh flowers ; while the sun shines **warm,**
And the Babe leaps up on his Mother's arm :—
   I hear, I hear, with joy I hear !
   —But there's a Tree, of many, one,
A single Field which I have looked upon,
Both of them speak of something that is gone **:**
   The Pansy at my feet
   Doth the same tale repeat :
Whither is fled the visionary gleam?
Where is it now, the glory and the dream **?**

5.

Our birth is but a sleep and a forgetting:
The Soul that rises with us, our life's Star,
  Hath had elsewhere its setting,
   And cometh from afar:
  Not in entire forgetfulness,
  And not in utter nakedness,
But trailing clouds of glory do we come
  From God, who is our home:
Heaven lies about us in our infancy!
Shades of the prison-house begin to close
  Upon the growing Boy,
But He beholds the light, and whence it flows
  He sees it in his joy;
The Youth, who daily farther from the east
  Must travel, still is Nature's Priest,
   And by the vision splendid
  Is on his way attended;
At length the Man perceives it die away,
And fade into the light of common day.

6.

Earth fills her lap with pleasures of her own;
Yearnings she hath in her own natural kind,
And even with something of a Mother's mind,
   And no unworthy aim,
  The homely Nurse doth all she can
To make her Foster-child, her Inmate Man,
  Forget the glories he hath known,
And that imperial palace whence he came.

7.

Behold the Child among his new-born blisses,
A six years' Darling of a pigmy size!
See, where 'mid work of his own hand he lies,
Fretted by sallies of his mother's kisses,

With light upon him from his father's eyes !
See, at his feet, some little plan or chart,
Some fragment from his dream of human life,
Shaped by himself with newly-learned art ;
  A wedding or a festival,
  A mourning or a funeral ;
   And this hath now his heart,
  And unto this he frames his song:
   Then will he fit his tongue
To dialogues of business, love, or strife :
   But it will not be long
   Ere this be thrown aside,
   And with new joy and pride
The little Actor cons another part ;
Filling from time to time his ' humorous stage '
With all the Persons, down to palsied Age,
That Life brings with her in her equipage ;
   As if his whole vocation
   Were endless imitation.

8.

Thou, whose exterior semblance doth belie
   Thy Soul's immensity ;
Thou best Philosopher, who yet dost keep
Thy heritage, thou Eye among the blind,
That, deaf and silent, read'st the eternal deep,
Haunted for ever by the eternal mind,—
   Mighty Prophet ! Seer blest !
   On whom those truths do rest,
Which we are toiling all our lives to find,
In darkness lost, the darkness of the grave ;
Thou, over whom thy Immortality
Broods like the Day, a Master o'er a Slave,
A Presence which is not to be put by ;
Thou little Child, yet glorious in the might
Of heaven-born freedom on thy being's height,
Why with such earnest pains dost thou provoke
The years to bring the inevitable yoke,

Thus blindly with thy blessedness at strife?
Ful! soon thy Soul shall have her earthly freight,
And custom lie upon thee with a weight,
Heavy as frost, and deep almost as life!

9.

> O joy! that in our embers
> Is something that doth live,
> That nature yet remembers
> What was so fugitive!

The thought of our past years in me doth breed
Perpetual benediction : not indeed
For that which is most worthy to be blest ;
Delight and liberty, the simple creed
Of Childhood, whether busy or at rest,
With new-fledged hope still fluttering in his breast :—

> Not for these I raise
> The song of thanks and praise ;
> But for those obstinate questionings
> Of sense and outward things,
> Fallings from us, vanishings ;
> Blank misgivings of a Creature

Moving about in worlds not realised,
High instincts before which our mortal Nature
Did tremble like a guilty thing surprised :

> But for those first affections,
> Those shadowy recollections,
> Which, be they what they may,

Are yet the fountain light of all our day,
Are yet a master light of all our seeing ;

> Uphold us, cherish, and have power to make

Our noisy years seem moments in the being
Of the eternal Silence : truths that wake,

> To perish never ;

Which neither listlessness, nor mad endeavour,

> Nor Man nor Boy.

Nor all that is at enmity with joy,
Can utterly abolish or destroy!

Hence in a season of calm weather
　　Though inland far we be,
Our Souls have sight of that immortal sea
　　Which brought us hither,
　　　Can in a moment travel thither,
And see the Children sport upon the shore,
And hear the mighty waters rolling evermore.

10.

Then sing, ye Birds, sing, sing a joyous song !
　　　And let the young Lambs bound
　　　As to the tabor's sound !
We in thought will join your throng,
　　　Ye that pipe and ye that play,
　　　Ye that through your hearts to-day
　　　Feel the gladness of the May !
What though the radiance which was once so bright
Be now for ever taken from my sight,
　　Though nothing can bring back the hour
Of splendour in the grass, of glory in the flower ;
　　　We will grieve not, rather find
　　　Strength in what remains behind ;
　　　In the primal sympathy
　　　Which having been must ever be ;
　　　In the soothing thoughts that spring
　　　Out of human suffering ;
　　　In the faith that looks through death,
In years that bring the philosophic mind.

11.

And O, ye Fountains, Meadows, Hills, and Groves,
Forebode not any severing of our loves !
Yet in my heart of hearts I feel your might ;
I only have relinquished one delight
To live beneath your more habitual sway.
I love the Brooks, which down their channels fret,
Even more than when I tripped lightly as they :
The innocent brightness of a new-born Day
　　　　Is lovely yet ;

The Clouds that gather round the setting sun
Do take a sober colouring from an eye
That hath kept watch o'er man's mortality;
Another race hath been, and other palms are won.
Thanks to the human heart by which we live,
Thanks to its tenderness, its joys, and fears,
To me the meanest flower that blows can give
Thoughts that do often lie too deep for tears.

(1803-1806.)

LAODAMIA.

'With sacrifice before the rising morn
Vows have I made by fruitless hope inspired:
And from the infernal Gods, 'mid shades forlorn
Of night, my slaughtered Lord have I required:
Celestial pity I again implore;—
Restore him to my sight—great Jove, restore!'

So speaking, and by fervent love endowed
With faith, the Suppliant heavenward lifts her hands;
While, like the sun emerging from a cloud,
Her countenance brightens—and her eye expands;
Her bosom heaves and spreads, her stature grows;
And she expects the issue in repose.

O terror! what hath she perceived?—O joy!
What doth she look on?—whom doth she behold?
Her Hero slain upon the beach of Troy?
His vital presence? his corporeal mould?
It is—if sense deceive her not—'tis he!
And a god leads him—winged Mercury!

Mild Hermes spake—and touched her with his wand
That calms all fear: 'Such grace hath crowned thy prayer,
Laodamía! that at Jove's command
Thy Husband walks the paths of upper air:
He comes to tarry with thee three hours' space;
Accept the gift, behold him face to face!'

Forth sprang the impassioned Queen her Lord to clasp :
Again that consummation she essayed :
But unsubstantial Form eludes her grasp
As often as that eager grasp was made.
The Phantom parts—but parts to reunite,
And reassume his place before her sight.

'Protesiláus, lo ! thy guide is gone !
Confirm, I pray, the vision with thy voice :
This is our palace,—yonder is thy throne ;
Speak, and the floor thou tread'st on will rejoice.
Not to appal me have the gods bestowed
This precious boon ; and blest a sad abode.'

'Great Jove, Laodamía ! doth not leave
His gifts imperfect :—Spectre though I be,
I am not sent to scare thee or deceive ;
But in reward of thy fidelity.
And something also did my worth obtain ;
For fearless virtue bringeth boundless gain.

Thou knowest, the Delphic oracle foretold
That the first Greek who touched the Trojan strand
Should die ; but me the threat could not withhold :
A generous cause a victim did demand ;
And forth I leapt upon the sandy plain ;
A self-devoted chief—by Hector slain.'

'Supreme of Heroes—bravest, noblest, best !
Thy matchless courage I bewail no more,
Which then, when tens of thousands were deprest
By doubt, propelled thee to the fatal shore ;
Thou found'st—and I forgive thee—here thou art—
A nobler counsellor than my poor heart.

But thou, though capable of sternest deed,
Wert kind as resolute, and good as brave ;
And he, whose power restores thee, hath decreed
Thou should'st elude the malice of the grave ;
Redundant are thy locks, thy lips as fair
As when their breath enriched Thessalian air.

No Spectre greets me,—no vain Shadow this:
Come, blooming Hero, place thee by my side!
Give, on this well-known couch, one nuptial kiss
To me, this day, a second time thy bride!'
Jove frowned in heaven: the conscious Parcæ threw
Upon those roseate lips a Stygian hue.

'This visage tells thee that my doom is past:
Nor should the change be mourned even if the joys
Of sense were able to return as fast
And surely as they vanish. Earth destroys
Those raptures duly—Erebus disdains:
Calm pleasures there abide—majestic pains.

Be taught, O faithful Consort, to control
Rebellious passion ; for the Gods approve
The depth, and not the tumult, of the soul ;
A fervent, not ungovernable, love.
Thy transports moderate ; and meekly mourn
When I depart, for brief is my sojourn——'

'Ah, wherefore?—Did not Hercules by force
Wrest from the guardian Monster of the tomb
Alcestis, a reanimated corse,
Given back to dwell on earth in vernal bloom?
Medea's spells dispersed the weight of years,
And Æson stood a youth 'mid youthful peers.

The Gods to us are merciful—and they
Yet further may relent : for mightier far
Than strength of nerve and sinew, or the sway
Of magic potent over sun and star,
Is love, though oft to agony distrest,
And though his favourite seat be feeble woman's breast.

But if thou goest, I follow——' 'Peace!' he said,—
She looked upon him and was calmed and cheered ;
The ghastly colour from his lips had fled ;
In his deportment, shape, and mien, appeared
Elysian beauty—melancholy grace—
Brought from a pensive though a happy place.

He spake of love, such love as Spirits feel
In worlds whose course is equable and pure ;
No fears to beat away—no strife to heal—
The past unsigh'd for, and the future sure ;
Spake of heroic hearts in graver mood
Revived, with finer harmony pursued ;

Of all that is most beauteous—imaged there
In happier beauty ; more pellucid streams,
An ampler ether, a diviner air,
And fields invested with purpureal gleams ;
Climes which the sun, who sheds the brightest day
Earth knows, is all unworthy to survey.

Yet there the Soul shall enter which hath earned
That privilege by virtue.—' Ill,' said he,
' The end of man's existence I discerned,
Who from ignoble games and revelry
Could draw, when we had parted, vain delight,
While tears were thy best pastime, day and night :

' And while my youthful peers before my eyes
(Each here following his peculiar bent)
Prepared themselves for glorious enterprise
By martial sports,—or, seated in the tent,
Chieftains and kings in council were detained ;
What time the fleet at Aulis lay enchained.

' The wish'd-for wind was given :—I then revolved
The oracle, upon the silent sea ;
And, if no worthier led the way, resolved
That, of a thousand vessels, mine should be
The foremost prow in pressing to the strand,—
Mine the first blood that tinged the Trojan sand.

' Yet bitter, oft-times bitter, was the pang
When of thy loss I thought, belovèd Wife !
On thee too fondly did my memory hang,
And on the joys we shared in mortal life,—
The paths which we had trod—these fountains,
My new-planned cities, and unfinished towers.

'But should suspense permit the Foe to cry,
"Behold, they tremble!—haughty their array,
Yet of their number no one dares to die"?
In soul I swept the indignity away:
Old frailties then recurred:—but lofty thought
In act embodied, my deliverance wrought.

'And Thou, though strong in love, art all too weak
In reason, in self-government too slow;
I counsel thee by fortitude to seek
Our blest re-union in the shades below.
The invisible world with thee hath sympathised:
Be thy affections raised and solemnised.

'Learn, by a mortal yearning, to ascend—
Seeking a higher object. Love was given,
Encouraged, sanctioned, chiefly for that end;
For this the passion to excess was driven—
That self might be annulled; her bondage prove
The fetters of a dream, opposed to love.'—

Aloud she shrieked! for Hermes reappears!
Round the dear Shade she would have clung—'tis vain.
The hours are past—too brief had they been years;
And him no mortal effort can detain:
Swift, toward the realms that know not earthly day,
He through the portal takes his silent way,
And on the palace-floor a lifeless corse she lay.

By no weak pity might the Gods be moved;
She who thus perished, not without the crime
Of lovers that in reason's spite have loved,
Was doomed to wear out her appointed time,
Apart from happy Ghosts—that gather flowers
Of blissful quiet 'mid unfading bowers.

—Yet tears to human suffering are due;
And mortal hopes defeated and o'erthrown
Are mourned by man, and not by man alone,
As fondly he believes.—Upon the side

Of Hellespont (such faith was entertained)
A knot of spiry trees for ages grew
From out the tomb of him for whom she died;
And ever, when such stature they had gained
That Ilium's walls were subject to their view,
The trees' tall summits withered at the sight;
A constant interchange of growth and blight!

(1814.)

To —— [Miss Blackett], on her First Ascent to the Summit of Helvellyn.

Inmate of a mountain-dwelling,
Thou hast clomb aloft, and gazed
From the watch-towers of Helvellyn;
Awed, delighted, and amazed!

Potent was the spell that bound thee
Not unwilling to obey:
For blue Ether's arms, flung round thee,
Stilled the pantings of dismay.

Lo! the dwindled woods and meadows;
What a vast abyss is there!
Lo! the clouds, the solemn shadows,
And the glistenings—heavenly fair!

And a record of commotion
Which a thousand ridges yield;
Ridge, and gulf, and distant ocean
Gleaming like a silver shield!

Maiden! now take flight;—inherit
Alps or Andes—they are thine!
With the morning's roseate Spirit,
Sweep their length of snowy line;

Or survey their bright dominions
In the gorgeous colours drest
Flung from off the purple pinions,
Evening spreads throughout the west!

Thine are all the coral fountains
Warbling in each sparry vault
Of the untrodden lunar mountains;
Listen to their songs!—or halt,

To Niphates' top invited,
Whither spiteful Satan steered;
Or descend where the ark alighted,
When the green earth re-appeared;

For the power of hills is on thee,
As was witnessed through thine eye
Then when old Helvellyn won thee
To confess their majesty!

(1816.)

EVENING VOLUNTARY.

[Composed upon an Evening of extraordinary Splendour and Beauty.]

I.

Had this effulgence disappeared
With flying haste, I might have sent,
Among the speechless clouds, a look
Of blank astonishment;
But 'tis endued with power to stay,
And sanctify one closing day,
That frail Mortality may see—
What is?—ah no, but what *can* be!
Time was when field and watery cove
With modulated echoes rang,
While choirs of fervent Angels sang
Their vespers in the grove;

Or, crowning, star-like, each some sovereign height,
Warbled, for heaven above and earth below,
Strains suitable to both.—Such holy rite,
Methinks, if audibly repeated now
From hill or valley, could not move
Sublimer transport, purer love,
Than doth this silent spectacle—the gleam—
The shadow—and the peace supreme!

2.

No sound is uttered,—but a deep
And solemn harmony pervades
The hollow vale from steep to steep,
And penetrates the glades.
Far-distant images draw nigh,
Called forth by wondrous potency
Of beamy radiance, that imbues
Whate'er it strikes with gem-like hues!
In vision exquisitely clear,
Herds range along the mountain side;
And glistening antlers are descried;
And gilded flocks appear.
Thine is the tranquil hour, purpureal Eve!
But long as god-like wish, or hope divine,
Informs my spirit, ne'er can I believe
That this magnificence is wholly thine!
—From worlds not quickened by the sun
A portion of the gift is won;
An intermingling of Heaven's pomp is spread
On ground which British shepherds tread!

3.

And, if there be whom broken ties
Afflict, or injuries assail,
Yon hazy ridges to their eyes
Present a glorious scale,
Climbing suffused with sunny air,
To stop—no record hath told where!

And tempting Fancy to ascend,
And with immortal Spirits blend !
—Wings at my shoulders seem to play ;
But, rooted here, I stand and gaze
On those bright steps that heaven-ward raise
Their practicable way.
Come forth, ye drooping old men, look abroad,
And see to what fair countries ye are bound !
And if some traveller, weary of his road,
Hath slept since noon-tide on the grassy ground,
Ye Genii ! to his covert speed ;
And wake him with such gentle heed
As may attune his soul to meet the dower
Bestowed on this transcendent hour !

4.

Such hues from their celestial Urn
Were wont to stream before mine eye,
Where'er it wandered in the morn
Of blissful infancy.
This glimpse of glory, why renewed ?
Nay, rather speak with gratitude ;
For, if a vestige of those gleams
Survived, 'twas only in my dreams.
Dread Power ! whom peace and calmness serve
No less than Nature's threatening voice,
If aught unworthy be my choice,
From THEE if I would swerve ;
Oh, let thy grace remind me of the light
Full early lost, and fruitlessly deplored ;
Which, at this moment, on my waking sight
Appears to shine, by miracle restored ;
My soul, though yet confined to earth,
Rejoices in a second birth !
—'Tis past, the visionary splendour fades ;
And right approaches with her shades.

(1818.)

[From the *Prelude.* 1799-1805.]

[APPARITION ON THE LAKE.]

Dust as we are, the immortal spirit grows
Like harmony in music ; there is a dark
Inscrutable workmanship that reconciles
Discordant elements, makes them cling together
In one society. How strange that all
The terrors, pains, and early miseries,
Regrets, vexations, lassitudes interfused
Within my mind, should e'er have borne a part,
And that a needful part, in making up
The calm existence that is mine when I
Am worthy of myself ! Praise to the end !
Thanks to the means which Nature deigned to employ ;
Whether her fearless visitings, or those
That came with soft alarm, like hurtless light
Opening the peaceful clouds ; or she may use
Severer interventions, ministry
More palpable, as best might suit her aim.

One summer evening (led by her) I found
A little boat tied to a willow tree
Within a rocky cave, its usual home.
Straight I unloosed her chain, and stepping in
Pushed from the shore. It was an act of stealth
And troubled pleasure, nor without the voice
Of mountain-echoes did my boat move on ;
Leaving behind her still, on either side,
Small circles glittering idly in the moon,
Until they melted all into one track
Of sparkling light. But now, like one who rows,
Proud of his skill, to reach a chosen point
With an unswerving line, I fixed my view

Upon the summit of a craggy ridge,
The horizon's utmost boundary ; far above
Was nothing but the stars and the grey sky.
She was an elfin pinnace ; lustily
I dipped my oars into the silent lake,
And, as I rose upon the stroke, my boat
Went heaving through the water like a swan ;
When, from behind that craggy steep till then
The horizon's bound, a huge peak, black and huge,
As if with voluntary power instinct
Upreared its head. I struck and struck again,
And growing still in stature the grim shape
Towered up between me and the stars, and still,
For so it seemed, with purpose of its own
And measured motion like a living thing,
Strode after me. With trembling oars I turned,
And through the silent water stole my way
Back to the covert of the willow tree ;
There in her mooring-place I left my bark,—
And through the meadows homeward went, in grave
And serious mood ; but after I had seen
That spectacle, for many days, my brain
Worked with a dim and undetermined sense
Of unknown modes of being ; o'er my thoughts
There hung a darkness, call it solitude
Or blank desertion. No familiar shapes
Remained, no pleasant images of trees,
Of sea or sky, no colours of green fields ;
But huge and mighty forms, that do not live
Like living men, moved slowly through the mind
By day, and were a trouble to my dreams.

[MORNING AFTER THE BALL.]

And yet, for chastisement of these regrets,
The memory of one particular hour
Doth here rise up against me. 'Mid a throng
Of maids and youths, old men, and matrons staid,
A medley of all tempers, I had passed
The night in dancing, gaiety, and mirth,
With din of instruments and shuffling feet,
And glancing forms, and tapers glittering,
And unaimed prattle flying up and down ;
Spirits upon the stretch, and here and there
Slight shocks of young love-liking interspersed,
Whose transient pleasure mounted to the head,
And tingled through the veins. Ere we retired,
The cock had crowed, and now the eastern sky
Was kindling, not unseen, from humble copse
And open field, through which the pathway wound,
And homeward led my steps. Magnificent
The morning rose, in memorable pomp,
Glorious as ere I had beheld—in front,
The sea lay laughing at a distance ; near,
The solid mountains shone, bright as the clouds,
Grain-tinctured, drenched in empyrean light ;
And in the meadows and the lower grounds
Was all the sweetness of a common dawn—
Dews, vapours, and the melody of birds,
And labourers going forth to till the fields.
Ah ! need I say, dear Friend ! that to the brim
My heart was full ; I made no vows, but vows
Were then made for me ; bond unknown to me
Was given, that I should be, else sinning greatly,
A dedicated Spirit. On I walked
In thankful blessedness, which yet survives.

[DEFILE OF GONDO.]

             The brook and road
Were fellow-travellers in this gloomy strait,
And with them did we journey several hours
At a slow pace. The immeasurable height
Of woods decaying, never to be decayed,
The stationary blasts of waterfalls,
And in the narrow rent at every turn
Winds thwarting winds, bewildered and forlorn,
The torrents shooting from the clear blue sky,
The rocks that muttered close upon our ears,
Black drizzling crags that spake by the way-side
As if a voice were in them, the sick sight
And giddy prospect of the raving stream,
The unfettered clouds and region of the Heavens,
Tumult and peace, the darkness and the light—
Were all like workings of one mind, the features
Of the same face, blossoms upon one tree ;
Characters of the great Apocalypse,
The types and symbols of Eternity,
Of first, and last, and midst, and without end.

[ASCENT OF SNOWDON.]

It was a close, warm, breezeless summer night,
Wan, dull, and glaring, with a dripping fog
Low-hung and thick that covered all the sky ;
But, undiscouraged, we began to climb
The mountain-side. The mist soon girt us round,
And, after ordinary travellers' talk
With our conductor, pensively we sank
Each into commerce with his private thoughts :
Thus did we breast the ascent, and by myself
Was nothing either seen or heard that checked
Those musings or diverted, save that once
The shepherd's lurcher, who, among the crags
Had to his joy unearthed a hedgehog, teased

His coiled-up prey with barkings turbulent.
This small adventure, for even such it seemed
In that wild place and at the dead of night,
Being over and forgotten, on we wound
In silence as before. With forehead bent
Earthward, as if in opposition set
Against an enemy, I panted up
With eager pace, and no less eager thoughts.
Thus might we wear a midnight hour away,
Ascending at loose distance each from each,
And I, as chanced, the foremost of the band ;
When at my feet the ground appeared to brighten,
And with a step or two seemed brighter still ;
Nor was time given to ask or learn the cause,
For instantly a light upon the turf
Fell like a flash, and lo ! as I looked up,
The Moon hung naked in a firmament
Of azure without cloud, and at my feet
Rested a silent sea of hoary mist.
A hundred hills their dusky backs upheaved
All over this still ocean ; and beyond,
Far, far beyond, the solid vapours stretched
In headlands, tongues, and promontory sha
Into the main Atlantic, that appeared
To dwindle, and give up his majesty,
Usurped upon far as the sight could reach.
Not so the ethereal vault ; encroachment none
Was there, nor loss ; only the inferior stars
Had disappeared, or shed a fainter light
In the clear presence of the full-orbed Moon,
Who, from her sovereign elevation, gazed
Upon the billowy ocean, as it lay
All meek and silent, save that through a rift—
Not distant from the shore whereon we stood
A fixed, abysmal, gloomy, breathing-place—
Mounted the roar of waters, torrents, streams
Innumerable, roaring with one voice !
Heard over earth and sea, and, in that hour,
For so it seemed, felt by the starry heavens.

When into air had partially dissolved
That vision, given to spirits of the night
And three chance human wanderers, in calm thought
Reflected, it appeared to me the type
Of a majestic intellect, its acts
And its possessions, what it has and craves,
What in itself it is, and would become.
There I beheld the emblem of a mind
That feeds upon infinity, that broods
Over the dark abyss, intent to hear
Its voices issuing forth to silent light
In one continuous stream ; a mind sustained
By recognitions of transcendent power,
In sense conducting to ideal form,
In soul of more than mortal privilege.
One function, above all, of such a mind
Had Nature shadowed there, by putting forth,
'Mid circumstances awful and sublime,
That mutual domination which she loves
To exert upon the face of outward things,
So moulded, joined, abstracted, so endowed
With interchangeable supremacy,
That men, least sensitive, see, hear, perceive,
And cannot choose but feel. The power, which all
Acknowledge when thus moved, which Nature thus
To bodily sense exhibits, is the express
Resemblance of that glorious faculty
That higher minds bear with them as their own.
This is the very spirit in which they deal
With the whole compass of the universe :
They from their native selves can send abroad
Kindred mutations ; for themselves create
A like existence ; and, whene'er it dawns
Created for them, catch it, or are caught
By its inevitable mastery,
Like angels stopped upon the wing by sound
Of harmony from Heaven's remotest spheres.
Them the enduring and the transient both
Serve to exalt ; they build up greatest things

From least suggestions ; ever on the watch,
Willing to work and to be wrought upon,
They need not extraordinary calls
To rouse them ; in a world of life they live,
By sensible impressions not enthralled,
But by their quickening impulse made more prompt
To hold fit converse with the spiritual world,
And with the generations of mankind
Spread over time, past, present, and to come,
Age after age, till Time shall be no more.

[From the *Excursion.* 1795-1813.]

[TWIN PEAKS OF THE VALLEY.]

                    In genial mood,
While at our pastoral banquet thus we sate
I could not, ever and anon, forbear
To glance an upward look on two huge Peaks,
That from some other vale peered into this.
'Those lusty twins,' exclaimed our host, 'if here
It were your lot to dwell, would soon become
Your prized companions.—Many are the notes
Which, in his tuneful course, the wind draws forth
From rocks, woods, caverns, heaths, and dashing shores ;
And well those lofty brethren bear their part
In the wild concert—chiefly when the storm
Rides high ; then all the upper air they fill
With roaring sound, that ceases not to flow,
Like smoke, along the level of the blast,
In mighty current ; theirs, too, is the song
Of stream and headlong flood that seldom fails ;
And, in the grim and breathless hour of noon,
Methinks that I have heard them echo back
The thunder's greeting. Nor have nature's laws
Left them ungifted with a power to yield
Music of finer tone ; a harmony,
So do I call it, though it be the hand
Of silence, though there be no voice ;—the clouds,

The mist, the shadows, light of golden suns,
Motions of moonlight, all come thither—touch,
And have an answer—thither come, and shape
A language not unwelcome to sick hearts
And idle spirits :—there the sun himself,
At the calm close of summer's longest day,
Rests his substantial orb ;—between those heights
And on the top of either pinnacle,
More keenly than elsewhere in night's blue vault,
Sparkle the stars, as of their station proud.
Thoughts are not busier in the mind of man
Than the mute agents stirring there :—alone
Here do I sit and watch.'

[MIST OPENING IN THE HILLS.]

So was he lifted gently from the ground,
And with their freight homeward the shepherds **moved**
Through the dull mist, I following—when a step,
A single step, that freed me from the skirts
Of the blind vapour, opened to my view
Glory beyond all glory ever seen
By waking sense or by the dreaming soul !
The appearance, instantaneously disclosed,
Was of a mighty city—boldly say
A wilderness of building, sinking far
And self-withdrawn into a boundless depth
Far sinking into splendour—without end !
Fabric it seemed of diamond and of gold,
With alabaster domes, and silver spires,
And blazing terrace upon terrace, high
Uplifted ; here, serene pavilions bright,
In avenues disposed ; there, towers begirt
With battlements that on their restless fronts
Bore stars—illumination of all gems !
By earthly nature had the effect been **wrought**
Upon the dark materials of the storm
Now pacified : on them, and on the cove
And mountain-steeps and summits, whereunto

The vapours had receded, taking there
Their station under a cerulean sky.
Oh, 'twas an unimaginable sight !
Clouds, mists, streams, watery rocks and emerald turf,
Clouds of all tincture, rocks and sapphire sky
Confused, commingled, mutually inflamed,
Molten together, and composing thus,
Each lost in each, that marvellous array
Of temple, palace, citadel, and huge
Fantastic pomp of structure without name,
In fleecy folds voluminous enwrapped.
Right in the midst, where interspace appeared
Of open court, an object like a throne
Under a shining canopy of state
Stood fixed ; and fixed resemblance were seen
To implements of ordinary use,
But vast in size, in substance glorified ;
Such as by Hebrew Prophets were beheld
In vision—forms uncouth of mightiest power
For admiration and mysterious awe.
This little Vale, a dwelling-place of Man,
Lay low beneath my feet ; 'twas visible—
I saw not, but I felt that it was there.
That which I *saw* was the revealed abode
Of Spirits in beatitude.

[AMONG THE MOUNTAINS.]

(Greek Divinities.)

Once more to distant ages of the world
Let us revert, and place before our thoughts
The face which rural solitude might wear
To the unenlightened swains of pagan Greece.
—In that fair clime, the lonely herdsman, stretched
On the soft grass through half a summer's day,
With music lulled his indolent repose :
And, in some fit of weariness, if he
When his own breath was silent, chanced to hear

A distant strain, far sweeter than the sounds
Which his poor skill could make, his fancy fetched,
Even from the blazing chariot of the sun,
A beardless Youth, who touched a golden lute,
And filled the illumined groves with ravishment.
The nightly hunter, lifting a bright eye
Up towards the crescent moon, with grateful heart
Called on the lovely wanderer who bestowed
That timely light, to share his joyous sport :
And hence, a beaming Goddess with her Nymphs,
Across the lawn and through the darksome grove.
Not unaccompanied with tuneful notes
By echo multiplied from rock or cave,
Swept in the storm of chase ; as moon and stars
Glance rapidly along the clouded heaven,
When winds are blowing strong. The traveller slaked
His thirst from rill or gushing fount, and thanked
The Naiad. Sunbeams, upon distant hills
Gliding apace, with shadows in their train,
Might, with small help from fancy, be transformed
Into fleet Oreads sporting visibly.
The Zephyrs fanning, as they passed, their wings,
Lacked not, for love, fair objects whom they wooed
With gentle whisper. Withered boughs grotesque,
Stripped of their leaves and twigs by hoary age,
From depth of shaggy covert peeping forth
In the low vale, or on steep mountain side ;
And, sometimes, intermixed with stirring horns
Of the live deer, or goat's depending beard,—
These were the lurking Satyrs, a wild brood
Of gamesome Deities ; or Pan himself,
The simple shepherd's awe-inspiring God !

[THE MOON AMONG TREES.]

Within the soul a faculty abides,
That with interpositions, which would hide
And darken, so can deal that they become
Contingencies of pomp ; and serve to exalt

Her native brightness. As the ample moon,
In the deep stillness of a summer even
Rising behind a thick and lofty grove,
Burns, like an unconsuming fire of light,
In the green trees ; and, kindling on all sides
Their leafy umbrage, turns the dusky veil
Into a substance glorious as her own,
Yea, with her own incorporated, by power
Capacious and serene :—Like power abides
In man's celestial spirit ; virtue thus
Sets forth and magnifies herself ; thus feeds
A calm, a beautiful, and silent fire,
From the encumbrances of mortal life,
From error, disappointment—nay, from guilt ;
And sometimes, so relenting justice wills,
From palpable oppressions of despair.'

[THE SEA SHELL.]

                                    I have seen
A curious child, who dwelt upon a tract
Of inland ground, applying to his ear
The convolutions of a smooth-lipped shell ;
To which, in silence hushed, his very soul
Listened intensely ; and his countenance soon
Brightened with joy ; for from within were heard
Murmurings, whereby the monitor expressed
Mysterious union with its native sea.
Even such a shell the universe itself
Is to the ear of Faith ; and there are times,
I doubt not, when to you it doth impart
Authentic tidings of invisible things ;
Of ebb and flow, and ever-during power ;
And central peace, subsisting at the heart
Of endless agitation. Here you stand,
Adore, and worship, when you know it not ;
Pious beyond the intention of your thought ;
Devout above the meaning of your will.
—Yes, you have felt, and may not cease to feel

The estate of man would be indeed forlorn
If false conclusions of the reasoning power
Made the eye blind, and closed the passages
Through which the ear converses with the heart.
Has not the soul, the being of your life,
Received a shock of awful consciousness,
In some calm season, when these lofty rocks
At night's approach bring down the unclouded sky,
To rest upon their circumambient walls ;
A temple framing of dimensions vast,
And yet not too enormous for the sound
Of human anthems,—choral song, or burst
Sublime of instrumental harmony,
To glorify the Eternal ! What if these
Did never break the stillness that prevails
Here,—if the solemn nightingale be mute,
And the soft woodlark here did never chant
Her vespers,—Nature fails not to provide
Impulse and utterance. The whispering air
Sends inspiration from the shadowy heights,
And blind recesses of the caverned rocks ;
The little rills, and waters numberless,
Inaudible by daylight, blend their notes
With the loud streams : and often, at the hour
When issue forth the first pale stars, is heard,
Within the circuit of this fabric huge,
One voice—the solitary raven, flying
Athwart the concave of the dark blue dome,
Unseen, perchance above all power of sight—
An iron knell ! with echoes from afar
Faint—and still fainter—as the cry, with which
The wanderer accompanies her flight
Through the calm region, fades upon the ear,
Diminishing by distance till it seemed
To expire ; yet from the abyss is caught again,
And yet again recovered !

SONNETS.

[THE GAINS OF RESTRAINT.]

Nuns fret not at their convent's narrow room;
And hermits are contented with their cells;
And students with their pensive citadels;
Maids at the wheel, the weaver at his loom,
Sit blithe and happy; bees that soar for bloom,
High as the highest Peak of Furness-fells,
Will murmur by the hour in foxglove bells:
In truth the prison, unto which we doom
Ourselves, no prison is: and hence for me,
In sundry moods, 'twas pastime to be bound
Within the Sonnet's scanty plot of ground;
Pleased if some Souls (for such there needs must be)
Who have felt the weight of too much liberty,
Should find brief solace there, as I have found.

[ON THE BEACH AT CALAIS.]

It is a beauteous evening, calm and free;
The holy time is quiet as a Nun
Breathless with adoration; the broad sun
Is sinking down in its tranquillity;
The gentleness of heaven broods o'er the Sea:
Listen! the mighty Being is awake,
And doth with his eternal motion make
A sound like thunder—everlastingly.
Dear Child! dear Girl! that walkest with me here,
If thou appear untouched by solemn thought,
Thy nature is not therefore less divine:
Thou liest in Abraham's bosom all the year;
And worship'st at the Temple's inner shrine,
God being with thee when we know it not.

(1802.)

Composed upon Westminster Bridge, Sept. 3, 1802 [? 1803]

Earth has not any thing to show more fair :
Dull would he be of soul who could pass by
A sight so touching in its majesty :
This City now doth, like a garment, wear
The beauty of the morning ; silent, bare,
Ships, towers, domes, theatres, and temples lie
Open unto the fields, and to the sky ;
All bright and glittering in the smokeless air.
Never did sun more beautifully steep
In his first splendour, valley, rock, or hill ;
Ne'er saw I, never felt, a calm so deep !
The river glideth at his own sweet will :
Dear God ! the very houses seem asleep ;
And all that mighty heart is lying still !

Thought of a Briton on the Subjugation of Switzerland.

Two Voices are there ; one is of the sea,
One of the mountains ; each a mighty Voice :
In both from age to age thou didst rejoice,
They were thy chosen music, Liberty !
There came a Tyrant, and with holy glee
Thou fought'st against him ; but hast vainly striven :
Thou from thy Alpine holds at length art driven,
Where not a torrent murmurs heard by thee.
Of one deep bliss thine ear hath been bereft :
Then cleave, O cleave to that which still is left ;
For, high-souled Maid, what sorrow would it be
That Mountain floods should thunder as before,
And Ocean bellow from his rocky shore,
And neither awful Voice be heard by thee !

(1802 or 1803 ?)

MILTON,

WRITTEN IN LONDON, SEPTEMBER 1802.

Milton! thou should'st be living at this hour:
England hath need of thee: she is a fen
Of stagnant waters: altar, sword, and pen,
Fireside, the heroic wealth of hall and bower,
Have forfeited their ancient English dower
Of inward happiness. We are selfish men;
Oh! raise us up, return to us again;
And give us manners, virtue, freedom, power.
Thy soul was like a Star, and dwelt apart:
Thou hadst a voice whose sound was like the sea
Pure as the naked heavens, majestic, free,
So didst thou travel on life's common way,
In cheerful godliness; and yet thy heart
The lowliest duties on herself did lay.

[THE WORLD'S RAVAGES.]

The world is too much with us: late and soon.
Getting and spending, we lay waste our powers:
Little we see in Nature that is ours;
We have given our hearts away, a sordid boon!
This Sea that bares her bosom to the moon;
The winds that will be howling at all hours,
And are up-gathered now like sleeping flowers;
For this, for every thing, we are out of tune;
It moves us not.—Great God! I'd rather be
A Pagan suckled in a creed outworn:
So might I, standing on this pleasant lea,
Have glimpses that would make me less forlorn;
Have sight of Proteus rising from the sea;
Or hear old Triton blow his wreathèd horn.

(1806?)

[THE THRONE OF DEATH.]

Methought I saw the footsteps of a throne
Which mists and vapours from mine eyes did shroud—
Nor view of who might sit thereon allowed ;
But all the steps and ground about were strown
With sights the ruefullest that flesh and bone
Ever put on ; a miserable crowd,
Sick, hale, old, young, who cried before that cloud,
'Thou art our king, O Death ! to thee we groan.'
Those steps I clomb ; the mists before me gave
Smooth way: and I beheld the face of one
Sleeping alone within a mossy cave,
With her face up to heaven ; that seemed to have
Pleasing remembrance of a thought foregone ;
A lovely Beauty in a summer grave !

(1806 ?)

[THE SHOCK OF BEREAVEMENT.]

Surprised by joy—impatient as the Wind
I turned to share the transport—Oh ! with whom
But Thee, deep buried in the silent tomb,
That spot which no vicissitude can find ?
Love, faithful love, recalled thee to my mind—
But how could I forget thee ? Through what power,
Even for the least division of an hour,
Have I been so beguiled as to be blind
To my most grievous loss ?—That thought's return
Was the worst pang that sorrow ever bore,
Save one, one only, when I stood forlorn,
Knowing my heart's best treasure was no more ;
That neither present time, nor years unborn
Could to my sight that heavenly face restore.

(1806 ?)

AFTER-THOUGHT

[Concluding sonnet of the series ' To the River Duddon,' 1820]

I thought of Thee, my partner and my guide,
As being past away.—Vain sympathies !
For, backward, Duddon ! as I cast my eyes,
I see what was, and is, and will abide ;
Still glides the Stream, and shall for ever glide ;
The Form remains, the Function never dies ;
While we, the brave, the mighty, and the wise,
We Men, who in our morn of youth defied
The elements, must vanish ;—be it so !
Enough, if something from our hands have power
To live, and act, and serve the future hour ;
And if, as toward the silent tomb we go,
Through love, through hope, and faith's transcendent
　　dower,
We feel that we are greater than we know.

MUTABILITY.

From low to high doth dissolution climb,
And sink from high to low, along a scale
Of awful notes, whose concord shall not fail ;
A musical but melancholy chime,
Which they can hear who meddle not with crime,
Nor avarice, nor over-anxious care.
Truth fails not ; but her outward forms that bear
The longest date do melt like frosty rime,
That in the morning whitened hill and plain
And is no more ; drop like the tower sublime
Of yesterday, which royally did wear
His crown of weeds, but could not even sustain
Some casual shout that broke the silent air,
Or the unimaginable touch of Time.

(1822.)

To Lady Fitzgerald, in her Seventieth Year.

Such age how beautiful! O Lady bright,
Whose mortal lineaments seem all refined
By favouring Nature and a saintly Mind
To something purer and more exquisite
Than flesh and blood; whene'er thou meet'st my sight,
When I behold thy blanched unwithered cheek,
Thy temples fringed with locks of gleaming white,
And head that droops because the soul is meek,
Thee with the welcome Snowdrop I compare;
That child of winter, prompting thoughts that climb
From desolation toward the genial prime;
Or with the Moon conquering earth's misty air,
And filling more and more with crystal light
As pensive Evening deepens into night.

                   (1827.)

On the Departure of Sir Walter Scott from Abbotsford, for Naples. [1831.]

A trouble, not of clouds, or weeping rain,
Nor of the setting sun's pathetic light
Engendered, hangs o'er Eildon's triple height:
Spirits of Power, assembled there, complain
For kindred Power departing from their sight;
While Tweed, best pleased in chanting a blithe strain,
Saddens his voice again, and yet again
Lift up your hearts, ye Mourners! for the might
Of the whole world's good wishes with him goes;
Blessings and prayers in nobler retinue
Than sceptred king or laurelled conqueror knows,
Follow this wondrous Potentate. Be true,
Ye winds of ocean, and the midland sea,
Wafting your Charge to soft Parthenope!

[Past Years of Home.]

Wansfell![1] this Household has a favoured lot,
Living with liberty on thee to gaze,
To watch while Morn first crowns thee with her rays,
Or when along thy breast serenely float
Evening's angelic clouds.   Yet ne'er a note
Hath sounded (shame upon the Bard!) thy praise
For all that thou, as if from heaven, hast brought
Of glory lavished on our quiet days.
Bountiful Son of Earth! when we are gone
From every object dear to mortal sight,
As soon we shall be, may these words attest
How oft, to elevate our spirits, shone
Thy visionary majesties of light,
How in thy pensive glooms our hearts found rest.

(Dec. 24, 1842)

[1] The Hill that rises to the south east, above Ambleside.

SAMUEL ROGERS.

[SAMUEL ROGERS was born at **Stoke Newington** in 1763 and died in 1855. The dates of his principal poems are—*Pleasures of Memory* 1793, *Epistle to a Friend* 1798, *Human Life* 1819, *Italy* (complete edition) 1834.]

When a poet has become a poet of the past and in the natural course of things his poetry has ceased to be talked about, it is not easy to ascertain how far it may or may not have ceased to be read. Has it ceased to be bought? The answer to that question might be accepted in most cases as answering the other. But in the case of Rogers an element of ambiguity was introduced long since. When a well-known firm some fifty years ago expressed a doubt whether the public would provide a market for a volume he wished them to publish, Rogers, in a tone half serious, half comic, said—'I will *make* them buy it;' and being a rich man and a great lover of art, he sent for Turner and Stothard, and a volume appeared with such adornments as have never been equalled before or since. It was called by a sarcastic friend of mine 'Turner illustrated.'

The Pleasures of Memory is an excellent specimen of what Wordsworth calls 'the *accomplishment* of verse'; and it was well worthy to attract attention and admiration at the time when it appeared; for at that time poetry, with few exceptions, was to be distinguished from prose by versification and little else. *The Pleasures of Memory* is an essay in verse, not wanting in tender sentiment and just reflection, expressed, gracefully no doubt, but with a formal and elaborate grace, and in studiously pointed and carefully poised diction, such as the heroic couplet had been trained to assume since the days of Pope. In 1793 very different days were approaching—days in which poetry was to break its chains, and formality to be thrown to the winds. The didactic dullness of the eighteenth century was presently to be supplanted by the romantic spirit and easy animation of Scott, the amorous appeals of Moore, and the passion of Byron ; whilst mere tenderness, thoughtfulnes and grace were to share its fate, and be trampled in the dust.

An author's name will generally continue long to be associated with that of the work which has first made him known to the world, whether or not it be his best. *The Pleasures of Memory* is probably to this day the best known by name of the author's principal poems. They were seven in number – an *Ode to Superstition, The Pleasures of Memory, An Epistle to a Friend, Columbus, Jacqueline, Human Life,* and *Italy* ; and they were written, the earliest at twenty-two years of age, the latest at seventy-one.

Human Life is a poem of the same type as *The Pleasures of Memory,* and in the same verse. The fault of such poems is that they are about nothing in particular. Their range and scope is so wide that one theme is almost as apposite as another. The poet sets himself to work to think thoughts and devise episodes, and to give them what coherency he can ; the result being, that some are forced and others commonplace. But if such poems are to be written by a poet who is not a philosopher, they could not well be executed by any one with more care and skill than by Rogers.

The subject of *Italy* was better chosen. The poet travels from Geneva to Naples ; and his itinerary brings picturesque features, alternately with romantic traditions and memorable facts in history, into a natural sequence of poetic themes. They are described and related always in a way to please, often with striking effect ; and any one who travels the same road and desires to see with the eyes of a poet what is best worth seeing, and to be reminded of what is best worth remembering, can have no better companion.

The heroic couplet, moreover, is left behind. For before the first of the fifteen years occupied in the composition of *Italy* (1819–34) Spenserian stanzas, *ottava rima,* octosyllabic verse, blank verse, any verse, had found itself to be more in harmony with the poetic spirit of the time. *Italy* is the longest of the author's poems ; and for a poem of such length, blank verse is best. It is a form of verse which, since the Elizabethans, no poet except Milton had hitherto used with what could be called signal success ; and the abrupt contrasts and startling significance of which it was capable in their hands, will always find a place more naturally in dramatic than in narrative poetry. But the blank verse written by Rogers, though not very expressive, flows with an easy and gentle melody, sufficiently varied, and almost free from faults.

Of the other poems, the *Epistle to a Friend* will perhaps be read with the most pleasure. It is short, familiar, and graceful. The subject is entirely within his powers, though wholly remote from his experience. 'Every reader,' he says in the preface, 'turns with pleasure to those passages of Horace, Pope, and Boileau, which describe how they lived and where they dwelt ; and which, being interspersed among their satirical writings, derive a secret and irresistible grace from the contrast, and are admirable examples of what in painting is termed repose ;' and he proceeds to describe a sort of Sabine Farm in which he supposes himself to pass his days in studious seclusion and absolute repose. His real life was the reverse of all this. His house in St. James's Place did indeed exemplify the classic ideal described in his poem ; it was adorned with exquisite works of art, and with these only ; rejecting as inconsistent with purity of taste all ornaments which are ornaments and nothing more ; and in its interior it might be said to be a work of art in itself. But his life was a life of society ; and in the circles which he frequented, including all who were eminent in literature as well as celebrities in every other walk of life, he was more conspicuous by his conversation and by his wit, than admired as a poet. He had kindness of heart, benevolence, and tender emotions : but his wit was a bitter wit ; and it found its way into verse only in the shape of epigrams, too personal and pungent for publication. It may be matter of regret that he did not adopt the converse of the examples he quotes, of Horace, Pope, and Boileau, and intersperse some satirical writings amongst his other works. His poetic gifts were surpassed by half a dozen or more of his contemporaries ; his gift of wit equalled by only one or two. His deliberate and quiet manner of speaking made it the more effective. I remember one occasion on which he threw a satire into a sentence :—' They tell me I say ill-natured things. I have a very weak voice : if I did not say ill-natured things, no one would hear what I said.'

If it is true that he said ill-natured things, it is equally so that he did kind and charitable and generous things, and that he did them in large measure, though, to his credit, with less notoriety.

HENRY TAYLOR.

From 'The Pleasures of Memory.'

Oft may the spirits of the dead descend
To watch the silent slumbers of a friend;
To hover round his evening-walk unseen,
And hold sweet converse on the dusky green;
To hail the spot where first their friendship grew,
And heaven and nature opened to their view!
Oft, when he trims his cheerful hearth, and sees
A smiling circle emulous to please;
There may these gentle guests delight to dwell,
And bless the scene they loved in life so well!
 Oh thou! with whom my heart was wont to share
From Reason's dawn each pleasure and each care;
With whom, alas! I fondly hoped to know
The humble walks of happiness below;
If thy blest nature now unites above
An angel's pity with a brother's love,
Still o'er my life preserve thy mild controul,
Correct my views, and elevate my soul;
Grant me thy peace and purity of mind,
Devout yet cheerful, active yet resigned;
Grant me, like thee, whose heart knew no disguise,
Whose blameless wishes never aimed to rise,
To meet the changes Time and Chance present
With modest dignity and calm content.
When thy last breath, ere Nature sunk to rest,
Thy meek submission to thy God expressed,
When thy last look, ere thought and feeling fled,
A mingled gleam of hope and triumph shed,
What to thy soul its glad assurance gave,
Its hope in death, its triumph o'er the grave?
The sweet Remembrance of unblemished youth,
The still inspiring voice of Innocence and Truth!
 Hail, Memory, hail! in thy exhaustless mine
From age to age unnumbered treasures shine!
Thought and her shadowy brood thy call obey,
And Place and Time are subject to thy sway!

Thy pleasures most we feel, when most alone;
The only pleasures we can call our own.
Lighter than air, Hope's summer-visions die,
If but a fleeting cloud obscure the sky;
If but a beam of sober Reason play,
Lo, Fancy's fairy frost-work melts away!
But can the wiles of Art, the grasp of Power,
Snatch the rich relics of a well-spent hour?
These, when the trembling spirit wings her flight,
Pour round her path a stream of living light,
And gild those pure and perfect realms of rest
Where Virtue triumphs and her sons are blest!

FROM 'HUMAN LIFE.'

When by a good man's grave I muse alone,
Methinks an Angel sits upon the stone,
Like those of old, on that thrice-hallowed night,
Who sate and watched in raiment heavenly bright,
And, with a voice inspiring joy not fear,
Says, pointing upward, 'Know, He is not here;
He is risen!'
        But the day is almost spent;
And stars are kindling in the firmament,
To us how silent—though like ours perchance
Busy and full of life and circumstance;
Where some the paths of Wealth and Power pursue,
Of Pleasure some, of Happiness a few;
And, as the sun goes round—a sun not ours—
While from her lap another Nature showers
Gifts of her own, some from the crowd retire,
Think on themselves, within, without inquire;
At distance dwell on all that passes there,
All that their world reveals of good and fair;
And, as they wander, picturing things, like me,
Not as they are but as they ought to be,
Trace out the journey through their little day,
And fondly dream an idle hour away.

From 'Italy.'

But who comes,
Brushing the floor with what was once, methinks,
A hat of ceremony? On he glides,
Slip-shod, ungartered ; his long suit of black
Dingy, thread-bare, tho', patch by patch, renewed
Till it has almost ceased to be the same.
At length arrived, and with a shrug that pleads
''Tis my necessity !' he stops and speaks,
Screwing a smile into his dinnerless face.
' Blame not a Poet, Signor, for his zeal—
When all are on the wing, who would be last ?
The splendour of thy name has gone before thee ;
And Italy from sea to sea exults,
As well indeed she may ! But I transgress.
He, who has known the weight of praise himself,
Should spare another.' Saying so, he laid
His sonnet, an impromptu, at my feet,
(If his, then Petrarch must have stolen it from him)
And bowed and left me ; in his hollow hand
Receiving my small tribute, a zecchine,
Unconsciously, as doctors do their fees.

My omelet, and a flagon of hill-wine,
Pure as the virgin-spring, had happily
Fled from all eyes ; or, in a waking dream,
I might have sat as many a great man has,
And many a small, like him of Santillane,
Bartering my bread and salt for empty praise.

Am I in Italy? Is this the Mincius?
Are those the distant turrets of Verona?
And shall I sup where Juliet at the Masque
Saw her loved Montague, and now sleeps by him?
Such questions hourly do I ask myself ;
And not a stone, in a cross-way, inscribed
' To Mantua'—' To Ferrara'—but excites
Surprise, and doubt, and self-congratulation.

O Italy, how beautiful thou art!
Yet I could weep—tor thou art lying, alas,
Low in the dust; and we admire thee now
As we admire the beautiful in death.
Thine was a dangerous gift, when thou wast born,
The gift of Beauty. Would thou hadst it not;
Or wert as once, awing the caitiffs vile
That now beset thee, making thee their slave!
Would they had loved thee less, or feared thee more!
——But why despair? Twice hast thou lived already;
Twice shone among the nations of the world,
As the sun shines among the lesser lights
Of heaven; and shalt again. The hour shall come,
When they who think to bind the ethereal spirit,
Who, like the eagle cowering o'er his prey,
Watch with quick eye, and strike and strike again
If but a sinew vibrate, shall confess
Their wisdom folly. Even now the flame
Bursts forth where once it burnt so gloriously,
And, dying, left a splendour like the day,
That like the day diffused itself, and still
Blesses the earth—the light of genius, virtue,
Greatness in thought and act, contempt of death,
God-like example. Echoes that have slept
Since Athens, Lacedæmon, were Themselves,
Since men invoked 'By Those in Marathon!'
Awake along the Ægean; and the dead,
They of that sacred shore, have heard the call,
And thro' the ranks, from wing to wing, are seen
Moving as once they were—instead of rage
Breathing deliberate valour.

CINEVRA.

[From the same.]

If thou shouldst ever come by choice or chance
To Modena, where still religiously
Among her ancient trophies is preserved
Bologna's bucket (in its chain it hangs
Within that reverend tower, the Guirlandine)

Stop at a Palace near the Reggio-gate,
Dwelt in of old by one of the Orsini.
Its noble gardens, terrace above terrace,
And rich in fountains, statues, cypresses,
'Will long detain thee; thro' their arched walks,
Dim at noon-day, discovering many a glimpse
Of knights and dames, such as in old romance,
And lovers, such as in heroic song,
Perhaps the two, for groves were their delight,
That in the spring-time, as alone they sat,
Venturing together on a tale of love,
Read only part that day.——A summer-sun
Sets ere one half is seen; but, ere thou go,
Enter the house—prythee, forget it not—
And look awhile upon a picture there.

'Tis of a Lady in her earliest youth,
The very last of that illustrious race,
Done by Zampieri—but I care not whom.
He, who observes it—ere he passes on,
Gazes his fill, and comes and comes again,
That he may call it up, when far away.

She sits, inclining forward as to speak,
Her lips half-open, and her finger up,
As tho' she said 'Beware!' her vest of gold
Broidered with flowers, and clasped from head to foot,
An emerald-stone in every golden clasp;
And on her brow, fairer than alabaster,
A coronet of pearls. But then her face,
So lovely, yet so arch, so full of mirth,
The overflowings of an innocent heart—
It haunts me still, tho' many a year has fled,
Like some wild melody!

                              Alone it hangs
Over a mouldering heir-loom, its companion,
An oaken-chest, half-eaten by the worm,
But richly carved by Anthony of Trent
With scripture-stories from the Life of Christ;
A chest that came from Venice, and had held
The ducal robes of some old Ancestor.

That by the way—it may be true or false—
But don't forget the picture ; and thou wilt not,
When thou hast heard the tale they told me there.

 She was an only child ; from infancy
The joy, the pride of an indulgent Sire.
Her Mother dying of the gift she gave,
That precious gift, what else remained to him ?
The young Ginevra was his all in life,
Still as she grew, for ever in his sight ;
And in her fifteenth year became a bride,
Marrying an only son, Francesco Doria,
Her playmate from her birth, and her first love.

 Just as she looks there in her bridal dress,
She was all gentleness, all gaiety ;
Her pranks the favourite theme of every tongue.
But now the day was come, the day, the hour,
Now, frowning, smiling, for the hundredth time,
The nurse, that ancient lady, preached decorum ;
And, in the lustre of her youth, she gave
Her hand, with her heart in it, to Francesco.

 Great was the joy; but at the Bridal feast,
When all sat down, the Bride was wanting there.
Nor was she to be found ! Her Father cried
''Tis but to make a trial of our love !'
And filled his glass to all ; but his hand shook,
And soon from guest to guest the panic spread.
'Twas but that instant she had left Francesco,
Laughing and looking back and flying still,
Her ivory tooth imprinted on his finger.
But now, alas, she was not to be found ;
Nor from that hour could anything be guessed,
But that she was not !

     Weary of his life,
Francesco flew to Venice, and forthwith
Flung it away in battle with the Turk.
Orsini lived ; and long might'st thou have seen
An old man wandering as in quest of something,
Something he could not find—he knew not what.
When he was gone the house remained awhile

Silent and tenantless—then went to strangers.
　Full fifty years were past, and all forgot,
When on an idle day, a day of search
Mid the old lumber in the Gallery,
That mouldering chest was noticed ; and 'twas **said**
By one as young, as thoughtless as Ginevra,
' Why not remove it from its lurking place !'
'Twas done as soon as said ; but on the **way**
It burst, it fell ; and lo, a skeleton,
With here and there a pearl, an emerald-sto**ne,**
A golden clasp, clasping a shred of gold.
All else had perished—save a nuptial ring,
And a small seal, her mother's legacy,
Engraven with **a name, the name of both,**
' **Ginevra.** '

WILLIAM LISLE BOWLES.

[THE REV. WILLIAM LISLE BOWLES was born at King's Sutton in 1762. His chief work is his *Sonnets*, first published in 1789. He died at Salisbury in 1850.]

It was the candle of Bowles that lit the fire of Coleridge. We have it on record in the *Biographia Literaria* that to the author of *The Ancient Mariner*, bewildered at seventeen between metaphysics and theological controversy, and utterly out of sympathy with the artificialities of the Popesque school, the early sonnets of Bowles came almost in the light of a revelation. In a copy preserved at South Kensington he writes of them later as 'having done his heart more good than all the other books he ever read excepting his Bible.' Those who to-day turn to the much-praised verses will scarcely find in their pensive amenity that enduring charm which they presented to the hungry and restless soul of Coleridge, seeking its fitting food in unpropitious places. They exhibit a grace of expression, a delicate sensibility, and above all a 'musical sweet melancholy' that is especially grateful in certain moods of mind ; but with lapse of time and change of fashion they have grown a little thin and faint and colourless. Of Bowles's remaining works it is not necessary to speak. He was overmatched in his controversy with Byron as to Pope, and the blunt

'Stick to thy sonnets, Bowles,—at least they pay'

of the former must be accepted as the final word upon the poetical efforts of the cultivated and amiable Canon of Salisbury.

AUSTIN DOBSON.

WRITTEN AT OSTEND.

How sweet the tuneful bells responsive peal!
As when at opening morn, the fragrant breeze
Breathes on the trembling sense of pale disease,
So piercing to my heart their force I feel!
And hark! with lessening cadence now they fall!
And now along the white and level tide,
They fling their melancholy music wide;
Bidding me many a tender thought recall
Of summer-days, and those delightful years
When from an ancient tower in life's fair prime,
The mournful magic of their mingling chime
First waked my wondering childhood into tears!
But seeming now, when all those days are o'er,
The sounds of joy once heard and heard no more.

INFLUENCE OF TIME ON GRIEF.

O Time! who know'st a lenient hand to lay
Softest on sorrow's wound, and slowly thence,
Lulling to sad repose the weary sense,
The faint pang stealest unperceived away;
On thee I rest my only hope at last,
And think, when thou hast dried the bitter tear
That flows in vain o'er all my soul held dear,
I may look back on every sorrow past,
And meet life's peaceful evening with a smile;—
As some lone bird, at day's departing hour,
Sings in the sunbeam, of the transient shower
Forgetful, though its wings are wet the while;—
Yet ah! how much must that poor heart endure
Which hopes from thee, and thee alone, a cure.

NOVEMBER, 1793.

There is strange music in the stirring wind,
When lowers the autumnal eve, and all alone
To the dark wood's cold covert thou art gone,
Whose ancient trees on the rough slope reclined
Rock, and at times scatter their tresses sere.
If in such shades, beneath their murmuring,
Thou late hast passed the happier hours of spring,
With sadness thou wilt mark the fading year;
Chiefly if one, with whom such sweets at morn
Or evening thou hast shared, far off shall stray.
O Spring, return! return, auspicious May!
But sad will be thy coming, and forlorn,
If she return not with thy cheering ray,
Who from these shades is gone, gone far away.

BEREAVEMENT.

Whose was that gentle voice, that, whispering sweet,
Promised methought long days of bliss sincere!
Soothing it stole on my deluded ear,
Most like soft music, that might sometimes cheat
Thoughts dark and drooping! 'Twas the voice of Hope.
Of love, and social scenes, it seemed to speak,
Of truth, of friendship, of affection meek;
That oh! poor friend, might to life's downward slope
Lead us in peace, and bless our latest hours.
Ah me! the prospect saddened as she sung;
Loud on my startled ear the death-bell rung;
Chill darkness wrapt the pleasurable bowers,
Whilst Horror pointing to yon breathless clay,
'No peace be thine,' exclaimed, 'away, away!'

SAMUEL TAYLOR COLERIDGE.

[SAMUEL TAYLOR COLERIDGE was born at Ottery Saint Mary in the year 1772, was educated at Christ's Hospital and Jesus College, Cambridge, and died in 1834, at Highgate, in the house of Mr. Gillman, under whose friendly care he had passed the last eighteen years of his life, during which years he wrote but little. His first volume of poems was published at Bristol in 1796, and in 1798, Wordsworth's famous volume of *Lyrical Ballads*, to which Coleridge contributed *The Ancient Mariner*, together with some other pieces. *Christabel*, after lying long in manuscript, was printed in 1816, three editions of it appearing in one year; and in the next year Coleridge published a collection of his chief poems, under the title of *Sibylline Leaves*, 'in allusion,' as he says, 'to the fragmentary and wildly-scattered state in which they had been long suffered to remain.' A desultory writer both in prose and verse, he published the first really collective edition of his *Poetical and Dramatic Works* in the year 1828, in three volumes arranged by himself; a third and more complete issue of which, arranged by another hand, appeared in 1834, the year of his death. The latest reprint[1], with notes and an excellent memoir, and some poems not included in any earlier collection, is founded on that final edition of 1834.]

Coleridge's prose writings on philosophy, politics, religion and criticism, were but one element in a whole life-time of endeavours to present the then recent metaphysics of Germany to English readers, as a legitimate expansion of the older, classical and native, masters of what has been variously called the *à priori*, or absolute, or spiritual, or Platonic view of things. To introduce that spiritual philosophy, as represented by the more transcendental parts of Kant, and by Schelling, into all subjects, as a system of reason in them, one and ever identical with itself, however various the matter through which it was diffused, became with him the motive of an unflagging enthusiasm, which seems to have been the one thread of continuity in a life otherwise

[1] London: Basil Montagu Pickering, 1877.

singularly wanting in unity of purpose, and in which he was
certainly far from uniformly at his best. Fragmentary and
obscure, but often eloquent, and always at once earnest and
ingenious, those writings, supplementing his remarkable gift of
conversation, were directly and indirectly influential, even on
some the furthest removed from Coleridge's own masters; on
John Stuart Mill, for instance, and some of the earlier writers of
the *high-church* school. Like his verse, they display him also in
two other characters—as a student of words, and as a psychologist,
that is, as a more minute observer than other men of the phenomena of mind. To note the recondite associations of words, old
or new; to expound the logic, the reasonable soul, of their various
uses; to recover the interest of older writers who had had a
phraseology of their own—this was a vein of enquiry allied to
his undoubted gift of tracking out and analysing curious modes
of thought. A quaint fragment on *Human Life* might serve to
illustrate his study of the earlier English philosophical poetry.
The latter gift, that power of the 'subtle-souled psychologist,' as
Shelley calls him, seems to have been connected with a tendency
to disease in the physical temperament, to something of a morbid
want of balance in the parts where the physical and intellectual
elements mix most intimately together, with a kind of languid
visionariness, deep-seated in the very constitution of the 'nar-
cotist' who had quite a gift for 'plucking the poisons of self-harm,'
and which the actual habit of taking opium, accidentally acquired,
did but reinforce. This morbid languor of nature, connected both
with his fitfulness of purpose and his rich delicate dreaminess,
qualifies Coleridge's poetic composition even more than his prose;
his verse, with the exception of his avowedly political poems,
being, unlike that of the 'Lake School,' to which in some respects
he belongs, singularly unaffected by any moral, or professional, or
personal effort and ambition,—'written,' as he says, 'after the
more violent emotions of sorrow, to give him pleasure, when
perhaps nothing else could;' but coming thus, indeed, very close
to his own most intimately personal characteristics, and having
a certain languidly soothing grace or cadence, for its most fixed
quality, from first to last. After some Platonic soliloquy on a
flower opening on a fine day in February, he goes on—

> ' Dim similitudes
> Weaving in mortal strains, I've stolen one hour
> From anxious self, life's cruel task-master!

And the warm wooings of this sunny day
Tremble along my frame and harmonise
The attempered organ, that even saddest thoughts
Mix with some sweet sensations, like harsh tunes
Played deftly on a soft-toned instrument.'

The expression of two opposed yet allied elements of sensibility in these lines is very true to Coleridge ;—the grievous agitation, the grievous listlessness, almost never entirely relieved, with a certain physical voluptuousness. He has spoken several times of the scent of the bean-field in the air : the tropical notes in a chilly climate—his is a nature which will make the most of these, which finds a sort of caress in these things. *Kubla Khan,* a fragment of a poem actually composed in some certainly not quite healthy sleep, is perhaps chiefly interesting as showing, by the mode of its composition, how physical, how much a matter of a diseased and valetudinarian temperament in its moments of relief, Coleridge's happiest gift really was ; and, side by side with *Kubla Khan,* should be read, as Coleridge placed it, the *Pains of Sleep,* to illustrate that retarding physical burden in his temperament, that 'unimpassioned grief,' the source of which was so near the source of those pleasures. Connected also with this, and again in contrast with Wordsworth, is the limited quantity of his poetical performance, which he himself regrets so eloquently in the lines addressed to Wordsworth after his recitation of *The Prelude.* It is like some exotic plant just managing to blossom a little in the somewhat un-English air of Coleridge's own birth-place, but never quite well there.

The period of Coleridge's residence at Nether Stowey, 1797–1798, was his *annus mirabilis.* Nearly all the chief works by which his poetic fame will live were then composed or planned. What shapes itself for criticism as the main phenomenon of Coleridge's poetic life, is not, as with most poets, the gradual development of a poetic gift, determined, enriched, retarded, by the circumstances of the poet's life, but the sudden blossoming, through one short season, of such a gift already perfect in its kind, which thereafter deteriorates as suddenly, with something like premature old age. Connecting this phenomenon with the leading motive of his prose writings, we might note it as the deterioration of a productive or creative power into one merely metaphysical or discursive. In the unambitious conception of his function as a poet, and in the limited quantity of his poetical performance, as

I have said, he was a contrast to his friend Wordsworth. That friendship with Wordsworth, the chief 'developing' circumstance of his poetic life, comprehended a very close intellectual sympathy ; and in this association chiefly, lies whatever truth there may be in the popular classification of Coleridge as a member of what is called the 'Lake School.' Coleridge's philosophical speculations do really turn on the ideas which underlay Wordsworth's poetical practice. His prose works are one long explanation of all that is involved in that famous distinction between the Fancy and the Imagination. Of what is understood by both as the imaginative quality in the use of mere poetic figures, we may take some words of Shakespeare as an example :—

> 'My cousin Suffolk,
> My soul shall thine keep company to heaven:
> Tarry, sweet soul, for mine, then fly abreast.'

The complete infusion here, of the figure into the thought, so vividly realised that though the birds are not actually mentioned yet the sense of their flight, conveyed to us by the single word 'abreast,' comes to be more than half of the thought itself ;— this, as the expression of exalted feeling, is an instance of what Coleridge meant by Imagination. And this sort of identification of the poet's thought, of himself, with the image or figure which serves him, is the secret, sometimes, of a singularly entire realisation of that image, which makes this figure of Coleridge's, for instance, 'imaginative' :—

> 'Amid the howl of more than wintry storms,
> The halcyon hears the voice of vernal hours
> Already on the wing.'

There are many such figures both in Coleridge's prose and verse. He has too his passages of that sort of impassioned contemplation on the permanent and elementary conditions of nature and humanity, which Wordsworth held to be the essence of the poetic life, and its object to awaken in other men—those 'moments, as Coleridge says, addressing him,—

> 'Moments awful,
> Now in thy inner life, and now abroad,
> When power streamed from thee, and thy soul received
> The light reflected, as a light bestowed.'

The whole of the poem from which those lines are taken, ' composed on the night after Wordsworth's recitation of a poem on the growth of an individual mind,' is, in its strain of impassioned contemplation, and in the combined justness and elevation of its philosophical expression—

> ' high and passionate thoughts
> To their own music chanted ; '—

entirely sympathetic with *The Prelude* which it celebrates, and of which the subject is, in effect, the generation of the spirit of the ' Lake poetry.' The *Lines to Joseph Cottle* have the same philosophically imaginative character ; the *Ode to Dejection* being Coleridge's most sustained effort of this sort.

It is in a highly sensitive apprehension of the aspects of external nature that Coleridge identifies himself most closely with one of the main tendencies of the ' Lake School ; ' a tendency instinctive, and no mere matter of theory, in him as in Wordsworth. That record of the

> ' green light
> Which lingers in the west,'

and again, of

> ' the western sky
> And its peculiar tint of yellow green,'

which Byron found ludicrously untrue, but which surely needs no defence, is a characteristic example of a singular watchfulness for the minute fact and expression of natural scenery, pervading all he writes—a closeness to the exact physiognomy of nature, having something to do with that idealistic philosophy, which sees in the external world no mere concurrence of mechanical agencies, but an animated body, informed and made expressive, like the body of man, by an indwelling intelligence. It was a tendency, doubtless, in the air, for Shelley too is affected by it, and Turner, with the school of landscape which followed him. ' I had found,' Coleridge tells us,

> ' That outward forms, the loftiest, still receive
> Their finer influence from the world within ;
> Fair ciphers of vague import, where the eye
> Traces no spot, in which the heart may read
> History and prophecy . . . .'

and this induces in him no indifference to actual colour and form and process, but such minute realism as this—

> 'The thin grey cloud is spread on high,
> It covers but not hides the sky.
> The moon is behind and at the full;
> And yet she looks both small and dull;'

or this, which has a touch of 'romantic' weirdness—

> 'Nought was green upon the oak
> But moss and rarest misletoe;'

or this—

> 'There is not wind enough to twirl
> The one red leaf, the last of its clan,
> That dances as often as dance it can,
> Hanging so light, and hanging so high,
> On the topmost twig that looks up at the sky;'—

or this, with a weirdness again, like that of some wild French etcher—

> 'Lo! the new-moon winter-bright!
> And over-spread with phantom light,
> (With swimming phantom light o'erspread,
> But rimmed and circled with a silver thread,)
> I see the old moon in her lap, foretelling
> The coming on of rain and squally blast.'

He has the same imaginative apprehension of the silent and unseen processes of nature, its 'ministries' of dew and frost, for instance; **as when he writes in April**—

> 'A balmy night! and though the stars be dim,
> Yet let us think upon the vernal showers
> That gladden the green earth, and we shall find
> A pleasure in the dimness of the stars.'

Of such imaginative treatment of landscape there is no better instance than in the description of *the Dell*, in *Fears in Solitude*—

> 'A green and silent spot amid the hills,
> A small and silent dell! O'er stiller place
> No singing sky-lark ever poised himself—
>   'But the dell,
> Bathed by the mist is fresh and delicate
> As vernal cornfield, or the unripe flax
> When, through its half-transparent stalks, **at eve,**
> The level sunshine glimmers with green light—

> ' The gust that roared and died away
> To the distant tree '—
>   ' heard and only heard
> In this low dell, bowed not the delicate grass.'

This curious dwelling of the mind on one particular spot, till it seems to attain real expression and a sort of soul in it—a mood so characteristic of the 'Lake School'—occurs in an earnest political poem, 'written in April, 1798, during the alarm of an invasion ;' and that silent dell is the background against which the tumultuous fears of the poet are in strong relief, while the quiet sense of it, maintained all through them, gives a real poetic unity to the piece. Good political poetry—political poetry that shall be permanently moving—can, perhaps, only be written on motives which, for those whom they concern, have ceased to be open questions and are really beyond argument ; and Coleridge's political poems are for the most part on open questions. For although it was a great part of his intellectual ambition to subject political questions to the action of the fundamental ideas of his philosophy, he was still an ardent partisan, first on one side, then on the other, of the actual politics of the end of the last and the beginning of the present century, where there is still room for much difference of opinion. Yet *The Destiny of Nations*, though formless as a whole, and unfinished, has many traces of his most elevated speculation, cast into that sort of imaginative philosophical expression, in which, in effect, the language itself is inseparable from, or a part of the thought. *France, an Ode*, begins with the famous apostrophe to Liberty :—

> ' Ye Clouds ! that far above me float and pause,
>   Whose pathless march no mortal may control !
>   Ye Ocean-Waves ! that wheresoe'er ye roll,
> Yield homage only to eternal laws !
> Ye Woods ! that listen to the night-bird's singing,
>   Midway the smooth and perilous slope reclined,
> Save when your own imperious branches swinging,
>   Have made a solemn music of the wind !
> Where like a man beloved of God,
> Through glooms which never woodman trod,
>   How oft, pursuing fancies holy,
> My moonlight way o'er flowering weeds I wound,
> Inspired, beyond the guess of folly,
> By each rude shape and wild unconquerable sound !

> O ye loud Waves! and O ye Forests high!
>   And O ye Clouds that far above me soar'd!
> Thou rising Sun! thou blue rejoicing Sky!
> Yea. everything that is and will be free!
> Bear witness for me, wheresoe'er ye be,
> With what deep worship I have still adored
>   The spirit of divinest liberty.'

And the whole ode, though, in Coleridge's way, not quite equal
to that exordium, is an example of strong national sentiment, partly
in indignant reaction against his own earlier sympathy with the
French republic, inspiring a composition which, in spite of some
turgid lines, really justifies itself as poetry, and has that true unity
of effect which the ode requires. Liberty, after all his hopes of
young France, is only to be found in nature :—

> 'Thou speedest on thy subtle pinions
>   The guide of homeless winds, and playmate of the waves!'

In his changes of political sentiment Coleridge was associated
with the 'Lake School;' and there is yet one other very different
sort of sentiment in which he is one with that school, yet all
himself, his sympathy, namely, with the animal world. That was
a sentiment connected at once with the love of outward nature
in himself and in the 'Lake School,' and its assertion of the natural
affections in their simplicity ; with the homeliness and pity, conse-
quent upon that assertion. The *Lines to a Young Ass*, tethered,

> 'Where the close-eaten grass is scarcely seen,
>   While sweet around her waves the tempting green,'

which had seemed merely whimsical in their day, indicate a vein
of interest constant in Coleridge's poems, and at its height in his
chief poems—in *Christabel*, where it has its effect, as it were anti-
pathetically, in the vivid realisation of the serpentine element in
Geraldine's nature ; and in *The Ancient Mariner*, whose fate is
interwoven with that of the wonderful bird, the curse for whose
death begins to pass away at the Mariner's blessing of the water-
snakes, and where the moral of the love of all creatures, as a sort of
religious duty, is definitely expressed.

Christabel, though not printed till 1816, was written mainly in
the year 1797. *The Rime of the Ancient Mariner* was printed
as a contribution to the *Lyrical Ballads*, in 1798. These two
poems belong to the great year of Coleridge's poetic production,

his twenty-fifth year. In poetic quality, above all in that most
poetic of all qualities, a keen sense of and delight in beauty, the
infection of which lays hold upon the reader, they are quite out
of proportion to all his other composition. The form in both is
that of the ballad, with some of its terminology, and some also
of its quaint conceits. They connect themselves with that revival
of ballad literature, of which Percy's *Relics*, and, in another way,
Macpherson's *Ossian* are monuments, and which afterwards so
powerfully affected Scott.

> 'Young-eyed poesy
> All deftly masked as hoar antiquity,'—

The Ancient Mariner, as also in its measure *Christabel*, is a
'romantic' poem, impressing us by bold invention, and appeal-
ing to that taste for the supernatural, that longing for a *shudder*,
to which the 'romantic' school in Germany, and its derivatives
in England and France, directly ministered. In Coleridge personally, this taste had been encouraged by his odd and out-of-
the-way reading in the old-fashioned literature of the marvellous—
books like Purchas's *Pilgrims*, early voyages like Hakluyt's, old
naturalists and visionary moralists like Thomas Burnet, from whom
he quotes the motto of *The Ancient Mariner—Facile credo, plures
esse naturas invisibiles quam visibiles in rerum universitate, &c.*
Fancies of the strange things which may very well happen, even
in broad daylight, to men shut up alone in ships far off on the sea,
seem to have arisen in the human mind in all ages with a peculiar
readiness, and often have about them, from the story of the theft
of Dionysus downwards, the fascination of a certain dreamy
grace, which distinguishes them from other kinds of marvellous
inventions. This sort of fascination *The Ancient Mariner* brings
to its highest degree ; it is the delicacy, the dreamy grace in his
presentation of the marvellous, which makes Coleridge's work so
remarkable. The too palpable intruders from a spiritual world,
in almost all ghost literature, in Scott and Shakespeare even, have
a kind of coarseness or crudeness. Coleridge's power is in the
very fineness with which, as with some really ghostly finger, he
brings home to our inmost sense his inventions, daring as they
are—the skeleton ship, the polar spirit, the inspiriting of the dead
bodies of the ship's crew ; *The Rime of the Ancient Mariner* has
the plausibility, the perfect adaptation to reason and the general
aspect of life, which belongs to the marvellous when actually
presented as part of a credible experience, in our dreams. Doubt

less the mere experience of the opium-eater, the habit he must almost necessarily fall into of noting the more elusive phenomena of dreams, had something to do with that ; in its essence, however, it is connected with a more purely intellectual circumstance in the development of Coleridge's poetic gift. Some one once asked William Blake, to whom Coleridge has many resemblances, when either is at his best, (that whole episode of the inspiriting of the ship's crew in *The Ancient Mariner* being comparable to Blake's well-known design of the morning stars singing together,) whether he had ever seen a ghost, and was surprised when the famous seer, who ought, one might think, to have seen so many, answered frankly, 'Only once!' His 'spirits,' at once more delicate, and so much more real than any ghost—at once the burden and the privilege of his temperament — like it, were an integral element in his every-day life. And the difference of mood expressed in that question and its answer, is indicative of a change of temper in regard to the supernatural, which has passed over the whole modern mind, and of which the true measure is the influence of the writings of Swedenborg : and what that change is we may see, if we compare the vision by which Swedenborg was called, as he thought, to his work, with the ghost which *called* Hamlet ; or the spells of Marlowe's *Faust* with those of Goethe's. The modern mind, so minutely self-scrutinising, if it is to be affected at all by a sense of the supernatural, requires to be more finely touched than was possible in the older romantic presentment of it. The spectral object, so crude, so impossible, has become plausible, as ' the spot upon the brain that will show itself without,' and is understood to be but a condition of one's own mind, for which, according to the scepticism latent at least in so much of our modern philosophy, the so-called real things themselves are but *spectra,* after all.

It is this finer, more delicately marvellous supernaturalism, the fruit of his more delicate psychology, which Coleridge infuses into romantic narrative, itself also then a new, or revived thing in English literature ; and with a fineness of weird effect in *The Ancient Mariner,* unknown in those old, more simple, romantic legends and ballads. It is a flower of medieval, or later German romance, growing up in the peculiarly compounded atmosphere of modern psychological speculation, and putting forth in it wholly new qualities. The quaint prose commentary, which runs side by side with the verse of *The Ancient Mariner,* illustrates this—

a composition of quite a different shade of beauty and merit from that of the verse which it accompanies, connecting this the chief poem of Coleridge with his philosophy, and emphasizing in it that psychological element of which I have spoken, its curious soul-lore.

Completeness, the perfectly rounded unity and wholeness of the impression it leaves on the mind of a reader who really gives himself to it,—that, too, is one of the characteristics of a really excellent work, in the poetic, as in every other kind of art; and by this completeness *The Ancient Mariner* certainly gains upon *Christabel*,—a completeness, entire as that of Wordsworth's *Leech-gatherer*, or Keats's *Saint Agnes' Eve*, each typical in its way of such wholeness or entirety of effect on a careful reader. It is Coleridge's own great complete work, the one really finished thing, in a life of many beginnings. *Christabel* remained a fragment—the first, and portions of a second, part, on which two other parts should have followed, each with its own 'conclusion'; and we seem to have lost more by its incompleteness than the mere amount of excellent verse; for what Coleridge tells us about it suggests the notion of a very exquisitely limited design, with that pleasing sense of unity, which is secured in the *The Ancient Mariner*, partly by the skill with which the incidents of the marriage-feast break in, dreamily, from time to time, upon the main story; and with which the whole night-mare story itself is made to end, so pleasantly and reassuringly, among the clear, fresh sounds and lights of the bay, where it began, with

> 'The moon-light steeped in silentness
> The steady weather-cock.'

So different from *The Rime of the Ancient Mariner* in regard to this completeness of effect, *Christabel* illustrates the same complexion of motives, the same intellectual situation. Here too the work is that peculiar to one who touches the characteristic motives of the old romantic ballad in a spirit made subtle and fine by modern reflexion, and which we feel, I think, in such passages as—

> 'But though my slumber had gone by,
> This dream it would not pass away—
> It seems to live upon mine eye;'—

and—

> 'For she belike, hath drunken deep
> Of all the blessedness of sleep;'—

and again—

> ' With such perplexity of mind
> As dreams too lively leave behind.'

And the gift of handling the finer passages of human feeling, at once with power and delicacy, which was another of the results of that finer psychology, of his exquisitely refined habit of self-reflexion, is illustrated by a passage on Friendship in the *Second Part :*—

> ' Alas ! they had been friends in youth ;
> But whispering tongues can poison truth ;
> And constancy lives in realms above ;
> And life is thorny ; and youth is vain ;
> And to be wroth with one we love,
> Doth work like madness in the brain.
> And thus it chanced, as I divine,
> With Roland and Sir Leoline.
> Each spake words of high disdain
> And insult to his heart's best brother :
> They parted—ne'er to meet again !
> But never either found another
> To free the hollow heart from paining—
> They stood aloof the scars remaining,
> Like cliffs which had been rent asunder ;
> A dreary sea now flows between ;—
> But neither heat, nor frost. nor thunder,
> Shall wholly do away, I ween,
> The marks of that which once hath been.'

I suppose these lines leave almost every reader with a quickened sense of the beauty and compass of human feeling ; and it is the sense of such richness and beauty which, in spite of his ' dejection,' in spite of that burden of his morbid lassitude, accompanies Coleridge himself through life. A warm poetic joy in every thing beautiful, whether it be a moral sentiment, like the friendship of Roland or Leoline, or only the flakes of falling light from the water-snakes—this joy, visiting him, now and again, after sickly dreams, waking or sleeping, as a relief not to be forgotten, and with such a power of felicitous expression that the infection of it passes irresistibly to the reader,—this is the predominant quality in the matter of his poetry, as cadence is the predominant quality of its form. ' We bless Thee for our creation ! ' he might have said, in his later period of definite religious assent, ' because the world is so beautiful ; the world of ideas—living spirits, detached from the divine nature itself, to inform and lift the heavy mass of material things; the world of man, above all in his melodious and intelligible speech ; the world of living creatures and natural scenery; the world of dreams. What he really did say, by way of a *Tombless Epitaph*, is true enough of himself—

> 'Sickness, 'tis true,
> Whole years of weary days, besieged him close,
> Even to the gates and inlets of his life!
> But it is true, no less, that strenuous, firm,
> And with a natural gladness, he maintained
> The citadel unconquered, and in joy
> Was strong to follow the delightful Muse.
> For not a hidden path, that to the shades
> Of the beloved Parnassian forest leads,
> Lurked undiscovered by him; not a rill
> There issues from the fount of Hippocrene,
> But he had traced it upward to its source,
> Through open glade, dark glen, and secret dell,
> Knew the gay wild flowers on its banks, and culled
> Its med'cinable herbs. Yea, oft alone,
> Piercing the long-neglected holy cave,
> The haunt obscure of old Philosophy,
> He bade with lifted torch its starry walls
> Sparkle, as erst they sparkled to the flame
> Of odorous lamps tended by Saint and Sage.
> O framed for calmer times and nobler hearts !
> O studious Poet, eloquent for truth !
> Philosopher ! contemning wealth and death,
> Yet docile, childlike, full of Life and Love !

WALTER H. PATER.

Time, Real and Imaginary.

An Allegory.

On the wide level of a mountain's head,
(I knew not where, but 'twas some faery place)
Their pinions, ostrich-like, for sails outspread,
Two lovely children run an endless race,
  A sister and a brother!
  That far outstripped the other;
 Yet ever runs she with reverted face,
 And looks and listens for the boy behind:
  For he, alas! is blind!
O'er rough and smooth with even step he passed,
And knows not whether he be first or last.

Love.

All thoughts, all passions, all delights,
Whatever stirs this mortal frame,
All are but ministers of Love,
 And feed his sacred flame.

Oft in my waking dreams do I
Live o'er again that happy hour,
When midway on the mount I lay,
 Beside the ruined tower.

The moonshine, stealing o'er the scene,
Had blended with the lights of eve;
And she was there, my hope, my joy,
 My own dear Genevieve!

She leaned against the armed man,
The statue of the armed knight;
She stood and listened to my lay,
 Amid the lingering light.

Few sorrows hath she of her own,
My hope! my joy! my Genevieve!
She loves me best, whene'er I sing
    The songs that make her grieve.

I played a soft and doleful air,
I sang an old and moving story—
An old rude song, that suited well
    That ruin wild and hoary.

She listened with a flitting blush,
With downcast eyes and modest grace;
For well she knew, I could not choose
    But gaze upon her face.

I told her of the Knight that wore
Upon his shield a burning brand;
And that for ten long years he wooed
    The Lady of the Land.

I told her how he pined; and ah!
The deep, the low, the pleading tone
With which I sang another's love,
    Interpreted my own.

She listened with a flitting blush,
With downcast eyes, and modest grace;
And she forgave me, that I gazed
    Too fondly on her face!

But when I told the cruel scorn
That crazed that bold and lovely Knight,
And that he crossed the mountain-woods,
    Nor rested day nor night;

That sometimes from the savage den,
And sometimes from the darksome shade,
And sometimes starting up at once
    In green and sunny glade,—

There came and looked him in the face
An angel beautiful and bright;
And that he knew it was a Fiend,
    This miserable Knight!

And that unknowing what he did,
He leaped amid a murderous band,
And saved from outrage worse than death
    The Lady of the Land;—

And how she wept, and clasped his knees;
And how she tended him in vain—
And ever strove to expiate
    The scorn that crazed his brain;—

And that she nursed him in a cave;
And how his madness went away,
When on the yellow forest leaves
    A dying man he lay;—

His dying words—but when I reached
That tenderest strain of all the ditty,
My faltering voice and pausing harp
    Disturbed her soul with pity!

All impulses of soul and sense
Had thrilled my guileless Genevieve;
The music, and the doleful tale,
    The rich and balmy eve;

And hopes, and fears that kindle hope,
An undistinguishable throng,
And gentle wishes, long subdued,
    Subdued and cherished long!

She wept with pity and delight,
She blushed with love, and virgin shame;
And like the murmur of a dream,
    I heard her breathe my name.

Her bosom heaved—she stept aside,
As conscious of my look she stept—
Then suddenly, with timorous eye
    She fled to me and wept.

She half enclosed me with her arms,
She pressed me with a meek embrace;
And bending back her head, looked up,
    And gazed upon my face.

'Twas partly love, and partly fear,
And partly 'twas a bashful art,
That I might rather feel, than see,
    The swelling of her heart.

I calmed her fears, and she was calm,
And told her love with virgin-pride;
And so I won my Genevieve,
    My bright and beauteous Bride.

SONNET.

As when far off the warbled strains are heard,
That soar on Morning's wing the vales among,
Within his cage the imprisoned matin bird
Swells the full chorus with a generous song:
He bathes no pinion in the dewy light,
No father's joy, no lover's bliss he shares,
Yet still the rising radiance cheers his sight;
His fellows' freedom soothes the captive's cares!
Thou, Fayette! who didst wake with startling voice
Life's better sun from that long wintry night,
Thus in thy country's triumphs shalt rejoice,
And mock with raptures high the dungeon's might:
For lo! the morning struggles into day,
And Slavery's spectres shriek and vanish from the ray!

The Eolian Harp.

[Composed at Clevedon, Somersetshire.]

My pensive Sara! thy soft cheek reclined
Thus on mine arm, most soothing sweet it is
To sit beside our cot, our cot o'ergrown
With white-flowered jasmin, and the broad-leaved myrtle,
(Meet emblems they of Innocence and Love!)
And watch the clouds, that late were rich with light,
Slow saddening round, and mark the star of eve
Serenely brilliant (such should wisdom be)
Shine opposite! How exquisite the scents
Snatched from yon bean-field! and the world so hushed!
The stilly murmur of the distant sea
Tells us of silence. And that simplest lute,
Placed length-ways in the clasping casement, hark!
How by the desultory breeze caressed,
Like some coy maid half-yielding to her lover,
It pours such sweet upbraiding, as must needs
Tempt to repeat the wrong! And now, its strings
Boldlier swept, the long sequacious notes
Over delicious surges sink and rise,
Such a soft floating witchery of sound
As twilight Elfins make, when they at eve
Voyage on gentle gales from Fairy-Land,
Where melodies round honey-dropping flowers,
Footless and wild, like birds of Paradise,
Nor pause, nor perch, hovering on untamed wing!
O! the one life, within us and abroad,
Which meets all motion, and becomes its soul,
A light in sound, a sound-like power in light,
Rhythm in all thought, and joyance everywhere.
Methinks, it should have been impossible
Not to love all things in a world so filled,

Where the breeze warbles and the mute still **air,**
Is Music slumbering on her instrument!

And thus, my love! as on the midway slope
Of yonder hill I stretch my limbs at noon,
Whilst through my half-closed eye-lids I behold
The sunbeams dance, like diamonds, on the **main,**
And tranquil muse upon tranquillity;
Full many a thought uncalled and undetained,
And many idle flitting phantasies,
Traverse my indolent and passive brain,
As wild and various as the random gales
That swell and flutter on this subject lute!

And what if all of animated nature
Be but organic harps diversely framed,
That tremble into thought, as o'er them **sweeps**
Plastic and vast, one intellectual breeze,
At once the Soul of each, and God of all?

But thy more serious eye a mild reproof
Darts, O beloved woman! nor such **thoughts**
Dim and unhallowed dost thou not reject,
And biddest me walk humbly with my God.
Meek daughter in the family of Christ!
Well hast thou said and holily dispraised
These shapings of the unregenerate mind,
Bubbles that glitter as they rise and break
On vain Philosophy's aye-babbling spring.
For never guiltless may I speak of Him,
The Incomprehensible! save when with awe
I praise Him, and with faith that inly feels;
Who with His saving mercies healed me,
A sinful and most miserable man,
Wildered and dark, and gave me to possess
Peace, and this cot, and thee, heart-honoured Maid!

FROST AT MIDNIGHT.

The Frost performs its secret ministry,
Unhelped by any wind. The owlet's cry
Came loud—and hark, again ! loud as before.
The inmates of my cottage, all at rest,
Have left me to that solitude, which suits
Abstruser musings : save that at my side
My cradled infant slumbers peacefully.
'Tis calm indeed ! so calm, that it disturbs
And vexes meditation with its strange
And extreme silentness. Sea, hill, and wood,
This populous village ! Sea, and hill, and wood,
With all the numberless goings on of life,
Inaudible as dreams ! the thin blue flame
Lies on my low burnt fire, and quivers not ;
Only that film, which fluttered on the grate,
Still flutters there, the sole unquiet thing.
Methinks, its motion in this hush of nature
Gives it dim sympathies with me who live,
Making it a companionable form,
Whose puny flaps and freaks, the idling spirit
By its own mood interprets, every where
Echo or mirror seeking of itself,
And makes a toy of thought.
                        But O ! how oft,
How oft, at school, with most believing mind,
Presageful, have I gazed upon the bars,
To watch that fluttering stranger ! and as oft
With unclosed lids, already had I dreamt
Of my sweet birth-place, and the old church-tower,
Whose bells, the poor man's only music, rang
From morn to evening, all the hot fair-day,
So sweetly, that they stirred and haunted me
With a wild pleasure, falling on mine ear
Most like articulate sounds of things to come !
So gazed I, till the soothing things I dreamt,
Lulled me to sleep, and sleep prolonged my dreams
And so I brooded all the following morn,

Awed by the stern preceptor's face, mine eye
Fixed with mock study on my swimming book:
Save if the door half opened, and I snatched
A hasty glance, and still my heart leaped up,
For still I hoped to see the stranger's face,
Townsman, or aunt, or sister more beloved,
My play-mate when we both were clothed alike!

   Dear Babe, that sleepest cradled by my side,
Whose gentle breathings, heard in this deep calm,
Fill up the interspersed vacancies
And momentary pauses of the thought!
My babe so beautiful! it thrills my heart
With tender gladness, thus to look at thee,
And think that thou shalt learn far other lore
And in far other scenes! For I was reared
In the great city, pent 'mid cloisters dim,
And saw nought lovely but the sky and stars.
But thou, my babe! shalt wander like a breeze
By lakes and sandy shores, beneath the crags
Of ancient mountain, and beneath the clouds
Which image in their bulk both lakes and shores
And mountain crags: so shalt thou see and hear
The lovely shapes and sounds intelligible
Of that eternal language, which thy God
Utters, who from eternity doth teach
Himself in all, and all things in Himself.
Great universal Teacher! He shall mould
Thy spirit, and by giving make it ask.

   Therefore all seasons shall be sweet to thee,
Whether the summer clothe the general earth
With greenness, or the redbreast sit and sing
Betwixt the tufts of snow on the bare branch
Of mossy apple-tree, while the nigh thatch
Smokes in the sun-thaw; whether the eave-drops fall,
Heard only in the trances of the blast,
Or if the secret ministry of frost
Shall hang them up in silent icicles,
Quietly shining to the quiet Moon.

DEJECTION. AN ODE.

> 'Late, late yestreen I saw the new Moon,
> With the old Moon in her arms;
> And I fear, I fear, my Master dear!
> We shall have a deadly storm.'
>
> *Ballad of Sir Patrick Spence.*

I.

Well! if the Bard was weather-wise, who made
  The grand old ballad of Sir Patrick Spence,
  This night, so tranquil now, will not go hence
Unroused by winds, that ply a busier trade
Than those which mould yon clouds in lazy flakes,
Or the dull sobbing draft, that moans and rakes
    Upon the strings of this Eolian lute,
    Which better far were mute.
  For lo! the New-moon winter-bright!
  And overspread with phantom light,
  (With swimming phantom light o'erspread
  But rimmed and circled by a silver thread)
I see the old Moon in her lap, foretelling
  The coming on of rain and squally blast.
And oh! that even now the gust were swelling,
  And the slant night-shower driving loud and fast!
Those sounds which oft have raised me, whilst they awed,
    And sent my soul abroad,
Might now perhaps their wonted impulse give,
Might startle this dull pain, and make it move and live!

II.

A grief without a pang, void, dark, and drear,
  A stifled, drowsy, unimpassioned grief,
  Which finds no natural outlet, no relief,
    In word, or sigh, or tear—
O Lady! in this wan and heartless mood,
To other thoughts by yonder throstle wooed,

All this long eve, so balmy and serene,
Have I been gazing on the western sky,
    And its peculiar tint of yellow green :
And still I gaze—and with how blank an eye!
And those thin clouds above, in flakes and bars,
That give away their motion to the stars ;
Those stars, that glide behind them or between,
Now sparkling, now bedimmed, but always seen ;
Yon crescent Moon, as fixed as if it grew
In its own cloudless, starless lake of blue ;
I see them all so excellently fair,
I *see*, not *feel* how beautiful they are!

III.

My genial spirits fail ;
    And what can these avail,
To lift the smothering weight from off my breast?
    It were a vain endeavour,
    Though I should gaze for ever
On that green light that lingers in the west :
I may not hope from outward forms to win
The passion and the life, whose fountains are within.

IV.

O Lady! we receive but what we give,
And in our life alone does nature live :
Ours is her wedding-garment, ours her shroud!
    And would we aught behold, of higher worth,
Than that inanimate cold world allowed
To the poor loveless ever-anxious crowd,
    Ah! from the soul itself must issue forth,
A light, a glory, a fair luminous cloud
        Enveloping the Earth—
And from the soul itself must there be sent
    A sweet and potent voice, of its own birth,
Of all sweet sounds the life and element.

V.

O pure of heart! thou need'st not ask of me
What this strong music in the soul may be!
What, and wherein it doth exist,
This light, this glory, this fair luminous mist,
This beautiful, and beauty-making power.
  Joy, virtuous Lady! Joy that ne'er was given,
Save to the pure, and in their purest hour,
Life, and Life's effluence, cloud at once and shower,
Joy, Lady! is the spirit and the power,
Which wedding Nature to us gives in dower
  A new Earth and new Heaven,
Undreamt of by the sensual and the proud—
Joy is the sweet voice, Joy the luminous cloud—
  We in ourselves rejoice!
And thence flows all that charms or ear or sight,
  All melodies the echoes of that voice,
All colours a suffusion from that light.

VI.

There was a time when, though my path was rough,
  This joy within me dallied with distress,
And all misfortunes were but as the stuff
  Whence Fancy made me dreams of happiness:
For hope grew round me, like the twining vine,
  And fruits, and foliage, not my own, seemed mine.
But now afflictions bow me down to earth:
Nor care I that they rob me of my mirth,
  But oh! each visitation
Suspends what nature gave me at my birth,
  My shaping spirit of Imagination.
For not to think of what I needs must feel,
  But to be still and patient, all I can;
And haply by abstruse research to steal
  From my own nature all the natural man—
  This was my sole resource, my only plan:
Till that which suits a part infects the whole,
And now is almost grown the habit of my soul.

VII.

Hence, viper thoughts, that coil around my mind,
    Reality's dark dream!
I turn from you, and listen to the wind,
    Which long has raved unnoticed.   What a scream
Of agony by torture lengthened out
That lute sent forth!   Thou Wind, that ravest without,
    Bare crag, or mountain-tairn, or blasted tree,
Or pine-grove whither woodman never clomb,
Or lonely house, long held the witches' home,
    Methinks were fitter instruments for thee,
Mad Lutanist! who in this month of showers,
Of dark brown gardens, and of peeping flowers,
Mak'st Devils' yule, with worse than wintry song,
The blossoms, buds, and timorous leaves among.
    Thou Actor, perfect in all tragic sounds!
Thou mighty Poet, e'en to frenzy bold!
        What tell'st thou now about?
        'Tis of the rushing of a host in rout,
    With groans of trampled men, with smarting wounds—
At once they groan with pain, and shudder with the cold!
But hush! there is a pause of deepest silence!
    And all that noise, as of a rushing crowd,
With groans and tremulous shudderings—all is over—
    It tells another tale, with sounds less deep and loud!
        A tale of less affright,
        And tempered with delight,
As Otway's self had framed the tender lay—
        'Tis of a little child
        Upon a lonesome wild,
Not far from home, but she hath lost her way:
And now moans low in bitter grief and fear,
And now screams loud, and hopes to make her mother hear

VIII.

'Tis midnight, but small thoughts have I of sleep:
Full seldom may my friend such vigils keep!
Visit her, gentle Sleep! with wings of healing,
  And may this storm be but a mountain-birth,
May all the stars hang bright above her dwelling,
  Silent as though they watched the sleeping Earth!
    With light heart may she rise,
    Gay fancy, cheerful eyes,
  Joy lift her spirit, Joy attune her voice:
To her may all things live, from pole to pole,
Their life the eddying of her living soul!
  O simple spirit, guided from above,
Dear Lady! friend devoutest of my choice,
Thus mayst thou ever, evermore rejoice.

SONNET. COMPOSED ON A JOURNEY HOMEWARD ; THE AUTHOR
HAVING RECEIVED INTELLIGENCE OF THE BIRTH OF A SON,
SEPT. 20, 1796.

Oft o'er my brain does that strange fancy roll
  Which makes the present (while the flash doth last)
  Seem a mere semblance of some unknown past,
Mixed with such feelings, as perplex the soul
Self-questioned in her sleep : and some have said
  We lived, ere yet this robe of flesh we wore.
  O my sweet baby! when I reach my door,
If heavy looks should tell me thou art dead
(As sometimes, through excess of hope, I fear)
I think, that I should struggle to believe
  Thou wert a spirit, to this nether sphere
Sentenced for some more venial crime to grieve ;
Did'st scream, then spring to meet Heaven's quick reprieve,
  While we wept idly o'er thy little bier!

First Part of Christabel.

'Tis the middle of night by the castle clock,
And the owls have awaken'd the crowing cock,
Tu—whit !——Tu—whoo !
And hark, again ! the crowing cock,
How drowsily it crew.

Sir Leoline, the Baron rich,
Hath a toothless mastiff bitch ;
From her kennel beneath the rock
She maketh answer to the clock,
Four for the quarters, and twelve for the hour ;
Ever and aye, by shine and shower,
Sixteen short howls, not over loud ;
Some say, she sees my lady's shroud.

Is the night chilly and dark ?
The night is chilly, but not dark.
The thin gray cloud is spread on high,
It covers but not hides the sky.
The moon is behind, and at the full ;
And yet she looks both small and dull.
The night is chill, the cloud is gray :
'Tis a month before the month of May,
And the Spring comes slowly up this way.

The lovely lady, Christabel,
Whom her father loves so well,
What makes her in the wood so late,
A furlong from the castle gate ?
She had dreams all yesternight
Of her own betrothed knight ;
Dreams that made her moan and leap
As on her bed she lay in sleep ;
And she in the midnight wood will pray
For the weal of her lover that 's far away.

She stole along, she nothing spoke,
The sighs she heaved were soft and low,
And naught was green upon the oak
But moss and rarest mistletoe:
She kneels beneath the huge oak tree,
And in silence prayeth she.

The lady sprang up suddenly,
The lovely lady, Christabel!
It moaned as near as near can be,
But what it is she cannot tell.—
On the other side it seems to be
Of the huge, broad-breasted, old oak tree.

The night is chill; the forest bare;
Is it the wind that moaneth bleak?
There is not wind enough in the air
To move away the ringlet curl
From the lovely lady's cheek—
There is not wind enough to twirl
The one red leaf, the last of its clan,
That dances as often as dance it can,
Hanging so light, and hanging so high,
On the topmost twig that looks up at the sky.

Hush, beating heart of Christabel!
Jesu Maria, shield her well!
She folded her arms beneath her cloak,
And stole to the other side of the oak.
　　What sees she there?

There she sees a damsel bright,
Drest in a silken robe of white,
That shadowy in the moonlight shone:
The neck that made that white robe wan,
Her stately neck and arms were bare;
Her blue-vein'd feet unsandal'd were,
And wildly glitter'd here and there.
The gems entangled in her hair.

I guess, 'twas frightful there to see
A lady so richly clad as she—
Beautiful exceedingly!

'Mary mother, save me now!'
(Said Christabel,) 'And who art thou?'

The lady strange made answer meet,
And her voice was faint and sweet :—
'Have pity on my sore distress,
I scarce can speak for weariness :
Stretch forth thy hand, and have no fear!'
Said Christabel, 'How camest thou here?'
And the lady, whose voice was faint and sweet,
Did thus pursue her answer meet :—
'My sire is of a noble line,
And my name is Geraldine :
Five warriors seized me yestermorn,
Me, even me, a maid forlorn :
They choked my cries with force and fright,
And tied me on a palfrey white.
The palfrey was as fleet as wind,
And they rode furiously behind.
They spurred amain, their steeds were white :
And once we cross'd the shade of night.
As sure as Heaven shall rescue me,
I have no thought what men they be ;
Nor do I know how long it is
(For I have lain entranced I wis)
Since one, the tallest of the five,
Took me from the palfrey's back,
A weary woman, scarce alive.
Some mutter'd words his comrades spoke :
He placed me underneath this oak ;
He swore they would return with haste ;
Whither they went I cannot tell—
I thought I heard, some minutes past,
Sounds as of a castle bell.
Stretch forth thy hand' (thus ended she),
'And help a wretched maid to flee.'

Then Christabel stretch'd forth her hand
And comforted fair Geraldine :
'O well, bright dame! may you command
The service of Sir Leoline ;
And gladly our stout chivalry
Will he send forth and friends withal
To guide and guard you safe and free
Home to your noble father's hall.'

She rose : and forth with steps they pass'd
That strove to be, and were not, fast.
Her gracious stars the lady blest,
And thus spake on sweet Christabel :
'All our household are at rest,
The hall as silent as the cell ;
Sir Leoline is weak in health,
And may not well awaken'd be,
But we will move as if in stealth,
And I beseech your courtesy,
This night, to share your couch with me.'

They cross'd the moat, and Christabel
Took the key that fitted well ;
A little door she open'd straight,
All in the middle of the gate ;
The gate that was iron'd within and without,
Where an army in battle array had march'd out.
The lady sank, belike through pain,
And Christabel with might and main
Lifted her up, a weary weight,
Over the threshold of the gate :
Then the lady rose again,
And moved, as she were not in pain.

So free from danger, free from fear,
They cross'd the court : right glad they were.
And Christabel devoutly cried
To the lady by her side ;
'Praise we the Virgin all divine
Who hath rescued thee from thy distress!'

'Alas, alas!' said Geraldine,
'I cannot speak for weariness.'
So free from danger, free from fear,
They crossed the court: right glad they were.

Outside her kennel the mastiff old
Lay fast asleep, in moonshine cold.
The mastiff old did not awake,
Yet she an angry moan did make!
And what can ail the mastiff bitch?
Never till now she utter'd yell
Beneath the eye of Christabel.
Perhaps it is the owlet's scritch:
For what can ail the mastiff bitch?

They pass'd the hall, that echoes still,
Pass as lightly as you will!
The brands were flat, the brands were dying,
Amid their own white ashes lying;
But when the lady pass'd, there came
A tongue of light, a fit of flame;
And Christabel saw the lady's eye,
And nothing else saw she thereby,
Save the boss of the shield of Sir Leoline tall,
Which hung in a murky old niche in the wall.
'O softly tread,' said Christabel,
'My father seldom sleepeth well.'

Sweet Christabel her feet doth bare,
And, jealous of the listening air,
They steal their way from stair to stair,
Now in glimmer, and now in gloom,
And now they pass the Baron's room,
And still as death, with stifled breath!
And now have reach'd her chamber door;
And now doth Geraldine press down
The rushes of the chamber floor.

The moon shines dim in the open air,
And not a moonbeam enters here.

But they without its light can see
The chamber carved so curiously,
Carved with figures strange and sweet,
All made out of the carver's brain,
For a lady's chamber meet :
The lamp with twofold silver chain
Is fastened to an angel's feet.

The silver lamp burns dead and dim;
But Christabel the lamp will trim.
She trimm'd the lamp, and made it bright,
And left it swinging to and fro,
While Geraldine, in wretched plight,
Sank down upon the floor below.

'O weary lady, Geraldine,
I pray you, drink this cordial wine!
It is a wine of virtuous powers ;
My mother made it of wild flowers.'

'And will your mother pity me,
Who am a maiden most forlorn?'
Christabel answered—'Woe is me!
She died the hour that I was born.
I have heard the grey-hair'd friar tell,
How on her death-bed she did say,
That she should hear the castle-bell
Strike twelve upon my wedding-day.
O mother dear! that thou wert here!'
'I would,' said Geraldine, 'she were!'

But soon with altered voice, said she—
'Off, wandering mother! Peak and pine!
I have power to bid thee flee.'
Alas! what ails poor Geraldine?
Why stares she with unsettled eye?
Can she the bodiless dead espy?
And why with hollow voice cries she,
'Off, woman, off! this hour is mine—
Though thou her guardian spirit be,
Off, woman, off! 'tis given to me.'

Then Christabel knelt by the lady's side,
And raised to heaven her eyes so blue—
'Alas!' said she, 'this ghastly ride—
Dear lady! it hath wilder'd you!'
The lady wiped her moist cold brow,
And faintly said, ''Tis over now!'

Again the wild-flower wine she drank:
Her fair large eyes 'gan glitter bright,
And from the floor whereon she sank,
The lofty lady stood upright:
She was most beautiful to see,
Like a lady of a far countrée.

And thus the lofty lady spake—
'All they who live in the upper sky,
Do love you, holy Christabel!
And you love them, and for their sake
And for the good which me befell,
Even I in my degree will try,
Fair maiden, to requite you well.
But now unrobe yourself; for I
Must pray, ere yet in bed I lie.'

Quoth Christabel, 'So let it be!'
And as the lady bade, did she.
Her gentle limbs did she undress,
And lay down in her loveliness.

But through her brain of weal and woe
So many thoughts moved to and fro,
That vain it were her lids to close;
So half-way from the bed she rose,
And on her elbow did recline
To look at the lady Geraldine.

Beneath the lamp the lady bow'd,
And slowly roll'd her eyes around;
Then drawing in her breath aloud
Like one that shudder'd, she unbound

The cincture from beneath her breast :
Her silken robe, and inner vest,
Dropt to her feet, and full in view,
Behold! her bosom and half her side——
A sight to dream of, not to tell!
O shield her! shield sweet Christabel!

Yet Geraldine nor speaks nor stirs ;
Ah! what a stricken look was hers!
Deep from within she seems half-way
To lift some weight with sick assay,
And eyes the maid and seeks delay ;
Then suddenly, as one defied,
Collects herself in scorn and pride,
And lay down by the maiden's side!—
And in her arms the maid she took,
     Ah well-a-day!
And with low voice and doleful look
These words did say :
'In the touch of this bosom there worketh a spell,
Which is lord of thy utterance, Christabel!
Thou knowest to-night, and wilt know to-morrow,
This mark of my shame, this seal of my sorrow ;
    But vainly thou warrest,
      For this is alone in
    Thy power to declare,
      That in the dim forest
    Thou heard'st a low moaning,
And found'st a bright lady, surpassingly fair ;
And didst bring her home with thee in love
    and in charity,
To shield her and shelter her from the damp air.

The Rime of the Ancient Mariner.

In Seven Parts.

PART I.

An ancient Mariner meeteth three Gallants bidden to a wedding-feast, and detaineth one.

It is an ancient Mariner,
And he stoppeth one of three.
'By thy long grey beard and glittering eye,
Now wherefore stopp'st thou me?

'The Bridegroom's doors are open'd wide,
And I am next of kin;
The guests are met, the feast is set:
May'st hear the merry din.'

He holds him with his skinny hand,
'There was a ship,' quoth he.
'Hold off! unhand me, grey-beard loon!'
Eftsoons his hand dropt he.

The Wedding-Guest is spell-bound by the eye of the old seafaring-man, and constrained to hear his tale.

He holds him with his glittering eye—
The Wedding-Guest stood still,
And listens like a three years' child:
The Mariner hath his will.

The Wedding-Guest sat on a stone:
He cannot choose but hear;
And thus spake on that ancient man,
The bright-eyed Mariner.

'The ship was cheer'd, the harbour clear'd,
Merrily did we drop
Below the kirk, below the hill,
Below the light-house top.

The Mariner tells how the ship sailed southward with a good wind and fair weather, till it reached the line.

'The sun came up upon the left,
Out of the sea came he!
And he shone bright, and on the right
Went down into the sea.

'Higher and higher every day,
Till over the mast at noon—'
The Wedding-Guest here beat his breast,
For he heard the loud bassoon.

The bride hath paced into the hall,
Red as a rose is she ;
Nodding their heads before her goes
The merry minstrelsy.

The Wedding-Guest heareth the bridal music; but the Mariner continueth his tale.

The Wedding-Guest he beat his breast,
Yet he cannot choose but hear ;
And thus spake on that ancient man,
The bright-eyed Mariner.

'And now the storm-blast came, and he
Was tyrannous and strong :
He struck with his o'ertaking wings,
And chased us south along.

The ship drawn by a storm toward the south pole.

With sloping masts and dipping prow,
As who pursued with yell and blow
Still treads the shadow of his foe,
And forward bends his head,
The ship drove fast, loud roar'd the blast,
And southward aye we fled.

And now there came both mist and snow,
And it grew wondrous cold :
And ice, mast-high, came floating by,
As green as emerald.

And through the drifts the snowy clifts
Did send a dismal sheen :
Nor shapes of men nor beasts we ken—
The ice was all between.

The land of ice, and of fearful sounds, where no living thing was to be seen.

The ice was here, the ice was there,
The ice was all around :
It crack'd and growl'd, and roar'd and howl'd,
Like noises in a swound !

Till a great
sea-bird,
called the
Albatross,
came through
the snow-fog,
and was
received with
great joy and
hospitality.

At length did cross an Albatross:
Thorough the fog it came;
As if it had been a Christian soul,
We hail'd it in God's name.

It ate the food it ne'er had eat,
And round and round it flew.
The ice did split with a thunder-fit;
The helmsman steer'd us through!

And lo! the
Albatross
proveth a bird
of good omen,
and followeth
the ship as it
returned
northward
through fog
and floating
ice.

And a good south wind sprung up behind;
The Albatross did follow,
And every day, for food or play,
Came to the mariners' hollo!

In mist or cloud, on mast or shroud,
It perch'd for vespers nine;   [white,
Whiles all the night, through fog-smoke
Glimmer'd the white moon-shine.

The ancient
Mariner
inhospitably
killeth the
pious bird of
good omen.

'God save thee, ancient Mariner!
From the fiends, that plague thee thus!—
Why look'st thou so?'—'With my cross-bow
I shot the Albatross!'

PART II.

The Sun now rose upon the right:
Out of the sea came he,
Still hid in mist, and on the left
Went down into the sea.

And the good south wind still blew behind,
But no sweet bird did follow,
Nor any day for food or play
Came to the mariners' hollo!

His ship-
mates cry out
against the
ancient Mari-
ner for kill-
ing the bird
of good luck.

And I had done a hellish thing,
And it would work 'em woe;
For all averr'd, I had kill'd the bird
That made the breeze to blow.
Ah wretch! said they, the bird to slay,
That made the breeze to blow!

Nor dim nor red, like God's own head,
The glorious Sun uprist :
Then all averr'd, I had kill'd the bird
That brought the fog and mist.
'Twas right, said they, such birds to slay,
That bring the fog and mist.

But when the fog cleared off, they justify the same, and thus make themselves accomplices in the crime.

The fair breeze blew, the white foam flew,
The furrow stream'd off free ;
We were the first that ever burst
Into that silent sea.

The fair breeze continues, the ship enters the Pacific Ocean, and sails northward, even till it reaches the Line.

Down dropt the breeze, the sails dropt
'Twas sad as sad could be ;   [down,
And we did speak only to break
The silence of the sea !

The ship hath been suddenly becalmed.

All in a hot and copper sky,
The bloody Sun, at noon,
Right up above the mast did stand,
No bigger than the Moon.

Day after day, day after day,
We stuck, nor breath nor motion ;
As idle as a painted ship
Upon a painted ocean.

Water, water, every where,
And all the boards did shrink ;
Water, water, every where,
Nor any drop to drink.

And the Albatross begins to be avenged.

The very deep did rot : O Christ !
That ever this should be !
Yea, slimy things did crawl with legs
Upon the slimy sea.

About, about, in reel and rout
The death-fires danced at night ;
The water, like a witch's oils,
Burnt green and blue and white.

A spirit had followed them; one of the invisible inhabitants of this planet, neither departed souls nor angels; concerning whom the learned Jew, Josephus, and the Platonic Constantinopolitan, Michael Psellus, may be consulted. They are very numerous, and there is no climate or element without one or more.

And some in dreams assured were
Of the spirit that plagued us so :
Nine fathom deep he had followed us
From the land of mist and snow.

And every tongue, through utter drouth,
Was wither'd at the root ;
We could not speak, no more than if
We had been choked with soot.

The shipmates, in their sore distress, would fain throw the whole guilt on the ancient Mariner ; in sign whereof they hang the dead sea-bird round his neck.

Ah ! well a-day ! what evil looks
Had I from old and young !
Instead of the Cross, the Albatross
About my neck was hung.

PART III.

There pass'd a weary time. Each throat
Was parch'd, and glazed each eye.
A weary time ! A weary time !
How glazed each weary eye !

The ancient Mariner beholdeth a sign in the element afar off.

When looking westward, I beheld
A something in the sky.

At first it seem'd a little speck,
And then it seem'd a mist ;
It moved and moved, and took at last
A certain shape, I wist.

A speck, a mist, a shape, I wist !
And still it near'd and near'd :
And as if it dodged a water-sprite,
It plunged and tack'd and veer'd.

At its nearer approach, it seemeth him to be a ship ; and at a dear ransom he freeth his speech from the bonds of thirst.

With throats unslaked, with black lips baked,
We could nor laugh nor wail ;
Through utter drought all dumb we stood !
I bit my arm, I suck'd the blood,
And cried, A sail ! a sail !

With throats unslaked, with black lips
Agape they heard me call :   [baked,
Gramercy! they for joy did grin,
And all at once their breath drew in,
As they were drinking all.

A flash of joy :

See! see! (I cried) she tacks no more!
Hither to work us weal ;
Without a breeze, without a tide,
She steadies with upright keel!

And horror
follows. For
can it be a
ship that
comes on-
ward without
wind or tide !

The western wave was all a-flame,
The day was well-nigh done !
Almost upon the western wave
Rested the broad bright Sun ;
When that strange shape drove suddenly
Betwixt us and the Sun.

And straight the Sun was fleck'd with bars,
(Heaven's Mother send us grace !)
As if through a dungeon-grate he peer'd,
With broad and burning face.

It seemeth
him but the
skeleton of a
ship.

Alas! (thought I, and my heart beat loud)
How fast she nears and nears !
Are those *her* sails that glance in the Sun,
Like restless gossameres ?

Are those *her* ribs through which the Sun
Did peer, as through a grate ?
And is that Woman all her crew ?
Is that a Death ? and are there two ?
Is Death that woman's mate ?

And its ribs
are seen as
bars on the
face of the
setting Sun.
The spectre-
woman and
her death-
mate, and no
other on
board the
skeleton ship.
Like vessel,
like crew !

Her lips were red, her looks were free,
Her locks were yellow as gold :
Her skin was as white as leprosy,
The Night-mare Life-in-Death was she,
Who thicks man's blood with cold.

Death and Life-in-Death have diced for the ship's crew, and she (the latter) winneth the ancient Mariner.

The naked hulk alongside came,
And the twain were casting dice;
'The game is done! I've won, I've **won**!'
Quoth she, and whistles thrice.

No twilight within the courts of the sun.

The Sun's rim dips; the stars rush **out**:
At one stride comes the dark;
With far-heard whisper, o'er the sea,
Off shot the spectre-bark.

We listen'd and look'd sideways up!
Fear at my heart, as at a cup,
My life-blood seem'd to sip!
The stars were dim, and thick the ni**ght**,
The steersman's face by his lamp gleam'**d**
　　white;
From the sails the dew did drip—

At the rising of the Moon,

Till clomb above the eastern bar
The horned Moon, with one bright sta**r**
Within the nether tip.

One after another,

One after one, by the star-dogg'd **Moon,**
Too quick for groan or sigh,
Each turn'd his face with a ghastly pan**g,**
And cursed me with his eye.

His shipmates drop down dead.

Four times fifty living men,
(And I heard nor sigh nor groan)
With heavy thump, a lifeless lump,
They dropp'd down one by one.

But Life-in-Death begins her work on the ancient Mariner.

The souls did from their bodies fly,**—**
They fled to bliss or woe!
And every soul, it pass'd me **by,**
Like the whizz of my cross-bow!

PART IV.

'I fear thee, ancient Mariner!
I fear thy skinny hand!
And thou art long, and lank, and brown,
As is the ribb'd sea-sand.

The Wedding-Guest feareth that a spirit is talking to him;

I fear thee and thy glittering eye,
And thy skinny hand, so brown.'—
Fear not, fear not, thou Wedding-Guest!
This body dropt not down.

But the ancient Mariner assureth him of his bodily life, and proceedeth to relate his horrible penance.

Alone, alone, all all alone,
Alone on a wide wide sea!
And never a saint took pity on
My soul in agony.

The many men, so beautiful!
And they all dead did lie:
And a thousand thousand slimy things
Lived on; and so did I.

He despiseth the creatures of the calm.

I look'd upon the rotting sea,
And drew my eyes away;
I look'd upon the rotting deck,
And there the dead men lay.

And envieth that they should live, and so many lie dead.

I look'd to Heaven, and tried to pray;
But or ever a prayer had gusht,
A wicked whisper came, and made
My heart as dry as dust.

I closed my lids, and kept them close,
And the balls like pulses beat;
For the sky and the sea, and the sea and
the sky
Lay like a load on my weary eye,
And the dead were at my feet.

The cold sweat melted from their limbs,
Nor rot nor reek did they:
The look with which they look'd on me
Had never pass'd away.

But the curse liveth for him in the eye of the dead men.

An orphan's curse would drag to Hell
A spirit from on high;
But oh! more horrible than that
Is the curse in a dead man's eye!
Seven days, seven nights, I saw that curse,
And yet I could not die.

In his loneli-
ness and
fixedness he
yearneth
towards the
journeying
Moon, and
the stars
that still
sojourn, yet
still move
onward; and
everywhere
the blue sky
belongs to
them, and is

The moving Moon went up the sky,
And no where did abide:
Softly she was going up,
And a star or two beside—
Her beams bemock'd the sultry main,
Like April hoar-frost spread;
But where the ship's huge shadow lay,
The charmed water burnt alway
A still and awful red.

their appointed rest, and their native country and their own natural home,
which they enter unannounced, as lords that are certainly expected, and yet
there is a silent joy at their arrival.

By the light
of the Moon
he beholdeth
God's crea-
tures of the
great calm.

Beyond the shadow of the ship,
I watch'd the water-snakes:
They moved in tracks of shining white,
And when they rear'd, the elfish light
Fell off in hoary flakes.

Within the shadow of the ship
I watch'd their rich attire:
Blue, glossy green, and velvet black,
They coil'd and swam; and every track
Was a flash of golden fire.

Their beauty
and their
happiness.

He blesseth
them in his
heart.

O happy living things! no tongue
Their beauty might declare:
A spring of love gush'd from my heart,
And I bless'd them unaware!
Sure my kind saint took pity on me,
And I bless'd them unaware!

The spell
begins to
break.

The self-same moment I could pray;
And from my neck so free
The Albatross fell off, and sank
Like lead into the sea.

PART V

Oh sleep! it is a gentle thing,
Beloved from pole to pole!
To Mary Queen the praise be given!
She sent the gentle sleep from Heaven,
That slid into my soul.

The silly buckets on the deck,
That had so long remain'd,
I dreamt that they were fill'd with dew;
And when I awoke, it rain'd.

By grace of the holy Mother, the ancient Mariner is refreshed with rain.

My lips were wet, my throat was cold,
My garments all were dank;
Sure I had drunken in my dreams,
And still my body drank.

I moved, and could not feel my limbs:
I was so light—almost
I thought that I had died in sleep,
And was a blessed ghost.

And soon I heard a roaring wind:
It did not come anear;
But with its sound it shook the sails,
That were so thin and sere.

He heareth sounds and seeth strange sights and commotions in the sky and the element.

The upper air burst into life!
And a hundred fire-flags sheen,
To and fro they were hurried about;
And to and fro, and in and out,
The wan stars danced between.

And the coming wind did roar more loud,
And the sails did sigh like sedge;
And the rain pour'd down from one black
The Moon was at its edge.   [cloud;

The thick black cloud was cleft, and still
The Moon was at its side:
Like waters shot from some high crag,
The lightning fell with never a jag,
A river steep and wide.

The bodies of
the ship's
crew are in-
spirited, and
the ship
moves on;

The loud wind never reach'd the ship,
Yet now the ship moved on!
Beneath the lightning and the moon
The dead men gave a groan.

They groan'd, they stirr'd, they all uprose,
Nor spake, nor moved their eyes;
It had been strange, even in a dream
To have seen those dead men rise.

The helmsman steer'd, the ship moved on;
Yet never a breeze up-blew;
The mariners all 'gan work the ropes,
Where they were wont to do:
They raised their limbs like lifeless tools—
We were a ghastly crew.

The body of my brother's son
Stood by me, knee to knee:
The body and I pull'd at one rope,
But he said nought to me.

But not by
the souls of
the men, nor
by demons of
earth or mid-
dle air, but
by a blessed
troop of an-
gelic spirits,
sent down by
the invoca-
tion of the
guardian
saint.

'I fear thee, ancient Mariner!'
Be calm, thou Wedding-Guest!
'Twas not those souls that fled in pain,
Which to their corses came again,
But a troop of spirits blest:

For when it dawn'd—they dropp'd their arms,
And cluster'd round the mast;
Sweet sounds rose slowly through their
And from their bodies passed.   [mouths,

Around, around, flew each sweet sound,
Then darted to the Sun;
Slowly the sounds came back again,
Now mix'd, now one by one.

Sometimes a-dropping from the sky
I heard the sky-lark sing;
Sometimes all little birds that are,
How they seem'd to fill the sea and air
With their sweet jargoning!

And now 'twas like all instruments,
Now like a lonely flute ;
And now it is an angel's song,
That makes the heavens be mute.

It ceased ; yet still the sails made on
A pleasant noise till noon,
A noise like of a hidden brook
In the leafy month of June,
That to the sleeping woods all night
Singeth a quiet tune.

Till noon we quietly sailed on,
Yet never a breeze did breathe :
Slowly and smoothly went the ship,
Moved onward from beneath.

Under the keel nine fathom deep,
From the land of mist and snow,
The spirit slid ; and it was he
That made the ship to go.
The sails at noon left off their tune,
And the ship stood still also.

The lonesome spirit from the south-pole carries on the ship as far as the line, in obedience to the angelic troop, but still requireth vengeance.

The Sun, right up above the mast,
Had fix'd her to the ocean ;
But in a minute she 'gan stir,
With a short uneasy motion—
Backwards and forwards half her length
With a short uneasy motion.

Then like a pawing horse let go,
She made a sudden bound :
It flung the blood into my head,
And I fell down in a swound.

How long in that same fit I lay,
I have not to declare ;
But ere my living life return'd,
I heard, and in my soul discern'd
Two voices in the air.

The Polar Spirit's fellow demons, the invisible inhabitants of the element, take part in his

wrong ; and two of them relate, one to the other, that penance long and heavy for the ancient Mariner hath been accorded to the Polar Spirit, who returneth southward.

L 2

'Is it he?' quoth one, 'Is this the man?
By Him who died on cross,
With his cruel bow he laid full low,
The harmless Albatross.

'The spirit who bideth by himself
In the land of mist and snow,
He loved the bird that loved the man
Who shot him with his bow.'

The other was a softer voice,
As soft as honey-dew:
Quoth he, 'The man hath penance done,
And penance more will do.'

PART VI.

First Voice.

But tell me, tell me! speak again,
Thy soft response renewing—
What makes that ship drive on so fast?
What is the Ocean doing?

Second Voice.

Still as a slave before his lord,
The Ocean hath no blast;
His great bright eye most silently
Up to the Moon is cast—

If he may know which way to go;
For she guides him smooth or grim.
See, brother, see! how graciously
She looketh down on him.

First Voice.

The Mariner hath been cast into a trance; for the angelic power causeth the vessel to drive northward faster than human life could endure.

But why drives on that ship so fast,
Without or wave or wind?

Second Voice.

The air is cut away before,
And closes from behind.

Fly, brother, fly! more high, more high!
Or we shall be belated:
For slow and slow that ship will go,
When the Mariner's trance is abated.

I woke, and we were sailing on
As in a gentle weather:
'Twas night, calm night, the Moon was
The dead men stood together.   [high;

The super-natural motion is retarded; the Mariner awakes, and his penance begins anew.

All stood together on the deck,
For a charnel-dungeon fitter:
All fixed on me their stony eyes,
That in the Moon did glitter.

The pang, the curse, with which they died,
Had never pass'd away:
I could not draw my eyes from theirs,
Nor turn them up to pray.

And now this spell was snapt: once more
I view'd the ocean green,
And look'd far forth, yet little saw
Of what had else been seen—

The curse is finally expiated.

Like one that on a lonesome road
Doth walk in fear and dread,
And having once turn'd round, walks on,
And turns no more his head;
Because he knows, a frightful fiend
Doth close behind him tread.

But soon there breathed a wind on me
Nor sound nor motion made:
Its path was not upon the sea,
In ripple or in shade.

It raised my hair, it fann'd my cheek
Like a meadow-gale of spring—
It mingled strangely with my fears,
Yet it felt like a welcoming.

Swiftly, swiftly flew the ship,
Yet she sail'd softly too:
Sweetly, sweetly blew the breeze—
On me alone it blew.

And the ancient Mariner beholdeth his native country.

Oh! dream of joy! is this indeed
The light-house top I see?
Is this the hill? is this the kirk?
Is this mine own countree?

We drifted o'er the harbour-bar,
And I with sobs did pray—
'O let me be awake, my God!
Or let me sleep alway.'

The harbour-bay was clear as glass,
So smoothly it was strewn!
And on the bay the moonlight lay,
And the shadow of the moon.

The rock shone bright, the kirk no less,
That stands above the rock:
The moonlight steeped in silentness
The steady weathercock.

The angelic spirits leave the dead bodies,

And the bay was white with silent light,
Till rising from the same,
Full many shapes, that shadows were,
In crimson colours came.

And appear in their own forms of light,

A little distance from the prow
Those crimson shadows were:
I turn'd my eyes upon the deck—
Oh, Christ! what saw I there!

Each corse lay flat, lifeless and flat,
And, by the holy rood!
A man all light, a seraph-man,
On every corse there stood.

This seraph-band, each waved his hand:
It was a heavenly sight!
They stood as signals to the land,
Each one a lovely light:

This seraph-band, each waved his hand,
No voice did they impart—
No voice; but oh! the silence sank
Like music on my heart.

But soon I heard the dash of oars,
I heard the Pilot's cheer;
My head was turn'd perforce away,
And I saw a boat appear.

The Pilot, and the Pilot's boy,
I heard them coming fast:
Dear Lord in Heaven! it was a joy
The dead men could not blast.

I saw a third—I heard his voice:
It is the Hermit good!
He singeth loud his godly hymns
That he makes in the wood.
He'll shrieve my soul, he'll wash away
The Albatross's blood.

PART VII.

This Hermit good lives in that wood   *The Hermit*
Which slopes down to the sea.   *of the wood.*
How loudly his sweet voice he rears!
He loves to talk with marineres
That come from a far countree.

He kneels at morn, and noon, and eve—
He hath a cushion plump:
It is the moss that wholly hides
The rotted old oak stump.

The skiff-boat near'd : I heard them talk,
'Why, this is strange, I trow!
Where are those lights so many and fair,
That signal made but now ?'

Approacheth
the ship with
wonder.

'Strange, by my faith!' the Hermit said—
'And they answer'd not our cheer!
The planks look warp'd! and see those   [sails,
How thin they are and sere!
I never saw aught like to them,
Unless perchance it were

Brown skeletons of leaves that lag
My forest-brook along ;
When the ivy-tod is heavy with snow,
And the owlet whoops to the wolf below,
That eats the she-wolf's young.'

'Dear Lord! it hath a fiendish look'—
(The Pilot made reply)
'I am a-fear'd'—'Push on, push on!'
Said the Hermit cheerily.

The boat came closer to the ship,
But I nor spake nor stirr'd ;
The boat came close beneath the ship,
And straight a sound was heard.

The ship sud-
denly sink-
eth.

Under the water it rumbled on,
Still louder and more dread :
It reach'd the ship, it split the bay ;
The ship went down like lead.

The ancient
Mariner is
saved in the
Pilot's boat.

Stunn'd by that loud and dreadful sound,
Which sky and ocean smote,
Like one that hath been seven days drown'd
My body lay afloat ;
But swift as dreams, myself I found
Within the Pilot's boat.

Upon the whirl, where sank the ship,
The boat spun round and round ;
And all was still, save that the hill
Was telling of the sound.

I moved my lips—the Pilot shriek'd
And fell down in a fit;
The holy Hermit raised his eyes,
And pray'd where he did sit.

I took the oars: the Pilot's boy,
Who now doth crazy go,
Laugh'd loud and long, and all the while
His eyes went to and fro.
'Ha! ha!' quoth he, 'full plain I see
The Devil knows how to row.'

And now, all in my own countree,
I stood on the firm land!
The Hermit stepped forth from the boat,
And scarcely he could stand.

'O shrieve me, shrieve me, holy man!'
The Hermit crossed his brow.
'Say quick,' quoth he, ' I bid thee say—
What manner of man art thou?'

The ancient Mariner earnestly entreateth the Hermit to shrieve him; and the penance of life falls on him.

Forthwith this frame of mine was wrench'd
With a woful agony,
Which forced me to begin my tale;
And then it left me free.

Since then, at an uncertain hour,
That agony returns;
And till my ghastly tale is told,
This heart within me burns.

And ever and anon throughout his future life and agony constraineth him to travel from land to land;

I pass, like night, from land to land;
I have strange power of speech;
The moment that his face I see,
I know the man that must hear me:
To him my tale I teach.

What loud uproar bursts from that door!
The wedding-guests are there:
But in the garden-bower the bride
And bride-maids singing are:
And hark the little vesper bell,
Which biddeth me to prayer!

O Wedding-Guest! this soul hath **been**
Alone on a wide wide sea:
So lonely 'twas, that God himself
Scarce seemed there to be.

O sweeter than the marriage-**feast,**
'Tis sweeter far to me,
To walk together to the **kirk**
With a goodly company!—

To walk together to the kirk,
And all together pray,
While each to his great Father bends,
Old men, and babes, and loving friends,
And youths and maidens gay!

And to teach, by his own example, love and reverence to all things that God made and loveth.

Farewell, farewell! but this I tell
To thee, thou Wedding-Guest!
He prayeth well who loveth well
Both man and bird and beast.

He prayeth best, who loveth best
All things both great and small;
For the dear God who loveth us,
He made and loveth all.

The Mariner, whose eye is bright,
Whose beard with age is hoar,
Is gone: and now the Wedding-Guest
Turn'd from the bridegroom's door.

He went like one that hath been **stunn'd,**
And is of sense forlorn:
A sadder and a wiser man,
He rose the morrow **morn.**

ROBERT SOUTHEY.

[ROBERT SOUTHEY was born at Bristol on Aug. 12, 1774. He was educated at Westminster School and at Balliol College, Oxford; and after some
years of wandering and unsettlement he went to live, in 1803, at Greta Hall,
near Keswick, which remained his home till his death in 1843. In 1813 he
was made poet laureate. Besides his countless prose works, his volumes of
verse were very numerous; the chief of them are:—*Poems by Robert Lovell
and Robert Southey, of Balliol College, Oxford*, 2 vols., 1795-9; *Joan of Arc*,
1796; *Poems*, 1797; *Thalaba the Destroyer*, 1801; *Madoc*, 1805; *Metrical
Tales and other Poems*, 1805; *The Curse of Kehama*, 1810; *Roderick, the last
of the Goths*, 1814; *A Vision of Judgment*, 1821.]

In the year 1837, two years before his brain softened and his
mind went to ruin, Southey superintended a collective edition of
his poems in ten volumes.

Of his five narrative poems, *Joan of Arc*, written at nineteen
years of age (1793-94), was, in his own just estimation, the least
worthy to succeed; and yet it gave him what he calls a 'Baxter's
shove into his right place in the world.'

Thalaba came next; 'the wild and wondrous song;' delightful
in its kind, as a Tale of the Arabian Nights is delightful; but
wanting, as all stories in which supernatural agencies play a
leading part must be, in one sort of charm,—that which results
from a sense of art exercised in the fulfilment of a law. For when
the law of Nature is set aside, the poet's fancy may 'wander at its
own sweet will.'

To a poem thus lawless in its incidents and accidents, Southey
thought that a rythmic structure of blank verse almost equally
lawless was appropriate. He does not deny that regular blank
verse is superior; he says of it in one of his prefaces,—'Take it in
all its gradations, from the elaborate rhythm of Milton, down to its
loosest structure in the early dramatists, I believe there is no
measure comparable to it, either in our own or in any other

language, for might, and majesty, and flexibility and compass.¹ But for *Thalaba* he prefers a blank verse of his own, in which the decasyllabic rule is renounced, and the lines, following a spontaneous melody, divide themselves into every variety of length, with the ordinary iambic cadence interrupted from time to time by some trochaic or dactylic movement, springing up as a pleasant surprise :—

> Years of his youth, how rapidly ye fled
> In that beloved solitude!
> Is the morn fair and doth the freshening breeze
> Flow with cool current o'er his cheek?
> Lo! underneath the broad-leaved sycamore
> With lids half closed he lies,
> Dreaming of days to come.
> His dog beside him in mute blandishment
> Now licks his listless hand;
> Now lifts an anxious and expectant eye,
> *Courting the wonted caress.*
>
> Book III. 17.

Southey in his school-days at Westminster had conceived the design of founding a poem on each of the more important mythologies known to the world. *Thalaba* was founded on the Mahometan ; and *Kehama* followed, founded on the Hindoo. For *Kehama* he had less expectation of success, inasmuch as it rambles farther still beyond the range of human sympathies. It had an advantage, however, of which he seems to have been unconscious,—that of being in rhyme. This he valued by its cost to himself, which was apparently next to nothing ; he says in a letter to me that 'rhyme suggests more thoughts than it baulks ;' but it is to rhyme probably that the greater success of *Kehama* was owing.

In the one poem, as well as in the other, though we are carried far and wide into other worlds than this, we meet from time to time with some penetrating insight into human life and nature as it exists here below :—

> 'Be of good heart, and may thy sleep be sweet,
> Ladurlad said; . . . Alas! that cannot be
> To one whose days are days of misery.
> How often did she stretch her hands to greet
> Ereenia, rescued in the dreams of night!
> How oft, amid the vision of delight,

Fear in her heart all is not as it seems;
  Then from unsettled slumber start, and hear
The winds that moan above, the waves below!
  Thou hast been called, oh Sleep! the friend of Woe,
  But 'tis the happy who have called thee so.'

                                                    XV. 12.

Kehama was begun in 1801-2, resumed in 1806, and completed in 1809. *Madoc* had been written before *Kehama* was begun ; but mistaking it in those days for the greatest poem he should ever write, he laid it aside till he should have time to reconstruct and in great part to rewrite it ; and it was not published till 1805. It has the merit of a varied melody and an easy, fluent and graceful narrative diction ; but of his long poems it was the least successful.

Roderick was the most so. Perhaps the moral grandeur of the theme may have given it that pre-eminence, as much as its tragic interests. The subjugation, for a season, of a whole people, resulting from a single and momentary sin of the passions,—what may be charitably called a *casualty* of sin,—on the part of an otherwise virtuous sovereign,—the slaughter of the Christians by the Moors in the eight days' fight on the banks of Chrysus, —the unknown and almost unwilling escape of the King when the battle was over,—his deep remorse and self-inflicted penance of years in a solitary hermitage whilst supposed to have been killed,—the dream in which his mother appeared to him and bade him to go forth and deliver his country from the Moors, —his departure and encounter with Adosinda, sole survivor of the massacre of Auria,—her story and the passion for revenge, both personal and patriotic, with which it inspired him,—are all sublimely conceived and admirably told. Scarcely less so are his adventures when, wasted by austerities and in the habit of a priest, he passed through the country on his mission, meeting many old friends, but known for the man he was only by his dog,—his ultimate triumph over the Moors in the battle in which, on the inadvertent utterance of his once familiar war-cry, he was enthusiastically recognised by his army,—and thereupon his instant disappearance, whither no one knew, till, after the lapse of some centuries, a humble tomb was discovered within a hermitage in the neighbourhood of Viseu with his name inscribed upon it.

In the versification, Southey has availed himself with singular skill of names belonging to three languages, Spanish, Moorish and

Gothic, to vary his rhythmic effects. English itself is a language
derived from divers roots, and therefore, if competently dealt with,
the more capable of composite and contrasted melodies. But
auxiliaries from even one alien tongue may do excellent service;
as Milton well knew when he sounded his roll-call of devils in the
first book of *Paradise Lost.* The concluding lines of the passage
which follows will exemplify the advantage taken by Southey of
Spanish names in *Roderick:*—

> 'So saying Adosinda left the King
> Alone amid the ruins. There he stood,
> As when Elisha, on the further bank
> Of Jordan, saw that elder prophet mount
> The fiery chariot, and the steeds of fire,
> Trampling the whirlwind, bear him up the sky:
> Thus gazing after her did Roderick stand;
> And as the immortal Tishbite left behind
> His mantle and prophetic powers, even so
> Had her inspiring presence left infused
> The spirit which she breathed. Gazing he stood
> As at a Heavenly visitation there
> Vouchsafed in mercy to himself and Spain;
> And when the heroic mourner from his sight
> Had passed away, still reverential awe
> Held him suspended there and motionless.
> Then, turning from the ghastly scene of death,
> Up murmuring *Lona,* he began toward
> The holy *Bierzo* his obedient way.
> *Sil's* ample stream he crossed, where thro' the vale
> Of *Orras,* from that sacred land it bears
> The whole collected waters; northward then,
> Skirting the heights of *Aguiar,* he reached
> That consecrated pile amid the wild
> Which sainted *Fructuoso* in his zeal
> Reared to *St. Felix,* on *Visonia's* banks.'

> *Roderick,* **IV.**

The picturesque element enters largely into *Roderick;* and in
poems of such length, descriptions of natural scenery are invaluable
as resting-places. Rest from action and passion,—rest even from
intellectual effort,—cannot be dispensed with after prolonged
strains in one or another mood of emotion or exaltation; nor is it
to be obtained in any better way than by occupying the mind's
eye with natural beauty and the mind's ear with the gentle melodies

by which it is most aptly accompanied. This exercise of art is nowhere more conspicuous than in *Roderick*.

Of minor poems Southey wrote many more than he had any desire to write. And how he came to write them is easily explained. In his first youth he says he 'often walked the streets for want of a dinner, not having eighteen pence for the ordinary nor bread and cheese at his lodgings [1].' After twenty-one years of age he had a family to provide for, as well as certain relatives whom he could not allow to suffer from penury, though some of them may have deserved so to suffer. In 1835, when he was sixty-one years of age, he writes to Sir R. Peel (in a letter declining the offer of a baronetcy [2]), 'Last year for the first time in my life I was provided with a year's expenditure beforehand.' Under such circumstances, much as it may have been his desire to write only from impulse and aspiration, it was his duty to write for money too. In his earlier years minor poems were marketable ; a large proportion of his ballads and metrical tales were written for the *Morning Post* at a guinea a week ; and when they were republished in a book, it was still for money, and with the motto, ' Nos haec novimus esse nihil.' There was no humiliation in this, and he knew that there was none. When he found his means again failing in 1807, he writes that, if necessary, he will seek more review employment, write in more magazines, and scribble verses for the newspapers ; adding, 'as long as I can keep half my time for labours worthy of myself and of posterity I shall not feel debased by sacrificing the other, however unworthily it may be employed.' And the fact is that, laborious and exuberant as he was from first to last, the great works which he was always longing and preparing, and in his sanguine heart hoping, to accomplish,— the history of Portugal, the history of English Literature, and the history of the Monastic Orders,—were postponed again and again and for ever.

As time passed on, his poetry, whether written for the market or not, became less saleable ; and in 1820 he writes to Landor,— ' My poems hang on hand. I want no monitor to tell me it is time to leave off. I shall force myself to finish what I have begun, and then — good night. Had circumstances favoured I might have done more in this way, and better. But I have done enough to be remembered among poets, though my proper place will be

[1] **Letter to G. Bedford.**   [2] **Life and Letters, vol. vi. p. 256.**

among the historians, if I live to complete the works upon yonder shelves : '—which most unhappily he did not.

Every generation has a pet poet or two of its own ; and the generation which had now arisen worshipped a Muse instinct with amorous or personal passion,—a Muse of a very different order from Southey's. His *Clio*, even in his first youth, had administered a scornful rebuke when he uttered a few words that seemed akin to sentimental softness :—

> 'I spake, when Lo !
> There stood before me in her majesty
> Clio, the strong-eyed Muse   Upon her brow
> Sate a calm anger. Go, young man, she cried,
> Sigh among myrtle bowers, and let thy soul
> Effuse itself in strains so sorrowful sweet,
> That lovesick maids may weep upon thy page
> Soothed with delicious sorrow.'

That was *not* the way he went ; but in his own way and in some of his poems—certainly in *Roderick*—passion, though governed and severe, and couchant, as it were, in the language of reserve, is by no means wanting ; and how far it would be a mistake to assume that, because he was of a happy and cheerful temperament, he was a stranger to imaginative emotion, may be gathered from what he says of himself in a letter to Landor :—'You wonder that I can think of two poems at once. It proceeds from weakness, not from strength. I could not stand the continuous excitement which you have gone through in your tragedy : in me it would not work itself off in tears ; the tears would flow while in the act of composition, and would leave behind a throbbing head and a whole system in the highest state of nervous exciteability, which would soon induce disease in one of its most fearful forms. From such a state I recovered in 1800 by going to Portugal and suddenly changing climate, occupation, and all internal objects ; and I have kept it off since by a good intellectual regimen[1].' How much reason he had to be careful was shown by the disease of the brain which followed his domestic calamities, and brought his literary life to a close at sixty-five years of age.

Of poetic passion then there was enough and to spare in his nature, though he took no pleasure in it, or none which he could afford to indulge. But along with this there was an imaginative vehe-

---

[1] Life and Letters, vol. iii. p. 300.

mence and power partaking of passion, which, on one occasion at
least, he did not care to keep within the bounds of his 'intellectual
regimen.' He had a passionate hatred of Bonaparte, growing out
of moral as well as political and patriotic feelings, and no doubt
exasperated by the antagonism of those who fell down in worship
before the wonders of his success. Wordsworth has told us,—

> 'How an accursèd thing it is to gaze
> On prosperous tyrants with a dazzled eye,'—

and on one of the two occasions on which Southey and Byron
met, Bonaparte was spoken of; and when Byron gave some
indications of the dazzled eye, Southey replied that Bonaparte was
'a *mean* tyrant.' But his meanness was by no means the worst
part of him. Some of his political murders, secret or avowed,
were regarded by Southey (justly, may it not be said?) as private
and personal crimes for which it was right that, when circumstances rendered it possible, he should be made to answer with
his life. He writes to Landor (9th March 1814),—'For five years
I have been preaching the policy, the duty, the necessity, of
declaring Bonaparte under the ban of human nature.' These
feelings and opinions gave birth to the *Ode written during the
Negociations for Peace in* 1814; and since Milton's immortal
imprecation,—

> 'Avenge, oh Lord, thy slaughtered Saints whose bones
> Lie scattered on the Alpine mountains cold' . . . .

there has been no occasional poem equal to it in grandeur and
power. Nor any indeed equal to it in art ; witness the expressive
change of tone and temper when, at the fifth line of the third
stanza, the denunciations are arrested for a few moments, and a
vision arises of what the tyrant's career might have been had he
chosen the better part.

Occasional poems on great public events are very rarely great
poems. The facts are too strong for the imaginative effects, and
take the place of them. But there is one other of Southey's,—
that on the death of the Princess Charlotte,—with the grace and
beauty of which no facts could compete.

Of the minor poems other than occasional, the varieties are too
numerous to be even so much as indicated here ; but some of
them are examples of the humour, sometimes light and playful,
sometimes grotesque, which was strongly characteristic of Southey.
Humour is an element which cannot but widen the field of a poet's

imagination, though it has been utterly wanting in some of our greatest poets,—in Wordsworth and Coleridge, as well as in Milton. It is commonly and perhaps correctly said to be the gift of a gloomy rather than of a cheerful temperament ; and no doubt the humour which breaks through the clouds is the most enlarging and enriching :—

> ' The richest mirth, the richest sadness too,
> Stands from a groundwork of its opposite;
> For these extremes upon the way to meet
> Take a wide sweep of Nature, gathering in
> Harvests of sundry seasons.'

This was not Southey's kind ; but his had a charm of its own. Much of it belonged to his daily life, and it was often out of this that it found its way into his poetry. His life was a singular combination of gaiety with steady industry and laborious research. Some trivial incident occurred, and his fireside was enlivened by verses like those which follow[1], almost conversational in their easy pleasantry :—

> *' Inscription for a Coffee-pot.*
>
> ' A golden medal was voted to me
> By a certain Royal Society.
> 'Twas not a thing at which to scoff,
> For fifty guineas were the cost thereof.
> On the one side the head of the King you might see,
> And on the other was Mercury.
> But I was scant of worldly riches,
> And moreover the Mercury had no breeches.
> So, thinking of honour and utility too,
> And having modesty also in view,
> I sold the medal,—why should I not?
> And with the money which for it I got
> I purchased this silver coffee-pot ;
> Which I trust my son will preserve with care,
> To be handed down from heir to heir.
> These verses are engraven here,
> That the truth of the matter may appear;
> And I hope the Society will be so wise
> As in future to dress their Mercuries.'

As to the place and rank to be assigned to Southey amongst the poetic souls of our literature, the time has hardly yet arrived for

[1] I was at his fireside when they were written, and took a copy of them

forming a judgment. ' Do not ask yourself,' he says in a letter to Ebenezer Elliot, ' what are the causes of the failure or success of your contemporaries ; their failure or success is not determined yet ; a generation, an age, a century, will not suffice to determine it [1].' This is a truth to which past history will be found to testify. We read now with astonishment the opinion which Dryden, evidently conscious that he was flying in the face of prevailing sentiments, ventured to express, towards the end of the seventeenth century, about two poets who had written in the beginning of it · —' *For my own part, I consider Shakespeare equal to Ben Jonson, if not superior.*'

Southey's belief in his own posthumous renown has led some persons to call him conceited. In his youth he was sanguine and presumptuous ; in his after-life sanguine and confident ; at no time of life was he ever vain. He took great delight in his own works. Why should he not ? Wordsworth once spoke to me of the value he had himself attached to ethical poetry as possibly excessive, but not on that account to be found fault with ; inasmuch as it had given encouragement and animation to his endeavours. Southey in a letter to Grosvenor Bedford (Feb. 12, 1809) says,—' Young lady never felt more desirous to see herself in a new ball-dress than I do to see my own performances in print. . . . There are a great many philosophical reasons for this fancy of mine, and one of the best of all reasons is, that I hold it good to make everything a pleasure which it is possible to make so.' And in a letter to me (April 13, 1829) twenty years later, he illustrates the same principle by a story of a Spaniard he had known who ' always put on his spectacles when he was about to eat cherries, that they might look the bigger and more tempting.'

He was not in the habit of guarding himself against misconstruction. Except on rare occasions,—such as Lord Byron's invectives in the Press or those of Mr. W. Smith in the House of Commons,—he left his character to take care of itself. He had a high opinion, especially in his earlier years, of his powers. He believed too in the high and permanent place which some portion of his work would take in the literature of his country. Such expectations are probably indulged by many young poets who make no mention of it. As abstinence is easier than moderation, and egoism in soliloquy than outspoken egoism, so is it not seldom the

---

[1] Life and Letters, vol. iv. Jan. 30, 1819.

refuge of the weak. And whether the aspirants be weak or strong, their aspirations are not ignoble, and their hopes make them happy. If they succeed, the world is the better ; if they fail, it is no worse.

Whatever tendency to excess there may have been on Southey's part in the estimate of his own works will be found to prevail quite as much in his estimate of the works of his friends, or indeed of many other works, old and new, which he approved and admired. In a letter to me of Oct. 1829, he writes,—' A greater poet than Wordsworth there never has been nor ever will be.' And if he expected for himself a larger measure of attention from posterity than may now seem likely to be accorded him, it should be remembered, that though as long as his mind lasted he 'lived laborious days' for the sake of his family and of others whom, in the generosity of his heart, he helped to support, yet all the labours of all the days did not enable him to do more than make preparations for the three great works which it was the object and ambition of his life to accomplish.

Of what he did accomplish, a portion will not soon be forgotten. There were greater poets in his generation, and there were men of a deeper and more far-reaching philosophic faculty ; but take him for all in all,—his ardent and genial piety, his moral strength, the magnitude and variety of his powers, the field which he covered in literature, and the beauty of his life,—it may be said of him, justly and with no straining of the truth, that of all his contemporaries he was the greatest MAN.

HENRY TAYLOR.

From 'Roderick.'

[The King is in disguise on his final mission to exterminate the Moors.]

On foot they came,
Chieftains and men alike ; the Oaken Cross,
'Triumphant borne on high, precedes their march,
And broad and bright the argent banner shone.
Roderick, who dealing death from side to side,
Had through the Moorish army now made way,
Beheld it flash, and judging well what aid
Approach'd, with sudden impulse that way rode,
To tell of what had pass'd, . . lest in the strife
They should engage with Julian's men, and mar
The mighty consummation. One ran on
To meet him fleet of foot, and having given
His tale to this swift messenger, the Goth
Halted awhile to let Orelio breathe.
Siverian, quoth Pelayo, if mine eyes
Deceive me not, yon horse, whose reeking sides
Are red with slaughter, is the same on whom
The apostate Orpas in his vauntery
Wont to parade the streets of Cordoba.
But thou shouldst know him best ; regard him well ;
Is 't not Orelio?
Either it is he,
The old man replied, or one so like to him,
Whom all thought matchless, that similitude
Would be the greater wonder. But behold,
What man is he who in that disarray
Doth with such power and majesty bestride
The noble steed, as if he felt himself
In his own proper seat ? Look how he leans
To cherish him ; and how the gallant horse
Curves up his stately neck, and bends his head,
As if again to court that gentle touch,
And answer to the voice which praises him.
Can it be Maccabee? rejoin'd the King,
Or are the secret wishes of my soul

Indeed fulfill'd, and hath the grave given up
Its dead? . . . So saying, on the old man he turn'd
Eyes full of wide astonishment, which told
The incipient thought that for incredible
He spake no farther. But enough had past;
For old Siverian started at the words
Like one who sees a spectre, and exclaim'd,
Blind that I was to know him not till now!
My Master, O my Master!

                He meantime
With easy pace moved on to meet their march.
King, to Pelayo he began, this day
By means scarce less than miracle, thy throne
Is stablish'd, and the wrongs of Spain revenged.
Orpas the accursed, upon yonder field
Lies ready for the ravens. By the Moors
Treacherously slain, Count Julian will be found
Before Saint Peter's altar; unto him
Grace was vouchsafed; and by that holy power
Which at Visonia from the Primate's hand
Of his own proper act to me was given,
Unworthy as I am, . . yet sure I think
Not without mystery, as the event hath shown, . .
Did I accept Count Julian's penitence,
And reconcile the dying man to Heaven.
Beside him hath his daughter fallen asleep;
Deal honourably with his remains, and let
One grave with Christian rites receive them both.
Is it not written that as falls the Tree
So it shall lie?

              In this and all things else,
Pelayo answered, looking wistfully
Upon the Goth, thy pleasure shall be done.
Then Roderick saw that he was known, and turn'd
His head away in silence. But the old man
Laid hold upon his bridle, and look'd up
In his master's face, weeping and silently.
Thereat the Goth with fervent pressure took
His hand, and bending down toward him, said,

My good Siverian, go not thou this day
To war! I charge thee keep thyself from harm!
Thou art past the age for battles, and with whom
Hereafter should thy mistress talk of me
If thou wert gone? . . Thou seest I am unarm'd ;
Thus disarray'd as thou beholdest me,
Clean through yon miscreant army have I cut
My way unhurt ; but being once by Heaven
Preserved, I would not perish with the guilt
Of having wilfully provoked my death.
Give me thy helmet and thy cuirass! . . nay, . .
Thou wert not wont to let me ask in vain,
Nor to gainsay me when my will was known!
To thee methinks I should be still the King. . . .

O who could tell what deeds were wrought that day,
Or who endure to hear the tale of rage,
Hatred, and madness, and despair, and fear,
Horror, and wounds, and agony, and death,
The cries, the blasphemies, the shrieks, and groans,
And prayers, which mingled with the din of arms
In one wild uproar of terrific sounds ;
While over all predominant was heard,
Reiterate from the conquerors o'er the field,
Roderick the Goth! Roderick and Victory!
Roderick and Vengeance! . . .

The evening darken'd, but the avenging sword
Turned not away its edge till night had closed
Upon the field of blood. The Chieftains then
Blew the recall, and from their perfect work
Return'd rejoicing, all but he for whom
All look'd with most expectance. He full sure
Had thought upon that field to find his end
Desired, and with Florinda in the grave
Rest, in indissoluble union joined.
But still where through the press of war he went
Half-arm'd, and like a lover seeking death,
The arrows past him by to right and left,

The spear-point pierced him not, the scymitar
Glanced from his helmet ; he, when he beheld
The rout complete, saw that the shield of Heaven
Had been extended over him once more,
And bowed before its will. Upon the banks
Of Sella was Orelio found, his legs
And flanks incarnadined, his poitral smeared
With froth and foam and gore, his silver mane
Sprinkled with blood, which hung on every hair,
Aspersed like dew-drops ; trembling there he stood
From the toil of battle, and at times sent forth
His tremulous voice far echoing loud and shrill,
A frequent anxious cry, with which he seem'd
To call the master whom he loved so well,
And who had thus again forsaken him.
Siverian's helm and cuirass on the grass
Lay near ; and Julian's sword, its hilt and chain
Clotted with blood ; but where was he whose hand
Had wielded it so well that glorious day ? . . .

Days, months, and years, and generations pass'd,
And centuries held their course, before, far off
Within a hermitage near Viseu's walls
A humble tomb was found, which bore inscribed
In ancient characters King Roderick's name.

FROM 'THALABA.'

He found a Woman in the cave,
A solitary Woman,
Who by the fire was spinning,
And singing as she spun.
The pine boughs were cheerfully blazing,
And her face was bright with the flame ;
Her face was as a Damsel's face,
And yet her hair was grey.
She bade him welcome with a smile,
And still continued spinning,
And singing as she spun. . . .

The thread she spun it gleam'd like gold
In the light of the odorous fire,
Yet was it so wonderously thin,
That, save when it shone in the light,
You might look for it closely in vain.
The youth sate watching it,
And she observed his wonder,
And then again she spake,
And still her speech was song;
'Now twine it round thy hands I say,
Now twine it round thy hands I pray;
My thread is small, my thread is fine,
But he must be
A stronger than thee,
Who can break this thread of mine!'

And up she raised her bright blue eyes,
And sweetly she smiled on him,
And he conceived no ill;
And round and round his right hand,
And round and round his left,
He wound the thread so fine.
And then again the Woman spake,
And still her speech was song,
'Now thy strength, O Stranger, strain!
Now then break the slender chain.'

Thalaba strove, but the thread
By magic hands was spun,
And in his cheek the flush of shame
Arose, commixt with fear.
She beheld and laugh'd at him,
And then again she sung,
'My thread is small, my thread is fine,
But he must be
A stronger than thee,
Who can break this thread of mine!'

And up she raised her bright blue eyes,
And fiercely she smiled on him:

'I thank thee, I thank thee, Hodeirah's son!
I thank thee for doing what can't be undone,
For binding thyself in the chain I have spun!'
Then from his head she wrench'd
A lock of his raven hair,
And cast it in the fire,
And cried aloud as it burnt,
'Sister! Sister! hear my voice!
'Sister! Sister! come and rejoice!
The thread is spun,
The prize is won,
The work is done,
For I have made captive Hodeirah's Son.'

FROM 'KEHAMA.'

O force of faith! O strength of virtuous will!
Behold him in his endless martyrdom,
Triumphant still!
The Curse still burning in his heart and brain,
And yet doth he remain
Patient the while, and tranquil, and content!
The pious soul hath framed unto itself
A second nature, to exist in pain
As in its own allotted element.

Such strength the will reveal'd had given
This holy pair, such influxes of grace,
That to their solitary resting place
They brought the peace of Heaven.
Yea, all around was hallow'd! Danger, Fear,
Nor thought of evil ever enter'd here.
A charm was on the Leopard when he came
Within the circle of that mystic glade;
Submiss he crouch'd before the heavenly maid,
And offer'd to her touch his speckled side;
Or with arch'd back erect, and bending head,
And eyes half-closed for pleasure, would he stand
Courting the pressure of her gentle hand.

Trampling his path through wood and brake,
And canes which crackling fall before his way,
And tassel-grass, whose silvery feathers play
O'ertopping the young trees,
On comes the Elephant, to slake
His thirst at noon in yon pellucid springs.
Lo! from his trunk upturn'd, aloft he flings
The grateful shower ; and now
Plucking the broad-leaved bough
Of yonder plane, with wavey motion slow,
Fanning the languid air,
He moves it to and fro.
But when that form of beauty meets his sight,
The trunk its undulating motion stops,
From his forgetful hold the plane-branch drops,
Reverent he kneels, and lifts his rational eyes
To her as if in prayer ;
And when she pours her angel voice in song
Entranced he listens to the thrilling notes,
Till his strong temples, bathed with sudden dews,
Their fragrance of delight and love diffuse.

Lo! as the voice melodious floats around,
The Antelope draws near,
The Tigress leaves her toothless cubs to hear ;
The Snake comes gliding from the secret brake,
Himself in fascination forced along
By that enchanting song ;
The antic Monkeys, whose wild gambols late,
When not a breeze waved the tall jungle grass,
Shook the whole wood, are hush'd, and silently
Hang on the cluster'd tree.
All things in wonder and delight are still ;
Only at times the Nightingale is heard,
Not that in emulous skill that sweetest bird
Her rival strain would try,
A mighty songster, with the Maid to vie ;
She only bore her part in powerful sympathy.

Well might they thus adore that heavenly Maid!
　　For never Nymph of Mountain,
　　Or Grove, or Lake, or Fountain,
With a diviner presence fill'd the shade.
　　　No idle ornaments deface
　　　Her natural grace,
Musk-spot, nor sandal-streak, nor scarlet stain,
Ear-drop nor chain, nor arm nor ankle-ring,
Nor trinketry on front, or neck, or breast,
Marring the perfect form : she seem'd a thing
Of Heaven's prime uncorrupted work, a child
　　　Of early nature undefiled,
　　A daughter of the years of innocence.
And therefore all things loved her. When she stood
　Beside the glassy pool, the fish, that flies
　Quick as an arrow from all other eyes,
Hover'd to gaze on her. The mother bird,
　　When Kailyal's step she heard,
Sought not to tempt her from her secret nest,
But hastening to the dear retreat, would fly
To meet and welcome her benignant eye.

ODE, WRITTEN DURING THE NEGOCIATIONS WITH
BUONAPARTE, IN JANUARY, 1814.

I.

Who counsels peace at this momentous hour,
When God hath given deliverance to the oppress'd,
　　And to the injured power?
Who counsels peace, when Vengeance like a flood
　Rolls on, no longer now to be repress'd;
　　When innocent blood
From the four corners of the world cries out
　For justice upon one accursed head;
When Freedom hath her holy banner spread
　Over all nations, now in one just cause
　United; when with one sublime accord
　Europe throws off the yoke abhorr'd,
And Loyalty and Faith and Ancient Laws
　Follow the avenging sword!

2.

Woe, woe to England! woe and endless shame,
  If this heroic land,
False to her feelings and unspotted fame,
Hold out the olive to the Tyrant's hand!
Woe to the world, if Buonaparte's throne
  Be suffer'd still to stand!
For by what names shall Right and Wrong be known, . .
What new and courtly phrases must we feign
For Falsehood, Murder, and all monstrous crimes,
  If that perfidious Corsican maintain
  Still his detested reign,
And France, who yearns even now to break her chain,
Beneath his iron rule be left to groan?
  No! by the innumerable dead
Whose blood hath for his lust of power been shed,
Death only can for his foul deeds atone;
That peace which Death and Judgment can bestow,
That peace be Buonaparte's . . that alone!

3.

For sooner shall the Ethiop change his skin,
Or from the Leopard shall her spots depart,
Than this man change his old flagitious heart.
Have ye not seen him in the balance weighed,
And there found wanting?—On the stage of blood
  Foremost the resolute adventurer stood;
  And when, by many a battle won,
  He placed upon his brow the crown,
Curbing delirious France beneath his sway,
  Then, like Octavius in old time,
  Fair name might he have handed down,
Effacing many a stain of former crime.
Fool! should he cast away that bright renown!
Fool! the redemption proffer'd should he lose!
When Heaven such grace vouchsafed him that the way
  To Good and Evil lay
  Before him, which to choose.

4.

But Evil was his Good,
For all too long in blood had he been nurst,
And ne'er was earth with verier tyrant curst.
Bold man and bad,
Remorseless, godless, full of fraud and lies,
And black with murders and with perjuries,
Himself in Hell's whole panoply he clad;
No law but his own headstrong will he knew,
No counsellor but his own wicked heart.
From evil thus portentous strength he drew,
And trampled under foot all human ties,
All holy laws, all natural charities.

5.

O France! beneath this fierce Barbarian's sway
Disgraced thou art to all succeeding times;
Rapine, and blood, and fire have mark'd thy way,
All loathsome, all unutterable crimes.
A curse is on thee, France! from far and wide
It hath gone up to Heaven; all lands have cried
For vengeance upon thy detested head;
All nations curse thee, France! for wheresoe'er
In peace or war thy banner hath been spread,
All forms of human woe have follow'd there:
The Living and the Dead
Cry out alike against thee! They who bear,
Crouching beneath its weight, thine iron yoke,
Join in the bitterness of secret prayer
The voice of that innumerable throng
Whose slaughtered spirits day and night invoke
The everlasting Judge of right and wrong,
How long, O Lord! Holy and Just, how long!

6.

A merciless oppressor hast thou been,
Thyself remorselessly oppress'd meantime;
Greedy of war, when all that thou couldst gain
Was but to dye thy soul with deeper crime,
And rivet faster round thyself the chain.

O blind to honour, and to interest blind,
  When thus in abject servitude resign'd
To this barbarian upstart, thou couldst brave
God's justice, and the heart of humankind!
Madly thou thoughtest to enslave the world,
  Thyself the while a miserable slave;
  Behold the flag of vengeance is unfurl'd!
The dreadful armies of the North advance;
While England, Portugal, and Spain combined
Give their triumphant banners to the wind,
And stand victorious in the fields of France.

7.

One man hath been for ten long wretched years
The cause of all this blood and all these tears;
One man in this most aweful point of time
Draws on thy danger, as he caused thy crime.
    Wait not too long the event,
For now whole Europe comes against thee bent;
His wiles and their own strength the nations know;
Wise from past wrongs, on future peace intent,
  The People and the Princes, with one mind,
From all parts move against the general foe:
  One act of justice, one atoning blow,
    One execrable head laid low,
Even yet, O France! averts thy punishment:
Open thine eyes! too long hast thou been blind;
Take vengeance for thyself, and for mankind!

8.

France! if thou lov'st thine ancient fame,
Revenge thy sufferings and thy shame!
By the bones that bleach on Jaffa's beach;
By the blood which on Domingo's shore
Hath clogg'd the carrion-birds with gore;
By the flesh that gorged the wolves of Spain,
  Or stiffen'd on the snowy plain
    Of frozen Muscovy;

By the bodies that lie all open to the sky,
Tracking from Elbe to Rhine the Tyrant's flight;
By the widow's and the orphan's cry,
By the childless parent's misery,
By the lives which he hath shed,
By the ruin he hath spread,
By the prayers that rise for curses on his head,
Redeem, O France! thine ancient fame,
Revenge thy sufferings and thy shame;
Open thine eyes! . . too long hast thou been blind;
Take vengeance for thyself, and for mankind!

9.

By those horrors which the night
Witness'd, when the torches' light
To the assembled murderers show'd
Where the blood of Condé flow'd;
By thy murder'd Pichegru's fame;
By murder'd Wright, . . an English name;
By murder'd Palm's atrocious doom;
By murder'd Hofer's martyrdom;
Oh! by the virtuous blood thus vilely spilt,
The Villain's own peculiar private guilt,
Open thine eyes! too long hast thou been blind!
Take vengeance for thyself and for mankind!

FUNERAL ODE ON THE DEATH OF THE PRINCESS CHARLOTTE.

In its summer pride array'd,
Low our Tree of Hope is laid!
Low it lies: . . in evil hour,
Visiting the bridal bower,
Death hath levell'd root and flower.
Windsor, in thy sacred shade,
(This the end of pomp and power!)
Have the rites of death been paid:
Windsor, in thy sacred shade
Is the Flower of Brunswick laid!

Ye whose relics rest around,
Tenants of this funeral ground!
Know ye, Spirits, who is come,
By immitigable doom
Summon'd to the untimely tomb?
Late with youth and splendour crown'd,
Late in beauty's vernal bloom,
Late with love and joyaunce blest;
Never more lamented guest
Was in Windsor laid to rest.

Henry, thou of saintly worth,
Thou, to whom thy Windsor gave
Nativity and name, and grave;
Thou art in this hallowed earth
Cradled for the immortal birth!
Heavily upon his head
Ancestral crimes were visited:
He, in spirit like a child,
Meek of heart and undefiled,
Patiently his crown resign'd,
And fix'd on heaven his heavenly mind,
Blessing, while he kiss'd the rod,
His Redeemer and his God.
Now may he in realms of bliss
Greet a soul as pure as his.

Passive as that humble spirit,
Lies his bold dethroner too;
A dreadful debt did he inherit
To his injured lineage due;
Ill-starr'd prince, whose martial merit
His own England long might rue!
Mournful was that Edward's fame,
Won in fields contested well,
While he sought his rightful claim:
Witness Aire's unhappy water,
Where the ruthless Clifford fell;
And when Wharfe ran red with slaughter,

On the day of Towton's field,
Gathering, in its guilty flood,
The carnage and the ill-spilt blood
That forty thousand lives could yield.
Cressy was to this but sport,—
Poictiers but a pageant vain;
And the victory of Spain
Seem'd a strife for pastime meant,
And the work of Agincourt
Only like a tournament;
Half the blood which there was spent
Had sufficed again to gain
Anjou and ill-yielded Maine,
Normandy and Aquitaine;
And Our Lady's Ancient towers,
Maugre all the Valois' powers,
Had a second time been ours.—
A gentle daughter of thy line,
Edward, lays her dust with thine.

Thou, Elizabeth, art here;
Thou to whom all griefs were known;
Who wert placed upon the bier
In happier hour than on the throne.
Fatal daughter, fatal mother,
Raised to that ill-omen'd station,
Father, uncle, sons, and brother,
Mourn'd in blood her elevation!
Woodville, in the realms of bliss,
To thine offspring thou may'st say,
Early death is happiness;
And favour'd in their lot are they
Who are not left to learn below
That length of life is length of woe.
Lightly let this ground be prest;
A broken heart is here at rest.

But thou, Seymour, with a greeting,
Such as sisters use at meeting,
Joy, and sympathy, and love,
Wilt hail her in the seats above.

Like in loveliness were ye,
By a like lamented doom,
Hurried to an early tomb.
While together, spirits blest,
Here your earthly relics rest,
Fellow angels shall ye be
In the angelic company.

Henry, too, hath here his part;
At the gentle Seymour's side,
With his best beloved bride,
Cold and quiet, here are laid
The ashes of that fiery heart.
Not with his tyrannic spirit
Shall our Charlotte's soul inherit;
No, by Fisher's hoary head,—
By More, the learned and the good,—
By Katharine's wrongs and Boleyn's blood,—
By the life so basely shed
Of the pride of Norfolk's line,
By the axe so often red,
By the fire with martyrs fed,
Hateful Henry, not with thee
May her happy spirit be!

And here lies one whose tragic name
A reverential thought may claim;
That murder'd Monarch, whom the grave,
Revealing its long secret, gave
Again to sight, that we might spy
His comely face and waking eye!
There, thrice fifty years, it lay,
Exempt from natural decay,
Unclosed and bright, as if to say,
A plague, of bloodier, baser birth,
Than that beneath whose rage he bled,
Was loose upon our guilty earth;—
Such awful warning from the dead,
Was given by that portentous eye;
Then it closed eternally.

Ye whose relics rest around,
Tenants of this funeral ground;
Even in your immortal spheres,
What fresh yearnings will ye feel,
When this earthly guest appears!
Us she leaves in grief and tears;
But to you will she reveal
Tidings of old England's weal;
Of a righteous war pursued,
Long, through evil and through good,
With unshaken fortitude;
Of peace, in battle twice achieved;
Of her fiercest foe subdued,
And Europe from the yoke reliev'd,
Upon that Brabantine plain!
Such the proud, the virtuous story,
Such the great, the endless glory
Of her father's splendid reign!
He who wore the sable mail,
Might at this heroic tale,
Wish himself on earth again.

One who reverently, for thee,
Raised the strain of bridal verse,
Flower of Brunswick! mournfully
Lays a garland on thy herse.

THE HOLLY TREE.

I.

O Reader! hast thou ever stood to see
      The Holly Tree?
The eye that contemplates it well perceives
      Its glossy leaves
Order'd by an intelligence so wise,
As might confound the Atheist's sophistries.

2.

Below, a circling fence, its leaves are seen
    Wrinkled and keen ;
No grazing cattle through their prickly round
    Can reach to wound ;
But as they grow where nothing is to fear,
Smooth and unarm'd the pointless leaves appear.

3.

I love to view these things with curious eyes,
    And moralize :
And in this wisdom of the Holly Tree
    Can emblems see
Wherewith perchance to make a pleasant rhyme,
One which may profit in the after time.

4.

Thus, though abroad perchance I might appear
    Harsh and austere,
To those who on my leisure would intrude
    Reserved and rude,
Gentle at home amid my friends I'd be
Like the high leaves upon the Holly Tree.

5.

And should my youth, as youth is apt I know,
    Some harshness show,
All vain asperities I day by day
    Would wear away,
Till the smooth temper of my age should be
Like the high leaves upon the Holly Tree.

6.

And as when all the summer trees are seen
    So bright and green,
The Holly leaves a sober hue display
    Less bright than they,
But when the bare and wintry woods we see,
What then so cheerful as the Holly Tree?

7.

So serious should my youth appear among
 The thoughtless throng,
So would I seem amid the young and gay
 More grave than they,
That in my age as cheerful I might be
As the green winter of the Holly Tree.

THE BATTLE OF BLENHEIM.

1.

It was a summer evening,
 Old Kaspar's work was done,
And he before his cottage door
 Was sitting in the sun,
And by him sported on the green
His little grandchild Wilhelmine.

2.

She saw her brother Peterkin
 Roll something large and round,
Which he beside the rivulet
 In playing there had found;
He came to ask what he had found,
That was so large, and smooth, and round.

3.

Old Kaspar took it from the boy,
 Who stood expectant by;
And then the old man shook his head,
 And with a natural sigh,
'''Tis some poor fellow's skull,' said he,
'Who fell in the great victory.

4.

'I find them in the garden,
 For there's many here about;
And often when I go to plough,
 The ploughshare turns them out!
For many thousand men,' said he,
'Were slain in that great victory.'

5.

'Now tell us what 't was all about,'
  Young Peterkin, he cries ;
And little Wilhelmine looks up
  With wonder-waiting eyes ;
'Now tell us all about the war,
And what they fought each other for.'

6.

'It was the English,' Kaspar cried,
  'Who put the French to rout ;
But what they fought each other for,
  I could not well make out ;
But every body said,' quoth he,
'That 't was a famous victory.

7.

'My father lived at Blenheim then,
  Yon little stream hard by ;
They burnt his dwelling to the ground,
  And he was forced to fly ;
So with his wife and child he fled,
Nor had he where to rest his head.

8.

'With fire and sword the country round
  Was wasted far and wide,
And many a childing mother then,
  And new-born baby died ;
But things like that, you know, must be
At every famous victory.

9.

'They say it was a shocking sight
  After the field was won ;
For many thousand bodies here
  Lay rotting in the sun ;
But things like that, you know, must be
After a famous victory.

10.

'Great praise the Duke of Marlbro' won,
   And our good Prince Eugene.'
'Why 't was a very wicked thing!'
   Said little Wilhelmine.
'Nay . . nay . . my little girl,' quoth he.
'It was a famous victory.

11.

'And everybody praised the Duke
   Who this great fight did win.'
'But what good came of it at last?'
   Quoth little Peterkin.
'Why that I cannot tell,' said he,
'But 't was a famous victory.'

STANZAS WRITTEN IN HIS LIBRARY.

1.

My days among the Dead are past;
   Around me I behold,
Where'er these casual eyes are cast.
   The mighty minds of old;
My never failing friends are they,
With whom I converse day by day.

2.

With them I take delight in weal,
   And seek relief in woe;
And while I understand and feel
   How much to them I owe,
My cheeks have often been bedew'd
With tears of thoughtful gratitude.

3.

My thoughts are with the Dead, with them
　　I live in long-past years,
Their virtues love, their faults condemn,
　　Partake their hopes and fears,
And from their lessons seek and find
Instruction with an humble mind.

4.

My hopes are with the Dead, anon
　　My place with them will be,
And I with them shall travel on
　　Through all Futurity;
Yet leaving here a name, I trust,
That will not perish in the dust.

WALTER SCOTT.

[WALTER SCOTT, the son of a Writer to the Signet, was born in Edinburgh on August 15, 1771, and was educated at the High School and the College. In 1792 he became an advocate, but soon began to occupy himself seriously with literature, publishing in 1799 a translation of Goethe's *Goetz von Berlichingen*, and in 1802 his *Border Minstrelsy*. As Sheriff of Selkirkshire he went in 1804 to live at Ashestiel on the banks of the Tweed, and there produced *The Lay of the Last Minstrel*, 1805; *Marmion*, 1808; *The Lady of the Lake*, 1810; *Don Roderick*, 1811; *Triermain* and *Rokeby*, 1813. At his new house at Abbotsford he wrote *The Lord of the Isles*, 1815; and *Harold the Dauntless*, 1817. Before these last two were published *Waverley* appeared, and henceforth Scott wrote no more poetry, save a few short lyrics, ending with his *Farewell to the Muse*, 1822. He was made a baronet in 1820, but in 1826 commercial disaster came upon him, and his last ten years were a time of struggle and overwork. He died at Abbotsford, September 21, 1836.]

Walter Scott ranks in imaginative power hardly below any writer save Homer and Shakespeare. His best works are his novels ; but he holds a high place as a poet in virtue of his metrical romances and of his lyrical pieces and ballads. He was the first great British writer of the Romantic school, and the first who turned the thoughts and hearts of his countrymen towards the Middle Ages. The author of *The Castle of Otranto* and the builder of Strawberry Hill was his feeble precursor : Bishop Percy with his *Reliques* had lighted the way : Ellis with his *Specimens of Early English Poems and Romances* ministered to the same taste. In Germany the Romantic school prevailed at the same time over the Classical. There is in the poetry of Coleridge an element derived from that school ; and Scott's earliest works were translations from the German ballads of Bürger and of a romantic tragedy by Goethe, though the rill of foreign influence was soon lost in a river which flowed from a more abundant spring.

It is always said of Scott that he was above all things a Scotchman. The pride of Scotland he was indeed ; and by the varied scenery and rich stores of romance, Lowland and Highland, Island and Border, which lie within the compass of that small realm, his creative genius was awakened and the materials for its exercise were supplied. But his culture, connections, and interests were British, and for the British public he wrote. To the Highland Celts, whose picturesqueness made them the special darlings of his patriotic fancy, he was, like other Lowlanders, really an alien. In his poems, at least, there is little which, so far as language or sentiment is concerned, might not have been written by a native of any part of the island. Even the scenes and characters of his great poems are partly English, and only to a small extent taken from Scott's own Lowlands. The Lowland Scotch generally were Presbyterians and Whigs : Scott was an Episcopalian and a Tory. He descended and loved to trace his descent from the wild Borderers who were not more Scotch than English. His solidity of character, his geniality, his shrewdness, like his massive head and shaggy brows, were of Southern Scotland ; but a Southern Scotchman is a Northern Englishman. On the other hand, his genius and education were in an important sense Scotch, as not being classical : he knew no Greek, and his Latin was not so much classical as mediæval. He belonged entirely either to his own day or to the feudal age. Of Italian and Spanish Romance he had a tincture, but no deep dye.

The poetry of Scott flowed from a nature in which strength, high spirit, and active energy were united with tender sensibility and with an imagination wonderfully lively and directed by historic and antiquarian surroundings and by personal associations towards the feudal past. Homer may have been a warrior debarred from battle by blindness : Scott would perhaps have been a soldier if he had not been lame. War and its pageantry were his delight. He was the ardent quarter-master of a volunteer corps, and rode a hundred miles in twenty-four hours to muster, composing a poem by the way. It was not the only poem he composed on horseback. 'Oh ! man, I had many a grand gallop among those braes when I was thinking of Marmion.' In boyhood, despite his lameness, he was renowned as a pugilist, both 'in single fight and mixed affray,' and in after-life he was a keen sportsman, though he liked the chase best when it took him to historic scenes.

He loved to be and to be thought a man of action. Set to the law, though he did not love it, he faced the hard work gallantly, and could boast that when he was at the oar, no man pulled it harder : in fact it seems that had not his literary genius called him away he might have been a good lawyer. Of literature as a profession he was not so proud as he ought to have been, though no man ever pursued it more steadily or made more by it. He thought much of his pedigree, which connected him through Border chiefs with the House of Buccleuch, and above all things he desired to be a gentleman. 'Author as I am, I wish these good people would recollect that I began with being a gentleman and don't mean to give up the character.' In his eagerness to become the owner of a lordship and of the rank attached to it, which had a romantic as well as a social value in his eyes, he wrecked his fortune and brought on his declining age tragic calamity, which he faced with unquailing courage. The character of the strong and proud man with the weaknesses attendant on pride underlies all his productions.

The Violet is the memorial of an early cross in love, which perhaps left its trace on Scott's character in a shade of pensiveness. He afterwards made a marriage of intellectual disparagement, but in his family as in his social relations he was happy. Loved by all, men and animals, he embraced in his sympathies everything that was not mean or cowardly. Though himself a keen Tory, he reconciled in his art Tory and Whig, Cavalier and Covenanter, Catholic and Puritan. He loves to depict the mutual courtesies of generous foes. Once he forgot his chivalry in attacking Fox ; but in the introduction to the first canto of *Marmion* he made full amends.

A nature so joyous, a life so happy, so full of physical as well as of mental enjoyment, social success so great excluded all questionings about the mystery of being and all sympathy with the desire of change. There is not in Scott's poems a particle of the philosophy which we find in Wordsworth, Byron, and Shelley, or a shade of the melancholy which we find in the last two. He is as purely pictorial as Homer. The Revolution politically was his aversion ; it seemed to him merely vulgar and levelling. He wished 'to cleave the politic pates' of its Cobbetts as Homer revelled in the drubbing of Thersites. Intellectually it has left no more trace upon his poems than upon the waters of Loch Katrine.

Our generation has seen a strong current of religious reaction

setting towards the Middle Ages. Of this there is nothing in
Scott. The things which he loved in mediæval life were the
chivalry, the adventure, the feudal force of character, the aristo-
cratic sentiment, the military picturesqueness. For Dante he
cared little, while he cared much for Ariosto. Roman Catholicism
he contemned as a weak and effeminate superstition. Asceticism
was utterly alien to him ; in the Guard-room Song in *The Lady of
the Lake* he is anti-ascetic to the verge of coarseness. A boon
companion was in his eyes 'worth the whole Bernardine brood.'
In his writings the churchman appears only as the chaplain of the
warrior. His priests and friars are either jolly fellows who patter a
hasty mass for lords and knights impatient to be in their saddles, or
wizards like Michael Scott. Ecclesiastical ruins, though he loves
them as an antiquary, do not seem to move his reverence. At
Kirkwall and Iona he thinks much more about the tombs of
chieftains than about the monuments of religion. In Kirkwall
Cathedral, the Canterbury of the Orkneys, he says : 'The church
is as well fitted up as could be expected ; much of the old carved
oak remains, but with a motley mixture of modern deal pews : all
however is neat and clean, and does great honour to the Kirk
Session who maintain its decency.' Not so would he have spoken
of a famous castle of the Middle Ages.

The poet first drew the breath of mental life at Sandy Knowe,
the home of his grandfather. There he looked on a district 'in
which every field has its battle and every rivulet its song ;' on the
ruined tower of Smailholme, the scene of *The Eve of St. John*,
Mertoune and Hume Castle, Dryburgh and Melrose, the purple
bosks of Eildon, the hill of Faerie, the distant mountain region
of the Gala, the Ettrick and the Yarrow. Edinburgh, in which he
lived while reading law, he might well call 'his own romantic
town.' In his vacations it was his delight to ramble through the
dales of the Border, above all through Teviotdale, living with the
dalesmen, drinking whiskey with them—sometimes too much, for
there was an element of coarse conviviality as well as of popular
joviality in his character—and garnering in his eager mind their
Border tales and ballads. The fruits were a collection of *Border
Minstrelsy* (1802), with which he published some ballads of his
own. Being asked by Lady Dalkeith, wife of the heir of his
'chieftain,' the Duke of Buccleuch, to write her a ballad on the
legend of Gilpin Horner, and finding the subject grow under his
pen, he in a happy hour developed the ballad into the metrical

romance and produced *The Lay of the Last Minstrel.* The Last Minstrel is the poet himself, who revives in a prosaic and degenerate age the heroic memories of the olden time. Of those which followed *The Lady of the Lake* was the first revelation to the world of the lovely scenery and the poetry of clan life which lay enclasped and unknown to the cultivated world in the Highlands, into the fastnesses of which, physical and social, he had penetrated on a legal errand. This gave the poem an immense popularity. Otherwise *Marmion* is the greatest of his poems, while the *Lay* is the freshest. *Rokeby* and *The Lord of the Isles* show exhaustion, the last in a sad degree. Two minor romances, *The Bridal of Triermain* and *Harold the Dauntless*, have not taken rank with the five : *Harold the Dauntless* is weak ; but *Triermain*, in narrative skill and picturesqueness, is certainly superior to *The Lord of the Isles.* *The Vision of Don Roderick* has been justly described by Mr. Palgrave as an unsuccessful attempt to blend the past history of Spain with the interests of the Peninsular War. The Epistles introductory to the cantos of *Marmion* have been deemed out of place ; but they are in themselves charming pictures of Scott among his literary friends. They seem also to show that he well knew he was living in the present while he amused himself and his readers with the romantic past ; although he was sometimes enough under the illusion to be taken with ravishment by the mock-feudalism of George the Fourth's coronation, and to play with heart and soul the cockney Highlander on the occasion of the same monarch's farcical visit to Scotland.

Before *The Lord of the Isles, Waverley* appeared. Scott's career as a novelist began as his career as a poet ended. His vein was worked out, his popularity flagged, he was being eclipsed by Byron, one part of whose talisman the high-minded and self-repressing gentleman certainly would not have condescended to borrow.

Scott has vindicated the metre of his tales as preferable to Pope's couplet : in the case of a romance which was a development of the ballad, the vindication was needless. Scott's metre is the true English counterpart, if there be one, of Homer. In *The Lady of the Lake* and *Rokeby* it is the simple eight-syllable couplet. In the other poems variations are freely introduced with the best effect. Scott had no ear for music, but he had an ear for verse.

In each of the romances, *The Lord of the Isles* perhaps excepted, there is an exciting story, well told, for Scott was a thorough master of narration. In *The Lay of the Last Minstrel*, it is true, the *diablerie* sits lorn on the general plot ; but it was an imposed task, not his own idea. We are always carried on, as the writer was himself when he was composing *Marmion*, by the elastic stride of a strong horse over green turf and in the freshest air. Abounding power alike of invention and expression is always there ; and we feel throughout the influence of Scott's strong though genial and sympathetic character and the control of his masculine sense, which never permits bad taste or extravagance. The language however, always good and flowing, is never very choice or memorable. There is not seldom a want of finish ; and under the seductive influence of the facile measure, the wonderful ease not seldom runs into diffuseness, and sometimes, in the weaker poems, into a prolixity of common-place.

> 'Though wild as cloud. as stream, as gale,
> Flow forth, flow unrestrained, my tale!'

Scott was a little too fond of unrestrained flow ; and perhaps it rather pleased him to think that his works were carelessly thrown off, by a gentleman writing for his amusement, not laboured by a professional writer.

He was a painter of action rather than of character, at least in its higher grades. Something of insight and experience which Homer had he wanted. All the heroes of his novels are insipid except the Master of Ravenswood, who interests not by his character but by his circumstances ; all the heroines except Di Vernon, who interests by her circumstances and her horsemanship. So it is with the heroes and heroines of the poems. Margaret, in the *Lay of the Last Minstrel*, comes on with a charming movement, but she remains merely the fairest maid of Teviotdale. The best characters are heroic scoundrels, such as Marmion the stately forger, and Bertram Risingham the buccaneer with a vein of good in his evil nature. 'The worst of all my undertakings,' says Scott himself, 'is that my rogue always in despite of me turns out my hero.' The author of *Paradise Lost* met with the same misfortune. Marmion is an almost impossible mixture of majesty and felony ; but he is better than a seraph of a gentleman. There is not a happier passage in the poems than that in which, as a gentle judgment on his career of criminal ambition, the peasant takes his place in the baronial tomb. It is marred by the moralising at the end. Scott did not know when enough had been said.

'To write a modern romance of chivalry,' said Jeffrey in his review of *Marmion,* 'seems to be much such a phantasy as to build a modern abbey or an English pagoda.' Restorations are forced and therefore they are weak, even when the mind of the restorer is so steeped in the lore of the past as was that of Scott. His best works, after all, are his novels of contemporary or nearly contemporary life. A revival, whether in fiction or in painting, is a masquerade. Scott knew the Middle Ages better perhaps than any other man of his time; but he did not know them as they are known now; and an antiquary would pick many holes in his costume. His baronial mansion at Abbotsford was bastard Gothic, and so are many details of his poems. The pageantry not seldom makes us think of the circus, while in the sentiment there is too often a strain of the historical melodrama. The Convent Scene in Marmion is injured by the melodramatic passage in the speech of Constance about the impending dissolution of the monasteries.

All that a reviver could do by love of his period Scott did. He shows his passionate desire of realising feudal life, and at the same time his circumstantial vividness of fancy, by a minuteness of detail like that which we find in Homer, who perhaps was also a Last Minstrel. He resembles Homer too in his love of local names, which to him were full of associations.

Scott has said of himself—'To me the wandering over the field of Bannockburn was the source of more exquisite pleasure than gazing upon the celebrated landscape from the battlements of Stirling Castle. I do not by any means infer that I was dead to the feeling of picturesque scenery; on the contrary, few delighted more in its general effect. But I was unable with the eye of a painter to dissect the various parts of the scene, to comprehend how the one bore on the other, to estimate the effect which various features of the view had in producing its leading and general effect.' It is true that he had not a painter's eye any more than he had a musician's ear; and we may be sure that the landscape charmed him most when it was the scene of some famous deed or the setting of some legendary tower. Yet he had a passionate love of the beauties of nature and communicated it to his readers. He turned the Highlands from a wilderness at the thought of which culture shuddered into a place of universal pilgrimage. He was conscientious in his study of nature, going over the scene of *Rokeby* with book in hand and taking down all the plants and shrubs, though he sometimes lapsed into a closet description, as in saying of the buttresses of Melrose in the moonlight that they seem framed alternately of ebon and ivory. Many of his pictures, such as that of Coriskin, are examples of pure landscape painting without the aid of historical accessories. In a nature so warm, feeling for colour was sure not to be wanting; the best judges have pronounced that Scott possessed this gift in an eminent degree; and his picture of Edinburgh and the Camp in *Marmion* has been given as an example. He never thought of lending a soul to Nature like the author of *Tintern Abbey*, to whose genius he paid hearty homage across a wide gulf of difference. But he could give her life; and he could make her sympathise with the human drama, as in the lines at the end of the Convent Canto of *Marmion* and in the opening of *Rokeby*, which rivals the opening of *Hamlet* in the cold winter night on the lonely platform of Elsinore.

Of the ballads and lyrical pieces some were Scott's earliest productions; among these is the *Eve of St. John*, in which his romantic imagination is at its height. Others are scattered through the romances and novels. In the ballads, even when they are most successful as imitations of the antique, there is inevitably something modern: but so, it may be said, there is in the old ballads themselves, or they would not touch us as they do. Edmund's song in *Rokeby* is an old ballad, only with a finer grace and a more tender pathos. There is nothing in Scott's lyrical poetry deep or spiritual; the same fresh, joyous unphilosophising character runs through all his works: but in 'County Guy' he shows a true lyrical power of awakening by suggestion thoughts which would suffer by distinct expression.

GOLDWIN SMITH.

The Last Minstrel.

[From *The Lay of the Last Minstrel.* Introduction to Canto I.]

The way was long, the wind was cold,
The Minstrel was infirm and old;
His wither'd cheek, and tresses grey,
Seem'd to have known a better day;
The harp, his sole remaining joy,
Was carried by an orphan boy.
The last of all the Bards was he,
Who sung of Border chivalry;
For, welladay! their date was fled,
His tuneful brethren all were dead;
And he, neglected and oppress'd,
Wish'd to be with them, and at rest.
No more on prancing palfrey borne,
He carolled light as lark at morn:
No longer courted and caress'd,
High placed in hall, a welcome guest,
He pour'd, to lord and lady gay,
The unpremeditated lay:
Old times were changed, old manners gone;
A stranger filled the Stuarts' throne;
The bigots of the iron time
Had call'd his harmless art a crime.
A wandering Harper, scorn'd and poor,
He begg'd his bread from door to door,
And tuned, to please a peasant's ear,
The harp a king had loved to hear.

He pass'd where Newark's stately tower
Looks out from Yarrow's birchen bower:
The Minstrel gazed with wishful eye—
No humbler resting-place was nigh:
With hesitating step at last,
The embattled portal arch he pass'd,

Whose ponderous grate and massy bar
Had oft roll'd back the tide of war,
But never closed the iron door
Against the desolate and poor.
The Duchess [1] mark'd his weary pace,
His timid mien, and reverend face,
And bade her page the menials tell
That they should tend the old man well
For she had known adversity,
Though born in such a high degree;
In pride of power, in beauty's bloom,
Had wept o'er Monmouth's bloody tomb!

When kindness had his wants supplied,
And the old man was gratified,
Began to rise his minstrel pride;
And he began to talk anon,
Of good Earl Francis [2], dead and gone,
And of Earl Walter [3], rest him, God!
A braver ne'er to battle rode;
And how full many a tale he knew
Of the old warriors of Buccleuch;
And, would the noble Duchess deign
To listen to an old man's strain,
Though stiff his hand, his voice though weak,
He thought even yet, the sooth to speak,
That, if she loved the harp to hear,
He could make music to her ear.

The humble boon was soon obtain'd;
The aged Minstrel audience gain'd.
But, when he reach'd the room of state,
Where she, with all her ladies, sate,

[1] Anne, Duchess of Buccleuch and Monmouth, representative of the ancient Lords of Buccleuch, and widow of the unfortunate James, Duke of Monmouth, who was beheaded in 1685.

[2] Francis Scott, Earl of Buccleuch, father of the Duchess.

[3] Walter, Earl of Buccleuch, grandfather of the Duchess, and a celebrated warrior.

Perchance he wish'd his boon denied:
For, when to tune his harp he tried,
His trembling hand had lost the ease
Which marks security to please;
And scenes, long past, of joy and pain,
Came wildering o'er his aged brain—
He tried to tune his harp in vain!
The pitying Duchess praised its chime,
And gave him heart, and gave him time,
Till every string's according glee
Was blended into harmony.
And then, he said, he would full fain
He could recall an ancient strain,
He never thought to sing again.
It was not framed for village churls,
But for high dames and mighty earls;
He had play'd it to King Charles the good,
When he kept court in Holyrood;
And much he wish'd, yet fear'd, to try
The long-forgotten melody.

Amid the strings his finger stray'd,
And an uncertain warbling made,
And oft he shook his hoary head.
But when he caught the measure wild,
The old man raised his face, and smiled;
And lighten'd up his faded eye,
With all a poet's ecstasy!
In varying cadence, soft or strong,
He swept the sounding chords along:
The present scene, the future lot,
His toils, his wants, were all forgot:
Cold diffidence, and age's frost,
In the full tide of song were lost;
Each blank in faithless memory void,
The poet's glowing thought supplied:
And, while his harp responsive rung,
'T was thus the Latest Minstrel sung.

The Camp.

[From *Marmion,* Canto IV.]

[Marmion and Sir David Lindesay survey the Scottish Camp from
Blackford Hill.]

Early they took Dun-Edin's road,
And I could trace each step they trode :
Hill, brook, nor dell, nor rock, nor stone,
Lies on the path to me unknown.
Much might it boast of storied lore ;
But, passing such digression o'er,
Suffice it that their route was laid
Across the furzy hills of Braid.
They pass'd the glen and scanty rill,
And climb'd the opposing bank, until
They gain'd the top of Blackford Hill.

Blackford ! on whose uncultured breast,
    Among the broom, and thorn, and whin,
A truant-boy, I sought the nest,
Or listed, as I lay at rest,
    While rose on breezes thin,
The murmur of the city crowd,
And, from his steeple jangling loud,
    Saint Giles's mingling din.
Now, from the summit to the plain,
Waves all the hill with yellow grain ;
    And o'er the landscape as I look,
Nought do I see unchanged remain,
    Save the rude cliffs and chiming brook.
To me they make a heavy moan,
Of early friendships past and gone.

But different far the change has been,
    Since Marmion, from the crown
Of Blackford, saw that martial scene
    Upon the bent so brown :

Thousand pavilions, white as snow,
Spread all the Borough-moor below,
  Upland, and dale, and down :—
A thousand, did I say? I ween,
Thousands on thousands there were seen,
That chequer'd all the heath between
  The streamlet and the town ;
In crossing ranks extending far,
Forming a camp irregular ;
Oft giving way, where still there stood
Some relics of the old oak wood,
That darkly huge did intervene,
And tamed the glaring white with green :
In these extended lines there lay
A martial kingdom's vast array.

Far from Hebudes, dark with rain,
To eastern Lodon's fertile plain,
And from the southern Redswire edge,
To farthest Rosse's rocky ledge ;
From west to east, from south to north,
Scotland sent all her warriors forth.
Marmion might hear the mingled hum
Of myriads up the mountain come ;
The horses' tramp, and tingling clank,
Where chiefs review'd their vassal rank,
  And charger's shrilling neigh ;
And see the shifting lines advance
While frequent flash'd, from shield and lance,
  The sun's reflected ray.

Thin curling in the morning air,
The wreaths of failing smoke declare
To embers now the brands decay'd,
Where the night-watch their fires had made.
They saw, slow rolling on the plain,
Full many a baggage-cart and wain,
And dire artillery's clumsy car,
By sluggish oxen tugg'd to war ;

And there were Borthwick's Sisters Seven [1],
And culverins which France had given.
Ill-omen'd gift! the guns remain
The conqueror's spoil on Flodden plain.

Nor mark'd they less, where in the air
A thousand streamers flaunted fair;
  Various in shape, device, and hue,
  Green, sanguine, purple, red, and blue,
Broad, narrow, swallow-tailed, and square,
Scroll, pennon, pensil, bandrol [2], there
  O'er the pavilions flew.
Highest and midmost, was descried
The royal banner floating wide;
  The staff, a pine-tree, strong and straight,
Pitch'd deeply in a massive stone,
Which still in memory is shown,
  Yet bent beneath the standard's weight
  Whene'er the western wind unroll'd,
  With toil, the huge and cumbrous fold,
And gave to view the dazzling field,
Where, in proud Scotland's royal shield,
  The ruddy Lion ramp'd in gold.

Lord Marmion view'd the landscape bright,—
He view'd it with a chief's delight,—
  Until within him burn'd his heart,
  And lightning from his eye did part,
    As on the battle-day;
  Such glance did falcon never dart,
    When stooping on his prey
'Oh! well, Lord-Lion, hast thou said,
Thy King from warfare to dissuade
  Were but a vain essay:

[1] Seven culverins so called, cast by one Borthwick.
[2] Each of these feudal ensigns intimated the different rank of those entitled to display them.

For, by St. George, were that host **mine,**
Not power infernal, nor divine,
Should once to peace my soul incline,
Till I had dimm'd their armour's shin**e**
   In glorious battle fray!'
Answer'd the Bard, of milder mood,—
'Fair is the sight,—and yet 'twere goo**d,**
   That Kings would think withal,
When peace and wealth their land **has bless'd,**
'Tis better to sit still at rest,
   Than rise, perchance **to** fall.'

Still on the spot Lord Marmion stay'**d,**
For fairer scene he ne'er survey'd.
   When sated with the martial show
   That peopled all the plain below,
   The wandering eye could o'er it g**o,**
   And mark the distant city glow
     With gloomy splendour red ;
   For on the smoke-wreaths, huge and **slow,**
   That round her sable turrets flow,
     The morning beams were shed,
   And tinged them with a lustre proud,
   Like that which streaks a thunder-cloud.
Such dusky grandeur clothed the height,
Where the huge Castle holds its state,
   And all the deep slope down,
Whose ridgy back heaves to the sky,
Piled deep and massy, close and hig**h,**
   Mine own romantic town !
But northward far, with purer blaz**e,**
On Ochil mountains fell the rays,
And as each heathy top they kiss'**d,**
   It gleam'd a purple amethyst.
Yonder the shores of Fife you saw **;**
Here Preston-Bay and Berwick-Law **;**
   And, broad between them rolled,
The gallant Frith the eye migh**t** note,

Whose islands on its bosom float,
  Like emeralds chased in gold.
Fitz-Eustace' heart felt closely pent;
As if to give his rapture vent,
The spur he to his charger lent,
  And raised his bridle hand,
And making demi-volte in air,
Cried, 'Where's the coward that would not dare
  To fight for such a land!'
The Lindesay smiled his joy to see;
Nor Marmion's frown repress'd his glee.

Thus while they look'd, a flourish proud,
Where mingled trump, and clarion loud,
  And fife, and kettle-drum,
And sacbut deep, and psaltery,
And war-pipe with discordant cry,
And cymbal clattering to the sky,
Making wild music bold and high,
  Did up the mountain come;
The whilst the bells, with distant chime,
Merrily toll'd the hour of prime,
  And thus the Lindesay spoke:
'Thus clamour still the war-notes when
The King to mass his way has ta'en,
Or to St. Katharine's of Sienne,
  Or Chapel of Saint Rocque.
To you they speak of martial fame;
But me remind of peaceful game,
  When blither was their cheer,
Thrilling in Falkland-woods the air,
In signal none his steed should spare,
But strive which foremost might repair
  To the downfall of the deer.

BATTLE OF BEAL' AN DUINE.

[From *The Lady of the Lake*, Canto VI.]

[The Minstrel relates to the dying Roderick Dhu, Chief of Clan Alpine, the
story of the battle between the royal forces and those of the Clan.]

The Minstrel came once more to view
The eastern ridge of Benvenue,
For ere he parted, he would say
Farewell to lovely Loch Achray—
Where shall he find, in foreign land,
So lone a lake, so sweet a strand!—
There is no breeze upon the fern,
 Nor ripple on the lake,
Upon her eyry nods the erne,
 The deer has sought the brake;
The small birds will not sing aloud,
 The springing trout lies still,
So darkly glooms yon thunder cloud,
That swathes, as with a purple shroud,
 Benledi's distant hill.
Is it the thunder's solemn sound
 That mutters deep and dread,
Or echoes from the groaning ground
 The warrior's measured tread?
Is it the lightning's quivering glance
 That on the thicket streams,
Or do they flash on spear and lance—
 The sun's retiring beams?—
I see the dagger-crest of Mar,
I see the Moray's silver star,
Wave o'er the cloud of Saxon war,
That up the lake comes winding far!
 To hero bound for battle-strife,
  Or bard of martial lay,
 'Twere worth ten years of peaceful life,
  One glance at their array!

Their light-arm'd archers far and near
  Survey'd the tangled ground,
Their centre ranks, with pike and spear,
  A twilight forest frown'd,
Their barbed horsemen, in the rear,
  The stern battalia crown'd.
No cymbal clash'd, no clarion rang,
  Still were the pipe and drum;
Save heavy tread, and armour's clang,
  The sullen march was dumb.
There breathed no wind their crests to shake,
  Or wave their flags abroad;
Scarce the frail aspen seem'd to quake,
  That shadow'd o'er their road.
Their vaward scouts no tidings bring,
  Can rouse no lurking foe,
Nor spy a trace of living thing,
  Save when they stirr'd the roe;
The host moves like a deep-sea wave,
Where rise no rocks its power to brave,
  High-swelling, dark, and slow.
The lake is pass'd, and now they gain
A narrow and a broken plain,
Before the Trosach's rugged jaws;
And here the horse and spearmen pause,
While, to explore the dangerous glen,
Dive through the pass the archer-men.

At once there rose so wild a yell
Within that dark and narrow dell,
As all the fiends, from heaven that fell,
Had peal'd the banner-cry of hell!
  Forth from the pass in tumult driven,
  Like chaff before the wind of heaven,
    The archery appear:
  For life! for life! their plight they ply—
  And shriek, and shout, and battle-cry,
  And plaids and bonnets waving high,

And broad-swords flashing to the sky,
　　Are maddening in the rear.
Onward they drive, in dreadful race,
　　Pursuers and pursued;
Before that tide of flight and chase,
How shall it keep its rooted place,
　　The spearmen's twilight wood?—
'Down, down,' cried Mar, 'your lances down!
　　Bear back both friend and foe!'
Like reeds before the tempest's frown,
That serried grove of lances brown
　　At once lay levell'd low;
And closely shouldering side to side,
The bristling ranks the onset bide.—
'We'll quell the savage mountaineer,
　　As their Tinchel[1] cows the game!
They come as fleet as forest deer,
　　We'll drive them back as tame.'

Bearing before them, in their course,
The relics of the archer force,
Like wave with crest of sparkling foam,
Right onward did Clan-Alpine come.
　　Above the tide, each broadsword bright
　　Was brandishing like beam of light,
　　　Each targe was dark below;
　　And with the ocean's mighty swing,
　　When heaving to the tempest's wing,
　　　They hurl'd them on the foe.
I heard the lance's shivering crash,
As when the whirlwind rends the ash;
I heard the broadsword's deadly clang,
As if an hundred anvils rang!
But Moray wheel'd his rearward rank
Of horsemen on Clan Alpine's flank,—
　　'My banner-man, advance!
　　I see,' he cried, 'their column shake.
　　Now, gallants! for your ladies' sake,
　　　Upon them with the lance!'—

[1] A gradually narrowing circle of sportsmen closing in the game.

The horsemen dash'd among the rout,
  As deer break through the broom ;
Their steeds are stout, their swords are out,
  They soon make lightsome room.
Clan-Alpine's best are backward borne—
  Where, where was Roderick then !
One blast upon his bugle horn
  Were worth a thousand men.
And refluent through the pass of fear
  The battle's tide was pour'd ;
Vanish'd the Saxon's struggling spear,
  Vanish'd the mountain-sword.
As Bracklinn's chasm, so black and steep,
  Receives her roaring linn,
As the dark caverns of the deep
  Suck the wild whirlpool in,
So did the deep and darksome pass
Devour the battle's mingled mass :
None linger now upon the plain,
Save those who ne'er shall fight again.

THE BUCCANEER.

[From *Rokeby*, Canto I.]

[Bertram Risingham, the Buccaneer, brings the tidings of Marston Moor, and of his murder of Philip Mortham in the battle, to Oswald Wycliffe, his accomplice, then holding Barnard Castle for the Parliament.]

Far town-ward sounds a distant tread,
And Oswald, starting from his bed,
Hath caught it, though no human ear,
Unsharpen'd by revenge and fear,
Could e'er distinguish horse's clank,
Until it reach'd the castle bank.
Now nigh and plain the sound appears,
The warder's challenge now he hears,
Then clanking chains and levers tell,
That o'er the moat the drawbridge fell,
And, in the castle court below,
Voices are heard, and torches glow,

As marshalling the stranger's way,
Straight for the room where Oswald lay;
The cry was,—'Tidings from the host,
Of weight—a messenger comes post.'
Stifling the tumult of his breast,
His answer Oswald thus express'd—
'Bring food and wine, and trim the fire;
Admit the stranger, and retire.'

The stranger came with heavy stride;
The morion's plumes his visage hide,
And the buff-coat, an ample fold,
Mantles his form's gigantic mould.
Full slender answer deigned he
To Oswald's anxious courtesy,
But mark'd, by a disdainful smile,
He saw and scorn'd the petty wile,
When Oswald changed the torch's place,
Anxious that on the soldier's face
Its partial lustre might be thrown,
To show his looks, yet hide his own.
His guest, the while, laid low aside
The ponderous cloak of tough bull's hide,
And to the torch glanced broad and clear
The corslet of a cuirassier;
Then from his brows the casque he drew,
And from the dank plume dash'd the dew,
From gloves of mail relieved his hands,
And spread them to the kindling brands,
And, turning to the genial board,
Without a health, or pledge, or word
Of meet and social reverence said,
Deeply he drank, and fiercely fed;
As free from ceremony's sway,
As famish'd wolf that tears his prey.

With deep impatience, tinged with fear,
His host beheld him gorge his cheer,
And quaff the full carouse, that lent
His brow a fiercer hardiment.

Now Oswald stood a space aside,
Now paced the room with hasty stride,
In feverish agony to learn
Tidings of deep and dread concern,
Cursing each moment that his guest
Protracted o'er his ruffian feast.
Yet, viewing with alarm, at last,
The end of that uncouth repast,
Almost he seem'd their haste to rue,
As, at his sign, his train withdrew,
And left him with the stranger, free
To question of his mystery.
Then did his silence long proclaim
A struggle between fear and shame.
Much in the stranger's mien appears,
To justify suspicious fears.
On his dark face a scorching clime,
And toil, had done the work of time,
Roughen'd the brow, the temples bared,
And sable hairs with silver shared,
Yet left—what age alone could tame—
The lip of pride, the eye of flame ;
The full-drawn lip that upward curl'd,
The eye that seem'd to scorn the world.
That lip had terror never blench'd :
Ne'er in that eye had tear-drop quench'd
The flash severe of swarthy glow,
That mock'd at pain, and knew not woe.
Inured to danger's direst form,
Tornade and earthquake, flood and storm,
Death had he seen by sudden blow,
By wasting plague, by tortures slow,
By mine or breach, by steel or ball,
Knew all his shapes, and scorn'd them all.

But yet, though Bertram's hardened look,
Unmoved, could blood and danger brook,
Still worse than apathy had place
On his swart brow and callous face ;

For evil passions, cherish'd long,
Had plough'd them with impressions strong.
All that gives gloss to sin, all gay
Light folly, past with youth away,
But rooted stood, in manhood's hour,
The weeds of vice without their flower,
And yet the soil in which they grew,
Had it been tamed when life was new,
Had depth and vigour to bring forth
The hardier fruits of virtuous worth.
Not that, e'en then, his heart had known
The gentler feelings' kindly tone ;
But lavish waste had been refined
To bounty in his chasten'd mind,
And lust of gold, that waste to feed,
Been lost in love of glory's meed,
And, frantic then no more, his pride
Had ta'en fair virtue for its guide.
Even now, by conscience unrestrain'd,
Clogg'd by gross vice, by slaughter stain'd,
Still knew his daring soul to soar,
And mastery o'er the mind he bore ;
For meaner guilt, or heart less hard,
Quail'd beneath Bertram's bold regard.
And this felt Oswald, while in vain
He strove, by many a winding train,
To lure his sullen guest to show,
Unask'd, the news he long'd to know,
While on far other subject hung
His heart, than falter'd from his tongue.
Yet nought for that his guest did deign
To note or spare his secret pain,
But still, in stern and stubborn sort,
Return'd him answer dark and short,
Or started from the theme, to range
In loose digression wild and strange,
And forced the embarrass'd host to buy,
By query close, direct reply.

Lake Coriskin.

[From *The Lord of the Isles*, Canto III.]

A while their route they silent made,
 As men who stalk for mountain-deer,
Till the good Bruce to Ronald said,—
 'Saint Mary! what a scene is here!
I've traversed many a mountain-strand,
Abroad and in my native land,
And it has been my lot to tread
Where safety more than pleasure led ;
Thus, many a waste I've wandered o'er,
Clombe many a crag, cross'd many a moor,
 But, by my halidome,
A scene so rude, so wild as this,
Yet so sublime in barrenness,
Ne'er did my wandering footsteps press,
 Where'er I happ'd to roam.'

No marvel thus the Monarch spake ;
 For rarely human eye has known
A scene so stern as that dread lake,
 With its dark ledge of barren stone.
Seems that primeval earthquake's sway
Hath rent a strange and shatter'd way
 Through the rude bosom of the hill,
And that each naked precipice,
Sable ravine, and dark abyss,
 Tells of the outrage still.
The wildest glen, but this, can show
Some touch of Nature's genial glow ;
On high Benmore green mosses grow,
And heath-bells bud in deep Glencroe,
 And copse on Cruchan-Ben ;
But here,—above, around, below,
 On mountain or in glen,

Nor tree, nor shrub, nor plant, nor flower,
Nor aught of vegetative power,
    The weary eye may ken.
For all is rocks at random thrown,
Black waves, bare crags, and banks of stone,
    As if were here denied
The summer sun, the spring's sweet dew,
That clothe with many a varied hue
    The bleakest mountain-side.

And wilder, forward as they wound,
Were the proud cliffs and lake profound.
Huge terraces of granite black
Afforded rude and cumber'd track ;
    For from the mountain hoar,
Hurl'd headlong in some night of fear,
When yell'd the wolf, and fled the deer,
    Loose crags had toppled o'er ;
And some, chance-poised and balanced, lay
So that a stripling arm might sway
    A mass no host could raise,
In Nature's rage at random thrown,
Yet trembling like the Druid's stone
    On its precarious base.
The evening mists, with ceaseless change,
Now clothed the mountains' lofty range,
    Now left their foreheads bare,
And round the skirts their mantle furl'd,
Or on the sable waters curl'd,
Or on the eddying breezes whirl'd,
    Dispersed in middle air.
And oft, condensed, at once they lower,
When, brief and fierce, the mountain shower
    Pours like a torrent down,
And when return the sun's glad beams,
Whiten'd with foam a thousand streams
    Leap from the mountain's crown.

'This lake,' said Bruce, 'whose barriers drear
Are precipices sharp and sheer.
Yielding no track for goat or deer,
    Save the black shelves we tread,
How term you its dark waves? and how
Yon northern mountain's pathless brow,
    And yonder peak of dread,
That to the evening sun uplifts
The griesly gulfs and slaty rifts,
    Which seam its shiver'd head?'—
'Coriskin call the dark lake's name,
Coolin the ridge, as bards proclaim,
From old Cuchullin, chief of fame.
But bards, familiar in our isles
Rather with Nature's frowns than smiles,
Full oft their careless humours please
By sportive names from scenes like these.
I would old Torquil were to show
His maidens with their breasts of snow,
Or that my noble Liege were nigh
To hear his Nurse sing lullaby!
(The Maids—tall cliffs with breakers white,
The Nurse—a torrent's roaring might,)
Or that your eye could see the mood
Of Corryvrekin's whirlpool rude,
When dons the Hag her whiten'd hood—
'Tis thus our islesmen's fancy frames,
For scenes so stern, fantastic names.'

THE EVE OF ST. JOHN.

The Baron of Smaylho'me rose with day,
    He spurred his courser on,
Without stop or stay, down the rocky way,
    That leads to Brotherstone.

He went not with the bold Buccleuch,
    His banner broad to rear;
He went not 'gainst the English yew,
    To lift the Scottish spear.

Yet his plate-jack[1] was braced, and his helmet was laced,
  And his vaunt-brace of proof he wore ;
At his saddle-gerthe was a good steel sperthe,
  Full ten pound weight and more.

The Baron returned in three days' space,
  And his looks were sad and sour ;
And weary was his courser's pace,
  As he reached his rocky tower.

He came rot from where Ancram Moor
  Ran red with English blood ;
Where the Douglas true, and the bold Buccleuch,
  'Gainst keen Lord Evers stood.

Yet was his helmet hacked and hewed,
  His acton pierced and tore,
His axe and his dagger with blood imbrued,—
  But it was not English gore.

He lighted at the Chapellage,
  He held him close and still ;
And he whistled thrice for his little foot-page,
  His name was English Will.

'Come thou hither, my little foot-page,
  Come hither to my knee ;
Though thou art young, and tender of age,
  I think thou art true to me.

'Come, tell me all that thou hast seen,
  And look thou tell me true !
Since I from Smaylho'me tower have been,
  What did my lady do?'—

'My lady, each night, sought the lonely light
  That burns on the wild Watchfold ;
For, from height to height, the beacons bright
  Of the English foemen told.

---

[1] The plate-jack is coat armour ; the vaunt-brace, or wam-brace armour
for the body ; the sperthe, a battle-axe.

'The bittern clamoured from the moss,
  The wind blew loud and shrill ;
Yet the craggy pathway she did cross,
  To the eiry Beacon Hill.

'I watched her steps, and silent came
  Where she sat her on a stone ;
No watchman stood by the dreary flame ;
  It burned all alone.

'The second night I kept her in sight,
  Till to the fire she came,
And, by Mary's might ! an armèd Knight
  Stood by the lonely flame.

'And many a word that warlike lord
  Did speak to my lady there ;
But the rain fell fast, and loud blew the blast,
  And I heard not what they were.

'The third night there the sky was fair,
  And the mountain-blast was still,
As again I watched the secret pair,
  On the lonesome Beacon Hill.

'And I heard her name the midnight hour,
  And name this holy eve ;
And say, "Come this night to thy lady's bower ;
  Ask no bold Baron's leave.

'"He lifts his spear with the bold Buccleuch ;
  His lady is all alone ;
The door she'll undo to her knight so true,
  On the eve of good St. John."—

'"I cannot come ; I must not come ;
  I dare not come to thee ;
On the eve of St. John I must wander alone ;
  In thy bower I may not be."—

'"Now, out on thee, faint-hearted knight !
  Thou shouldst not say me nay ;
For the eve is sweet, and when lovers meet,
  Is worth the whole summer's day.

'" And I'll chain the blood-hound, and the warder shall not
　　 sound,
　 And rushes shall be strewed on the stair ;
So, by the black rood-stone ¹, and by holy St. John,
　 I conjure thee, my love, to be there ! "

'" Though the blood-hound be mute, and the rush beneath
　　 my foot,
　 And the warder his bugle should not blow,
Yet there sleepeth a priest in the chamber to the east,
　 And my footstep he would know."

'" O fear not the priest, who sleepeth to the east ;
　 For to Dryburgh the way he has ta'en ;
And there to say mass, till three days do pass,
　 For the soul of a knight that is slain."—

'He turned him around, and grimly he frowned ;
　 Then he laughed right scornfully—
" He who says the mass-rite for the soul of that knight,
　 May as well say mass for me :

'" At the lone midnight hour, when bad spirits have power,
　 In thy chamber will I be."—
With that he was gone, and my lady left alone,
　 And no more did I see.'—

Then changed, I trow, was that bold Baron's brow,
　 From the dark to the blood-red high ;
' Now tell me the mien of the knight thou hast seen,
　 For, by Mary, he shall die !'—

' His arms shone full bright, in the beacon's red light ;
　 His plume it was scarlet and blue ;
On his shield was a hound, in a silver leash bound,
　 And his crest was a branch of the yew.'—

¹ The black-rood of Melrose was a crucifix of black marble, and of
superior sanctity.

'Thou liest, thou liest, thou little foot-page,
   Loud dost thou lie to me!
For that knight is cold, and low laid in the mould,
   All under the Eildon-tree [1].'—

'Yet hear but my word, my noble lord!
   For I heard her name his name;
And that lady bright, she called the knight,
   Sir Richard of Coldinghame.'

The bold Baron's brow then changed, I trow,
   From high blood-red to pale—
'The grave is deep and dark—and the corpse is stiff and stark—
   So I may not trust thy tale.

'Where fair Tweed flows round holy Melrose,
   And Eildon slopes to the plain,
Full three nights ago, by some secret foe,
   That gay gallant was slain.

'The varying light deceived thy sight,
   And the wild winds drowned the name;
For the Dryburgh bells ring, and the white monks do sing,
   For Sir Richard of Coldinghame!'

He passed the court-gate, and he oped the tower grate,
   And he mounted the narrow stair
To the bartizan-seat, where, with maids that on her wait,
   He found his lady fair.

That lady sat in mournful mood;
   Looked over hill and vale;
Over Tweed's fair flood, and Mertoun's wood,
   And all down Teviotdale.

[1] Eildon is a high hill, terminating in three conical summits, immediately above the town of Melrose, where are the admired ruins of a magnificent monastery. Eildon-tree is said to be the spot where Thomas the Rhymer uttered his prophecies.

'Now hail, now hail, thou lady bright!'—
   'Now hail, thou Baron true!
What news, what news from Ancram fight?
   What news from the bold Buccleuch?'—

'The Ancram Moor is red with gore,
   For many a Southron fell;
And Buccleuch has charged us, evermore
   To watch our beacons well.'

The lady blushed red, but nothing she said;
   Nor added the Baron a word;
Then she stepped down the stair to her chamber fair,
   And so did her moody lord.

In sleep the lady mourned, and the Baron tossed and turned,
   And oft to himself he said—
'The worms around him creep, and his bloody grave is deep , ,
   It cannot give up the dead!'

It was near the ringing of matin-bell,
   The night was wellnigh done,
When a heavy sleep on that Baron fell,
   On the eve of good St. John.

The lady looked through the chamber fair
   By the light of a dying flame;
And she was aware of a knight stood there—
   Sir Richard of Coldinghame!

'Alas! away, away!' she cried,
   'For the holy Virgin's sake!'—
'Lady, I know who sleeps by thy side;
   But, lady, he will not awake.

'By Eildon-tree, for long nights three,
   In bloody grave have I lain;
The mass and the death-prayer are said for me,
   But lady, they are said in vain.

'By the Baron's brand, near Tweed's fair strand,
  Most foully slain I fell;
And my restless sprite on the beacon's height
  For a space is doomed to dwell.

'At our trysting-place, for a certain space
  I must wander to and fro;
But I had not had power to come to thy bower,
  Hadst thou not conjured me so.'—

Love mastered fear—her brow she crossed;
  'How, Richard, hast thou sped?
And art thou saved, or art thou lost?'—
  The Vision shook his head!

'Who spilleth life, shall forfeit life,
  So bid my lord believe;
That lawless love is guilt above,
  This awful sign receive.'

He laid his left palm on an oaken beam;
  His right upon her hand;
The lady shrunk, and fainting sunk,
  For it scorched like a fiery brand.

The sable score, of fingers four,
  Remains on that board impressed;
And for evermore that lady wore
  A covering on her wrist.

There is a Nun in Dryburgh bower,
  Ne'er looks upon the sun:
There is a Monk in Melrose tower,
  He speaketh word to none.

That Nun, who ne'er beholds the day,
  That Monk, who speaks to none—
That Nun was Smaylho'me's Lady gay,
  That Monk the bold Baron.

EDMUND'S SONG.

[From *Rokeby*.]

O, Brignall banks are wild and fair,
    And Greta woods are green,
And you may gather garlands there,
    Would grace a summer queen.

And as I rode by Dalton-hall.
    Beneath the turrets high.
A Maiden on the castle wall
    Was singing merrily,—

Chorus.

'O, Brignall banks are fresh and fair,
    And Greta woods are green;
I'd rather rove with Edmund there,
    Than reign our English queen.'—

'If, maiden, thou would'st wend with me,
    To leave both tower and town,
Thou first must guess what life lead we,
    That dwell by dale and down:
And if thou canst that riddle read,
    As read full well you may,
Then to the greenwood shalt thou speed,
    As blithe as Queen of May.'—

Chorus.

Yet sung she, 'Brignal banks are fair,
    And Greta woods are green;
I'd rather rove with Edmund there,
    Than reign our English queen.

'I read you, by your bugle-horn,
    And by your palfrey good,
I read you for a ranger sworn,
    To keep the king's greenwood.'—

'A ranger, lady, winds his horn,
  And 'tis at peep of light;
His blast is heard at merry morn,
  And mine at dead of night.'—

Chorus.

Yet sung she, 'Brignall banks are fair,
  And Greta woods are gay;
I would I were with Edmund there,
  To reign his Queen of May!

'With burnished brand and musketoon,
  So gallantly you come,
I read you for a bold dragoon,
  That lists the tuck of drum.'—
'I list no more the tuck of drum,
  No more the trumpet hear;
But when the beetle sounds his hum,
  My comrades take the spear.

Chorus.

And, O! though Brignall banks be fair,
  And Greta woods be gay,
Yet mickle must the maiden dare,
  Would reign my Queen of May!

'Maiden! a nameless life I lead,
  A nameless death I'll die;
The fiend, whose lantern lights the mead,
  Were better mate than I!
And when I'm with my comrades met,
  Beneath the greenwood bough,
What once we were we all forget,
  Nor think what we are now.

Chorus.

'Yet Brignall banks are fresh and fair,
  And Greta woods are green,
And you may gather garlands there
  Would grace a summer queen.'—

COUNTY GUY.

[From *Quentin Durward.*]

Ah! County Guy, the hour is nigh,
    The sun has left the lea,
The orange-flower perfumes the bower,
    The breeze is on the sea.
The lark, his lay who trill'd all day,
    Sits hush'd his partner nigh;
Breeze, bird, and flower, confess the hour,
    But where is County Guy?

The village maid steals through the shade,
    Her shepherd's suit to hear;
To beauty shy, by lattice high,
    Sings high-born Cavalier.
The star of Love, all stars above,
    Now reigns o'er earth and sky;
And high and low the influence know—
    But where is County Guy?

THE VIOLET.

[Published in the *Edinburgh Annual Register* for 1808.]

The violet in her greenwood bower,
    Where birchen boughs with hazels mingle,
May boast itself the fairest flower
    In glen, or copse, or forest dingle.

Though fair her gems of azure hue,
    Beneath the dewdrop's weight reclining.
I've seen an eye of lovelier blue,
    More sweet through watery lustre shining.

The summer sun that dew shall dry,
    Ere yet the day be past its morrow;
Nor longer in my false love's eye
    Remained the tear of parting sorrow.

JOANNA BAILLIE.

[BORN at Bothwell Manse, Lanarkshire, Sept. 11, 1762; came to live in London, 1784. Published *Plays on the Passions*, vol. i., 1798; vol. ii., 1802; vol. iii., 1812; *Miscellaneous Dramas*. 1804; *The Family Legend*, 1810; *Dramas*, 3 vols., 1836; *Fugitive Verses*, 1840. Died at Hampstead, Feb. 23, 1851.]

In reading Joanna Baillie's poetry we find her to possess a quickness of observation that nearly supplies the place of insight; a strongly moralised temperament delighting in natural things; a vigorous, simple style. These are not especially dramatic qualities, and although she won her reputation through her plays, the poetry by which she is remembered is chiefly of a pastoral kind. She described herself, with justice, as 'a poet of a simple and homely character,' and her truest poems deal with simple and homely things: had she not persuaded herself that she possessed a more ambitious vocation she could have taken an honourable place among idyllic poets. About the year 1790 Miss Baillie published her first little book of poems. It met with little notice, being, as she said, too rustic for those times when Mr. Hayley and Miss Seward were the chief poets south of the Tweed. Before the publication of her next work the great wave of German romanticism had burst on our literature, an impulse inspiring Scott and Southey with the spirit of heroic chivalry, and moving even this quiet singer of woods and fields to tell of supernatural horrors and of 'the great explosions of Passion.'

In 1798 appeared the earliest volume of a 'Series of Plays, in which it is attempted to delineate the stronger passions of the mind —each passion being the subject of a tragedy and a comedy.' These dramas are noticeable for the sustained vigour of their style and for the beautiful lyrics with which they are interspersed, but they have neither passion, interest, nor character. Few women possess the faculty of construction, and Joanna Baillie was not one of these ; nor had she qualities rare enough to cover the sins of a wandering story. Even in the revelation of a passion she is more occupied with the moral to be inferred than with the feeling itself, and few of her *dramatis personæ* are more than the means to bring the moral to its conclusion. Late in life Miss Baillie pro duced a book of *Metrical Legends* in the style of Scott, but without his fine romance and fervour, and quite at the end of her career she republished her earliest poems with the addition of some Scottish songs under the title of *Fugitive Verses.* The little book, with its modest name and prefaced apology, is nevertheless the most enduring of her works. Her country songs, written in the language of her early home, have the best qualities of Scottish national poetry ; their simplicity, their cautious humour, endeared them at once to the national heart ; they have the shrewdness and the freshness of the morning airs, the homeliness of unsophisticated feeling. Such songs as *Woo'd and Married and a'*, *The weary pund o' Tow*, *My Nanny O*, and the lovely trysting song beginning 'The gowan glitters on the sward' are among the treasures of Scottish minstrelsy. Only less delightful than these are her earlier sketches of country life, of cottage homes on summer and on winter days, of husbandman and housewife, of lovers happy and unhappy, of idle little village girls and boys—sketches touched with a certain homely grace whose greatest charm is its sincerity. Among these poems are a series of Farewells—the melancholy, the cheerful-tempered, the proud lover, each bids in turn an adieu to his mistress. Last of all comes the 'poetical or sound-hearted' lover, and even while we smile at the unusual synonym we remember how natural a truth it must have been to her that used it.

A. MARY F. ROBINSON.

THE CHOUGH AND CROW.

The chough and crow to roost are gone,
  The owl sits on the tree,
The hush'd wind wails with feeble moan,
  Like infant charity.
The wild fire dances on the fen,
  The red star sheds its ray,
Uprouse ye, then, my merry men!
  It is our opening day.

Both child and nurse are fast asleep,
  And closed is every flower,
The winking tapers faintly peep
  High from my lady's bower;
Bewildered hinds with shortened ken
  Shrink in their murky way.
Uprouse ye, then, my merry men!
  It is our opening day.

Nor board nor garner own we now,
  Nor roof nor latched door,
Nor kind mate bound by holy vow
  To bless a good man's store;
Noon lulls us in a gloomy den,
  And night is grown our day;
Uprouse ye, then, my merry men!
  It is our opening day.

FISHERMAN'S SONG.

No fish stir in our heaving net,
And the sky is dark and the night is wet;
And we must ply the lusty oar,
For the tide is ebbing from the shore;
And sad are they whose faggots burn,
So kindly stored for our return.

Our boat is small, and the tempest raves,
And nought is heard but the lashing waves
And the sullen roar of the angry sea
And the wild winds piping drearily;
Yet sea and tempest rise in vain,
We'll bless our blazing hearths again.

Push bravely, mates! Our guiding star
Now from its towerlet streameth far,
And now along the nearing strand,
See, swiftly moves yon flaming brand;
Before the midnight watch be past
We'll quaff our bowl and mock the blast.

SONG.

They who may tell love's wistful tale
    Of half its cares are lightened;
Their bark is tacking to the gale,
    The severed cloud is brightened.

Love like the silent stream is found
    Beneath the willows lurking,
The deeper that it hath no sound
    To tell its ceaseless working.

Submit, my heart; thy lot is cast,
    I feel its inward token;
I feel this misery will not last,
    Yet last till thou art broken.

SONG.

[Version taken from an old song, *Woo'd and married and a'*.]

The bride she is winsome and bonny,
　Her hair it is snooded sae sleek,
And faithfu' and kind is her Johnny,
　Yet fast fa' the tears on her cheek.
New pearlins [1] are cause of her sorrow,
　New pearlins and plenishing too ;
The bride that has a' to borrow
　Has e'en right mickle ado.
　　Woo'd and married and a' !
　　Woo'd and married and a' !
　Is na' she very weel aff
　　To be woo'd and married at a' ?

Her mither then hastily spak,
　'The lassie is glaikit [2] wi' pride ;
In my pouch I had never a plack
　On the day when I was a bride.
E'en tak to your wheel and be clever,
　And draw out your thread in the sun ;
The gear that is gifted it never
　Will last like the gear that is won.
　　Woo'd and married and a' !
　　Wi' havins and tocher [3] sae sma' !
　I think ye are very weel aff
　　To be woo'd and married at a'.'

'Toot, toot,' quo' her grey-headed faither,
　'She's less o' a bride than a bairn,
She's ta'en like a cout [4] frae the heather,
　Wi' sense and discretion to learn.
Half husband, I trow, and half daddy,
　As humour inconstantly leans,
The chiel maun be patient and steady
　That yokes wi' a mate in her teens.

---

[1] finery, lace.　　[2] silly.　　[3] goods and dowry.　　[4] colt.

A kerchief sae douce and sae neat
    O'er her locks that the wind used to blaw!
I'm baith like to laugh and to greet
    When I think of her married at a'!'

Then out spak the wily bridegroom,
    Weel waled were his wordies, I ween,
'I'm rich, though my coffer be toom[1],
    Wi' the blinks o' your bonny blue e'en.
I'm prouder o' thee by my side
    Though thy ruffles or ribbons be few,
Than if Kate o' the Croft were my bride
    Wi' purfles and pearlins enow.
        Dear and dearest of ony!
        Ye 're woo'd and buikit and a'!
    And do ye think scorn o' your Johnny,
        And grieve to be married at a'?'

She turn'd, and she blush'd, and she smiled,
    And she looked sae bashfully down;
The pride o' her heart was beguiled,
    And she played wi' the sleeves o' her gown.
She twirled the tag o' her lace,
    And she nipped her boddice sae blue,
Syne blinkit sae sweet in his face,
    And aff like a maukin[2] she flew.
        Woo'd and married and a'!
        Wi' Johnny to roose her and a'!
    She thinks hersel very weel aff
        To be woo'd and married at a'!

[1] empty.   [2] hare.

JAMES HOGG.

[THE 'Ettrick Shepherd,' born in 1770 in Selkirkshire, where his fore-fathers had been sheep-farmers for generations, was 'discovered' by Sir Walter Scott very much in the same way in which Allan Cunningham was discovered by Cromek. Scott struck across him while engaged in his search for *The Minstrelsy of the Scottish Border.* The living minstrel, in this case however, was not under the necessity of passing off his own poems as relics of an older time; Scott at once recognised his talent, and gave him a helping hand. Hogg threw aside the crook for the pen, migrated to Edinburgh, and wrote for the magazines and the booksellers. He was one of the projectors of *Blackwood's Magazine* in 1817, and became famous as one of the interlocutors in the *Noctes Ambrosianae.* The *Queen's Wake,* on which his poetic reputation chiefly rests, was published in 1813. He died in 1835.]

Hogg owed his introduction to letters to the same sort of acci-dent as Cunningham, and there was not a little similarity besides in their careers. Of both it may be said that there was as much of the elements of poetry in their lives as in their books. Hogg was a more boisterous character, with a much less firm grip of reality, and most at home in wild burlesque and the realms of unrestrained fancy. The combination of rough humour with sweetness and purity of sentiment is by no means rare; but Hogg is one of most eminent examples of it; all the more striking that both qualities were in him strongly accentuated by his demonstra-tive temperament. His humour often degenerates into deliberate loutishness, affected oddity; and his tenderness of fancy sometimes approaches 'childishness,' or, as the Scotch call it, 'bairnliness.' But with all his extravagances, there is a marked individuality in the Shepherd's songs and poems; he was a singer by genuine impulse, and there was an open-air freshness in his note.

W. MINTO.

A Boy's Song.

Where the pools are bright and deep,
Where the grey trout lies asleep,
Up the river and o'er the lea,
That's the way for Billy and me.

Where the blackbird sings the latest,
Where the hawthorn blooms the sweetest,
Where the nestlings chirp and flee,
That's the way for Billy and me.

Where the mowers mow the cleanest,
Where the hay lies thick and greenest;
There to trace the homeward bee,
That's the way for Billy and me.

Where the hazel bank is steepest,
Where the shadow falls the deepest,
Where the clustering nuts fall free,
That's the way for Billy and me.

Why the boys should drive away
Little maidens from their play,
Or love to banter and fight so well,
That's the thing I never could tell.

But this I know, I love to play,
Through the meadow, among the hay:
Up the water and o'er the lea,
That's the way for Billy and me.

THOMAS CAMPBELL.

[THOMAS CAMPBELL was born at Glasgow in 1777 of a good Scotch family. He was educated at the Glasgow Grammar School and University, and after one or two tutorships proceeded to Edinburgh to try his fortunes in literature. He published *The Pleasures of Hope* at the age of twenty-one, and from that date forward his career was one of literary success sufficient, with a pension of £200 from the Crown, to secure him from pecuniary anxiety. He contested successfully the Rectorship of his University with Sir Walter Scott in 1827, and was re-elected the two following years. He removed to London in 1840, but the last years of his life were spent at Boulogne, where he died in 1844. He was buried in Westminster Abbey.]

Campbell's poetry is by no means voluminous, and yet the greater part of it has ceased to be much read.

Two or three admirable ballads are well known to the present generation and will probably continue to be known beyond it, and a few lines out of his other poems have taken the place they so well deserve to hold among current quotations.

His first poem, *The Pleasures of Hope*, published in 1798, was modelled no doubt upon *The Pleasures of Memory*, published in 1793, and though Rogers was nearly thirty years of age when he wrote, and Campbell only twenty-one, there are finer passages to be found in the work of the younger poet. But there is the same fault of a prevailing didactic tameness in the one poem as in the other, and Campbell had to learn and to listen for a year or two more before he caught the livelier spirit of song which rang in the new century.

It was at this point of time that our poetry was about to 'breathe a second spring.' Wordsworth said[1] that Coleridge 'was in blossom from 1796 to 1800.' Southey wrote[2] in 1837—'Many volumes of

---

[1] In conversation with the writer.   [2] In a letter to the writer.

poems are now published every year without attracting public attention, any one of which, if it had appeared half a century ago, would have obtained a high reputation for its author.'

The Pleasures of Hope did obtain a high reputation for its author. It passed through four editions within one year of its publication. And on that reputation, and on its merits rather than its charms, it lived for half a century more or less ; and if it is now in a way to be dead and buried, there will be no small amount of poetic *material* to be buried with it. As in the case of its predecessor and model, it is the dull movement and desultory design which brings it in peril of its life.

When his songs took the place of what may be called poetical lectures, Campbell's diction was no longer so scrupulously correct. Perhaps absolute correctness of diction is less to be insisted upon in what is ejaculated than what is concocted : and Campbell's ballads have so much life and animation in them that the reader who is happy enough not to be a critic may well overlook one or two trifling faults of grammar,—carried away by their salient metrical effects and the force of the feeling that inspires them. Faults of sound, it is true, cannot so easily escape notice, and the rhymes are not always what they should be.

Of the ballads, *Hohenlinden* and *Ye Mariners of England* were written in 1800, and *The Battle of the Baltic* in 1809. In the latter year was published *Gertrude of Wyoming*, a narrative poem of ninety-two Spenserian stanzas, divided into three parts. If this poem had been the first to appear it would probably have taken and kept a higher place than *The Pleasures of Hope* in popular estimation. There is no search after something to say in this, and the story is told with a simple and pathetic as well as poetical sweetness which could scarcely have failed to take effect if the field of narrative poetry had not been preoccupied by poets of more varied powers. And though the Spenserian stanza is commonly supposed to be the most difficult in the language, it is written by Campbell with such a graceful fluency that it seems like the poet's natural way of expressing himself, and the difficulty is to suppose that it costs him any trouble.

One disadvantage that it had to contend with was the *locus in quo*. The scene is laid in America. Now there is no people on the face of the earth who have a quicker sense of what is poetical and romantic than the Americans. But they themselves would desire to forget their own country when their imaginations are to be invoked and they are to lose themselves in the regions of romance. They are affected quite as much as we are, if not more, by what is old and unfamiliar [1].

Campbell may have assumed, perhaps, that the same unfamiliarity which makes an old country most interesting to the natives of a new one, will make the new one most interesting to the natives of the old. Socially and politically it may be so, but in its relations with poetry and romance it is otherwise. 'On Susquehana's side fair Wyoming' may be as beautiful as it is beautifully described in the opening of the poem, but the picturesque effect would have gained in imaginative associations if Wyoming had been in the old world instead of the new. There is however one impressive figure of the new world which the old could not have afforded—that of the Indian Outalissi. He brings into the story at his first, and still more at his last appearance, an element of wildness which is employed with excellent effect.

Campbell wrote one other long story, *Theodoric* by name, which he calls 'domestic,' and in which he resumes the old heroic couplet (why called 'heroic' it is hard to understand), stumping along as if with two wooden legs. It is a commonplace tragedy of real life prosaically related, into which a plainness of speech not usually met with in poetry is occasionally introduced, with a view no doubt to give the effect of reality and truth. Such language might have fulfilled its purpose had the story been written in prose ; but being in verse of a stiff and pompous form, the effect is that of incongruity, combining two affectations, an affectation of poetic elevation with an affectation of simplicity. In short, the poem is altogether unworthy of its author.

And if anything could show *how* unworthy, it would be the poem next in succession, *O'Connor's Child;* for this is the very soul of song—tragic, romantic and passionate. Nor are there wanting among the minor poems a few more tales—*The Spectre Boat, Glenara, The Ritter Bann, Lord Ullin's Daughter*—which have a like, if not an equal charm ; and others, good of their kind,

---

[1] The writer was personally a witness to one example. He breakfasted in company with Mr. Webster on his first arrival in London. Mr. Webster was a man of a weighty and imposing presence and appearance, with a grave and stern expression of countenance, silent and self-possessed. After breakfast we took him to Westminster Abbey. He walked in, looked about him, and burst into tears.

short, well told in ballad metre, but with epigrammatic rather than poetic effect. Those which are *not* good of their kind are songs or ballads which Dame Nature seems to have intended for ebullitions, and which probably were so in their birth, but which Stepdame Art has laboured to improve.

For the rest, the complete editions of Campbell's poems, like those of most poets renowned in their day, contain a proportion of juvenile and senile efforts which might have been spared with advantage to the collection as a whole ; and the same may be said of certain occasional poems written because they were wanted. Some verses on Marie Antoinette, of no very great merit in themselves, are remarkable in having been written at fifteen years of age. And there is another poem, included in the edition published by Moxon in 1837, which is remarkable *amongst* Campbell's poems for not being Campbell's. It is Wordsworth's well-known poem beginning

'There is a change,—and I am poor.'

It is singular that such a misappropriation should have happened when both the poets were still living.

HENRY TAYLOR.

HOHENLINDEN.

On Linden, when the sun was low,
All bloodless lay the untrodden snow,
And dark as winter was the flow
Of Iser, rolling rapidly.

But Linden saw another sight,
When the drum beat at dead of night,
Commanding fires of death to light
The darkness of her scenery.

By torch and trumpet fast arrayed,
Each horseman drew his battle blade,
And furious every charger neighed,
To join the dreadful revelry.

Then shook the hills with thunder riven,
Then rushed the steed to battle driven,
And louder than the bolts of heaven,
Far flashed the red artillery.

But redder yet that light shall glow,
On Linden's hills of stained snow,
And bloodier yet the torrent flow
Of Iser, rolling rapidly.

'Tis morn, but scarce yon level sun
Can pierce the war-clouds, rolling dun,
Where furious Frank, and fiery Hun,
Shout in their sulphurous canopy.

The combat deepens. On, ye brave,
Who rush to glory, or the grave!
Wave, Munich! all thy banners wave!
And charge with all thy chivalry!

Few, few, shall part where many meet!
The snow shall be their winding sheet,
And every turf beneath their feet
Shall be a soldier's sepulchre.

YE MARINERS OF ENGLAND.   A NAVAL ODE.

Ye Mariners of England
That guard our native seas,
Whose flag has braved a thousand years
The battle and the breeze!
Your glorious standard launch again
To match another foe,
And sweep through the deep,
While the stormy winds do[1] blow;
While the battle rages loud and long,
And the stormy winds do blow.

The spirits of your fathers
Shall start from every wave!—
For the deck it was their field of fame,
And Ocean was their grave:
Where Blake and mighty Nelson fell
Your manly hearts shall glow,
As ye sweep through the deep,
While the stormy winds do blow;
While the battle rages loud and long,
And the stormy winds do blow.

Britannia needs no bulwark,
No towers along the steep;
Her march is o'er the mountain waves,
Her home is on the deep.
With thunders from her native oak
She quells the floods below—
As they roar on the shore,
When the stormy winds do blow;
When the battle rages loud and long,
And the stormy winds do blow.

[1] The earl'er editions have 'while the stormy *tempests* blow' throughout

The meteor flag of England
Shall yet terrific burn,
Till danger's troubled night depart
And the star of peace return.
Then, then, ye ocean-warriors!
Our song and feast shall flow
To the fame of your name,
When the storm has ceased to blow;
When the fiery fight is heard no more,
And the storm has ceased to blow.

BATTLE OF THE BALTIC.

Of Nelson and the North
Sing the glorious day's renown,
When to battle fierce came forth
All the might of Denmark's crown,
And her arms along the deep proudly shone;
By each gun the lighted brand
In a bold determin'd hand,
And the Prince of all the land
Led them on.

Like leviathans afloat
Lay their bulwarks on the brine,
While the sign of battle flew
On the lofty British line:
It was ten of April morn by the chime:
As they drifted on their path,
There was silence deep as death,
And the boldest held his breath
For a time.

But the might of England flushed
To anticipate the scene,
And her van the fleeter rushed
O'er the deadly space between—

'Hearts of oak,' our captains cried, when each gun
From its adamantine lips
Spread a death-shade round the ships,
Like the hurricane eclipse
Of the sun.

Again ! again ! again !
And the havoc did not slack,
Till a feeble cheer the Dane
To our cheering sent us back ;—
Their shots along the deep slowly boom :—
Then ceased—and all is wail,
As they strike the shattered sail,
Or in conflagration pale
Light the gloom.

Out spoke the victor then,
As he hailed them o'er the wave;
'Ye are brothers ! ye are men !
And we conquer but to save ;
So peace instead of death let us bring:
But yield, proud foe, thy fleet
With the crews at England's feet,
And make submission meet
To our King.'

Then Denmark blest our chief,
That he gave her wounds repose ;
And the sounds of joy and grief,
From her people wildly rose,
As death withdrew his shades from the day;
While the sun looked smiling bright
O'er a wide and woeful sight,
Where the fires of funeral light
Died away.

Now joy, old England, raise
For the tidings of thy might,
By the festal cities' blaze,
While the wine cup shines in light;

And yet amidst that joy and uproar,
Let us think of them that sleep,
Full many a fathom deep,
By thy wild and stormy steep,
Elsinore !

Brave hearts ! to Britain's pride.
Once so faithful and so true,
On the deck of fame that died,—
With the gallant good Riou,
Soft sigh the winds of heaven o'er their grave !
While the billow mournful rolls,
And the mermaid's song condoles,
Singing glory to the souls
Of the brave !

THE ONEYDA'S DEATH-SONG.

[From *Gertrude of Wyoming*, Part III.]

Hushed were his Gertrude's lips, but still their bland
And beautiful expression seemed to melt
With love that could not die ; and still his hand
She presses to the heart no more that felt.
Ah heart ! where once each fond affection dwelt,
And features yet that spoke a soul more fair.
Mute, gazing, agonizing as he knelt,—
Of them that stood encircling his despair,
He heard some friendly words ;—but knew not what they were

For now, to mourn their judge and child, arrives
A faithful band. With solemn rites between,
'Twas sung, how they were lovely in their lives,
And in their deaths had not divided been.
Touch'd by the music, and the melting scene,
Was scarce one tearless eye amidst the crowd :—
Stern warriors, resting on their swords, were seen
To veil their eyes, as pass'd each much-loved shroud—
While woman's softer soul in woe dissolved aloud.

Then mournfully the parting bugle bid
Its farewell, o'er the grave of worth and truth;
Prone to the dust, afflicted Waldegrave hid
His face on earth;—him watched in gloomy ruth
His woodland guide; but words had none to soothe
The grief that knew not consolation's name:
Casting his Indian mantle o'er the youth,
He watch'd, beneath its folds, each burst that came
Convulsive, ague-like across his shuddering frame!

'And I could weep;'—th' Oneyda chief
His descant wildly thus begun;
'But that I may not stain with grief
The death-song of my father's son,
Or bow this head in woe;
For by my wrongs and by my wrath
To-morrow Areouski's breath
(That fires you heav'n with storms of death)
Shall light us to the foe;
And we shall share, my Christian boy,
The foeman's blood, the avenger's joy!

'But thee, my flower, whose breath was given
By milder genii o'er the deep,
The spirits of the white man's heaven
Forbid not thee to weep;
Nor will the Christian host,
Nor will thy father's spirit grieve
To see thee, on the battle's eve,
Lamenting, take a mournful leave
Of her who loved thee most:
She was the rainbow to thy sight!
Thy sun—thy heaven—of lost delight!—

'To-morrow let us do or die!
But when the bolt of death is hurled,
Ah! whither then with thee to fly
Shall Outalissi roam the world?

Seek we thy once-loved home?—
The hand is gone that cropt its flowers,
Unheard their clock repeats its hours,
Cold is the hearth within their bowers,
And should we thither roam,
Its echoes and its empty tread
Would sound like voices from the dead.

'Or shall we cross yon mountains blue,
Whose streams my kindred nation quaff'd,
And by my side, in battle true,
A thousand warriors drew the shaft?
Ah! there in desolation cold
The desert serpent dwells alone,
Where grass o'ergrows each mouldering bone,
And stones themselves to ruin grown,
Like me, are death-like old:
Then seek we not their camp—for there
The silence dwells of my despair.

'But hark, the trump!—to-morrow thou
In glory's fires shalt dry thy tears:
Ev'n from the land of shadows now
My father's awful ghost appears
Amidst the clouds that round us roll;
He bids my soul for battle thirst,
He bids me dry the last—the first—
The only tears that ever burst
From Outalissi's soul;
Because I may not stain with grief
The death-song of an Indian chief.'

JOHN HOOKHAM FRERE.

[JOHN HOOKHAM FRERE was born in London in 1769, and died at Malta in 1846. The first part of his *Whistlecraft* poem was published in 1817 as the *Prospectus and Specimen of an intended National Work, by William and Robert Whistlecraft of Stow-Market in Suffolk, Harness and Collar Makers*. In the following year a second part was issued with the first under the title of *The Monks and the Giants*; but the work was never completed. Frere contributed much to the *Anti-Jacobin*, 1797-8, and translated several of the plays of Aristophanes. His *Works in Verse and Prose*, with a prefatory Memoir, were published in 1872 by his nephews, W. E., and Sir Bartle Frere.]

Frere's versions of the Aristophanic Comedy have an established reputation for spirit of rendering and mastery of metre. His translations from the *Poema del Cid*, which were printed in Southey's *Chronicle*, have also a fine balladic lilt ; but their literal fidelity to the Spanish has been lately challenged. Of his original work, the best examples are to be found in the *Anti-Jacobin* and the *Whistlecraft* fragment. He had a hand in all the great successes of the former,—notably the immortal *Needy Knife-Grinder* and the excellent imitations of Darwin and Schiller in the *Loves of the Triangles* and *The Rovers*. For *The Monks and the Giants* he adopted an eight-line stanza based upon that of the Italians. It had already been used by Harrington, Drayton, Fairfax, and (as we have seen) in later times by Gay ; it had even been used by Frere's contemporary, William Tennant ; but to Frere belongs the honour of giving it the special characteristics which Byron afterwards popularised in *Beppo* and *Don Juan*. Structurally the *ottava rima* of Frere singularly resembles that of Byron, who admitted that *Whistlecraft* was his 'immediate model.' But notwithstanding the cleverness and versatility of *The Monks and the Giants*, its interest was too remote and its plan too uncertain to command any but an eclectic audience. Moreover, it was almost immediately eclipsed by *Beppo*. Byron, taking up the stanza with equal skill and greater genius, filled it with the vigour of his personality, and made it a measure of his own, which it has ever since been hazardous for inferior poets to attempt.

AUSTIN DOBSON.

From 'The Monks and the Giants.'

And certainly they say, for fine behaving
King Arthur's Court has never had its match ;
True point of honour, without pride or braving,
Strict etiquette for ever on the watch :
Their manners were refined and perfect—saving
Some modern graces, which they could not catch,
As spitting through the teeth, and driving stages,
Accomplishments reserved for distant ages.

They looked a manly, generous generation ;
Beards, shoulders, eyebrows, broad, and square, and thick,
Their accents firm and loud in conversation,
Their eyes and gestures eager, sharp, and quick,
Showed them prepared, on proper provocation,
To give the lie, pull noses, stab and kick ;
And for that very reason, it is said,
They were so very courteous and well-bred.

The ladies looked of an heroic race—
At first a general likeness struck your eye,
Tall figures, open features, oval face,
Large eyes, with ample eyebrows arched and high ;
Their manners had an odd, peculiar grace,
Neither repulsive, affable, nor shy,
Majestical, reserved, and somewhat sullen ;
Their dresses partly silk, and partly woollen.

  *   *   *   *   *

Sir Gawain may be painted in a word—
He was a perfect loyal Cavalier ;
His courteous manners stand upon record,
A stranger to the very thought of fear.
The proverb says, *As brave as his own sword;*
And like his weapon was that worthy Peer,
Of admirable temper, clear and bright,
Polished yet keen, though pliant yet upright.

On every point, in earnest or in jest,
His judgment, and his prudence, and his wit,
Were deemed the very touchstone a..d the test
Of what was proper, graceful, just, and fit ;
A word from him set everything at rest,
His short decisions never failed to hit ;
His silence, his reserve, his inattention,
Were felt as the severest reprehension ;

His memory was the magazine and hoard,
Where claims and grievances, from year to year,
And confidences and complaints were stored
From dame and knight, from damsel, boor, and peer.
Loved by his friends, and trusted by his Lord,
A generous courtier, secret and sincere,
Adviser-general to the whole community,
He served his friend, but watched his opportunity.

     *   *   *   *   *

Meanwhile the solemn mountains that surrounded
The silent valley where the convent lay,
With tintinnabular uproar were astounded,
When the first peal burst forth at break of day :
Feeling their granite ears severely wounded,
They scarce knew what to think, or what to say ;
And (though large mountains commonly conceal
Their sentiments, dissembling what they feel,

Yet) Cader-Gibbrish from his cloudy throne
To huge Loblommon gave an intimation,
Of this strange rumour, with an awful tone,
Thundering his deep surprise and indignation ;
The lesser hills, in language of their own,
Discussed the topic by reverberation ;
Discoursing with their echoes all day long,
Their only conversation was, ' ding dong.'

Those giant-mountains inwardly were moved,
But never made an outward change of place :
Not so the mountain-giants—(as behoved
A more alert and locomotive race).

Hearing a clatter which they disapproved,
They ran straight forward to besiege the place
With a discordant universal yell,
Like house-dogs howling at a dinner-bell.

     *   *   *   *   *

As Bees, that when the skies are calm and fair,
In June, or the beginning of July,
Launch forth colonial settlers in the air,
Round, round, and round about, they whiz, they fly,
With eager worry whirling here and there,
They know not whence, nor whither, where, nor why
In utter hurry-scurry, going, coming,
Maddening the summer air with ceaseless humming;

Till the strong Frying-pan's energic jangle
With thrilling thrum their feebler hum doth drown,
Then passive and appeased, they drop and dangle,
Clinging together close, and clustering down,
Linked in a multitudinous living tangle
Like an old Tassel of a dingy brown;—
The joyful Farmer sees and spreads his hay,
And reckons on a settled sultry day:—

E'en so the Monks, as wild as sparks of fire,
(Or swarms unpacified by pan or kettle),
Ran restless round the Cloisters and the Quire,
Till those huge masses of sonorous metal
Attracted them towards the Tower and Spire;
There you might see them cluster, crowd, and settle,
Thronged in the hollow tintinnabular Hive;
The Belfry swarmed with Monks; it seemed alive.

LORD BYRON.

[BORN Jan 22, 1788. Educated at Harrow, and Trinity College, Cam-
bridge. Published *Hours of Idleness* in 1807. A review of this book in
the *Edinburgh* provoked the Satire *English Bards and Scotch Reviewers*, which
was published in March 1809. After this date Byron travelled in Spain,
Greece and Turkey for two years. On his return he published the two first
Cantos of *Childe Harold* in 1812. During the years 1813-1815 he wrote
*The Giaour, Bride of Abydos, Corsair, Lara, Hebrew Melodies, Siege of Corinth,
Parisina.* The two last were published in the spring of 1816 shortly after
Byron's separation from the wife whom he had married on Jan. 2, 1815.
This year, 1816, was the most important epoch in his life. He left England
never to return; settled first at Geneva, where he made the acquaintance of
Shelley, composed the Third Canto of *Childe Harold, Prisoner of Chillon,*
and *Prometheus*, and began *Manfred*. In 1817 he removed to Venice, finished
Manfred, wrote the *Lament of Tasso*, the Fourth Canto of *Childe Harold*, and
Beppo. In the years 1818 and 1819, still residing at Venice, he produced the
Ode on Venice, Mazeppa, and the first four Cantos of *Don Juan*. In 1820 and
1821, while living at Ravenna, he wrote the *Prophecy of Dante, Marino Faliero,
Sardanapalus, The Two Foscari, Cain, Heaven and Earth*, and *A Vision of Judgment.* Part of the two next years was spent at Pisa in close intimacy with
Shelley. *Werner, The Deformed Transformed, The Island*, and the remaining
Cantos of *Don Juan*, on which Byron had been from time to time at work
during his Ravenna residence, were completed. On July 13, 1823, Byron
sailed from Genoa for Greece, in order to take active part in the liberation
of that country from Turkish rule. He died of fever at Missolonghi on the
19th of April, 1824, at the age of thirty-six years and three months.]

The first thing that strikes a student of Byron's collected works
is the quantity of poetry produced by him in a short lifetime. The
second is the variety of forms attempted—the scope and range of
intellectual power displayed. The third is the inequality of the

performance, due apparently in certain cases to haste of composition, in others to imperfect sympathy with the subjects treated, or again to some contemptuous compliance with a fashion which the author only tolerated.

Byron's character is stamped upon his work in a remarkable degree ; and his character was powerfully biassed by external circumstance. The critic cannot therefore neglect his biography. In early childhood he was left to the sole care of a violent and injudicious mother. Impressed with the importance of the title to which he succeeded at the age of ten, he yet had neither friends nor connections of his own rank, and but slender means for sustaining its dignity. Handsome, active, and ambitious, he was debarred from engaging in field-sports by the malformation of his ankle. Thus, from the first, he lived under conditions eminently unfavourable for the growth of an equable temperament or for the acquisition of just views about society. His mental powers were acute and vigorous ; his emotions sincere and direct ; the impressions made upon his sensitive nature by the persons with whom he came in contact were vivid and indelible. Yet his judgment of the world was prematurely warped, while his naturally earnest feelings were overlaid with affectations and prejudices which he never succeeded in shaking off. He was constitutionally shy, uncertain in society, preferring the solitude of hills and woods and water, to the men and women whom he learned to misconceive and misinterpret. Though he strove to conceal this shyness beneath an assumption of off-handed ease, his manners to the last were awkward. It was his misfortune to be well-born but ill-bred, combining the pride of a peer with the self-consciousness of a *parvenu*. He rarely suffered his true opinions and emotions to be visible. What he proffered his acquaintance in their stead was stamped with artificiality. Trelawny thought that Byron was what London in the days of the Prince Regent made him. But we must go further back, and recognise that from his boyhood he began to construct and wear a masquerade costume that could not be abandoned. When Shelley discerned the 'canker of aristocracy' and 'perverse ideas' in one whom he admired but never made his friend ; when Goethe complained of his 'Empeiria' or taint of worldliness, they laid their fingers on this radical blot. The ostentation which repels us in Byron's correspondence and in the records left of him by his associates, the swaggering tone that spoils so much of his best work and makes it impossible to love the man as we should like to do, may be ascribed to a habit early acquired of self-sophistication. He venered the true and noble self which gave life to his poetry with a layer of imperfectly com-prehended cynicism and weak misanthropy, that passed with him for worldly wisdom. There are two distinct Byrons, interpene-trative, blended in his life and work. To disentangle them is wellnigh impossible ; for he cherished his inferior self, and mis-took its weakness and its falsehood for strength and sincerity of insight.

Byron began to write verse while still a boy. He published *Hours of Idleness* at the age of nineteen. Though this collection of juvenile lyrics did not deserve high commendation, it might have been spared the mangling it received from the blunt toma-hawk of the *Edinburgh Review*. His next essay was the product of mere rage against his critics and against the men of letters who, he thought, had neglected him. *English Bards and Scotch Reviewers* is an imitation of Gifford's satirical style, full of such stinging epigrams as proved that the poet of *Hours of Idleness* had thenceforth to be reckoned with. At the present time it is chiefly valuable for the light it throws on Byron's psychological develop-ment. Being of an exceptionally retentive temperament, each style that he essayed left something ineffaceable upon his habit of composition. The satire in question was begotten by indignation, and dealt in invective. We trace an element of indignation, not seldom of a less than sterling alloy, in nearly all his subsequent poems, which break too frequently into invectives against un-worthy or mistaken objects of his spleen. Byron, it may be said at once, was destitute of critical insight. Therefore not only are the judgments of *English Bards and Scotch Reviewers* worthless, but his maturest works are marred by strictures on contemporaries which now appear ridiculous. If Byron desired fame, he achieved it in fair and full measure by his satire. But disappointed by his reception into London society, he resolved on leaving England. His genius received its first true awakening upon his travels. Greece made him a poet, and he returned to England with two Cantos of *Childe Harold* ready for publication. It is difficult to speak in measured terms of a poem which has suffered more from eulogy and popularity than any other poem of equal excellence from depreciation or neglect. The celebrated passages of *Childe Harold*, quoted, extracted, learned by heart at school, and incor-porated into guide-books, have become a bye-word and a weariness to the present generation. We do not know how to render justice to the sonorous rhetoric and the often magnificent poetry of a masterpiece that has been subjected to processes so vulgarising. Some deductions, on sounder critical grounds, must also be made from the first enthusiasm that welcomed *Childe Harold.* The poem is written in a declamatory style, which savours of an age when Campbell's *Pleasures of Hope* was thought to soar above the level of prize poetry. The Pilgrim is a *rococo* creation, to whom Byron failed to communicate the breath of life. When this fictitious hero disappears from the scene, the stanzas invariably improve. Therefore the third and fourth Cantos, written in the plenitude of Byron's power, where Childe Harold has been all but forgotten, might pass for a separate composition. With the person of the Pilgrim, the affectation of Spenserian language, sparely but awkwardly employed in the first Canto, is dropped. The vein of meditation is richer, deeper, more dignified in utterance. The personal emotion of the poet, saddened and elevated by his cruel experience of life, finds vent in larger harmonies and more impassioned bursts of eloquence. His sympathy with the oppressed, and his sense of the world's past greatness, attain the altitude of lyrical inspiration in the apostrophe to Rome; while his enjoyment of nature in her grander aspects, and the consolation he received from her amid the solitudes of sea and lake and mountain, are expressed with sublimity in the passages upon the Ocean and the Jura thunderstorm.

After the publication of the first two Cantos, Byron woke in London and 'found himself famous.' What was far worse for him than fame, fashion claimed the new poet for her own. Though still isolated from true friends and family connections, he became the darling of society, poured forth for its amusement those Oriental tales, of which *The Giaour* alone retains sufficient vitality or perfume of true poetry to make its perusal at the present day desirable. Byron did not excel in the art of telling a simple story, unvaried by digressions, unassisted by contrasts of pathos and humour. One of his latest compositions in the narrative style, *The Island,* is a total failure. The best of his earlier tales, *The Prisoner of Chillon* and *Mazeppa,* were produced after the period of his fashionable fame, when, in the quietude of exile, he wrote with sobered feelings for himself. They owe, moreover, their greater purity of outline and sincerity of feeling to the form of monologue adopted. For the moment Byron becomes Bonnivard and Mazeppa, speaking through their lips of sufferings with which he felt the liveliest sympathy.

The life he led in London between 1812 and 1816, confirmed Byron's affectations and increased his tendency to cynicism. But while warping his character and enslaving his genius to trumpery standards of taste, it supplied him with much of the material which was to be wrought up into *Don Juan.* We have therefore no reason to deplore the fact that he lived through it. On the other hand we may perhaps be thankful that his uncongenial union with Lady Byron came to an abrupt conclusion at the beginning of 1816. His temper needed to be deepened by pain ; nor was it till the blow of Lady Byron's separation struck him, that the gravest chords of his genius uttered a note. From that time forward, in the ennobled Cantos of *Childe Harold,* no less than in occasional lyrics, the sorrow which drove him into exile and flung him for repose and consolation upon Nature, formed one of the principal topics of his purest poetry. The public who raved about *Lara* and *The Corsair,* must have felt that there was yet a greater Byron to arise, when they read the *Domestic Pieces,* so indiscreetly committed by friends to the pages of the London newspapers. Even though we may condemn, on principles of taste, the self-revelation which from this time forward became one of Byron's habits, though we may fail to appreciate the professed scorn of the world which he mingled with a free recourse to its confidence and sympathy upon delicate matters of his private life, there is no disputing the energy communicated to his genius by these trials.

The formation of Shelley's friendship at this epoch must be reckoned one of the most fortunate and decisive events of Byron's life. The immediate result of their intercourse at Geneva was evident in the poems composed during 1816 and 1817 ; in the loftier inspiration of *Childe Harold,* in the lyrical gravity of *Prometheus,* and in the maturer reflections of *Manfred.* The reading of Goethe's *Faust* was not without its share of influence, manifest in the general conception of both *Manfred* and *The Deformed Transformed.* Yet neither of these plays can be said to have been modelled upon *Faust.* Byron's genius could not work upon the same lines as Goethe's ; nor can dramas, hurriedly conceived and rapidly executed, without a distinct philosophical intention, be compared with the slowly elaborated masterpiece of a lifetime, which condenses and anticipates the profoundest thoughts of the nineteenth century. In *Manfred* the type of character which had previously been sketched by Byron in his romantic poems, receives more concentrated expression. Manfred is the incarnation of a defiant, guilty, self-reliant personality, preserved from despair by its disdainful pride, linked to the common joys and sorrows of humanity by the slender but still vital thread of a passion which is also an unforgotten and unforgivable crime. The egotism which is the source and secret of his vaunted strength, foredooms Manfred to destruction ; yet at the close of his course, he does not flinch. Such self-sustained stubbornness was Byron's ideal. But he infected the type with something melodramatic, which lowered it below the defiance of the Greek Prometheus, and he prepared no reconciliation of opposing motives in his dramatic scheme. Tested by common experience, the character he created in Manfred was soon found wanting in the essential elements of reality.

Byron's removal to Venice in 1817 marks a no less important epoch in his career than the meeting with Shelley at Geneva. He now came into close contact with the Italian genius in its raciest expression. He studied the writers of burlesque, and fastened with partiality on Pulci, two books of whose *Morgante Maggiore* he afterwards translated. It must not be imagined that the new form he was about to invent for English literature was borrowed from the Italian. Hookham Frere, in the octave stanzas of *Whistlecraft*, had already naturalised the Tuscan humoristic style. But neither the example of Frere nor the far more powerful influence of the Italian poets will suffice to account for *Beppo* and *Don Juan*. The blending of satire with description, of realism with imagination, of drollery with ideal beauty, were Italian possessions before Byron seized on them. But he added something characteristically his own. In *Beppo* he treated the incidents of a Venetian *novella*. At the same time he stood so completely. outside his subject, and informed it with humour at once so far more pungent and so far more universal than pervades the best work of his supposed models, that Europe received at his hands a species hitherto unguessed and undiscovered. *Beppo* seems to have revealed to Byron the power that had been latent in him from the earliest days of boyhood ; but which, partly from modesty and partly from the misdirection of his faculties, due to critical incapacity, had lain dormant. He found that he possessed an unrivalled command of comedy. *Beppo* was but a prelude to the two great works, *Don Juan* and *The Vision of Judgment*, on which his fame will ultimately rest, and last as long as there are minds to comprehend their many-sided excellence.

In the year 1818 Byron began *Don Juan*. Until his death in 1824 he used it as the channel of expression for the varied reminiscences of past experience, and for the miscellaneous pictures of society and human life with which his mind was stored. It was a poem without a plan, and for this very reason well adapted to his purpose. Juan is a name: the fact that his parentage and earliest adventures are Spanish does not bring him into competition with the Don Juan of Spanish legend. He has but little in common with the hero of Molière's play or Mozart's opera. Juan's biography is the thread on which Byron hangs descriptions, episodes, satirical digressions, and reflective passages of brilliant audacity. That *Don Juan*, as Byron began it in the extant sixteen cantos, should have arrived at a conclusion, seems inconceivable. It was therefore scarcely a misfortune that death cut the poet short, when he had closed the fourth chapter of his hero's adventures. Byron, it may be observed, was essentially an occasional poet. He needed some substratum of fact or personal emotion for his imaginative edifices, and wrote best when he was least hampered by self-imposed theories of art. *Childe Harold* and *Don Juan* may therefore be regarded as continuous poetic journals. He used them as receptacles for the ideas that every passing day suggested. 'If things are farcical,' he once said to Trelawny, during their voyage to Greece, 'they will do for *Don Juan*; if heroical, you shall have another canto of *Childe Harold*.' This accounts for the defect of structure in both poems. But while the change of style and tone in *Childe Harold* has been already pointed out, no such failure can be indicated in *Don Juan*. Within itself, and judged by the laws of its own nature, it is vigorously organised. The flux and reflux of contrasted incidents, —the balance of emotions between pathos and comedy, humour and satire,—the correspondence of voluptuous and piquant, sensual and tender, touches,—the passage from Donna Julia to Haidee and Dudu,—the siege succeeding to the shipwreck,—the picture of St. Petersburgh under Catherine followed by that of England ruled by Whig and Tory peers ;—this counterpoise of interests, this rapid modulation from key to key, gives to *Don Juan*, fragment as it is, a fine artistic coherence.

The Drama lies outside the scope of this book. It is not therefore necessary to speak in detail about the tragedies, which occupied

much of Byron's time at Venice and Ravenna, but which, neither
as acting plays nor as poems, can be reckoned among his masterpieces *Cain* and *Heaven and Earth,* called ' Mysteries' by their
author, detach themselves from the rest, because Byron's insuffi-
ciency as a dramatist was in both these cases covered by the
peculiar piquancy of the subject-matter. *Cain,* on its first appearance, had a veritable success of scandal ; but, since its day, our
advance in religious toleration and freedom of speech has shorn
its daring scenes of half their lustre. The case is very different
with the *Vision of Judgment.* In this poem, composed upon an
event of so ephemeral importance as George III's funeral, and
inspired by so trivial a passion as spite against Southey, Byron
displayed in short compass the range and scope of his peculiar
powers. His humour, common sense, inventive faculty, and
luminous imagination, are here, as nowhere else, combined in
perfect fusion. We only miss the pathos and the sympathy with
nature displayed in previous compositions of a different purpose.
The octave stanza, which he had essayed in *Beppo,* and perfected
in *Don Juan,* is used with unrivalled command of its resources.
Like some elemental substance taking shape beneath a spirit-
touch, the metre obeys his will, and from the slightest bias of his
fancy assumes imperishable form. Satire, which at the outset of
Byron's career crawled like a serpent, has here acquired the
wings and mailed panoply of a dragon. The poetry of the *Vision
of Judgment,* sustained by the companion pictures of Lucifer and
Michael, is no less brilliant than its burlesque, expressed in
St. Peter and the King.

Byron's best poetry admits of no selections being made from it.
He was deficient in those qualities of ear and taste which are necessary for the production of studied perfection on a small scale. We
must admire him for the sweep and strength of his genius, or not
at all. With the exception of a few personal lyrics, characterised
by simplicity of feeling and limpidity of style, his shorter pieces do
not adequately represent him. He succeeded best in all the mixed
specimens he attempted. But precisely because those poems
blend so many qualities, contrasted and assimilated by the poet's
power, they cannot be perused in fragments. We may reckon
this impossibility of doing justice to Byron by selections among
the reasons for his present comparative neglect. Yet the change
of opinion which has taken place among cultivated people during
the last half century in this respect, is so striking, that no critic of

Byron can avoid discussing it. To do so is in fact the simplest way of ascertaining his place in literature. During his lifetime he enjoyed a renown which has rarely fallen to the lot of any living writer. At the present day it is common to hear people asserting that Byron was not a true poet. Some causes of this revolution are patent. In the first place he cannot be called a moral poet. His collected works are not of a kind to be recom-mended for family reading ; and the poems in which his genius shines most clearly, are precisely those which lie open to the charges of cynicism, unorthodoxy, or licentiousness. Again, he suffers from the very range and versatility of his performance. Like the Roman Empire, *magnitudine laborat suâ.* His masterpieces are long, and make considerable demands upon the reader's patience. Byron has suffered even more from the mixed quality of his work. Not only are his poems voluminous, but they are exceedingly unequal ; nor is it so easy, as in the case of Words-worth, to separate what is worthless from the imperishable creations of his genius. The sudden burst of glory which followed upon the publication of *Childe Harold,* and the indiscriminate enthusiasm of his admirers, injured Byron during his lifetime by establishing the certainty that whatever he wrote would be read. It has injured him still more with posterity by stirring a reaction against claims in some respects so obviously ill-founded. Instead of subjecting the whole mass of Byron's poetry to a careful criticism, the world has been contented lately to reckon it among the nine days' wonders of a previous age. This injustice would, however, have been impossible, unless a current of taste inimical to Byron had set in soon after his death. Students of literature in England began about that period to assimilate Wordsworth, Coleridge, Keats, Shelley, Landor—those very poets whom Byron, in his uncritical arrogance, had despised or neglected. Their ears be-came accustomed to versification more exquisite and careful, to harmonies deeper and more refined if less resonant and brilliant. They learned to demand a more patient and studied delineation of natural beauty, passion more reserved, artistic aims at once more sober and more earnest, and emotions of a less obtrusively personal type. Tennyson and Browning, with all the poet-artists of the present generation, represent as sheer a departure from Byronian precedent as it is possible to take in literature. The very greatness of Byron has unfitted him for an audience educated in this different school of poetry. That greatness was his truth to fact, conceived as action, feeling, energy ; not as the material for picture-painting, reflection, or analysis. Men nursed on the idyllic or the analytic kinds of poetry can hardly do him justice ; not because he is exactly greater, or they indisputably less, but because he makes his best points in a region which is alien to their sympathy. The idyll was a species invented by the Greeks in their decline, when the passion, action and practical energy—the lyrical emotion and the dramatic fervour of their past literature—had become fit subjects for little pictures, jewels of verse, refracting the light cast on them by culture, and returning it to the eyes of the beholder in a prism of suggestive hues. Our age is in a somewhat similar sense idyllic. We are now accustomed to the art which appeals to educated sensibilities, by suggestions and reflections, by careful workmanship and attentive study of form, by artistically finished epitomes of feeling, by picturesquely blended reminiscences of realism, culture, and poetical idealism. Byron's work is too primitive, too like the raw material of poetry, in its crudity and inequality, to suit our Neo-Alexandrian taste. He wounds our sympathies ; he violates our canons of correctness ; he fails to satisfy our subtlest sense of art. He showers upon us in profusion what we do not want, and withholds the things for which we have been trained to crave. His personality inspires no love, like that which makes the devotees of Shelley as faithful to the man as they are loyal to the poet. His intellect, though robust and masculine, is not of the kind to which we willingly submit. As a man, as a thinker, as an artist, he is out of harmony with us. Nevertheless nothing can be more certain than Byron's commanding place in English literature. He is the only British poet of the nineteenth century who is also European ; nor will the lapse of time fail to make his greatness clearer to his fellow-countrymen, when a just critical judgment finally dominates the fluctuations of fashion to which he has been subject.

It is desirable in all disputed cases to readjust the balance of criticism by reference to authorities who command attention. This disposes me to quote the opinions of Byron's most eminent contemporaries, not because they seem to represent the final truth about his poetry, but because their deliberate enthusiasm must force the reader to a reconsideration of his merits. Shelley, who was no mean critic, and who was certainly not blinded to Byron's faults by their close intimacy, wrote of him in private correspondence thus : ' He touched the chord to which a million hearts responded, and the coarse music which he produced to please them, disciplined him to the perfection to which he now approaches.' This was in 1822. Again, in an earlier letter of the same year : 'Space wondered less at the swift and fair creations of God when he grew weary of vacancy, than ! at this spirit of an angel in the mortal paradise of a decaying body.' Goethe, in conversation with Eckermann, after death had removed the English peer and poet above all reach of flattery, said : 'The English may think of Byron as they please ; but this is certain, that they can show no poet who is to be compared with him. He is different from all the others, and for the most part, greater.' That this was no hasty utterance, is proved by Euphorion's part, assigned to Byron, in *Faust*, as the typical modern poet, and by many parallel passages in Eckermann's book of *Table Talk*. Mazzini, to quote an authority of a different type, breaks, at the end of his essay on Goethe and Byron, into the following vindication of the poet's claim : 'The day will come when Democracy will remember all that it owes to Byron. England too will, I hope, one day remember the mission—so entirely English, yet hitherto overlooked by her— which Byron fulfilled on the continent ; the European rôle given by him to English literature, and the appreciation and sympathy for England which he awakened amongst us. Before he came, all that was known of English literature was the French translation of Shakespeare, and the anathema hurled by Voltaire against the "intoxicated barbarian." It it since Byron that we Continentalists have learned to study Shakespeare and other English writers. From him dates the sympathy of all the true-hearted amongst us for this land of liberty, whose true vocation he so worthily represented among the oppressed. He led the genius of Britain on a pilgrimage throughout all Europe.'

The judgments I have cited are of value when we seek to discern Byron's merits with eyes unblinded by contemporary prejudice. If we measure him from the standpoint of British literature, where of absolute perfection in verse there is perhaps less than we desire, he will scarcely bear the test of niceness to which our present rules of taste expose him. But if we try him by the standards of universal literature, where of finish and exactitude in execution there is plenty, we shall find that he has qualities of strength and elasticity, of elemental sweep and energy, which condone all defects in technical achievement. Such power, sincerity and radiance, such directness of generous enthusiasm and disengagement from local or patriotic prepossessions, such sympathy with the forces of humanity in movement after freedom, such play of humour and passion, as Byron pours into the common stock, are no slight contributions. Europe does not need to make the discount upon Byron's claims to greatness that are made by his own country.

J. A. SYMONDS.

WHEN WE TWO PARTED.

When we two parted
　　In silence and tears,
Half broken-hearted
　　To sever for years,
Pale grew thy cheek and cold,
　　Colder thy kiss ;
Truly that hour foretold
　　Sorrow to this.

The dew of the morning
　　Sunk chill on my brow—
It felt like the warning
　　Of what I feel now.
Thy vows are all broken,
　　And light is thy fame :
I hear thy name spoken,
　　And share in its shame.

They name thee before me,
　　A knell to mine ear ;
A shudder comes o'er me—
　　Why wert thou so dear?
They know not I knew thee,
　　Who knew thee too well :—
Long, long shall I rue thee,
　　Too deeply to tell.

In secret we met—
　　In silence I grieve,
That thy heart could forget,
　　Thy spirit deceive.
If I should meet thee
　　After long years,
How should I greet thee?
　　With silence and tears.

(1808.)

AND THOU ART DEAD, AS YOUNG AND FAIR.

And thou art dead, as young and fair
   As aught of mortal birth ;
And form so soft, and charms so rare,
   Too soon return'd to Earth !
Though Earth received them in her bed,
And o'er the spot the crowd may tread
   In carelessness or mirth,
There is an eye which could not brook
A moment on that grave to look.

I will not ask where thou liest low,
   Nor gaze upon the spot ;
There flowers or weeds at will may grow,
   So I behold them not :
It is enough for me to prove
That what I loved, and long must love,
   Like common earth can rot ;
To me there needs no stone to tell,
'Tis Nothing that I loved so well.

Yet did I love thee to the last
   As fervently as thou,
Who didst not change through all the past,
   And canst not alter now.
The love where Death has set his seal,
Nor age can chill, nor rival steal,
   Nor falsehood disavow :
And, what were worse, thou canst not see
Or wrong, or change, or fault in me.

The better days of life were ours ;
   The worst can be but mine :
The sun that cheers, the storm that lowers,
   Shall never more be thine.
The silence of that dreamless sleep
I envy now too much to weep ;
   Nor need I to repine,
That all those charms have pass'd away ;
I might have watch'd through long decay.

The flower in ripen'd bloom unmatch'd
　Must fall the earliest prey ;
Though by no hand untimely snatch'd,
　The leaves must drop away :
And yet it were a greater grief
To watch it withering, leaf by leaf,
　Than see it pluck'd to-day ;
Since earthly eye but ill can bear
To trace the change to foul from fair.

I know not if I could have borne
　To see thy beauties fade ;
The night that follow'd such a morn
　Had worn a deeper shade :
Thy day without a cloud hath pass'd,
And thou wert lovely to the last ;
　Extinguish'd, not decay'd ;
As stars that shoot along the sky
Shine brightest as they fall from high.

As once I wept, if I could weep,
　My tears might well be shed,
To think I was not near to keep
　One vigil o'er thy bed ;
To gaze, how fondly ! on thy face,
To fold thee in a faint embrace,
　Uphold thy drooping head ;
And show that love, however vain,
Nor thou nor I can feel again.

Yet how much less it were to gain,
　Though thou hast left me free,
The loveliest things that still remain,
　Than thus remember thee !
The all of thine that cannot die
Through dark and dread Eternity
　Returns again to me,
And more thy buried love endears
Than aught, except its living years.

February, 1812.

From 'The Bride of Abydos.'

Know ye the land where the cypress and myrtle
  Are emblems of deeds that are done in their clime?
Where the rage of the vulture, the love of the turtle,
  Now melt into sorrow, now madden to crime!
Know ye the land of the cedar and vine,
Where the flowers ever blossom, the beams ever shine;
Where the light wings of Zephyr, oppress'd with perfume,
Wax faint o'er the gardens of Gúl in her bloom;
Where the citron and olive are fairest of fruit,
And the voice of the nightingale never is mute;
Where the tints of the earth, and the hues of the sky,
In colour though varied, in beauty may vie,
And the purple of ocean is deepest in dye;
Where the virgins are soft as the roses they twine,
And all, save the spirit of man, is divine?
'Tis the clime of the East; 'tis the land of the Sun—
Can he smile on such deeds as his children have done?
Oh! wild as the accents of lovers' farewell
Are the hearts which they bear, and the tales which they tell

[From *The Hebrew Melodies.*]

I.

She walks in Beauty.

She walks in beauty, like the night
  Of cloudless climes and starry skies;
And all that's best of dark and bright
  Meet in her aspect and her eyes:
Thus mellow'd to that tender light
  Which heaven to gaudy day denies.

One shade the more, one ray the less,
　　Had half impair'd the nameless grace
Which waves in every raven tress,
　　Or softly lightens o'er her face;
Where thoughts serenely sweet express
　　How pure, how dear their dwelling-place.

And on that cheek, and o'er that brow,
　　So soft, so calm, yet eloquent,
The smiles that win, the tints that glow,
　　But tell of days in goodness spent,
A mind at peace with all below,
　　A heart whose love is innocent!

II.

OH! SNATCH'D AWAY IN BEAUTY'S BLOOM.

Oh! snatch'd away in beauty's bloom,
On thee shall press no ponderous tomb;
　　But on thy turf shall roses rear
　　Their leaves, the earliest of the year;
And the wild cypress wave in tender gloom:

And oft by yon blue gushing stream
　　Shall Sorrow lean her drooping head,
And feed deep thought with many a dream,
　　And lingering pause and lightly tread;
　　Fond wretch! as if her step disturb'd the dead!

Away! we know that tears are vain,
　　That death nor heeds nor hears distress:
Will this unteach us to complain?
　　Or make one mourner weep the less?
And thou—who tell'st me to forget,
Thy looks are wan, thine eyes are wet.

FROM 'PARISINA.'

It is the hour when from the boughs
  The nightingale's high note is heard;
It is the hour when lovers' vows
  Seem sweet in every whisper'd word;
And gentle winds, and waters near,
Make music to the lonely ear
Each flower the dews have lightly wet,
And in the sky the stars are met,
And on the wave is deeper blue,
And on the leaf a browner hue,
And in the heaven that clear obscure,
So softly dark, and darkly pure,
Which follows the decline of day,
As twilight melts beneath the moon away.

STANZAS FOR MUSIC.

There be none of Beauty's daughters
  With a magic like thee;
And like music on the waters
  Is thy sweet voice to me:
When, as if its sound were causing
The charmed ocean's pausing,
The waves lie still and gleaming,
And the lull'd winds seem dreaming:

And the midnight moon is weaving
  Her bright chain o'er the deep;
Whose breast is gently heaving,
  As an infant's asleep:
So the spirit bows before thee,
To listen and adore thee;
With a full but soft emotion,
Like the swell of Summer's ocean.

STANZAS FOR MUSIC.

There's not a joy the world can give like that it takes away,
When the glow of early thought declines in feeling's dull decay:
'Tis not on youth's smooth cheek the blush alone, which fades
    so fast,
But the tender bloom of heart is gone, ere youth itself be past.

Then the few whose spirits float above the wreck of happiness,
Are driven o'er the shoals of guilt or ocean of excess :
The magnet of their course is gone, or only points in vain
The shore to which their shiver'd sail shall never stretch again.

Then the mortal coldness of the soul like death itself comes
    down ;
It cannot feel for others' woes, it dare not dream its own ;
That heavy chill has frozen o'er the fountain of our tears,
And though the eye may sparkle still, 'tis where the ice appears.

Though wit may flash from fluent lips, and mirth distract the
    breast,
Through midnight hours that yield no more their former hope
    of rest ;
'Tis but as ivy-leaves around the ruin'd turret wreath,
All green and wildly fresh without, but worn and grey beneath.

Oh could I feel as I have felt,—or be what I have been,
Or weep as I could once have wept o'er many a vanish'd scene ;
As springs in deserts found seem sweet, all brackish though
    they be,
So, midst the wither'd waste of life, those tears would flow to me
                           March, 1815.

FARE THEE WELL.

Fare thee well! and if for ever,
  Still for ever, fare the well:
Even though unforgiving, never
  'Gainst thee shall my heart rebel.

Would that breast were bared before thee
  Where thy head so oft hath lain,
While that placid sleep came o'er thee
  Which thou ne'er canst know again:

Would that breast, by thee glanced over,
  Every inmost thought could show!
Then thou wouldst at last discover
  'Twas not well to spurn it so.

Though the world for this commend thee—
  Though it smile upon the blow,
Even its praises must offend thee,
  Founded on another's woe:

Though my many faults defaced me,
  Could no other arm be found,
Than the one which once embraced me,
  To inflict a cureless wound?

Yet, oh yet, thyself deceive not;
  Love may sink by slow decay,
But by sudden wrench, believe not
  Hearts can thus be torn away:

Still thine own its life retaineth,
  Still must mine, though bleeding, beat;
And the undying thought which paineth
  Is—that we no more may meet.

These are words of deeper sorrow
  Than the wail above the dead;
Both shall live, but every morrow
  Wake us from a widow'd bed.

And when thou wouldst solace gather,
  When our child's first accents flow,
Wilt thou teach her to say 'Father!'
  Though his care she must forego?

When her little hands sh⁻ll press thee,
  When her lip to thine is press'd,
Think of him whose prayer shall bless thee,
  Think of him thy love had bless'd!

Should her lineaments resemble
  Those thou never more may'st see,
Then thy heart will softly tremble
  With a pulse yet true to me.

All my faults perchance thou knowest,
  All my madness none can know;
All my hopes, where'er thou goest,
  Wither, yet with *thee* they go.

Every feeling hath been shaken;
  Pride, which not a world could bow,
Bows to thee—by thee forsaken,
  Even my soul forsakes me now:

But 'tis done—all words are idle—
  Words from me are vainer still;
But the thoughts we cannot bridle
  Force their way without the will.

Fare thee well! thus disunited,
  Torn from every nearer tie,
Sear'd in heart, and lone, and blighted,
  More than this I scarce can die.

                              March 17, 1816.

STANZAS TO AUGUSTA.

Though the day of my destiny's over,
    And the star of my fate hath declined,
Thy soft heart refused to discover
    The faults which so many could find ;
Though thy soul with my grief was acquainted,
    It shrunk not to share it with me,
And the love which my spirit hath painted
    It never hath found but in *thee.*

Then when nature around me is smiling,
    The last smile which answers to mine,
I do not believe it beguiling,
    Because it reminds me of thine ;
And when winds are at war with the ocean,
    As the breasts I believed in with me,
If their billows excite an emotion,
    It is that they bear me from *thee.*

Though the rock of my last hope is shiver'd,
    And its fragments are sunk in the wave,
Though I feel that my soul is deliver'd
    To pain—it shall not be its slave.
There is many a pang to pursue me :
    They may crush, but they shall not contemn ;
They may torture, but shall not subdue me ;
    'Tis of *thee* that I think—not of them.

Though human, thou didst not deceive me,
    Though woman, thou didst not forsake,
Though loved, thou forborest to grieve me,
    Though slander'd, thou never couldst shake ;
Though trusted, thou didst not disclaim me,
    Though parted, it was not to fly,
Though watchful, 'twas not to defame me,
    Nor mute, that the world might belie.

Yet I blame not the world, nor despise **it,**
  Nor the war of the many with one **;**
If my soul was not fitted to prize it,
  'Twas folly not sooner to shun :
And if dearly that error hath cost **me,**
  And more than I once could foresee**,**
I have found that, whatever it lost me,
  It could not deprive me of *thee.*

From the wreck of the past, which hath **perish'd,**
  Thus much I at least may recall,
It hath taught me that what I most cherish'd
  Deserved to be dearest of all :
In the desert a fountain is springing,
  In the wide waste there still is a tree,
And a bird in the solitude singing,
  Which speaks to my spirit of *thee.*

July 24, **1816.**

Epistle to Augusta.

My sister ! my sweet sister ! if a name
Dearer and purer were, it should be thine ;
Mountains and seas divide us, but I claim
No tears, but tenderness to answer mine :
Go where I will, to me thou art the same—
A loved regret which I would not resign.
There yet are two things in my destiny,—
A world to roam through, and a home with **thee.**

The first were nothing—had I still the last**,**
It were the haven of my happiness ;
But other claims and other ties thou hast**,**
And mine is not the wish to make them less.
A strange doom is thy father's son's, and past
Recalling, as it lies beyond redress ;
Reversed for him our grandsire's fate of **yore,—**
He had no rest at sea, nor I on shore.

If my inheritance of storms hath been
In other elements, and on the rocks

Of perils, overlook'd or unforeseen,
I have sustain'd my share of worldly shocks,
The fault was mine ; nor do I seek to screen,
My errors with defensive paradox ;
I have been cunning in mine overthrow,
The careful pilot of my proper woe.

Mine were my faults, and mine be their reward.
My whole life was a contest, since the day
That gave me being, gave me that which marr'd
The gift,—a fate, or will, that walk'd astray;
And I at times have found the struggle hard,
And thought of shaking off my bonds of clay:
But now I fain would for a time survive,
If but to see what next can well arrive.

Kingdoms and empires in my little day
I have outlived, and yet I am not old ;
And when I look on this, the petty spray
Of my own years of trouble, which have roll'd
Like a wild bay of breakers, melts away;
Something—I know not what—does still uphold
A spirit of slight patience ;—not in vain,
Even for its own sake, do we purchase pain.

Perhaps the workings of defiance stir
Within me—or perhaps a cold despair,
Brought on when ills habitually recur,—
Perhaps a kinder clime, or purer air,
(For even to this may change of soul refer,
And with light armour we may learn to bear,)
Have taught me a strange quiet, which was not
The chief companion of a calmer lot.

I feel almost at times as I have felt
In happy childhood ; trees, and flowers, and brooks,
Which do remember me of where I dwelt
Ere my young mind was sacrificed to books,
Come as of yore upon me, and can melt
My heart with recognition of their looks ;
And even at moments I think I could see
Some living thing to love—but none like thee.

Here are the Alpine landscapes which create
A fund for contemplation ;—to admire
Is a brief feeling of a trivial date :
But something worthier do such scenes inspire:
Here to be lonely is not desolate,
For much I view which I could most desire,
And, above all, a lake I can behold
Lovelier, not dearer, than our own of old.

Oh that thou wert but with me !—but I grow
The fool of my own wishes, and forget
The solitude which I have vaunted so
Has lost its praise in this but one regret ;
There may be others which I less may show ;—
I am not of the plaintive mood, and yet·
I feel an ebb in my philosophy,
And the tide rising in my alter'd eye.

I did remind thee of our own dear Lake,
By the old Hall which may be mine no more.
Leman's is fair ; but think not I forsake
The sweet remembrance of a dearer shore :
Sad havoc Time must with my memory make
Ere *that* or *thou* can fade these eyes before ;
Though, like all things which I have loved, they are
Resign'd for ever, or divided far.

The world is all before me ; but I ask
Of Nature that with which she will comply—
It is but in her summer's sun to bask,
To mingle with the quiet of her sky,
To see her gentle face without a mask,
And never gaze on it with apathy.
She was my early friend, and now shall be
My sister—till I look again on thee.

I can reduce all feelings but this one ;
And that I would not ;—for at length I see
Such scenes as those wherein my life begun.
The earliest—even the only paths for me—

Had I but sooner learnt the crown to shun,
I had been better than I now can be;
The passions which have torn me would have slept;
I had not suffer'd, and *thou* hadst not wept.

With false Ambition what had I to do?
Little with Love, and least of all with Fame;
And yet they came unsought, and with me grew,
And made me all which they can make—a name.
Yet this was not the end I did pursue;
Surely I once beheld a nobler aim.
But all is over—I am one the more
To baffled millions which have gone before.

And for the future, this world's future may
From me demand but little of my care;
I have outlived myself by many a day;
Having survived so many things that were;
My years have been no slumber, but the prey
Of ceaseless vigils; for I had the share
Of life which might have fill'd a century,
Before its fourth in time had pass'd me by.

And for the remnant which may be to come
I am content; and for the past I feel
Not thankless,—for within the crowded sum
Of struggles, happiness at times would steal,
And for the present, I would not benumb
My feelings further.—Nor shall I conceal
That with all this I still can look around,
And worship Nature with a thought profound.

For thee, my own sweet sister, in thy heart
I know myself secure, as thou in mine;
We were and are—I am, even as thou art—
Beings who ne'er each other can resign;
It is the same, together or apart,
From life's commencement to its slow decline
We are entwined—let death come slow or fast,
The tie which bound the first endures the last!

THE DREAM.

I.

Our life is two fold : Sleep hath its own world,
A boundary between the things misnamed
Death and existence : Sleep hath its own world,
And a wide realm of wild reality.
And dreams in their development have breath,
And tears, and tortures, and the touch of joy;
They leave a weight upon our waking thoughts,
They take a weight from off our waking toils,
They do divide our being ; they become
A portion of ourselves as of our time,
And look like heralds of eternity;
They pass like spirits of the past,—they speak
Like Sibyls of the future : they have power—
The tyranny of pleasure and of pain ;
They make us what we were not—what they will,
And shake us with the vision that 's gone by,
The dream of vanish'd shadows—Are they so?
Is not the past all shadow?—What are they?
Creations of the mind?—The mind can make
Substance, and people planets of its own
With beings brighter than have been, and give
A breath to forms which can outlive all flesh.
I would recall a vision which I dream'd
Perchance in sleep—for in itself a thought,
A slumbering thought, is capable of years,
And curdles a long life into one hour.

II.

I saw two beings in the hues of youth
Standing upon a hill, a gentle hill,
Green, and of mild declivity, the last
As 't were the cape of a long ridge of such,

Save that there was no sea to lave its base,
But a most living landscape, and the wave
Of woods and corn-fields, and the abodes of men
Scatter'd at intervals, and wreathing smoke
Arising from such rustic roofs ;—the hill
Was crown'd with a peculiar diadem
Of trees, in circular array, so fix'd,
Not by the sport of nature, but of man :
These two, a maiden and a youth, were there
Gazing—the one on all that was beneath
Fair as herself—but the boy gazed on her ;
And both were young, and one was beautiful :
And both were young—yet not alike in youth,
As the sweet moon on the horizon's verge,
The maid was on the eve of womanhood ;
The boy had fewer summers, but his heart
Had far outgrown his years, and to his eye
There was but one beloved face on earth,
And that was shining on him : he had look'd
Upon it till it could not pass away;
He had no breath, no being, but in hers ;
She was his voice ; he did not speak to her,
But trembled on her words ; she was his sight,
For his eye follow'd hers, and saw with hers,
Which colour'd all his objects : he had ceased
To live within himself ; she was his life,
The ocean to the river of his thoughts,
Which terminated all : upon a tone,
A touch of hers, his blood would ebb and flow,
And his cheek change tempestuously—his heart
Unknowing of its cause of agony.
But she in these fond feelings had no share :
Her sighs were not for him ; to her he was
Even as a brother—but no more ; 't was much,
For brotherless she was, save in the name
Her infant friendship had bestowed on him ;
Herself the solitary scion left
Of a time-honour'd race.— It was a name
Which pleased him, and yet pleased him not—and why?

Time taught him a deep answer—when she loved
Another; even *now* she loved another,
And on the summit of that hill she stood
Looking afar if yet her lover's steed
Kept pace with her expectancy, and flew.

III.

A change came o'er the spirit of my dream.
There was an ancient mansion, and before
Its walls there was a steed caparison'd :
Within an antique Oratory stood
The Boy of whom I spake ;—he was alone,
And pale, and pacing to and fro : anon
He sate him down, and seized a pen, and traced
Words which I could not guess of ; then he lean'd
His bow'd head on his hands, and shook as 't were
With a convulsion—then arose again,
And with his teeth and quivering hands did tear
What he had written, but he shed no tears,
And he did calm himself, and fix his brow
Into a kind of quiet : as he paused,
The Lady of his love re-entered there ;
She was serene and smiling then, and yet
She knew she was by him beloved,—she knew,
For quickly comes such knowledge, that his heart
Was darken'd with her shadow, and she saw
That he was wretched, but she saw not all.
He rose, and with a cold and gentle grasp
He took her hand ; a moment o'er his face
A tablet of unutterable thoughts
Was traced, and then it faded, as it came ;
He dropp'd the hand he held, and with slow steps
Retired, but not as bidding her adieu,
For they did part with mutual smiles ; he pass'd
From out the massy gate of that old Hall,
And mounting on his steed he went his way ;
And ne'er repass'd that hoary threshold more.

IV.

A change came o'er the spirit of my dream.
The Boy was sprung to manhood: in the wilds
Of fiery climes he made himself a home,
And his soul drank their sunbeams : he was girt
With strange and dusky aspects ; he was not
Himself like what he had been ; on the sea
And on the shore he was a wanderer ;
There was a mass of many images
Crowded like waves upon me, but he was
A part of all ; and in the last he lay
Reposing from the noontide sultriness,
Couch'd among fallen columns, in the shade
Of ruin'd walls that had survived the names
Of those who rear'd them ; by his sleeping side
Stood camels grazing, and some goodly steeds
Were fasten'd near a fountain ; and a man
Clad in a flowing garb did watch the while,
While many of his tribe slumber'd around :
And they were canopied by the blue sky,
So cloudless, clear, and purely beautiful,
That God alone was to be seen in heaven.

V.

A change came o'er the spirit of my dream.
The Lady of his love was wed with One
Who did not love her better :—in her home,
A thousand leagues from his,—her native home,
She dwelt, begirt with growing Infancy,
Daughters and sons of Beauty,—but behold !
Upon her face there was the tint of grief,
The settled shadow of an inward strife,
And an unquiet drooping of the eye,
As if its lid were charged with unshed tears.
What could her grief be ?—she had all she loved,
And he who had so loved her was not there
To trouble with bad hopes, or evil wish,
Or ill-repress'd affliction, her pure thoughts.

What could her grief be?—she had loved him not,
Nor given him cause to deem himself beloved,
Nor could he be a part of that which prey'd
Upon her mind—a spectre of the past.

VI.

A change came o'er the spirit of my dream.
The Wanderer was return'd.—I saw him stand
Before an Altar—with a gentle bride ;
Her face was fair, but was not that which made
The Starlight of his Boyhood ;—as he stood
Even at the altar, o'er his brow there came
The self-same aspect, and the quivering shock
That in the antique Oratory shook
His bosom in its solitude ; and then—
As in that hour—a moment o'er his face
The tablet of unutterable thoughts
Was traced,—and then it faded as it came,
And he stood calm and quiet, and he spoke
The fitting vows, but heard not his own words,
And all things reel'd around him ; he could see
Not that which was, nor that which should have been—
But the old mansion, and the accustom'd hall,
And the remember'd chambers, and the place,
The day, the hour, the sunshine, and the shade,
All things pertaining to that place and hour,
And her who was his destiny,—came back
And thrust themselves between him and the light :
What business had they there at such a time?

VII.

A change came o'er the spirit of my dream.
The Lady of his love ;—Oh ! she was changed
As by the sickness of the soul ; her mind
Had wander'd from its dwelling, and her eyes
They had not their own lustre, but the look
Which is not of the earth ; she was become
The queen of a fantastic realm ; her thoughts

Were combinations of disjointed things;
And forms impalpable and unperceived
Of others' sight familiar were to hers.
And this the world calls frenzy; but the wise
Have a far deeper madness, and the glance
Of melancholy is a fearful gift;
What is it but the telescope of truth?
Which strips the distance of its fantasies,
And brings life near in utter nakedness,
Making the cold reality too real!

VIII.

A change came o'er the spirit of my dream.
The Wanderer was alone as heretofore,
The beings which surrounded him were gone,
Or were at war with him; he was a mark
For blight and desolation, compass'd round
With Hatred and Contention; Pain was mix'd
In all which was served up to him, until,
Like to the Pontic monarch of old days,
He fed on poisons, and they had no power,
But where a kind of nutriment; he lived
Through that which had been death to many men,
And made him friends of mountains: with the stars
And the quick Spirit of the Universe
He held his dialogues; and they did teach
To him the magic of their mysteries;
To him the book of Night was open'd wide,
And voices from the deep abyss reveal'd
A marvel and a secret—Be it so.

IX.

My dream was past; it had no further change.
It was of a strange order, that the doom
Of these two creatures should be thus traced out
Almost like a reality—the one
To end in madness—both in misery.

July, 1816.

[From *Childe Harold's Pilgrimage.* **Canto III.**]

HAROLD THE WANDERER.

Is thy face like thy mother's, my fair child!
ADA! sole daughter of my house and heart?
When last I saw thy young blue eyes they smiled,
And then we parted,—not as now we part,
But with a hope.—
            Awaking with a start,
The waters heave around me; and on high
The winds lift up their voices: I depart,
Whither I know not; but the hour's gone by,
When Albion's lessening shores should grieve or glad mine eye

Once more upon the waters! yet once more!
And the waves bound beneath me as a steed
That knows his rider. Welcome to their roar!
Swift be their guidance, wheresoe'er it lead!
Though the strain'd mast should quiver as a reed,
And the rent canvas fluttering strew the gale,
Still must I on; for I am as a weed,
Flung from the rock, on Ocean's foam to sail
Where'er the surge may sweep, the tempest's breath prevail.

In my youth's summer I did sing of One,
The wandering outlaw of his own dark mind;
Again I seize the theme, then but begun,
And bear it with me, as the rushing wind
Bears the cloud onwards: in that Tale I find
The furrows of long thought, and dried-up tears,
Which, ebbing, leave a sterile track behind,
O'er which all heavily the journeying years
Plod the last sands of life,—where not a flower appears.

Since my young days of passion—joy, or pain,
Perchance my heart and harp have lost a string,

And both may jar: it may be, that in vain
I would essay as I have sung to sing.
Yet, though a dreary strain, to this I cling;
So that it wean me from the weary dream
Of selfish grief or gladness—so it fling
Forgetfulness around me—it shall seem
To me, though no one else, a not ungrateful theme.

He, who grown aged in this world of woe,
In deeds, not years, piercing the depths of life,
So that no wonder waits him; nor below
Can love or sorrow, fame, ambition, strife,
Cut to his heart again with the keen knife
Of silent, sharp endurance: he can tell
Why thought seeks refuge in lone caves, yet rife
With airy images, and shapes which dwell
Still unimpair'd, though old, in the soul's haunted cell.

'Tis to create, and in creating live
A being more intense that we endow
With form our fancy, gaining as we give
The life we image, even as I do now.
What am I? Nothing: but not so art thou,
Soul of my thought! with whom I traverse earth,
Invisible but gazing, as I glow
Mix'd with thy spirit, blended with thy birth,
And feeling still with thee in my crush'd feelings' death.

Yet must I think less wildly:—I *have* thought
Too long and darkly, till my brain became,
In its own eddy boiling and o'erwrought,
A whirling gulf of fantasy and flame:
And thus, untaught in youth my heart to tame,
My springs of life were poison'd. 'Tis too late!
Yet am I changed; though still enough the same
In strength to bear what time cannot abate,
And feed on bitter fruits without accusing Fate.

Something too much of this :—but now 'tis past,
And the spell closes with its silent seal.
Long absent HAROLD re-appears at last ;
He of the breast which fain no more would feel,
Wrung with the wounds which kill not, but ne'er heal ;
Yet Time, who changes all, had alter'd him
In soul and aspect as in age : years steal
Fire from the mind as vigour from the limb ;
And life's enchanted cup but sparkles near the brim.

His had been quaff'd too quickly, and he found
The dregs were wormwood ; but he fill'd again,
And from a purer fount, on holier ground,
And deem'd its spring perpetual ; but in vain !
Still round him clung invisibly a chain
Which gall'd for ever, fettering though unseen,
And heavy though it clank'd not ; worn with pain,
Which pined although it spoke not, and grew keen,
Entering with every step he took through many a scene.

Secure in guarded coldness, he had mix'd
Again in fancied safety with his kind,
And deem'd his spirit now so firmly fix'd
And sheath'd with an invulnerable mind,
That, if no joy, no sorrow lurk'd behind ;
And he, as one, might 'midst the many stand
Unheeded, searching through the crowd to find
Fit speculation ; such as in strange land
He found in wonder-works of God and Nature's hand.

But who can view the ripen'd rose, nor seek
To wear it ? who can curiously behold
The smoothness and the sheen of beauty's cheek,
Nor feel the heart can never all grow old ?
Who can contemplate Fame through clouds unfold
The star which rises o'er her steep, nor climb ?
Harold, once more within the vortex, roll'd
On with the giddy circle, chasing Time,
Yet with a nobler aim than in his youth's fond prime.

But soon he knew himself the most unfit
Of men to herd with Man ; with whom he held
Little in common ; untaught to submit
His thoughts to others, though his soul was quell'd
In youth by his own thoughts ; still uncompell'd,
He would not yield dominion of his mind
To spirits against whom his own rebell'd ;
Proud though in desolation ; which could find
A life within itself, to breathe without mankind.

Where rose the mountains, there to him were friends;
Where roll'd the ocean, thereon was his home ;
Where a blue sky, and glowing clime, extends,
He had the passion and the power to roam ;
The desert, forest, cavern, breaker's foam,
Were unto him companionship ; they spake
A mutual language, clearer than the tome
Of his land's tongue, which he would oft forsake
For Nature's pages glass'd by sunbeams on the lake.

Like the Chaldean, he could watch the stars,
Till he had peopled them with beings bright
As their own beams ; and earth, and earth-born jars,
And human frailties, were forgotten quite :
Could he have kept his spirit to that flight
He had been happy ; but this clay will sink
Its spark immortal, envying it the light
To which it mounts, as if to break the link
That keeps us from yon heaven which woos us to its brink.

But in Man's dwellings he became a thing
Restless and worn, and stern and wearisome,
Droop'd as a wild-born falcon with clipt wing,
To whom the boundless air alone were home :
Then came his fit again, which to o'ercome,
As eagerly the barr'd-up bird will beat
His breast and beak against his wiry dome
Till the blood tinge his plumage, so the heat
Of his impeded soul would through his bosom eat.

LONGING.

The castled crag of Drachenfels
Frowns o'er the wide and winding Rhine,
Whose breast of waters broadly swells
Between the banks which bear the vine,
And hills all rich with blossom'd trees,
And fields which promise corn and wine,
And scatter'd cities crowning these,
Whose far white walls along them shine,
Have strew'd a scene, which I should see
With double joy wert *thou* with me.

And peasant girls, with deep blue eyes,
And hands which offer early flowers,
Walk smiling o'er this paradise ;
Above, the frequent feudal towers
Through green leaves lift their walls of gray ;
And many a rock which steeply lowers,
And noble arch in proud decay,
Look o'er this vale of vintage-bowers ;
But one thing want these banks of Rhine,—
Thy gentle hand to clasp in mine !

I send the lilies given to me ;
Though long before thy hand they touch,
I know that they must wither'd be,
But yet reject them not as such ;
For I have cherish'd them as dear,
Because they yet may meet thine eye,
And guide thy soul to mine even here,
When thou behold'st them drooping nigh,
And know'st them gather'd by the Rhine,
And offer'd from my heart to thine !

The river nobly foams and flows,
The charm of this enchanted ground,
And all its thousand turns disclose
Some fresher beauty varying round :

The haughtiest breast its wish might bound
Through life to dwell delighted here ;
Nor could on earth a spot be found
To nature and to me so dear,
Could thy dear eyes in following mine
Still sweeten more these banks of Rhine !

NIGHT AND TEMPEST.

Clear, placid Leman ! thy contrasted lake,
With the wild world I dwelt in, is a thing
Which warns me, with its stillness, to forsake
Earth's troubled waters for a purer spring.
This quiet sail is as a noiseless wing
To waft me from distraction ; once I loved
Torn ocean's roar, but thy soft murmuring
Sounds sweet as if a Sister's voice reproved,
That I with stern delights should e'er have been so moved.

It is the hush of night, and all between
Thy margin and the mountains, dusk, yet clear,
Mellow'd and mingling, yet distinctly seen,
Save darken'd Jura, whose capt heights appear
Precipitously steep ; and drawing near,
There breathes a living fragrance from the shore,
Of flowers yet fresh with childhood ; on the ear
Drops the light drip of the suspended oar,
Or chirps the grasshopper one good-night carol more ;

He is an evening reveller, who makes
His life an infancy, and sings his fill ;
At intervals, some bird from out the brakes
Starts into voice a moment, then is still.
There seems a floating whisper on the hill,
But that is fancy, for the starlight dews
All silently their tears of love instil,
Weeping themselves away, till they infuse
Deep into nature's breast the spirit of her hues.

Ye stars! which are the poetry of heaven!
If in your bright leaves we would read the fate
Of men and empires,—'tis to be forgiven,
That in our aspirations to be great,
Our destinies o'erleap their mortal state,
And claim a kindred with you; for ye are
A beauty and a mystery, and create
In us such love and reverence from afar,
That fortune, fame, power, life, have named themselves a star

All heaven and earth are still—though not in sleep,
But breathless, as we grow when feeling most;
And silent, as we stand in thoughts too deep:—
All heaven and earth are still: From the high host
Of stars, to the lull'd lake and mountain-coast,
All is concenter'd in a life intense,
Where not a beam, nor air, nor leaf is lost,
But hath a part of being, and a sense
Of that which is of all Creator and defence.

Then stirs the feeling infinite, so felt
In solitude, where we are *least* alone;
A truth, which through our being then doth melt,
And purifies from self: it is a tone,
The soul and source of music, which makes known
Eternal harmony, and sheds a charm
Like to the fabled Cytherea's zone,
Binding all things with beauty;—'t would disarm
The spectre Death, had he substantial power to harm.

Not vainly did the early Persian make
His altar the high places, and the peak
Of earth-o'ergazing mountains, and thus take
A fit and unwall'd temple, there to seek
The Spirit, in whose honour shrines are weak,
Uprear'd of human hands. Come, and compare
Columns and idol-dwellings, Goth or Greek,
With Nature's realms of worship, earth and air,
Nor fix on fond abodes to circumscribe thy pray'r!

The sky is changed!—and such a change! Oh night,
And storm, and darkness, ye are wondrous strong,
Yet lovely in your strength, as is the light
Of a dark eye in woman! Far along,
From peak to peak, the rattling crags among
Leaps the live thunder! Not from one lone cloud,
But every mountain now hath found a tongue,
And Jura answers, through her misty shroud,
Back to the joyous Alps, who call to her aloud!

And this is in the night:—Most glorious night!
Thou wert not sent for slumber! let me be
A sharer in thy fierce and far delight,—
A portion of the tempest and of thee!
How the lit lake shines, a phosphoric sea,
And the big rain comes dancing to the earth!
And now again 'tis black,—and now, the glee
Of the loud hills shakes with its mountain-mirth,
As if they did rejoice o'er a young earthquake's birth.

Now, where the swift Rhone cleaves his way between
Heights which appear as lovers who have parted
In hate, whose mining depths so intervene,
That they can meet no more, though broken-hearted;
Though in their souls, which thus each other thwarted,
Love was the very root of the fond rage
Which blighted their life's bloom, and then departed:
Itself expired, but leaving them an age
Of years all winters,—war within themselves to wage.

Now, where the quick Rhone thus hath cleft his way,
The mightiest of the storms hath ta'en his stand:
For here, not one, but many, make their play,
And fling their thunder-bolts from hand to hand,
Flashing and cast around: of all the band,
The brightest through these parted hills hath fork'd
His lightnings,—as if he did understand,
That in such gaps as desolation work'd,
There the hot shaft should blast whatever therein lurk'd.

Sky, mountains, river, winds, lake, lightnings' ye!
With night, and clouds, and thunder, and a soul
To make these felt and feeling, well may be
Things that have made me watchful ; the far roll
Of your departing voices, is the knoll
Of what in me is sleepless,—if I rest.
But where of ye, O tempests ! is the goal?
Are ye like those within the human breast?
Or do ye find, at length, like eagles, some high nest?

Could I embody and unbosom now
That which is most within me,—could I wreak
My thoughts upon expression, and thus throw
. Soul, heart, mind, passions, feelings, strong or weak,
All that I would have sought, and all I seek,
Bear, know, feel, and yet breathe—into *one* word,
And that one word were Lightning, I would speak ;
But as it is, I live and die unheard,
With a most voiceless thought, sheathing it as a sword.

[From *Childe Harold's Pilgrimage.* Canto IV.]

OCEAN.

There is a pleasure in the pathless woods,
There is a rapture on the lonely shore,
There is society, where none intrudes,
By the deep Sea, and music in its roar:
I love not Man the less, but Nature more,
From these our interviews, in which I steal
From all I may be, or have been before,
To mingle with the Universe, and feel
What I can ne'er express, yet cannot all conceal.

Roll on, thou deep and dark blue Ocean—roll!
Ten thousand fleets sweep over thee in vain ;
Man marks the earth with ruin—his control
Stops with the shore ; upon the watery plain
The wrecks are all thy deed, nor doth remain

A shadow of man's ravage, save his own,
When, in a moment, like a drop of rain,
He sinks into thy depths with bubbling groan,
Without a grave, unknell'd, uncoffin'd, and unknown.

His steps are not upon thy paths,—thy fields
Are not a spoil for him,—thou dost arise
And shake him from thee ; the vile strength he wields
For earth's destruction thou dost all despise,
Spurning him from thy bosom to the skies,
And send'st him, shivering in thy playful spray
And howling, to his Gods, where haply lies
His petty hope in some near port or bay,
And dashest him again to earth :—there let him lay.

The armaments which thunderstrike the walls
Of rock-built cities, bidding nations quake,
And monarchs tremble in their capitals,
The oak leviathans, whose huge ribs make
Their clay creator the vain title take
Of lord of thee, and arbiter of war —
These are thy toys, and, as the snowy flake,
They melt into thy yeast of waves, which mar
Alike the Armada's pride or spoils of Trafalgar.

Thy shores are empires, changed in all save thee—
Assyria, Greece, Rome, Carthage, what are they?
Thy waters wash'd them power while they were free,
And many a tyrant since ; their shores obey
The stranger, slave, or savage ; their decay
Has dried up realms to deserts :—not so thou ;—
Unchangeable, save to thy wild waves' play,
Time writes no wrinkle on thine azure brow :
Such as creation's dawn beheld, thou rollest now.

Thou glorious mirror, where the Almighty's form
Glasses itself in tempests ; in all time,—
Calm or convulsed, in breeze, or gale, or storm,
Icing the pole, or in the torrid clime
Dark-heaving—boundless, endless, and sublime.

The image of eternity, the throne
Of the invisible ; even from out thy slime
The monsters of the deep are made ; each zone
Obeys thee ; thou goest forth, dread, fathomless, alone.

And i have loved thee, Ocean! and my joy
Of youthful sports was on thy breast to be
Borne, like thy bubbles, onward : from a boy
I wanton'd with thy breakers—they to me
Were a delight ; and if the freshening sea
Made them a terror—'t was a pleasing fear,
For I was as it were a child of thee,
And trusted to thy billows far and near,
And laid my hand upon thy mane—as I do here.

PROMETHEUS.

I.

Titan ! to whose immortal eyes
  The sufferings of mortality,
  Seen in their sad reality,
Were not as things that gods despise,
What was thy pity's recompense ?
A silent suffering, and intense ;
The rock, the vulture, and the chain,
All that the proud can feel of pain,
The agony they do not show,
The suffocating sense of woe,
  Which speaks but in its loneliness,
And then is jealous lest the sky
Should have a listener, nor will sigh
  Until its voice is echoless.

II.

Titan ! to thee the strife was given
  Between the suffering and the will,
  Which torture where they cannot kill ;
And the inexorable Heaven,

And the deaf tyranny of Fate,
The ruling principle of Hate,
Which for its pleasure doth create
The things it may annihilate,
Refused thee even the boon to die:
The wretched gift eternity
Was thine—and thou hast borne it well.
All that the Thunderer wrung from thee
Was but the menace which flung back
Of him the torments of thy rack;
The fate thou didst so well foresee,
But would not to appease him tell;
And in thy Silence was his Sentence,
And in his Soul a vain repentance,
And evil dread so ill dissembled,
That in his hand the lightnings trembled.

III.

Thy Godlike crime was to be kind,
  To render with thy precepts less
  The sum of human wretchedness,
And strengthen Man with his own mind;
But baffled as thou wert from high,
Still in thy patient energy,
In the endurance, and repulse
  Of thine impenetrable Spirit,
Which Earth and Heaven could not convulse,
  A mighty lesson we inherit:
Thou art a symbol and a sign
  To Mortals of their fate and force;
Like thee, Man is in part divine,
  A troubled stream from a pure source;
And Man in portions can foresee
His own funereal destiny;
His wretchedness, and his resistance,
And his sad unallied existence:
To which his Spirit may oppose
Itself—and equal to all woes,

And a firm will, and a deep sense,
Which even in torture can descry
   Its own concenter'd recompense,
Triumphant where it dares defy,
And making Death a Victory.

                DIODATI, *July* 1816.

SONNET ON CHILLON.

Eternal Spirit of the chainless Mind!
   Brightest in dungeons, Liberty! thou art,
   For there thy habitation is the heart—
The heart which love of thee alone can bind;
And when thy sons to fetters are consign'd—
   To fetters, and the damp vault's dayless gloom,
   Their country conquers with their martyrdom,
And Freedom's fame finds wings on every wind.
Chillon! thy prison is a holy place,
   And thy sad floor an altar—for 'twas trod,
Until his very steps have left a trace
   Worn, as if thy cold pavement were a sod,
By Bonnivard! May none those marks efface!
   For they appeal from tyranny to God.

STANZAS FOR MUSIC.

I.

They say that Hope is happiness;
   But genuine Love must prize the past,
And Memory wakes the thoughts that bless:
   They rose the first—they set the last;

II.

And all that Memory loves the most
   Was once our only Hope to be,
And all that Hope adored and lost
   Hath melted into Memory.

III.

Alas! it is delusion all:
  The future cheats us from afar,
Nor can we be what we recall,
  Nor dare we think on what we **are**.

SO, WE'LL GO NO MORE A ROVING.

I.

So, we'll go no more a roving
  So late into the night,
Though the heart be still as loving,
  And the moon be still as bright.

II.

For the sword outwears its sheath,
  And the soul wears out the breast,
And the heart must pause to breathe,
  And love itself have rest.

III.

Though the night was made for loving,
  And the day returns too soon,
Yet we'll go no more a roving
  By the light of the moon.

(1817.)

STANZAS WRITTEN ON THE ROAD BETWEEN FLORENCE AND PISA.

Oh, talk not to me of a name great in story;
The days of our youth are the days of our glory;
And the myrtle and ivy of sweet two-and-twenty
Are worth all your laurels, though ever so plenty.

What are garlands and crowns to the brow that is wrinkled?
'Tis but as a dead flower with May-dew besprinkled.
Then away with all such from the head that is hoary!
What care I for the wreaths that can *only* give glory!

Oh FAME!—if I e'er took delight in thy praises,
'Twas less for the sake of thy high-sounding phrases,
Than to see the bright eyes of the dear one discover,
She thought that I was not unworthy to love her.

There chiefly I sought thee, *there* only I found thee;
Her glance was the best of the rays that surround thee;
When it sparkled o'er aught that was bright in my story,
I knew it was love, and I felt it was glory.

November, 1821.

STANZAS.

Could Love for ever
Run like a river,
And Time's endeavour
Be tried in vain—
No other pleasure
With this could measure;
And like a treasure
We'd hug the chain.
But since our sighing
Ends not in dying,
And, form'd for flying,
Love plumes his wing;
Then for this reason
Let's love a season;
But let that season be only Spring.

When lovers parted
Feel broken-hearted,
And, all hopes thwarted,
Expect to die;
A few years older,
Ah! how much colder
They might behold her
For whom they sigh!

When link'd together,
In every weather,
They pluck Love's feather
From out his wing—
He'll stay for ever,
But sadly shiver
Without his plumage, when past the Spring.

(1819.)

Donna Julia's Letter.

[From *Don Juan.* Canto I.]

They tell me 'tis decided you depart :
  'Tis wise—'tis well, but not the less a pain ;
I have no further claim on your young heart,
  Mine is the victim, and would be again :
To love too much has been the only art
  I used ;—I write in haste, and if a stain
Be on this sheet, 'tis not what it appears ;
My eyeballs burn and throb, but have no tears.

I loved, I love you ; for this love have lost
  State, station, heaven, mankind's, my own esteem,
And yet cannot regret what it hath cost,
  So dear is still the memory of that dream ;
Yet, if I name my guilt, 'tis not to boast,
  None can deem harshlier of me than I deem :
I trace this scrawl because I cannot rest—
I've nothing to reproach or to request.

Man's love is of man's life a thing apart,
  'Tis woman's whole existence ; man may range
The court, camp, church, the vessel, and the mart ;
  Sword, gown, gain, glory, offer in exchange
Pride, fame, ambition, to fill up his heart,
  And few there are whom these cannot estrange ;
Men have all these resources, we but one,
To love again, and be again undone.

U 2

You will proceed in pleasure, and in pride,
  Beloved and loving many; all is o'er
For me on earth, except some years to hide
  My shame and sorrow deep in my heart's **core:**
These I could bear, but cannot cast aside
  The passion which still rages as before,—
And so farewell—forgive me, love me—No,
That word is idle now—but let it go.

My breast has been all weakness, is so yet;
  But still I think I can collect my mind;
My blood still rushes where my spirit's set,
  As roll the waves before the settled wind;
My heart is feminine, nor can forget—
  To all, except one image, madly blind,
So shakes the needle, and so stands the pole,
As vibrates my fond heart to my fix'd soul.

I have no more to say, but linger still,
  And dare not set my seal upon this sheet,
And yet I may as well the task fulfil,
  My misery can scarce be more complete:
I had not lived till now, could sorrow kill;
  Death shuns the wretch who fain the blow would **meet,**
And I must even survive this last adieu,
And bear with life, to love and pray for you!

FIRST LOVE.

[From the same.]

       'Tis sweet to hear
  At midnight on the blue and moonlit deep
The song and oar of Adria's gondolier,
  By distance mellow'd, o'er the waters sweep;
'Tis sweet to see the evening star appear;
  'Tis sweet to listen as the night-winds creep
From leaf to leaf; 'tis sweet to view on high
The rainbow, based on ocean, span the sky.

'Tis sweet to hear the watch-dog's honest bark
  Bay deep-mouth'd welcome as we draw near home;
'Tis sweet to know there is an eye will mark
  Our coming, and look brighter when we come;
'Tis sweet to be awaken'd by the lark,
  Or lull'd by falling waters; sweet the hum
Of bees, the voice of girls, the song of birds,
The lisp of children, and their earliest words.

Sweet is the vintage, when the showering grapes
  In Bacchanal profusion reel to earth,
Purple and gushing; sweet are our escapes
  From civic revelry to rural mirth;
Sweet to the miser are his glittering heaps,
  Sweet to the father is his first-born's birth,
Sweet is revenge—especially to women,
Pillage to soldiers, prize-money to seamen.

Sweet is a legacy, and passing sweet
  The unexpected death of some old lady
Or gentleman of seventy years complete,
  Who 've made ' us youth ' wait too—too long already
For an estate, or cash, or country seat,
  Still breaking, but with stamina so steady
That all the Israelites are fit to mob its
Next owner for their double-damn'd post-obits.

'Tis sweet to win, no matter how, one's laurels,
  By blood or ink; 'tis sweet to put an end
To strife; 'tis sometimes sweet to have our quarrels,
  Particularly with a tiresome friend:
Sweet is old wine in bottles, ale in barrels;
  Dear is the helpless creature we defend
Against the world; and dear the schoolboy spot
We ne'er forget, though there we are forgot.

But sweeter still than this, than these, than all,
  Is first and passionate love—it stands alone,
Like Adam's recollection of his fall;
  The tree of knowledge has been pluck'd—all 's known—

And life yields nothing further to recall
  Worthy of this ambrosial sin, so shown,
No doubt in fable, as the unforgiven
Fire which Prometheus filch'd for us from heaven.

THE ISLES OF GREECE.

[From *Don Juan.* Canto III.]

The isles of Greece! the isles of Greece!
  Where burning Sappho loved and sung,
Where grew the arts of war and peace,
  Where Delos rose, and Phœbus sprung!
Eternal summer gilds them yet,
But all, except their sun, is set.

The Scian and the Teian muse,
  The hero's harp, the lover's lute,
Have found the fame your shores refuse:
  Their place of birth alone is mute
To sounds which echo further west
Than your sires' 'Islands of the Blest.'

The mountains look on Marathon—
  And Marathon looks on the sea;
And musing there an hour alone,
  I dreamed that Greece might still be free;
For standing on the Persians' grave,
I could not deem myself a slave.

A king sate on the rocky brow
  Which looks o'er sea-born Salamis;
And ships, by thousands, lay below,
  And men in nations;—all were his!
He counted them at break of day—
And when the sun set, where were they?

And where are they? and where art thou,
  My country? On thy voiceless shore
The heroic lay is tuneless now—
  The heroic bosom beats no more!
And must thy lyre, so long divine,
Degenerate into hands like mine?

'Tis something, in the dearth of fame,
  Though link'd among a fetter'd race,
To feel at least a patriot's shame,
  Even as I sing, suffuse my face ;
For what is left the poet here ?
For Greeks a blush—for Greece a tear.

Must *we* but weep o'er days more blest ?
  Must *we* but blush ?—Our fathers bled.
Earth ! render back from out thy breast
  A remnant of our Spartan dead !
Of the three hundred grant but three,
To make a new Thermopylæ !

What, silent still ? and silent all ?
  Ah ! no ;—the voices of the dead
Sound like a distant torrent's fall,
  And answer, ' Let one living head,
But one arise,—we come, we come !'
'Tis but the living who are dumb.

In vain—in vain : strike other chords ;
  Fill high the cup with Samian wine!
Leave battles to the Turkish hordes,
  And shed the blood of Scio's vine !
Hark ! rising to the ignoble call—
How answers each bold Bacchanal !

You have the Pyrrhic dance as yet ;
  Where is the Pyrrhic phalanx gone ?
Of two such lessons, why forget
  The nobler and the manlier one ?
You have the letters Cadmus gave—
Think ye he meant them for a slave ?

Fill high the bowl with Samian wine !
  We will not think of themes like these!
It made Anacreon's song divine :
  He served—but served Polycrates—
A tyrant ; but our masters then
Were still, at least, our countrymen.

The tyrant of the Chersonese
 Was freedom's best and bravest friend ;
That tyrant was Miltiades !
 Oh ! that the present hour would lend
Another despot of the kind !
Such chains as his were sure to bind.

Fill high the bowl with Samian wine !
 On Suli's rock, and Parga's shore,
Exists the remnant of a line
 Such as the Doric mothers bore ;
And there, perhaps, some seed is sown,
The Heracleidan blood might own.

Trust not for freedom to the Franks—
 They have a king who buys and sells ;
In native swords, and native ranks,
 The only hope of courage dwells :
But Turkish force, and Latin fraud,
Would break your shield, however broad.

Fill high the bowl with Samian wine !
 Our virgins dance beneath the shade—
I see their glorious black eyes shine ;
 But gazing on each glowing maid,
My own the burning tear-drop laves,
To think such breasts must suckle slaves

Place me on Sunium's marbled steep,
 Where nothing, save the waves and I,
May hear our mutual murmurs sweep ;
 There, swan-like, let me sing and die :
A land of slaves shall ne'er be mine—
Dash down yon cup of Samian wine !

HAIDEE AND JUAN.

[From *Don Juan.* Canto IV.]

Nothing so difficult as a beginning
  In poesy, unless perhaps the end ;
For oftentimes when Pegasus seems winning
  The race, he sprains a wing, and down we tend,
Like Lucifer when hurl'd from heaven for sinning ;
  Our sin the same, and hard as his to mend,
Being pride, which leads the mind to soar too far,
Till our own weakness shows us what we are.

But time, which brings all beings to their level,
  And sharp Adversity, will teach at last
Man,—and, as we would hope,—perhaps the devil,
  That neither of their intellects are vast :
While youth's hot wishes in our red veins revel,
  We know not this—the blood flows on too fast :
But as the torrent widens towards the ocean,
We ponder deeply on each past emotion.

As boy, I thought myself a clever fellow,
  And wish'd that others held the same opinion :
They took it up when my days grew more mellow,
  And other minds acknowledged my dominion ;
Now my sere fancy ' falls into the yellow
  Leaf,' and Imagination droops her pinion,
And the sad truth which hovers o'er my desk
Turns what was once romantic to burlesque.

And if I laugh at any mortal thing,
  'Tis that I may not weep ; and if I weep,
'Tis that our nature cannot always bring
  Itself to apathy, for we must steep
Our hearts first in the depths of Lethe's spring,
  Ere what we least wish to behold will sleep :
Thetis baptized her mortal son in Styx ;
A mortal mother would on Lethe fix.

Some have accused me of a strange design
   Against the creed and morals of the land,
And trace it in this poem every line,
   I don't pretend that I quite understand
My own meaning when I would be *very* fine;
   But the fact is that I have nothing plann'd,
Unless it were to be a moment merry,
A novel word in my vocabulary.

To the kind reader of our sober clime
   This way of writing will appear exotic;
Pulci was sire of the half-serious rhyme,
   Who sang when chivalry was more Quixotic,
And revell'd in the fancies of the time,
   True knights, chaste dames, huge giants, kings despotic,
But all these, save the last, being obsolete,
I chose a modern subject as more meet.

How I have treated it, I do not know;
   Perhaps no better than they have treated me,
Who have imputed such designs as show
   Not what they saw, but what they wished to see;
But if it gives them pleasure, be it so,
   This is a liberal age, and thoughts are free:
Meantime Apollo plucks me by the ear,
And tells me to resume my story here.

Young Juan and his lady-love were left
   To their own hearts' most sweet society;
Even Time the pitiless in sorrow cleft
   With his rude scythe such gentle bosoms; he
Sigh'd to behold them of their hours bereft,
   Though foe to love; and yet they could not be
Meant to grow old, but die in happy spring,
Before one harm or hope had taken wing.

Their faces were not made for wrinkles, their
   Pure blood to stagnate, their great hearts to fail;
The blank grey was not made to blast their hair,
   But like the climes that know nor snow nor hail,

They were all summer; lightning might assail
  And shiver them to ashes, but to trail
A long and snake-like life of dull decay
Was not for them—they had too little clay.

They were alone once more; for them to be
  Thus was another Eden; they were never
Weary, unless when separate: the tree
  Cut from its forest root of years—the river
Damm'd from its fountain—the child from the knee
  And breast maternal wean'd at once for ever,—
Would wither less than these two torn apart;
Alas! there is no instinct like the heart—

The heart—which may be broken: happy they!
  Thrice fortunate! who of that fragile mould,
The precious porcelain of human clay,
  Break with the first fall: they can ne'er behold ·
The long year link'd with heavy day on day,
  And all which must be borne, and never told;
While life's strange principle will often lie
Deepest in those who long the most to die.

'Whom the gods love die young' was said of yore,
  And many deaths do they escape by this:
The death of friends, and that which slays even more—
  The death of friendship, love, youth, all that is,
Except mere breath; and since the silent shore
  Awaits at last even those who longest miss
The old archer's shafts, perhaps the early grave
Which men weep over may be meant to save.

Haidée and Juan thought not of the dead.
  The heavens, and earth, and air, seem'd made for them;
They found no fault with Time, save that he fled;
  They saw not in themselves aught to condemn;
Each was the other's mirror, and but read
  Joy sparkling in their dark eyes like a gem,
And knew such brightness was but the reflection
Of their exchanging glances of affection.

The gentle pressure, and the thrilling touch,
    The least glance better understood than words,
Which still said all, and ne'er could say too much ;
    A language, too, but like to that of birds,
Known but to them, at least appearing such
    As but to lovers a true sense affords ;
Sweet playful phrases, which would seem absurd
To those who have ceased to hear such, or ne'er heard.

All these were theirs, for they were children still,
    And children still they should have ever been ;
They were not made in the real world to fill
    A busy character in the dull scene,
But like two beings born from out a rill,
    A nymph and her beloved, all unseen
To pass their lives in fountains and on flowers,
And never know the weight of human hours.

Moons changing had roll'd on, and changeless found
    Those their bright rise had lighted to such joys
As rarely they beheld throughout their round ;
    And these were not of the vain kind which cloys,
For theirs were buoyant spirits, never bound
    By the mere senses ; and that which destroys
Most love, possession, unto them appear'd
A thing which each endearment more endear'd.

INVOCATION TO THE SPIRIT OF ACHILLES.

[From *The Deformed Transformed.*]

Beautiful shadow
    Of Thetis's boy !
Who sleeps in the meadow
    Whose grass grows o'er Troy :
From the red earth, like Adam,
    Thy likeness I shape,
As the being who made him,
    Whose actions I ape.

Thou clay, be all glowing,
   Till the rose in his cheek
Be as fair as, when blowing,
   It wears its first streak !
Ye violets, I scatter,
   Now turn into eyes !
And thou, sunshiny water,
   Of blood take the guise !
Let these hyacinth boughs
   Be his long flowing hair,
And wave o'er his brows
   As thou wavest in air !
Let his heart be this marble
   I tear from the rock !
But his voice as the warble
   Of birds on yon oak !
Let his flesh be the purest
   Of mould, in which grew
The lily-root surest,
   And drank the best dew !
Let his limbs be the lightest
   Which clay can compound,
And his aspect the brightest
   On earth to be found !
Elements, near me,
   Be mingled and stirr'd,
Know me, and hear me,
   And leap to my word !
Sunbeams, awaken
   This earth's animation !
'Tis done ! He hath taken
   His stand in creation !

ON THIS DAY I COMPLETE MY THIRTY-SIXTH YEAR.

Missolonghi, *Jan.* 22, 1824

'Tis time this heart should be unmoved,
　　Since others it hath ceased to move:
Yet, though I cannot be beloved,
　　　　Still let me love!

My days are in the yellow leaf;
　　The flowers and fruits of love are gone;
The worm, the canker, and the grief
　　　　Are mine alone!

The fire that on my bosom preys
　　Is lone as some volcanic isle;
No torch is kindled at its blaze—
　　　　A funeral pile.

The hope, the fear, the jealous care,
　　The exalted portion of the pain
And power of love, I cannot share,
　　　　But wear the chain.

But 'tis not *thus*—and 'tis not *here*—
　　Such thoughts should shake my soul, nor *now*,
Where glory decks the hero's bier,
　　　　Or binds his brow.

The sword, the banner, and the field,
　　Glory and Greece, around me see!
The Spartan, borne upon his shield,
　　　　Was not more free.

Awake! (not Greece—she *is* awake!)
　　Awake, my spirit! Think through *whom*
Thy life-blood tracks its parent lake,
　　　　And then strike home!

Tread those reviving passions down,
　　Unworthy manhood!—unto thee
Indifferent should the smile or frown
　　　　Of beauty be.

If thou regrett'st thy youth, *why live?*
  The land of honourable death
Is here :—up to the field, and give
    Away thy breath!

Seek out—less often sought than found—
  A soldier's grave, for thee the best;
Then look around, and choose thy ground,
    And take thy rest.

WILLIAM TENNANT.

[TENNANT, born at Anstruther, Fifeshire, in 1786, was in early life a school-master, and later on Professor of Oriental Languages at St. Andrew's. *Anster Fair*, by which he is known to poetry, was written in 1811 and published in 1812. *The Thane of Fife*, a long narrative poem, published in 1822, was a failure, and the same may be said of his *Hebrew Dramas* and his tragedies of *Cardinal Bethune* and *John Balliol*. He died in 1848.]

The author of *Anster Fair* is an extraordinary instance of a single-poem poet. When Byron translated the first Canto of Pulci's *Morgante Maggiore*, he spoke of the Italian poet as 'the founder of a new style of poetry lately sprung up in England,' explaining that he 'alluded to that of the ingenious Whistlecraft.' Tennant, however, anticipated the ingenious Whistlecraft in the introduction of this new style into the English poetry of the nineteenth century. He was the first to use with masterly effect the style which Byron associated for all time with *Don Juan*. After taking rank at an early age among the masters of mock-heroic, he abandoned this field, essayed the true-heroic, and failed, but never returned to his first love.

Whether Tennant's poetic vein was exhausted, or crushed beneath his weight of learning, or simply abandoned as out of keeping with his grave and reverend professorial character, we have no means of knowing. The abundance and freshness of the vein almost negatives the hypothesis of exhaustion. Even when read after *Don Juan*, *Anster Fair* must excite admiration by the flexibility and rapid freedom of its verse. There is no trace of poverty in the ornaments embroidered on the fantastically cut garment ; the artist runs riot in the wealth of his fantastic imagination, spending prodigally as if from an inexhaustible purse. Tennant has told us himself that it was in laughing over *Peebles to the Play* the humorous extravaganza ascribed to James I of Scotland, that the first thought of *Auster Fair* occurred to him, and his diction shows that he was a delighted student of Spenser and Shakespeare. It was probably from these native sources and not from the Italian masters that he drew his inspiration. His discipleship to Spenser is proclaimed in the Alexandrine with which he closes his eight-rhyme stanza. But he was no mere imitator and copyist; home-grown popular legends and popular sports supplied him with his materials, and he handled them boldly in his own fashion, trans-porting them into a many-coloured atmosphere of humorous imagination. The specimen here quoted will give some idea of his powers of imaginative description.

W. MINTO.

RAB THE RANTER'S BAG-PIPE PLAYING.

[From *Anster Fair*.]

Nodded his liege assent, and straightway bade
  Him stand a-top o' th' hillock at his side;
A-top he stood; and first a bow he made
  To all the crowd that shouted far and wide;
Then like a piper dexterous at his trade,
  His pipes to play adjusted and applied;
Each finger rested on its proper bore,
His arm appeared half-raised to wake the bag's uproar.

A space he silent stood, and cast his eye
  In meditation upwards to the pole,
As if he prayed some fairy power in sky
  To guide his fingers right o'er bore and hole;
Then pressing down his arm, he gracefully
  Awaked the merry bag-pipes' slumbering soul,
And piped and blew, and played so sweet a tune
As well might have unsphered the reeling midnight moon.

His every finger, to its place assigned,
  Moved quivering like the leaf of aspen tree,
Now shutting up the skittish squeaking wind,
  Now opening to the music passage free;
His cheeks, with windy puffs therein confined,
  Were swol'n into a red rotundity
As from his lungs into the bag was blown
Supply of needful air to feed the growling drone.

And such a potent tune did never greet
  The drum of human ear with lively strain,
So merry, that from dancing on his feet
  No man, undeaf, could stockishly refrain;

So loud, 'twas heard a dozen miles complete,
  Making old Echo pipe and hum again ;
So sweet, that all the birds in air that fly
Charmed into new delight came sailing through the sky.

*　*　*　*　*　*　*　*

Nor was its influence less on human ear :
  First from their gilded chairs upstart at once,
The royal James and Maggie, seated near,
  Enthusiastic both and mad to dance :
Her hand he snatched and looked a merry leer,
  Then capered high in wild extravagance,
And on the grassy summit of the knoll,
Wagged each monarchial leg in galliard strange and droll.

As when a sunbeam from the waving face
  Of well-filled water-pail reflected bright
Varies upon the chamber walls its place,
  And quivering tries to cheat and foil the sight ;
So quick did Maggie with a nimble grace,
  Skip pattering to and fro, alert and light,
And with her noble colleague in the reel
Haughtily tossed her arms, and shook her glancing heel.

The Lords and Ladies next, who sat or stood
  Near to the Piper and the King around,
Smitten with that contagious dancing mood
  'Gan hand in hand in high lavolt to bound,
And jigged it on as featly as they could,
  Circling in sheeny rows the rising ground,
Each sworded Lord a Lady's soft palm griping,
And to his mettle roused at such unwonted piping.

Then did the infectious hopping mania seize
  The circles of the crowd that stood more near,
Till round and round, far spreading by degrees,
  It maddened all the Loan to kick and rear :
Men, women, children, lilt and ramp and squeeze,
  Such fascination takes the general ear,
Even babes that at their mothers' bosoms hung
Their little willing limbs fantastically flung

And hoar-haired men and wives, whose marrow age
　　Hath from their hollow bones sucked out and drunk,
Canary in unconscionable rage,
　　Nor feel their sinews withered now and shrunk;
Pell-mell, in random couples they engage,
　　And boisterously wag feet, arms, and trunk,
As if they strove, in capering so brisk,
To heave their aged knees up to the solar disk.

And cripples from beneath their shoulders fling
　　Their despicable crutches far away,
Then, yoked with those of stouter limbs, upspring
　　In hobbling merriment, uncouthly gay;
And some on one leg stand y-gambolling;
　　For why? the other short and frail had they;
Some, both whose legs distorted were and weak,
Dance on their poor knee-pans in mad preposterous freak.

So on they trip, King, Maggie, Knight and Earl,
　　Green-coated courtier, satin-snooded dame,
Old men and maidens, man, wife, boy, and girl,
　　The stiff, the supple, bandy-legged, and lame,—
All suckt and wrapt into the dance's whirl,
　　Inevitably witched within the same;
Whilst Rab far-seen, o'erlooks the huddling Loan,
Rejoices in his pipes and squeals serenely on.

THOMAS MOORE.

[THOMAS MOORE was born at No. 12, Aungier Street, Dublin, on May 28, 1779. He began to print verses at the age of thirteen, and became popular in early youth as a precocious genius. He came to London in 1799, and was received into fashionable society. In 1803 he was made Admiralty Registrar at Bermuda, a post he soon resigned to a deputy and returned to England after travelling in Canada and the United States. In 1819 he was involved in financial ruin by the embezzlements of his Bermuda agent, and left England in company with Lord John Russell. He came back to England in 1822. After a very quiet life, the end of which was saddened by the deaths of his five children, he died at Sloperton on Feb. 25, 1852. His chief poetical works are—*Odes of Anacreon*, 1800 ; *Little's Poems*, 1801 ; *Odes and Epistles*, 1806 ; *Irish Melodies*, 1807 to 1834 ; *Lalla Rookh*, 1817 ; *The Fudge Family in Paris*, 1818 ; *Rhymes on the Road*, 1819 ; *The Loves of the Angels*, 1823.]

When Moore wrote his *Life of Byron* in 1830 and casually spoke of Mr. Shelley as a finer poet than himself, the world admired his generous modesty, but smiled at the exaggerated instance of it. Yet, even then, close observers like Leigh Hunt noticed that the dazzling reputation of the Irish lyrist was on the wane, and that his supremacy as a singer was by no means likely to remain long unchallenged. A few years earlier Christopher North had said, in his autocratical manner, ' of all the song-writers that ever warbled, the best is Thomas Moore.' A few years later, as Keats and Tennyson came before the world with a richer and more artistic growth of verse, the author of *The Loves of the Angels* passed more and more into the background, until at last in our own day critics have dared to deny him all merit, and even to treat him as a kind of lyrical Pariah, an outcast at whom every one is welcome to cast a stone.

As usual in the case of such vicissitudes of taste, the truth seems to lie midway between the extremes, and as in 1830 it would have been salutary to point out how limited in interest, poor in execution, and tawdry in ornament much of Moore's work was, it is now quite as necessary to recall to the minds of readers of poetry the great claims that he possesses to our respect and allegiance. When Moore began to publish,—and it must be remembered that his earliest printed verses show much of his peculiar individuality,— the genius of Burns alone reminded the public of that day of the existence of a singing element in literature. Neither Crabbe nor Rogers, the two poets then most prominently before the world, knew what it was to write a song, and it was into an atmosphere of refined and frigid reflection that Tom Moore brought the fervour of his Irish heart and the liquid numbers of his Irish tongue. He heralded a new age of poetic song, for although the *Lyrical Ballads* two years before had, in a far truer sense, announced a fresh epoch, yet their voice had been heard only by one or two. The easy muse of Moore conquered the town ; he popularised the use of bright and varied measures, sparkling rhymes, and all the bewitching panoply of artistic form in which Shelley, the true songwriter, was to array himself. In a larger sense than he himself was conscious of, he was a pioneer in letters. He boasted, with no more gaiety than truth, that he originated modern Irish poetry :—

> 'Dear Harp of my Country ! in darkness I found thee,
>   The cold chain of silence had hung o'er thee long,
> When proudly, my own Island Harp, I unbound thee,
>   And gave all thy chords to light, freedom and song.'

He might have applied these words to the harp of England also, for if he was not destined to strike from it the noblest music, he it was at least who took it down from the wall, and tuned it for the service of greater poets than himself.

It is still possible to read *Lalla Rookh* with pleasure, and even with a sort of indulgent enthusiasm. Rococo prettiness could hardly reach a higher point of accomplishment, and the sham-oriental is perhaps not more hopelessly antiquated than our own sham-mediæval will be sixty years hence. The brilliance of Moore's voluptuous scenes has faded ; he gilded them too much with the gold of Mrs. Tighe's *Psyche*, a preparation that was expressly made to tarnish. But underneath the smooth and faded surface lie much tenderness and pathos in the story of the Peri, much genuine patriotism in the fate of the Fire-Worshippers, much tropical sweetness in the adventures of the 'Light of the Haram.' These narratives possess more worth, for instance, than all but the very best of Byron's tales, and would be read with more pleasure than those, were they not overburdened by sensuous richness of style. This quality, which Moore considered his chief claim to immortality, was in point of fact a great snare to him. His idealism, so far from allowing the presence of coarse and passionate touches, expunges them with incessant care, so that throughout the gush and glow of his descriptive scenes the eye and ear alike are conscious of no salient point, no break or discord by which the beauty of the whole can be tested. The reader sympathises with the French gentleman who said that he admired the pastorals of M. de Florian very much, but that he considered a wolf would improve them. In the *Loves of the Angels* this honeyed elegance degenerates into a tiresome mannerism ; in *Lalla Rookh* it is still tempered by the vigour of the narrative, the freshness of the scenes, and the skill of the artist. The latter poem, indeed, is constructed with consummate cleverness ; the prose story, in which the poetical episodes are enshrined, is both interesting and amusing, so that the whole work leaves on the mind of the reader a greater sense of completeness than any other of Moore's books. In versification it displays him at his best and at his worst, it shows his mellifluous charm, his ardent flow of verse, and his weak, uncertain wing.

In one only of his writings Moore attained a positive perfection of style. Those homely and sentimental lyrics which have endeared themselves to thousands of hearts under the name of the *Irish Melodies* form a part and parcel of our literature the extinction of which would leave a sad blank behind it. When they were first produced, in slender instalments spread over a period of more than twenty five years, they seemed universally brilliant and fascinating to the ears on whom their fresh tunes and dulcet numbers fell in a most amiable union. Here for once, it seemed, music and sweet poetry agreed in complete harmony, the one not brighter or more dainty than the other. Exposed to the wear and tear of sixty years, all the jewels in the casket do not now, any longer, look equally brilliant. Some have wholly faded, others have become weak or crude in colouring, while a few, perhaps one eighth of the whole, are as glowing and exquisite as ever, and shine like real stones in a heap of false jewellery. It is upon these fifteen or sixteen songs, amatory, patriotic and jocose, that Moore's fame mainly rests, but though the support has become slender. it **is lifted beyond** all further fear of disintegration. The *Irish*

Melodies belong preeminently to that minor and less ambitious school of lyrics which of set purpose dedicates itself to vocal singing. The highest lyrical poetry, of course, appeals to the inner ear alone, in that silent singing which is a sweeter thing than any triumph of the vocalist. No tune of the most transcendent aptness could throw fresh charm into the finest stanzas of Shelley, while the most clear-voiced and sympathetic singer would probably fail to make so subtle a scheme of words intelligible to any audience previously ignorant of them. But Moore is a master in that ritual of which Burns is the high priest, in which words of a commonplace character are so strung together as to form poetry easily grasped and enjoyed by the ear, while sometimes the *Melodies* reach a higher pitch, and may be judged by a more severe standard than the improvisatore ever knows. When his genuine and burning love of Irish liberty inspires him, the little amatory bard rises for a moment to the level of Tyrtæus and Campbell.

It is difficult at the present day to revive an interest in Moore's satirical and humourous collections of verse, yet their gaiety was hailed with great enjoyment by a generation accustomed to Wolcot's sturdy fun and the heavy hand of Gifford. In fact the public was excessively entertained by these brisk, smart epistles, in which the Horatian manner was carried to its last excess of levity, and in which witty personalities against public individuals were as thick as plums in a pudding. The *Fables for the Holy Alliance* were more serious and more trenchant than the rest, and perhaps just because their effect was greater at the time, it is less now. It is precisely the lightness of *The Twopenny Post-Bag* that supports it still on the stream of literature. In *Rhymes on the Road* Moore seems to be emulating Byron in his rapid interchange of cynical with romantic reflection, but he has not the muscular strength needed to draw the bow of Byron, and when he describes the view of Lake Leman from the Jura we miss almost painfully the note of the master. He is infinitely more at home in describing the gay world of Florence, and sentimentally regretting the domestic pleasures of an English home. Nor is the modern reader much scandalised, but only very much amused, to find little Mr. Moore inditing a long poem at Les Charmettes merely to insist upon the fact that he was *not* roused by reminiscences of Rousseau.

EDMUND W. GOSSE.

THE LIGHT OF THE HARAM.

[From *Lalla Rookh.*]

Who has not heard of the Vale of Cashmere,
  With its roses the brightest that earth ever gave,
Its temples, and grottos, and fountains as clear
  As the love-lighted eyes that hang over their wave?

Oh! to see it at sunset,—when warm o'er the Lake
  Its splendour at parting a summer eve throws,
Like a bride, full of blushes, when ling'ring to take
  A last look of her mirror at night ere she goes!—
When the shrines through the foliage are gleaming half shown,
And each hallows the hour by some rites of its own.
Here the music of prayer from a minaret swells,
  Here the Magian his urn, full of perfume, is swinging,
And here, at the altar, a zone of sweet bells
  Round the waist of some fair Indian dancer is ringing.
Or to see it by moonlight,—when mellowly shines
The light o'er its palaces, gardens, and shrines;
When the water-falls gleam, like a quick fall of stars,
And the nightingale's hymn from the Isle of Chenars
Is broken by laughs and light echoes of feet
From the cool, shining walks where the young people meet.—
Or at morn, when the magic of daylight awakes
A new wonder each minute, as slowly it breaks,
Hills, cupolas, fountains, called forth every one
Out of darkness, as if but just born of the Sun.
When the Spirit of Fragrance is up with the day,
From his Haram of night-flowers stealing away;
And the wind, full of wantonness, woos like a lover
The young aspen-trees, till they tremble all over.
When the East is as warm as the light of first hopes,
  And Day, with his banner of radiance unfurled,
Shines in through the mountainous portal that opes,
  Sublime, from that Valley of bliss to the world!

THE FIRE-WORSHIPPERS.

[From the same.]

'How sweetly,' said the trembling maid,
Of her own gentle voice afraid,
So long had they in silence stood,
Looking upon that tranquil flood—
'How sweetly does the moonbeam smile
To-night upon yon leafy isle!
Oft, in my fancy's wanderings,
I've wish'd that little isle had wings,
And we, within its fairy bowers,
　　Were wafted off to seas unknown,
Where not a pulse should beat but ours,
　　And we might live, love, die alone!
Far from the cruel and the cold,—
　　Where the bright eyes of angels only
Should come around us, to behold
　　A paradise so pure and lonely!
Would this be world enough for thee?'
Playful she turned, that he might see
　　The passing smile her cheek put on;
But when she marked how mournfully
　　His eyes met hers, that smile was gone;
And, bursting into heartfelt tears,
'Yes, yes,' she cried, 'my hourly fears,
My dreams, have boded all too right—
We part—for ever part—to-night!—
I knew, I knew it *could* not last—
'Twas bright, 'twas heavenly, but 'tis past!
Oh! ever thus, from childhood's hour,
　　I've seen my fondest hopes decay;
I never loved a tree or flower,
　　But 'twas the first to fade away.
I never nursed a dear gazelle,
　　To glad me with its soft black eye,

But when it came to know me well,
  And love me, it was sure to die!
Now too—the joy most like divine
  Of all I ever dreamt or knew,
To see thee, hear thee, call thee mine,—
  Oh, misery! must I lose *that* too?
Yet go—on peril's brink we meet;—
  Those frightful rocks—that treacherous sea—
No, never come again—though sweet,
  Though heaven, it may be death to thee.
Farewell—and blessings on thy way,
  Where'er thou go'st, beloved stranger!
Better to sit and watch that ray,
And think thee safe, though far away,
  Than have thee near me, and in danger!'

WHEN HE, WHO ADORES THEE.

When he, who adores thee, has left but the name
  Of his fault and his sorrows behind,
Oh! say wilt thou weep, when they darken the fame
  Of a life that for thee was resigned?
Yes, weep, and however my foes may condemn,
  Thy tears shall efface their decree;
For Heaven can witness, though guilty to them,
  I have been but too faithful to thee.

With thee were the dreams of my earliest love;
  Every thought of my reason was thine;
In my last humble prayer to the Spirit above,
  Thy name shall be mingled with mine.
Oh! blest are the lovers and friends who shall live
  The days of thy glory to see;
But the next dearest blessing that Heaven can give
  Is the pride of thus dying for thee.

BELIEVE ME, IF ALL THOSE ENDEARING YOUNG CHARMS

Believe me, if all those endearing young charms,
  Which I gaze on so fondly to-day,
Were to change by to-morrow, and fleet in my arms,
  Like fairy-gifts fading away,
Thou wouldst still be ador'd, as this moment thou art,
  Let thy loveliness fade as it will,
And around the dear ruin each wish of my heart
  Would entwine itself verdantly still.

It is not while beauty and youth are thine own,
  And thy cheeks unprofan'd by a tear,
That the fervour and faith of a soul can be known,
  To which time will but make thee more dear ;
No, the heart that has truly lov'd never forgets,
  But as truly loves on to the close,
As the sun-flower turns on her god, when he sets,
  The same look which she turn'd when he rose.

BY THAT LAKE, WHOSE GLOOMY SHORE[1].

By that Lake, whose gloomy shore
Sky-lark never warbles o'er,
Where the cliff hangs high and steep,
Young Saint Kevin stole to sleep.
' Here, at least,' he calmly said,
' Woman ne'er shall find my bed.'
Ah ! the good Saint little knew,
What that wily sex can do.

'Twas from Kathleen's eyes he flew,—
Eyes of most unholy blue !
She had lov'd him well and long,
Wish'd him hers, nor thought it wrong.

[1] This ballad is founded upon one of the many stories related of St. Kevin, whose bed in the rock is to be seen at Glendalough, a most gloomy and romantic spot in the county of Wicklow.

Wheresoe'er the Saint would fly,
Still he heard her light foot nigh ;
East or west, where'er he turn'd,
Still her eyes before him burn'd.

On the bold cliff's bosom cast,
Tranquil now he sleeps at last ;
Dreams of heav'n, nor thinks that e'er
Woman's smile can haunt him there.
But nor earth nor heaven is free
From her power, if fond she be :
Even now, while calm he sleeps,
Kathleen o'er him leans and weeps.

Fearless she had tracked his feet
To this rocky, wild retreat ;
And when morning met his view,
Her mild glances met it too.
Ah, your Saints have cruel hearts !
Sternly from his bed he starts,
And with rude, repulsive shock,
Hurls her from the beetling rock.

Glendalough, thy gloomy wave
Soon was gentle Kathleen's grave !
Soon the saint (yet ah ! too late,)
Felt her love, and mourn'd her fate.
When he said, 'Heav'n rest her soul !'
Round the Lake light music stole ;
And her ghost was seen to glide,
Smiling o'er the fatal tide.

LESBIA HATH A BEAMING EYE.

Lesbia hath a beaming eye,
  But no one knows for whom it beameth ;
Right and left its arrows fly,
  But what they aim at no one dreameth.

Sweeter 'tis to gaze upon
  My Nora's lid that seldom rises;
Few its looks, but every one,
  Like unexpected light, surprises!
    Oh, my Nora Creina, dear,
  My gentle, bashful Nora Creina,
      Beauty lies
      In many eyes,
But Love in yours, my Nora Creina.

Lesbia wears a robe of gold,
  But all so close the nymph hath laced it,
Not a charm of beauty's mould
  Presumes to stay where nature placed it.
Oh! my Nora's gown for me,
  That floats as wild as mountain breezes,
Leaving every beauty free
  To sink or swell as Heaven pleases.
    Yes, my Nora Creina, dear,
  My simple, graceful Nora Creina,
      Nature's dress
      Is loveliness—
The dress *you* wear, my Nora Creina.

Lesbia hath a wit refin'd,
  But, when its points are gleaming round us,
Who can tell if they 're design'd
  To dazzle merely, or to wound us?
Pillowed on my Nora's heart,
  In safer slumber Love reposes—
Bed of peace! whose roughest part
  Is but the crumpling of the roses
    Oh! my Nora Creina dear,
  My mild, my artless Nora Creina!
      Wit, tho' bright,
      Hath no such light,
As warms your eyes, my Nora Creina.

At the Mid Hour of Night.

At the mid hour of night, when stars are weeping, I fly
To the lone vale we lov'd, when life shone warm in thine eye;
   And I think oft, if spirits can steal from the regions of air
   To revisit past scenes of delight, thou wilt come to me there,
And tell me our love is remembered, even in the sky.

Then I sing the wild song 'twas once such pleasure to hear!
When our voices commingling breathed, like one, on the ear;
   And, as Echo far off through the vale my sad orison rolls,
   I think, oh my love! 'tis thy voice from the Kingdom of Souls,
Faintly answering still the notes that once were so dear.

The Young May Moon.

The young May moon is beaming, love,
The glow-worm's lamp is gleaming, love,
    How sweet to rove
    Through Morna's grove,
When the drowsy world is dreaming, love!
Then awake!—the heavens look bright, my dear,
'Tis never too late for delight, my dear,
    And the best of all ways
    To lengthen our days,
Is to steal a few hours from the night, my dear!

Now all the world is sleeping, love,
But the Sage, his star-watch keeping, love,
    And I, whose star,
    More glorious far,
Is the eye from that casement peeping, love.
Then awake!—till rise of sun, my dear,
The Sage's glass we'll shun, my dear,
    Or, in watching the flight
    Of bodies of light,
He might happen to take thee for one, my dear.

The Time I've lost in Wooing.

The time I've lost in wooing,
In watching and pursuing
　　The light, that lies
　　In woman's eyes,
Has been my heart's undoing.
Tho' Wisdom oft has sought me,
I scorn'd the lore she brought me,
　　My only books
　　Were woman's looks,
And folly's all they've taught me.

Her smile when Beauty granted,
I hung with gaze enchanted,
　　Like him the Sprite,
　　Whom maids by night
Oft meet in glen that's haunted.
Like him, too, Beauty won me,
But while her eyes were on me,
　　If once their ray
　　Was turned away
O! winds could not outrun me.

And are those follies going?
And is my proud heart growing
　　Too cold or wise
　　For brilliant eyes
Again to set it glowing?
No, vain, alas! th' endeavour
From bonds so sweet to sever:
　　Poor Wisdom's chance
　　Against a glance
Is now as weak as ever.

DEAR HARP OF MY COUNTRY.

Dear Harp of my Country! in darkness I found thee,
  The cold chain of silence had hung o'er thee long,
When proudly, my own Island Harp, I unbound thee,
  And gave all thy chords to light, freedom, and song!

The warm lay of love and the light note of gladness
  Have waken'd thy fondest, thy liveliest thrill;
But, so oft hast thou echoed the deep sigh of sadness,
  That ev'n in thy mirth it will steal from thee still.

Dear Harp of my Country! farewell to thy numbers,
  This sweet wreath of song is the last we shall twine!
Go, sleep with the sunshine of Fame on thy slumbers,
  Till touch'd by some hand less unworthy than mine;

If the pulse of the patriot, soldier, or lover,
  Have throbb'd at our lay, 'tis thy glory alone;
I was *but* as the wind, passing heedlessly over,
  And all the wild sweetness I wak'd was thy own.

ECHO.

How sweet the answer Echo makes
    To music at night,
When, roused by lute or horn, she wakes,
And far away, o'er lawns and lakes,
    Goes answering light.

Yet Love hath echoes truer far,
    And far more sweet,
Than e'er beneath the moonlight's star,
Of horn or lute, or soft guitar,
    The songs repeat.

'Tis when the sigh, in youth sincere,
    And only then,—
The sigh that's breath'd for one to hear,
Is by that one, that only dear,
    Breathed back again!

OFT IN THE STILLY NIGHT.

[From *National Airs.*]

Oft, in the stilly night,
  Ere Slumber's chain has bound me,
Fond Memory brings the light
  Of other days around me;
    The smiles, the tears,
    Of boyhood's years,
  The words of love then spoken;
    The eyes that shone,
    Now dimm'd and gone,
  The cheerful hearts now broken!
Thus, in the stilly night,
  Ere Slumber's chain has bound me,
Sad Memory brings the light
  Of other days around me.

When I remember all
  The friends, so link'd together,
I've seen around me fall,
  Like leaves in wintry weather;
    I feel like one
    Who treads alone
  Some banquet-hall deserted,
    Whose lights are fled,
    Whose garlands dead,
  And all but he departed!
Thus, in the stilly night,
  Ere Slumber's chain has bound me,
Sad Memory brings the light
  Of other days around me.

CHARLES WOLFE.

[CHARLES WOLFE was born in Dublin, Dec. 14, 1791. He was educated at the University of Dublin, was ordained in 1817, became Curate of Donoughmore in Downshire, and died at the Cove of Cork, Feb. 21. 1823. He printed no book during his life-time, but his slender remains in prose and verse were collected some years after his death by Archdeacon Russell.]

The famous ode on *The Burial of Sir John Moore* was first printed in *The Newry Telegraph*, an Ulster newspaper, in 1817, with the initials C. W. It was copied into the English papers, and won an instant popularity, but the slight evidence of authorship seems to have dropped out of sight at once. Byron's friends charged him with its composition, but he regretfully disowned it, reading it meanwhile to all his friends with enthusiasm, among others to Shelley, who remarked, 'I should have taken the whole for a rough sketch of Campbell's.' Almost immediately it took its place among the four or five best martial poems in our language, preeminent for simplicity, patriotic fervour, and manly pathos. It was presently discovered that this poem had been written some years before it was printed, by a young Irishman of much promise who died of a decline in his thirty-second year[1]. When this fact became known, public curiosity was attracted to his name, and an attempt was made by one of his early friends to collect what he had written. Only twelve short pieces, besides the ode, could be discovered ; they were mostly songs of love and friendship, full of ardour, and not uninfluenced by the popular Irish manner of Moore. We give one of these, as a favourable specimen of Wolfe's ordinary style.

EDMUND W. GOSSE.

---

[1] It has been usually said that Wolfe paraphrased very closely the report of the death of Sir John Moore in the *Edinburgh Annual Register* for 1808. A reference to the report in question relegates this statement to the province of fable ; the newspaper account is quite bald and commonplace, and the poet has supplied all the salient points out of his own imagination.

The Burial of Sir John Moore at Corunna.

Not a drum was heard, not a funeral note,
    As his corse to the rampart we hurried;
Not a soldier discharged his farewell shot
    O'er the grave where our hero we buried.

We buried him darkly at dead of night,
    The sods with our bayonets turning;
By the struggling moonbeam's misty light,
    And the lantern dimly burning.

No useless coffin enclosed his breast,
    Not in sheet nor in shroud we wound him;
But he lay like a warrior taking his rest
    With his martial cloak around him.

Few and short were the prayers we said,
    And we spoke not a word of sorrow;
But we stedfastly gazed on the face that was dead,
    And we bitterly thought of the morrow.

We thought as we hollowed his narrow bed,
    And smoothed down his lonely pillow,
That the foe and the stranger would tread o'er his head,
    And we far away on the billow!

Lightly they'll talk of the spirit that gone,
    And o'er his cold ashes upbraid him,—
But little he'll reck, if they let him sleep on
    In the grave where a Briton has laid him.

But half of our weary task was done
    When the clock struck the hour for retiring;
And we heard the distant and random gun
    That the foe was sullenly firing.

Slowly and sadly we laid him down,
    From the field of his fame fresh and gory;
We carved not a line, and we raised not a stone—
    But we left him alone with his glory.

Song.

O say not that my heart is cold
   To aught that once could warm it;
That Nature's form, so dear of old,
   No more has power to charm it;
Or that the ungenerous world can chill
   One glow of fond emotion
For those who made it dearer still,
   And shared my wild devotion.

Still oft those solemn scenes I view
   In rapt and dreamy sadness;
Oft look on those who loved them too
   With Fancy's idle gladness;
Again I longed to view the light
   In Nature's features glowing,
Again to tread the mountain's height,
   And taste the soul's o'erflowing.

Stern Duty rose, and frowning flung
   His leaden chain around me;
With iron look and sullen tongue
   He muttered as he bound me:
'The mountain breeze, the boundless heaven,
   Unfit for toil the creature;
These for the free alone were given,—
   But what have slaves with Nature?'

CHARLES LAMB.

[Born in the Temple, London, February 10, 1775; was educated at Christ's Hospital, with Coleridge for a school-fellow; became clerk in the India House, 1792; retired on a pension, 1825; died December 27, 1834. His poetry is as follows:—*Poems by S. T. Coleridge, second edition, to which are now added Poems by Charles Lamb and Charles Lloyd*, 1797. *Blank Verse, by Charles Lloyd and Charles Lamb*, 1798. *Poetry for Children, entirely original; by the Author of Mrs. Leicester's School*, 1809. *Poems in The Works of Charles Lamb*, 1818. *Album Verses, with a few others, by Charles Lamb*, 1830.]

Charles Lamb's nosegay of verse may be held by the small hand of a maiden, and there is not in it one flaunting, gallant flower; it is, however, fragrant with the charities of home, like blossoms gathered in some old cottage croft. To know his varying subtleties, his play of intellect, his lambent humour, one must turn to his prose writings; but the gentle heart, the unworldly temper, the fine courtesy, betray themselves in every utterance of Lamb. It was in early manhood and in snatches of time that his first verses were written; he speaks of them as creatures of the fancy and the feeling in life's more vacant hours, as derivatives from the poetry of Coleridge. And certainly there is less in them of Lamb's own favourite, Burns, than of Bowles, whom Coleridge at one time idolised. In Coleridge's volume they modestly made their appearance. 'My friend Lloyd and myself came into our first battle under cover of the greater Ajax.' The larger number of his poems are occasional; a few are interesting as records of a love in idleness that gave unusual charm to the memory of some months in Lamb's prime of youth. From the India House desk it was pleasant to wander in fancy along some forest-glade by the side of fair-haired Anna. But after all, his dear sister, even his good and pious grandame, was closer to Lamb than any beloved 'mild-eyed maid.' And did there not remain to console him that life-long comrade, his pipe, the parting from which for a season he celebrates in a piece of mirthful fantasy that would readily run from verse into the quaint prose of Elia? For less pensive companionship he had now and again little Hartley Coleridge, or Thornton Hunt, a guileless traitor enduring imprisonment with his father when Lamb addressed him in verse. Nor in those innocent days of albums was Elia unacquainted with maiden-petitioners — Edith Southey, Dora Wordsworth, Lucy Barton—bashful yet intent to acquire the autograph. Lamb's deeper and sadder heart lay for the most part in quiet concealment ; but once at least in the mournful music of his *Old Familiar Faces*, its monody is heard.

EDWARD DOWDEN.

HESTER.

When maidens such as Hester die,
Their place ye may not well supply,
Though ye among a thousand try,
　　　With vain endeavour.

A month or more hath she been dead,
Yet cannot I by force be led
To think upon the wormy bed,
　　　And her together.

A springy motion in her gait,
A rising step, did indicate
Of pride and joy no common rate,
　　　That flushed her spirit.

I know not by what name beside
I shall it call :—if 'twas not pride,
It was a joy to that allied,
　　　She did inherit.

Her parents held the Quaker rule,
Which doth the human feeling cool,
But she was train'd in Nature's school,
　　　Nature had blest her.

A waking eye, a prying mind,
A heart that stirs, is hard to bind,
A hawk's keen sight ye cannot blind,
　　　Ye could not Hester.

My sprightly neighbour, gone before
To that unknown and silent shore,
Shall we not meet, as heretofore,
　　　Some summer morning,

When from thy cheerful eyes a ray
Hath struck a bliss upon the day,
A bliss that would not go away,
　　　A sweet fore-warning?

THE OLD FAMILIAR FACES.

I have had playmates, I have had companions,
In my days of childhood, in my joyful school-days;
All, all are gone, the old familiar faces.

I have been laughing, I have been carousing,
Drinking late, sitting late, with my bosom cronies;
All, all are gone, the old familiar faces.

I loved a love once, fairest among women;
Closed are her doors on me, I must not see her—
All, all are gone, the old familiar faces.

I have a friend, a kinder friend has no man;
Like an ingrate, I left my friend abruptly;
Left him, to muse on the old familiar faces.

Ghost-like I paced round the haunts of my childhood,
Earth seemed a desert I was bound to traverse,
Seeking to find the old familiar faces.

Friend of my bosom, thou more than a brother,
Why wert not thou born in my father's dwelling?
So might we talk of the old familiar faces—

How some they have died, and some they have left me,
And some are taken from me; all are departed;
All, all are gone, the old familiar faces.

THE GRANDAME.

On the green hill top,
Hard by the house of prayer, a modest roof,
And not distinguished from its neighbour-barn,
Save by a slender-tapering length of spire,
The Grandame sleeps. A plain stone barely tells
The name and date to the chance passenger.

For lowly born was she, and long had eat,
Well-earned, the bread of service :—hers was else
A mounting spirit, one that entertained
Scorn of base action, deed dishonourable,
Or aught unseemly. I remember well
Her reverend image : I remember, too,
With what a zeal she served her master's house :
And how the prattling tongue of garrulous age
Delighted to recount the oft-told tale
Or anecdote domestic. Wise she was,
And wondrous skilled in genealogies,
And could in apt and voluble terms discourse
Of births, of titles, and alliances ;
Of marriages, and intermarriages ;
Relationship remote, or near of kin ;
Of friends offended, family disgraced—
Maiden high-born, but wayward, disobeying
Parental strict injunction, and regardless
Of unmixed blood, and ancestry remote,
Stooping to wed with one of low degree.
But these are not thy praises ; and I wrong
Thy honoured memory, recording chiefly
Things light or trivial. Better 'twere to tell,
How with a nobler zeal, and warmer love,
She served her *heavenly master*. I have seen
That reverend form bent down with age and pain
And rankling malady. Yet not for this
Ceased she to praise her Maker, or withdrew
Her trust in him, her faith, and humble hope—
So meekly had she learned to bear her cross—
For she had studied patience in the school
Of Christ, much comfort she had thence derived,
And was a follower of the Nazarene.

On an Infant Dying as soon as Born.

I saw where in the shroud did lurk
A curious frame of Nature's work.
A floweret crushed in the bud,
A nameless piece of Babyhood,
Was in her cradle-coffin lying;
Extinct, with scarce the sense of dying:
So soon to exchange the imprisoning womb
For darker closets of the tomb!
She did but ope an eye, and put
A clear beam forth, then straight up shut
For the long dark: ne'er more to see
Through glasses of mortality.
Riddle of destiny, who can show
What thy short visit meant, or know
What thy errand here below?
Shall we say, that Nature blind
Checked her hand, and changed her mind,
Just when she had exactly wrought
A finished pattern without fault?
Could she flag, or could she tire,
Or lacked she the Promethean fire
(With her nine moons' long workings sickened)
That should thy little limbs have quickened?
Limbs so firm, they seemed to assure
Life of health, and days mature:
Woman's self in miniature!
Limbs so fair, they might supply
(Themselves now but cold imagery)
The sculptor to make Beauty by.
Or did the stern-eyed Fate descry,
That babe, or mother, one must die;
So in mercy left the stock,
And cut the branch; to save the shock
Of young years widowed; and the pain,
When Single State comes back again

To the lone man who, reft of wife,
Thenceforward drags a maimed life?
The economy of Heaven is dark;
And wisest clerks have missed the mark,
Why human buds, like this, should fall,
More brief than fly ephemeral,
That has his day; while shrivelled crones
Stiffen with age to stocks and stones;
And crabbed use the conscience sears
In sinners of an hundred years.
Mother's prattle, mother's kiss,
Baby fond, thou ne'er will miss.
Rites, which custom does impose,
Silver bells and baby clothes;
Coral redder than those lips,
Which pale death did late eclipse;
Music framed for infants' glee,
Whistle never tuned for thee;
Though thou want'st not, thou shalt have them,
Loving hearts were they which gave them.
Let not one be missing; nurse,
See them laid upon the hearse
Of infant slain by doom perverse.
Why should kings and nobles have
Pictured trophies to their grave;
And we, churls, to thee deny
Thy pretty toys with thee to lie,
A more harmless vanity?

WORK.

Who first invented work, and bound the free
And holyday-rejoicing spirit down
To the ever-haunting importunity
Of business in the green fields, and the town—
To plough, loom, anvil, spade—and oh! most sad,
To that dry drudgery at the desk's dead wood?
Who but the Being unblest, alien from good,

Sabbathless Satan! he who his unglad
Task ever plies 'mid rotatory burnings,
That round and round incalculably reel—
For wrath divine hath made him like a wheel—
In that red realm from which are no returnings;
  Where toiling, and turmoiling, ever and aye
  He, and his thoughts, keep pensive working-day.

PARENTAL RECOLLECTIONS.

[From *Poetry for Children,* by Charles and Mary **Lamb.**]

    A child's a plaything for an hour;
      Its pretty tricks we try
    For that or for a longer space;
      Then tire, and lay it by.

    But I knew one that to itself
      All seasons could control;
    That would have mocked the sense of pain
      Out of a grieved soul.

    Thou straggler into loving arms,
      Young climber up of knees,
    When I forget thy thousand ways
      Then life and all shall cease.

FELICIA HEMANS.

[FELICIA DOROTHEA BROWNE was born in Liverpool Sept. 25, 1793, and published her first poems in 1803. She married Captain Hemans, 1812, and died in Dublin May 16, 1835. Her principal works are:—*Tales and Historic Scenes*. 1816; *The Forest Sanctuary*, 1826; *Lays of Many Lands*. 1826; *Records of Woman*, 1828; *Songs of the Affections*, 1830; *Scenes and Hymns of Life*, 1834. She also published various dramas and translations.]

Fifty years ago few poets were more popular than Mrs. Hemans; her verses were familiar to all hearts, and won praise from such fastidious critics as Gifford and Jeffrey, no less than from Wordsworth, Scott and Byron. Yet now they are chiefly forgotten, and without injustice. Her tedious romantic tales, her dramas characterless and without invention, are more frequently below than above the mean of merit. Her lyric poetry is more memorable; yet this, even, is less to be valued for its own sake than as the revelation of a delicate and attractive personality. Sprung from a talent expressive not creative, her verses are stamped with feminine qualities. In their familiar pathos, their love of brilliant adventure, their moral earnestness and habit of obvious reflection, no Pythian enthusiasm fills the poet and compels us to forget her womanhood. The inspiring genius of Mrs. Hemans is neither personal nor artistic passion, but a mild Anglican variety of Christianity. She was a woman of wide culture, yet her acquaintance with the civilisations of the past served only to heighten in her eyes the superiority of Protestant England. For the cause of faith she lays her timidity aside, and in a long and feeble poem, *The Sceptic*, attempts to scale the fastnesses of unbelief. Happily her religion has a gentler side; a side revealing her to be, as Wordsworth said, 'a holy spirit.' And as a spirit she passed through the world. This life to her, with all its keenly-felt endearments of natural beauty and of human love, is but the prelude to an infinite future. Not in nature, not in art, not in sympathy must the weary spirit hope for rest.

> ' Earth has *no* heart, fond dreamer, with a tone
> To send thee back the spirit of thine own;
> Seek it in heaven.'

The transitoriness of this world is the dominant note of her music; loudest in all the chords of warning, consolation, and regret.

This is the chief distinction of Mrs. Hemans' poetry. Her other qualities may be referred to the influence of contemporary writers. The knowledge of many literatures preserved her from the servile adoption of any master's manner, but her early romantic poems are certainly suggested by those of Scott and of Southey; and the beauty of *Childe Harold* probably guided her choice of subject when she wrote a poem *On the Restoration of the Arts to Italy,* and another on *Modern Greece.* The last is a long attempt at loftiness of style whose passion for the beautiful burns with the warmth of painted fire. Mrs. Hemans was little qualified for such ambitious efforts. The habit of improvisation, never disciplined, disposed her to a looseness of style, an incoherence of thought, that no after revision corrected. Even her sweetest lyrics are somewhere imperfect, but to her more aspiring poems these weaknesses are fatal.

After the year 1828, when she fell in with Wordsworth's poetry, a simpler spirit moved her, and her gifts developed on a line more suited to their scope. Her simplicity was never the result of an inspired clearness of vision, as with Wordsworth or with Blake, but was rather the expression of a nature whose vistas were not wide enough to be indistinct, and whose plan of the globe ignored the unseen side. Still, such as it is, it counts for a merit. Her domestic lyrics are often spirited and tender. Some of these, *The Child's First Grief, Casabianca,* and others, are household words among our children. In such work, simple, chivalrous pathetic, her real strength lies, and only by such poems can she assert a claim on our remembrance.

A. MARY F. ROBINSON.

A BALLAD OF RONCESVALLES.

'Thou hast not been with the festal throng
  At the pouring of the wine,
Men bear not from the hall of song
  So dark a mien as thine!
    There's blood upon thy shield,
    There's dust upon thy plume,
Thou hast brought from some disastrous field
    That brow of wrath and gloom.'

'And is there blood upon my shield?
  Maiden, it well may be!
We have sent the streams from our battle field
  All darkened to the sea!
    We have given the founts a stain
    Midst their woods of ancient pine ;
And the ground is wet—but not with rain,
    Deep dyed—but not with wine.

'The ground is wet—but not with rain ;
  We have been in war array,
And the noblest blood of Christian Spain
  Hath bathed her soil to-day.
    I have seen the strong man die,
    And the stripling meet his fate,
Where the mountain winds go sounding by
    In the Roncesvalles' Strait.

'In the gloomy Roncesvalles' Strait
  There are helms and lances cleft ;
And they that moved at morn elate
  On a bed of heath are left!
    There's many a fair young face
    Which the war-steed hath gone o'er ;
At many a board there is kept a place
    For those that come no more !'

'Alas for love, for woman's breast,
  If woe like this must be!
Hast thou seen a youth with an eagle crest
  And a white plume waving free?
    With his proud quick-flashing eye,
    And his mien of kingly state,
Doth he come from where the swords flashed **high**
  In the Roncesvalles' Strait?'

'In the gloomy Roncesvalles' Strait
  I saw, and marked him well;
For nobly on his steed he sate
  When the pride of manhood fell.
    But it is not youth which turns
    From the field of spears again;
For the boy's high heart too wildly **burns**
  Till it rests among the slain.'

'Thou canst not say that *he* lies low,
  The lovely and the brave?
Oh none could look on his joyous **brow**
  And think upon the grave!
    Dark, dark perchance the day
    Hath been with valour's fate;
But he is on his homeward way
  From the Roncesvalles' Strait.'

'There is dust upon his joyous brow,
  And o'er his graceful head,
And the warhorse will not wake him **now,**
  Though it browse his greensward bed.
    I have seen the stripling die,
    And the strong man meet his fate,
Where the mountain winds go sounding **by,**
  In the Roncesvalles' Strait.'

A DIRGE.

Calm on the bosom of thy God,
  Fair spirit, rest thee now!
E'en while with ours thy footsteps trod
  His seal was on thy brow.

Dust, to its narrow house beneath!
  Soul, to its place on high!
They that have seen thy look in death
  No more may fear to die.

CASABIANCA.

The boy stood on the burning deck,
  Whence all but he had fled;
The flame that lit the battle's wreck,
  Shone round him o'er the dead;
Yet beautiful and bright he stood
  As born to rule the storm!
A creature of heroic blood,
  A proud, though child-like form!

The flames roll'd on—he would not go
  Without his Father's word;
That Father, faint in death below,
  His voice no longer heard.
He call'd aloud: 'Say, father, say
  If yet my task is done!'
He knew not that the chieftain lay
  Unconscious of his son.

'Speak, father!' once again he cried,
  'If I may yet be gone!'
And but the booming shots replied,
  And fast the flames roll'd on.
Upon his brow he felt their breath,
  And in his waving hair;
And look'd from that lone post of death
  In still, yet brave, despair;

And shouted but once more aloud,
  'My father! must I stay?'
While o'er him fast through sail and shroud,
  The wreathing fires made way.
They wrapt the ship in splendour wild,
  They caught the flag on high,
And stream'd above the gallant child
  Like banners in the sky.

There came a burst of thunder-sound—
  The boy—O! where was he?
—Ask of the winds that far around
  With fragments strewed the sea,
With mast, and helm, and pennon fair,
  That well had borne their part;
But the noblest thing which perish'd there
  Was that young faithful heart!

LEIGH HUNT.

[Born at Southgate, Middlesex, October 19, 1784; was educated at Christ's Hospital; contributed to various periodicals; was an editor of *The Examiner*, 1808; was imprisoned for libel on the Prince Regent, 1811; visited Byron and Shelley in Italy, 1822; received a pension from the Crown, 1847; died August 28 1859. Besides many works in prose, he published *Juvenilia*, 1801; *The Feast of the Poet*, 1814; *The Descent of Liberty, A Mask*, 1815; *The Story of Rimini*, 1816; *Foliage*, 1818; *Poetical Works*, 1832; *Captain Sword and Captain Pen*, 1835; *A Legend of Florence*, 1840; *The Palfrey*, 1842; *Stories in Verse*, 1855. For the bibliography of Leigh Hunt see 'List of the Writings of William Hazlitt and Leigh Hunt, chronologically arranged with notes, &c., by Alexander Ireland,' 1868.]

Leigh Hunt's distinction as a poet is to be inspired by pleasure which never steals from his senses the freshness of boyhood, and never darkens his heart with the shadow of unsatisfied desire. Hazlitt spoke of 'the *vinous* quality of his mind,' which, with his natural gaiety and sprightliness of manner and his high animal spirits, 'produce an immediate fascination and intoxication in those who come in contact with him.' This vinous quality is in all Leigh Hunt's verse, but it is not that of the heady liquor Hazlitt describes; it is a bright, light wine,

> 'Tasting of Flora, and the country green,
> Dance, and Provençal song, and sun-burnt mirth.'

For his chief poem, *The Story of Rimini*, he chose a passionate and piteous theme; but it was, as he says, to steady his felicity when, released from imprisonment, he visited the English south coast with his wife and their first beloved child.

A clear bright happiness in duty Leigh Hunt found; his industry was that of a bird building its nest. He had dared in a troubled time to libel the girth of the first gentleman in Europe, to call Adonis corpulent ; and when sentence of two years' imprisonment was pronounced, there was some sinking at his heart. But by and by his room in the prison infirmary began to blossom into an Arcadian bower—' I papered the wall with a trellis of roses ; I had the ceiling covered with clouds and sky ; the barred windows I screened with Venetian blinds ; and when my book-cases were set up with their busts, and flowers and a pianoforte made their appearance, perhaps there was not a handsomer room on that side the water.' It must have come out of a fairy tale, said Charles Lamb. On one bookshelf lay a solid 'lump of sunshine,' the *Parnaso Italiano* in fifty-six duodecimo volumes. All Mount Hybla and the Vale of Enna were in his cell.

The *Parnaso Italiano* accompanied him later to Italy. His earlier masters had been Spenser, the youthful Milton, and, in chief, Dryden. He speaks of his ' first manner,' and of his growth in inward perception of poetical requirement ; as he advanced in years he became fastidious, rejecting altogether many charming pieces of earlier date. But in truth, although sallies of vivid phraseology were less frequent as his animal spirits lost the licence of boyhood, his style was from first to last in essentials one and the same. The wine was the same, but it had grown mellower. His poetry was not the poetry of thought and passion, which we have in Shakespeare ; nor—to use Leigh Hunt's own words—that of ' scholarship and a rapt ambition,' which we have in Milton. He could have passed his whole life writing eternal new stories in verse, part grave, part gay, of no great length, but ' just sufficient,' he says, ' to vent the pleasure with which I am stung on meeting with some touching adventure, and which haunts me till I can speak of it somehow.'

Strolling in the meadows near northern London, a *Spenser* or a volume of the *Parnaso* under his arm, Leigh Hunt—a Cockney poet, as were Milton, Chaucer, and Spenser—gathered honey for his hive. When seated at his desk a blissful still excitement possessed him ; his cheek flushed, his breath came irregularly, yet all seemed to be calmed and harmonised by some sweet necessity. In such a vivid composure the fine phrase, the subtle image emerged, to be welcomed and caressed :—

> ' A ghastly castle, that eternally
> Holds its blind visage out to the lone sea '

—after such words the poet's breast might drink a deep inspiration.

'A few cattle looking up askance
  With ruminant meek mouths and sleepy glance'—

there again he had liberated his perception and his pleasure, and might pause for a happy moment. So he flitted on with steady purpose, and a happy industrious imagination storing his hive. His verses, though less rich and deep in loveliness than those of Keats, seem, as he so finely said of Keats's lines, 'to take pleasure in the progress of their own beauty, like sea-nymphs luxuriating in the water.' He loved the triplet because it prolonged this luxury.

Leigh Hunt's reverence for literature was of the finest temper. It would have pleased him to be a servant in the train of Ariosto. His loyalty to Keats was generous and constant, untouched by a shadow of ignoble rivalry. To him, the elder of the two, Keats offered his first printed verses. And Shelley withdrew, as fearing by sigh or tear to wrong the deeper grief of him, the 'gentlest of the wise,' who 'taught, soothed, loved, honoured' dead Adonais.

EDWARD DOWDEN.

A Garden and Summer House.

[From *The Story of Rimini*.]

A noble range it was, of many a rood,
Walled and tree-girt, and ending in a wood.
A small sweet house o'erlooked it from a nest
Of pines :—all wood and garden was the rest,
Lawn, and green lane, and covert :—and it had
A winding stream about it, clear and glad,
With here and there a swan, the creature born
To be the only graceful shape of scorn.
The flower-beds all were liberal of delight :
Roses in heaps were there, both red and white,
Lilies angelical, and gorgeous glooms
Of wall-flowers, and blue hyacinths, and blooms
Hanging thick clusters from light boughs ; in short,
All the sweet cups to which the bees resort,
With plots of grass, and leafier walks between
Of red geraniums, and of jessamine,
And orange, whose warm leaves so finely suit,
And look as if they shade a golden fruit ;
And midst the flowers, turfed round beneath a shade
Of darksome pines, a babbling fountain played,
And 'twixt their shafts you saw the water bright,
Which through the tops glimmered with showering light.
So now you stood to think what odours best
Made the air happy in that lovely nest ;
And now you went beside the flowers, with eyes
Earnest as bees, restless as butterflies ;
And then turned off into a shadier walk,
Close and continuous, fit for lover's talk ;
And then pursued the stream, and as you trod
Onward and onward o'er the velvet sod,
Felt on your face an air, watery and sweet,
And a new sense in your soft-lighting feet.

At last you entered shades indeed, the wood,
Broken with glens and pits, and glades far-viewed,
Through which the distant palace now and then
Look'd lordly forth with many-windowed ken ;
A land of trees,—which reaching round about
In shady blessing stretched their old arms out ;
With spots of sunny openings, and with nooks
To lie and read in, sloping into brooks,
Where at her drink you startled the slim deer,
Retreating lightly with a lovely fear.
And all about, the birds kept leafy house,
And sung and darted in and out the boughs ;
And all about, a lovely sky of blue
Clearly was felt, or down the leaves laughed through ;
And here and there, in every part, were seats,
Some in the open walks, some in retreats,—
With bowering leaves o'erhead, to which the eye
Looked up half sweetly and half awfully,—
Places of nestling green, for poets made,
Where, when the sunshine struck a yellow shade,
The rugged trunks, to inward peeping sight,
Thronged in dark pillars up the gold green light.

But 'twixt the wood and flowery walks, half-way,
And formed of both, the loveliest portion lay,—
A spot, that struck you like enchanted ground :—
It was a shallow dell, set in a mound
Of sloping orchards,—fig, and almond trees,
Cherry and pine, with some few cypresses ;
Down by whose roots, descending darkly still,
(You saw it not, but heard) there gushed a rill,
Whose low sweet talking seemed as if it said,
Something eternal to that happy shade.
The ground within was lawn, with fruits and flowers
Heaped towards the centre, half of citron bowers ;
And in the middle of those golden trees,
Half seen amidst the globy oranges,
Lurked a rare summer-house, a lovely sight,—
Small, marble, well-proportioned, creamy white,

Its top with vine leaves sprinkled,—but no more,—
And a young bay-tree either side the door.
The door was to the wood, forward and square,
The rest was domed at top, and circular ;
And through the dome the only light came in,
Tinged as it entered by the vine-leaves thin.

It was a beauteous piece of ancient skill,
Spared from the rage of war, and perfect still ;
By some supposed the work of fairy hands,—
Famed for luxurious taste, and choice of lands,
Alcina or Morgana,—who from fights
And errant fame inveigled amorous knights,
And lived with them in a long round of blisses,
Feasts, concerts, baths, and bower-enshaded kisses.
But 'twas a temple, as its sculpture told,
Built to the Nymphs that haunted there of old ;
For o'er the door was carved a sacrifice
By girls and shepherds brought, with reverend eyes,
Of sylvan drinks and foods, simple and sweet,
And goats with struggling horns and planted feet :
And round about, ran, on a line with this,
In like relief, a world of pagan bliss,
That shewed, in various scenes, the nymphs themselves ;
Some by the water-side, on bowery shelves
Leaning at will,—some in the stream at play,—
Some pelting the young Fauns with buds of May,—
Or half-asleep, pretending not to see
The latter in the brakes come creepingly,
While from their careless urns, lying aside
In the long grass, the straggling waters glide.
Never, be sure, before or since was seen
A summer-house so fine in such a nest of green.

Rondeau.

Jenny kissed me when we met,
    Jumping from the chair she sat in ;
Time, you thief, who love to get
    Sweets into your list, put that in :
Say I'm weary, say I'm sad,
    Say that health and wealth have missed me,
Say I'm growing old, but add,
    Jenny kissed me.

To the Grasshopper and the Cricket.

Green little vaulter in the sunny grass,
Catching your heart up at the feel of June,
Sole voice that's heard amidst the lazy noon,
When even the bees lag at the summoning brass ;
And you, warm little housekeeper, who class
With those who think the candles come too soon,
Loving the fire, and with your tricksome tune
Nick the glad silent moments as they pass ;

O sweet and tiny cousins, that belong,
One to the fields, the other to the hearth,
Both have your sunshine ; both, though small, are strong
At your clear hearts ; and both seem given to earth
To ring in thoughtful ears this natural song—
In doors and out, summer and winter, Mirth.

The Fish, the Man, and the Spirit.

To Fish.

You strange, astonished-looking, angle-faced,
Dreary-mouthed, gaping wretches of the sea,
Gulping salt-water everlastingly,
Cold-blooded, though with red your blood be graced,
And mute, though dwellers in the roaring waste ;
And you, all shapes beside, that fishy be,—
Some round, some flat, some long, all devilry,
Legless, unloving, infamously chaste :—

O scaly, slippery, wet, swift, staring wights,
What is 't ye do? what life lead? eh, dull goggles?
How do ye vary your vile days and nights?
How pass your Sundays? Are ye still but joggles
In ceaseless wash? Still nought but gapes, and bites,
And drinks, and stares, diversified with boggles?

A Fish answers.

Amazing monster! that, for aught I know,
With the first sight of thee didst make our race
For ever stare! O flat and shocking face,
Grimly divided from the breast below!
Thou that on dry land horribly dost go
With a split body and most ridiculous pace,
Prong after prong, disgracer of all grace,
Long-useless-finned, haired, upright, unwet, slow!

O breather of unbreathable, sword-sharp air,
How canst exist? How bear thyself, thou dry
And dreary sloth! What particle canst share
Of the only blessed life, the watery?
I sometimes see of ye an actual *pair*
Go by! linked fin by fin! most odiously.

The Fish turns into a Man, and then into a Spirit, and again speaks.

Indulge thy smiling scorn, if smiling still,
O man! and loathe, but with a sort of love:
For difference must its use by difference prove,
And, in sweet clang, the spheres with music fill.
One of the spirits am I, that at his will
Live in whate'er has life—fish, eagle, dove—
No hate, no pride, beneath nought, nor above,
A visitor of the rounds of God's sweet skill.

Man's life is warm, glad, sad, 'twixt loves and graves,
Boundless in hope, honoured with pangs austere,
Heaven-gazing; and his angel-wings he craves:—
The fish is swift, small-needing, vague yet clear,
A cold, sweet, silver life, wrapp'd in round waves,
Quickened with touches of transporting fear.

PERCY BYSSHE SHELLEY.

[PERCY BYSSHE SHELLEY, eldest son of Timothy Shelley (afterwards Sir
Timothy Shelley, Bart.), was born at Field Place, near Horsham in Sussex,
August 4. 1792. He was educated at Eton and at University College,
Oxford ; but was expelled from Oxford in 1811 on account of his authorship
of a tract on *The Necessity of Atheism*. In the same year he married
Harriet Westbrook, a girl of sixteen, daughter of a coffee house keeper, but
separated from her in 1814. His intimacy with Mary Godwin, daughter of
William Godwin, author of *Political Justice*, and of Mary Wollstonecraft, led
to a marriage with her after his first wife's death in 1816. In 1817 he was
deprived by Lord Eldon of the custody of his children by his first marriage,
and in 1818 he left England for Italy, in which country he resided, mainly
at Naples, Leghorn, and Pisa, till his death by drowning in the gulf of
Spezia, July 8. 1822. *Queen Mab*, his first work of any note, was privately
printed in 1813; *Alastor* was published in 1816; and *Laon* and *Cythna*,
published and withdrawn in 1817, was reissued as *The Revolt of Islam* in
1818. The *Cenci* and *Prometheus Unbound* were both published in 1820.
Epipsychidion was printed, and *Adonais* published in 1821, and the list is
ended by *Hellas* published in 1822,—the year of the poet's untimely death.]

The title of ' the poets' poet,' which has been bestowed for various
reasons on very different authors, applies perhaps with a truer fitness to Shelley than to any of the rest. For all students of Shelley
must in a manner feel that they have before them an extreme,
almost an extravagant, specimen of the poetic character ; and the
enthusiastic love, or contemptuous aversion, which his works have
inspired has depended mainly on the reader's sympathy or distaste
for that character when exhibited in its unmixed intensity.

And if a brief introductory notice is to be prefixed to a selection
from those poems, it becomes speedily obvious that it is on Shelley's
individual nature, rather than on his historical position, that stress
must be laid. Considered as a link in the chain of English literature, his poetry is of less importance than we might expect. It is
not closely affiliated to the work of any preceding school, nor,

with one or two brilliant exceptions, has it modified subsequent poetry in any conspicuous way. It is no doubt true that Shelley, belonging to that group of poets whose genius was awakened by the stirring years which ushered in this century, shows traces of the influence of more than one contemporary. There are echoes of Wordsworth in *Alastor*, echoes of Moore in the lyrics, echoes even of Byron in the later poems. But, with the possible exception of Wordsworth, whose fresh revelation of Nature supplied poetic nutriment even to minds quite alien from his own, none of these can be said to have perceptibly modified either the substance or the style of Shelley's works as a whole.

Nor, again, will it be useful to dwell at length here on the special characteristics of each of his poems in order. They show indeed much apparent diversity both of form and content. *Alastor* is the early reflection of the dreamy and solitary side of its author's nature. *The Revolt of Islam* embodies in a fantastic tale the poet's eager rebellion against the cruelties and oppressions of the world. In *Prometheus Unbound* these two strains mingle in their highest intensity. The drama of *The Cenci* shows Shelley's power of dealing objectively with the thoughts and passions of natures other than his own. *Adonais*, his elegy on the death of Keats, is the most carefully finished, and the most generally popular, of his longer pieces. And in the songs and odes which he poured forth during his last years, his genius, essentially lyrical, found its most unmixed and spontaneous expression. But in fact the forms which Shelley's poems assumed, or the occasions which gave them birth, are not the points on which it is most important to linger. It is in 'the one Spirit's plastic stress' which pervades them all,—in the exciting and elevating quality which all in common possess,—that the strange potency of Shelley lies.

For although the directly traceable instances of this great poet's influence on the style of his successors may be few or unimportant, it by no means follows that the impression left by his personality has been small. On the contrary, it has, I believe, been deeply felt by most of those who since his day have had any share of poetic sensibility as at once an explanation and a justification of the points in which they feel themselves different from the mass of mankind. His character and his story,—more chequered and romantic than Wordsworth's, purer and loftier than Byron's,—are such as to call forth in men of ardent and poetic temper the maximum at once of sympathetic pity and sympathetic triumph.

For such men are apt to feel that they have a controversy with the world. Their virtue,—because it is original rather than re-flected,—because it rests on impulse rather than on tradition,—seems too often to be counted for nothing at all by those whose highest achievement is to walk mechanically along the ancient ways. Their eagerness to face the reality of things, without some touch of which religion is but a cajoling dream, is denounced as heresy or atheism. Their enthusiasm for ideal beauty, without some touch of which love is but a selfish instinct, is referred to the promptings of a less dignified passion. The very name of their master Plato is vulgarised into an easy sneer. And nevertheless the wisest among them perceive that all this must be, and is better thus. The world must be arranged to suit the ordinary man, for though the man of genius is more capable of being *pained*, the ordinary man is more likely to be really *injured* by surroundings unfitted for his development. In society, as in nature, the tests which any exceptional variation has to encounter should be prompt and severe. It is better that poets should be

'Cradled into poesy by wrong,
And learn in suffering what they teach in song,'

than that a door should be opened to those who are the shadow of that of which the poet is the reality,—who are only sentimental, only revolutionary, only uncontrolled. It is better that the world should persecute a Shelley than that it should endure a St. Just.

But in whatever mood the man of poetic temper may contem-plate his own relation to society, he will be tempted to dwell upon, even to idealise, the character and achievements of Shelley. Perhaps he is dreaming, as many men have innocently dreamt who had not strength enough to make their dream come true, of the delight of justifying what the world calls restless indolence by some apparition of unlooked-for power ; of revealing the central force of self-control which has guided those eager impulses along an ordered way,

'As the sun rules, even with a tyrant's gaze
The unquiet republic of the maze
Of Planets struggling fierce toward Heaven's free wilderness';—

of giving, in short, to motives misconstrued and character maligned the noble vindication of some work whose sincerity and virtue enshrine it in the heart of a great people. In such a mood he will turn proudly to Shelley as to one who knew to the uttermost the poet's sorrow, and has received the poet's reward; one who, assailed by obloquy, misjudged, abandoned and accursed, replied by strains which have become a part of the highest moments of all after generations, an element (if I may be allowed the expression) in the religion of mankind.

Or if the mood in which the lover of poetry turns to Shelley be merely one in which that true world in which he fain would dwell seems in danger of fading into a remote unreality amid the gross and pressing cares of every day, he will still be tempted to cling to and magnify the poet of *Prometheus Unbound*, because he offers so uncompromising a testimony to the validity of the poetic vision, because he carries as it were the accredited message of a dweller among unspeakable things.

We need not therefore wonder if among poets and imaginative critics we find the worship of Shelley carried to an extraordinary height. I quote as a specimen some words of a living poet himself closely akin to Shelley in the character of his genius. 'Shelley outsang all poets on record but some two or three throughout all time; his depths and heights of inner and outer music are as divine as nature's, and not sooner exhaustible. He was alone the perfect singing-god; his thoughts, words, deeds, all sang together. . . . The master singer of our modern race and age; the poet beloved above all other poets, being beyond all other poets—in one word, and the only proper word—divine.'

The tone of this eulogy presupposes that there will be many readers to agree and to enjoy. And, in fact, the representatives of this school of criticism are now so strong, and their utterance so confident, that the easiest course in treating of Shelley would be simply to accept their general view, and to ignore that opposite opinion which, if not less widely held, finds at any rate less eloquent exposition. But it is surely not satisfactory that literary judgments should thus become merely the utterances of the imaginative to the imaginative, of the aesthetic to the aesthetic, that 'poetry and criticism,' in Pope's words, should be 'by no means the universal concern of the world, but only the affair of idle men who write in their closets, and of idle men who read there.'

We should surely desire that poetry should become 'the universal concern of the world' at least thus far; that those who delight in its deeper mysteries should also be ready to meet plain men on the common ground of plain good sense; should see what they see, listen to what they say, and explain their own superior insight in terms intelligible to all. If clear-headed but unimaginative readers are practically told that the realm of poetry is a fairy-land which they cannot enter, they will retaliate by calling it a 'Cloud-cuckoo-town' built in the air. The sight of our esoteric raptures will only incite them to use the term 'poetry' as the antithesis, not of prose, but of common-sense and right reason.

And there is much indeed both in the matter and style of Shelley's poems to which readers of this uninitiated class are apt to take exception. 'We had always supposed,' they say,—if I may condense many floating criticisms into an argument, as it were, of the *advocatus diaboli* in the case of Shelley's canonisation,—'we had always supposed that one main function of poetry, at least, was to irradiate human virtue with its proper, but often hidden, charm ; that she depicts to us the inspiring triumph of man's higher over his lower self ; that (in Plato's words) "by adorning ten-thousand deeds of men long gone she educates the men that are to be." But we find Shelley telling us, "You might as well go to a gin-shop for a leg of mutton as expect anything human or earthly from me." And his poems bear out this self-criticism. He is indeed fond of painting a golden age of human happiness ; but of what does his millennium consist ? and how is it attained ? In the *Witch of Atlas* it is the fantastic paradise of a child's day-dream, summoned, like the transformation-scene in a pantomime, by the capricious touch of a fairy. In the *Prometheus* an attempt is made to deal more seriously with the sins and sorrows of men. But even there the knot of human destinies is cut and not unravelled ; the arbitrary catastrophes of an improvised and chaotic mythology bring about a change in human affairs depending in no way on moral struggle or moral achievement,—on which every real change in human affairs *must* depend,—but effected apparently by the simple re-moval of priests and kings,—of the persons, that is to say, in whom the race, however mistakenly, has hitherto embodied its instincts of reverence and of order. And further,—to illustrate by one striking instance the pervading unreality of Shelley's ideals,—what does Prometheus himself, the vaunted substitute for any other Redeemer, propose to do in this long-expected and culminant hour ? He begins at once "There is a cave," and proposes to retire thither straightway with the mysterious Asia, and "*entangle buds and flowers and beams.*" "Ask for this great Deliverer now, and find him,"—not surely occupied as a Milton or an Æschylus would have left that bringer of light to men! Nay, so constantly does this idea of a cave-life of beatific seclusion recur in Shelley's mind that it is even left uncertain whether Asia, amid competing offers of the same kind, can obey Prometheus' call. For hardly is *his* description over when Earth in her turn begins " There is a cavern," —and invites the mystic goddess to this alternative retreat. Nor is Asia's choice of caves ended here. For we have already heard of her as occupying with Ione a submarine cavern,—as well as an Indian solitude, styled indeed a *vale*, but differing from the caves above-mentioned in no essential particular. And if this unreality, this aloofness from the real facts of life, pervades Shelley's crowning composition, what are we to say of *Queen Mab* and the *Revolt of Islam*? If we compare their characters and incidents with anything which earth has really to show we should be tempted to argue that their author had never seen a human being. And the one dramatic situation in which Shelley is so strong,—the situation which gives tragic intensity alike to his *Cenci* and his *Prometheus*,—hardly assures us of any more searching knowledge of mankind. For it is simply the opposition of absolute wickedness to absolute virtue.

'For the most part, then, Shelley's conception of the actual world seems to us boyish and visionary. Nor, on the other hand, does he offer us much more of wisdom when we desert the actual world for the ideal,—the realm of observation and experience for the realm of conjecture and intuition. We cannot, in fact, discover what he thought on the main spiritual problems which occupy mankind, while in his treatment of the beliefs of others there is often a violent crudity which boyishness can scarcely excuse. Now we do not demand of a poet a definite religion or a definite philosophy. But we are disappointed to find in so much lofty verse so little substance,—nothing, we may almost say, save a few crumbs from the banquet of Plato. The lark who so scorned our earth and heaven might have brought us, we think, some more convincing message from his empyrean air.

'And now as regards his style. We perceive and admit that Shelley's style is unique and inimitable. But it often seems to us inimitable only as Turner's latest pictures are inimitable ; the work obviously of a great master, but work so diffused and deflected as to bear quite too remote a relation to the reality of things. We can believe that Shelley's descriptions of natural scenes, for instance, are full of delightful suggestiveness for the imaginative reader. But considered simply as descriptions we cannot admit that they describe. The objects on which our eyes have rested are certainly not so *crystalline* or so *marmoreal,* so *amethystine, pellucid,* or *resplendent,* as the objects which meet us in Shelley's song. Nature never seems to be enough for him as she *is,* and yet we do not think that he has really improved on her.

'Again ; we know that it is characteristic of the poetic mind to be fertile in imagery, and to pass from one thought to another by an emotional rather than a logical link of connection. But as regards imagery we think that Shelley might with advantage have remembered Corinna's advice to Pindar in a somewhat similar case, —"to sow with the hand, and not with the whole sack"; while as regards the connection of parts we think that though the poet (like one of his own magic pinnaces) may be in reality impelled by a rushing impulse peculiar to himself, he should nevertheless (like those pinnaces) carry a rag of sail, so that some breath of reason may at least seem to be bearing him along. We are aware that this hurrying spontaneity of style is often cited as a proof of Shelley's wealth of imagination. Yet in desiring from him more concentration, more finish, more self-control, we are not desiring that he should have had less imagination but more ; that he should have had the power of renewing his inspiration on the same theme and employing it for the perfection of the same passage ; so as to leave us less of melodious incoherence,—less of that which is perhaps poetry but is certainly nothing *but* poetry,— and more of what the greatest poets have left us, namely high ideas and noble emotions enshrined in a form so complete and exquisite that the ideas seem to derive a new truth, the emotions a new dignity, from the intensity with which they have existed in those master minds.'

Some such words as these will express the thoughts of many men whose opinions we cannot disregard without a risk of weakening, by our literary exclusiveness, the hold of poetry on the mass of mankind. But neither need we admit that such criticisms as these are unanswerable. Some measure of truth they do no doubt contain, and herein we must plead our poet's youth and immaturity as our best reply. That immaturity, as we believe, was lessening with every season that passed over his head. With the exception of *Alastor* (1815),—the first and most pathetic of Shelley's portraits of himself,—all his poems that possess much

value were written in the last four and a-half years of his life
(1818–22), and during those years a great, though not a uniform,
progress is surely discernible. As his hand gains in cunning we
see him retaining all his earliest magic, but also able from time to
time to dismiss that excess of individuality which would be mannerism were it less spontaneous. The drama of *Hellas*, the last
long poem which he finished, illustrates this irregular advance
in power. It is for the most part among the slightest of his compositions, but in its concluding chorus,—Shelley's version of the
ancient theme, *Alter erit tum Tiphys et altera quæ vehat Argo,*—
—we recognise, more plainly perhaps than ever before in his lyrics,
that solidity and simplicity of treatment which we associate with
classical masterpieces. And the lyrics of the last year of his life
are the very crown of all that he has bequeathed. The delight
indeed with which we hear them too quickly passes into regret,
so plainly do they tell us that we have but looked on the poet's
opening blossom ; his full flower and glory have been reserved as
a θέαμα εὐδαιμόνων θεατῶν, a sight for the blest to see.

But there is much that has been said in Shelley's dispraise
to which we shall need to plead no demurrer. We shall admit it ;
but in such fashion that our admission constitutes a different or a
higher claim. If we are told of the crudity of his teaching and of
his conceptions of life, we answer that what we find in him is
neither a code nor a philosophy, but a rarer thing,—an example,
namely (as it were in an angel or in a child), of the manner in
which the littleness and the crimes of men shock a pure spirit
which has never compromised with their ignobility nor been tainted
with their decay. And in the one dramatic situation in which
Shelley is confessedly so great,—the attitude of Beatrice resisting
her father, of Prometheus resisting Zeus,—we say that we discern
the noble image of that courageous and enduring element in the
poet himself which gives force to his gentleness and dignity to his
innocence, and which through all his errors, his sufferings, his
inward and outward storms, leaves us at last with the conviction
that 'there is nothing which a spirit of such magnitude cannot
overcome or undergo.'

Again, if we are told of the vagueness or incoherence of Shelley's
language, we answer that poetic language must always be a com-
promise between the things which can definitely be said and the
things which the poet fain would say ; and that when poet or
painter desires to fill us with the sense of the vibrating worlds

of spiritual intelligences which interpenetrate the world we see,—
of those

> 'Ten thousand orbs involving and involved, . . .
> Peopled with unimaginable shapes, . . .
> Yet each intertranspicuous,'—

it must needs be that the reflection of these transcendent things
should come to us in forms that luxuriate into arabesque, in colours
that shimmer into iridescence, in speech that kindles into imagery;
while yet we can with little doubt discern whether he who addresses us is merely illuminating the mists of his own mind, or
'has beheld' (as Plato has it) 'and been initiated into the most
blessed of initiations, gazing on simple and imperishable and
happy visions in a stainless day.'

And, finally, if we are told that, whatever these visions or
mysteries may be, Shelley has not revealed them; that he has
contributed nothing to the common faith and creed of men,—has
only added to their aspiring anthem one keen melodious cry ;—
we answer that this common religion of all the world advances
by many kinds of prophecy, and is spread abroad by the flying
flames of pure emotion as well as by the solid incandescence of
eternal truth. Some few souls indeed there are,—a Plato, a Dante, a
Wordsworth,—whom we may without extravagance call stars of the
spiritual firmament, so sure and lasting seems their testimony to
those realities which life hides from us as sunlight hides the depth
of heaven. But we affirm that in Shelley too there is a testimony
of like kind, though it has less of substance and definition, and
seems to float diffused in an ethereal loveliness. We may rather
liken him to the dewdrop of his own song, which

> 'becomes a winged mist
> And wanders up the vault of the blue day,
> Outlives the noon, and in the sun's last ray
> Hangs o'er the sea, a fleece of fire and amethyst.'

For the hues of sunset also have for us their revelation. We look,
and the conviction steals over us that such a spectacle can be no
accident in the scheme of things ; that the whole universe is
tending to beauty; and that the apocalypse of that crimsoned
heaven may be not the less authentic because it is so fugitive, not
the less real because it comes to us in a fantasy wrought but of
light and air.

FREDERIC W. H. MYERS.

STANZAS — APRIL 1814.

Away! the moor is dark beneath the moon,
Rapid clouds have drunk the last pale beam of even:
  Away! the gathering winds will call the darkness soon,
  And profoundest midnight shroud the serene lights of heaven.
Pause not! the time is past! Every voice cries 'Away!'
  Tempt not with one last tear thy friend's ungentle mood:
Thy lover's eye, so glazed and cold, dares not entreat thy stay:
Duty and dereliction guide thee back to solitude.

    Away, away! to thy sad and silent home;
      Pour bitter tears on its desolated hearth;
    Watch the dim shades as like ghosts they go and come,
    And complicate strange webs of melancholy mirth.
The leaves of wasted autumn woods shall float around thine head,
  The blooms of dewy Spring shall gleam beneath thy feet:
  But thy soul or this world must fade in the frost that binds
      the dead,
Ere midnight's frown and morning's smile, ere thou and peace,
    may meet.

    The cloud-shadows of midnight possess their own repose,
For the weary winds are silent, or the moon is in the deep;
    Some respite to its turbulence unresting ocean knows:
Whatever moves or toils or grieves hath its appointed sleep.
    Thou in the grave shalt rest:—yet, till the phantoms flee
    Which that house and heath and garden made dear to thee
      erewhile,
Thy remembrance and repentance and deep musings are not free
From the music of two voices, and the light of one sweet smile.

From 'Alastor; or, The Spirit of Solitude.'

Nondum amabam, et amare amabam, quaerebam quid amarem amans amare
Confess. St. August.

Earth, Ocean, Air, beloved brotherhood!
If our great mother has imbued my soul
With aught of natural piety to feel
Your love, and recompense the boon with mine;
If dewy morn, and odorous noon, and even,
With sunset and its gorgeous ministers,
And solemn midnight's tingling silentness;
If Autumn's hollow sighs in the sere wood,
And Winter robing with pure snow and crowns
Of starry ice the grey grass and bare boughs—
If Spring's voluptuous pantings when she breathes
Her first sweet kisses—have been dear to me;
If no bright bird, insect, or gentle beast,
I consciously have injured, but still loved
And cherished these my kindred;—then forgive
This boast, beloved brethren, and withdraw
No portion of your wonted favour now!

Mother of this unfathomable world,
Favour my solemn song! for I have loved
Thee ever, and thee only; I have watched
Thy shadow, and the darkness of thy steps,
And my heart ever gazes on the depth
Of thy deep mysteries. I have made my bed
In charnels and on coffins, where black Death
Keeps record of the trophies won from thee;
Hoping to still these obstinate questionings
Of thee and thine by forcing some lone ghost,
Thy messenger, to render up the tale
Of what we are. In lone and silent hours,
When night makes a weird sound of its own stillness,
Like an inspired and desperate alchemist
Staking his very life on some dark hope,

Have I mixed awful talk and asking looks
With my most innocent love; until strange tears,
Uniting with those breathless kisses, made
Such magic as compels the charmèd night
To render up thy charge. And, though ne'er yet
Thou hast unveiled thy inmost sanctuary,
Enough from incommunicable dream,
And twilight phantasms, and deep noonday thought,
Has shone within me, that serenely now
And moveless (as a long-forgotten lyre
Suspended in the solitary dome
Of some mysterious and deserted fane)
I wait thy breath, Great Parent; that my strain
May modulate with murmurs of the air,
And motions of the forests and the sea,
And voice of living beings, and woven hymns
Of night and day, and the deep heart of man.

There was a Poet whose untimely tomb
No human hand with pious reverence reared,
But the charmed eddies of autumnal winds
Built o'er his mouldering bones a pyramid
Of mouldering leaves in the waste wilderness.
A lovely youth, no mourning maiden decked
With weeping flowers or votive cypress-wreath
The lone couch of his everlasting sleep:
Gentle and brave and generous, no lorn bard
Breathed o'er his dark fate one melodious sigh:
He lived, he died, he sang, in solitude.
Strangers have wept to hear his passionate notes,
And virgins, as unknown he passed, have pined
And wasted for fond love of his wild eyes.
The fire of those soft orbs has ceased to burn,
And Silence, too enamoured of that voice,
Locks its mute music in her rugged cell.

By solemn vision and bright silver dream
His infancy was nurtured. Every sight
And sound from the vast earth and ambient air

Sent to his heart its choicest impulses.
The fountains of divine philosophy
Fled not his thirsting lips : and all of great
Or good or lovely which the sacred past
In truth or fable consecrates he felt
And knew. When early youth had passed, he left
His cold fireside and alienated home,
To seek strange truths in undiscovered lands.
Many a wide waste and tangled wilderness
Has lured his fearless steps ; and he has bought
With his sweet voice and eyes, from savage men,
His rest and food. Nature's most secret steps
He like her shadow has pursued, where'er
The red volcano overcanopies
Its fields of snow and pinnacles of ice
With burning smoke ; or where bitumen-lakes
On black bare pointed islets ever beat
With sluggish surge ; or where the secret caves
Rugged and dark, winding among the springs
Of fire and poison, inaccessible
To avarice or pride, their starry domes
Of diamond and of gold expand above
Numberless and immeasurable halls,
Frequent with crystal column, and clear shrines
Of pearl, and thrones radiant with chrysolite.
Nor had that scene of ampler majesty
Than gems or gold, the varying roof of heaven
And the green earth, lost in his heart its claims
To love and wonder. He would linger long
In lonesome vales, making the wild his home ;
Until the doves and squirrels would partake
From his innocuous hand his bloodless food,
Lured by the gentle meaning of his looks,—
And the wild antelope, that starts whene'er
The dry leaf rustles in the brake, suspend
Her timid steps, to gaze upon a form
More graceful than her own.

                                  His wandering step,
Obedient to high thoughts, has visited

The awful ruins of the days of old :
Athens, and Tyre, and Balbec, and the waste
Where stood Jerusalem, the fallen towers
Of Babylon, the eternal pyramids,
Memphis and Thebes, and whatsoe'er of strange,
Sculptured on alabaster obelisk,
Or jasper tomb, or mutilated sphinx,
Dark Ethiopia in her desert hills
Conceals. Among the ruined temples there,
Stupendous columns, and wild images
Of more than man, where marble dæmons watch
The zodiac's brazen mystery, and dead men
Hang their mute thoughts on the mute walls around
He lingered, poring on memorials
Of the world's youth ; through the long burning day
Gazed on those speechless shapes ; nor, when the moon
Filled the mysterious halls with floating shades,
Suspended he that task, but ever gazed
And gazed, till meaning on his vacant mind
Flashed like strong inspiration, and he saw
The thrilling secrets of the birth of time.

Meanwhile an Arab maiden brought his food,
Her daily portion, from her father's tent,
And spread her matting for his couch, and stole
From duties and repose to tend his steps :
Enamoured, yet not daring for deep awe
To speak her love :—and watched his nightly sleep,
Sleepless herself to gaze upon his lips
Parted in slumber, whence the regular breath
Of innocent dreams arose. Then, when red morn
Made paler the pale moon, to her cold home,
Wildered and wan and panting, she returned.

The poet, wandering on, through Arabie,
And Persia, and the wild Carmanian waste,
And o'er the aërial mountains which pour down
Indus and Oxus from their icy caves.
In joy and exultation held his way ;

Till in the vale of Cashmire, far within
Its loneliest dell, where odorous plants entwine
Beneath the hollow rocks a natural bower,
Beside a sparkling rivulet he stretched
His languid limbs. A vision on his sleep
There came, a dream of hopes that never yet
Had flushed his cheek. He dreamed a veilèd maid
Sate near him, talking in low solemn tones.
Her voice was like the voice of his own soul
Heard in the calm of thought; its music long,
Like woven sounds of streams and breezes, held
His inmost sense suspended in its web
Of many-coloured woof and shifting hues.
Knowledge and truth and virtue were her theme,
And lofty hopes of divine liberty,
Thoughts the most dear to him, and poesy,
Herself a poet. Soon the solemn mood
Of her pure mind kindled through all her frame
A permeating fire. Wild numbers then
She raised, with voice stifled in tremulous sobs
Subdued by its own pathos : her fair hands
Were bare alone, sweeping from some strange harp
Strange symphony, and in their branching veins
The eloquent blood told an ineffable tale.
The beating of her heart was heard to fill
The pauses of her music, and her breath
Tumultuously accorded with those fits
Of intermitted song. Sudden she rose,
As if her heart impatiently endured
Its bursting burden. At the sound he turned,
And saw, by the warm light of their own life,
Her glowing limbs beneath the sinuous veil
Of woven wind ; her outspread arms now bare,
Her dark locks floating in the breath of night,
Her beamy bending eyes, her parted lips
Outstretched, and pale, and quivering eagerly.
His strong heart sank and sickened with excess
Of love. He reared his shuddering limbs, and quelled
His gasping breath, and spread his arms to meet

Her panting bosom :—she drew back awhile,
Then, yielding to the irresistible joy,
With frantic gesture and short breathless cry
Folded his frame in her dissolving arms.
Now blackness veiled his dizzy eyes, and night
Involved and swallowed-up the vision ; sleep,
Like a dark flood suspended in its course,
Rolled back its impulse on his vacant brain.

Roused by the shock, he started from his trance.
The cold white light of morning, the blue moon
Low in the west, the clear and garish hills,
The distinct valley and the vacant woods,
Spread round him where he stood. Whither have fled
The hues of heaven that canopied his bower
Of yesternight? the sounds that soothed his sleep,
The mystery and the majesty of earth,
The joy, the exultation? His wan eyes
Gaze on the empty scene as vacantly
As ocean's moon looks on the moon in heaven.
The Spirit of sweet Human Love has sent
A vision to the sleep of him who spurned
Her choicest gifts. He eagerly pursues
Beyond the realms of dream that fleeting shade ;
He overleaps the bounds. Alas! alas!
Were limbs and breath and being intertwined
Thus treacherously? Lost, lost, for ever lost
In the wide pathless desert of dim Sleep,
That beautiful shape! Does the dark gate of Death
Conduct to thy mysterious paradise,
O Sleep? Does the bright arch of rainbow clouds,
And pendent mountains seen in the calm lake,
Lead only to a black and watery depth,—
While Death's blue vault with loathliest vapours hung,
Where every shade which the foul grave exhales
Hides its dead eye from the detested day,
Conducts, O Sleep, to thy delightful realms?
This doubt with sudden tide flowed on his heart ;
The insatiate hope which it awakened stung

His brain even like despair.

　　　　　　　While daylight held
The sky, the Poet kept mute conference
With his still soul. At night the passion came,
Like the fierce fiend of a distempered dream,
And shook him from his rest, and led him forth
Into the darkness.—As an eagle, grasped
In folds of the green serpent, feels her breast
Burn with the poison, and precipitates,
Through night and day, tempest and calm and cloud,
Frantic with dizzying anguish, her blind flight
O'er the wide aëry wilderness; thus, driven
By the bright shadow of that lovely dream,
Beneath the cold glare of the desolate night,
Through tangled swamps and deep precipitous dells,
Startling with careless step the moonlight snake,
He fled. Red morning dawned upon his flight,
Shedding the mockery of its vital hues
Upon his cheek of death. He wandered on,
Till vast Aornos, seen from Petra's steep,
Hung o'er the low horizon like a cloud;
Through Balk, and where the desolated tombs
Of Parthian kings scatter to every wind
Their wasting dust, wildly he wandered on,
Day after day, a weary waste of hours,
Bearing within his life the brooding care
That ever fed on its decaying flame.
And now his limbs were lean; his scattered hair,
Sered by the autumn of strange suffering,
Sung dirges in the wind; his listless hand
Hung like dead bone within its withered skin;
Life, and the lustre that consumed it, shone,
As in a furnace burning secretly,
From his dark eyes alone. The cottagers,
Who ministered with human charity
His human wants, beheld with wondering awe
Their fleeting visitant. The mountaineer,
Encountering on some dizzy precipice
That spectral form, deemed that the Spirit of Wind,

With lightning eyes, and eager breath, and feet
Disturbing not the drifted snow, had paused
In his career. The infant would conceal
His troubled visage in his mother's robe
In terror at the glare of those wild eyes,
To remember their strange light in many a dream
Of after times. But youthful maidens, taught
By Nature, would interpret half the woe
That wasted him, would call him with false names,
Brother and friend, would press his pallid hand
At parting, and watch, dim through tears, the path
Of his departure from their father's door.

At length upon the lone Chorasmian shore
He paused, a wide and melancholy waste
Of putrid marshes. A strong impulse urged
His steps to the sea-shore. A swan was there,
Beside a sluggish stream among the reeds.
It rose as he approached, and, with strong wings
Scaling the upward sky, bent its bright course
High over the immeasurable main.
His eyes pursued its flight:—'Thou hast a home,
Beautiful bird! thou voyagest to thine home,
Where thy sweet mate will twine her downy neck
With thine, and welcome thy return with eyes
Bright in the lustre of their own fond joy.
And what am I that I should linger here,
With voice far sweeter than thy dying notes,
Spirit more vast than thine, frame more attuned
To beauty, wasting these surpassing powers
In the deaf air, to the blind earth, and heaven
That echoes not my thoughts?' A gloomy smile
Of desperate hope wrinkled his quivering lips.
For Sleep, he knew, kept most relentlessly
Its precious charge; and silent Death exposed,
Faithless perhaps as Sleep, a shadowy lure,
With doubtful smile mocking its own strange charms.

Startled by his own thoughts, he looked around:
There was no fair fiend near him, not a sight

Or sound of awe but in his own deep mind.
A little shallop floating near the shore
Caught the impatient wandering of his gaze.
It had been long abandoned, for its sides
Gaped wide with many a rift, and its frail joints
Swayed with the undulations of the tide.
A restless impulse urged him to embark.
And meet lone Death on the drear ocean's waste;
For well he knew that mighty shadow loves
The slimy caverns of the populous deep.

The day was fair and sunny: sea and sky
Drank its inspiring radiance, and the wind
Swept strongly from the shore, blackening the waves.
Following his eager soul, the wanderer
Leapt in the boat; he spread his cloak aloft
On the bare mast, and took his lonely seat,
And felt the boat speed o'er the tranquil sea
Like a torn cloud before the hurricane.

As one that in a silver vision floats
Obedient to the sweep of odorous winds
Upon resplendent clouds, so rapidly
Along the dark and ruffled waters fled
The straining boat. A whirlwind swept it on,
With fierce gusts and precipitating force,
Through the white ridges of the chafèd sea.
The waves arose. Higher and higher still
Their fierce necks writhed beneath the tempest's scourge,
Like serpents struggling in a vulture's grasp.
Calm, and rejoicing in the fearful war
Of wave ruining on wave, and blast on blast
Descending, and black flood on whirlpool driven
With dark obliterating course, he sate:
As if their genii were the ministers
Appointed to conduct him to the light
Of those beloved eyes, the Poet sate
Holding the steady helm. Evening came on;
The beams of sunset hung their rainbow hues
High mid the shifting domes of sheeted spray

That canopied his path o'er the waste deep;
Twilight, ascending slowly from the east,
Entwined in duskier wreaths her braided locks
O'er the fair front and radiant eyes of Day;
Night followed clad with stars. On every side
More horribly the multitudinous streams
Of ocean's mountainous waste to mutual war
Rushed in dark tumult thundering, as to mock
The calm and spangled sky. The little boat
Still fled before the storm , still fled, like foam
Down the steep cataract of a wintry river;
Now pausing on the edge of the riven wave;
Now leaving far behind the bursting mass,
That fell, convulsing ocean ;—safely fled—
As if that frail and wasted human form
Had been an elemental god.

                              At midnight
The moon arose: and lo! the ethereal cliffs
Of Caucasus, whose icy summits shone
Among the stars like sunlight, and around
Whose caverned base the whirlpools and the waves,
Bursting and eddying irresistibly,
Rage and resound for ever.—Who shall save?—
The boat fled on,—the boiling torrent drove,—
The crags closed round with black and jagged arms,
The shattered mountain overhung the sea ;
And faster still, beyond all human speed,
Suspended on the sweep of the smooth wave,
The little boat was driven. A cavern there
Yawned, and amid its slant and winding depths
Engulfed the rushing sea. The boat fled on
With unrelaxing speed. 'Vision and Love!'
The Poet cried aloud, 'I have beheld
The path of thy departure. Sleep and Death
Shall not divide us long.'

                              The boat pursued
The windings of the cavern. Daylight shone
At length upon that gloomy river's flow.
Now, where the fiercest war among the waves

Is calm, on the unfathomable stream
The boat moved slowly. Where the mountain, riven,
Exposed those black depths to the azure sky,
Ere yet the flood's enormous volume fell
Even to the base of Caucasus, with sound
That shook the everlasting rocks, the mass
Filled with one whirlpool all that ample chasm ;
Stair above stair the eddying waters rose,
Circling immeasurably fast, and laved
With alternating dash the gnarlèd roots
Of mighty trees that stretched their giant arms
In darkness over it. I' the midst was left,
Reflecting yet distorting every cloud,
A pool of treacherous and tremendous calm.
Seized by the sway of the ascending stream,
With dizzy swiftness, round and round and round,
Ridge after ridge the straining boat arose ;
Till on the verge of the extremest curve,
Where through an opening of the rocky bank
The waters overflow, and a smooth spot
Of glassy quiet mid those battling tides
Is left, the boat paused shuddering. Shall it sink
Down the abyss ? shall the reverting stress
Of that resistless gulf embosom it ?
Now shall it fall ?—A wandering stream of wind,
Breathed from the west, has caught the expanded sail ;
And lo! with gentle motion, between banks
Of mossy slope, and on a placid stream,
Beneath a woven grove, it sails : and, hark !
The ghastly torrent mingles its far roar
With the breeze murmuring in the musical woods.
Where the embowering trees recede, and leave
A little space of green expanse, the cove
Is closed by meeting banks, whose yellow flowers
For ever gaze on their own drooping eyes
Reflected in the crystal calm. The wave
Of the boat's motion marred their pensive task,
Which nought but vagrant bird, or wanton wind,
Or falling spear-grass, or their own decay,

Had e'er disturbed before. The Poet longed
To deck with their bright hues his withered hair;
But on his heart its solitude returned,
And he forbore. Not the strong impulse hid
In those flushed cheeks, bent eyes, and shadowy frame,
Had yet performed its ministry: it hung
Upon his life, as lightning in a cloud
Gleams, hovering ere it vanish, ere the floods
Of night close over it.

     The noonday sun
Now shone upon the forest, one vast mass
Of mingling shade, whose brown magnificence
A narrow vale embosoms. There, huge caves,
Scooped in the dark base of their aëry rocks,
Mocking its moans respond and roar for ever.
The meeting boughs and implicated leaves
Wove twilight o'er the Poet's path, as, led
By love, or dream, or god, or mightier Death,
He sought in Nature's dearest haunt some bank,
Her cradle, and his sepulchre. More dark
And dark the shades accumulate. The oak,
Expanding its immense and knotty arms,
Embraces the light beech. The pyramids
Of the tall cedar, overarching, frame
Most solemn domes within; and far below,
Like clouds suspended in an emerald sky,
The ash and the acacia floating hang,
Tremulous and pale. Like restless serpents clothed
In rainbow and in fire, the parasites,
Starred with ten-thousand blossoms, flow around
The grey trunks; and, as gamesome infants' eyes,
With gentle meanings and most innocent wiles,
Fold their beams round the hearts of those that love,
These twine their tendrils with the wedded boughs,
Uniting their close union; the woven leaves
Make network of the dark-blue light of day
And the night's noontide clearness, mutable
As shapes in the weird clouds. Soft mossy lawns
Beneath these canopies extend their swells,

Fragrant with perfumed herbs, and eyed with blooms
Minute yet beautiful. One darkest glen
Sends from its woods of musk-rose twined with jasmine
A soul-dissolving odour, to invite
To some more lovely mystery. Through the dell,
Silence and Twilight here, twin sisters, keep
Their noonday watch, and sail among the shades,
Like vaporous shapes half-seen. Beyond, a well,
Dark, gleaming, and of most translucent wave,
Images all the woven boughs above,
And each depending leaf, and every speck
Of azure sky darting between their chasms;
Nor aught else in the liquid mirror laves
Its portraiture, but some inconstant star
Between one foliaged lattice twinkling fair,
Or painted bird sleeping beneath the moon,
Or gorgeous insect floating motionless,
Unconscious of the day, ere yet his wings
Have spread their glories to the gaze of noon.

Hither the Poet came. His eyes beheld
Their own wan light through the reflected lines
Of his thin hair, distinct in the dark depth
Of that still fountain; as the human heart,
Gazing in dreams over the gloomy grave,
Sees its own treacherous likeness there. He heard
The motion of the leaves; the grass that sprung
Startled, and glanced and trembled, even to feel
An unaccustomed presence; and the sound
Of the sweet brook that from the secret springs
Of that dark fountain rose. A Spirit seemed
To stand beside him—clothed in no bright robes
Of shadowy silver or enshrining light
Borrowed from aught the visible world affords
Of grace or majesty or mystery;
But,—undulating woods, and silent well,
And leaping rivulet, and evening gloom
Now deepening the dark shades, for speech assuming,—
Held commune with him, as if he and it

Were all that was. Only—when his regard
Was raised by intense pensiveness—two eyes,
Two starry eyes, hung in the gloom of thought
And seemed with their serene and azure smiles
To beckon him.

*   *   *   *   *

When on the threshold of the green recess
The wanderer's footsteps fell, he knew that death
Was on him. Yet a little, ere it fled,
Did he resign his high and holy soul
To images of the majestic past,
That paused within his passive being now,
Like winds that bear sweet music when they breathe
Through some dim latticed chamber. He did place
His pale lean hand upon the rugged trunk
Of the old pine. Upon an ivied stone
Reclined his languid head; his limbs did rest,
Diffused and motionless, on the smooth brink
Of that obscurest chasm;—and thus he lay,
Surrendering to their final impulses
The hovering powers of life. Hope and Despair,
The torturers, slept : no mortal pain or fear
Marred his repose ; the influxes of sense,
And his own being unalloyed by pain,
Yet feebler and more feeble, calmly fed
The stream of thought, till he lay breathing there
At peace, and faintly smiling. His last sight
Was the great moon, which o'er the western line
Of the wide world her mighty horn suspended,
With whose dun beams inwoven darkness seemed
To mingle. Now upon the jagged hills
It rests ; and still, as the divided frame
Of the vast meteor sunk, the Poet's blood,
That ever beat in mystic sympathy
With Nature's ebb and flow, grew feebler still.
And, when two lessening points of light alone
Gleamed through the darkness, the alternate gasp
Of his faint respiration scarce did stir

The stagnate night :—till the minutest ray
Was quenched, the pulse yet lingered in his heart.
It paused—it fluttered. But, when heaven remained
Utterly black, the murky shades involved
An image silent, cold, and motionless,
As their own voiceless earth and vacant air.
Even as a vapour fed with golden beams
That ministered on sunlight, ere the west
Eclipses it, was now that wondrous frame—
No sense, no motion, no divinity—
A fragile lute, on whose harmonious strings
The breath of heaven did wander—a bright stream
Once fed with many-voicèd waves—a dream
Of youth which night and time have quenched for ever—
Still, dark and dry, and unremembered now.

Oh for Medea's wondrous alchemy,
Which, wheresoe'er it fell, made the earth gleam
With bright flowers, and the wintry boughs exhale
From vernal blooms fresh fragrance ! Oh that God,
Profuse of poisons, would concede the chalice
Which but one living man has drained, who now,
Vessel of deathless wrath, a slave that feels
No proud exemption in the blighting curse
He bears, over the world wanders for ever,
Lone as incarnate death ! Oh that the dream
Of dark magician in his visioned cave,
Raking the cinders of a crucible
For life and power even when his feeble hand
Shakes in its last decay, were the true law
Of this so lovely world !—But thou art fled,
Like some frail exhalation which the dawn
Robes in its golden beams,—ah thou hast fled !
The brave, the gentle, and the beautiful,
The child of grace and genius ! Heartless things
Are done and said i' the world, and many worms
And beasts and men live on, and mighty earth,
From sea and mountain, city and wilderness,
In vesper low or joyous orison,

Lifts still its solemn voice :—but thou art fled—
Thou canst no longer know or love the shapes
Of this phantasmal scene, who have to thee
Been purest ministers, who are, alas !
Now thou art not ! Upon those pallid lips,
So sweet even in their silence, on those eyes
That image sleep in death, upon that form
Yet safe from the worm's outrage, let no tear
Be shed—not even in thought.   Nor, when those hues
Are gone, and those divinest lineaments,
Worn by the senseless wind, shall live alone
In the frail pauses of this simple strain,
Let not high verse mourning the memory
Of that which is no more, or painting's woe,
Or sculpture, speak in feeble imagery
Their own cold powers.   Art and eloquence,
And all the shows o' the world, are frail and vain
To weep a loss that turns their lights to shade.
It is a woe 'too deep for tears' when all
Is reft at once, when some surpassing Spirit,
Whose light adorned the world around it, leaves
Those who remain behind, not sobs or groans,
The passionate tumult of a clinging hope,—
But pale despair and cold tranquillity,
Nature's vast frame, the web of human things,
Birth and the grave, that are not as they were.

(1815.)

Stanzas written in Dejection near Naples.

I.

The sun is warm, the sky is clear,
　　The waves are dancing fast and bright,
Blue isles and snowy mountains wear
　　The purple noon's transparent might;
　　The breath of the moist earth is light
Around its unexpanded buds;
　　Like many a voice of one delight,
The winds', the birds', the ocean-floods',
The city's voice itself is soft like Solitude's.

II.

I see the deep's untrampled floor
　　With green and purple sea-weeds strown;
I see the waves upon the shore,
　　Like light dissolved in star-showers, thrown.
　　I sit upon the sands alone.
The lightning of the noontide ocean
　　Is flashing round me, and a tone
Arises from its measured motion,—
How sweet, did any heart now share in my emotion!

III.

Alas! I have nor hope nor health,
　　Nor peace within nor calm around;
Nor that content, surpassing wealth,
　　The sage in meditation found,
　　And walked with inward glory crowned;
Nor fame nor power nor love nor leisure.
　　Others I see whom these surround—
Smiling they live, and call life pleasure;—
To me that cup has been dealt in another measure.

IV.

Yet now despair itself is mild,
    Even as the winds and waters are;
I could lie down like a tired child,
    And weep away the life of care
    Which I have borne and yet must bear,—
Till death like sleep might steal on me,
    And I might feel in the warm air
My cheek grow cold, and hear the sea
Breathe o'er my dying brain its last monotony.

V.

Some might lament that I were cold,
    As I when this sweet day is gone,
Which my lost heart, too soon grown old,
    Insults with this untimely moan.
    They might lament—for I am one
Whom men love not, and yet regret;
    Unlike this day, which, when the sun
Shall on its stainless glory set,
Will linger, though enjoyed, like joy in memory yet.

                    (December, 1818.)

ODE TO THE WEST WIND.

I.

O wild West Wind, thou breath of Autumn's being,
    Thou from whose unseen presence the leaves dead
Are driven like ghosts from an enchanter fleeing,

    Yellow, and black, and pale, and hectic red,
Pestilence-stricken multitudes! O thou
    Who chariotest to their dark wintry bed

The wingèd seeds, where they lie cold and low,
    Each like a corpse within its grave, until
Thine azure sister of the Spring shall blow

    Her clarion o'er the dreaming earth, and fill
(Driving sweet buds like flocks to feed in air)
    With living hues and odours plain and hill;

Wild Spirit which art moving everywhere;
Destroyer and preserver; hear, oh hear!

II.

Thou on whose stream, mid the steep sky's commotion,
   Loose clouds like earth's decaying leaves are shed,
Shook from the tangled boughs of heaven and ocean,

   Angels of rain and lightning! there are spread
On the blue surface of thine airy surge,
   Like the bright hair uplifted from the head

Of some fierce Mænad, even from the dim verge
   Of the horizon to the zenith's height,
The locks of the approaching storm. Thou dirge

   Of the dying year, to which this closing night
Will be the dome of a vast sepulchre,
   Vaulted with all thy congregated might

Of vapours, from whose solid atmosphere
Black rain, and fire, and hail, will burst: Oh hear!

III.

Thou who didst waken from his summer dreams
   The blue Mediterranean, where he lay,
Lulled by the coil of his crystalline streams,

   Beside a pumice isle in Baiæ's bay,
And saw in sleep old palaces and towers
   Quivering within the wave's intenser day,

All overgrown with azure moss, and flowers
   So sweet the sense faints picturing them! Thou
For whose path the Atlantic's level powers

   Cleave themselves into chasms, while far below
The sea-blooms and the oozy woods which wear
   The sapless foliage of the ocean know

Thy voice, and suddenly grow grey with fear,
And tremble and despoil themselves: Oh hear!

IV.

If I were a dead leaf thou mightest bear;
  If I were a swift cloud to fly with thee;
A wave to pant beneath thy power, and share

  The impulse of thy strength, only less free
Than thou, O uncontrollable! if even
  I were as in my boyhood, and could be

The comrade of thy wanderings over heaven,
  As then, when to outstrip thy skiey speed
Scarce seemed a vision,—I would ne'er have striven

  As thus with thee in prayer in my sore need.
Oh lift me as a wave, a leaf, a cloud!
  I fall upon the thorns of life! I bleed!

A heavy weight of hours has chained and bowed
One too like thee—tameless, and swift, and proud.

V.

Make me thy lyre, even as the forest is:
  What if my leaves are falling like its own?
The tumult of thy mighty harmonies

  Will take from both a deep autumnal tone,
Sweet though in sadness. Be thou, Spirit fierce,
  My spirit! Be thou me, impetuous one!

Drive my dead thoughts over the universe,
  Like withered leaves, to quicken a new birth;
And, by the incantation of this verse,

  Scatter, as from an unextinguished hearth
Ashes and sparks, my words among mankind!
  Be through my lips to unawakened earth

The trumpet of a prophecy! O Wind,
If Winter comes, can Spring be far behind?

(1819.)

From 'Prometheus Unbound.'

Semichorus I. of Spirits (as Asia and Panthea pass into the forest)

The path through which that lovely twain
  Have passed, by cedar, pine, and yew,
  And each dark tree that ever grew,
  Is curtained out from heaven's wide blue.
Nor sun nor moon nor wind nor rain
Can pierce its interwoven bowers ;
  Nor aught save where some cloud of dew,
    Drifted along the earth-creeping breeze
    Between the trunks of the hoar trees,
Hangs each a pearl in the pale flowers
  Of the green laurel blown anew,
And bends, and then fades silently,
One frail and fair anemone.
Or, when some star, of many a one
  That climbs and wanders through steep night,
Has found the cleft through which alone
Beams fall from high those depths upon,—
Ere it is borne away, away,
By the swift heavens that cannot stay,—
  It scatters drops of golden light,
  Like lines of rain that ne'er unite :
And the gloom divine is all around,
And underneath is the mossy ground.

Semichorus II.

There the voluptuous nightingales
  Are awake through all the broad noonday.
When one with bliss or sadness fails,
And through the windless ivy-boughs,
  Sick with sweet love, droops dying away
  On its mate's music-panting bosom ;
  Another, from the swinging blossom

Watching to catch the languid close
Of the last strain, then lifts on high
The wings of the weak melody,—
Till some new strain of feeling bear
    The song, and all the woods are mute;
When there is heard through the dim air
The rush of wings, and, rising there
    Like many a lake-surrounded flute,
Sounds overflow the listener's brain
So sweet that joy is almost pain.

[From the same.]

VOICE *in the air, singing.*

Life of Life! thy lips enkindle
    With their love the breath between them;
And thy smiles, before they dwindle,
    Make the cold air fire,—then screen them
In those looks where whoso gazes
Faints, entangled in their mazes.

Child of Light! thy limbs are burning
    Through the vest which seems to hide them,
As the radiant lines of morning
    Through the clouds, ere they divide them;
And this atmosphere divinest
Shrouds thee wheresoe'er thou shinest.

Fair are others; none beholds thee
    (But thy voice sounds low and tender,
Like the fairest), for it folds thee
    From the sight—that liquid splendour;
And all feel, yet see thee never,
As I feel now, lost for ever!

Lamp of Earth! where'er thou movest,
    Its dim shapes are clad with brightness,
And the souls of whom thou lovest
    Walk upon the winds with lightness,
Till they fail, as I am failing,
Dizzy, lost, yet unbewailing!

(1820.)

HYMN OF PAN.

From the forests and highlands
  We come, we come ;
From the river-girt islands,
  Where loud waves are dumb
Listening to my sweet pipings.
  The wind in the reeds and the rushes,
    The bees on the bells of thyme,
  The birds on the myrtle-bushes,
    The cicale above in the lime,
  And the lizards below in the grass,
Were as silent as ever old Tmolus was,
  Listening to my sweet pipings.

Liquid Peneus was flowing,
  And all dark Tempe lay
In Pelion's shadow, outgrowing
  The light of the dying day,
Speeded by my sweet pipings.
  The Sileni and Sylvans and Fauns,
    And the Nymphs of the woods and waves,
  To the edge of the moist river-lawns,
    And the brink of the dewy caves,
  And all that did then attend and follow,
Were silent with love,—as you now, Apollo,
  With envy of my sweet pipings.

I sang of the dancing stars,
  I sang of the dædal earth,
And of heaven, and the Giant wars,
  And love, and death, and birth.
And then I changed my pipings,—
Singing how down the vale of Mænalus
  I pursued a maiden, and clasped a reed :
Gods and men, we are all deluded thus ;
  It breaks in our bosom, and then we bleed.
All wept—as I think both ye now would,
If envy or age had not frozen your blood—-
  At the sorrow of my sweet pipings.

(1820.)

The Cloud.

I.

I bring fresh showers for the thirsting flowers
    From the seas and the streams ;
I bear light shade for the leaves when laid
    In their noonday dreams.
From my wings are shaken the dews that waken
    The sweet buds every one,
When rocked to rest on their Mother's breast,
    As she dances about the sun.
I wield the flail of the lashing hail,
    And whiten the green plains under ;
And then again I dissolve it in rain,
    And laugh as I pass in thunder.

II.

I sift the snow on the mountains below,
    And their great pines groan aghast ;
And all the night 'tis my pillow white,
    While I sleep in the arms of the Blast.
Sublime on the towers of my skiey bowers
    Lightning my pilot sits ;
In a cavern under is fettered the Thunder,
    It struggles and howls at fits.
Over earth and ocean with gentle motion
    This pilot is guiding me,
Lured by the love of the Genii that move
    In the depths of the purple sea ;
Over the rills and the crags and the hills,
    Over the lakes and the plains,
Wherever he dream under mountain or stream
    The Spirit he loves remains ;
And I all the while bask in heaven's blue smile,
    Whilst he is dissolving in rains.

III.

The sanguine Sunrise, with his meteor eyes,
    And his burning plumes outspread,
Leaps on the back of my sailing rack,
    When the morning star shines dead :
As on the jag of a mountain-crag
    Which an earthquake rocks and swings
An eagle alit one moment may sit
    In the light of its golden wings.
And, when Sunset may breathe, from the lit sea beneath,
    Its ardour of rest and of love,
And the crimson pall of eve may fall
    From the depth of heaven above,
With wings folded I rest on mine airy nest,
    As still as a brooding dove.

IV.

That orbèd maiden with white fire laden
    Whom mortals call the Moon
Glides glimmering o'er my fleece-like floor
    By the midnight breezes strewn ;
And wherever the beat of her unseen feet,
    Which only the angels hear,
May have broken the woof of my tent's thin roof
    The Stars peep behind her and peer.
And I laugh to see them whirl and flee
    Like a swarm of golden bees,
When I widen the rent in my wind-built tent,—
    Till the calm rivers, lakes, and seas,
Like strips of the sky fallen through me on high,
    Are each paved with the moon and these.

V.

I bind the Sun's throne with a burning zone,
    And the Moon's with a girdle of pearl ;
The volcanoes are dim, and the Stars reel and swim,
    When the Whirlwinds my banner unfurl.

From cape to cape, with a bridge-like shape,
    Over a torrent sea,
Sunbeam-proof, I hang like a roof;
    The mountains its columns be.
The triumphal arch through which I march,
    With hurricane, fire, and snow,
When the Powers of the air are chained to my chair,
    Is the million-coloured bow;
The Sphere-fire above its soft colours wove,
    While the moist Earth was laughing below.

VI.

I am the daughter of Earth and Water,
    And the nursling of the Sky:
I pass through the pores of the ocean and shores;
    I change, but I cannot die.
For after the rain, when with never a stain
    The pavilion of heaven is bare,
And the winds and sunbeams with their convex gleams
    Build up the blue dome of air,
I silently laugh at my own cenotaph,—
    And out of the caverns of rain,
Like a child from the womb, like a ghost from the tomb,
    I arise, and unbuild it again.

                        (1820.)

To a Skylark.

I.

Hail to thee, blithe spirit—
    Bird thou never wert—
That from heaven or near it
    Pourest thy full heart
In profuse strains of unpremeditated art.

II.

Higher still and higher
    From the earth thou springest,
Like a cloud of fire;
    The blue deep thou wingest,
And singing still dost soar, and soaring ever singest.

III.

In the golden lightning
    Of the sunken sun,
O'er which clouds are bright'ning,
    Thou dost float and run,
Like an unbodied joy whose race is just begun.

IV.

The pale purple even
    Melts around thy flight;
Like a star of heaven,
    In the broad daylight
Thou art unseen, but yet I hear thy shrill delight—

V.

Keen as are the arrows
    Of that silver sphere
Whose intense lamp narrows
    In the white dawn clear,
Until we hardly see, we feel, that it is there.

VI.

All the earth and air
    With thy voice is loud,
As, when night is bare,
    From one lonely cloud
The moon rains out her beams, and heaven is overflowed

VII.

What thou art we know not;
    What is most like thee?
From rainbow-clouds there flow not
    Drops so bright to see
As from thy presence showers a rain of melody:—

VIII.

Like a poet hidden
    In the light of thought,
Singing hymns unbidden,
    Till the world is wrought
To sympathy with hopes and fears it heeded not:

IX.

Like a high-born maiden
In a palace tower,
Soothing her love-laden
Soul in secret hour
With music sweet as love which overflows her bower:

X.

Like a glow-worm golden
In a dell of dew,
Scattering unbeholden
Its aërial hue
Among the flowers and grass which screen it from the view:

XI.

Like a rose embowered
In its own green leaves,
By warm winds deflowered,
Till the scent it gives
Makes faint with too much sweet these heavy-wingèd thieves.

XII.

Sound of vernal showers
On the twinkling grass,
Rain-awakened flowers,—
All that ever was,
Joyous and clear and fresh,—thy music doth surpass.

XIII.

Teach us, sprite or bird,
What sweet thoughts are thine:
I have never heard
Praise of love or wine
That panted forth a flood of rapture so divine.

XIV.

Chorus hymeneal
Or triumphal chaunt,
Matched with thine, would be all
But an empty vaunt—
A thing wherein we feel there is some hidden want.

XV.

What objects are the fountains
Of thy happy strain?
What fields, or waves, or mountains?
What shapes of sky or plain?
What love of thine own kind? what ignorance of pain?

XVI.

With thy clear keen joyance
Languor cannot be:
Shadow of annoyance
Never came near thee:
Thou lovest, but ne'er knew love's sad satiety.

XVII.

Waking or asleep,
Thou of death must deem
Things more true and deep
Than we mortals dream,
Or how could thy notes flow in such a crystal stream?

XVIII.

We look before and after,
And pine for what is not:
Our sincerest laughter
With some pain is fraught;
Our sweetest songs are those that tell of saddest thought.

XIX.

Yet, if we could scorn
Hate and pride and fear,
If we were things born
Not to shed a tear,
I know not how thy joy we ever should come near.

XX.

Better than all measures
Of delightful sound,
Better than all treasures
That in books are found,
Thy skill to poet were, thou scorner of the ground?

XXI.

Teach me half the gladness
    That thy brain must know;
Such harmonious madness
    From my lips would flow
The world should listen then as I am listening now.

(1820.)

FROM 'EPIPSYCHIDION: VERSES ADDRESSED TO THE NOBLE AND
UNFORTUNATE LADY EMILIA VIVIANI, NOW IMPRISONED IN
THE CONVENT OF ST. ANNE, PISA.'

Spouse! sister! angel! pilot of the fate
Whose course has been so starless! O too late
Beloved, O too soon adored, by me!
For in the fields of immortality
My spirit should at first have worshipped thine,
A divine presence in a place divine;
Or should have moved beside it on this earth,
A shadow of that substance, from its birth:
But not as now.—I love thee; yes, I feel
That on the fountain of my heart a seal
Is set, to keep its waters pure and bright
For thee, since in those tears thou hast delight.
We —are we not formed, as notes of music are,
For one another, though dissimilar?
Such difference without discord as can make
Those sweetest sounds in which all spirits shake,
As trembling leaves in a continuous air.

Thy wisdom speaks in me, and bids me dare
Beacon the rocks on which high hearts are wrecked.
I never was attached to that great sect
Whose doctrine is that each one should select
Out of the crowd a mistress or a friend,
And all the rest, though fair and wise, commend
To cold oblivion; though it is in the code
Of modern morals, and the beaten road

C c 2

Which those poor slaves with weary footsteps tread
Who travel to their home among the dead
By the broad highway of the world, and so
With one chained friend, perhaps a jealous foe,
The dreariest and the longest journey go.

True love in this differs from gold and clay,
That to divide is not to take away.
Love is like understanding, that grows bright,
Gazing on many truths ; 'tis like thy light,
Imagination, which from earth and sky,
And from the depths of human fantasy,
As from a thousand prisms and mirrors, fills
The universe with glorious beams, and kills
Error the worm with many a sunlike arrow
Of its reverberated lightning.   Narrow
The heart that loves, the brain that contemplates,
The life that wears, the spirit that creates,
One object and one form, and builds thereby
A sepulchre for its eternity !

Mind from its object differs most in this :
Evil from good ; misery from happiness ;
The baser from the nobler ; the impure
And frail from what is clear and must endure.
If you divide suffering and dross, you may
Diminish till it is consumed away ;
If you divide pleasure and love and thought,
Each part exceeds the whole ; and we know not
How much, while any yet remains unshared,
Of pleasure may be gained, of sorrow spared.
This truth is that deep well whence sages draw
The unenvied light of hope ; the eternal law
By which those live to whom this world of life
Is as a garden ravaged, and whose strife
Tills for the promise of a later birth
The wilderness of this elysian earth.

*   *   *   *   *

The day is come, and thou wilt fly with me!
To whatsoe'er of dull mortality
Is mine remain a vestal sister still ;
To the intense, the deep, the imperishable—
Not mine, but me—henceforth be thou united,
Even as a bride, delighting and delighted.
The hour is come :—the destined star has risen
Which shall descend upon a vacant prison.
The walls are high, the gates are strong, thick set
The sentinels—but true Love never yet
Was thus constrained. It overleaps all fence :
Like lightning, with invisible violence
Piercing its continents ; like heaven's free breath,
Which he who grasps can hold not ; liker Death,
Who rides upon a thought, and makes his way
Through temple, tower, and palace, and the array
Of arms. More strength has Love than he or they;
For it can burst his charnel, and make free
The limbs in chains, the heart in agony,
The soul in dust and chaos.

                    Emily,
A ship is floating in the harbour now ;
A wind is hovering o'er the mountain's brow ;
There is a path on the sea's azure floor,
No keel has ever ploughed that path before ;
The halcyons brood around the foamless isles ;
The treacherous ocean has forsworn its wiles ;
The merry mariners are bold and free :
Say, my heart's sister, wilt thou sail with me?
Our bark is as an albatross whose nest
Is a far Eden of the purple east ;
And we between her wings will sit, while Night
And Day and Storm and Calm pursue their flight,
Our ministers, along the boundless sea,
Treading each other's heels, unheededly.
It is an isle under Ionian skies,
Beautiful as a wreck of paradise ;
And, for the harbours are not safe and good,
This land would have remained a solitude

But for some pastoral people native there,
Who from the elysian, clear, and golden air
Draw the last spirit of the age of gold,—
Simple and spirited, innocent and bold.
The blue Ægean girds this chosen home,
With ever-changing sound and light and foam
Kissing the sifted sands and caverns hoar ;
And all the winds wandering along the shore
Undulate with the undulating tide.
There are thick woods where sylvan forms abide ;
And many a fountain, rivulet, and pond,
As clear as elemental diamond,
Or serene morning air. And far beyond,
The mossy tracks made by the goats and deer
(Which the rough shepherd treads but once a year)
Pierce into glades, caverns, and bowers, and halls
Built round with ivy, which the waterfalls
Illumining, with sound that never fails,
Accompany the noonday nightingales.
And all the place is peopled with sweet airs.
The light clear element which the isle wears
Is heavy with the scent of lemon-flowers,
Which floats like mist laden with unseen showers,
And falls upon the eyelids like faint sleep ;
And from the moss violets and jonquils peep,
And dart their arrowy odour through the brain,
Till you might faint with that delicious pain.
And every motion, odour, beam, and tone,
With that deep music is in unison :
Which is a soul within the soul,—they seem
Like echoes of an antenatal dream.
It is an isle 'twixt heaven, air, earth, and sea,
Cradled, and hung in clear tranquillity ;
Bright as that wandering Eden, Lucifer,
Washed by the soft blue oceans of young air.
It is a favoured place. Famine or blight,
Pestilence, war, and earthquake, never light
Upon its mountain-peaks ; blind vultures, they
Sail onward far upon their fatal way.

The wingèd storms, chaunting their thunder-psalm
To other lands, leave azure chasms of calm
Over this isle, or weep themselves in dew,
From which its fields and woods ever renew
Their green and golden immortality.
And from the sea there rise, and from the sky
There fall, clear exhalations, soft and bright,
Veil after veil, each hiding some delight :
Which sun or moon or zephyr draw aside,
Till the isle's beauty, like a naked bride
Glowing at once with love and loveliness,
Blushes and trembles at its own excess.
Yet, like a buried lamp, a soul no less
Burns in the heart of this delicious isle,
An atom of the Eternal, whose own smile
Unfolds itself, and may be felt not seen
O'er the grey rocks, blue waves, and forests green,
Filling their bare and void interstices.

    *   *   *   *   *

This isle and house are mine, and I have vowed
Thee to be lady of the solitude.
And I have fitted up some chambers there
Looking towards the golden eastern air,
And level with the living winds which flow
Like waves above the living waves below.
I have sent books and music there, and all
Those instruments with which high spirits call
The future from its cradle, and the past
Out of its grave, and make the present last
In thoughts and joys which sleep but cannot die,
Folded within their own eternity.
Our simple life wants little, and true taste
Hires not the pale drudge Luxury to waste
The scene it would adorn ; and therefore still
Nature with all her children haunts the hill.
The ringdove in the embowering ivy yet
Keeps up her love-lament ; and the owls flit
Round the evening tower ; and the young stars glance
Between the quick bats in their twilight dance ;

The spotted deer bask in the fresh moonlight
Before our gate ; and the slow silent night
Is measured by the pants of their calm sleep.
Be this our home in life ; and, when years heap
Their withered hours like leaves on our decay,
Let us become the overhanging day,
The living soul, of this elysian isle—
Conscious, inseparable, one. Meanwhile
We two will rise and sit and walk together
Under the roof of blue Ionian weather ;
And wander in the meadows ; or ascend
The mossy mountains, where the blue heavens bend
With lightest winds to touch their paramour ;
Or linger where the pebble-paven shore
Under the quick faint kisses of the sea
Trembles and sparkles as with ecstasy ;—
Possessing and possessed by all that is
Within that calm circumference of bliss,
And by each other, till to love and live
Be one ;—or at the noontide hour arrive
Where some old cavern hoar seems yet to keep
The moonlight of the expired Night asleep,
Through which the awakened Day can never peep ;
A veil for our seclusion, close as Night's,
Where secure sleep may kill thine innocent lights—
Sleep, the fresh dew of languid love, the rain
Whose drops quench kisses till they burn again.
And we will talk, until thought's melody
Become too sweet for utterance, and it die
In words, to live again in looks, which dart
With thrilling tone into the voiceless heart,
Harmonising silence without a sound.
Our breath shall intermix, our bosoms bound,
And our veins beat together ; and our lips,
With other eloquence than words, eclipse
The soul that burns between them ; and the wells
Which boil under our being's inmost cells,
The fountains of our deepest life, shall be
Confused in passion's golden purity.

As mountain-springs under the morning sun.
We shall become the same, we shall be one
Spirit within two frames, oh wherefore two?
One passion in twin hearts, which grows and grew
Till, like two meteors of expanding flame,
Those spheres instinct with it become the same,
Touch, mingle, are transfigured; ever still
Burning, yet ever inconsumable;
In one another's substance finding food,
Light flames too pure and light and unimbued
To nourish their bright lives with baser prey,
Which point to heaven and cannot pass away:
One hope within two wills, one will beneath
Two overshadowing minds, one life, one death,
One heaven, one hell, one immortality,
And one annihilation!

> Woe is me!
The wingèd words on which my soul would pierce
Into the height of Love's rare universe
Are chains of lead around its flight of fire—
I pant, I sink, I tremble, I expire!

ADONAIS; AN ELEGY ON THE DEATH OF JOHN KEATS.

I.

I weep for Adonais—he is dead!
    Oh weep for Adonais, though our tears
Thaw not the frost which binds so dear a head!
    And thou, sad Hour selected from all years
    To mourn our loss, rouse thy obscure compeers,
And teach them thine own sorrow! Say: 'With me
    Died Adonais! Till the future dares
Forget the past, his fate and fame shall be
An echo and a light unto eternity.'

II.

Where wert thou, mighty Mother, when he lay,
  When thy son lay, pierced by the shaft which flies
In darkness? Where was lorn Urania
  When Adonais died? With veilèd eyes,
  Mid listening Echoes, in her paradise
She sate, while one, with soft enamoured breath,
  Rekindled all the fading melodies
With which, like flowers that mock the corse beneath,
He had adorned and hid the coming bulk of Death.

III.

Oh weep for Adonais—he is dead!
  Wake, melancholy Mother, wake and weep!—
Yet wherefore? Quench within their burning bed
  Thy fiery tears, and let thy loud heart keep,
  Like his, a mute and uncomplaining sleep;
For he is gone where all things wise and fair
  Descend. Oh dream not that the amorous deep
Will yet restore him to the vital air;
Death feeds on his mute voice, and laughs at our despair.

IV.

Most musical of mourners, weep again!
  Lament anew, Urania!—He died
Who was the sire of an immortal strain,
  Blind, old, and lonely, when his country's pride
  The priest, the slave, and the liberticide,
Trampled and mocked with many a loathèd rite
  Of lust and blood. He went unterrified
Into the gulf of death; but his clear sprite
Yet reigns o'er earth, the third among the Sons of light.

V.

Most musical of mourners, weep anew!
  Not all to that bright station dared to climb:
And happier they their happiness who knew,
  Whose tapers yet burn through that night of time

In which suns perished. Others more sublime,
Struck by the envious wrath of man or god,
    Have sunk, extinct in their refulgent prime ;
And some yet live, treading the thorny road
Which leads, through toil and hate, to Fame's serene abode.

VI.

But now thy youngest, dearest one has perished,
    The nursling of thy widowhood, who grew,
Like a pale flower by some sad maiden cherished,
    And fed with true-love tears instead of dew.
    Most musical of mourners, weep anew !
Thy extreme hope, the loveliest and the last,
    The bloom whose petals, nipped before they blew,
Died on the promise of the fruit, is waste ;
The broken lily lies—the storm is overpast.

VII.

To that high Capital where kingly Death
    Keeps his pale court in beauty and decay
He came ; and bought, with price of purest breath,
    A grave among the eternal.—Come away !
    Haste, while the vault of blue Italian day
Is yet his fitting charnel-roof, while still
    He lies as if in dewy sleep he lay.
Awake him not ! surely he takes his fill
Of deep and liquid rest, forgetful of all ill.

VIII.

He will awake no more, oh never more !
    Within the twilight chamber spreads apace
The shadow of white Death, and at the door
    Invisible Corruption waits to trace
    His extreme way to her dim dwelling-place ;
The eternal Hunger sits, but pity and awe
    Soothe her pale rage, nor dares she to deface
So fair a prey, till darkness and the law
Of change shall o'er his sleep the mortal curtain draw.

IX.

Oh weep for Adonais!—The quick Dreams,
    The passion-wingèd ministers of thought,
Who were his flocks, whom near the living streams
    Of his young spirit he fed, and whom he taught
    The love which was its music, wander not—
Wander no more from kindling brain to brain,
    But droop there whence they sprung; and mourn their lot
Round the cold heart where, after their sweet pain,
They ne'er will gather strength or find a home again.

X.

And one with trembling hands clasps his cold head,
    And fans him with her moonlight wings, and cries,
'Our love, our hope, our sorrow, is not dead!
    See, on the silken fringe of his faint eyes,
    Like dew upon a sleeping flower, there lies
A tear some dream has loosened from his brain.'
    Lost angel of a ruined paradise!
She knew not 'twas her own,—as with no stain
She faded, like a cloud which had outwept its rain.

XI.

One from a lucid urn of starry dew
    Washed his light limbs, as if embalming them;
Another clipped her profuse locks, and threw
    The wreath upon him, like an anadem
    Which frozen tears instead of pearls begem;
Another in her wilful grief would break
    Her bow and wingèd reeds, as if to stem
A greater loss with one which was more weak,—
And dull the barbèd fire against his frozen cheek.

XII.

Another Splendour on his mouth alit,
    That mouth whence it was wont to draw the breath
Which gave it strength to pierce the guarded wit,
    And pass into the panting heart beneath

With lightning and with music : the damp death
Quenched its caress upon his icy lips ;
  And, as a dying meteor stains a wreath
Of moonlight vapour which the cold night clips,
It flushed through his pale limbs, and passed to its eclipse.

XIII.

And others came. Desires and Adorations ;
  Wingèd Persuasions, and veiled Destinies ;
Splendours, and Glooms, and glimmering incarnations
  Of Hopes and Fears, and twilight Fantasies ;
  And Sorrow, with her family of Sighs ;
And Pleasure, blind with tears, led by the gleam
  Of her own dying smile instead of eyes,—
Came in slow pomp ;—the moving pomp might seem
Like pageantry of mist on an autumnal stream.

XIV.

All he had loved, and moulded into thought
  From shape and hue and odour and sweet sound,
Lamented Adonais. Morning sought
  Her eastern watch-tower, and her hair unbound,
  Wet with the tears which should adorn the ground,
Dimmed the aërial eyes that kindle day ;
  Afar the melancholy Thunder moaned,
Pale Ocean in unquiet slumber lay,
And the wild Winds flew round, sobbing in their dismay.

XV.

Lost Echo sits amid the voiceless mountains,
  And feeds her grief with his remembered lay,
And will no more reply to winds or fountains,
  Or amorous birds perched on the young green spray,
  Or herdsman's horn, or bell at closing day ;
Since she can mimic not his lips, more dear
  Than those for whose disdain she pined away
Into a shadow of all sounds :—a drear
Murmur, between their songs, is all the woodmen hear.

XVI.

Grief made the young Spring wild, and she threw down
  Her kindling buds, as if she Autumn were,
Or they dead leaves; since her delight is flown,
  For whom should she have waked the sullen Year?
  To Phœbus was not Hyacinth so dear,
Nor to himself Narcissus, as to both
  Thou, Adonais; wan they stand and sere
Amid the faint companions of their youth,
With dew all turned to tears,—odour, to sighing ruth.

XVII.

Thy spirit's sister, the lorn nightingale,
  Mourns not her mate with such melodious pain;
Not so the eagle, who like thee could scale
  Heaven, and could nourish in the sun's domain
  Her mighty youth with morning, doth complain,
Soaring and screaming round her empty nest,
  As Albion wails for thee: the curse of Cain
Light on his head who pierced thy innocent breast,
And scared the angel soul that was its earthly guest!

XVIII.

Ah woe is me! Winter is come and gone,
  But grief returns with the revolving year.
The airs and streams renew their joyous tone;
  The ants, the bees, the swallows, re-appear;
  Fresh leaves and flowers deck the dead Seasons' bier;
The amorous birds now pair in every brake,
  And build their mossy homes in field and brere;
And the green lizard and the golden snake,
Like unimprisoned flames, out of their trance awake.

XIX.

Through wood and stream and field and hill and ocean
  A quickening life from the Earth's heart has burst,
As it has ever done, with change and motion,
  From the great morning of the world when first

God dawned on chaos In its stream immersed,
The lamps of heaven flash with a softer light ;
  All baser things pant with life's sacred thirst,
Diffuse themselves, and spend in love's delight
The beauty and the joy of their renewèd might.

XX.

The leprous corpse, touched by this spirit tender,
  Exhales itself in flowers of gentle breath ;
Like incarnations of the stars, when splendour
  Is changed to fragrance, they illumine death,
  And mock the merry worm that wakes beneath.
Nought we know dies : shall that alone which knows
  Be as a sword consumed before the sheath
By sightless lightning? The intense atom glows
A moment, then is quenched in a most cold repose.

XXI.

Alas that all we loved of him should be,
  But for our grief, as if it had not been,
And grief itself be mortal ! Woe is me !
  Whence are we, and why are we? of what scene
  The actors or spectators ? Great and mean
Meet massed in death, who lends what life must borrow.
  As long as skies are blue and fields are green,
Evening must usher night, night urge the morrow,
Month follow month with woe, and year wake year to sorrow.

XXII.

He will awake no more, oh never more !
  'Wake thou,' cried Misery, 'childless Mother ! Rise
Out of thy sleep, and slake in thy heart's core
  A wound more fierce than his, with tears and sighs.'
  And all the Dreams that watched Urania's eyes,
And all the Echoes whom their Sister's song
  Had held in holy silence, cried 'Arise';
Swift as a thought by the snake Memory stung,
From her ambrosial rest the fading Splendour sprung.

XXIII.

She rose like an autumnal Night that springs
    Out of the east, and follows wild and drear
The golden Day, which, on eternal wings,
    Even as a ghost abandoning a bier,
    Had left the Earth a corpse. Sorrow and fear
So struck, so roused, so rapt, Urania ;
    So saddened round her like an atmosphere
Of stormy mist ; so swept her on her way,
Even to the mournful place where Adonais lay.

XXIV.

Out of her secret paradise she sped,
    Through camps and cities rough with stone and steel
And human hearts, which, to her aery tread
    Yielding not, wounded the invisible
    Palms of her tender feet where'er they fell.
And barbèd tongues, and thoughts more sharp than they,
    Rent the soft form they never could repel,
Whose sacred blood, like the young tears of May,
Paved with eternal flowers that undeserving way.

XXV.

In the death-chamber for a moment Death,
    Shamed by the presence of that living Might,
Blushed to annihilation, and the breath
    Revisited those lips, and life's pale light
    Flashed through those limbs so late her dear delight.
'Leave me not wild and drear and comfortless,
    As silent lightning leaves the starless night !
Leave me not !' cried Urania. Her distress
Roused Death : Death rose and smiled, and met her vain caress

XXVI.

'Stay yet awhile ! speak to me once again !
    Kiss me, so long but as a kiss may live !
And in my heartless breast and burning brain
    That word, that kiss, shall all thoughts else survive,

With food of saddest memory kept alive,
Now thou art dead, as if it were a part
Of thee, my Adonais! I would give
All that I am, to be as thou now art :—
But I am chained to Time, and cannot thence depart.

XXVII.

'O gentle child, beautiful as thou wert,
Why didst thou leave the trodden paths of men
Too soon, and with weak hands though mighty heart
Dare the unpastured dragon in his den?
Defenceless as thou wert, oh where was then
Wisdom the mirrored shield, or Scorn the spear?—
Or, hadst thou waited the full cycle when
Thy spirit should have filled its crescent sphere,
The monsters of life's waste had fled from thee like deer.

XXVIII.

'The herded wolves bold only to pursue,
The obscene ravens clamorous o'er the dead,
The vultures to the conqueror's banner true,
Who feed where Desolation first has fed,
And whose wings rain contagion,—how they fled,
When, like Apollo from his golden bow,
The Pythian of the age one arrow sped,
And smiled!—The spoilers tempt no second blow,
They fawn on the proud feet that spurn them lying low.

XXIX.

'The sun comes forth, and many reptiles spawn;
He sets, and each ephemeral insect then
Is gathered into death without a dawn,
And the immortal stars awake again.
So is it in the world of living men:
A godlike mind soars forth, in its delight
Making earth bare and veiling heaven; and, when
It sinks, the swarms that dimmed or shared its light
Leave to its kindred lamps the spirit's awful night.'

XXX.

Thus ceased she : and the Mountain Shepherds[1] came,
  Their garlands sere, their magic mantles rent.
The Pilgrim of Eternity, whose fame
  Over his living head like heaven is bent,
  An early but enduring monument,
Came, veiling all the lightnings of his song
  In sorrow. From her wilds Ierne sent
The sweetest lyrist of her saddest wrong,
And love taught grief to fall like music from his tongue.

XXXI.

Midst others of less note came one frail form,
  A phantom among men, companionless
As the last cloud of an expiring storm,
  Whose thunder is its knell. He, as I guess,
  Had gazed on Nature's naked loveliness
Actæon-like ; and now he fled astray
  With feeble steps o'er the world's wilderness,
And his own thoughts along that rugged way
Pursued like raging hounds their father and their prey.

XXXII.

A pard-like Spirit beautiful and swift—
  A love in desolation masked—a power
Girt round with weakness ; it can scarce uplift
  The weight of the superincumbent hour.
  It is a dying lamp, a falling shower,
A breaking billow ;—even whilst we speak
  Is it not broken ? On the withering flower
The killing sun smiles brightly : on a cheek
The life can burn in blood even while the heart may break.

XXXIII.

His head was bound with pansies overblown,
  And faded violets, white and pied and blue ;
And a light spear topped with a cypress-cone,
  Round whose rude shaft dark ivy-tresses grew

---

[1] The poets referred to (stanzas xxx-xxxv) are Byron, Moore, Shelley
himself, and Leigh Hunt.

Yet dripping with the forest's noonday dew,
Vibrated, as the ever-beating heart
  Shook the weak hand that grasped it. Of that crew
He came the last, neglected and apart;
A herd-abandoned deer struck by the hunter's dart.

XXXIV.

All stood aloof, and at his partial moan
  Smiled through their tears. Well knew that gentle band
Who in another's fate now wept his own.
  As in the accents of an unknown land
  He sang new sorrow, sad Urania scanned
The Stranger's mien, and murmured 'Who art thou?'
  He answered not, but with a sudden hand
Made bare his branded and ensanguined brow,
Which was like Cain's or Christ's—oh that it should be so!

XXXV.

What softer voice is hushed over the dead?
  Athwart what brow is that dark mantle thrown?
What form leans sadly o'er the white death-bed,
  In mockery of monumental stone,
  The heavy heart heaving without a moan?
If it be he who, gentlest of the wise,
  Taught, soothed, loved, honoured, the departed one,
Let me not vex with inharmonious sighs
The silence of that heart's accepted sacrifice.

XXXVI.

Our Adonais has drunk poison—oh
  What deaf and viperous murderer could crown
Life's early cup with such a draught of woe?
  The nameless worm would now itself disown;
  It felt, yet could escape, the magic tone
Whose prelude held all envy, hate, and wrong,
  But what was howling in one breast alone,
Silent with expectation of the song
Whose master's hand is cold, whose silver lyre unstrung.

XXXVII.

Live thou, whose infamy is not thy fame!
  Live! fear no heavier chastisement from me,
Thou noteless blot on a remembered name!
  But be thyself, and know thyself to be!
  And ever at thy season be thou free
To spill the venom which thy fangs o'erflow:
  Remorse and self-contempt shall cling to thee,
Hot shame shall burn upon thy secret brow,
And like a beaten hound tremble thou shalt—as now.

XXXVIII.

Nor let us weep that our delight is fled
  Far from these carrion-kites that scream below.
He wakes or sleeps with the enduring dead;
  Thou canst not soar where he is sitting now.
  Dust to the dust: but the pure spirit shall flow
Back to the burning fountain whence it came,
  A portion of the Eternal, which must glow
Through time and change, unquenchably the same,
Whilst thy cold embers choke the sordid hearth of shame.

XXXIX.

Peace, peace! he is not dead, he doth not sleep!
  He hath awakened from the dream of life.
'Tis we who, lost in stormy visions, keep
  With phantoms an unprofitable strife,
  And in mad trance strike with our spirit's knife
Invulnerable nothings.   *We* decay
  Like corpses in a charnel; fear and grief
Convulse us and consume us day by day,
And cold hopes swarm like worms within our living clay

XL.

He has outsoared the shadow of our night.
  Envy and calumny and hate and pain,
And that unrest which men miscall delight,
  Can touch him not and torture not again.

From the contagion of the world's slow stain
He is secure ; and now can never mourn
    A heart grown cold, a head grown grey, in vain—
Nor, when the spirit's self has ceased to burn,
With sparkless ashes load an unlamented urn.

XLI.

He lives, he wakes—'tis Death is dead, not he;
    Mourn not for Adonais.—Thou young Dawn,
Turn all thy dew to splendour, for from thee
    The spirit thou lamentest is not gone !
    Ye caverns and ye forests, cease to moan !
Cease, ye faint flowers and fountains ! and, thou Air,
    Which like a mourning-veil thy scarf hadst thrown
O'er the abandoned Earth, now leave it bare
Even to the joyous stars which smile on its despair !

XLII.

He is made one with Nature. There is heard
    His voice in all her music, from the moan
Of thunder to the song of night's sweet bird.
    He is a presence to be felt and known
    In darkness and in light, from herb and stone,—
Spreading itself where'er that Power may move
    Which has withdrawn his being to its own,
Which wields the world with never-wearied love,
Sustains it from beneath, and kindles it above.

XLIII.

He is a portion of the loveliness
    Which once he made more lovely. He doth bear
His part, while the One Spirit's plastic stress
    Sweeps through the dull dense world ; compelling there
    All new successions to the forms they wear ;
Torturing the unwilling dross, that checks its flight,
    To its own likeness, as each mass may bear ;
And bursting in its beauty and its might
From trees and beasts and men into the heaven's light.

XLIV.

The splendours of the firmament of time
  May be eclipsed, but are extinguished not;
Like stars to their appointed height they climb,
  And death is a low mist which cannot blot
  The brightness it may veil. When lofty thought
Lifts a young heart above its mortal lair,
  And love and life contend in it for what
Shall be its earthly doom, the dead live there,
And move like winds of light on dark and stormy air.

XLV.

The inheritors of unfulfilled renown
  Rose from their thrones, built beyond mortal thought
Far in the unapparent. Chatterton
  Rose pale, his solemn agony had not
  Yet faded from him : Sidney, as he fought,
And as he fell, and as he lived and loved,
  Sublimely mild, a spirit without spot,
Arose ; and Lucan, by his death approved ;—
Oblivion as they rose shrank like a thing reproved.

XLVI.

And many more, whose names on earth are dark,
  But whose transmitted effluence cannot die
So long as fire outlives the parent spark,
  Rose, robed in dazzling immortality.
  'Thou art become as one of us,' they cry;
'It was for thee yon kingless sphere has long
  Swung blind in unascended majesty,
Silent alone amid an heaven of song.
Assume thy wingèd throne, thou Vesper of our throng!'

XLVII.

Who mourns for Adonais? Oh come forth,
  Fond wretch, and know thyself and him aright.
Clasp with thy panting soul the pendulous earth ;
  As from a centre, dart thy spirit's light

Beyond all worlds, until its spacious might
Satiate the void circumference : then shrink
Even to a point within our day and night ;
And keep thy heart light, lest it make thee sink,
When hope has kindled hope, and lured thee to the brink.

XLVIII.

Or go to Rome, which is the sepulchre,
Oh not of him, but of our joy. 'Tis nought
That ages, empires, and religions, there
Lie buried in the ravage they have wrought ;
For such as he can lend—they borrow not
Glory from those who made the world their prey ;
And he is gathered to the kings of thought
Who waged contention with their time's decay,
And of the past are all that cannot pass away.

XLIX.

Go thou to Rome,—at once the paradise,
The grave, the city, and the wilderness ;
And where its wrecks like shattered mountains rise,
And flowering weeds and fragrant copses dress
The bones of Desolation's nakedness,
Pass, till the Spirit of the spot shall lead
Thy footsteps to a slope of green access,
Where, like an infant's smile, over the dead
A light of laughing flowers along the grass is spread.

L.

And grey walls moulder round, on which dull Time
Feeds, like slow fire upon a hoary brand ;
And one keen pyramid with wedge sublime,
Pavilioning the dust of him who planned
This refuge for his memory, doth stand
Like flame transformed to marble ; and beneath
A field is spread, on which a newer band
Have pitched in heaven's smile their camp of death,
Welcoming him we lose with scarce-extinguished breath.

LI.

Here pause. These graves are all too young as yet
  To have outgrown the sorrow which consigned
Its charge to each ; and, if the seal is set
  Here on one fountain of a mourning mind,
  Break it not thou ! too surely shalt thou find
Thine own well full, if thou returnest home,
  Of tears and gall. From the world's bitter wind
Seek shelter in the shadow of the tomb.
What Adonais is why fear we to become?

LII.

The One remains, the many change and pass ;
  Heaven's light for ever shines, earth's shadows fly ;
Life, like a dome of many-coloured glass,
  Stains the white radiance of eternity,
  Until Death tramples it to fragments.—Die,
If thou wouldst be with that which thou dost seek !
  Follow where all is fled !—Rome's azure sky,
Flowers, ruins, statues, music, words, are weak
The glory they transfuse with fitting truth to speak.

LIII.

Why linger, why turn back, why shrink, my heart ?
  Thy hopes are gone before : from all things here
They have departed ; thou shouldst now depart.
  A light is past from the revolving year,
  And man and woman ; and what still is dear
Attracts to crush, repels to make thee wither.
  The soft sky smiles, the low wind whispers near :
'Tis Adonais calls ! Oh hasten thither !
No more let life divide what death can join together.

LIV.

That light whose smile kindles the universe,
  That beauty in which all things work and move,
That benediction which the eclipsing curse
  Of birth can quench not, that sustaining Love

Which, through the web of being blindly wove
By man and beast and earth and air and sea,
  Burns bright or dim, as each are mirrors of
The fire for which all thirst, now beams on me,
Consuming the last clouds of cold mortality.

LV.

The breath whose might I have invoked in song
  Descends on me ; my spirit's bark is driven
Far from the shore, far from the trembling throng
  Whose sails were never to the tempest given.
  The massy earth and spherèd skies are riven !
I am borne darkly, fearfully, afar !
  Whilst, burning through the inmost veil of heaven,
The soul of Adonais, like a star,
Beacons from the abode where the Eternal are.

                                    (1821.)

To Night.

I.

Swiftly walk over the western wave,
        Spirit of Night !
Out of the misty eastern cave
      Where, all the long and lone daylight,
Thou wovest dreams of joy and fear
Which make thee terrible and dear,
        Swift be thy flight !

II.

Wrap thy form in a mantle grey,
        Star-inwrought ;
Blind with thine hair the eyes of Day;
      Kiss her until she be wearied out.
Then wander o'er city and sea and land,
Touching all with thine opiate wand—
        Come, long-sought !

III.

When I arose and saw the dawn,
    I sighed for thee;
When light rode high, and the dew was gone,
    And noon lay heavy on flower and tree,
And the weary Day turned to his rest,
Lingering like an unloved guest,
    I sighed for thee.

IV.

Thy brother Death came, and cried,
    'Wouldst thou me?'
Thy sweet child Sleep, the filmy-eyed,
    Murmured like a noontide bee,
'Shall I nestle near thy side?
Wouldst thou me?'—And I replied,
    'No, not thee.'

V.

Death will come when thou art dead,
    Soon, too soon—
Sleep will come when thou art fled.
    Of neither would I ask the boon
I ask of thee, beloved Night—
Swift be thine approaching flight,
    Come soon, soon!

(1821.)

To ——.

Music, when soft voices die,
Vibrates in the memory;
Odours, when sweet violets sicken,
Live within the sense they quicken;

Rose-leaves, when the rose is dead,
Are heaped for the beloved's bed;
And so thy thoughts, when thou art gone,
Love itself shall slumber on.

(1821.)

A Lament.

O World! O life! O time!
    On whose last steps I climb,
Trembling at that where I had stood before,—
When will return the glory of your prime?
    No more—oh never more!

    Out of the day and night
    A joy has taken flight;
Fresh Spring, and Summer, and Winter hoar,
Move my faint heart with grief,—but with delight
    No more—oh never more!

                                    (1821.)

To ——.

One word is too often profaned
    For me to profane it;
One feeling too falsely disdained
    For thee to disdain it;
One hope is too like despair
    For prudence to smother;
And pity from thee more dear
    Than that from another.

I can give not what men call love:
    But wilt thou accept not
The worship the heart lifts above,
    And the Heavens reject not:
The desire of the moth for the star,
    Of the night for the morrow,
The devotion to something afar
    From the sphere of our sorrow?

                                    (1821.)

LAST CHORUS OF 'HELLAS.'

The world's great age begins anew,
  The golden years return,
The earth doth like a snake renew
  Her winter weeds outworn :
Heaven smiles, and faiths and empires gleam
Like wrecks of a dissolving dream.

A brighter Hellas rears its mountains
  From waves serener far ;
A new Peneus rolls his fountains
  Against the morning star ;
Where fairer Tempes bloom, there sleep
Young Cyclads on a sunnier deep.

A loftier Argo cleaves the main,
  Fraught with a later prize ;
Another Orpheus sings again,
  And loves, and weeps, and dies ;
A new Ulysses leaves once more
Calypso for his native shore.

Oh write no more the tale of Troy,
  If earth Death's scroll must be—
Nor mix with Laian rage the joy
  Which dawns upon the free,
Although a subtler Sphinx renew
Riddles of death Thebes never knew.

Another Athens shall arise,
  And to remoter time
Bequeath, like sunset to the skies,
  The splendour of its prime ;
And leave, if nought so bright may live,
All earth can take or heaven can give.

Saturn and Love their long repose
  Shall burst, more bright and good
Than all who fell, than one who rose,
  Than many unsubdued:
Not gold, not blood, their altar dowers,
But votive tears and symbol flowers.

Oh cease! must hate and death return?
  Cease! must men kill and die?
Cease! drain not to its dregs the urn
  Of bitter prophecy!
The world is weary of the past,—
Oh might it die or rest at last!

(1822.)

LINES.

I.

When the lamp is shattered
The light in the dust lies dead;
  When the cloud is scattered,
The rainbow's glory is shed;
  When the lute is broken,
Sweet notes are remembered not;
  When the lips have spoken,
Loved accents are soon forgot.

II.

As music and splendour
Survive not the lamp and the lute,
  The heart's echoes render
No song when the spirit is mute:—
  No song but sad dirges,
Like the wind in a ruined cell,
  Or the mournful surges
That ring the dead seaman's knell.

III.

When hearts have once mingled,
Love first leaves the well-built nest;
　　The weak one is singled
To endure what it once possessed.
　　O Love, who bewailest
The frailty of all things here,
　　Why choose you the frailest
For your cradle, your home, and your bier?

IV.

Its passions will rock thee,
As the storms rock the ravens on high;
　　Bright reason will mock thee,
Like the sun from a wintry sky.
　　From thy nest every rafter
Will rot, and thine eagle home
　　Leave thee naked to laughter
When leaves fall and cold winds come.

(1822.)

To Jane—The Recollection.

I.

We wandered to the pine-forest
　　That skirts the ocean's foam;
The lightest wind was in its nest,
　　The tempest in its home.
The whispering waves were half asleep,
　　The clouds were gone to play,
And on the bosom of the deep
　　The smile of heaven lay;
It seemed as if the hour were one
　　Sent from beyond the skies,
Which scattered from above the sun
　　A light of paradise.

II.

We paused amid the pines that stood
    The giants of the waste,
Tortured by storms to shapes as rude
    As serpents interlaced ;
And soothed, by every azure breath
    That under heaven is blown,
To harmonies and hues beneath,
    As tender as its own ;
Now all the tree-tops lay asleep
    Like green waves on the sea,
As still as in the silent deep
    The ocean-woods may be.

III.

How calm it was !—The silence there
    By such a chain was bound,
That even the busy woodpecker
    Made stiller with her sound
The inviolable quietness ;
    The breath of peace we drew
With its soft motion made not less
    The calm that round us grew.
There seemed, from the remotest seat
    Of the white mountain-waste,
To the soft flower beneath our feet,
    A magic circle traced,—
A spirit interfused around,
    A thrilling silent life :
To momentary peace it bound
    Our mortal nature's strife.
And still, I felt, the centre of
    The magic circle there
Was one fair form that filled with love
    The lifeless atmosphere.

IV.

We paused beside the pools that lie
    Under the forest-bough.
Each seemed as 't were a little sky
    Gulfed in a world below :
A firmament of purple light
    Which in the dark earth lay,
More boundless than the depth of night,
    And purer than the day—
In which the lovely forests grew
    As in the upper air,
More perfect both in shape and hue
    Than any spreading there.
There lay the glade, the neighbouring lawn,
    And through the dark-green wood
The white sun twinkling like the dawn
    Out of a speckled cloud.
Sweet views which in our world above
    Can never well be seen,
Were imaged by the water's love
    Of that fair forest green ;
And all was interfused beneath
    With an elysian glow,
An atmosphere without a breath,
    A softer day below.
Like one beloved, the scene had lent
    To the dark water's breast
Its every leaf and lineament
    With more than truth expressed ;
Until an envious wind crept by,—
    Like an unwelcome thought,
Which from the mind's too faithful eye
    Blots one dear image out.
Though thou art ever fair and kind,
    And forests ever green,
Less oft is peace in Shelley's mind
    Than calm in water seen.

              (*February* 2, 1822.)

THOMAS LOVE PEACOCK.

[THOMAS LOVE PEACOCK was born at Weymouth, October 18, 1785. In 1808 he was made under-secretary to Sir Home Popham, and served at Flushing. In 1820 he married the Welsh lady celebrated by Shelley as 'the Snowdonia Antelope;' he had made the acquaintance of that poet in 1812. He became a clerk to the East India Company in 1819, from which post he retired in 1856. His first novel, *Headlong Hall*, appeared in 1816; his last, *Gryll Grange*, in 1861. Peacock died at Halliford, near Shepperton, on January 23, 1866. His poetical publications were *Palmyra*, 1806; *The Genius of the Thames*, 1810; *Rhododaphne*, 1818; *Paper Money Lyrics*, 1837.]

The fame of Peacock as a prose humourist of incomparable vivacity has tended to overshadow and stunt his reputation as a poet. It is time, however, that his claims in verse should be vindicated, and a place demanded for him as an independent figure in the crowded Parnassus of his age,—a place a little below the highest, and somewhat isolated, at the extreme right of the composition. He has certain relations, not wholly accidental, with Shelley, who stands above him, and with such minor figures as Horace Smith and Thomas Haynes Bayly, who stand no less obviously below him ; but in the main he is chiefly notable for his isolation. His ironical and caustic songs are unique in our literature, illuminated by too much fancy to be savage, but crackling with a kind of ghastly merriment that inspires quite as much terror as amusement. In parody he has produced at least one specimen, 'There is a fever of the spirit,' which does not possess its equal for combined sympathy and malice. When we pass to his serious and sentimental lyrics, our praise cannot be so un- measured. Peacock possessed too much literary refinement, too little personal sensibility to write with passion or to risk a fall by flying ; yet his consummate purity of style seldom fails to give a subdued charm to the quietest of his songs. The snatches and refrains which are poured over the novel of *Maid Marian*, like a shower of seed pearl, are full of the very essence of spontaneous song, as opposed to deliberate lyrical writing ; while the corresponding chants and ballads in *The Misfortunes of Elphin* show with equal distinctness Peacock's limitations as a poetical artist. Once or twice he has succeeded in writing a lyric that is almost perfect ; ' I dug beneath the cypress shade' would, for instance, be worthy of Landor in Landor's best manner, but for a little stiffness in starting.

Twice in mature life Peacock attempted a long flight in poetry, and each time without attracting any serious attention from the public of his own time or from posterity. In one of these cases I hope to show that this neglect has been deeply unjust ; for the other I find an excuse in the extreme languor which it has produced on myself to read once more *The Genius of the Thames*. This poem, written just before the general revival of poetic style, may almost be called the last production of the eighteenth century. It contains all the wintry charms and hypocritical graces of the school of Collins in its last dissolution ; it proceeds with mingled pomp and elegance along the conventional path, in the usual genteel manner, until suddenly the reader, familiar with the temperament of Peacock, starts and rubs his eyes to read an invocation of

> ' Sun-crowned Science ! child of heaven !
> To wandering man by angels given !
> Still, nymph divine ! on mortal sight
> Diffuse thy intellectual light.'

from the man to whom the whole spirit of scientific enquiry was entirely hostile.

Rhododaphne, which Peacock published eight years later, is a performance of a very different kind. While somewhat indebted to Akenside for matter, to Byron for style, to Shelley for phraseology, the essential part of this poem is as original as it is delicate and fascinating. There is little plot or action in the piece. A youth Anthemion loves a mortal maiden Calliroë, but is courted and subdued by a supernatural being named Rhododaphne, who exercises over him the poisonous spell of the rose-laurel. Calliroë dies and Rhododaphne triumphs, but in the end the doom is reversed, Calliroë returns to life, and the charms of the rose-laurel are evaded. It is curious to compare *Rhododaphne* with *Endymion*, which was published in the same year. Peacock leaves Keats far behind in knowledge of English language and of Greek manners, in grace and learning of every kind, but Keats, as by a diviner instinct, is led by his very ignorance into a mood more truly antique than Peacock attains by such pedantries as—

> 'The rose and myrtle blend in beauty
> Round Thespian Love's *hypæthric* fane.'

Still *Rhododaphne* is a poem full of eminent beauties and touches of true art. It would be absolutely and not comparatively great were it not that the whole structure of the work is spoiled by a tone of Georgian sentiment which we should scarcely have expected from so genuine a Pagan as 'Greeky-Peeky.' The ethics of the poem are not merely modern, they are positively provincial. In short, *Rhododaphne* may be best compared to a series of charming friezes in antique story carved by some sculptor of the beginning of the present century, some craftsman less soft than Canova, less breezy than Thorwaldsen. The marble is excellently chosen, the artist's touch sharp and delicate, the design flowing and refined, but the figures have the most provoking resemblance to those in the fashion-books of the last age but one.

EDMUND W. GOSSE.

[From *Rhododaphne*.]

THE SPELL OF THE LAUREL-ROSE.

Oh youth, beware! that laurel-rose
Around Larissa's evil walls
In tufts of rank luxuriance grows,
'Mid dreary valleys, by the falls
Of haunted streams; and magic knows
No herb or plant of deadlier might,
When impious footsteps wake by night
The echoes of those dismal dells,
What time the murky midnight dew
Trembles on many a leaf and blossom,
That draws from earth's polluted bosom
Mysterious virtue, to imbue
The chalice of unnatural spells.
Oft, those dreary rocks among,
The murmurs of unholy song,
Breathed by lips as fair as hers
By whose false hands that flower was given,
The solid earth's firm breast have riven,
And burst the silent sepulchres,
And called strange shapes of ghastly fear,
To hold, beneath the sickening moon,
Portentous parle, at night's deep noon,
With beauty skilled in mysteries drear.
Oh, youth! Larissa's maids are fair;
But the dæmons of the earth and air
Their spells obey, their councils share,
And wide o'er earth and ocean bear
Their mandates to the storms that tear
The rock-enrooted oak, and sweep
With whirlwind wings the labouring deep.

Their words of power can make the streams
Roll refluent on their mountain-springs,
Can torture sleep with direful dreams,
And on the shapes of earthly things,
Man, beast, bird, fish, with influence strange,
Breathe foul and fearful interchange,
And fix in marble bonds the form
Erewhile with natural being warm,
And give to senseless stones and stocks
Motion, and breath, and shape that mocks,
As far as nicest eye can scan,
The action and the life of man.
Beware! yet once again beware!
Ere round thy inexperienced mind,
With voice and semblance falsely fair,
A chain Thessalian magic bind,
Which never more, oh youth! believe,
Shall either earth or heaven unweave.

THE VENGEANCE OF BACCHUS.

Bacchus by the lonely ocean
Stood in youthful semblance fair:
Summer winds, with gentle motion,
Waved his black and curling hair.
Streaming from his manly shoulders
Robes of gold and purple dye
Told of spoil to fierce beholders
In their black ship sailing by.
On the vessel's deck they placed him
Strongly bound in triple bands;
But the iron rings that braced him
Melted, wax-like from his hands.
Then the pilot spake in terror:
''Tis a god in mortal form!
Seek the land; repair your error
Ere his wrath invoke the storm.'

'Silence!' cried the frowning master,
'Mind the helm, the breeze is fair:
Coward! cease to bode disaster:
Leave to men the captive's care.'
While he speaks, and fiercely tightens
In the full free breeze the sail,
From the deck wine bubbling lightens,
Winy fragrance fills the gale.
Gurgling in ambrosial lustre
Flows the purple-eddying wine:
O'er the yard-arms trail and cluster
Tendrils of the mantling vine:
Grapes, beneath the broad leaves springing,
Blushing as in vintage-hours,
Droop, while round the tall mast clinging
Ivy twines its buds and flowers,
Fast with graceful berries blackening:—
Garlands hang on every oar:
Then in fear the cordage slackening,
One and all, they cry, 'To shore!'
Bacchus changed his shape, and glaring
With a lion's eye-balls wide,
Roared: the pirate-crew, despairing,
Plunged amid the foaming tide.
Through the azure depths they flitted
Dolphins by transforming fate:
But the god the pilot pitied,
Saved, and made him rich and great.

The War-Song of Dinas Vawr.

[From *The Misfortunes of Elphin.*]

The mountain sheep are sweeter,
But the valley sheep are fatter;
We therefore deemed it meeter
To carry off the latter.
We made an expedition;
We met an host and quelled it;
We forced a strong position,
And killed the men who held it.

On Dyfed's richest valley,
Where herds of kine were browsing,
We made a mighty sally,
To furnish our carousing.
Fierce warriors rushed to meet us;
We met them, and o'erthrew them:
They struggled hard to beat us;
But we conquered them, and slew them.

As we drove our prize at leisure,
The king marched forth to catch us:
His rage surpassed all measure,
But his people could not match us.
He fled to his hall pillars;
And, ere our force we led off,
Some sacked his house and cellars,
While others cut his head off.

We there, in strife bewildering,
Spilt blood enough to swim in:
We orphaned many children,
And widowed many women.
The eagles and the ravens
We glutted with our foemen:
The heroes and the cravens,
The spearmen and the bowmen.

We brought away from battle,
And much their land bemoaned them,
Two thousand head of cattle,
And the head of him who owned them :
Ednyfed, King of Dyfed,
His head was borne before us ;
His wine and beasts supplied our feasts,
And his overthrow, our chorus.

THE MEN OF GOTHAM.

[From *Nightmare Abbey*.]

Seamen three ! What men be ye ?
Gotham's three wise men we be.
Whither in your bowl so free ?
To rake the moon from out the sea.
The bowl goes trim.   The moon doth **shine.**
And our ballast is old wine ;
And your ballast is old wine.

Who art thou, so fast adrift ?
I am he they call Old Care.
Here on board we will thee lift.
 No : I may not enter there.
Wherefore so ? 'Tis Jove's decree,
In a bowl Care may not be ;
In a bowl Care may not be.

Fear ye not the waves that roll ?
No : in charmed bowl we swim.
What the charm that floats the bowl ?
Water may not pass the brim.
The bowl goes trim.   The moon doth **shine.**
And our ballast is old wine ;
And your ballast is old wine.

[From *Melincourt.*]

THE FLOWER OF LOVE.

'Tis said the rose is Love's own flower,
Its blush so bright, its thorns so many;
And winter on its bloom has power,
But has not on its sweetness any.
For though young Love's ethereal rose
Will droop on Age's wintry bosom,
Yet still its faded leaves disclose
The fragrance of their earliest blossom.

But ah! the fragrance lingering there
Is like the sweets that mournful duty
Bestows with sadly-soothing care,
To deck the grave of bloom and beauty.
For when its leaves are shrunk and dry,
Its blush extinct, to kindle never,
That fragrance is but Memory's sigh,
That breathes of pleasures past for ever.

Why did not Love the amaranth choose,
That bears no thorns, and cannot perish?
Alas! no sweets its flowers diffuse,
And only sweets Love's life can cherish.
But be the rose and amaranth twined,
And Love, their mingled powers assuming,
Shall round his brows a chaplet bind,
For ever sweet, for ever blooming.

The Grave of Love.

I dug, beneath the cypress shade,
　　What well might seem an elfin's grave;
And every pledge in earth I laid,
　　That erst thy false affection gave.

I pressed them down the sod beneath;
　　I placed one mossy stone above;
And twined the rose's fading wreath
　　Around the sepulchre of love.

Frail as thy love, the flowers were dead,
　　Ere yet the evening sun was set:
But years shall see the cypress spread,
　　Immutable as my regret.

Mr. Cypress's Song in Ridicule of Lord Byron.

[From *Nightmare Abbey*.]

There is a fever of the spirit,
　　The brand of Cain's unresting doom,
Which in the lone dark souls that bear it
　　Glows like the lamp in Tullia's tomb:
Unlike that lamp, its subtle fire
　　Burns, blasts, consumes its cell, the heart,
Till, one by one, hope, joy, desire,
　　Like dreams of shadowy smoke depart.

When hope, love, like itself, are only
　　Dust—spectral memories—dead and cold—
The unfed fire burns bright and lonely,
　　Like that undying lamp of old:
And by that dreary illumination,
　　Till time its clay-built home has rent,
Thought broods on feeling's desolation—
　　The soul is its own monument.

JOHN KEATS.

[JOHN KEATS was born in London on the 29th of October, 1795. His father was in the employment of a livery-stable keeper in Moorfields, whose daughter he married. Our poet was born prematurely. He lost his father when he was nine years old, and his mother when he was fifteen. He and his brothers were sent to a good school at Enfield kept by Mr. Clarke, whose son, Charles Cowden Clarke, well known afterwards from his connexion with letters and literary men, was a valuable friend to John Keats As a schoolboy, Keats seems to have been at first remarked chiefly for his pugnacity and high spirit, but he soon showed a love of reading. On leaving school in 1810 he was apprenticed for five years to a surgeon at Edmonton; he was thus still in the neighbourhood of the Clarkes, who continued to see him, took interest in his awakening powers, and lent him books,—amongst them the *Fairy Queen* of Spenser, the poet whose influence has left on the poetry of Keats so deep an impression. The young surgeon's apprentice took to verse-making; when he went to London to walk the hospitals, he was introduced by the Clarkes to their literary friends there, and knew Leigh Hunt, Hazlitt, Basil Montagu, Haydon, Shelley, and Godwin. In 1817 he brought out his first volume of verse, and abandoned the profession of surgery, for which however, disagreeable though it was to him, he had shown aptitude and dexterity. His first volume contained the *Epistles,* which we now read amongst his collected poems; it had no success. But his friends saluted his genius with warm admiration and confidence, and in 1818 he published his *Endymion.* It was mercilessly treated by *Blackwood's Edinburgh Magazine* and by the *Quarterly Review.* Meanwhile Keats's small fortune was melting away, and signs of disease began to show themselves in him. Nevertheless, in the next year or two he produced his best poems; but his health and circumstances did not mend, while a passionate attachment, with which he was at this time seized, added another cause of agitation. The seeds of consumption were in him, he had the temperament of the consumptive; his poetry fevered him, his embarrassments fretted him, his love-passion shook him to pieces. He had an attack of bleeding from the lungs; he got better, but it returned; change of climate was recommended, and after publishing his third volume, *Lamia, Isabella, and other Poems*, he sailed for Italy in September 1820, accompanied by his friend Severn. Italy could not restore him. He established himself at Rome with Severn, but in spite of the devoted care and kindness of this admirable friend, he rapidly grew worse, and on the 23rd of February, 1821, he died. He was twenty-five years old. John Keats was buried in the Protestant cemetery at Rome, and on his gravestone is the inscription which he himself told his friend to place there: *Here lies one whose name was writ in water.*]

Poetry, according to Milton's famous saying, should be 'simple, sensuous, impassioned.' No one can question the eminency, in Keats's poetry, of the quality of sensuousness. Keats as a poet is abundantly and enchantingly sensuous; the question with some people will be, whether he is anything else. Many things may be brought forward which seem to show him as under the fascination and sole dominion of sense, and desiring nothing better. There is the exclamation in one of his letters: 'O for a life of sensations rather than of thoughts!' There is the thesis, in another, 'that with a great Poet the sense of Beauty overcomes every other consideration, or rather obliterates all consideration.' There is Haydon's story of him, how 'he once covered his tongue and throat as far as he could reach with Cayenne pepper, in order to appreciate the delicious coldness of claret in all its glory—his own expression.' One is not much surprised when Haydon further tells us, of the hero of such a story, that once for six weeks together he was hardly ever sober. 'He had no decision of character,' Haydon adds, 'no object upon which to direct his great powers.'

Character and self-control, the *virtus verusque labor* so necessary for every kind of greatness, and for the great artist, too, indispensable, appear to be wanting, certainly, to this Keats of Haydon's portraiture. They are wanting also to the Keats of the *Letters to Fanny Brawne*. These letters make as unpleasing an impression as Haydon's anecdotes. The editor of Haydon's journals could not well omit what Haydon said of his friend, but for the publication of the *Letters to Fanny Brawne* I can see no good reason whatever. Their publication appears to me, I confess, inexcusable; they ought never to have been published. But published they are, and we have to take notice of them. Letters written when Keats was near his end, under the throttling and unmanning grasp of mortal disease, we will not judge. But here is a letter written some months before he was taken ill. It is printed just as Keats wrote it.

'You have absorb'd me. I have a sensation at the present moment as though I was dissolving—I should be exquisitely miserable without the hope of soon seeing you. I should be afraid to separate myself far from you. My sweet Fanny will your heart never change? My love, will it? I have no limit now to my love .... Your note came in just here. I cannot be happier away from you. 'Tis richer than an Argosy of Pearles. Do not threat me even in jest. I have been astonished that Men could die Martyrs for religion—I have shuddered at it. I shudder no more—I could be martyred for my Religion—Love is my religion—I could die for that. I could die for you. My Creed is Love and you are its only tenet. You have ravished me away by a Power I cannot resist; and yet I could resist till I saw you; and even since I have seen you I have endeavoured often "to reason against the reasons of my Love." I can do that no more—the pain would be too great. My love is selfish. I cannot breathe without you.'

A man who writes love-letters in this strain is probably pre-destined, one may observe, to misfortune in his love-affairs ; but that is nothing. The complete enervation of the writer is the real point for remark. We have the tone, or rather the entire want of tone, the abandonment of all reticence and all dignity, of the merely sensuous man, of the man who 'is passion's slave.' Nay, we have them in such wise that one is tempted to speak even as *Blackwood* or the *Quarterly* were in the old days wont to speak ; one is tempted to say that Keats's love-letter is the love-letter of a surgeon's apprentice. It has in its relaxed self-abandonment something underbred and ignoble, as of a youth ill brought up, without the training which teaches us that we must put some constraint upon our feelings and upon the expression of them. It is the sort of love letter of a surgeon's apprentice which one might hear read out in a breach of promise case, or in the Divorce Court. The sensuous man speaks in it, and the sensuous man of a badly bred and badly trained sort. That many who are themselves, also, badly bred and badly trained should enjoy it, and should even think it a beautiful and characteristic production of him whom they call their 'lovely and beloved Keats,' does not make it better. These are the admirers whose pawing and fondness does not good but harm to the fame of Keats ; who concentrate attention upon what in him is least wholesome and most questionable ;

who worship him, and would have the world worship him too, as the poet of

> 'Light feet, dark violet eyes, and parted hair,
>　Soft dimpled hands, white neck, and creamy breast.'

This sensuous strain Keats had, and a man of his poetic powers could not, whatever his strain, but show his talent in it. But he has something more, and something better. We who believe Keats to have been by his promise, at any rate, if not fully by his performance, one of the very greatest of English poets, and who believe also that a merely sensuous man cannot either by promise or by performance be a very great poet, because poetry interprets life, and so large and noble a part of life is outside of such a man's ken,—we cannot but look for signs in him of something more than sensuousness, for signs of character and virtue. And indeed the elements of high character Keats undoubtedly has, and the effort to develope them ; the effort is frustrated and cut short by misfortune, and disease, and time, but for the due understanding of Keats's worth the recognition of this effort, and of the elements on which it worked, is necessary.

Lord Houghton, who praises very discriminatingly the poetry of Keats, has on his character, also, a remark full of discrimination. He says : ' The faults of Keats's disposition were precisely the contrary of those attributed to him by common opinion.' And he gives a letter written after the death of Keats by his brother George, in which the writer, speaking of the fantastic *Johnny Keats* invented for common opinion by Lord Byron and by the reviewers, declares indignantly : ' John was the very soul of manliness and courage, and as much like the Holy Ghost as *Johnny Keats.*' It is important to note this testimony, and to look well for whatever illustrates and confirms it.

Great weight is laid by Lord Houghton on such a direct profession of faith as the following. ' That sort of probity and disinterestedness,' Keats writes to his brothers, ' which such men as Bailey possess, does hold and grasp the tip-top of any spiritual honours that can be paid to anything in this world.' Lord Houghton says that ' never have words more effectively expressed the conviction of the superiority of virtue above beauty than those.' But merely to make a profession of faith of the kind here made by Keats is not difficult ; what we should rather look for, is some evidence of the instinct for character, for virtue, passing into the man's life, passing into his work.

Signs of virtue, in the true and large sense of the word, the instinct for virtue passing into the life of Keats and strengthening it, I find in the admirable wisdom and temper of what he says to his friend Bailey on the occasion of a quarrel between Reynolds and Haydon :—

'Things have happened lately of great perplexity; you must have heard of them ; Reynolds and Haydon retorting and recriminating, and parting for ever. The same thing has happened between Haydon and Hunt. It is unfortunate ; men should bear with each other ; there lives not the man who may not be cut up, aye, lashed to pieces, on his weakest side. The best of men have but a portion of good in them. . . . The sure way, Bailey, is first to know a man's faults, and then be passive. If, after that, he insensibly draws you towards him, then you have no power to break the link. Before I felt interested in either Reynolds or Haydon, I was well read in their faults ; yet knowing them, I have been cementing gradually with both. I have an affection for them both, for reasons almost opposite ; and to both must I of necessity cling, supported always by the hope that when a little time, a few years, shall have tried me more fully in their esteem, I may be able to bring them together.'

Butler has well said that ' endeavouring to enforce upon our own minds a practical sense of virtue, or to beget in others that practical sense of it which a man really has himself, is a virtuous *act.*' And such an ' endeavouring' is that of Keats in those words written to Bailey. It is more than mere words ; so justly thought and so discreetly urged as it is, it rises to the height of a virtuous *act.* It is proof of character.

The same thing may be said of some words written to his friend Charles Brown, whose kindness, willingly exerted whenever Keats chose to avail himself of it, seemed to free him from any pressing necessity of earning his own living. Keats felt that he must not allow this state of things to continue. He determined to set himself to ' fag on as others do' at periodical literature, rather than to endanger his independence and his self-respect ; and he writes to Brown :—

'I had got into a habit of mind of looking towards you as a help in all difficulties. This very habit would be the parent of idleness and difficulties. You will see it is a duty I owe to myself to break the neck of it. I do nothing for my subsistence—make no exertion. At the end of another year you shall applaud me, not for verses, but for conduct.'

He had not, alas, another year of health before him when he announced that wholesome resolve ; it then wanted but six months of the day of his fatal attack. But in the brief time allowed to him he did what he could to keep his word.

What character, again, what strength and clearness of judgment, in his criticism of his own productions, of the public, and of 'the literary circles'! His words after the severe reviews of *Endymion* have often been quoted ; they cannot be quoted too often :—

'Praise or blame has but a momentary effect on the man whose love of beauty in the abstract makes him a severe critic on his own works. My own criticism has given me pain without comparison beyond what *Blackwood* or the *Quarterly* could possibly inflict; and also, when I feel I am right. no external praise can give me such a glow as my own solitary reperception and ratification of what is fine. J. S. is perfectly right in regard to the "slip-shod Endymion." That it is so is no fault of mine. No! though it may sound a little paradoxical, it is as good as I had power to make it by myself.'

And again, as if he had foreseen certain of his admirers gushing over him, and was resolved to disengage his responsibility :—

'I have done nothing, except for the amusement of a few people who refine upon their feelings till anything in the un-understandable way will go down with them. I have no cause to complain, because I am certain anything really fine will in these days be felt. I have no doubt that if I had written *Othello* I should have been cheered. I shall go on with patience.'

Young poets almost inevitably over-rate what they call 'the might of poesy,' and its power over the world which now is. Keats is not a dupe on this matter any more than he is a dupe about the merit of his own performances :—

'I have no trust whatever in poetry. I don't wonder at it ; the marvel is to me how people read so much of it.'

His attitude towards the public is that of a strong man, not of a weakling avid of praise, and made to 'be snuff'd out by an article' :—

'I shall ever consider the public as debtors to me for verses, not myself to them for admiration, which I can do without.'

And again, in a passage where one may perhaps find fault with the capital letters, but surely with nothing else :—

'I have not the slightest feel of humility towards the public or to anything in existence but the Eternal Being, the Principle of Beauty, and the Memory of great Men. . . . I would be subdued before my friends, and thank them for subduing me; but among multitudes of men I have no feel of stooping; I hate the idea of humility to them. I never wrote one single line of poetry with the least shadow of thought about their opinion. Forgive me for vexing you, but it eases me to tell you: I could not live without the love of my friends; I would jump down Etna for any great public good — but I hate a mawkish popularity. I cannot be subdued before them. My glory would be to daunt and dazzle the thousand jabberers about pictures and books'

Against these artistic and literary 'jabberers,' amongst whom Byron fancied Keats, probably, to be always living, flattering them and flattered by them, he has yet another outburst :—

'Just so much as I am humbled by the genius above my grasp, am I exalted and look with hate and contempt upon the literary world. Who could wish to be among the common place crowd of the little famous, who are each individually lost in a throng made up of themselves?'

And he loves Fanny Brawne the more, he tells her, because he believes that she has liked him for his own sake and for nothing else. 'I have met with women who I really think would like to be married to a Poem and to be given away by a Novel.'

There is a tone of too much bitterness and defiance in all this, a tone which he with great propriety subdued and corrected when he wrote his beautiful preface to *Endymion.* But the thing to be seized is, that Keats had flint and iron in him, that he had character; that he was, as his brother George says, 'as much like the Holy Ghost as *Johnny Keats*,'—as that imagined sensuous weakling, the delight of the literary circles of Hampstead.

It is a pity that Byron, who so misconceived Keats, should never have known how shrewdly Keats, on the other hand, had characterised *him*, as 'a fine thing' in the sphere of 'the worldly, theatrical, and pantomimical.' But indeed nothing is more remarkable in Keats than his clear-sightedness, his lucidity; and lucidity is in itself akin to character and to high and severe work. In spite, therefore, of his overpowering feeling for beauty, in spite of his sensuousness, in spite of his facility, in spite of his gift of expression, Keats could say resolutely :—

'I know nothing, I have read nothing; and I mean to follow Solomon's directions: "Get learning, get understanding." There is but one way for me. The road lies through application, study, and thought. I will pursue it.'

And of Milton, instead of resting in Milton's incomparable

F f

phrases, Keats could say, although indeed all the while 'looking upon fine phrases,' as he himself tells us, 'like a lover' :—

'Milton had an exquisite passion for what is properly, in the sense of ease and pleasure, poetical luxury; and with that, it appears to me, he would fain have been content, if he could, so doing, preserve his self-respect and feeling of duty performed ; but there was working in him, as it were, that same sort of thing which operates in the great world to the end of a prophecy's being accomplished   Therefore he devoted himself rather to the ardours than the pleasures of song, solacing himself at intervals with cups of old wine.'

In his own poetry, too, Keats felt that place must be found for 'the ardours rather than the pleasures of song,' although he was aware that he was not yet ripe for it :—

> 'But my flag is not unfurl'd
> On the Admiral-staff, and to philosophise
> I dare not yet.'

Even in his pursuit of 'the pleasures of song,' however, there is that stamp of high work which is akin to character, which is character passing into intellectual production. '*The best sort of poetry*—that,' he truly says, 'is all I care for, all I live for.' It is curious to observe how this severe addiction of his to the best sort of poetry affects him with a certain coldness, as if the addiction had been to mathematics, towards those prime objects of a sensuous and passionate poet's regard, love and women. He speaks of 'the opinion I have formed of the generality of women, who appear to me as children to whom I would rather give a sugar-plum than my time.' He confesses 'a tendency to class women in my books with roses and sweetmeats—they never see themselves dominant'; and he can understand how the unpopularity of his poems may be in part due to 'the offence which the ladies,' not unnaturally, 'take at him' from this cause. Even to Fanny Brawne he can write 'a flint-worded letter,' when his 'mind is heaped to the full' with poetry :—

'I know the generality of women would hate me for this; that I should have so unsoftened, so hard a mind as to forget them ; forget the brightest realities for the dull imaginations of my own brain. . . . My heart seems now made of iron—I could not write a proper answer to an invitation to Idalia.'

The truth is that 'the yearning passion for the Beautiful,' which was with Keats, as he himself truly says, the master-passion, is not a passion of the sensuous or sentimental man, is not a passion of the sensuous or sentimental poet. It is an intellectual and spiritual passion. It is 'connected and made one,' as Keats declares that in his case it was, 'with the ambition of the intellect.' It is, as he again says, 'the mighty *abstract idea* of Beauty in all things.' And in his last days Keats wrote: 'If I should die, I have left no immortal work behind me—nothing to make my friends proud of my memory; *but I have loved the principle of beauty in all things,* and if I had had time I would have made myself remembered.' He *has* made himself remembered, and remembered as no merely sensuous poet could be; and he has done it by having 'loved the principle of beauty in all things.'

For to see things in their beauty is to see things in their truth, and Keats knew it. 'What the Imagination seizes as Beauty must be Truth,' he says in prose; and in immortal verse he has said the same thing :—

> 'Beauty is truth, truth beauty,—that is all
> Ye know on earth, and all ye need to know.'

No, it is not all; but it is true, deeply true, and we have deep need to know it. And with beauty goes not only truth, joy goes with her also; and this too Keats saw and said, as in the famous first line of his *Endymion* it stands written :—

> 'A thing of beauty is a joy for ever.'

It is no small thing to have so loved the principle of beauty as to perceive the necessary relation of beauty with truth, and of both with joy. Keats was a great spirit, and counts for far more than many even of his admirers suppose, because this just and high perception made itself clear to him. Therefore a dignity and a glory shed gleams over his life, and happiness, too, was not a stranger to it. 'Nothing startles me beyond the moment,' he says; 'the setting sun will always set me to rights, or if a sparrow come before my window I take part in its existence and pick about the gravel.' But he had terrible bafflers,—consuming disease and early death. 'I think,' he writes to Reynolds, 'if I had a free and healthy and lasting organisation of heart, and lungs as strong as an ox's, so as to be able to bear unhurt the shock of extreme thought and sensation without weariness, I could pass my life very nearly alone, though it should last eighty years. But I feel my body too weak to support me to the height ; I am obliged continually to check myself, and be nothing.' He had against him even more than this ; he had against him the blind power which we call Fortune. ' O that something fortunate,' he cries in the closing months of his life, ' had ever happened to me or my brothers !—then I might hope,—but despair is forced upon me as a habit.' So baffled and so sorely tried,—while laden, at the same time, with a mighty formative thought requiring health, and many days, and favouring circumstances, for its adequate manifestation,—what wonder if the achievement of Keats be partial and incomplete ?

Nevertheless, let and hindered as he was, and with a short term and imperfect experience,—' young,' as he says of himself, 'and writing at random, straining after particles of light in the midst of a great darkness, without knowing the bearing of any one assertion, of any one opinion,'—notwithstanding all this, by virtue of his feeling for beauty and of his perception of the vital connexion of beauty with truth, Keats accomplished so much in poetry, that in one of the two great modes by which poetry interprets, in the faculty of naturalistic interpretation, in what we call natural magic, he ranks with Shakespeare. ' The tongue of Kean,' he says in an admirable criticism of that great actor and of his enchanting elocution, ' the tongue of Kean must seem to have robbed the Hybla bees and left them honeyless. There is an indescribable *gusto* in his voice ;—in Richard, " Be stirring with the lark to-morrow, gentle Norfolk !" comes from him as through the morning atmosphere towards which he yearns.' This magic, this 'indescribable *gusto* in the voice,' Keats himself, too, exhibits in his poetic expression. No one else in English poetry, save Shakespeare, has in expression quite the fascinating felicity of Keats, his perfection of loveliness. ' I think,' he said humbly, ' I shall be among the English poets after my death.' He is ; he is with Shakespeare.

For the second great half of poetic interpretation, for that faculty of moral interpretation which is in Shakespeare, and is informed by him with the same power of beauty as his naturalistic interpretation, Keats was not ripe. For the architectonics of poetry, the faculty which presides at the evolution of works like the *Agamemnon* or *Lear*, he was not ripe. His *Endymion*, as he himself well saw, is a failure, and his *Hyperion*, fine things as it contains, is not a success. But in shorter things, where the matured power of moral interpretation, and the high architectonics which go with complete poetic development, are not required, he is perfect. The poems which follow prove it,—prove it far better by themselves than anything which can be said about them will prove it. Therefore I have chiefly spoken here of the man, and of the elements in him which explain the production of such work. Shakespearian work it is; not imitative, indeed, of Shakespeare, but Shakespearian, because its expression has that rounded perfection and felicity of loveliness of which Shakespeare is the great master. To show such work is to praise it. Let us now end by delighting ourselves with a fragment of it, too broken to find a place among the pieces which follow, but far too beautiful to be lost. It is a fragment of an ode for May-day. O might I, he cries to May, O might I

> . . . . ' thy smiles
> Seek as they once were sought, in Grecian isles,
> By bards who died content on pleasant sward,
> Leaving great verse unto a little clan!
> O, give me their old vigour, and unheard
> Save of the quiet primrose, and the span
> Of heaven, and few ears,
> Rounded by thee, my song should die away,
> Content as theirs,
> Rich in the simple worship of a day!'

MATTHEW ARNOLD.

[From *Endymion*, Book **I.**]

BEAUTY.

A thing of beauty is a joy for ever :
Its loveliness increases ; it will never
Pass into nothingness ; but still will keep
A bower quiet for us, and a sleep
Full of sweet dreams, and health, and quiet breathing
Therefore, on every morrow, are we wreathing
A flowery band to bind us to the earth,
Spite of despondence, of the inhuman dearth
Of noble natures, of the gloomy days,
Of all the unhealthy and o'er-darkened ways
Made for our searching : yes, in spite of all,
Some shape of beauty moves away the pall
From our dark spirits. Such the sun, the moon,
Trees old and young, sprouting a shady boon
For simple sheep ; and such are daffodils
With the green world they live in ; and clear rills
That for themselves a cooling covert make
'Gainst the hot season ; the mid-forest brake,
Rich with a sprinkling of fair musk-rose blooms ;
And such too is the grandeur of the dooms
We have imagined for the mighty dead ;
All lovely tales that we have heard or read :
An endless fountain of immortal drink,
Pouring unto us from the heaven's brink.

[From *Miscellaneous Poems.*]

ENDYMION.

He was a Poet, sure a lover too,
Who stood on Latmus' top, what time there blew
Soft breezes from the myrtle vale below,
And brought, in faintness solemn, sweet, and slow,
A hymn from Dian's temple ; while upswelling,
The incense went to her own starry dwelling.

But though her face was clear as infants' eyes,
Though she stood smiling o'er the sacrifice,
The poet wept at her so piteous fate,
Wept that such beauty should be desolate.
So in fine wrath some golden sounds he won,
And gave meek Cynthia her Endymion.

[From *Endymion*, Book I.]

HYMN TO PAN.

O Hearkener to the loud clapping shears,
While ever and anon to his shorn peers
A ram goes bleating : Winder of the horn,
When snouted wild-boars routing tender corn
Anger our huntsman : Breather round our farms,
To keep off mildews, and all weather harms :
Strange ministrant of undescribed sounds,
That come a-swooning over hollow grounds,
And wither drearily on barren moors :
Dread opener of the mysterious doors
Leading to universal knowledge—see,
Great son of Dryope,
The many that are come to pay their vows
With leaves about their brows !

[From *Endymion*, Book IV.]

BACCHUS.

And as I sat, over the light blue hills
There came a noise of revellers : the rills
Into the wide stream came of purple hue—
　　'Twas Bacchus and his crew !
The earnest trumpet spake, and silver thrills
From kissing cymbals made a merry din—
　　'Twas Bacchus and his kin!
Like to a moving vintage down they came,
Crown'd with green leaves, and faces all on flame ;
All madly dancing through the pleasant valley,
　　To scare thee, Melancholy !

[From *Miscellaneous Poems.*]

CYNTHIA'S BRIDAL EVENING.

The evening weather was so bright and clear,
That men of health were of unusual cheer;
Stepping like Homer at the trumpet's call,
Or young Apollo on the pedestal:
And lovely women were as fair and warm,
As Venus looking sideways in alarm.
The breezes were ethereal and pure,
And crept through half closed lattices to cure
The languid sick; it cooled their fevered sleep,
And soothed them into slumbers full and deep.
Soon they awoke clear-eyed: nor burned with thirsting,
Nor with hot fingers, nor with temples bursting:
And springing up, they met the wondering sight
Of their dear friends, nigh foolish with delight;
Who feel their arms and breasts, and kiss, and stare,
And on their placid foreheads part the hair.
Young men and maidens at each other gazed,
With hands held back, and motionless, amazed
To see the brightness in each other's eyes;
And so they stood, filled with a sweet surprise,
Until their tongues were loosed in poesy.
Therefore no lover did of anguish die:
But the soft numbers, in that moment spoken,
Made silken ties, that never may be broken.

[From *Hyperion*, Book I.]

SATURN.

Deep in the shady sadness of a vale
Far sunken from the healthy breath of morn,
Far from the fiery noon, and eve's one star,
Sat grey-hair'd Saturn, quiet as a stone,
Still as the silence round about his lair;

Forest on forest hung about his head
Like cloud on cloud. No stir of air was there,
Not so much life as on a summer's day
Robs not one light seed from the feathered grass,
But where the dead leaf fell, there did it rest.
A stream went voiceless by, still deadened more
By reason of his fallen divinity
Spreading a shade : the Naiad 'mid her reeds
Pressed her cold finger closer to her lips.

Along the margin-sand large foot-marks went,
No further than to where his feet had strayed,
And slept there since. Upon the sodden ground
His old right hand lay nerveless, listless, dead,
Unsceptred ; and his realmless eyes were closed ;
While his bowed head seem'd listening to the Earth,
His ancient mother, for some comfort yet.

It seem'd no force could wake him from his place ;
But there came one, who with a kindred hand
Touched his wide shoulders, after bending low
With reverence, though to one who knew it not.
She was a Goddess of the infant world ;
By her in stature the tall Amazon
Had stood a pigmy's height : she would have ta'en
Achilles by the hair and bent his neck ;
Or with a finger stayed Ixion's wheel.
Her face was large as that of Memphian sphinx,
Pedestal'd haply in a palace-court,
When sages look'd to Egypt for their lore.
But oh ! how unlike marble was that face :
How beautiful, if sorrow had not made
Sorrow more beautiful than Beauty's self.
There was a listening fear in her regard,
As if calamity had but begun ;
As if the vanward clouds of evil days
Had spent their malice, and the sullen rear
Was with its stored thunder labouring up.
One hand she pressed upon that aching spot

Where beats the human heart, as if just there,
Though an immortal, she felt cruel pain :
The other upon Saturn's bended neck
She laid, and to the level of his ear
Leaning with parted lips, some words she spake
In solemn tenour and deep organ tone :
Some mourning words, which in our feeble tongue
Would come in these like accents ; O how frail
To that large utterance of the early Gods !

Cœlus to Hyperion.

¹O brightest of my children dear, earth-born
And sky-engendered, Son of Mysteries !
All unrevealed even to the powers
Which met at thy creating ! at whose joys,
And palpitations sweet, and pleasures soft,
I, Cœlus, wonder how they came and whence ;
And at the fruits thereof what shapes they be,
Distinct, and visible ; symbols divine,
Manifestations of that beauteous life
Diffused unseen throughout eternal space ;
Of these new-formed art thou, O brightest child !
Of these, thy brethren and the Goddesses !
There is sad feud among ye, and rebellion
Of son against his sire. I saw him fall,
I saw my firstborn tumbled from his throne !
To me his arms were spread, to me his voice
Found way from forth the thunders round his head !
Pale wox I, and in vapours hid my face.
Art thou, too, near such doom ? vague fear there is ·
For I have seen my sons most unlike Gods.
Divine ye were created, and divine
In sad demeanour, solemn, undisturbed,
Unruffled, like high Gods, ye lived and ruled :
Now I behold in you fear, hope, and wrath ;
Actions of rage and passion ; even as
I see them, on the mortal world beneath,

In men who die.—This is the grief, O Son!
Sad sign of ruin, sudden dismay, and fall!
Yet do thou strive; as thou art capable,
As thou canst move about, an evident God,
And canst oppose to each malignant hour
Ethereal presence.—I am but a voice;
My life is but the life of winds and tides;
No more than winds and tides can I avail;—
But thou canst.—Be thou therefore in the van
Of circumstance; yea, seize the arrow's barb
Before the tense string murmur.—To the earth!
For there thou wilt find Saturn, and his woes.
Meantime I will keep watch on thy bright sun,
And of thy seasons be a careful nurse.'—
Ere half this region-whisper had come down
Hyperion arose, and on the stars
Lifted his curved lids, and kept them wide
Until it ceased; and still he kept them wide:
And still they were the same bright, patient stars.
Then with a slow incline of his broad breast,
Like to a diver in the pearly seas,
Forward he stooped over the airy shore,
And plunged all noiseless into the deep night.

[From *Hyperion*, Book II.]

OCEANUS.

So ended Saturn; and the God of the Sea,
Sophist and sage, from no Athenian grove,
But cogitation in his watery shades,
Arose, with locks not oozy, and began,
In murmurs, which his first endeavouring tongue
Caught infant-like from the far-foamed sands.
'O ye, whom wrath consumes! who, passion-stung,
Writhe at defeat, and nurse your agonies!
Shut up your senses, stifle up your ears,
My voice is not a bellows unto ire.

Yet listen, ye who will, whilst I bring proof
How ye, perforce, must be content to stoop :
And in the proof much comfort will I give,
If ye will take that comfort in its truth.
We fall by course of Nature's law, not force
Of thunder, or of Jove. Great Saturn, thou
Hast sifted well the atom-universe ;
But for this reason, that thou art the King,
And only blind from sheer supremacy,
One avenue was shaded from thine eyes,
Through which I wandered to eternal truth.
And first, as thou wast not the first of powers,
So art thou not the last ; it cannot be.
Thou art not the beginning nor the end.
From chaos and parental darkness came
Light, the first fruits of that intestine broil,
That sullen ferment, which for wondrous ends
Was ripening in itself. The ripe hour came,
And with it light, and light engendering
Upon its own producer, forthwith touched
The whole enormous matter into life.
Upon that very hour, our parentage,
The Heavens and the Earth, were manifest :
Then thou first-born, and we the giant-race,
Found ourselves ruling new and beauteous realms.
Now comes the pain of truth, to whom 'tis pain ;
O folly ! for to bear all naked truths,
And to envisage circumstance, all calm,
That is the top of sovereignty. Mark well !
As Heaven and Earth are fairer, fairer far
Than Chaos and blank Darkness, though once chiefs ;
And as we show beyond that Heaven and Earth
In form and shape compact and beautiful,
In will, in action free, companionship,
And thousand other signs of purer life ;
So on our heels a fresh perfection treads,
A power more strong in beauty, born of us
And fated to excel us, as we pass
In glory that old Darkness : nor are we

Thereby more conquered than by us the rule
Of shapeless Chaos. Say, doth the dull soil
Quarrel with the proud forests it hath fed,
And feedeth still, more comely than itself?
Can it deny the chiefdom of green groves?
Or shall the tree be envious of the dove
Because it cooeth, and hath snowy wings
To wander wherewithal and find its joys?
We are such forest-trees, and our fair boughs
Have bred forth, not pale solitary doves,
But eagles golden-feathered, who do tower
Above us in their beauty, and must reign
In right thereof; for 'tis the eternal law
That first in beauty should be first in might:
Yea, by that law, another race may drive
Our conquerors to mourn as we do now.
Have ye beheld the young God of the Seas,
My dispossessor? Have ye seen his face?
Have ye beheld his chariot, foam'd along
By noble winged creatures he hath made?
I saw him on the calmed waters scud,
With such a glow of beauty in his eyes,
That it enforced me to bid sad farewell
To all my empire: farewell sad I took,
And hither came, to see how dolorous fate
Had wrought upon ye; and how I might best
Give consolation in this woe extreme.
Receive the truth, and let it be your balm.'

HYPERION'S ARRIVAL.

All eyes were on Enceladus's face,
And they beheld, while still Hyperion's name
Flew from his lips up to the vaulted rocks,
A pallid gleam across his features stern:
Not savage, for he saw full many a God
Wroth as himself. He locked upon them all,
And in each face he saw a gleam of light,
But splendider in Saturn's whose hoar locks

Shone like the bubbling foam about a keel
When the prow sweeps into a midnight cove.
In pale and silver silence they remained,
Till suddenly a splendour, like the morn,
Pervaded all the beetling gloomy steeps,
All the sad spaces of oblivion,
And every gulf, and every chasm old,
And every height, and every sullen depth,
Voiceless, or hoarse with loud tormented streams:
And all the everlasting cataracts,
And all the headlong torrents far and near,
Mantled before in darkness and huge shade,
Now saw the light and made it terrible.
It was Hyperion:—a granite peak
His bright feet touched, and there he stayed to view
The misery his brilliance had betrayed
To the most hateful seeing of itself.
Golden his hair of short Numidian curl,
Regal his shape majestic, a vast shade
In midst of his own brightness, like the bulk
Of Memnon's image at the set of sun
To one who travels from the dusking East:
Sighs, too, as mournful as that Memnon's harp,
He uttered, while his hands, contemplative,
He pressed together, and in silence stood.

[From *The Eve of St. Agnes.*]

THE FLIGHT.

Full on this casement shone the wintry moon,
And threw warm gules on Madeline's fair breast,
As down she knelt for heaven's grace and boon;
Rose-bloom fell on her hands, together prest,
And on her silver cross soft amethyst,
And on her hair a glory, like a saint:
She seem'd a splendid angel, newly drest,
Save wings, for heaven:—Porphyro grew faint:
She knelt, so pure a thing, so free from mortal taint.

Anon his heart revives : her vespers done,
Of all its wreathed pearls her hair she frees ;
Unclasps her warmed jewels one by one ;
Loosens her fragrant boddice ; by degrees
Her rich attire creeps rustling to her knees :
Half-hidden, like a mermaid in sea-weed,
Pensive awhile she dreams awake, and sees,
In fancy, fair St. Agnes in her bed,
But dares not look behind, or all the charm is fled.

Soon, trembling in her soft and chilly nest,
In sort of wakeful swoon, perplexed she lay,
Until the poppied warmth of sleep oppressed
Her soothed limbs, and soul fatigued away ;
Flown, like a thought, until the morrow-day ;
Blissfully havened both from joy and pain ;
Clasped like a missal where swart Paynims pray :
Blinded alike from sunshine and from rain,
As though a rose should shut, and be a bud again.

Stolen to this paradise, and so entranced,
Porphyro gazed upon her empty dress,
And listened to her breathing, if it chanced
To wake into a slumberous tenderness ;
Which when he heard, that minute did he bless,
And breathed himself : then from the closet crept,
Noiseless as fear in a wide wilderness,
And over the hushed carpet, silent, stept,
And 'tween the curtains peeped, where, lo!—how fast she
    slept.

Then by the bed-side, where the faded moon
Made a dim, silver twilight, soft he set
A table, and, half anguished, threw thereon
A cloth of woven crimson, gold, and jet :—
O for some drowsy Morphean amulet !
The boisterous, midnight, festive clarion,
The kettle-drum, and far-heard clarionet,
Affray his ears, though but in dying tone :—
The hall-door shuts again, and all the noise is gone.

And still she slept an azure-lidded sleep,
In blanched linen, smooth, and lavendered,
While he from forth the closet brought a heap
Of candied apple, quince, and plum, and gourd;
With jellies soother than the creamy curd,
And lucent syrops, tinct with cinnamon;
Manna and dates, in argosy transferred
From Fez; and spiced dainties, every one,
From silken Samarcand to cedared Lebanon.

These delicates he heaped with glowing hand
On golden dishes and in baskets bright
Of wreathed silver: sumptuous they stand
In the retired quiet of the night,
Filling the chilly room with perfume light.—
'And now, my love, my seraph fair, awake!
Thou art my heaven, and I thine eremite:
Open thine eyes, for meek St. Agnes' sake,
Or I shall drowse beside thee, so my soul doth ache.'

Thus whispering, his warm, unnerved arm
Sank in her pillow. Shaded was her dream
By the dusk curtains:—'twas a midnight charm
Impossible to melt as iced stream:
The lustrous salvers in the moonlight gleam;
Broad golden fringe upon the carpet lies:
It seemed he never, never could redeem
From such a steadfast spell his lady's eyes;
So mused awhile, entoiled in woofed phantasies.

Awakening up, he took her hollow lute,—
Tumultuous,—and, in chords that tenderest be,
He play'd an ancient ditty, long since mute,
In Provence called 'La belle dame sans mercy':
Close to her ear touching the melody;—
Wherewith disturbed, she uttered a soft moan:
He ceased—she panted quick—and suddenly
Her blue affrayed eyes wide open shone:
Upon his knees he sank, pale as smooth-sculptured stone

Her eyes were open, but she still beheld,
Now wide awake, the vision of her sleep :
There was a painful change, that nigh expelled
The blisses of her dream so pure and deep.
At which fair Madeline began to weep,
And moan forth witless words with many a sigh ;
While still her gaze on Porphyro would keep ;
Who knelt, with joined hands and piteous eye,
Fearing to move or speak, she looked so dreamingly.

'Ah, Porphyro !' said she, 'but even now
Thy voice was at sweet tremble in mine ear,
Made tuneable with every sweetest vow ;
And those sad eyes were spiritual and clear :
How changed thou art ! how pallid, chill, and drear !
Give me that voice again, my Porphyro,
Those looks immortal, those complainings dear !
Oh leave me not in this eternal woe,
For if thou diest, my Love, I know not where to go.'

Beyond a mortal man impassioned far
At these voluptuous accents, he arose,
Ethereal, flushed, and like a throbbing star
Seen 'mid the sapphire heaven's deep repose ;
Into her dream he melted, as the rose
Blendeth its odour with the violet,—
Solution sweet : meantime the frost-wind blows
Like Love's alarum pattering the sharp sleet
Against the window-panes ; St. Agnes' moon hath set.

'Tis dark : quick pattereth the flaw-blown sleet :
'This is no dream, my bride, my Madeline !'
'Tis dark : the iced gusts still rave and beat :
'No dream, alas ! alas ! and woe is mine !
Porphyro will leave me here to fade and pine.—
Cruel ! what traitor could thee hither bring?
I curse not, for my heart is lost in thine,
Though thou forsakest a deceived thing ;—
A dove forlorn and lost with sick unpruned wing.'

'My Madeline! sweet dreamer! lovely bride!
Say, may 1 be for aye thy vassal blest?
Thy beauty's shield, heart-shaped and vermeil **dyed?**
Ah, silver shrine, here will I take my **rest**
After so many hours of toil and quest,
A famished pilgrim,—saved by miracle.
Though 1 have found, I will not rob thy **nest,**
Saving of thy sweet self; if thou think'st **well**
To trust, fair Madeline, to no rude infidel.'

'Hark! 'tis an elfin-storm from faery **land,**
Of haggard seeming, but a boon indeed :
Arise—arise! the morning is at hand ;—
The bloated wassailers will never heed :—
Let us away, my love, with happy speed ;
There are no ears to hear, or eyes to see,—
Drowned all in Rhenish and the sleepy mead :
Awake! arise! my love, and fearless be,
For o'er the southern moors I have a home for **thee.'**

She hurried at his words, beset with fears,
For there were sleeping dragons all around,
At glaring watch, perhaps with ready spears—
Down the wide stairs a darkling way they **found,**
In all the house was heard no human sound.
A chain-drooped lamp was flickering by each **door;**
The arras, rich with horseman, hawk, and **hound,**
Fluttered in the besieging wind's uproar ;
And the long carpets rose along the gusty floor.

They glide, like phantoms, into the wide hall!
Like phantoms to the iron porch they glide,
Where lay the Porter, in uneasy sprawl,
With a huge empty flagon by his side :
The wakeful bloodhound rose, and shook his **hide,**
But his sagacious eye an inmate owns :
By one, and one, the bolts full easy slide :—
The chains lie silent on the footworn stones ;
The key turns, and the door upon its hirges groans.

And they are gone : ay, ages long ago
These lovers fled away into the storm.
That night the Baron dreamt of many a woe,
And all his warrior-guests, with shade and form
Of witch, and demon, and large coffin-worm,
Were long be-nightmared. Angela the old
Died palsy-twitch'd, with meagre face deform ;
The Beadsman, after thousand aves told,
For aye unsought-for slept among his ashes cold.

ODE TO A NIGHTINGALE.

I.

My heart aches, and a drowsy numbness pains
  My sense, as though of hemlock I had drunk,
Or emptied some dull opiate to the drains
  One minute past, and Lethe-wards had sunk :
'Tis not through envy of thy happy lot,
  But being too happy in thy happiness,—
    That thou, light-winged Dryad of the trees,
      In some melodious plot
Of beechen green, and shadows numberless,
  Singest of summer in full-throated ease.

2.

O for a draught of vintage, that hath been
  Cooled a long age in the deep-delved earth,
Tasting of Flora and the country-green,
  Dance, and Provençal song, and sun-burnt mirth !
O for a beaker full of the warm South,
  Full of the true, the blushful Hippocrene,
    With beaded bubbles winking at the brim,
      And purple-stained mouth ;
'That I might drink, and leave the world unseen,
  And with thee fade away into the forest dim :

G g 2

3.

Fade far away, dissolve, and quite forget
  What thou among the leaves hast never known,
The weariness, the fever, and the fret
  Here, where men sit and hear each other groan;
Where palsy shakes a few, sad, last grey hairs,
  Where youth grows pale, and spectre-thin, and dies;
    Where but to think is to be full of sorrow
      And leaden-eyed despairs;
  Where Beauty cannot keep her lustrous eyes,
    Or new Love pine at them beyond to-morrow.

4.

Away! away! for I will fly to thee,
  Not charioted by Bacchus and his pards,
But on the viewless wings of Poesy,
  Though the dull brain perplexes and retards:
Already with thee! tender is the night,
  And haply the Queen-Moon is on her throne,
    Clustered around by all her starry Fays;
      But here there is no light,
  Save what from heaven is with the breezes blown
    Through verdurous glooms and winding mossy ways.

5.

I cannot see what flowers are at my feet,
  Nor what soft incense hangs upon the boughs,
But, in embalmed darkness, guess each sweet
  Wherewith the seasonable month endows
The grass, the thicket, and the fruit-tree wild;
  White hawthorn, and the pastoral eglantine;
    Fast-fading violets covered up in leaves;
      And mid-May's eldest child,
  The coming musk-rose, full of dewy wine,
    The murmurous haunt of flies on summer eves.

6.

Darkling I listen ; and for many a time
  I have been half in love with easeful Death,
Called him soft names in many a mused rhyme,
  To take into the air my quiet breath ;
Now more than ever seems it rich to die,
  To cease upon the midnight with no pain,
    While thou art pouring forth thy soul abroad
      In such an ecstasy !
  Still wouldst thou sing, and I have ears in vain—
    To thy high requiem become a sod.

7.

Thou wast not born for death, immortal Bird !
  No hungry generations tread thee down ;
The voice I hear this passing night was heard
  In ancient days by emperor and clown :
Perhaps the self-same song that found a path
  Through the sad heart of Ruth, when, sick for home,
    She stood in tears amid the alien corn ;
      The same that oft-times hath
  Charmed magic casements, opening on the foam
    Of perilous seas, in faery lands forlorn.

8.

Forlorn ! the very word is like a bell
  To toll me back from thee to my sole self !
Adieu ! the fancy cannot cheat so well
  As she is famed to do, deceiving elf.
Adieu ! adieu ! thy plaintive anthem fades
  Past the near meadows, over the still stream,
    Up the hill-side ; and now 'tis buried deep
      In the next valley-glades :
  Was it a vision, or a waking dream ?
    Fled is that music :—do I wake or sleep ?

ODE ON A GRECIAN URN.

1.

Thou still unravished bride of quietness!
 Thou foster-child of Silence and slow Time,
Sylvan historian, who canst thus express
 A flowery tale more sweetly than our rhyme:
What leaf-fringed legend haunts about thy shape
 Of deities or mortals, or of both,
  In Tempe or the dales of Arcady?
 What men or gods are these? What maidens loath?
What mad pursuit? What struggle to escape?
  What pipes and timbrels? What wild ecstasy?

2.

Heard melodies are sweet, but those unheard
 Are sweeter; therefore, ye soft pipes, play on;
Not to the sensual ear, but, more endeared,
 Pipe to the spirit ditties of no tone:
Fair youth, beneath the trees, thou canst not leave
 Thy song, nor ever can those trees be bare;
  Bold Lover, never, never canst thou kiss,
Though winning near the goal—yet, do not grieve;
  She cannot fade, though thou hast not thy bliss,
 For ever wilt thou love, and she be fair!

3.

Ah, happy, happy boughs! that cannot shed
 Your leaves, nor ever bid the Spring adieu;
And, happy melodist, unwearied,
 For ever piping songs for ever new;
More happy love! more happy, happy love!
 For ever warm and still to be enjoyed,
  For ever panting and for ever young;
All breathing human passion far above,
  That leaves a heart high sorrowful and cloyed,
  A burning forehead, and a parching tongue.

4.

Who are these coming to the sacrifice?
  To what green altar, O mysterious priest,
Lead'st thou that heifer lowing at the skies,
  And all her silken flanks with garlands drest?
What little town by river or sea-shore,
  Or mountain-built with peaceful citadel,
    Is emptied of its folk, this pious morn?
And, little town, thy streets for evermore
  Will silent be; and not a soul to tell
    Why thou art desolate, can e'er return.

5.

O Attic shape! Fair attitude! with brede
  Of marble men and maidens overwrought,
With forest branches and the trodden weed;
  Thou, silent form! dost tease us out of thought
As doth eternity. Cold Pastoral!
  When old age shall this generation waste,
    Thou shalt remain, in midst of other woe
  Than ours, a friend to man, to whom thou say'st:
'Beauty is truth, truth beauty,—that is all
    Ye know on earth, and all ye need to know.'

ODE.

  Bards of Passion and of Mirth,
  Ye have left your souls on earth!
  Have ye souls in heaven too,
  Double-lived in regions new?
  Yes, and those of heaven commune
  With the spheres of sun and moon;
  With the noise of fountains wondrous,
  And the parle of voices thunderous:

With the whisper of heaven's trees
And one another, in soft ease
Seated on Elysian lawns
Browsed by none but Dian's fawns;
Underneath large blue-bells tented,
Where the daisies are rose-scented,
And the rose herself has got
Perfume which on earth is not;
Where the nightingale doth sing
Not a senseless, tranced thing,
But divine melodious truth;
Philosophic numbers smooth;
Tales and golden histories
Of heaven and its mysteries.

Thus ye live on high, and then
On the earth ye live again;
And the souls ye left behind you
Teach us, here, the way to find you,
Where your other souls are joying,
Never slumbered, never cloying.
Here, your earth-born souls still speak
To mortals, of their little week;
Of their sorrows and delights;
Of their passions and their spites;
Of their glory and their shame:
What doth strengthen and what maim.
Thus ye teach us, every day,
Wisdom, though fled far away.

Bards of Passion and of Mirth,
Ye have left your souls on earth!
Ye have souls in heaven too,
Double-lived in regions new!

To Autumn.

Season of mists and mellow fruitfulness !
  Close bosom-friend of the maturing sun ;
Conspiring with him how to load and bless
  With fruit the vines that round the thatch-eaves **run** ;
To bend with apples the mossed cottage-trees,
  And fill all fruit with ripeness to the core ;
    To swell the gourd, and plump the hazel shells
  With a sweet kernel ; to set budding more,
And still more, later flowers for the bees,
Until they think warm days will never cease,
    For Summer has o'er-brimmed their clammy cells.

Who hath not seen thee oft amid thy store ?
  Sometimes whoever seeks abroad may find
Thee sitting careless on a granary floor,
  Thy hair soft-lifted by the winnowing wind ;
Or on a half-reaped furrow sound asleep,
  Drowsed with the fume of poppies, while thy hook
    Spares the next swath and all its twined flowers ;
And sometime like a gleaner thou dost keep
  Steady thy laden head across a brook ;
  Or by a cider-press, with patient look,
    Thou watchest the last oozings, hours by hours.

Where are the songs of Spring ? Ay, where are they ?
  Think not of them, thou hast thy music too,
While barred clouds bloom the soft-dying day,
  And touch the stubble-plains with rosy hue ;
Then in a wailful choir the small gnats mourn
  Among the river sallows, borne aloft
    Or sinking as the light wind lives or dies ;
And full-grown lambs loud bleat from hilly bourn ;
  Hedge-crickets sing ; and now with treble soft
  The redbreast whistles from a garden-croft,
    And gathering swallows twitter in the skies.

LINES ON THE MERMAID TAVERN.

Souls of poets dead and gone,
What Elysium have ye known,
Happy field or mossy cavern,
Choicer than the Mermaid Tavern?
Have ye tippled drink more fine
Than mine host's Canary wine?
Or are fruits of Paradise
Sweeter than those dainty pies
Of venison? O generous food!
Drest as though bold Robin Hood
Would, with his maid Marian,
Sup and bowse from horn and can.

I have heard that on a day
Mine host's sign-board flew away,
Nobody knew whither, till
An astrologer's old quill
To a sheepskin gave the story,—
Said he saw you in your glory,
Underneath a new old-sign
Sipping beverage divine,
And pledging with contented smack
The Mermaid in the Zodiac.

Souls of poets dead and gone,
What Elysium have ye known,
Happy field or mossy cavern,
Choicer than the Mermaid Tavern?

SCNNETS.

I. ON FIRST LOOKING INTO CHAPMAN'S HOMER.

Much have I travelled in the realms of gold,
And many goodly states and kingdoms seen ;
Round many western islands have I been
Which bards in fealty to Apollo hold.
Oft of one wide expanse had I been told
That deep-browed Homer ruled as his demesne :
Yet did I never breathe its pure serene
Till I heard Chapman speak out loud and bold :
Then felt I like some watcher of the skies
When a new planet swims into his ken ;
Or like stout Cortez when with eagle eyes
He stared at the Pacific—and all his men
Looked at each other with a wild surmise—
Silent, upon a peak in Darien.

II. WRITTEN IN JANUARY, 1817.

After dark vapours have oppressed our plains
For a long dreary season, comes a day
Born of the gentle South, and clears away
From the sick heavens all unseemly stains.
The anxious mouth, relieved from its pains,
Takes as a long-lost right the feel of May,
The eyelids with the passing coolness play,
Like rose leaves with the drip of summer rains.
And calmest thoughts come round us—as, of leaves
Budding,—fruit ripening in stillness,—autumn suns
Smiling at eve upon the quiet sheaves,—
Sweet Sappho's cheek,—a sleeping infant's breath,—
The gradual sand that through an hour-glass runs,—
A woodland rivulet,—a Poet's death.

III. Written in January, 1818.

When I have fears that I may cease to be
Before my pen has gleaned my teeming brain,
Before high piled books, in charact'ry,
Hold like full garners the full-ripened grain ;
When I behold, upon the night's starred face,
Huge cloudy symbols of a high romance,
And feel that I may never live to trace
Their shadows, with the magic hand of chance ;
And when I feel, fair creature of an hour !
That I shall never look upon thee more,
Never have relish in the faery power
Of unreflecting love !—then on the shore
Of the wide world I stand alone, and think
Till Love and Fame to nothingness do sink.

IV. Addressed to Haydon.

Great spirits now on earth are sojourning :
He of the cloud, the cataract, the lake,
Who on Helvellyn's summit, wide awake,
Catches his freshness from Archangel's wing :
He of the rose, the violet, the spring,
The social smile, the chain for Freedom's sake :
And lo ! whose steadfastness would never take
A meaner sound than Raphael's whispering.
And other spirits there are, standing apart
Upon the forehead of the age to come ;
These, these will give the world another heart,
And other pulses. Hear ye not the hum
Of mighty workings ?——
Listen awhile, ye nations, and be dumb.

V. ON THE GRASSHOPPER AND CRICKET.

The poetry of earth is never dead :
When all the birds are faint with the hot sun,
And hide in cooling trees, a voice will run
From hedge to hedge about the new-mown mead :
That is the grasshopper's—he takes the lead
In summer luxury,—he has never done
With his delights, for, when tired out with fun,
He rests at ease beneath some pleasant weed.
The poetry of earth is ceasing never :
On a lone winter evening, when the frost
Has wrought a silence, from the stove there shrills
The Cricket's song, in warmth increasing ever,
And seems to one in drowsiness half lost,
The Grasshopper's among some grassy hills.

VI THE HUMAN SEASONS.

Four Seasons fill the measure of the year ;
There are four seasons in the mind of man :
He has his lusty Spring, when fancy clear
Takes in all beauty with an easy span :
He has his Summer, when luxuriously
Spring's honeyed cud of youthful thought he loves
To ruminate, and by such dreaming high
Is nearest unto heaven : quiet coves
His soul has in its Autumn, when his wings
He furleth close ; contented so to look
On mists in idleness—to let fair things
Pass by unheeded as a threshold brook.
He has his Winter too of pale misfeature,
Or else he would forgo his mortal nature.

VII. On a Picture of Leander.

Come hither, all sweet maidens soberly,
Down-looking aye, and with a chastened light,
Hid in the fringes of your eyelids white,
And meekly let your fair hands joined be,
As if so gentle that ye could not see,
Untouched, a victim of your beauty bright,
Sinking away to his young spirit's night,
Sinking bewildered 'mid the dreary sea :
'Tis young Leander toiling to his death ;
Nigh swooning, he doth purse his weary lips
For Hero's cheek, and smiles against her smile.
O horrid dream ! see how his body dips
Dead-heavy ; arms and shoulders gleam awhile :
He's gone ; up bubbles all his amorous breath !

VIII. Keats's Last Sonnet.

Bright star ! would I were steadfast as thou art—
Not in lone splendour hung aloft the night,
And watching, with eternal lids apart,
Like Nature's patient sleepless Eremite,
The moving waters at their priestlike task
Of pure ablution round earth's human shores,
Or gazing on the new soft fallen mask
Of snow upon the mountains and the moors.—
No – yet still steadfast, still unchangeable,
Pillowed upon my fair love's ripening breast,
To feel for ever its soft fall and swell,
Awake for ever in a sweet unrest ;
Still, still to hear her tender-taken breath,
And so live ever—or else swoon to death.

THE BARD SPEAKS.

[From the Epistle to my Brother George.]

What though I leave this dull and earthly mould,
Yet shall my spirit lofty converse hold
With after times.—The patriot shall feel
My stern alarum, and unsheath his steel;
Or in the senate thunder out my numbers,
To startle princes from their easy slumbers.
The sage will mingle with each moral theme
My happy thoughts sententious: he will teem
With lofty periods when my verses fire him,
And then I'll stoop from heaven to inspire him.
Lays have I left of such a dear delight
That maids will sing them on their bridal-night
Gay villagers, upon a morn of May,
When they have tired their gentle limbs with play,
And formed a snowy circle on the grass,
And placed in midst of all that lovely lass
Who chosen is their queen,—with her fine head
Crowned with flowers purple, white, and red:
For there the lily and the musk-rose sighing,
Are emblems true of hapless lovers dying:
Between her breasts, that never yet felt trouble,
A bunch of violets full blown, and double,
Serenely sleep:—she from a casket takes
A little book, and then a joy awakes
About each youthful heart,—with stifled cries,
And rubbing of white hands, and sparkling eyes:
For she's to read a tale of hopes and fears;
One that I fostered in my youthful years:
The pearls, that on each glistening circlet sleep,
Gush ever and anon with silent creep,
Lured by the innocent dimples. To sweet rest
Shall the dear babe, upon its mother's breast,

Be lulled with songs of mine. Fair world, adieu!
Thy dales and hills are fading from my view:
Swiftly I mount, upon wide-spreading pinions,
Far from the narrow bounds of thy dominions.
Full joy I feel, while thus I cleave the air,
That my soft verse will charm thy daughters fair,
And warm thy sons!'

WALTER SAVAGE LANDOR.

[WALTER SAVAGE LANDOR was born at Warwick, Jan. 30. 1775; died at Florence, Dec. 17, 1864. He resided in Italy almost continuously from 1815 to 1835, and afterwards 21 years in Bath. His writings, the dates of which range from 1795 to almost the year of his death, were first collected by himself in two large volumes (1846), and afterwards (1876), with his Life, by Mr. John Forster, in eight vols. 8vo.]

There is always some difficulty in discussing the characteristics and merits of the poetry of an eminent writer in prose. There are indeed exceptions, in which the one production has no more to do with the other than the misletoe with the old oak to which it is attached, but in most cases there is sufficient analogy to compel comparison, and sufficient difference to disturb the clear comprehension of the literary character. But the prose and poetry of Landor are especially homogeneous, not only in the sense of the dominant imaginativeness that constitutes what is ordinarily called poetical power, but in the melody and determinateness of poetry that pervades so much of his simplest writing. If this selection had included dramatic pieces, many of the Imaginary Conversations might have taken their place in it as becomingly as if written in poetical rhythm, and there would be no difficulty in culling passages from them and in other works which recur to the memory of the reader rather as screeds of song than as passages of eloquence, beauty, or wisdom. In the limited sketch of the poet which is here attempted it will be seen that there is an unity of intellectual faculty and moral purpose which made this similarity of production almost a necessity. He lived in a past world of heroic thought, unaltered by the events of common life, commencing from his school and college days and enduring for some ninety years. He passed nearly through the most eventful century of the world without learning from experience and almost without adding to his ideas, and thus the conceit of his difference from, and superiority to, others never translated itself into fact, and, aided by his imperious temper, kept him aloof at once from the intrusion and sympathy of his contemporaries. The elder son of a physician of large practice in the town of Warwick, young Landor had all the advantages of good birth and of the best education of his time. Besides his father's property in Staffordshire, he inherited through his mother the ancient estates of the Savages of Ipsley Court and Tachbrooke. At Rugby, and at Trinity College, Oxford, the classical culture which at that period was all the gentleman's education, however artificial and enforced, seemed to find in him a natural affinity that in any other youth would have been the delight of his teachers and the gratification of a just ambition. But to his wayward temperament all competition was not only distasteful but repugnant, and the very sense of superiority was distorted into a contempt for success. He thus left both school and college not only without the ordinary distinctions of scholarship, but prematurely as an offender against ordinary discipline.

At about twenty years of age he settled himself at Tenby in South Wales, and between that secluded sea-place and Swansea, with an occasional visit to Warwick, he passed three years in continuous and lonely study. It was a thrifty and almost pastoral existence, and the sandy dells and dingles covered with moss-roses and golden snap-dragons were always associated in his mind with the production of *Gebir*.

'Play-day for Landor's Latin verses' is a remembrance of one of his Rugby contemporaries, and his first steps in English poetry had been translations and adaptations from the classics ; but a small volume published in 1795, suppressed and forgotten, contains original verse far above the juvenile standard, and distinguished by a satiric gaiety, with no trace of immaturity about it. To this is appended *Poematum Latinorum Libellus et Latine scribendi Defensio*, and there is extant a letter from one of the objects of his satire praising its ease and continuity, and curiously speaking of the *Hendecasyllabi*, many of which were reprinted in the Pisan edition of 1820, as worthy of Catullus, his lifelong model of the perfection of literary grace.

It was during the studious solitude in South Wales that he happened to light on a collection of tales by Clara Reeve, a now forgotten novelist, one of which, an Arabian romance, attracted his fancy. It related to the mythic founder of Gibraltar, and on this he constructed an epic in seven books, which still remains the only sustained poetic effort of his genius, and which, but for certain accidents of the poetic literature of the time, and its author's subsequent fame as a great prose writer, might have only survived as a curiosity of precocious intellectual power. It was composed under the double inspiration of the great classics and of Milton, fortuitously in Latin or in English as his inclination prompted, and it would be difficult if not impossible to discriminate the original medium of poetic thought. It has no interest of plot, and no delicate discrimination of character. Two brothers, representatives of the militant and peaceful natures, are each, after the ancient manner, assisted by sympathetic supernatural agencies, and display the old moralities of the barrenness of conquest and the omnipotence of love. There is the Virgilian descent to the world of future Destiny, with its ancestral and heroic shapes of doom, allegorizing among other objects of his reprobation, not only George the Third 'with eyebrows white and slanting brow,' and Louis Seize, who 'shrinks yelling from that sword there enginehung,' but 'William miscalled Deliverer,' contrasted curiously with a vision in another part of Bonaparte as ' a mortal man above all mortal praise,' but these are the only disturbances of the general unity and consistency of the poem[1]. The happy issue of the pastoral affection of Tamar, and the disastrous close of that of Gebir, afford occasion for an accumulated wealth of imagery which wants but some human relation to raise itself to the utmost heights of epic grandeur, and there are other salient passages, which we hear without wonder that Shelley was never tired of reciting, and which Coleridge could describe as 'eminences as excessively bright as the ground was dark around and between them.'

It was a dreary period of English poetic literature. The gentle voice of Cowper alone rose above a factitious and uninteresting mediocrity, and the small group of writers whose destiny it

[1] It is interesting to contrast with this the after-estimate of Napoleon in the only Greek epigram of his which is extant—

> Τίς ποτε Ναπόλεον τὰ σὰ πρῶτα καὶ ὕστατα γράψει
> Ἔργα ; Χρόνος τέκνων αἵματι τερπόμενος.

Translated by Mr. Algernon Swinburne—

> 'Thy life-long works, Napoleon, who shall write?
> Time, in his children's blood who takes delight.'

was to recall our verse to a truer sense of nature and a purer diction, were just struggling into existence through a hostile and contemptuous criticism. One of these, Robert Southey, who had been Landor's contemporary at Oxford, and who said that 'he would have sought his acquaintance from his Jacobinism, but was repelled by his eccentricity,' happened to light upon *Gebir*, and found in it 'some of the most exquisite poetry in the language. I would go a hundred miles to see the author.' He declared it more Homeric than anything in modern poetical writing. The attention of such men as Coleridge, Taylor of Norwich, the Hebers, and later De Quincey, and Shelley, was attracted to the poem, and what was far more important, that friendship with Southey was secured to him, which overcame every discrepancy of character, survived every change of political opinion, and, though little fostered by personal intercourse, was constant to the last. 'Landor, my Landor,' Southey repeated softly to himself, when almost every name had passed from his perception. And Landor wrote, with pathetic conceit,

> 'Southey and I have run in the same traces,
> When we break down, what pair shall fill our places?'

Five years after *Gebir*, Landor printed at Warwick a small volume containing the commencement of another epic, on the story of the Phocæans, the invaders of Gaul who built Marseilles, with the same power of fragmentary imagery and thought compressed into obscurity. The beautiful address *To Tacæa* (Tachbrooke) given in these extracts, first appeared in these pages, but henceforth Landor's poetic faculty seems to have found no serious exercise, though there is a record of another similar 'fasciculus' called *Simonidia*, containing some admirable Latin verse, afterwards collected, and some English pieces addressed to certain objects of his admiration at Bath, where he resided for some time, under the then conventional names of 'Ione' and 'Ianthe.'

An expedition in aid of Spanish freedom elicited the tragedy of *Count Julian*, in which, and in later dramatic pieces, he showed none of the power of transformation and self-forgetfulness essential to a great dramatic writer, but every page contains some passage of no common order of thought or expression. His correspondence with Southey during this period abounds in poetical criticism of much interest, interspersed with such paradoxical judgments as the 'jargon of the flimsy and fantastic Spenser.'

The story of the purchase of Llanthony Abbey at the sacrifice of Tachbrooke, and its speedy abandonment—his hasty and ill-assorted marriage, of which he wrote

> 'The brightest stars are not the **best**
> To follow on the way to rest.'

—his flight from his friends and country—his subsequent wanderings in France and Italy—and his ultimate settlement on the beautiful slopes of Fiesole, is told by Mr. Forster with a combination of affectionate interest and biographic tact such as has fallen to the lot of few men of letters to secure. It was during this time that the felicitous project of the *Imaginary Conversations* was conceived and matured—a form of composition cognate to both his intellectual and moral peculiarities, and the success of which was almost a compensation for all the mischances of his outward and inner life. With such a vehicle for thought and language, no wonder that poetry was abandoned, and all his energies devoted to this great and appropriate work. Not that the habit which he had acquired and cultivated of casting into verse any pleasant, picturesque, humorous, or tender thought that suggested itself as appropriate was discontinued. 'As I had never drunk wine,' he had written, 'I am forced every now and then to write half a dozen verses that I may forget what is passing round about.' Some of these exercises had appeared in the scattered 'opuscula,' but it was mainly in his letters that they were inserted, and his correspondence was frequent and large. After the completion of the main body of the *Conversations*, the practice grew upon him to such an extent that these lyric and epigrammatic forms of verse became his chief literary occupation, and are the substance of several volumes published under quaint designations, while there are no doubt many still in manuscript in the hands of his friends or their representatives. Of them the best are of the very best, perhaps unsurpassed in our language, and in foreign literature only equalled by Voltaire and Goethe. In his later years he was pained by the thought that he had wasted in such trivialities something of the genius which might have been concentrated on higher purposes, and gave expression to this feeling very characteristically in a passage of an *Imaginary Conversation* between himself and one of his truest friends :—

WALTER LANDOR

It is objected that most of my poems are occasional. . . . .

ARCHDEACON HARE.

Of your poems the smaller alone are occasional : now not only are the smaller, but the best of Catullus and Horace, and all of Pindar. Were not the speeches of Lysias, Aeschines, Demosthenes, occasional? Draw nearer home. What but occasional were the Letters of Junius? *Materiem superabat opus.*

WALTER LANDOR.

True. The ministers and their king are now mould and worms ; they were little better when aboveground ; but the bag-wig and point-lace of Junius are suspended aloft upon a golden peg for curiosity and admiration.

ARCHDEACON HARE.

Regarding the occasional in poetry ; is there less merit in taking and treating what is before us, than in seeking and wandering through an open field as we would for mushrooms ?

WALTER LANDOR.

I stand out a rude rock in the middle of a river, with no exotic or parasitical plant on it, and few others. Eddies and dimples and froth and bubbles pass rapidly by, without shaking me. Here indeed is little room for picnic and polka.

ARCHDEACON HARE.

Praise and censure are received by you with nearly the same indifference.

WALTER LANDOR.

Not yours. Praise on poetry, said to be the most exhilarating of all, affects my brain but little. Certainly I never attempted to snatch ' the peculiar graces so generally delightful.' My rusticity has at least thus much of modesty in it.

It is interesting to observe how large a portion of these occasional poems are personal. Landor affected, or rather persuaded himself, that he felt not only an entire contempt for the opinions of others, but even a dislike to the general commerce of mankind, and yet there is hardly any one, even of his casual acquaintance, with whom he does not link himself on by some token of poetical sympathy. He had indeed written over the entrance of his Villa—

Hominum satis superque
Multi viderunt naturae nemo
Hospes introgreditur.
Et in parvis eam ut in maximis mirabilem
Pio animo heic et ubique contemplator;

and he poured out on the humblest objects of Nature an abundant tenderness that in a less vigorous temperament would have had the character of a morbid sentimentalism. The beautiful lines in which he deprecates the plucking of flowers will be found in the *Faesulan Idyl*, and the destruction of some sparrows elicited this solemn reprobation.

> Ah me! what rumour do I hear?
> It makes me shrivel up with fear.
> Can it—it never can—be true,
> That poison is prepared for *you*,
> Who clear the blossoms as they shoot
> And watch the bud and save the fruit?
> Turn, turn again your sideling eyes
> On one more grateful and more wise.

This is not the place to enlarge on Landor's command of the Latin language, which enabled him to use it for every purpose, and to adapt it to every theme, from the fables of Greek mythology to the incidents and characters of his own day. ' His style,' wrote Bishop Thirlwall, ' is not that either of the golden or the silver or of any earlier or later age of Latinity. It is the style of Landor, and it is marked with the stamp not only of his intellect, but of his personal idiosyncrasy. This is the cause of that obscurity which must be felt, even by scholars, to mar to some extent the enjoyment of his Latin poetry [1].' The composition of two delightful reviews on Catullus and Theocritus about 1842, accompanied by the necessity of translating certain passages into English, produced a revival of that peculiar alternation of classic and English expressions of poetic thought of which *Gebir* was the early illustration

---

[1] Landor's Latin poems belong to English literature, and thus two of his most perfect epigrams may be here appropriately inserted.

> 'Non ut ames—ut amere, peto, da, dulcis Ianthe;
> Est mihi, si merear, plura datura dies.'
>
> In *Philological Museum*, 1832.

VISIS IMAGINIBUS ROMANORUM VETERUM.

> ' Vos nudo capite atque vos saluto,
> Quae saltem estis imagines proborum,
> Ne, multis patriá procul diebus,
> Oblitus male moris usitati,
> Viso quolibet aut probo aut amico,
> Dicar rusticus ad meos reversus.'

Of these **one** of the first was the *Hamadryad*, a dramatic idyl of
the time when to every man the shapes of Nature were but the
reflections of his own, and in the Collection of all his writings during
the next three years he not only added other similar pieces, such
as the *Cymodameia*, but translated most of the Latin idyls already
printed with a force and ingenuity that left no trace of their
original form. These again were brought together in a volume
under the title of *Hellenics*, and others later under that of *Heroic
Idyls*, after he had returned to England in consequence of domestic
discomforts and had established himself once more at Bath, the
scene of his happiest youthful days. He returned once more to
Italy, and died at Florence in his 90th year.

The consummate grace of many of Landor's smaller pieces will
ever recommend them to the general reader, but the bulk of his
poetry can only be appreciated by those who possess cognate tastes
and something of similar acquisitions. There remains however a
just interest in this signal example of the enduring dominion of
the old classic forms of thought not only over the young imagination but over the matured and most cultivated intelligence. To
Keats they assimilated themselves almost without learning by a
certain natural affinity ; to the industrious and scholarly Landor
they became the lifelong vital forces not only of poetic generation
but of moral sustenance. They gave to his character the heroic
influences which alone subdued the wilfulness of his temperament,
and amid all the confusions of life kept his heart high and his fancy
pure. But they did not limit the powers they controlled : in the
Examination of Shakespeare he is the Englishman of the Elizabethan age, in the *Pentameron* the Italian of that of Petrarch and
Boccaccio, as even when most Greek and most Latin he is ever
Landor himself alone.

HOUGHTON.

[The peculiar orthography has been preserved in these extracts : it was adopted by Julius Hare, and by Connop Thirlwall in his earlier writings.]

THE SHELL.

[From *Gebir*, Book I.]

I am not daunted, no ; I will engage.
But first, said she, what wager will you lay?
A sheep, I answered, add whate'er you will.
I cannot, she replied, make that return :
Our hided vessels in their pitchy round
Seldom, unless from rapine, hold a sheep.
But I have sinuous shells of pearly hue
Within, and they that lustre have imbibed
In the Sun's palace-porch, where when unyoked
His chariot-wheel stands midway in the wave :
Shake one and it awakens, then apply
Its polisht lips to your attentive ear
And it remembers its august abodes,
And murmurs as the ocean murmurs there.

PRAYERS.

[From Book V.]

Ye men of Gades, armed with brazen shields,
And ye of near Tartessus, where the shore
Stoops to receive the tribute which all owe
To Baetis and his banks for their attire,
Ye too whom Durius bore on level meads,
Inherent in your hearts is bravery :
For Earth contains no nation where abounds
The generous horse and not the warlike man.
But neither soldier now nor steed avails :
Nor steed nor soldier can oppose the Gods :
Nor is there aught above like Jove himself,
Nor weighs against his purpose, when once fixt,
Aught but, with supplicating knee, the Prayers.
Swifter than light are they, and every face,

Tho' different, glows with beauty; at the throne
Of mercy, when clouds shut it from mankind,
They fall bare-bosom'd, and indignant Jove
Drops at the soothing sweetness of their voice
The thunder from his hand: let us arise
On these high places daily, beat our breast,
Prostrate ourselves and deprecate his wrath.

TAMAR AND THE NYMPH.

[From Book VI.]

' Oh seek not destin'd evils to divine,
Found out at last too soon! cease here the search,
'Tis vain, 'tis impious, 'tis no gift of mine;
I will impart far better, will impart
What makes, when Winter comes, the Sun to rest
So soon on Ocean's bed his paler brow,
And Night to tarry so at Spring's return.
And I will tell sometimes the fate of men
Who loos'd from drooping neck the restless arm
Adventurous, ere long nights had satisfied
The sweet and honest avarice of love;
How whirlpools have absorb'd them, storms o'erwhelm'd,
And how amid their struggles and their prayers
The big wave blacken'd o'er the mouth supine:
Then, when my Tamar trembles at the tale,
Kissing his lips half open with surprise,
Glance from the gloomy story, and with glee
Light on the fairer fables of the Gods.
—Thus we may sport at leisure when we go
Where, loved by Neptune and the Naiad, loved
By pensive Dryad pale, and Oread
The sprightly nymph whom constant Zephyr woos,
Rhine rolls his beryl-colour'd wave; than Rhine
What river from the mountains ever came
More stately? most the simple crown adorns
Of rushes and of willows intertwined
With here and there a flower: his lofty brow

Shaded with vines and mistleto and oak
He rears, and mystic bards his fame resound.
Or gliding opposite, th' Illyrian gulf
Will harbour us from ill.' While thus she spake,
She toucht his eyelashes with libant lip,
And breath'd ambrosial odours, o'er his cheek
Celestial warmth suffusing : grief dispersed,
And strength and pleasure beam'd upon his brow.
Then pointed she before him : first arose
To his astonisht and delighted view
The sacred ile that shrines the queen of love.
It stood so near him, so acute each sense,
That not the symphony of lutes alone
Or coo serene or billing strife of doves,
But murmurs, whispers, nay the very sighs
Which he himself had utter'd once, he heard.
Next, but long after and far off, appear
The cloudlike cliffs and thousand towers of Crete,
And further to the right, the Cyclades :
Phoebus had rais'd and fixt them, to surround
His native Delos and aerial fane.
He saw the land of Pelops, host of Gods,
Saw the steep ridge where Corinth after stood
Beckoning the serious with the smiling Arts
Into the sunbright bay; unborn the maid
That to assure the bent-up hand unskilled
Lookt oft, but oftener tearing who might wake.
He heard the voice of rivers ; he descried
Pindan Peneus and the slender nymphs
That tread his banks but fear the thundering tide ;
These, and Amphrysos and Apidanus
And poplar-crown'd Spercheus, and reclined
On restless rocks Enipeus, where the winds
Scatter'd above the weeds his hoary hair.
Then, with Pirene and with Panope
Evenus, troubled from paternal tears,
And last was Achelous, king of iles.
Zacynthus here, above rose Ithaca,
Like a blue bubble floating in the bay.

Far onward to the left a glimm'ring light
Glanced out oblique, nor vanisht; he inquired
Whence that arose, his consort thus replied.
'Behold the vast Eridanus! ere long
We may again behold him and rejoice.
Of noble rivers none with mightier force
Rolls his unwearied torrent to the main.'
And now Sicanian Etna rose to view:
Darkness with light more horrid she confounds,
Baffles the breath and dims the sight of day.
Tamar grew giddy with astonishment
And, looking up, held fast the bridal vest;
He heard the roar above him, heard the roar
Beneath, and felt it too, as he beheld,
Hurl, from Earth's base, rocks, mountains, to the skies.

To Tacæa.

To-morrow, brightest-eyed of Avon's train,
To-morrow thou art slavelike bound and sold,
Another's and another's; haste away,
Winde through the willows, dart along the path,
It nought avails thee, nought our plaint avails.
O happy those before me, who could say,
'Short though thy period, sweet Tacæa, short
Ere thou art destined to the depths below,
Thou passest half thy sunny hours with me.'
I mourn not, envy not, what others gain,
Thee, and thy venerable elms I mourn,
Thy old protectors, ruthless was the pride,
And gaunt the need that bade their heads lie low.
I see the meadow's tender grass start back,
See from their prostrate trunks the gory glare.
Ah! pleasant was it once to watch thy waves
Swelling o'er pliant beds of glossy weed;
Pleasant to watch them dip amid the stones,
Chirp, and spring over, glance and gleam along,
And tripping light their wanton way pursue.

Methinks they now with mellow mournfulness
Bid their faint breezes chide my fond delay,
Nor suffer on the bridge nor on the knee
My poor irregularly pencilled page.
Alas, Tacæa, thou art sore deceived!
Here are no foren words, no fatal seal,
But thou and all who hear me shall avow
The simple notes of sorrow's song are here.

FÆSULAN IDYL.

Here, when precipitate Spring with one light bound
Into hot Summer's lusty arms expires;
And where go forth at morn, at eve, at night,
Soft airs, that want the lute to play with them,
And softer sighs, that know not what they want;
Under a wall, beneath an orange tree
Whose tallest flowers could tell the lowlier ones
Of sights in Fiesole right up above,
While I was gazing a few paces off
At what they seemed to show me with their nods,
Their frequent whispers and their pointing shoots,
A gentle maid came down the garden steps
And gathered the pure treasure in her lap.
I heard the branches rustle, and stept forth
To drive the ox away, or mule, or goat,
(Such I believed it must be); for sweet scents
Are the swift vehicles of still sweeter thoughts,
And nurse and pillow the dull memory
That would let drop without them her best stores.
They bring me tales of youth and tones of love,
And 'tis and ever was my wish and way
To let all flowers live freely, and all die,
Whene'er their Genius bids their souls depart,
Among their kindred in their native place.
I never pluck the rose; the violet's head
Hath shaken with my breath upon its bank
And not reproacht me; the ever-sacred cup

Of the pure lily hath between my hands
Felt safe, unsoiled, nor lost one grain of gold.
I saw the light that made the glossy leaves
More glossy; the fair arm, the fairer cheek
Warmed by the eye intent on its pursuit;
I saw the foot, that although half-erect
From its grey slippers, could not lift her up
To what she wanted; I held down a branch,
And gathered her some blossoms, since their hour
Was come, and bees had wounded them, and flies
Of harder wing were working their way through
And scattering them in fragments under foot.
So crisp were some, they rattled unevolved,
Others, ere broken off, fell into shells,
For such appear the petals when detacht,
Unbending, brittle, lucid, white like snow,
And like snow not seen through, by eye or sun;
Yet every one her gown received from me
Was fairer than the first; . . . . I thought not so,
But so she praised them to reward my care,
I said: *you find the largest.*

This indeed,

Cried she, *is large and sweet.*

She held one forth,

Whether for me to look at or to take
She knew not, nor did I; but taking it
Would best have solved (and this she felt) her doubts,
I dared not touch it; for it seemed a part
Of her own self; fresh, full, the most mature
Of blossoms, yet a blossom; with a touch
To fall, and yet unfallen.

She drew back

The boon she tendered, and then, finding not
The ribbon at her waist to fix it in,
Dropt it, as loth to drop it, on the rest.

IPHIGENEIA AND AGAMEMNON.

Iphigeneia, when she heard her doom
At Aulis, and when all beside the King
Had gone away, took his right hand, and said,
'O father! I am young and very happy.
I do not think the pious Calchas heard
Distinctly what the Goddess spake. Old-age
Obscures the senses. If my nurse, who knew
My voice so well, sometimes misunderstood
While I was resting on her knee both arms
And hitting it to make her mind my words,
And looking in her face, and she in mine,
Might he not also hear one word amiss,
Spoken from so far off, even from Olympus?'
The father placed his cheek upon her head,
And tears dropt down it, but the king of men
Replied not. Then the maiden spake once more.
'O father! sayst thou nothing? Hear'st thou not
Me, whom thou ever hast, until this hour,
Listened to fondly, and awakened me
To hear my voice amid the voice of birds,
When it was inarticulate as theirs,
And the down deadened it within the nest?'
He moved her gently from him, silent still,
And this, and this alone, brought tears from her,
Although she saw fate nearer: then with sighs,
'I thought to have laid down my hair before
Benignant Artemis, and not have dimmed
Her polisht altar with my virgin blood;
I thought to have selected the white flowers
To please the Nymphs, and to have asked of each
By name, and with no sorrowful regret,
Whether, since both my parents willed the change,
I might at Hymen's feet bend my clipt brow;
And (after those who mind us girls the most)
Adore our own Athena, that she would

Regard me mildly with her azure eyes.
But, father! to see you no more, and see
Your love, O father! go ere I am gone.' . . .
Gently he moved her off, and drew her back,
Bending his lofty head far over hers,
And the dark depths of nature heaved and burst.
He turned away; not far, but silent still.
She now first shuddered; for in him, so nigh,
So long a silence seemed the approach of death,
And like it. Once again she raised her voice.
'O father! if the ships are now detained,
And all your vows move not the Gods above,
When the knife strikes me there will be one prayer
The less to them: and purer can there be
Any, or more fervent than the daughter's prayer
For her dear father's safety and success?'
A groan that shook him shook not his resolve.
An aged man now entered, and without
One word, stept slowly on, and took the wrist
Of the pale maiden. She looked up, and saw
The fillet of the priest and calm cold eyes.
Then turned she where her parent stood, and cried
'O father! grieve no more: the ships can sail.'

THE DEATH OF ARTEMIDORA.

'Artemidora! Gods invisible,
  While thou art lying faint along the couch,
  Have tied the sandal to thy slender feet
And stand beside thee, ready to convey
  Thy weary steps where other rivers flow.
  Refreshing shades will waft thy weariness
  Away, and voices like thy own come near
And nearer, and solicit an embrace.'
Artemidora sighed, and would have prest
  The hand now pressing hers, but was too weak
Trio stood over her dark hair unseen
  While thus Elpenor spoke. He lookt into

Eyes that had given light and life erewhile
  To those above them, but now dim with tears
And wakefulness. Again he spake of joy
  Eternal. At that word, that sad word, *joy*,
Faithful and fond her bosom heaved once more ;
Her head fell back ; and now a loud deep sob
Swelled thro' the darkened chamber ; 'twas not hers.

CORINNA, FROM ATHENS, TO TANAGRA

[From *Pericles and Aspasia*.]

I.

Tanagra ! think not I forget
  Thy beautifully-storied streets;
Be sure my memory bathes yet
  In clear Thermodon, and yet greets
The blythe and liberal shepherd boy,
Whose sunny bosom swells with joy
When we accept his matted rushes
Upheaved with sylvan fruit ; away he bounds, and blushes.

2.

I promise to bring back with me
  What thou with transport will receive,
The only proper gift for thee,
  Of which no mortal shall bereave
In later times thy mouldering walls,
Until the last old turret falls ;
A crown, a crown from Athens won,
A crown no god can wear, beside Latona's son.

3.

There may be cities who refuse
  To their own child the honours due,
And look ungently on the Muse ;
  But ever shall those cities rue

The dry, unyielding, niggard breast,
Offering no nourishment, no rest,
To that young head which soon shall rise
Disdainfully, in might and glory, to the skies.

4.

Sweetly where caverned Dirce flows
    Do white-armed maidens chaunt my lay,
Flapping the while with laurel-rose
    The honey-gathering tribes away;
And sweetly, sweetly, Attick tongues
Lisp your Corinna's early songs;
To her with feet more graceful come
The verses that have dwelt in kindred breasts at home.

5.

O let thy children lean aslant
    Against the tender mother's knee,
And gaze into her face, and want
    To know what magic there can be
In words that urge some eyes to dance,
While others as in holy trance
Look up to heaven; be such my praise!
Why linger? I must haste, or lose the Delphick bays.

CLEONE TO ASPASIA.

We mind not how the sun in the mid-sky
    Is hastening on; but when the golden orb
Strikes the extreme of earth, and when the gulphs
    Of air and ocean open to receive him,
Dampness and gloom invade us; then we think
    Ah! thus it is with youth. Too fast his feet
Run on for sight; hour follows hour; fair maid
    Succeeds fair maid; bright eyes bestar his couch;
The cheerful horn awakens him; the feast,
    The revel, the entangling dance, allure,

And voices mellower than the Muse's own
  Heap up his buoyant bosom on their wave.
A little while, and then . . . . Ah youth! youth! **youth!**
  Listen not to my words . . . but stay with me!
When thou art gone, Life may go too ; the sigh
  That rises is for thee, and not for Life.

THE MAID'S LAMENT.

[From the *Examination of Shakespeare.*]

I loved him not ; and yet now he is gone
  I feel I am alone.
I checked him while he spoke ; yet could he speak,
  Alas, I would not check.
For reasons not to love him once I sought
  And wearied all my thought
To vex myself and him ; I now would give
  My love, could he but live
Who lately lived for me, and when he found
  'Twas vain, in holy ground
He hid his face amid the shades of death.
  I waste for him my breath
Who wasted his for me ; but mine returns,
  And this lorn bosom burns
With stifling heat, heaving it up in sleep,
  And waking me to weep
Tears that had melted his soft heart; for years
  Wept he as bitter tears.
'Merciful God!' such was his latest prayer,
  'These may she never share!'
Quieter is his breath, his breast more cold
  Than daisies in the mould,
Where children spell, athwart the churchyard gate,
  His name, and life's brief date.
Pray for him, gentle souls, whoe'er you be,
  And, O, pray too for me.

Ye who have toiled uphill to reach the haunt
Of other men who lived in other days,
Whether the ruins of a citadel
Raised on the summit by Pelasgic hands,
Or chamber of the distaff and the song . . . . .
Ye will not tell what treasure there ye found,
But I will.
         Ye found there the viper laid
Full-length, flat-headed, on a sunny slab,
Nor loth to hiss at ye while crawling down.
Ye saw the owl flap the loose ivy leaves
And, hooting, shake the berries on your heads.
  Now, was it worth your while to mount so high?
Merely to say ye did it, and to ask
If those about ye ever did the like?
Believe me, O my friends, 'twere better far
To stretch your limbs along the level sand
As they do, where small children scoop the drift,
Thinking it must be gold, where curlews soar
And scales drop glistening from the prey above.

Twenty years hence my eyes may grow
If not quite dim, yet rather so,
Yet yours from others they shall know
      Twenty years hence.

Twenty years hence, though it may hap
That I be called to take a nap
In a cool cell where thunder clap
      Was never heard,

There breathe but o'er my arch of grass,
A not too sadly sighed 'Alas!'
And I shall catch ere you can pass
      That wingèd word.

Lately our poets loitered in green lanes,
Content to catch the ballad of the plains;
　I fancied I had strength enough to climb
　A loftier station at no distant time,
And might securely from intrusion doze
　Upon the flowers thro' which Ilissus flows.
In those pale olive grounds all voices cease,
　And from afar dust fills the paths of Greece.
My slumber broken and my doublet torn,
　I find the laurel also bears a thorn.

When Helen first saw wrinkles in her face
('Twas when some fifty long had settled there
And intermarried and brancht off awide),
She threw herself upon her couch, and wept;
On this side hung her head, and over that
Listlessly she let fall the faithless brass
That made the men as faithless.

　　　　　　　　　　But when you
Found them, or fancied them, and would not hear
That they were only vestiges of smiles,
Or the impression of some amorous hair
Astray from cloistered curls and roseat band,
Which had been lying there all night perhaps
Upon a skin so soft　　*No, no*, you said,
Sure, they are coming, yes, are come, are here . . .
Well, and what matters it . . . while you are too!

Say ye, that years roll on and ne'er return?
Say ye, the Sun who leaves them all behind,
Their great creator, cannot bring one back
With all his force, tho' he draw worlds around?...
Witness me, little streams! that meet before
My happy dwelling; witness, Africo

And Mensola! that ye have seen at once
Twenty roll back, twenty as swift and bright
As are your swiftest and your brightest waves,
When the tall cypress o'er the Doccia
Hurls from his inmost boughs the latent snow.
　Go, and go happy, pride of my past days
And solace of my present, thou whom Fate
Alone hath severed from me! One step higher
Must yet be mounted, high as was the last;
Friendship, with faltering accent, says Depart!
And take the highest seat below the crowned.

FRIENDS.

How often, when life's summer day
　Is waning, and its sun descends,
Wisdom drives laughing wit away,
　And lovers shrivel into friends!

───────

You smiled, you spoke, and I believed,
By every word and smile deceived.
Another man would hope no more—
Nor hope I what I hoped before:
But let not this last wish be vain,
Deceive—deceive me once again!

───────

There are who say we are but dust,
　We may be soon, but are not yet,
Nor should be while in Love we trust
　And never what he taught forget.

───────

Why, why repine, my pensive friend,
　At pleasures slipt away?
Some the stern Fates will never lend,
　And all refuse to stay.

I see the rainbow in the sky,
    The dew upon the grass ;
I see them, and I ask not why
    They glimmer or they pass.

With folded arms I linger not
    To call them back—'twere vain :
In this, or in some other spot
    I know they'll shine again.

CHILDREN PLAYING IN A CHURCHYARD.

Children, keep up that harmless play,
Your kindred angels plainly say
By God's authority ye may.

Be prompt his Holy word to hear,
It teaches you to banish fear ·
The lesson lies on all sides near.

Ten summers hence the sprightliest lad
In Nature's face will look more sad,
And ask where are those smiles she had ?

Ere many days the last will close.
Play on, play on, for then (who knows ?)
Ye who play here may here repose.

———

Ah ! what avails the sceptered race !
    Ah ! what the form divine !
What every virtue, every grace !
    Rose Aylmer, all were thine.

Rose Aylmer, whom these wakeful eyes
    May weep, but never see,
A night of memories and sighs
    I consecrate to thee.

On Southey's Death.

Friends, hear the words my wandering thoughts would say
And cast them into shape some other day ;
Southey, my friend of forty years, is gone,
And, shattered by the fall, I stand alone.

———

An aged man who loved to doze away
An hour by daylight, for his eyes were dim,
And he had seen too many suns go down
And rise again, dreamt that he saw two forms
Of radiant beauty ; he would clasp them both,
But both flew stealthily away.   He cried
In his wild dream,
      ' I never thought, O youth,
That thou, altho' so cherisht, would'st return,
But I did think that he who came with thee,
Love, who could swear more sweetly than birds sing,
Would never leave me comfortless and lone.'
A sigh broke through his slumber, not the last.

For an Epitaph at Fiesole.

Lo! where the four mimosas blend their shade,
 In calm repose at last is Landor laid ;
For ere he slept he saw them planted here
 By her his soul had ever held most dear,
And he had lived enough when he had dried her tear.

BRYAN WALLER PROCTER.

[BRYAN WALLER PROCTER was born in London Nov. 21, 1787. He was educated, with Byron, at Harrow; studied as a solicitor in the country; returned to London to live in 1807. His period of literary activity extended from 1815 to 1823. In 1832 he was made Metropolitan Commissioner of Lunacy, a post which he resigned in 1861. He died Oct. 4, 1874. His principal works. all published under the pseudonym of Barry Cornwall, are *Dramatic Scenes,* 1819; *Marcian Colonna,* 1820; *A Sicilian Story,* 1821; *Mirandola,* 1821; *The Flood of Thessaly,* 1823; *English Songs,* 1832.]

Barry Cornwall was a very fluent and accomplished **artist in verse** rather than what we usually understand by a poet. He **had** nothing bardic or prophetic in his nature, he was burdened **with** no special message to mankind, and he gave no sign of ever feeling very strongly on any particular point or occasion. The critic is curiously baffled in seeking for a poetical or personal individuality in his verse, for he never seems to be expressing anything in his own person. This negative quality forms the chief characteristic of his best work, his *English Songs.* All other known lyrists have either recorded in their songs their personal experiences in emotion, or they have so framed their verses as to seem to do so ; Barry Cornwall alone has contrived to write songs of a purely and obviously impersonal and artificial kind, dealing dramatically with feelings which the poet does not himself pretend to experience. His fragments of drama are lyrical, his lyrics dramatic, and each class suffers somewhat from this intrusion into the domain of the other. We hardly do justice to the merit of verse which is so impartial as to become almost uninteresting, and Procter has suffered from his retiring modesty no less than other poets from their arrogance. His lyrics do not possess passion or real pathos or any very deep magic of melody, but he has written more songs that deserve the comparative praise of *good* than any other modern writer except Shelley and Tennyson. There is a sort of literary insincerity about Barry Cornwall's verse that found no counterpart in the beautiful character of Mr. Procter. We wonder at rapturous addresses to the ocean,

> 'I'm on the Sea! I'm on the Sea!
> I am where I would ever be,'

from the landsman who could never, in the course of a long life, venture on the voyage from Dover to Calais, and at bursts of vinous enthusiasm from the most temperate of valetudinarians ; but the poet would have defended his practice by his own curious theory that 'those songs are most natural which do not proceed from the author in person.' Procter's verse has been much admired and much neglected, and will never, in all probability, gain the ear of the public again to any great extent. His merits are more than considerable, but the mild lustrous beauty of his verse is scarcely vivid enough to attract much attention. There would be more to say about his writings if they were less faultless and refined.

EDMUND W. GOSSE.

For Music.

Now whilst he dreams, O Muses, wind him round !
  Send down thy silver words, O murmuring Rain !
Haunt him, sweet Music ! Fall, with gentlest sound,--
  Like dew, like night, upon his weary brain !
Come, Odours of the rose and violet,--bear
Into his charmed sleep all visions fair !
So may the lost be found,
So may his thoughts by tender Love be crowned,
And Hope come shining like a vernal morn,
And with its beams adorn
The Future, till he breathes diviner air,
In some soft Heaven of joy, beyond the range of Care !

The Sea.

The Sea ! the Sea ! the open Sea !
The blue, the fresh, the ever free !
Without a mark, without a bound,
It runneth the earth's wide regions 'round ;
It plays with the clouds ; it mocks the skies ;
Or like a cradled creature lies.

I'm on the Sea ! I'm on the Sea !
I am where I would ever be ;
With the blue above, and the blue below,
And silence wheresoe'er I go ;
If a storm should come and awake the deep,
What matter ? *I* shall ride and sleep.

I love (oh ! *how* I love) to ride
On the fierce foaming bursting tide,
When every mad wave drowns the moon,
Or whistles aloft his tempest tune,
And tells how goeth the world below,
And why the south-west blasts do blow.

I never was on the dull tame shore,
But I lov'd the great Sea more and more,
And backwards flew to her billowy breast,
Like a bird that seeketh its mother's nest ;
And a mother she *was*, and *is* to me ;
For I was born on the open Sea !

The waves were white, and red the morn,
In the noisy hour when I was born ;
And the whale it whistled, the porpoise rolled,
And the dolphins bared their backs of gold ;
And never was heard such an outcry wild
As welcomed to life the Ocean-child !

I've lived since then, in calm and strife,
Full fifty summers a sailor's life,
With wealth to spend and a power to range,
But never have sought, nor sighed for change ;
And Death, whenever he come to me,
Shall come on the wide unbounded Sea !

A Bacchanalian Song.

Sing !—Who sings
To her who weareth a hundred rings ?
　Ah, who is this lady fine ?
　The VINE, boys, the VINE !
　The mother of mighty Wine.
　　A roamer is she
　　O'er wall and tree,
And sometimes very good company.

Drink !—Who drinks
To her who blusheth and never thinks ?
　Ah ! who is this maid of thine ?
　The GRAPE, boys, the GRAPE !
　O, never let her escape
　Until she be turned to Wine !
　　For better is she,
　　Than vine can be,
And very very good company !

Dream !—who dreams
Of the God that governs a thousand streams ?
  Ah, who is this Spirit fine ?
  'Tis WINE, boys, 'tis WINE !
  God Bacchus, a friend of mine.
    O better is he
    Than grape or tree,
And the best of all good company.

A REPOSE.

She sleeps amongst her pillows soft,
  (A dove, now wearied with her flight),
And all around, and all aloft,
  Hang flutes and folds of virgin white :
Her hair out-darkens the dark night,
  Her glance out-shines the starry sky ;
But now her locks are hidden quite,
  And closed is her fringed eye !

She sleepeth : wherefore doth she start ?
  She sigheth ; doth she feel no pain ?
None, none ! the Dream is near her heart ;
  The Spirit of sleep is in her brain.
He cometh down like golden rain,
  Without a wish, without a sound ;
He cheers the sleeper (ne'er in vain),
  Like May, when earth is winter bound.

All day within some cave he lies,
  Dethroned from his nightly sway,—
Far fading when the dawning skies
  Our souls with wakening thoughts array.
Two Spirits of might doth man obey ;
  By each he's wrought, from each he learns ;
The one is Lord of life by day ;
  The other when starry Night returns.

INSCRIPTION FOR A FOUNTAIN.

Rest ! This little Fountain runs
   Thus for aye :—It never stays
For the look of summer suns,
   Nor the cold of winter days.
Whosoe'er shall wander near,
   When the Syrian heat is worst,
Let him hither come, nor fear
   Lest he may not slake his thirst :
He will find this little river
Running still, as bright as ever.
Let him drink, and onwards hie,
Bearing but in thought, that I,
EROTAS, bade the Naiad fall,
And thank the great god Pan for all !

A PETITION TO TIME.

Touch us gently, Time !
   Let us glide adown thy stream
Gently,—as we sometimes glide
   Through a quiet dream !
Humble voyagers are We,
Husband, wife, and children three—
(One is lost,—an angel, fled
To the azure overhead !)

Touch us gently, Time !
   We've not proud nor soaring wings ;
Our ambition, *our* content
   Lies in simple things.
Humble voyagers are We,
O'er Life's dim unsounded sea,
Seeking only some calm clime :—
Touch us *gently*, gentle Time !

EBENEZER ELLIOTT.

[Born 17th of March, 1781, at the New Foundry, Masbro', near Rother-
ham, Yorkshire; wrote in his seventeenth year *The Vernal Walk*; worked
in his father's foundry until 1804; made trials of business in Sheffield, of
which the first failed; published his first volume of verse, 1823; *Village
Patriarch*, 1829; *Corn Law Rhymer*, 1831; retired from business, 1841;
died 1st of December, 1849.]

'My feelings have been hammered until they have become *cold-
short*, and are apt to snap and fly off in sarcasms.' The betrayal
of sensitiveness, the apology for anger in these words, might lead
one to surmise that the writer, Ebenezer Elliott, steel-merchant
and poet, was no broad-thewed forger of the weapons of revolution
who took to his trade with a will. Had one met him, instead
of the 'burly ironmonger' described by an American visitor,
one would have seen a man slender and of middle stature, with
narrow forehead, bushy eyebrows under which gleamed the
vivid fire of grey-blue eyes, sensitive nostrils, and a mouth apt to
express love as much as scorn. It was not the bread-tax that first
made him a poet, but the picture of a primrose in Sowerby's
English Botany; this sent him to country lanes, the stream-side,
and the moor, and he found his friends in the dragon-fly, the king-
fisher, the green snake, and the nightingales of Basingthorpe
Spring. Sensitiveness was more Elliott's characteristic than
strength, and what strength he had was of an ardent, eager kind,
less muscular than nervous.

Elliott's imagination was ambitious, and imperfectly trained : he
accordingly dealt with large and passionate themes, entering into
them with complete *abandon*; and he was hurried on to passages
of genuine inspiration; real heights and depths were within his
range; heavenly lights alternate with nether darkness. Few of
his longer poems, however, possess imaginative ordonnance; from
the sublime he could pass to the turgid; from the pathetic to

the pseudo-romantic ; and therefore few of these longer poems can be read with satisfaction in each as a whole. Nothing of worth that Elliott wrote was caught out of the air ; each poem had its roots in fact ; but the colouring in his earlier pieces is sometimes extravagant : as he matured, his imagination gravitated from the romantic to the real. There are not many figures in English poetry drawn from real life worthier of regard than the Ranter, Elliott's pale preacher of reform on Shirecliffe height, and his Village Patriarch, the blind lone father, with wind-blown venerable hair, still unbowed after his hundred years ; though seeming coeval with the cliffs around, still a living and heroic pattern of English manhood.

The wild flowers and the free wild streams of Yorkshire never found a more eager and faithful lover than Ebenezer Elliott ; but mere sunlight and pure air delight him. The silence or living sounds of the fields or the moor bring healing and refreshment to an ear harassed by the din of machinery ; the wide peaceful brightness is a benediction to an eye smarting from blear haze of the myriad-chimneyed city. Animal refreshment rises, by degrees, to gratitude, exaltation, worship.

But from the wilderness his heart full of passionate tenderness drew him back to the troubled walks of men. His poetry could not be like

> ' The child
> That gathers daisies from the lap of May,
> With prattle sweeter than the bloomy wild.'

The indignation of the workers of England against the injustice of their lot found a voice in the Corn Law Rhymer. His anger is that of a sweet nature perforce turned bitter ; this strife, he feels, may for ever mar his better self, yet it cannot be abandoned :—

> 'My heart, once soft as woman's tear, is gnarled
> With gloating on the ills I cannot cure ;'

and still he ' wooes Contention,' for in the end ' her dower is sure.' The sorrows of oppressed toil were sung by Elliott with a sincerity which makes amends for some imaginative crudeness. His pathos is not hard and dry like that of Crabbe ; it is not that of a student of human misery, but that of a loving fellow-sufferer. And his ideal of happiness for the working man is simple and refined— some leisure, flowers, a good book, a neat home, a happy wife, and glad innocent children.

EDWARD DOWDEN.

An Excursion to the Mountains.

[From *The Village Patriarch.*]

I.

Come, Father of the Hamlet ! grasp again
Thy stern ash plant, cut when the woods were young ;
Come, let us leave the plough-subjected plain,
And rise, with freshened hearts, and nerves restrung,
Into the azure dome, that, haply, hung
O'er thoughtful power, ere suffering had begun.

II.

Flowers peep, trees bud, boughs tremble, rivers run ;
The redwing saith, it is a glorious morn.
Blue are thy Heavens, thou Highest ! and thy sun
Shines without cloud, all fire. How sweetly, borne
On wings of morning o'er the leafless thorn,
The tiny wren's small twitter warbles near !
How swiftly flashes in the stream the trout !
Woodbine ! our father's ever-watchful ear
Knows, by thy rustle, that thy leaves are out.
The trailing bramble hath not yet a sprout ;
Yet harshly to the wind the wanton prates,
Not with thy smooth lisp, woodbine of the fields !
Thou future treasure of the bee, that waits
Gladly on thee, spring's harbinger ! when yields
All bounteous earth her odorous flowers, and builds
The nightingale, in beauty's fairest land.

III.

Five rivers, like the fingers of a hand,
Flung from black mountains, mingle, and are one
Where sweetest valleys quit the wild and grand,
And eldest forests, o'er the silvan Don,
Bid their immortal brother journey on,

A stately pilgrim, watched by all the hills.
Say, shall we wander where, through warriors' graves,
The infant Yewden, mountain-cradled, trills
Her doric notes? Or, where the Locksley raves
Of broil and battle, and the rocks and caves
Dream yet of ancient days? Or, where the sky
Darkens o'er Rivilin, the clear and cold,
That throws his blue length, like a snake, from high?
Or, where deep azure brightens into gold
O'er Sheaf, that mourns in Eden? Or, where rolled
On tawny sands, through regions passion-wild,
And groves of love, in jealous beauty dark,
Complains the Porter, Nature's thwarted child,
Born in the waste, like headlong Wiming? Hark!
The poised hawk calls thee, Village Patriarch!
He calls thee to his mountains! Up, away!
Up, up, to Stanedge! higher still ascend,
Till kindred rivers, from the summit grey,
To distant seas their course in beauty bend,
And, like the lives of human millions, blend
Disparted waves in one immensity!

SONG.

Child, is thy father dead?
  Father is gone!
Why did they tax his bread?
  God's will be done!
Mother has sold her bed:
Better to die than wed!
Where shall she lay her head?
  Home we have none!

Father clammed[1] thrice a week—
  God's will be done!
Long for work did he seek,
  Work he found none.

  [1] Fasted; was hungry.

Tears on his hollow cheek
Told what no tongue could speak:
Why did his master break?
   God's will be done!

Doctor said air was best—
   Food we had none ;
Father, with panting breast,
   Groaned to be gone :
Now he is with the blest—
Mother says death is best !
We have no place of rest—
   Yes, we have one !

BATTLE SONG.

Day, like our souls, is fiercely dark ;
   What then ? 'Tis day !
We sleep no more ; the cock crows—hark !
   To arms ! away !
They come ! they come ! the knell is rung
   Of us or them ;
Wide o'er their march the pomp is flung
   Of gold and gem.
What collared hound of lawless sway,
   To famine dear—
What pensioned slave of Attila,
   Leads in the rear?
Come they from Scythian wilds afar,
   Our blood to spill ?
Wear they the livery of the Czar ?
   They do his will.
Nor tasselled silk, nor epaulette,
   Nor plume, nor torse—
No splendour gilds, all sternly met,
   Our foot and horse.
But, dark and still, we inly glow,
   Condensed in ire !

Strike, tawdry slaves, and ye shall know
    Our gloom is fire.
In vain your pomp, ye evil powers,
    Insults the land ;
Wrongs, vengeance, and *the cause* are ours,
    And God's right hand !
Madmen ! they trample into snakes
    The wormy clod,
Like fire, beneath their feet awakes
    The sword of God !
Behind, before, above, below,
    They rouse the brave ;
Where'er they go, they make a foe,
    Or find a grave.

A POET'S EPITAPH.

Stop, Mortal ! Here thy brother lies,
    The Poet of the Poor.
His books were rivers, woods, and skies,
    The meadow, and the moor ;
His teachers were the torn hearts' wail,
    The tyrant and the slave,
The street, the factory, the jail,
    The palace—and the grave !
The meanest thing, earth's feeblest worm,
    He feared to scorn or hate ;
And honoured in a peasant's form
    The equal of the great.
But if he loved the rich who make
    The poor man's little more,
Ill could he praise the rich who take
    From plundered labour's store.
A hand to do, a head to plan,
    A heart to feel and dare—
Tell man's worst foes, here lies the man
    Who drew them as they are.

THE THREE MARYS AT CASTLE HOWARD, IN 1812 AND 1837.

The lifeless son--the mother's agony,
O'erstrained till agony refused to feel—
That sinner too I *then* dry-eyed could see;
For I was hardened in my selfish weal,
And strength and joy had strung my soul with steel.
I knew not then what man may live to be,
A thing of life, that feels he lives in vain—
A taper, to be quenched in misery!
Forgive me, then, Caracci! if I seek
To look on this, thy tale of tears, again;
For now the swift is slow, the strong is weak.
Mother of Christ! how merciful is pain!
But if I longer view thy tear-stained cheek,
Heart-broken Magdalen! my heart will break.

PLAINT.

Dark, deep, and cold the current flows
Unto the sea where no wind blows,
Seeking the land which no one knows.

O'er its sad gloom still comes and goes
The mingled wail of friends and foes,
Borne to the land which no one knows.

Why shrieks for help yon wretch, who goes
With millions, from a world of woes,
Unto the land which no one knows?

Though myriads go with him who goes,
Alone he goes where no wind blows,
Unto the land which no one knows.

For all must go where no wind blows,
And none can go for him who goes;
None, none return whence no one knows.

Yet why should he who shrieking goes
With millions, from a world of woes,
Reunion seek with it or those ?

Alone with God, where no wind blows,
And Death, his shadow—doomed, he goes :
That God is there the shadow shows.

Oh, shoreless Deep, where no wind blows !
And, thou, oh, Land which no one knows !
That God is All, His shadow shows.

JOHN KEBLE[1]

[JOHN KEBLE was born on St. Mark's Day (April 25), 1792, at Fairford, in Gloucestershire. He was elected Scholar of Corpus, Oxford, in his fifteenth, and Fellow of Oriel in his nineteenth year. After a few years of tutorship at Oxford and curacy in the country, he became Vicar of Hursley in Hampshire in 1839, where he continued to minister till his death in 1866. He was with Dr. Newman and Dr. Pusey regarded as forming the Triumvirate of the Oxford Catholic movement. His prose works consist of an elaborate edition of *Hooker*, a careful *Life of Bishop Wilson*, and various theological treatises. But it is as a poet much more than a scholar or a controversialist that he is known; and of his poetical works, the *Lyra Innocentium*, the *Translation of the Psalter*, a posthumous volume of *Poems*, and *The Christian Year* (1827), it is by the last that he acquired an universal and undying fame in English literature. As Professor of Poetry at Oxford he wrote in Latin *Praelections on Poetry*, which are remarkable both for their subtlety and their exquisite Latinity.

His Life was written by his friend Mr. Justice Coleridge.]

Keble was not merely, like Isaac Watts or Charles Wesley, a writer of hymns. He was a real poet. Their works, no doubt, have occasional flashes of poetry, but their main object is didactic, devotional, theological. Not so the *Christian Year*, the *Lyra Innocentinm*, or the *Psalter*. Very few of his verses can be used in public worship. His hymns are the exception. His originality lies in the fact that whilst the subjects which he touches are for the most part consecrated by religious usage or Biblical allusion, yet he grasps them not chiefly or exclusively as a theologian, or a Churchman, but as a poet. The *Lyra Innocentium*, whilst its more limited range of subjects, and perhaps its more subtle turn of thought, will always exclude it from the rank occupied by the

---

[1] The bulk of this notice appeared in the writer's *Essays on Church and State*.

Christian Year, has more of the true fire of genius, more of the true rush of poetic diction. The *Psalter* again differs essentially from Sternhold and Hopkins, Tate and Brady, not merely in execution, but in design. It is the only English example of a rendering of Hebrew poetry by one who was himself a poet, with the full appreciation of the poetical thought as well as of the spiritual life which lies enshrined in the deep places of the *Psalter*. A striking instance of this is the version of the 93rd Psalm. The general subject of that Psalm must be obvious to every one in any translation, however meagre. But it required the magic touch of a kindred spirit to bring out of the rugged Hebrew sentences the splendour and beauty of the dashing and breaking waves, which doubtless was intended, though shrouded in that archaic tongue from less keen observers.

Keble was not a sacred but, in the best sense of the word, a secular poet. It is not David only, but the Sibyl, whose accents we catch in his inspirations. The 'sword in myrtle drest' of Harmodius and Aristogeiton, 'the many-twinkling smile of ocean' from Æschylus, are images as familiar to him as 'Bethlehem's glade,' or 'Carmel's haunted strand.' Not George Herbert, or Cowper, but Wordsworth, Scott, and perhaps more than all, Southey, are the English poets that kindled his flame, and coloured his diction. The beautiful stanza, 'Why so stately, maiden fair?' and the whole poem on 'May Garlands,' might have been written by the least theological of men. The allusions to nature are even superabundantly inwoven with the most sacred subjects. Occasionally a thought of much force and sublimity is lost by its entanglement in some merely passing phase of cloud or shadow. The descriptions of natural scenery display a depth of poetical intuition very rarely vouchsafed to any man. The exactness of the descriptions of Palestine, which he had never visited, have been noted and verified on the spot, as very few such descriptions ever have been. There are not above two or three failures, even in turns of expression. One example of this minute accuracy is so striking as to deserve special record. Amongst the features of the Lake of Gennesareth, one which most arrests the attention is the belt of oleanders which surrounds its shores. But this remarkable characteristic had, as far as we know, entirely escaped the observation of all travellers before the beginning of this century ; and, if we are not mistaken, the first published notice of it was in that line of the *Christian Year*—

> 'All through the summer night,
> Those blossoms [1] red and bright—'

by one who had never seen them, and who must have derived his
knowledge of them from careful cross-examination of some
traveller from the Holy Land. It was an instance of his curious
shyness that, when complimented on this singular accuracy of
description of the Holy Land, he replied, ' It was by a happy acci-
dent.' Not less precise, if we knew exactly where to look for the
original spots which suggested them, are his descriptions of the
scenery of England. With the single exception of the allusion
to the rocky isthmus at the Land's End said to be found in the
lines,

> 'Lo, on a narrow neck of land,
> 'Twixt two unbounded seas I stand,'

there is probably no local touch through the whole of the poems
of the two Wesleys. But Oxford, Bagley Wood, and the neighbourhood of Hursley, might, we are sure, be traced through
hundreds of lines, both in the *Christian Year* and the *Lyra Innocentium*.

Though Keble's pastoral life was retired and his ecclesiastical
life narrow, as a poet he not only touched the great world of
literature, but he was also a free-minded, free-speaking thinker.
Both in form and in doctrine his poetry has a broad and philosophical vein, the more striking from its contrast to his opposite
tendencies in connexion with his ecclesiastical party.

That eagerness to give the local colour of the sacred events,
which runs through these volumes, is the 'first step which costs
everything' in the attempt to treat these august topics historically,
and not dogmatically.

> 'The rude sandy lea,
> Where stately Jordan flows by many a palm—'

> 'Green lake, and cedar tuft, and spicy glade,
> Shaking their dewy tresses now the storm is laid;'

> ' The cell
> In Kedron's storied dell;'

---

[1] In all the early editions these were in a note erroneously called ' rhodo-
dendron.' It was not till after his attention had been called to it, that, we
think in the 72nd edition, it was altered to ' oleander.'

> ' The vaulted cells where martyr'd seers of old,
>   Far in the rocky walls of Sion sleep.'

The Biblical scenery is treated graphically as real scenery, the Biblical history and poetry as real history and poetry: the wall of partition between things sacred and things secular is broken down ; the dogmatist, the allegorist, have disappeared ; the critic and the poet have stepped into their place.

> ' O for a sculptor's hand,
>   That thou might'st take thy stand,
>   Thy wild hair floating on the Eastern breeze.'

This is the true poetic fire of Gray's ' Bard,' not the language of convention.

> ' The moist pearls now bestrewing
>   Thymy slope and rushy vale ;
> Comrades—what our sires have told us,
>   Watch and wait, for it will come ;
> Not by manna showers at morning
>   Shall our wants be then supplied ;
> But a strange pale gold adorning
>   Many a tufted mountain side.'

This is the tone, not of the mystical commentator, but of the creative poet.

In doctrine too, whether in points distinctive of high Anglicanism or in those common to Christian controversialists in general, it is noticeable how the view of the poet transcends the view of the theologian. The beautiful poem of the ' Waterfall ' in the *Lyra Innocentium* is a direct contradiction to the rigid opinions of its author, in his theological writings, on the hope expressed by Origen and Tillotson of the final restoration of lost souls. He speaks of the ancient world as Zwinglius or Spinoza regarded it, not as the scholastic divines spoke of it :—

> ' Now of Thy love we deem,
>   As of an ocean vast,
> Mounting in tides against the stream
>   Of ages gone and past.'

> ' That warning still and deep,
> At which high spirits of old would start
>   Even from their pagan sleep.'

In direct opposition to the spirit which would make not moral excellence but technical forms of belief the test of safety he writes such verses as these—

> '—— In one blaze of charity
> Care and remorse are lost, like motes in light divine; . . . .
> Whole years of folly we outlive
> In His unerring sight, who measures Life by Love.'

> '" Lord, and what shall this man do?"
>   Ask'st thou, Christian, for thy friend?
> If his love for Christ be true,
>   Christ hath told thee of his end:
> This is he whom God approves,
> This is he whom Jesus loves.'

> 'Wouldst thou the life of souls discern?
>   Nor human wisdom nor divine
> Helps thee by aught beside to learn;
>   Love is life's only sign.'

Again, the doubts and difficulties, which in the rude conflict of theological controversy are usually ascribed to corrupt motives and the like, are treated in his *Ode on St. Thomas's Day* with a tenderness worthy of the most advanced of modern thinkers :—

> 'Is there on earth a spirit frail,
>   Who fears to take their word;
> Scarce daring through the twilight pale
>   To think he sees the Lord?
> With eyes too tremblingly awake
> To bear with dimness for His sake?
> Read and confess the Hand Divine
> That drew thy likeness here so true in every line.'

And the beautiful analysis of the character and position of Barnabas, which is one of the masterpieces of Renan's work on the Apostles, is all but anticipated in the lines on that saint in the *Christian Year* :—

> 'Never so blest as when in Jesus' roll,
>   They write some hero-soul,
> More pleased upon his brightening road
> To wait, than if their own with all his radiance glow'd.'

Such a keen discrimination of the gifts and relations of the Apostles belongs to the true modern element of theology, not to the conventional theories of former days.

And with regard to the more special peculiarities of the High Church school, it is remarkable how at every turn he broke away from them in his poetry. It is enough to refer to the justification of marriage as against celibacy in the Ode on the Wednesday in Passion Week ; the glorification of the religion of common against conventual life in his Morning Hymn, and in his Ode on St. Matthew's Day. The contending polemic schools have themselves called attention to the well-known lines on the Eucharist in the poem on Gunpowder Treason. It is clear that, whatever may have been the subtle theological dogma which he may have held on the subject, the whole drift of that passage, which no verbal alteration can obliterate, is to exalt the moral and spiritual elements of that ordinance above those physical and local attributes on which later developments of his school have so exclusively dwelt.

These instances might be multiplied to any extent. It would, of course, be preposterous to press each line of poetry into an argument. But the whole result is to show how far nobler, purer, and loftier was what may be called the natural element of the poet's mind, than the artificial distinctions in which he became involved as a partisan and as a controversialist. This is no rare phenomenon. Who has not felt it hard to recognise the author of the *Paradise Lost* and of the *Penseroso* in the polemical treatises on Divorce and on the Execution of Charles I ? Who does not know the immeasurable contrast between Wordsworth the poet of nature and of the human heart, and Wordsworth the narrow Tory and High Churchman of his later years ? In all these cases it is the poet who is the real man—the theologian and politician only the temporary mask and phase.

A. P. **STANLEY.**

[From *The Christian Year.*]

THIRD SUNDAY IN LENT.

(The Christian Inheritance.)

See Lucifer like lightning fall,
    Dashed from his throne of pride ;
While, answering Thy victorious call,
    The Saints his spoils divide ;
This world of Thine, by him usurped too long,
Now opening all her stores to heal Thy servants' wrong.

So when the first-born of Thy foes
    Dead in the darkness lay,
When Thy redeemed at midnight rose
    And cast their bonds away,
The orphaned realm threw wide her gates, and told
Into freed Israel's lap her jewels and her gold.

And when their wondrous march was o'er,
    And they had won their homes,
Where Abraham fed his flock of yore,
    Among their fathers' tombs ;
A land that drinks the rain of Heaven at will,
Whose waters kiss the feet of many a vine-clad hill ;—

Oft as they watched, at thoughtful eve,
    A gale from bowers of balm
Sweep o'er the billowy corn, and heave
    The tresses of the palm,
Just as the lingering Sun had touched with gold,
Far o'er the cedar shade, some tower of giants old :

It was a fearful joy, I ween,
    To trace the Heathen's toil,
The limpid wells, the orchards green,
    Left ready for the spoil,
The household stores untouched, the roses bright
Wreathed o'er the cottage walls in garlands of delight

And now another Canaan yields
 To Thine all-conquering ark ;—
Fly from the ' old poetic' fields[1],
 Ye Paynim shadows dark !
Immortal Greece, dear land of glorious lays,
Lo ! here the 'unknown God' of thy unconscious praise !

The olive-wreath, the ivied wand,
 ' The sword in myrtles drest,'
Each legend of the shadowy strand
 Now wakes a vision blest ;
As little children lisp, and tell of Heaven,
So thoughts beyond their thought to those high Bards
  were given.

And these are ours : Thy partial grace
 The tempting treasure lends :
These relics of a guilty race
 Are forfeit to Thy friends ;
What seemed an idol hymn, now breathes of Thee,
Tuned by Faith's ear to some celestial melody.

There 's not a strain to Memory dear[2],
 Nor flower in classic grove,
There 's not a sweet note warbled here,
 But minds us of Thy Love,
O Lord, our Lord, and spoiler of our foes,
There is no light but Thine : with Thee all beauty glows

SECOND SUNDAY AFTER EASTER.

(Balaam's Prophecy.)

O for a sculptor's hand,
 That thou might'st take thy stand,
Thy wild hair floating on the eastern breeze,
 Thy tranced yet open gaze
 Fixed on the desert haze,
As one who deep in heaven some airy pageant sees.

---

[1] Where each old poetic mountain
  Inspiration breathed around. *Gray.*
[2] See Burns's Works, i. 293. Dr Currie's edition.

In outline dim and vast
Their fearful shadows cast
The giant forms of empires on their **way**
To ruin : one by one
They tower and they are gone,
Yet in the Prophet's soul the dreams of avarice **stay.**

No sun or star so bright
In all the world of light
That they should draw to Heaven his downward **eye :**
He hears th' Almighty's word,
He sees the angel's sword,
Yet low upon the earth his heart and treasure lie.

Lo! from yon argent field,
To him and us revealed,
One gentle Star glides down, on earth to **dwell.**
Chained as they are below
Our eyes may see it glow,
And as it mounts again, may track its brightness well.

To him it glared afar,
A token of wild war,
The banner of his Lord's victorious **wrath :**
But close to us it gleams,
Its soothing lustre streams
Around our home's green walls, and on our church-way path.

We in the tents abide
Which he at distance eyed
Like goodly cedars by the waters **spread,**
While seven red altar-fires
Rose up in wavy spires,
Where on the mount he watched his sorceries dark and dread.

He watched till morning's ray
On lake and meadow lay,
And willow-shaded streams, that silent sweep
Around the bannered lines,
Where by their several signs
The desert-wearied tribes in sight of Canaan sleep.

He watched till knowledge came
    Upon his soul like flame,
Not of those magic fires at random caught :
    But true Prophetic light
    Flashed o'er him, high and bright,
Flashed once, and died away, and left his darkened thought.

    And can he choose but fear,
    Who feels his God so near,
That when he fain would curse, his powerless tongue
    In blessing only moves ?—
    Alas ! the world he loves
Too close around his heart her tangling veil hath flung

    Sceptre and Star divine,
    Who in Thine inmost shrine
Hast made us worshippers, O claim Thine own ;
    More than Thy seers we know—
    O teach our love to grow
Up to Thy heavenly light, and reap what Thou has sown

FIFTEENTH SUNDAY AFTER TRINITY.

(The Lilies of the Field.)

Sweet nurslings of the vernal skies,
    Bathed in soft airs, and fed with dew,
What more than magic in you lies,
    To fill the heart's fond view ?
In childhood's sports, companions gay,
In sorrow, on Life's downward way,
How soothing ! in our last decay
    Memorials prompt and true.

Relics ye are of Eden's bowers,
    As pure, as fragrant, and as fair,
As when ye crowned the sunshine hours
    Of happy wanderers there.
Fall'n all beside—the world of life,
How is it stained with fear and strife !
In Reason's world what storms are rife,
    What passions range and glare !

But cheerful and unchanged the while
　Your first and perfect form ye show,
The same that won Eve's matron smile
　In the world's opening glow.
The stars of heaven a course are taught
Too high above our human thought;
Ye may be found if ye are sought,
　And as we gaze, we know.

Ye dwell beside our paths and homes,
　Our paths of sin, our homes of sorrow,
And guilty man, where'er he roams,
　Your innocent mirth may borrow.
The birds of air before us fleet,
They cannot brook our shame to meet—
But we may taste our solace sweet
　And come again to-morrow.

Ye fearless in your nests abide—
　Nor may we scorn, too proudly wise,
Your silent lessons, undescried
　By all but lowly eyes:
For ye could draw th' admiring gaze
Of Him who worlds and hearts surveys:
Your order wild, your fragrant maze,
　He taught us how to prize.

Ye felt your Maker's smile that hour,
　As when He paused and owned you good;
His blessing on earth's primal bower,
　Ye felt it all renewed.
What care ye now, if winter's storm
Sweep ruthless o'er each silken form?
Christ's blessing at your heart is warm,
　Ye fear no vexing mood.

Alas! of thousand bosoms kind,
　That daily court you and caress,
How few the happy secret find
　Of your calm loveliness!

'Live for to-day! to-morrow's light
To-morrow's cares shall bring to sight,
Go sleep like closing flowers at night,
And Heaven thy morn will bless.'

ALL SAINTS' DAY.

Why blow'st thou not, thou wintry wind,
    Now every leaf is brown and sere,
And idly droops, to thee resigned,
    The fading chaplet of the year?
Yet wears the pure aërial sky
Her summer veil, half drawn on high,
Of silvery haze, and dark and still
The shadows sleep on every slanting hill.

How quiet shews the woodland scene!
    Each flower and tree, its duty done,
Reposing in decay serene,
    Like weary men when age is won,
Such calm old age as conscience pure
And self-commanding hearts ensure,
Waiting their summons to the sky,
Content to live, but not afraid to die.

Sure if our eyes were purged to trace
    God's unseen armies hovering round,
We should behold by angels' grace
    The four strong winds of Heaven fast bound,
Their downward sweep a moment stayed
On ocean cove and forest glade,
Till the last flower of autumn shed
Her funeral odours on her dying bed.

So in Thine awful armoury, Lord,
    The lightnings of the judgment-day
Pause yet awhile, in mercy stored,
    Till willing hearts wear quite away

Their earthly stains; and spotless shine
On every brow in light divine
The Cross by angel hands impressed,
The seal of glory won and pledge of promised rest.

Little they dream, those haughty souls
   Whom empires own with bended knee,
What lowly fate their own controls,
   Together linked by Heaven's decree;—
As bloodhounds hush their baying wild
To wanton with some fearless child,
So Famine waits, and War with greedy eyes,
Till some repenting heart be ready for the skies.

Think ye the spires that glow so bright
   In front of yonder setting sun,
Stand by their own unshaken might?
   No—where th' upholding grace is won,
We dare not ask, nor Heaven would tell,
But sure from many a hidden dell,
From many a rural nook unthought of there,
Rises for that proud world the saints' prevailing prayer.

On Champions blest, in Jesus' name,
   Short be your strife, your triumph full,
Till every heart have caught your flame,
   And, lightened of the world's misrule,
Ye soar those elder saints to meet,
Gathered long since at Jesus' feet,
No world of passions to destroy,
Your prayers and struggles o'er, your task all praise and joy

UNITED STATES.

[From *Lyra Apostolica.*]

Tyre of the *farther* West! be thou too warned,
   Whose eagle wings thine own green world o'erspread,
Touching two Oceans: wherefore hast thou scorned
   Thy fathers' God, O proud and full of bread?

Why lies the Cross unhonoured on thy ground
  While in mid air thy stars and arrows flaunt?
That sheaf of darts, will it not fall unbound,
  Except, disrobed of thy vain earthly vaunt,
  Thou bring it to be blessed where Saints and Angels haunt?

The holy seed, by Heaven's peculiar grace.
  Is rooted here and there in thy dark woods;
But many a rank weed round it grows apace,
  And Mammon builds beside thy mighty floods,
O'ertopping Nature, braving Nature's God;
  O while thou yet hast room, fair fruitful land,
Ere war and want have stained thy virgin sod,
  Mark thee a place on high, a glorious stand,
  Whence Truth her sign may make o'er forest, lake, and strand

Eastward, this hour, perchance thou turn'st thine ear,
  Listening if haply with the surging sea,
Blend sounds of Ruin from a land once dear
  To thee and Heaven. O trying hour for thee!
Tyre mocked when Salem fell; where now is Tyre?
  Heaven was against her. Nations thick as waves,
Burst o'er her walls, to Ocean doomed and fire:
  And now the tideless water idly laves
  Her towers, and lone sands heap her crowned merchants'
    graves.

From 'The Waterfall.'

[*Lyra Innocentium.*]

Go where the waters fall,
  Sheer from the mountain's height—

Mark how a thousand streams in one,—
  One in a thousand on they fare,
    Now flashing to the sun,
    Now still as beast in lair.

Now round the rock, now mounting o'er,
  In lawless dance they win their way,
    Still seeming more and more
    To swell as we survey,

They rush and roar, they whirl and leap,
Not wilder drives the wintry storm.
  Yet a strong law they keep,
  Strange powers their course inform.

Even so the mighty skyborn stream
Its living waters from above,
  All marred and broken seem,
  No union and no love.

Yet in dim caves they softly b!end
In dreams of mortals unespied:
  One is their awful end,
  One their unfailing **Guide.**

HARTLEY COLERIDGE.

[HARTLEY COLERIDGE, son of Samuel Taylor Coleridge, was born 19th September, 1796; died, 6th January, 1849. Besides some prose writings, we have *Poems by Hartley Coleridge*, vol. i. (all published) Leeds, 1833; *Poems by Hartley Coleridge, with a Memoir of his Life by his Brother*, 2 vols, 1851.]

Hartley Coleridge always classed himself among 'the small poets,' and it is true he was not born for great and splendid achievements ; but there are some writers for whom our affection would be less if they were stronger, more daring, more successful ; and Hartley Coleridge is one of these. We think of him as the visionary boy, whom his father likened to the moon among thin clouds, moving in a circle of his own light,—as the fairy voyager of Wordsworth's prophetic poem, whose boat seemed rather

'To brood on air than on an earthly stream.'

We think of him as the elvish figure one might meet forty years later by Grasmere side, too soon an old man and white-haired, with now and then an expression of pain, a half-tone in his voice that betrayed some sense of incompleteness or failure, but with the full eye still bright and soft ; the speech still rippling out fancy and play and wisdom ; the heart, in spite of sorrow and the injuries of time, still as Wordsworth knew it,

'A young lamb's heart among the full-grown flocks.'

A great poet is a toiler, even when his toil is rapturous. Hartley Coleridge did not and perhaps could not toil. Good thoughts came to him as of free grace ; gentle pleasures possessed his senses ; loving-kindnesses flowed from his heart, and took as they flowed shadows and colours from his imagination ; and all these mingled and grew mellow. And so a poet's moods expressed themselves in his verse ; but he built no lofty rhyme. The sonnet, in which a thought and a feeling are wedded helpmates suited his genius ; and of his many delightful sonnets some of the best are immediate transcripts of the passing mood of joy or pain. ' To see him brandishing his pen,' a friend has written, ' and now and then beating time with his foot, and breaking out into a shout at any felicitous idea, was a thing never to be forgotten. . . . His sonnets were all written instantaneously, and never, to my knowledge, occupied more than ten minutes.' Perhaps because of this happy facility they often fall short of complete attainment ; sometimes the vigour of conception suddenly declines, sometimes the touch loses its precision ; nor is the poetic mood from which they originate always delivered by the imagination from its surrounding circumstance of prose, or its alloy of humbler feeling.

But all that Hartley Coleridge has written is genuine, full of nature, sweet, fresh, breathing charity and reconciliation. His poems of self-portrayal are many, and of these not a few are pathetic with sense of change and sorrowing self-condemnation ; yet his penitence had a silver side of hope, and one whose piety was so unaffected, whose faith though 'thinner far than vapour' had yet outlived all frowardness, could not desperately upbraid even his weaker self. For all that is sweet and venerable—for the charm of old age, for the comeliness of ancient use and wont, for the words of sacred poet or prophet, for the traditions of civility, for the heritage of English law and English freedom, for the simple humanities of earth, for fatherhood and motherhood, Hartley Coleridge had a heartfelt and tender reverence. And with a more exquisite devotion he cherished all frail, innocent, and dependent creatures ; small they should be or they could not look to their quaint little poet as a protector. To think of the humming-bird's or the cricket's glee made him happy ; he bowed over the forget-me-not blossom as if it were a sapphire amulet against all mortal taint, and over the eye-bright 'gold-eyed weedie,' which owns such holy, medicinal virtue. He loved with the naïveté of innocent-hearted old bachelorhood the paradise of maidenhood ; with all its sweet she-slips, in Shakespeare's play and Stothard's page, and, better still, on English lawn or by English fireside. And who has been laureate to as many baby boys and 'wee ladies sweet' as Hartley Coleridge ? Rounding the lives of all little children and all helpless things he felt a nearness of some strong protecting Love which called forth his deepest instincts of piety.

In Grasmere churchyard, close to the body of Wordsworth, rests that of Hartley Coleridge ; so a Presence of strength and plain heroic magnitude of mind environs him. And hard by a stream goes murmuring to the lake. As a mountain rivulet to a mountain lake, so is Hartley Coleridge's poetry to that of Wordsworth ; and the stream has a melodious life and a freshness of its own.

EDWARD DOWDEN.

SONNET.

Long time a child, and still a child, when years
Had painted manhood on my cheek, was I,—
For yet I lived like one not born to die ;
A thriftless prodigal of smiles and tears,
No hope I needed, and I knew no fears.
But sleep, though sweet, is only sleep, and waking,
I waked to sleep no more, at once o'ertaking
The vanguard of my age, with all arrears
Of duty on my back.   Nor child, nor man,
Nor youth, nor sage, I find my head is grey,
For I have lost the race I never ran :
A rathe December blights my lagging May ;
And still I am a child, though I be old,
Time is my debtor for my years untold.

TO A LOFTY BEAUTY, FROM HER POOR KINSMAN.

Fair maid, had I not heard thy baby cries,
Nor seen thy girlish, sweet vicissitude,
Thy mazy motions, striving to elude,
Yet wooing still a parent's watchful eyes,
Thy humours, many as the opal's dyes,
And lovely all ;—methinks thy scornful mood,
And bearing high of stately womanhood,—
Thy brow, where Beauty sits to tyrannize
O'er humble love, had made me sadly fear thee ;
For never sure was seen a royal bride,
Whose gentleness gave grace to so much pride—
My very thoughts would tremble to be near thee ,
But when I see thee at thy father's side,
Old times unqueen thee, and old loves endear thee.

MAY, 1840.

A lovely morn, so still, so very s..ll,
't hardly seems a growing day of Spring,
Though all the odorous buds are blossoming,
And the small matin birds were glad and shrill
Some hours ago ; but now the woodland rill
Murmurs along, the only vocal thing,
Save when the wee wren flits with stealthy wing,
And cons by fits and bits her evening trill.
Lovers might sit on such a morn as this
An hour together, looking at the sky,
Nor dare to break the silence with a kiss,
Long listening for the signal of a sigh ;
And the sweet Nun, diffused in voiceless prayer,
Feel her own soul through all the brooding air.

TO A DEAF AND DUMB LITTLE GIRL.

Like a loose island on the wide expanse,
Unconscious floating on the fickle sea,
Herself her all, she lives in privacy ;
Her waking life as lonely as a trance,
Doomed to behold the universal dance,
And never hear the music which expounds
The solemn step, coy slide, the merry bounds,
The vague, mute language of the countenance.
In vain for her I smooth my antic rhyme ;
She cannot hear it, all her little being
Concentred in her solitary seeing—
What can she know of beaut[eous] or sublime?
And yet methinks she looks so calm and good,
God must be with her in her solitude.

STANZAS.

She was a queen of noble Nature's **crowning,**
A smile of her's was like an act of grace ;
She had no winsome looks, no pretty frowning,
Like daily beauties of the vulgar race :
But if she smiled, a light was on her face,
A clear, cool kindliness, a lunar beam
Of peaceful radiance, silvering o'er the stream
Of human thought with unabiding glory ;
Not quite a waking truth, not quite a dream,
A visitation, bright and transitory.

But she is changed,—hath felt the touch of sorrow,
No love hath she, no understanding friend ;
Oh grief ! when heaven is forced of earth to borrow
What the poor niggard earth has not to lend ;
But when the stalk is snapt, the rose must bend.
The tallest flower that skyward rears its head,
Grows from the common ground, and there must **shed**
Its delicate petals. Cruel fate, too surely,
That they should find so base a bridal bed,
Who lived in virgin pride, so sweet and purely.

She had a brother, and a tender father,
And she was loved, but not as others are
From whom we ask return of love,—but rather
As one might love a dream ; a phantom fair
Of something exquisitely strange and rare,
Which all were glad to look on, men and maids,
Yet no one claimed—as oft, in dewy glades
The peering primrose, like a sudden gladness,
Gleams on the soul, yet unregarded fades ;—
The joy is ours, but all its own the sadness.

'Tis vain to say—her worst of grief is only
The common lot, which all the world have known ;
To her 'tis more, because her heart is lonely,
And yet she hath no strength to stand alone,—
Once she had playmates, fancies of her own,

And she did love them. They are past away
As Fairies vanish at the break of day ;
And like a spectre of an age departed,
Or unsphered Angel woefully astray,
She glides along—the solitary hearted.

SONG.

She is not fair to outward view
    As many maidens be,
Her loveliness I never knew
    Until she smiled on me ;
Oh! then I saw her eye was bright,
A well of love, a spring of light.

But now her looks are coy and cold,
    To mine they ne'er reply,
And yet I cease not to behold
    The love-light in her eye :
Her very frowns are fairer far,
Than smiles of other maidens are.

SUMMER RAIN.

Thick lay the dust, uncomfortably white,
In glaring mimicry of Arab sand.
The woods and mountains slept in hazy light ;
The meadows look'd athirst and tawny tanned ;
The little rills had left their channels bare,
With scarce a pool to witness what they were ;
And the shrunk river gleamed 'mid oozy stones,
That stared like any famished giant's bones.

Sudden the hills grew black, and hot as stove
The air beneath ; it was a toil to be.
There was a growling as of angry Jove,
Provoked by Juno's prying jealousy—
A flash—a crash—the firmament was split,
And down it came in drops—the smallest fit
To drown a bee in fox-glove bell conceal'd ;
Joy filled the brook, and comfort cheered the field.

WILLIAM MOTHERWELL.

[WILLIAM MOTHERWELL, born in Glasgow in 1797, became a 'limb of the law' in 1819, being then appointed to the office of Sheriff Clerk Depute at Paisley. In 1828 he put his literary talent at the service of his party, edited a Tory newspaper, *The Paisley Advertiser*, and afterwards *The Glasgow Courier*. The strain of journalism proved too much for him. and he died of apoplexy at the early age of thirty-seven. A small volume of poems, narrative and lyrical, published in 1832, was the only fruit of his fine poetic gifts.]

Motherwell's reputation in his own country as a poet was made by the plaintive song of *Jeanie Morrison*, a sweet and touching reminiscence of pleasant days spent with a school playfellow and child sweetheart. This and another song in the Scotch dialect, *My heid is like to break*, in which a betrayed damsel harrows up the feelings of her seducer with pitiless pathos, may be said to be the only two lyrics of his that have taken any hold of fame. They prove him to have been a man of keen sensibility ; he was also a man of vigorous intellect and large culture, more of a student and a scholar than any contemporary Scotch lyrist. He wrote but little in verse—after he reached the prime of manhood his powers were wasted in vehement partisan support of a hopeless cause—but the little that he did write was not in the minor key of the songs in his native dialect. The exploits of the Vikings fascinated his imagination, and as the bard of these sturdy warriors he sang with a vigour that entitles him to be named as a link between Gray and Collins and Mr. William Morris. Motherwell found in the mighty deeds and haughty spirit of the irresistible masters of the sea more congenial themes than the woes and the aspirations of the Jacobites of which the literary world by his time was becoming somewhat weary, and revelled in the fresh field with eager delight. The most touching of his poems in its personal emotion, *I am not sad*, shows him resigned to 'the sadness of a nameless tomb,' but it is hard to believe that the wealth and variety of power evidenced in such poems as *The Madman's Love*, and his two songs in the Scotch dialect could have rested unused.

W. MINTO.

True Love's Dirge.

Some love is light and fleets away,
　Heigho! the wind and rain;
Some love is deep and scorns decay,
　Ah, well-a-day! in vain.

Of loyal love I sing this lay,
　Heigho! the wind and rain;
'Tis of a knight and lady gay,
　Ah, well-a-day! bright twain.

He loved her,—heart loved ne'er so well,
　Heigho! the wind and rain;
She was a cold and proud damsel,
　Ah, well-a-day! and vain.

He loved her,—oh, he loved her long,
　Heigho! the wind and rain;
But she for love gave bitter wrong,
　Ah, well-a-day! Disdain!

It is not meet for knight like me,
　Heigho! the wind and rain;
Though scorned, love's recreant to be,
　Ah, well-a-day! Refrain.

That brave knight buckled on his brand,
　Heigho! the wind and rain;
And fast he sought a foreign strand,
　Ah, well-a-day! in pain.

He wandered wide by land and sea,
　Heigho! the wind and rain;
A mirror of bright constancy.
　Ah, well-a-day! in vain.

He would not chide, he would not blame,
　Heigho! the wind and rain,
But at each shrine he breathed her name,
　Ah, well-a-day! Amen!

He would not carp, he would not sing,
　Heigho! the wind and rain,
That broke his heart with love-longing.
　Ah, well-a-day! poor brain.

He scorned to weep, he scorned to sigh,
　Heigho! the wind and rain,
But like a true knight he could die,—
　Ah, well-a-day! life's vain.

The banner which that brave knight bore,
　Heigho! the wind and rain;
Had scrolled on it, 'Faith Evermore.'
　Ah, well-a-day! again.

That banner led the Christian van,
　Heigho! the wind and rain;
Against Seljuck and Turcoman.
　Ah, well-a-day! bright train.

The fight was o'er, the day was done,
　Heigho! the wind and rain;
But lacking was that loyal one,—
　Ah, well-a-day! sad pain.

They found him on the battle-field,
　Heigho: the wind and rain;
With broken sword and cloven shield,
　Ah, well-a-day! in twain.

They found him pillowed on the dead,
　Heigho! the wind and rain; '
The blood-soaked sod his bridal bed,
　Ah, well-a-day! the Slain.

And his pale brow and paler cheek,
　Heigho! the wind and rain;
The white moonshine did fall so meek,
　Ah! well-a-day! sad strain.

They lifted up the True and Brave,
　Heigho! the wind and rain;
And bore him to his lone cold grave,
　Ah! well-a-day! in pain.

They buried him on that far strand,
   Heigho! the wind and rain;
His face turned towards his love's own land,
   Ah, well-a-day! how vain.

The wearied heart was laid at rest,
   Heigho! the wind and rain;
The dream of her he liked best,
   Ah, well-a-day! again.

They nothing said, but many a tear,
   Heigho! the wind and rain;
Rained down on that knight's lowly bier,
   Ah, well-a-day! amain.

They nothing said, but many a sigh,
   Heigho! the wind and rain;
Told how they wished like him to die,
   Ah, well-a-day! sans stain.

With solemn mass and orison,
   Heigho! the wind and rain;
They reared to him a cross of stone,
   Ah, well-a-day! in pain.

And on it graved with daggers bright,
   Heigho! the wind and rain;
'Here lies a true and gentle knight.'
   Ah, well a day! Amen!

JEANIE MORRISON.

I've wandered east, I've wandered west,
   Through mony a weary way;
But never, never can forget
   The love o' life's young day!
The fire that's blawn on Beltane e'en
   May weel be black gin Yule;
But blacker fa' awaits the heart
   Where first fond luve grows cule.

Oh dear, dear Jeanie Morrison,
  The thochts o' bygane years
Still fling their shadows ower my path,
  And blind my een wi' tears !
They blind my een wi' saut, saut tears,
  And sair and sick I pine,
As memory idly summons up
  The blithe blinks o' langsyne.

'Twas then we luvit ilk ither weel,
  'Twas than we twa did part ;
Sweet time, sad time ! twa bairns at schule,
  Twa bairns, and but ae heart !
'Twas then we sat on ae high bink,
  To leir [1] ilk ither lear [2] :
And tones, and looks, and smiles were shed,
  Remembered ever mair.

I wonder, Jeanie, often yet
  When sitting on that bink,
Cheek touchin' cheek, loof [3] locked in loof,
  What our wee heads could think.
When baith bent doun ower ae braid page,
  Wi' ae buik on our knee,
Thy lips were on thy lesson, but
  My lesson was in thee.

Oh mind ye how we hung our heads,
  How cheeks brent red wi' shame,
Whene'er the school-weans laughin' said,
  We cleeked [4] thegither hame ?
And mind ye o' the Saturdays
  (The schule then skail't [5] at noon)
When we ran aft to speel [6] the braes—
  The broomy braes o' June ?

My head rins round and round about,
  My heart flows like a sea,
As ane by ane the thochts rush back
  O' schuletime and o' thee.

[1] learn.   [2] learning.   [3] palm.   [4] lit. hooked = clung.   [5] dispersed.   [6] climb

O mornin' life! O mornin' luve!
　O lichtsome days and lang,
When hinnied hopes around our hearts,
　Like summer blossoms sprang!

Oh, mind ye, luve, how oft we left
　The deavin' dinsome town,
To wander by the green burnside,
　And hear its water croon.
The summer leaves hung ower our heids,
　The flowers burst round our feet,
And in the gloamin' i' the wud
　The throstle whusslit sweet.

The throstle whusslit i' the wud,
　The burn sang to the trees,
And we with Nature's heart in tune,
　Concerted harmonies ;
And on the knowe abune the burn,
　For hours thegither sat
In the silentest o' joy, till baith
　Wi' very gladness grat !

Aye, aye, dear Jeanie Morrison,
　Tears trinkled down your cheek,
Like dew-beads on a rose, yet nane
　Had ony power to speak !
That was a time, a blessed time,
　When hearts were fresh and young,
When freely gushed all feelings forth
　Unsyllabled—unsung !

I marvel, Jeanie Morrison,
　Gin I hae been to thee,
As closely twined wi' earliest thochts
　As ye hae been to me?
Oh, tell me gin their music fills
　Thine ear as it does mine ;
Oh, say gin e'er your heart grows grit
　Wi' dreamings o' langsyne?

I 've wandered east, I 've wandered west,
  I 've borne a weary lot ;
But in my wanderings, far or near,
  Ye never were forgot.
The fount that first burst frae this heart,
  Still travels on its way ;
And channels deeper as it rins
  The luve o' life's long day.

O dear, dear Jeanie Morrison,
  Since we were sindered young,
I 've never seen your face, nor heard
  The music of your tongue ;
But I could hug all wretchedness,
  And happy could I die,
Did I but ken your heart still dreamed
  O' bygane days and me

THOMAS HOOD.

[THOMAS HOOD was born in London in May, 1799. His chief poetical works, scattered during his life-time in various publications, are contained in two volumes entitled respectively *Poems*, 1846, and *Poems of Wit and Humour*, 1847. A complete edition of his works appeared in 1862. He died in May, 1845, and was buried in Kensal Green Cemetery, where. some years after his death, a monument was erected to him by public subscription.]

Since the issue in 1860 of the delightful *Memorials of Thomas Hood* by his son and daughter, both of whom are now dead, it has not been easy to dissociate the poet from the touching picture of him which those pages present. Nor indeed does literature often afford the spectacle of a heroism so smiling as that of the inde-fatigable manufacturer of *Whims and Oddities, Comic Annuals,* and the like,—pumping up ceaseless fun for a subsistence,—fault-less in his relations of husband and father,—patient under sickness and 'lack of pence'—and concluding, at last, that the life which to him, as to Pope, had been 'a long disease,' was still worth living, and the world he was leaving a beautiful one, 'and not so bad, humanly speaking, even as people would make it out.' Whether, under favourable circumstances, he would have produced more work of a high character is a question that it is scarcely profitable to discuss ; but it is manifest that during his life-time the some-what coarse-palated public welcomed most keenly not so much his best as his second-best. The 'Tom Hood' they cared for was not the delicate and fanciful author of the *Plea of the Midsummer Fairies*, but the Hood of *Miss Kilmansegg and her Precious Leg*, —the master of broad-grin and equivoque, the delightful parodist, the irrepressible and irresistible joker and Merry-Andrew. It is not to be denied that much of his work in this way is excellent

M m 2

of its kind, admirable for its genuine drollery and whim, having often at its core, moreover, that subtle sense of the *lacrimæ rerum*, which lends a piquancy of sadness and almost a quality of permanence to much of our modern jesting. But the rest!—the larger part! Nothing except the record of his over-strained, over-burdened life can enable us to understand how the author of the *Ode to Rae Wilson*, the *Lament for Chivalry*, and the lines *On a distant Prospect of Clapham Academy* could ever have produced such mechanical and melancholy mirth as much of that which has been preserved appears to be. Yet his worst work is seldom without some point; it is better than the best of many others; and, with all its drawbacks, it is at least always pure. It should be remembered too that the fashions of fun pass away like other fashions.

It was fortunate, however, for his good fame that the public of his day could not wholly detain him in the jester's domain. He was from the first, and remained throughout his life, a poet of distinct individuality and delicacy of note. Side by side with the fugitive puns and work-a-day witticisms, he found leisure to produce a number of pieces worthy of something more than mere ephemeral life. Such are *Hero and Leander*, the galloping anapæsts of *Lycus the Centaur*, and the beautiful petition to 'all-devouring Time' for Titania and her fragile following. In these, his earlier works, we may trace the influence of the Elizabethans, or perhaps we should say of Lamb and Keats. But in 1829 he struck a note more intimately his own in the *Dream of Eugene Aram*, a poem of strange fascination, and exhibiting an extraordinary faculty for 'moving a horror skilfully' and laying bare the tortured human heart. Many of his sonnets are beautiful, and not a few of his detached songs and ballads (e.g. *Fair Inez, I remember, It was the time of Roses*) have that rare merit of tunefulness which is as much in the matter as in the metre. Here and there, too, as in the *Death-Bed*, he touches the keenest chord of pathos. But what is most noteworthy is that this purely poetical faculty does not seem to have declined in the popularity of his lesser labours, but rather to have increased in spite of it. His best pieces in this way were written in the last years of his life, when he may almost be said to have entered the Valley of the Shadow. In *Punch* for Christmas, 1843, appeared the *Song of the Shirt*, a poem with which his name is usually associated. It was the sharp and exceeding bitter cry of the hitherto inarticulate,—the sudden wail, not of the poor seamstress alone, but of the whole body of the under-paid and over-worked, fighting out their grim duel with Hunger. It rang through the length and breadth of the land, arousing and quickening a compassion which to this day has not wholly faded out. Such a production it is waste of time to criticise : it reaches its mark so surely and swiftly that mere questions of detail and technique seem to be impertinent super-fluities. But the *Bridge of Sighs*, which appeared a few months after in *Hood's Magazine*, is, in our opinion, superior as a work of art. The *Lady's Dream*, and the *Lay of the Labourer*, which belong to the same periodical, have less merit. The *Haunted House*, with which its pages opened in January, 1844, is a master-piece of a different order. It is an extraordinarily minute study of disuse and decay,—of the ghostliness and horror that broods and gathers about neglect :—

> ' With shatter'd panes the grassy court was starr'd ;
> The time-worn coping-stone had tumbled after ;
> And through the ragged roof the sky shone, barr'd
> With naked beam and rafter.

> ' O'er all there hung a shadow and a fear ;
> A sense of mystery the spirit daunted,
> And said, as plain as whisper in the ear,
> The place is Haunted !'

The latter verse recurs throughout the poem with singular effect. The length of the piece places it beyond the limits of quotation ; but the selection given will show sufficiently how simple and sincere,—how strong in the abiding elements of song were the more serious efforts of this gentlest and most patient of poets.

AUSTIN DOBSON.

THE BRIDGE OF SIGHS.

'Drown'd! drown'd!'—*Hamlet.*

One more Unfortunate,
Weary of breath,
Rashly importunate,
Gone to her death!

Take her up tenderly,
Lift her with care;
Fashioned so slenderly,
Young, and so fair!

Look at her garments
Clinging like cerements;
Whilst the wave constantly
Drips from her clothing;
Take her up instantly,
Loving, not loathing.—

Touch her not scornfully;
Think of her mournfully,
Gently and humanly;
Not of the stains of her,
All that remains of her
Now is pure womanly.

Make no deep scrutiny
Into her mutiny
Rash and undutiful:
Past all dishonour,
Death has left on her
Only the beautiful.

Still, for all slips of hers,
One of Eve's family—
Wipe those poor lips of hers
Oozing so clammily.

Loop up her tresses
Escaped from the comb,
Her fair auburn tresses ;
Whilst wonderment guesses
Where was her home ?

Who was her father ?
Who was her mother ?
Had she a sister ?
Had she a brother ?
Or was there a dearer one
Still, and a nearer one
Yet, than all other ?

Alas ! for the rarity
Of Christian charity
Under the sun !
Oh ! it was pitiful !
Near a whole city full,
Home she had none.

Sisterly, brotherly,
Fatherly, motherly
Feelings had changed :
Love, by harsh evidence,
Thrown from its eminence ;
Even God's providence
Seeming estranged.

Where the lamps quiver
So far in the river,
With many a light
From window and casement,
From garret to basement,
She stood, with amazement,
Houseless by night.

The bleak wind of March
Made her tremble and shiver ;
But not the dark arch,
Or the black flowing river :

Mad from life's history,
Glad to death's mystery,
Swift to be hurled—
Any where, any where
Out of the world!

In she plunged boldly,
No matter how coldly
The rough river ran,—
Over the brink of it,
Picture it—think of it,
Dissolute Man!
Lave in it, drink of it,
Then, if you can!

Take her up tenderly,
Lift her with care ;
Fashioned so slenderly,
Young, and so fair!

Ere her limbs frigidly
Stiffen too rigidly,
Decently,—kindly,—
Smooth, and compose them ;
And her eyes, close them,
Staring so blindly!

Dreadfully staring
Thro' muddy impurity,
As when with the daring
Last look of despairing
Fix'd on futurity.

Perishing gloomily,
Spurred by contumely,
Cold inhumanity,
Burning insanity,
Into her rest.—
Cross her hands humbly
As if praying dumbly,
Over her breast.

Owning her weakness,
Her evil behaviour,
And leaving, with meekness,
Her sins to her Saviour !

A Parental Ode to my Son, aged Three Years and Five Months.

Thou happy, happy elf !
(But stop,—first let me kiss away that tear)—
Thou tiny image of myself !
(My love, he 's poking peas into his ear !)
Thou merry, laughing sprite !
With spirits feather-light,
Untouched by sorrow, and unsoiled by sin—
(Good heavens ! the child is swallowing a pin !)

Thou little tricksy Puck !
With antic toys so funnily bestuck,
Light as the singing bird that wings the air—
(The door ! the door ! he 'll tumble down the stair !)
Thou darling of thy sire !
(Why, Jane, he 'll set his pinafore a-fire !)
Thou imp of mirth and joy !
In Love's dear chain so strong and bright a link,
Thou idol of thy parents—(Drat the boy !
There goes my ink !)

Thou cherub—but of earth ;
Fit playfellow for Fays, by moonlight pale,
In harmless sport and mirth,
(That dog will bite him if he pulls its tail !)
Thou human humming-bee extracting honey
From ev'ry blossom in the world that blows,
Singing in Youth's Elysium ever sunny,
(Another tumble !—that 's his precious nose !)

Thy father's pride and hope!
(He 'll break the mirror with that skipping-rope!)
With pure heart newly stamped from Nature's mint—
(Where did he learn that squint?)

Thou young domestic dove!
(He 'll have that jug off, with another shove!)
Dear nurseling of the hymeneal nest!
(Are those torn clothes his best!)
Little epitome of man!
(He 'll climb upon the table, that 's his plan!)
Touched with the beauteous tints of dawning life—
(He 's got a knife!)

Thou enviable being!
No storms, no clouds, in thy blue sky foreseeing,
Play on, play on,
My elfin John!
Toss the light ball—bestride the stick—
(I knew so many cakes would make him sick!)
With fancies buoyant as the thistle down,
Prompting the face grotesque, and antic brisk,
With many a lamb-like frisk,
(He 's got the scissors, snipping at your gown!)

Thou pretty opening rose!
(Go to your mother, child, and wipe your nose!)
Balmy, and breathing music like the South,
(He really brings my heart into my mouth!)
Fresh as the morn, and brilliant as its star,—
(I wish that window had an iron bar!)
Bold as the hawk, yet gentle as the dove,—
(I tell you what, my love,
I cannot write, unless he 's sent above!)

THE DEATH-BED.

We watched her breathing thro' the night,
 Her breathing soft and low,
As in her breast the wave of life
 Kept heaving to and fro.

So silently we seemed to speak,
 So slowly moved about,
As we had lent her half our powers
 To eke her living out.

Our very hopes belied our fears,
 Our fears our hopes belied—
We thought her dying when she slept,
 And sleeping when she died.

For when the morn came dim and sad,
 And chill with early showers,
Her quiet eyelids closed—she had
 Another morn than ours.

LORD MACAULAY.

[Thomas Babington Macaulay was born at Rothley Temple, Leicestershire, Oct. 25, 1800, and died at Holly Lodge, Campden Hill, Dec. 28, 1859. His *Lays of Ancient Rome* were published in 1843; other ballads and poems were written from time to time, his earliest published piece, an *Epitaph on Henry Mar:y* , being dated 1812.]

'You are very right in admiring Macaulay,' wrote Miss Elizabeth Barrett to Mr. Horne in 1843; 'he has a noble, clear, metallic note in his soul, and makes us ready by it for battle. I very much admire Mr. Macaulay, and could scarcely read his ballads and keep lying down. They seemed to draw me up to my feet as the mesmeric powers are said to do [1].' This testimony from so competent a judge as Mrs. Browning is all the more valuable because, great as is still the popularity of the *Lays* with the mass of those who read poetry, the higher critical authorities have pronounced against them, and are even teaching us to wonder whether they can be called poetry at all. They find in the *Lays* the same faults which mar the author's prose—commonplaceness of ideas, cheapness of sentiment and imagery, made to prevail by dint of the writer's irresistible command of a new rhetorical force; in a word, eloquent Philistinism. Against this too exclusive judgment it is well to set Miss Barrett's frank recognition of the power, the spirit, the vividness of historical imagination that informs all Macaulay's writing. One of her epithets, which she uses *honoris causâ*, we may accept as fairly characterising the evil element in his mind— the epithet *metallic*. His ballads have the clear resonance of the trumpet: they have its hardness too.

The *Lays* are in everybody's hands: and they do not lend themselves easily to selection. We have preferred to print the less known *Naseby*, written in 1824; and the pathetic *Epitaph on a Jacobite*—a work of the author's maturity.

EDITOR.

[1] *Letters of Elizabeth Barrett Browning, vol. i. p. 166.*

THE BATTLE OF NASEBY.

(By Obadiah Bind-their-kings-in-chains-and-their-nobles-with-links-of-iron, Sergeant in Ireton's Regiment.)

Oh ! wherefore come ye forth, in triumph from the North,
  With your hands, and your feet, and your raiment all red ?
And wherefore doth your rout send forth a joyous shout ?
  And whence be the grapes of the wine-press which ye tread ?

Oh evil was the root, and bitter was the fruit,
  And crimson was the juice of the vintage that we trod ;
For we trampled on the throng of the haughty and the strong,
  Who sate in the high places, and slew the saints of God.

It was about the noon of a glorious day of June,
  That we saw their banners dance, and their cuirasses shine,
And the Man of Blood was there, with his long essenced hair,
  And Astley, and Sir Marmaduke, and Rupert of the Rhine.

Like a servant of the Lord, with his Bible and his sword,
  The General rode along us to form us to the fight,
When a murmuring sound broke out, and swelled into a shout
  Among the godless horsemen upon the tyrant's right.

And hark ! like the roar of the billows on the shore,
  The cry of battle rises along their charging line !
For God ! for the Cause ! for the Church ! for the Laws !
  For Charles King of England, and Rupert of the Rhine !

The furious German comes, with his clarions and his drums,
  His bravoes of Alsatia, and pages of Whitehall ;
They are bursting on our flanks. Grasp your pikes, close your
    ranks ;
For Rupert never comes but to conquer or to fall.

They are here ! They rush on ! We are broken ! We are gone !
  Our left is borne before them like stubble on the blast.
O Lord, put forth thy might ! O Lord, defend the right !
  Stand back to back, in God's name, and fight it to the last.

Stout Skippon hath a wound ; the centre hath given ground :
   Hark ! hark !—What means the trampling of horsemen on our
     rear ?
Whose banner do I see, boys ? 'Tis he, thank God, 'tis he, boys.
   Bear up another minute : brave Oliver is here.

Their heads all stooping low, their points all in a row,
   Like a whirlwind on the trees, like a deluge on the dykes,
Our cuirassiers have burst on the ranks of the Accurst,
   And at a shock have scattered the forest of his pikes.

Fast, fast, the gallants ride, in some safe nook to hide
   Their coward heads, predestined to rot on Temple Bar :
And he—he turns, he flies :—shame on those cruel eyes
   That bore to look on torture, and dare not look on war !

Ho ! comrades, scour the plain ; and, ere ye strip the slain,
   First give another stab to make your search secure,
Then shake from sleeves and pockets their broad-pieces and
     lockets,
   The tokens of the wanton, the plunder of the poor.

Fools ! your doublets shone with gold, and your hearts were gay
     and bold,
   When you kissed your lily hands to your lemans to-day ;
And to-morrow shall the fox, from her chambers in the rocks,
   Lead forth her tawny cubs to howl above the prey.

Where be your tongues that late mocked at heaven and hell
     and fate,
   And the fingers that once were so busy with your blades,
Your perfumed satin clothes, your catches and your oaths,
   Your stage-plays and your sonnets, your diamonds and your
     spades ?

Down, down, for ever down with the mitre and the crown,
   With the Belial of the Court, and the Mammon of the Pope
There is woe in Oxford Halls : there is wail in Durham's Stalls ,
   The Jesuit smites his bosom : the Bishop rends his cope.

And She of the seven hills shall mourn her children's ills,
  And tremble when she thinks on the edge of England's sword ;
And the Kings of earth in fear shall shudder when they hear
  What the hand of God hath wrought for the Houses and the
    Word.

Epitaph on a Jacobite.

To my true king I offered free from stain
Courage and faith ; vain faith, and courage vain.
For him, I threw lands, honours, wealth, away,
And one dear hope, that was more prized than they.
For him I languished in a foreign clime,
Grey-haired with sorrow in my manhood's prime ;
Heard on Lavernia Scargill's whispering trees,
And pined by Arno for my lovelier Tees ;
Beheld each night my home in fevered sleep,
Each morning started from the dream to weep ;
Till God, who saw me tried too sorely, gave
The resting-place I asked, an early grave.
Oh thou, whom chance leads to this nameless stone,
From that proud country which was once mine own,
By those white cliffs I never more must see,
By that dear language which I spake like thee,
Forget all feuds, and shed one English tear
O'er English dust. A broken heart lies here.

WINTHROP MACKWORTH PRAED.

[WINTHROP MACKWORTH PRAED was born in London on the 26th of July, 1802. He was educated at Eton, and Trinity College, Cambridge. He died on the 15th of July, 1839. His verses, contributed chiefly to periodicals such as the *Etonian* and Knight's *Quarterly Magazine*, were not collected in this country until 1864, when they were published in two volumes, with a memoir by the Rev. Derwent Coleridge.]

'In a collection of short pieces,'—says Mr. Matthew Arnold in his preface to Wordsworth's selected poems, 'the impression made by one piece requires to be continued and sustained by the piece following.' The verses of Praed are in some sort an illustration of the justice of this remark. Had he himself prepared his book for the press he would doubtless have cancelled a good many poems which his representatives, naturally enough, hesitated to omit. But even the over-affluent character of his legacy to posterity has not much impaired his popularity, or influenced the critical estimate of his work. As a writer of 'society-verse' in its exacter sense, Praed is justly acknowledged to be supreme. We say 'exacter sense,' because it has of late become the fashion to apply this vague term in the vaguest possible way, so as indeed to include almost all verse but the highest and the lowest. This is manifestly a mistake. 'Society-verse,' as Praed understood it, and as we understand it in Praed, treats almost exclusively of the *votum, timor, ira, voluptas* (and especially the *voluptas*) of that charmed circle of uncertain limits known conventionally as 'good society,'—those latter-day Athenians, who, in town and country, spend their time in telling or hearing some new thing, and whose graver and deeper impulses are subordinated to a code of artificial manners. Of these Praed is the laureate-elect ; and the narrow world in which they move is the 'main haunt and region of his song.' Now and again, it may be, he appears to quit it ; but never in reality ; and even when he seems to do so, like Landor's shell remote from the sea, he still 'remembers its august abodes.'

Praed's chief characteristics are his sparkling wit, the clearness and finish of his style, and the flexibility and unflagging vivacity of his rhythm. He is a master of epigram and antithesis, especially of the kind exemplified by the following couplets :—

> 'He lay beside a rivulet,
>   And looked beside himself';

or,

> 'And some grow rich by telling lies,
>   And some by telling money [1].'

His defects are that he lacks sincerity and variety of theme,—that his brilliancy at times becomes mere glitter, and his manner mechanical. His biographer assures us that his nature had a deeper and graver side than would be suspected from his habitual tone of sportive irony : it is incontestable, however, that the indications of this in his works are faint compared with those which we find in Thackeray and Hood. *My own Araminta* is an admirable example of his lightest style ; the *Vicar* of his more pensive character-pieces ; whilst in *My little Cousins*, which our space does not permit us to quote, there is a rarer vein of playful tenderness. In many of his charades he almost manages to raise those metrical pastimes to the dignity of poetry.

AUSTIN DOBSON.

[1] **Praed** may perhaps have taken the hint of this device from the *Holy Fair*,—

> 'There 's some are fou o' love divine ;
>   There 's some are fou o' brandy.'

A LETTER OF ADVICE. FROM MISS MEDORA TREVILIAN, AT PADUA, TO MISS ARAMINTA VAVASOUR, IN LONDON.

You tell me you're promised a lover,
  My own Araminta, next week ;
Why cannot my fancy discover
  The hue of his coat and his cheek ?
Alas ! if he look like another,
  A vicar, a banker, a beau,
Be deaf to your father and mother,
  My own Araminta, say ' No !'

Miss Lane, at her Temple of Fashion,
  Taught us both how to sing and to speak,
And we loved one another with passion,
  Before we had been there a week :
You gave me a ring for a token ;
  I wear it wherever I go ;
I gave you a chain,—is it broken ?
  My own Araminta, say ' No !'

O think of our favourite cottage,
  And think of our dear Lalla Rookh !
How we shared with the milkmaids their pottage,
  And drank of the stream from the brook ;
How fondly our loving lips faltered,
  'What further can grandeur bestow ?'
My heart is the same ;—is yours altered ?
  My own Araminta, say ' No !'

Remember the thrilling romances
  We read on the bank in the glen ;
Remember the suitors our fancies
  Would picture for both of us then.
They wore the red cross on their shoulder,
  They had vanquished and pardoned their foe—
Sweet friend, are you wiser or colder ?
  My own Araminta, say ' No !'

You know, when Lord Rigmarole's carriage,
  Drove off with your Cousin Justine,
You wept, dearest girl, at the marriage,
  And whispered ' How base she has been !'
You said you were sure it would kill you,
  If ever your husband looked so ;
And you will not apostatize,—will you ?
  My own Araminta, say ' No !'

When I heard I was going abroad, love,
  I thought I was going to die ;
We walked arm in arm to the road, love,
  We looked arm in arm to the sky;
And I said ' When a foreign postilion
  Has hurried me off to the Po,
Forget not Medora Trevilian :
  My own Araminta, say " No " !'

We parted ! but sympathy's fetters
  Reach far over valley and hill ;
I muse o'er your exquisite letters,
  And feel that your heart is mine still ;
And he who would share it with me, love,—
  The richest of treasures below,—
If he 's not what Orlando should be, love,
  My own Araminta, say ' No !'

If he wears a top boot in his wooing,
  If he comes to you riding a cob,
If he talks of his baking or brewing,
  If he puts up his feet on the hob,
If he ever drinks port after dinner,
  If his brow or his breeding is low,
If he calls himself ' Thompson ' or ' Skinner,'
  My own Araminta, say ' No !'

If he studies the news in the papers
  While you are preparing the tea,
If he talks of the damps or the vapours
  While moonlight lies soft on the sea,

If he's sleepy while you are capricious,
 If he has not a musical 'Oh!'
If he does not call Werther delicious,—
 My own Araminta, say 'No!'

If he ever sets foot in the City
 Among the stockbrokers and Jews,
If he has not a heart full of pity,
 If he don't stand six feet in his shoes,
If his lips are not redder than roses,
 If his hands are not whiter than snow,
If he has not the model of noses,—
 My own Araminta, say 'No!'

If he speaks of a tax or a duty,
 If he does not look grand on his knees,
If he's blind to a landscape of beauty,
 Hills, valleys, rocks, waters, and trees,
If he dotes not on desolate towers,
 If he likes not to hear the blast blow,
If he knows not the language of flowers,—
 My own Araminta, say 'No!'

He must walk—like a god of old story
 Come down from the home of his rest;
He must smile—like the sun in his glory
 On the buds he loves ever the best;
And oh! from its ivory portal
 Like music his soft speech must flow!—
If he speak, smile, or walk like a mortal,
 My own Araminta, say 'No!'

Don't listen to tales of his bounty,
 Don't hear what they say of his birth,
Don't look at his seat in the county,
 Don't calculate what he is worth;
But give him a theme to write verse on,
 And see if he turns out his toe;
If he's only an excellent person,—
 My own Araminta, say 'No!'

The Vicar.

Some years ago, ere time and taste
  Had turned our parish topsy-turvy,
When Darnel Park was Darnel Waste,
  And roads as little known as scurvy,
The man who lost his way, between
  St. Mary's Hill and Sandy Thicket,
Was always shown across the green,
  And guided to the Parson's wicket.

Back flew the bolt of lissom lath ;
  Fair Margaret, in her tidy kirtle,
Led the lorn traveller up the path,
  Through clean-clipt rows of box and myrtle ;
And Don and Sancho, Tramp and Tray,
  Upon the parlour steps collected,
Wagged all their tails, and seemed to say—
  ' Our master knows you—you 're expected.'

Uprose the Reverend Dr. Brown,
  Uprose the Doctor's winsome marrow ;
The lady laid her knitting down,
  Her husband clasped his ponderous Barrow ;
Whate'er the stranger's caste or creed,
  Pundit or Papist, saint or sinner,
He found a stable for his steed,
  And welcome for himself, and dinner.

If, when he reached his journey's end,
  And warmed himself in Court or College,
He had not gained an honest friend
  And twenty curious scraps of knowledge,—
If he departed as he came,
  With no new light on love or liquor,—
Good sooth, the traveller was to blame,
  And not the Vicarage, nor the Vicar.

His talk was like a stream, which runs
  With rapid change from rocks to roses:
It slipped from politics to puns,
  It passed from Mahomet to Moses;
Beginning with the laws which keep
  The planets in their radiant courses,
And ending with some precept deep
  For dressing eels, or shoeing horses.

He was a shrewd and sound Divine,
  Of loud Dissent the mortal terror;
And when, by dint of page and line,
  He 'stablished Truth, or startled Error,
The Baptist found him far too deep;
  The Deist sighed with saving sorrow;
And the lean Levite went to sleep,
  And dreamed of tasting pork to-morrow.

His sermon never said or showed
  That Earth is foul, that Heaven is grac'ous,
Without refreshment on the road
  From Jerome, or from Athanasius:
And sure a righteous zeal inspired
  The hand and head that penned and planned them,
For all who understood admired,
  And some who did not understand them.

He wrote, too, in a quiet way,
  Small treatises, and smaller verses,
And sage remarks on chalk and clay,
  And hints to noble Lords—and nurses;
True histories of last year's ghost,
  Lines to a ringlet, or a turban,
And trifles for the Morning Post,
  And nothings for Sylvanus Urban.

He did not think all mischief fair,
  Although he had a knack of joking;
He did not make himself a bear,
  Although he had a taste for smoking;

And when religious sects ran mad,
   He held, in spite of all his learning,
That if a man's belief is bad,
   It will not be improved by burning.

And he was kind, and loved to sit
   In the low hut or garnished cottage,
And praise the farmer's homely wit,
   And share the widow's homelier pottage:
At his approach complaint grew mild;
   And when his hand unbarred the shutter,
The clammy lips of fever smiled
   The welcome which they could not utter.

He always had a tale for me
   Of Julius Caesar, or of Venus;
From him I learnt the rule of three,
   Cat's cradle, leap-frog, and *Quae genus:*
I used to singe his powdered wig,
   To steal the staff he put such trust in,
And make the puppy dance a jig,
   When he began to quote Augustine.

Alack the change! in vain I look
   For haunts in which my boyhood trifled,—
The level lawn, the trickling brook,
   The trees I climbed, the beds I rifled:
The church is larger than before;
   You reach it by a carriage entry;
It holds three hundred people more,
   And pews are fitted up for gentry.

Sit in the Vicar's seat: you'll hear
   The doctrine of a gentle Johnian,
Whose hand is white, whose tone is clear,
   Whose phrase is very Ciceronian.
Where is the old man laid?—look down,
   And construe on the slab before you,
'*Hic jacet* GVLIELMVS BROWN,
   Vir nullâ non donandus lauru.

THOMAS LOVELL BEDDOES.

[THOMAS LOVELL BEDDOES was born at Rodney Place, Clifton, on the 20th of July, 1803 ; he was the son of the famous physician Dr. Thomas Beddoes, and nephew of the no less famous Maria Edgeworth. He was educated at Bath, and at the Charterhouse, and entered Pembroke College, Oxford, in 1820. From 1825 to 1846 he resided in Germany and Switzerland. He left England again after a stay of a few months, and died under somewhat mysterious circumstances in the hospital at Basle, Jan. 26, 1849. He published during his lifetime *The Improvisatore*, 1821, and *The Bride's Tragedy*, 1822, besides various works in German ; after his death appeared *Death's Jest Book*, 1850, and *Poems*, 1851].

It has been the fate of Beddoes to be made the subject of praise and blame exaggerated enough to fill his proud and indifferent spirit, could he revisit the moonlit world of journalism, with a fund of sardonic merriment. He would certainly be the first to see the jest of his being treated as a profoundly original philosophic poet, and probably more amused than annoyed at being confounded with his own

> ' bodyless child-full of life in the gloom,
> Crying with frog-voice, " What shall I be ? " '

There is certainly nothing vague, nothing misty or dubious about the poetic entity of Beddoes ; he has scarcely left a page behind him of which it cannot be said that he alone in recent times could have written it. His own caustic definition of his poetry pronounces it to be ' entertaining, very unamiable, and utterly unpopular.' We may paraphrase this by saying that it is entertaining because so skilful and nervous in style, so full of surprises, and so unconventional in its aspect of life ; but unamiable because of its entire indifference to the ordinary interests of life, and unpopular because it deals with passions and events of a wholly foreign and unfamiliar type. Beddoes is in poetry what the Helsche Breughel is in painting. He dedicates himself to the service of Death, not with a brooding sense of the terror and shame of mortality, but from a love of the picturesque pageantry of it, the majesty and sombre beauty, the swift, theatrical transitions, the combined elegance and horror that wait upon the sudden decease of monarchs. He was scarcely a born singer ; he was a man of consummate natural ability, who chose to walk through the world in the masquerade of a tragic dramatist, and who carried his antique robes so consistently and so skilfully, that at last his artificial presentment was almost as interesting as the real thing would have been, and the mummer himself almost forgot that he was mumming. The reader who carefully analyses his passages of declamatory fancy, is equally startled by the unreality and by the consummate cleverness of the style. The blank verse of Beddoes is always admirable ; it was not as a craftsman that so accomplished a personage was likely to fail ; it is even more than admirable, it occasionally approaches closer to the grand manner of the Elizabethan iambic movement than almost any modern verse. But under it all there lies no deep murmur of poetry, no ground-swell of momentous music, making itself dimly heard when the march of the lines is silent, none of that wonderful mystery of sound that we catch in the best passages of Webster and Marston, and even of Cyril Tourneur. Beddoes succeeds, in my judgment, much more truly as a song-writer than as a constructor of blank verse. His songs are very plainly modelled upon two types, the one that of Shakespeare and his school, the other that of Shelley. It was no honour to Beddoes, it was merely characteristic of his extraordinary intellectual vigour and perspicacity, that he was the first Englishman, outside the circle of personal friends, to perceive the momentous character of Shelley's genius. In his lyrics he sat at Shelley's feet, always with too much cleverness to fall into the tricks of imitation ; and it would perhaps not be very easy to trace the likeness, if he had not unwarily left one palpable specimen of his method in the song ' The swallow leaves her nest,' where the movement of Shelley's verse is borrowed, not adapted. Yet, if we are content to take the best of his songs for what they are worth, as mar-vellously clever *tours de force,* they are as enjoyable as purely artificial exercises in verse can ever be.

Beddoes expended thought and labour for four years on the one poem which he meant to be his masterpiece, *Death's Jest Book.* It is a tragedy of the same class as the *Duchess of Malfy* and *Antonio and Mellida* ; indeed there are whole scenes which might have been taken bodily out of Marston. There is no doubt that *Death's Jest Book* is a poem which will reward perusal ; it can scarcely be said to invite it. The plot is founded on the story of a Duke Boleslaus of Münsterberg in Silesia, who was killed by his court-fool in 1377. Some months before Beddoes actually commenced the composition of the piece, he wrote, in one of his charming letters, the following extremely sage words about the mode in which to approach modern tragedy : ' Say what you will, I am convinced the man who is to awaken the drama must be a bold trampling fellow, no creeper into wormholes, no reviver even, however good. Such ghosts as Marlowe, Webster, etc., are better dramatists, better poets, I dare say, than any contemporary of ours, but they are ghosts ; the worm is in their pages ; and we want to see something that our great-grandsires did not know.' It would have been salutary indeed for the poor poet himself to have practised what he preached ; as it is, nothing is more curious than the contrast between what he wished to do and what he did. *Death's Jest Book* is the most eminent specimen existing of poetical spirit-rapping ; those very ghosts, whose presence on the modern boards Beddoes so wisely deprecated, were called up more lustily and pertinaciously by none than he. Sometimes, as notably in the scene where the Duke watches by his wife's grave, the modern poet almost attains to the genuine horror of his master's touch, but even here something mechanical reminds us of the deception. In *Death's Jest Book*, as elsewhere in Beddoes, the lyrics appear to me fresher and more enjoyable than the blank verse, and some of the grim and humorous songs have the spell of real genius upon them. That containing the stanza—

> ' From the old supper-giver's pole
> He tore the many-kingdomed mitre;
> To him, who cost him his son's soul,
> He gave it, to the Persian fighter,'

seems to me of an extraordinary force and horror. My friend Mr. Browning, from whose subtle pen we may yet hope to receive the final and authoritative judgment on Beddoes, informs me that many songs of this ghastly comic cast still remain unprinted, and throw an interesting light upon the character of this problem of a poet.

EDMUND W. GOSSE.

DIRGE FOR WOLFRAM.

[Death's Jest Book, Act ii.]

If thou wilt ease thine heart
Of love and all its smart,
   Then sleep, dear, sleep ;
And not a sorrow
  Hang any tear on your eyelashes ;
   Lie still and deep,
  Sad soul, until the sea-wave washes
The rim o' the sun to-morrow,
   In eastern sky.

But wilt thou cure thine heart
Of love and all its smart,
   Then die, dear, die ;
'Tis deeper, sweeter,
  Than on a rose-bank to lie dreaming
   With folded eye ;
  And there alone, amid the beaming
Of Love's stars, thou 'lt meet her
   In eastern sky.

SONG.

[Torrismond, Sc. iii.]

How many times do I love thee, dear ?
  Tell me how many thoughts there be
   In the atmosphere
   Of a new-fall'n year,
Whose white and sable hours appear
  The latest flake of Eternity :—
So many times do I love thee, dear.

How many times do I love, again?
  Tell me how many beads there are
    In a silver chain
    Of evening rain
  Unravelled from the tumbling main
    And threading the eye of a yellow star '—
So many times do I love again.

AMALA'S BRIDAL SONG.

[From *Death's Jest Book*, Act iv.]

Female Voices.

We have bathed, where none have seen us,
  In the lake and in the fountain,
    Underneath the charmëd statue
Of the timid, bending Venus,
  When the water-nymphs were counting
    In the waves the stars of night,
    And those maidens started at you,
Your limbs shone through so soft and bright.
    But no secrets dare we tell,
      For thy slaves unlace thee,
      And he, who shall embrace thee,
    Waits to try thy beauty's spell.

Male Voices.

We have crowned thee queen of women,
  Since love's love, the rose, hath kept her
    Court within thy lips and blushes,
And thine eye, in beauty swimming,
  Kissing, we rendered up the sceptre,
At whose touch the startled soul
    Like an ocean bounds and gushes,
And spirits bend at thy control.
    But no secrets dare we tell,
      For thy slaves unlace thee,
      And he, who shall embrace thee,
    Is at hand, and so farewell.

ATHULF'S SONG.

[From *Death's Jest Book*, Act **iv.**]

A cypress-bough, and a rose-wreath sweet,
A wedding-robe, and a winding-sheet,
    A bridal bed and a bier.
Thine be the kisses, maid,
    And smiling Love's alarms;
And thou, pale youth, be laid
    In the grave's cold arms.
    Each in his own charms,
      Death and Hymen both are here;
      So up with scythe and torch,
      And to the old church porch,
      While all the bells ring clear :
And rosy, rosy the bed shall bloom,
And earthy, earthy heap up the tomb.

Now tremble dimples on your cheek,
Sweet be your lips to taste and speak,
    For he who kisses is near :
By her the bride-god fair,
    In youthful power and force ;
By him the grizard bare,
    Pale knight on a pale horse,
    To woo him to a corse.
      Death and Hymen both are here,
      So up with scythe and torch,
      And to the old church porch,
      While all the bells ring clear :
And rosy, rosy the bed shall bloom,
And earthy, earthy heap up the tomb.

SAILORS' SONG.

[From *Death's Jest Book*, Act **i.**]

To sea, to sea! The calm is o'er;
  The wanton water leaps in sport,
And rattles down the pebbly shore;
  The dolphin wheels, the sea-cows snort,
And unseen mermaids' pearly song
Comes bubbling up, the weeds among.
  Fling broad the sail, dip deep the oar:
  To sea, to sea! the calm is o'er.

To sea, to sea! our wide-winged bark
  Shall billowy cleave its sunny way,
And with its shadow, fleet and dark,
  Break the caved Tritons' azure day,
Like mighty eagle soaring light
O'er antelopes on Alpine height.
  The anchor heaves, the ship swings free,
  The sails swell full. To sea, to sea!

HESPERUS' SONG.

[From *The Bride's Tragedy*, Act **i.**]

Poor old pilgrim Misery,
  Beneath the silent moon he sate,
A-listening to the screech-owl's cry,
  And the cold wind's goblin prate;
Beside him lay his staff of yew
  With withered willow twined,
His scant grey hair all wet with dew,
  His cheeks with grief ybrined;
    And his cry it was ever, alack!
    Alack, and woe is me!

Anon a wanton imp astray
  His piteous moaning hears,
And from his bosom steals away
  His rosary of tears :
With his plunder fled that urchin elf,
  And hid it in your eyes,
Then tell me back the stolen pelf,
  Give up the lawless prize ;
    Or your cry shall be ever, alack !
    Alack, and woe is me !

SONG OF THE STYGIAN NAIADES.

Proserpine may pull her flowers,
  Wet with dew or wet with tears,
  Red with anger, pale with fears,
Is it any fault of ours,
If Pluto be an amorous king,
  And comes home nightly, laden,
Underneath his broad bat-wing,
  With a gentle, mortal maiden ?
Is it so, Wind, is it so ?
All that you and I do know
Is, that we saw fly and fix
'Mongst the reeds and flowers of Styx,
      Yesterday,
Where the Furies made their hay
For a bed of tiger-cubs,
A great fly of Beelzebub's,
The bee of hearts, whom mortals name
Cupid, Love, and Fie for shame.

Proserpine may weep in rage,
  But, ere you and I have done
  Kissing, bathing in the sun,
What I have in yonder cage,

Bird or serpent, wild or tame,
  She shall guess, and ask in vain;
  But, if Pluto does't again,
It shall sing out loud his shame.
  What hast caught then? What hast caught?
  Nothing but a poet's thought,
  Which so light did fall and fix
  'Mongst the reeds and flowers of Styx,
          Yesterday,
  Where the Furies made their hay
  For a bed of tiger-cubs,—
  A great fly of Beelzebub's,
  The bee of hearts, whom mortals name
  Cupid, Love, and Fie for shame.

WOLFRAM'S SONG.

[From *Death's Jest Book*, Act v.]

Old Adam, the carrion crow,
  The old crow of Cairo;
He sat in the shower, and let it flow
  Under his tail and over his crest;
      And through every feather
      Leaked the wet weather;
  And the bough swung under his nest;
For his beak it was heavy with marrow.
      Is that the wind dying? O no;
      It's only two devils, that blow
      Through a murderer's bones, to and fro,
          In the ghosts' moonshine.

Ho! Eva, my grey carrion wife,
  When we have supped on kings' marrow,
Where shall we drink and make merry our life?
  Our nest it is Queen Cleopatra's skull,
      'Tis cloven and cracked,
      And battered and hacked,

But with tears of blue eyes it is full :
Let us drink then, my raven of Cairo.
   Is that the wind dying? O no ;
   It is only two devils, that blow
   Through a murderer's bones, to and fro,
     In the ghosts' moonshine,

FROM ' DREAM-PEDLARY.'

If there were dreams to sell
    What would you buy?
Some cost a passing bell ;
    Some a light sigh,
That shakes from Life's fresh crown
Only a rose-leaf down.
If there were dreams to sell,
Merry and sad to tell,
And the crier rang the bell,
    What would you buy?

A cottage lone and still,
    With bowers nigh,
Shadowy, my woes to still,
    Until I die.
Such pearl from Life's fresh crown
Fain would I shake me down.
Were dreams to have at will,
This would best heal my ill,
    This would I buy.

ELIZABETH BARRETT BROWNING.

[BORN 1809: died 1861. Published *Prometheus Bound* and other poems, 1835; the *Seraphim* and other poems, 1838; *Romaunt of the Page*, 1839; two volumes of *Poems*, 1844; married Robert Browning, 1846; published *Casa Guidi Windows*, 1848; *Aurora Leigh*, 1856; *Poems before Congress*, 1860. The *Last Poems* were published posthumously in 1862, with a dedication to 'grateful Florence,' in allusion to the inscription on the tablet which after her death the city of Florence had put up in her honour.]

Elizabeth Barrett began verse-making at a very early age. Besides the unacknowledged *Essay on Mind*, an attempt in the style of Pope, which was written when she was a mere girl, she translated *Prometheus Bound* before she was twenty. Writing to her friend Mr. Horne, under the date of Oct. 5, 1843, she says :—

'Most of my events and nearly all my intense pleasures have passed in my *thoughts*. I wrote verses—as I daresay many have done who never wrote any poems — very early; at eight years old and earlier. But, what is less common, the early fancy turned into a will, and remained with me, and from that day to this poetry has been a distinct object with me—an object to read, think, and live for. And I could make you laugh, although you could not make the public laugh, by the narrative of nascent odes, epics, and didactics crying aloud on obsolete Muses from childish lips.'

Her life seems to have been a happy one till she was growing into womanhood. Then two things happened, at no great distance of time from one another, which altered and saddened it. Of the impression she made upon all who saw her before her great trial and sorrow came upon her let her old and tried friend Miss Mitford speak :—

'My first acquaintance with Elizabeth Barrett commenced about fifteen years ago. She was certainly one of the most interesting persons that I had ever seen. Everybody who then saw her said the same; so that it is not merely the impression of my partiality or my enthusiasm. Of a slight, delicate figure, with a shower of dark curls falling on either side of a most expressive face, large tender eyes richly fringed by dark eyelashes, a smile like a sunbeam, and such a look of youthfulness, that I had some difficulty in persuading a friend in whose carriage we went together to Chiswick that the translatress of the *Prometheu* of Aeschylus, the authoress of the *Essay on Mind*, was old enough to be introduced into company, in technical language, was o t. Through the kindness of another invaluable friend, to whom I owe many obligations, but none so great as this, I saw much of her during my stay in town. We met so constantly and so familiarly, that in spite of the difference of age, intimacy ripened into friendship. and after my return into the country we corresponded freely and frequently her letters being just what letters ought to be—her own talk put upon paper.'

The beginning of her trials came next year, when she broke a blood-vessel upon the lungs, which refused to heal. On the approach of winter the family doctor ordered her to a warmer climate, and her elder brother, who seems by all accounts to have been worthy of his sister, accompanied her to Torquay. His death by drowning—the sailing boat in which he was sank in sight of the house, and the body was not recovered—nearly killed his sister. She conceived a horror of Torquay, and had to be brought back to London in an invalid carriage. 'Returned to London,' says Miss Mitford, 'she began the life which she continued for so many years, confined to one large and commodiously darkened chamber, admitting only her own affectionate family and a few devoted friends . . . . reading almost every book worth reading in almost every language, and giving herself heart and soul to that poetry of which she seemed born to be the priestess.' This way of life lasted for many years. It was dignified by high thinking and strenuous endeavour, and sweetened by the intercourse of a few congenial minds ; but it was wholly outside the main current of the world, and it threw the poetess to an excessive extent upon her own inner consciousness for the materials of her poetry. This fact explains some of the defects of which we are conscious in a sustained reading of her poetical works. If her muse seems to dwell in a somewhat transcendental atmosphere, a little remote from the realities of the work-a-day world, if her portrayal of human nature is a little wanting in complexity and variety, and hardly seems born of contact with men and women as they are, that is not to be wondered at. Her happy marriage lifted her out of the bookish seclusion in which she had lived for many years ; and the immediate strength and activity which happiness brought with it makes us suspect that hitherto her friends and relations had encouraged her into thinking herself more of an invalid than she really was. The new and stirring world of political and intellectul activity into which her residence in Italy now transported her, soon made its way into her poetry, and left its mark. But the effects of her long seclusion never wore out, though here and there we may find them obliterated for a moment ; and in the most ambitious of her later poems, *Aurora Leigh* (a noble and admirable effort, though we should hardly agree with Mr. Ruskin in calling it 'the greatest poem which the century has produced in any language'), we feel the lack of that sure and sane knowledge of human nature which, as Miss Mitford truly said,—though the remark was not intended to apply to her friend,—is 'the salt of literature.'

One thing at all events Elizabeth Barrett gained from her years of studious seclusion — an accurate knowledge of most of the great poetry of the world. Her knowledge of Greek was wide if not profound, and she was familiar with the chief modern literatures. She had read English poetry with a thoroughness and a dis-crimination which is testified as much by her *Vision of Poets* as by her *Essay on English Poetry*. The English poets of her own day were intimately known to her. Her first volume shows traces of study of Byron, Shelley, and Coleridge, and the study has been deep enough to result rather in assimilation than imitation. Later on she became a great admirer of Tennyson, whom she called 'a divine poet,' though she warmly disclaimed the charge of imitating him. She may be described essentially as a learned poetess, and her wide knowledge of poetical forms explains her readiness to invent or reproduce difficult and elaborate metres. With these difficulties she has not always contended successfully. Her rhymes are often illegitimate, her words often far-fetched, and occasionally even ungrammatical. The splendid dash and energy with which she throws herself at a difficult piece of work should not blind us to the fact that after all its difficulties are sometimes evaded rather than met. She will not have it that this is for any want of due care or industry on her part. Writing to Mr. Horne, she says in terms very similar to those employed by Wordsworth in rebutting a similar charge :—

'If I fail ultimately before the public—that is before the people, for an ephemeral popularity does not appear to me worth trying for—it will not be because I have shrunk from the amount of labour, where labour could do anything. I have *worked* at poetry ; it has not been with me reverie, but art. As the physician and lawyer work at their several professions. so have I, and so do I, apply to mine. And this I say, only to put by any charge of care-lessness which may rise up to the verge of your lips or thoughts.'

Nevertheless in that correspondence between herself and Mr. Horne on her system of rhyming, which forms perhaps the most valuable part of the work that Mr. Horne has dedicated to her memory, there can be no doubt that Mr. Horne gets the best of the argument. He maintained that the fact was, 'whether the poetess intended it or not, that she was introducing a system of rhyming the first syllables and leaving the rest to a question of euphonious quantity.' His criticism was particularly directed against the rhymes in the *Dead Pan*, which the authoress as energetically defended. Miss Mitford, who was always candid in her judgment of her friend, supported Mr. Horne's view.

It will of course be understood that we are not complaining of that occasional violation of exact rhyme which only adds to the general harmony. No one with an ear would think of complaining of such a stanza as this from the *Vision of Poets*—

> 'Cleaving the incense clouds that *rise*
> With winking unaccustomed *eyes*,
> And lovelocks smelling sweet of *spice*.'

But what of this from *The Lost Bower* ?—

> 'Face to face with the true *mountains*
> I stood silently and still,
> Drawing strength from fancy's *dauntings*,
> From the air about the hill,
> And from Nature's open mercies a most debonair **good will**.'

or this from *The Dead Pan* ?—

> 'Christ hath sent us down the *angels*;
> And the whole earth and the skies
> Are illumed by altar-*candles*
> Lit for blessèd mysteries.'

Take, again, the sonnet called *Patience taught by Nature*. There are only two rhymes in the octave, and one set of four is thus made up — *birds, herds, girds, swards*. 'Birds' is an almost impracticable rhyme for the octave of a Petrarchan sonnet, and obviously the poetess has not solved the difficulty implied in starting upon it. But licence in rhyming is not the only licence she permits herself. Her use of words is often capricious and extravagant. She turns substantives into adjectives, she adds an adverbial termination to an adverb, she invents outright dozens of words, is she is hard pressed for a rhyme. Here for instance she secures an admirable effect by a wrong use of a Chaucerian adjective :—

> 'And Keats the real
> Adonis with the hymeneal
> Fresh vernal buds half sunk between
> His youthful curls, kissed straight and *sheen*
> In his Rome-grave by Venus queen.'
>
> (*Vision of Poets.*)

In an exquisite stanza she finds a rhyme for 'morning' in 'many a mist's *inurning.*' In another place we have—

> 'When beneath the palace-lattice
> You ride slow as you have done,
> And you see a face there, that is
> Not the old familiar one,—
> Will you *oftly*
> Murmur softly,
> Here ye watched me morn and e'en,
> Sweetest eyes, were ever seen!'

That 'oftly' is terrible. This kind of catalogue could be extended indefinitely. Such words as 'fantasque,' 'percipiency,' 'humiliant,' 'vatic,' 'sentiency,' 'aspectable,' 'horrent' are current coin in her language, and often give it a fantastic air. She is a little spoilt by that 'over-effluence of music,' which she herself blamed in Barry Cornwall. The delight in beautifully sounding words is as great with her as it was with Keats ; but Keats, though he allowed himself considerable latitude in his blank verse (*Hyperion* is full of coined and curious words), was most rigorous with himself in his rhymed verse. A poet who is enamoured of perfection will allow himself liberties anywhere and everywhere except for the sake of evading a difficulty. Now enamoured of perfection Mrs. Browning was not. The poems which, from what may be called a technical point of view, may be counted irreproachable, may, if we except the Sonnets, almost be reckoned on the fingers. Her Sonnets are among the very best work she has produced. Perhaps indeed her greatest poetic success is to be found in the *Sonnets from the Portuguese,*—sonnets, it need hardly be said, which are not 'from the Portuguese' at all, but are the faintly disguised presentment of the writer's most intimate experience. Into the 'sonnet's narrow room' she has poured the full flood of her profoundest thought, and yet the minuteness and exquisiteness of the mould has at the same time compelled a rigorous pruning alike of superabundant imagery and of harmonious verbosity, which has had the happiest results. She is one of the greatest sonnet writers in our language, worthy for this at all events to be ranked side by side with Milton and with Wordsworth.

Our own generation is probably inclined to give the poetess less than her due, and for obvious reasons. The art of verse-making has been carried to a point of technical perfection that she hardly dreamt of, and her laxity offends. Moreover, her innocent and heartfelt enthusiasms fall a little dully on the ear of a perverse and critical generation. We should call her naive, almost silly, where she has merely been artless and confiding. Her enthusiasm for Bulwer Lytton's weaker work and the traces of his influence on her earlier poems we cannot easily away with. There are passages in *Aurora Leigh*, particularly the passages describing the bad people, which might make an unkindly critic describe the authoress as a hysterical school-girl ; and indeed it would not be easy to confute the critic, except by putting passage against passage, and showing how, with her, a lapse is always followed by a rise. What valuable and original elements her thought possesses have for the most part been absorbed long ago, have become common property, and are no longer recognisable as hers. The great struggle for Italian unity has inspired some of her best verses, and that struggle has already become very much a matter of ancient history. Yet in spite of all deductions that can be made—deductions, be it remembered, which are sometimes to be counted against the reader, and only sometimes against the poetess—she remains an attractive and delightful personage, and she has stamped enough of herself upon her poetry to give it an enduring charm. Her deep tenderness and genuineness of feeling, showing themselves in such poems as the *Cry of the Children* or *Cowper's Grave*, will never fail of their rightful power. She has touched all the chief human relationships, that of friend and friend, that of husband and wife, that of mother and child, with an exquisite insight and sensitiveness and delicacy, and her style, when she touches them, attains almost always that noble and severe simplicity which is so greatly to be preferred to her most luscious and copious versification. She has added a charm to motherhood only less than that added by Raffaelle himself, and the pleasant fate will be hers of being faithfully read by many a generation of youthful lovers.

WILLIAM T. ARNOLD.

IRREPARABLENESS.

I have been in the meadows all the day,
And gathered there the nosegay that you see,
Singing within myself as bird or bee
When such do field-work on a morn of May.
But, now I look upon my flowers, decay
Has met them in my hands more fatally
Because more warmly clasped,—and sobs are free
To come instead of songs. What you say,
Sweet counsellors, dear friends? that I should go
Back straightway to the fields and gather more?
Another, sooth, may do it, but not I!
My heart is very tired, my strength is low,
My hands are full of blossoms plucked before,
Held dead within them till myself shall die.

GRIEF.

I tell you, hopeless grief is passionless;
That only men incredulous of despair,
Half-taught in anguish, through the midnight air
Beat upward to God's throne in loud access
Of shrieking and reproach. Full desertness
In souls as countries lieth silent-bare
Under the blanching vertical eye-glare
Of the absolute heavens. Deep-hearted man, express
Grief for thy Dead in silence like to death—
Most like a monumental statue set
In everlasting watch and moveless woe,
Till itself crumble to the dust beneath.
Touch it; the marble eyelids are not wet:
If it could weep, it could arise and go.

SONNETS FROM THE PORTUGUESE.

I.

I thought once how Theocritus had sung
Of the sweet years, the dear and wished for years,
Who each one in a gracious hand appears

To bear a gift for mortals, old or young:
And, as I mused it in his antique tongue,
I saw, in gradual vision through my tears,
The sweet, sad years, the melancholy years,—
Those of my own life, who by turns had flung
A shadow across me.   Straightway I was 'ware,
So weeping, how a mystic Shape did move
Behind me, and drew me backward by the hair;
And a voice said in mastery while I strove,—
'Guess now who holds thee?'—'Death,' I said.   But, there,
The silver answer rang—'Not Death, but Love.'

IV.

Thou hast thy calling to some palace floor,
Most gracious singer of high poems! where
The dancers will break footing from the care
Of watching up thy pregnant lips for more.
And dost thou lift this house's latch too poor
For hand of thine? and canst thou think and bear
To let thy music drop here unaware
In folds of golden fulness at my door?
Look up and see the casement broken in,
The bats and owlets builders in the roof!
My cricket chirps against thy mandolin.
Hush! call no echo up in further proof
Of desolation! there's a voice within
That weeps—as thou must sing—alone, aloof.

VI.

Go from me.   Yet I feel that I shall stand
Henceforward in thy shadow.   Nevermore
Alone upon the threshold of my door
Of individual life, I shall command
The uses of my soul, nor lift my hand
Serenely in the sunshine as before,
Without the sense of that which I forbore,—
Thy touch upon the palm.   The widest land
Doom takes to part us, leaves thy heart in mine

With pulses that beat double. What I do
And what I dream include thee, as the wine
Must taste of its own grapes. And when I sue
God for myself, He hears that name of thine,
And sees within my eyes, the tears of two.

XXVII.

My own beloved, who hast lifted me
From this drear flat of earth where I was thrown,
And in betwixt the languid ringlets, blown
A life-breath, till the forehead hopefully
Shines out again, as all the angels see,
Before thy saving kiss! My own, my own,
Who camest to me when the world was gone,
And I who looked for only God, found *thee*!
I find thee; I am safe, and strong, and glad.
As one who stands in dewless asphodel,
Looks backward on the tedious time he had
In the upper life—so I, with bosom-swell,
Make witness, here, between the good and bad,
That Love, as strong as Death, retrieves as well

XXVIII.

My letters! all dead paper, mute and white!
And yet they seem alive and quivering
Against my tremulous hands which loose the string
And let them drop down on my knee to-night.
This said,—he wished to have me in his sight
Once, as a friend: this fixed a day in spring
To come and touch my hand—a simple thing,
Yet I wept for it! this—the paper's light—
Said, *Dear, I love thee*; and I sank and quailed
As if God's future thundered on my past.
This said, *I am thine*—and so its ink has paled
With lying at my heart that beat too fast:
And this—O Love, thy words have ill availed,
If, what this said, I dared repeat at last!

XLIII.

How do I love thee? Let me count the ways.
I love thee to the depth and breadth and height
My soul can reach, when feeling out of sight
For the ends of Being and Ideal Grace.
I love thee to the level of everyday's
Most quiet need, by sun and candlelight.
I love thee freely, as men strive for Right;
I love thee purely, as they turn from Praise;
I love thee with the passion put to use
In my old griefs, and with my childhood's faith;
I love thee with a love I seemed to lose
With my lost saints,—I love thee with the breath,
Smiles, tears, of all my life!—and, if God choose,
I shall but love thee better after death.

From 'Casa Guidi Windows.'

Then, gazing, I beheld the long-drawn street
Live out, from end to end, full in the sun,
With Austria's thousand; sword and bayonet,
Horse, foot, artillery,—cannons rolling on
Like blind slow storm-clouds gestant with the heat
Of undeveloped lightnings, each bestrode
By a single man, dust-white from head to heel,
Indifferent as the dreadful thing he rode,
Like sculptured Fate serene and terrible.
As some smooth river which has overflowed,
Will slow and silent down its current wheel
A loosened forest, all the pines erect,
So swept, in mute significance of storm,
The marshalled thousands; not an eye deflects
To left or right, to catch a novel form
Of Florence city adorned by architect
And carver, or of Beaut'es live and warm
Scared at the casements,—all, straightforward eyes
And faces, held as steadfast as their swords,
And cognizant of acts, not imageries.

The key, O Tuscans, too well fits the wards!
Ye asked for mimes,—these bring you tragedies:
For purple,—these shall wear it as your lords.
Ye played like children,—die like innocents.
Ye mimicked lightnings with a torch,—the crack
Of the actual bolt, your pastime circumvents.
Ye called up ghosts, believing they were slack
To follow any voice from Gilboa's tents, . . .
Here's Samuel!—and, so, Grand-dukes come back!

A MUSICAL INSTRUMENT.

What was he doing, the great God Pan,
  Down in the reeds by the river?
Spreading ruin and scattering ban,
Splashing and paddling with hoofs of a goat,
And breaking the golden lilies afloat
  With the dragon-fly on the river.

He tore out a reed, the great God Pan,
  From the deep cool bed of the river:
The limpid water turbidly ran,
And the broken lilies a-dying lay,
And the dragon-fly had fled away,
  Ere he brought it out of the river.

High on the shore sat the great God Pan,
  While turbidly flowed the river;
And hacked and hewed as a great God can,
With his hard bleak steel at the patient reed,
Till there was not a sign of the leaf indeed
  To prove it fresh from the river.

He cut it short, did the great God Pan,
  (How tall it stood in the river!)
Then drew the pith, like the heart of a man,
Steadily from the outside ring,
And notched the poor dry empty thing
  In holes, as he sat by the river.

'This is the way, laughed the great God Pan,
  (Laughed while he sat by the river,)
'The only way, since Gods began
To make sweet music, they could succeed.'
Then, dropping his mouth to a hole in the reed,
  He blew in power by the river.

Sweet, sweet, sweet, O Pan!
  Piercing sweet by the river!
Blinding sweet, O great God Pan!
The sun on the hill forgot to die,
And the lilies revived, and the dragon-fly
  Came back to dream on the river.

Yet half a beast is the great God Pan,
  To laugh as he sits by the river,
Making a poet out of a man:
The true Gods sigh for the cost and pain,—
For the reed which grows never more again
  As a reed with the reeds in the river.

THE FORCED RECRUIT.   SOLFERINO, 1859.

In the ranks of the Austrian you found him,
  He died with his face to you all;
Yet bury him here where around him
  You honour your bravest that fall.

Venetian, fair-featured and slender,
  He lies shot to death in his youth,
With a smile on his lips, over-tender
  For any mere soldier's dead mouth.

No stranger, and yet not a traitor,
  Though alien the cloth on his breast,
Underneath it how seldom a greater
  Young heart, has a shot sent to rest!

By your enemy tortured and goaded
  To march with them, stand in their file,
His musket (see) never was loaded,
  He facing your guns with that smile!

As orphans yearn on to their mothers,
  He yearned to your patriot bands ;—
'Let me die for our Italy, brothers,
  If not in your ranks, by your hands !

'Aim straightly, fire steadily ! spare me
  A ball in the body which may
Deliver my heart here, and tear me
  This badge of the Austrian away !'

So thought he, so died he this morning.
  What then ? many others have died.
Ay, but easy for men to die scorning
  The death-stroke, who fought side by side :—

One tricolor floating above them ;
  Struck down 'mid triumphant acclaims
Of an Italy rescued to love them
  And blazon the brass with their names.

But he—without witness or honour,
  There, shamed in his country's regard,
With the tyrants who march in upon her,
  Died faithful and passive : 't was hard.

'T was sublime. In a cruel restriction
  Cut off from the guerdon of sons,
With most filial obedience, conviction,
  His soul kissed the lips of her guns.

That moves you ? Nay, grudge not to show it,
  While digging a grave for him here :
The others who died, says your poet,
  Have glory,—let *him* have a tear.

[From *Aurora Leigh.*]

AURORA'S HOME.

I had a little chamber in the house,
As green as any privet-hedge a bird
Might choose to build in, though the nest itself
Could show but dead brown sticks and straws ; the walls
Were green, the carpet was pure green, the straight

Small bed was curtained greenly, and the folds
Hung green about the window which let in
The out-door world with all its greenery.
You could not push your head out and escape
A dash of dawn-dew from the honey-suckle,
But so you were baptized into the grace
And privilege of seeing. . . .

　　　　　　　First, the lime,
(I had enough there, of the lime, be sure,—
My morning-dream was often hummed away
By the bees in it); past the lime, the lawn,
Which, after sweeping broadly round the house,
Went trickling through the shrubberies in a stream
Of tender turf, and wore and lost itself
Among the acacias, over which you saw
The irregular line of elms by the deep lane
Which stopped the grounds and dammed the overflow
Of arbutus and laurel. Out of sight
The lane was ; sunk so deep, no foreign tramp
Nor drover of wild ponies out of Wales
Could guess if lady's hall or tenant's lodge
Dispensed such odours,—though his stick well-crooked
Might reach the lowest trail of blossoming briar
Which dipped upon the wall. Behind the elms,
And through their tops, you saw the folded hills
Striped up and down with hedges (burly oaks
Projecting from the line to show themselves)
Through which my cousin Romney's chimney smoked
As still as when a silent month in frost
Breathes, showing where the woodlands hid Leigh Hall ;
While, far above, a jut of table-land,
A promontory without water stretched,—
You could not catch it if the days were thick,
Or took it for a cloud ; but, otherwise,
The vigorous sun would catch it up at eve
And use it for an anvil till he had filled
The shelves of heaven with burning thunderbolts,
Protesting against night and darkness :—then,
When all his setting trouble was resolved

To a trance of passive glory, you might see
In apparition on the golden sky
(Alas, my Giotto's background!) the sheep run
Along the fine clear outline, small as mice
That run along a witch's scarlet thread.

THE BEAUTY OF ENGLAND.

I learnt to love that England. Very oft,
Before the day was born, or otherwise
Through secret windings of the afternoons,
I threw my hunters off and plunged myself
Among the deep hills, as a hunted stag
Will take the waters, shivering with the fear
And passion of the course. And when at last
Escaped, so many a green slope built on slope
Betwixt me and the evening's house behind,
I dared to rest, or wander, in a rest
Made sweeter for the step upon the grass,
And view the ground's most gentle dimplement,
(As if God's finger touched, but did not press
In making England) such an up and down
Of verdure,—nothing too much up or down,
A ripple of land; such little hills, the sky
Can stoop so tenderly and the wheatfields climb;
Such nooks of valleys lined with orchises,
Fed full of noises by invisible streams;
And open pastures where you scarcely tell
White daisies from white dew,—at intervals
The mythic oaks and elm-trees standing out
Self-poised upon their prodigy of shade,—
I thought my father's land was worthy too
Of being my Shakespeare's.
     *   *   *   *   *   *
                    Ofter we walked only two,
If cousin Romney pleased to walk with me.
We read, or talked, or quarrelled, as it chanced.
We were not lovers, nor even friends well-matched:
Say rather, scholars upon different tracks,
And thinkers disagreed, he, overfull

Of what is, and I, haply, overbold
For what might be.

      But then the thrushes sang,
And shook my pulses and the elms' new leaves;
At which I turned, and held my finger up,
And bade him mark that, howsoe'er the world
Went ill, as he related, certainly
The thrushes still sang in it. At the word
His brow would soften,—and he bore with me
In melancholy patience, not unkind,
While breaking into voluble ecstasy
I flattered all the beauteous country round,
As poets use, the skies, the clouds, the fields,
The happy violets hiding from the roads
The primroses run down to, carrying gold;
The tangled hedgerows, where the cows push out
Impatient horns and tolerant churning mouths
'Twixt dripping ash-boughs,—hedgerows all alive
With birds and gnats and large white butterflies,
Which look as if the May-flower had caught life
And palpitated forth upon the wind;
Hills, vales, woods, netted in a silver mist,
Farms, granges, doubled up among the hills;
And cattle grazing in the watered vales,
And cottage-chimneys smoking from the woods,
And cottage-gardens smelling everywhere,
Confused with smell of orchards. 'See,' I said,
'And see! is God not with us on the earth?
And shall we put him down by aught we do?
Who says there's nothing for the poor and vile
Save poverty and wickedness? behold!'
And ankle-deep in English grass I leaped
And clapped my hands, and called all very fair.

A SIMILE.

      Every age,
Through being beheld too close, is ill-discerned
By those who have not lived past it. We'll suppose
Mount Athos carved, as Alexander schemed,

To some colossal statue of a man.
The peasants, gathering brushwood in his ear,
Had guessed as little as the browsing goats
Of form or feature of humanity
Up there,—in fact, had travelled five miles off
Or ere the giant image broke on them,
Full human profile, nose and chin distinct,
Mouth, muttering rhythms of silence up the sky
And fed at evening with the blood of suns ;
Grand torso,—hand, that flung perpetually
The largesse of a silver river down
To all the country pastures. 'Tis even thus
With times we live in,—evermore too great
To be apprehended near.

MARIAN'S CHILD.

　　　　　　There he lay upon his back,
The yearling creature, warm and moist with life
To the bottom of his dimples,—to the ends
Of the lovely tumbled curls about his face ;
For since he had been covered over-much
To keep him from the light-glare, both his cheeks
Were hot and scarlet as the first live rose
The shepherd's heart-blood ebbed away into
The faster for his love. And love was here
As instant ; in the pretty baby-mouth,
Shut close as if for dreaming that it sucked,
The little naked feet, drawn up the way
Of nestled birdlings ; everything so soft
And tender,—to the tiny holdfast hands,
Which, closing on a finger into sleep,
Had kept the mould of 't.
　　　　　　　　　While we stood there dumb,
For oh, that it should take such innocence
To prove just guilt, I thought, and stood there dumb,—
The light upon his eyelids pricked them wide,
And, staring out at us with all their blue,

As half perplexed between the angelhood
He had been away to visit in his sleep,
And our most mortal presence, gradually
He saw his mother's face, accepting it
In change for heaven itself with such a smile
As might have well been learnt there,—never moved,
But smiled on, in a drowse of ecstasy,
So happy (half with her and half with heaven)
He could not have the trouble to be stirred,
But smiled and lay there. Like a rose, I said?
As red and still indeed as any rose,
That blows in all the silence of its leaves,
Content in blowing to fulfil its life.

THE JOURNEY SOUTH.

        I just knew it when we swept
Above the old roofs of Dijon : Lyons dropped
A spark into the night, half trodden out
Unseen. But presently the winding Rhone
Washed out the moonlight large along his banks,
Which strained their yielding curves out clear and clean
To hold it,—shadow of town and castle blurred
Upon the hurrying river. Such an air
Blew thence upon the forehead,—half an air
And half a water,—that I leaned and looked,
Then, turning back on Marian, smiled to mark
That she looked only on her child, who slept,
His face toward the moon too.
              So we passed
The liberal open country and the close,
And shot through tunnels, like a lightning-wedge
By great Thor-hammers driven through the rock,
Which, quivering through the intestine blackness, splits,
And lets it in at once : the train swept in
Athrob with effort, trembling with resolve,
The fierce denouncing whistle wailing on
And dying off smothered in the shuddering dark,
While we, self-awed, drew troubled breath, oppressed

As other Titans underneath the pile
And nightmare of the mountains. Out, at last,
To catch the dawn afloat upon the land !
—Hills, slung forth broadly and gauntly everywhere,
Not crampt in their foundations, pushing wide
Rich outspreads of the vineyards and the corn,
(As if they entertained i' the name of France)
While, down their straining sides, streamed manifest
A soil as red as Charlemagne's knightly blood,
To consecrate the verdure. Some one said,
' Marseilles !' And lo, the city of Marseilles,
With all her ships behind her, and beyond,
The scimitar of ever-shining sea
For right-hand use, bared blue against the sky !

*   *   *   *   *   *

I felt the wind soft from the land of souls ;
The old miraculous mountains heaved in sight,
One straining past another along the shore,
The way of grand dull Odyssean ghosts,
Athirst to drink the cool blue wine of seas
And stare on voyagers. Peak pushing peak
They stood : I watched, beyond that Tyrian belt
Of intense sea betwixt them and the ship,
Down all their sides the misty olive-woods
Dissolving in the weak congenial moon,
And still disclosing some brown convent-tower
That seems as if it grew from some brown rock,
Or many a little lighted village, dropt
Like a fallen star upon so high a point,
You wonder what can keep it in its place
From sliding headlong with the waterfalls
Which powder all the myrtle and orange groves
With spray of silver. Thus my Italy
Was stealing on us. Genoa broke with day,
The Doria's long pale palace striking out,
From green hills in advance of the white town,
A marble finger dominant to ships
Seen glimmering through the uncertain gray of dawn.

EMILY BRONTË.

[EMILY BRONTË was born at Hartshead-cum-Clifton, near Leeds, in 1819, and lived at the parsonage at Haworth from 1820 to her death. The monotony of this existence was broken only by a brief attempt to be a governess and by a short stay at Brussels in 1842, all exile from home being excessively painful and hurtful to her. She died of consumption at Haworth on the 19th of December, 1848. She published, in conjunction with her sisters, *Poems, by Currer, Ellis, and Acton Bell,* in 1846, and, alone, the novel of *Wuthering Heights* in 1847.

Not even the unstinted praise of three great and very dissimilar poets has given to Emily Brontë her due rank in popular esteem. Her work is not universally acceptable, even to imaginative readers; her personality is almost repulsive to many who have schooled themselves to endure the vehemence of genius but not its ominous self-restraint. Most people were afraid of Emily Brontë's 'whitening face and set mouth' when she was alive, and even now that she is dead her memory seems to inspire more terror than affection. Against an instinctive repugnance it is in vain to reason, and in discussing her poetical quality we must assume that her power has at least been felt and not disliked by the reader, since 'you must love her, ere to you she should seem worthy to be loved.' Those who have come under the spell of her genius will expect no apology for her intellectual rebellion, her stoic harshness of purpose, her more than manlike strength. She was a native blossom of those dreary and fascinating moorlands of which Charlotte has given, in a few brilliant phrases, so perfect a description, and like the acrid heaths and gentians that flourish in the peat, to transplant her was to kill her. Her actions, like her writings, were strange, but consistent in their strangeness. Even the dreadful incident of her death, which occurred as she stood upright in the little parlour at Haworth, refusing to go to bed, but just leaning one hand upon the table, seems to me to be no unfit ending for a life so impatient of constraint from others, so implacable in its slavery to its own principles.

The poetry of Emily Brontë is small in extent and conventional in form. Its burning thoughts are concealed for the most part in the tame and ambling measures dedicated to female verse by the practice of Felicia Hemans and Letitia Landon. That she was progressing to the last even in this matter of the form is shown by the little posthumous collection of her verses issued by Charlotte, consisting of early, and very weak pieces, and of two poems written in the last year of her life, which attain, for the first time, the majesty of rhythm demanded by such sublime emotions. But it is impossible not to regret that she missed that accomplishment in the art of poetry which gives an added force to the verse of her great French contemporary, Marceline Valmore, the only modern poetess who can fitly be compared with Emily Brontë for power of expressing passion in its simplicity. In the 1846 volume there are but few of the contributions of Ellis Bell in which the form is adequate to the thought. Even *The Prisoner*, certain lines of which have justly called forth Mr. Swinburne's admiration, is on the whole a disjointed and halting composition. The moving and tear-compelling elegy called *A Death-Scene*, in conception one of the most original and passionate poems in existence, is clothed in a measure that is like the livery of a charitable institution. This limitation of style does not interfere with the beauty of her three or four best poems, where indeed it does not exist, but it prevents the poetess in all but these superlative successes from attaining that harmony and directness of utterance which should characterise a song so unflinchingly sincere as hers.

It is difficult to praise Emily's three or four greatest poems without an air of exaggeration. Finest among them all is that outburst of agnostic faith that was found by Charlotte on her desk when she died, a 'last poem' not to be surpassed in dignity and self-reliance by any in the language. *The Old Stoic* might have prepared us for the *Last Lines* by its concentrated force and passion. But the 'chainless soul' of the author found its most characteristic utterance in the *Stanzas* which stand second in our selection, the two last of which contain in its quintessence the peculiar gospel that it was the mission of Emily Brontë to preach.

It was a message that brought no peace or happiness to the fiery soul that bore it. For her, in her own wonderful words,

> 'intense the agony—
> When the ear begins to hear, and the eye begins to see;
> When the pulse begins to throb, the brain to think again;
> The soul to feel the flesh, and the flesh to feel the chain.'

Under such a strain of being, no wonder that the pale and slender physical frame declined, and that our literature was deprived, at the age of twenty-nine, of an unrecognised, uncherished, undeveloped woman,

> 'whose soul
> Knew no fellow for might,
> Passion, vehemence, grief,
> Daring, since Byron died.'

EDMUND W. GOSSE.

LAST LINES.

No coward soul is mine,
No trembler in the world's storm-troubled sphere:
I see Heaven's glories shine,
And faith shines equal, arming me from fear.

O God within my breast,
Almighty, ever-present Deity!
Life—that in me has rest,
As I—undying Life—have power in thee!

Vain are the thousand creeds
That move men's hearts : unutterably vain ;
Worthless as withered weeds,
Or idlest froth amid the boundless main,

To waken doubt in one
Holding so fast by thine infinity;
So surely anchored on
The stedfast rock of immortality.

With wide-embracing love
Thy spirit animates eternal years,
Pervades and broods above,
Changes, sustains, dissolves, creates, and rears.

Though earth and man were gone,
And suns and universes ceased to be,
And Thou were left alone,
Every existence would exist in Thee.

There is not room for Death,
Nor atom that his might could render void :
Thou—THOU art Being and Breath,
And what THOU art may never be destroyed.

STANZAS.

Often rebuked, yet always back returning
  To those first feelings that were born with me,
And leaving busy chase of wealth and learning
  For idle dreams of things which cannot be :

To-day, I will seek not the shadowy region ;
  Its unsustaining vastness waxes drear ;
And visions rising, legion after legion,
  Bring the unreal world too strangely near.

I 'll walk, but not in old heroic traces,
  And not in paths of high morality,
And not among the half-distinguished faces,
  The clouded forms of long-past history.

I 'll walk where my own nature would be leading :
  It vexes me to choose another guide :
Where the grey flocks in ferny glens are feeding ;
  Where the wild wind blows on the mountain side.

REMEMBRANCE.

Cold in the earth—and the deep snow piled above thee,
Far, far removed, cold in the dreary grave !
Have I forgot, my only Love, to love thee,
Severed at last by Time's all-severing wave ?

Now, when alone, do my thoughts no longer hover
Over the mountains, on that northern shore,
Resting their wings where heath and fern-leaves cover
Thy noble heart for ever, ever more ?

Cold in the earth—and fifteen wild Decembers,
From those brown hills, have melted into spring :
Faithful, indeed, is the spirit that remembers
After such years of change and suffering !

Sweet Love of youth, forgive, if I forget thee,
While the world's tide is bearing me along;
Other desires and other hopes beset me,
Hopes which obscure, but cannot do thee wrong!

No later light has lightened up my heaven,
No second morn has ever shone for me;
All my life's bliss from thy dear life was given,
All my life's bliss is in the grave with thee.

But, when the days of golden dreams had perished,
And even Despair was powerless to destroy;
Then did I learn how existence could be cherished,
Strengthened, and fed without the aid of joy.

Then did I check the tears of useless passion—
Weaned my young soul from yearning after thine;
Sternly denied its burning wish to hasten
Down to that tomb already more than mine.

And, even yet, I dare not let it languish,
Dare not indulge in memory's rapturous pain;
Once drinking deep of that divinest anguish,
How could I seek the empty world again?

THE OLD STOIC.

Riches I hold in light esteem,
  And Love I laugh to scorn;
And lust of fame was but a dream,
  That vanished with the morn:

And if I pray, the only prayer
  That moves my lips for me
Is, 'Leave the heart that now I bear,
  And give me liberty!'

Yes, as my swift days near their goal,
  'Tis all that I implore;
In life and death, a chainless soul,
  With courage to endure.

A Death-Scene.

'O Day! he cannot die
When thou so fair art shining!
O Sun, in such a glorious sky,
So tranquilly declining;

He cannot leave thee now,
While fresh west winds are blowing,
And all around his youthful brow
Thy cheerful light is glowing!

Edward, awake, awake—
The golden evening gleams
Warm and bright on Arden's lake—
Arouse thee from thy dreams!

Beside thee, on my knee,
My dearest friend, I pray
That thou, to cross the eternal sea,
Wouldst yet one hour delay:

I hear its billows roar—
I see them foaming high;
But no glimpse of a further shore
Has blest my straining eye.

Believe not what they urge
Of Eden isles beyond;
Turn back, from that tempestuous surge,
To thy own native land.

It is not death, but pain
That struggles in thy breast—
Nay, rally, Edward, rouse again;
I cannot let thee rest!'

One long look, that sore reproved me
For the woe I could not bear—
One mute look of suffering moved me
To repent my useless prayer:

And, with sudden check, the heaving
Of distraction passed away ;
Not a sign of further grieving
Stirred my soul that awful day.

Paled, at length, the sweet sun setting ;
Sunk to peace the twilight breeze :
Summer dews fell softly, wetting
Glen, and glade, and silent trees.

Then his eyes began to weary,
Weighed beneath a mortal sleep ;
And their orbs grew strangely dreary,
Clouded, even as they would weep.

But they wept not, but they changed **not,**
Never moved, and never closed ;
Troubled still, and still they ranged **not—**
Wandered not, nor yet reposed !

So I knew that he was dying—
Stooped, and raised his languid **head ;**
Felt no breath, and heard no sighing.
So I knew that he was dead.

ARTHUR HUGH CLOUGH.

[BORN at Liverpool, Jan. 1, 1819; passed some years of his childhood at Charleston, in Virginia; was at school at Rugby from 1829 to 1837; was Scholar of Balliol and afterwards Fellow and Tutor of Oriel; resigned his offices in Oxford in 1848; was Principal of University Hall, London, for a short time afterwards; again went to America; returned in 1853 to take a post in the Education Office. He died at Florence, Nov. 13, 1861. His poems were chiefly written between 1840 and 1850, *The Bothie* being published in 1848, and many of the shorter poems appearing in a volume called *Ambarvalia* in the next year.]

'We have a foreboding,' says Mr. Lowell in one of his essays, 'that Clough, imperfect as he was in many respects, and dying before he had subdued his sensitive temperament to the sterner requirements of his art, will be thought a hundred years hence to have been the truest expression in verse of the moral and intellectual tendencies, the doubt and struggle towards settled convictions, of the period in which he lived.' If doubt and struggle were the ruling tendencies of Clough's time, this lofty estimate may well be true; for in no writer of that day are they more vividly reflected. They are the very substance of his verse, they give it strength, they impose upon it the limitations from which it suffers. Clough has never been a popular poet, and it may be doubted if he ever will be. His poetry has too much of the element of conflict, too much uncertainty, ever to become what the best of it ought to become, a household word. But from beginning to end it exhibits that devotion to truth which was in a special degree the characteristic of the finer minds of his epoch; a devotion which in his case was fostered by his early training under Arnold at Rugby, and by the atmosphere of theological controversy in which he found himself at Oxford. The warmth of his feelings, the width of his sympathies, the fineness of his physical sensibilities, made him a poet rather than a writer of prose treatises ; but the other element, that element of impassioned search for reality, gives his poems their distinctive quality—namely, an air of strenuous mental effort which is almost greater than verse can bear.

'Clough was a philosophic poet in a sense in which no man since Lucretius has been so [1].' This judgment, the judgment of a very competent critic, is at first unpalatable ; one is not used to this matching of the men of our own time, and the men who are not among the most famous, with the giants of antiquity. The comparison however is no mere phrase. 'These two men were philosophers, not from the desire of fame, not from the pleasure of intellectual discovery, not because they hoped that philosophy would suggest thoughts that would soothe some private grief of their own, but because it was to them an overpowering interest to have some key to the universe, because all even of their desires were suspected by them until they could find some central desire on which to link the rest ; and love and beauty, and the animation of life, were no pleasure to them, except as testifying to that *something beyond* of which they were in search.' The unlikeness between the two poets is far more apparent than the likeness ; for Lucretius has found his solution of the puzzle of existence, and Clough has not ; the ancient poet believes that he has reached the point at which all contradictions are harmonised, the modern poet is sure that he has done nothing of the kind. But in this they are one, that both are philosophic, are 'lovers of the knowledge which reveals to them real existence,' are content with nothing less. A reader of Clough's poetry, marked as so much of it is by indecision and manifoldness of view, is startled when he comes upon such passages as these from his American letters—

'I think I must have been getting into a little mysticism lately. It won't do : twice two are four, all the world over, and there's no harm in its being so ; 'tisn't the devil's doing that it is ; il faut s y soumettre, and all right.'

And again—

'What I mean by mysticism, is letting feelings run on without thinking of the reality of their object, letting them out merely like water. The plain rule in all matters is, not to think what you are thinking about the question, but to look straight out at the things and let them affect you ; otherwise how can you judge at all? look at them at any rate, and judge while looking.'

[1] *Quarterly Review*, April 1869.

This is not the most obvious feature of Clough's mind, but it is the most real ; and it explains much in his work that is otherwise difficult to account for. It explains, for example, the scantiness of his production ; as Mrs. Clough says in her memoir of him, 'his absolute sincerity of thought, his intense feeling of reality, ren. dered it impossible for him to produce anything superficial.' When taken together with his sense of the infinite complexity of human life, it explains the play of conflicting thoughts and feelings which is the very essence of *Dipsychus*, and gives *The Bothie* its truth and charm. These poems, however, present the struggle between opposing views so strongly, that it is only when looked at from close by that we detect the positive element in them. It is otherwise with those short lyrics, than which nothing can be more perfect in form or stronger and surer in matter, those lyrics *Say not the struggle nought availeth*, and *As ships becalmed at eve*, and *O stream descending to the sea*,—they have the note of certainty without which the poet, whatever else he may have, can have no message for mankind.

There will always be a great charm, especially for Oxford men, in the ' Long Vacation pastoral' *The Bothie of Tober-na-Vuolich*. Humour, pathos, clear character-drawing, real delight in nature and a power of rendering her beauties, above all a sense of life, of ' the joy of eventful living '—it has all these, and over the whole is thrown, through the associations of the hexameter, a hal -burlesque veil of academic illusion that produces the happiest effect. Yet throughout there runs a current of controversy with the world ; the hero ' Philip Hewson, the poet ; Hewson, a radical hot,' an idealist who ends by marrying a peasant girl and emigrating with her to New Zealand—this Philip is a type that is always present to Clough's mind, as much in *Dipsychus* and *Amours de Voyage* as in *The Bothie*. Idealism triumphs in him, indeed, whereas in Dipsychus it is finally defeated by the world-spirit, and in Claude it is checked and baffled by the sheer Hamlet-like weakness of the man. But the likeness which the three bear to one another is too strong to be accidental ; it springs from the unity of the poet's thought. Clough was in the true sense of the term a sceptic ; and his three heroes, whatever the difference of their destinies, are alike sceptics too.

Clough holds a high and permanent place among our poets, not only because, as Mr. Lowell says, he represents an epoch of thought, but because he represents it in a manner so rare, so individual. He is neither singer nor prophet ; but he is a poet in virtue of the depth and sincerity with which he felt certain great emotions, and the absolute veracity with which he expressed them. ' His mind seems habitually to have been swayed by large, slow, deep-sea currents,' says one of the best of his critics [1]—currents partly general in their operation on his time, partly special to himself ; and his utterances when so swayed are intensely real. But he never was driven by them into a want of sympathy with other natures ; and it was this extraordinary union of sincerity and sympathy, of depth and breadth, that so endeared him to his friends, and that make it difficult even now for the critic of his poetry not to be moved by the ' personal estimate.' We find in his poems all sorts of drawbacks ; we find a prevailing indecision that injures their moral effect in most cases ; we find fragmentariness, inequality, looseness of construction, occasional difficulty of rhythm. Yet what of this ? one is tempted to ask. In the presence of that sincerity, that delight in all that is best in the physical and moral world, that humour at once bold and delicate, that moral ardour, often baffled, never extinguished, we feel that the deductions of criticism are unwelcome : we are more than content to take Thyrsis as we find him, though

> ' the music of his rustic flute
> Kept not for long its happy country tone;
> Lost it too soon, and learnt a stormy note
> Of men contention-tost, of men who groan,
> Which tasked his pipe too sore, and tired his throat.'

EDITOR.

[1] *Westminster Review*, October 1869.

QUA CURSUM VENTUS.

As ships, becalmed at eve, that lay
    With canvas drooping, side by side,
Two towers of sail at dawn of day
    Are scarce long leagues apart descried;

When fell the night, upsprung the breeze,
    And all the darkling hours they plied,
Nor dreamt but each the self-same seas
    By each was cleaving, side by side:

E'en so—but why the tale reveal
    Of those, whom year by year unchanged,
Brief absence joined anew to feel,
    Astounded, soul from soul estranged?

At dead of night their sails were filled,
    And onward each rejoicing steered—
Ah, neither blame, for neither willed,
    Or wist, what first with dawn appeared!

To veer, how vain! On, onward strain,
    Brave barks! In light, in darkness too,
Through winds and tides one compass guides—
    To that, and your own selves, be true.

But O blithe breeze! and O great seas,
    Though ne'er, that earliest parting past,
On your wide plain they join again,
    Together lead them home at last.

One port, methought, alike they sought,
    One purpose hold where'er they fare,—
O bounding breeze, O rushing seas!
    At last, at last, unite them there!

QUI LABORAT, ORAT.

O only Source of all our light and life,
    Whom as our truth, our strength, we see and feel,
But whom the hours of mortal moral strife
    Alone aright reveal!

Mine inmost soul, before Thee inly brought,
　　Thy presence owns ineffable, divine ;
Chastised each rebel self-encentered thought,
　　My will adoreth Thine.

With eye down-dropt, if then this earthly mind
　　Speechless remain, or speechless e'en depart ;
Nor seek to see—for what of earthly kind
　　Can see Thee as Thou art?—

If well-assured 'tis but profanely bold
　　In thought's abstractest forms to seem to see,
It dare not dare the dread communion hold
　　In ways unworthy Thee,

O not unowned, thou shalt unnamed forgive,
　　In worldly walks the prayerless heart prepare ;
And if in work its life it seem to live,
　　Shalt make that work be prayer.

Nor times shall lack, when while the work it plies,
　　Unsummoned powers the blinding film shall part,
And scarce by happy tears made dim, the eyes
　　In recognition start.

But, as thou willest, give or e'en forbear
　　The beatific supersensual sight,
So, with Thy blessing blest, that humbler prayer
　　Approach Thee morn and night.

THE HIDDEN LOVE.

O let me love my love unto myself alone,
And know my knowledge to the world unknown ;
No witness to my vision call,
Beholding, unbeheld of all ;
And worship Thee, with Thee withdrawn apart,
Whoe'er, Whate'er Thou art,
Within the closest veil of mine most inmost heart.

What is it then to me
If others are inquisitive to see?
Why should I quit my place to go and ask
If other men are working at their task?
Leave my own buried roots to go
And see that brother plants shall grow;
And turn away from Thee, O Thou most Holy **Light,**
To look if other orbs their orbits keep aright,
Around their proper sun,
Deserting Thee, and being undone.

O let me love my love unto myself alone,
And know my knowledge to the world unknown;
And worship Thee, O hid One, O much sought,
As but man can or ought,
Within the abstracted'st shrine of my least breathed-on
    thought.

Better it were, thou sayest, to consent;
Feast while we may, and live ere life be spent;
Close up clear eyes, and call the unstable sure,
The unlovely lovely, and the filthy pure;
In self-belyings, self-deceivings roll,
And lose in Action, Passion, Talk, the soul.

Nay, better far to mark off thus much air,
And call it Heaven: place bliss and glory there:
Fix perfect homes in the unsubstantial sky,
And say, what is not, will be by-and-by.

'WITH WHOM IS NO VARIABLENESS, NEITHER SHADOW OF TURNING.'

It fortifies my soul to know
That, though I perish, Truth is so:
That, howsoe'er I stray and range,
Whate'er I do, Thou dost not change.
I steadier step when I recall
That, if I slip, Thou dost not fall.

'Perchè Pensa? Pensando s'invecchia.'

To spend uncounted years of pain,
Again, again, and yet again,
In working out in heart and brain
    The problem of our being here ;
To gather facts from far and near,
Upon the mind to hold them clear,
And, knowing more may yet appear,
Unto one's latest breath to fear
The premature result to draw—
Is this the object, end and law,
    And purpose of our being here ?

The Shadow [1].

I dreamed a dream : I dreamt that I espied,
Upon a stone that was not rolled aside,
A Shadow sit upon a grave—a Shade,
As thin, as unsubstantial, as of old
Came, the Greek poet told,
To lick the life-blood in the trench Ulysses made—
As pale, as thin, and said :
'I am the Resurrection of the Dead.
The night is past, the morning is at hand,
And I must in my proper semblance stand,
Appear brief space and vanish,—listen, this is true,
I am that Jesus whom they slew.'

And shadows dim, I dreamed, the dead apostles came,
And bent their heads for sorrow and for shame—
Sorrow for their great loss, and shame
For what they did in that vain name.

And in long ranges far behind there seemed
Pale vapoury angel forms ; or was it cloud ? that kept
Strange watch ; the women also stood beside and wept

[1] The MS. of this poem is incomplete.

And Peter spoke the word:
'O my own Lord,
What is it we must do?
Is it then all untrue?
Did we not see, and hear, and handle Thee,
Yea, for whole hours
Upon the Mount in Galilee,
On the lake shore, and here at Bethany,
When Thou ascended to Thy God and ours?'
And paler still became the distant cloud,
And at the word the women wept aloud.

And the Shade answered, 'What ye say I know not;
      But it is true
    I am that Jesus whom they slew,
Whom ye have preached, but in what way I know not.'

   *   *   *   *   *   *

And the great World, it chanced, came by that way,
And stopped, and looked, and spoke to the police,
And said the thing, for order's sake and peace,
Most certainly must be suppressed, the nuisance cease.
His wife and daughter must have where to pray,
And whom to pray to, at the least one day
In seven, and something sensible to say.

Whether the fact so many years ago
Had, or not, happened, how was he to know?
Yet he had always heard that it was so.
As for himself, perhaps it was all one;
And yet he found it not unpleasant, too,
On Sunday morning in the roomy pew,
To see the thing with such decorum done.
As for himself, perhaps it was all one;
Yet on one's death-bed all men always said
It was a comfortable thing to think upon
The atonement and the resurrection of the dead.
So the great World as having said his say,
Unto his country-house pursued his way.
And on the grave the Shadow sat all day.

* * * * * *

And the poor Pope was sure it must be so,
Else wherefore did the people kiss his toe?
The subtle Jesuit cardinal shook his head,
And mildly looked and said,
It mattered not a jot
Whether the thing, indeed, were so or not;
Religion must be kept up, and the Church preserved,
And for the people this best served.
And then he turned, and added most demurely,
'Whatever may befal,
We Catholics need no evidence at all,
The holy father is infallible, surely!'

And English canons heard,
And quietly demurred.
Religion rests on evidence, of course,
And on inquiry we must put no force.
Difficulties still, upon whatever ground,
Are likely, almost certain, to be found.
The Theist scheme, the Pantheist, one and all,
Must with, or e'en before, the Christian fall.
And till the thing were plainer to our eyes,
To disturb faith was surely most unwise.
As for the Shade, who trusted such narration?
Except, of course, in ancient revelation.

And dignitaries of the Church came by.
It had been worth to some of them, they said,
Some hundred thousand pounds a year a head.
If it fetched so much in the market, truly,
'Twas not a thing to be given up unduly.
It had been proved by Butler in one way,
By Paley better in a later day;
It had been proved in twenty ways at once,
By many a doctor plain to many a dunce;
There was no question but it must be so.
  And the Shade answered, that He did not know;
He had no reading, and might be deceived,
But still He was the Christ, as He believed.

And women, mild and pure,
Forth from still homes and village schools did pass,
And asked, if this indeed were thus, alas,
What should they teach their children and the poor?
  The Shade replied, He could not know,
But it was truth, the fact was so.

     *   *   *   *   *   *

     *   *   *   *   *   *

Who had kept all commandments from his youth
Yet still found one thing lacking,—even Truth:
And the Shade only answered, ' Go, make haste,
Enjoy thy great possessions as thou may'st.'

[From *Dipsychus.*]

ISOLATION.

Where are the great, whom thou would'st wish to praise thee?
Where are the pure, whom thou would'st choose to love thee!
Where are the brave, to stand supreme above thee,
Whose high commands would cheer, whose chidings raise thee?
  Seek, seeker, in thyself; submit to find
  In the stones, bread, and life in the blank mind.

IN VENICE; DIPSYCHUS SPEAKS.

O happy hours!
O compensation ample for long days
Of what impatient tongues call wretchedness!
O beautiful, beneath the magic moon,
To walk the watery way of palaces!
O beautiful, o'ervaulted with gemmed blue,
This spacious court, with colour and with gold,
With cupolas, and pinnacles, and points.
And crosses multiplex, and tips and balls
(Wherewith the bright stars unreproving mix,
Nor scorn by hasty eyes to be confused);
Fantastically perfect this low pile
Of Oriental glory; these long ranges
Of classic chiselling, this gay flickering crowd,

And the calm Campanile.   Beautiful !
O, beautiful ! and that seemed more profound,
This morning by the pillar when I sat
Under the great arcade, at the review,
And took, and held, and ordered on my brain
The faces, and the voices, and the whole mass
O' the motley facts of existence flowing by !
O perfect, if 'twere all ! But it is not ;
Hints haunt me ever of a more beyond :
I am rebuked by a sense of the incomplete,
Of a completion ever soon assumed,
Of adding up too soon. What we call sin,
I could believe a painful opening out
Of paths for ampler virtue. The bare field,
Scant with lean ears of harvest, long had mocked
The vext laborious farmer ; came at length
The deep plough in the lazy undersoil
Down-driving ; with a cry earth's fibres crack,
And a few months, and lo ! the golden leas,
And autumn's crowded shocks and loaded wains.
Let us look back on life ; was any change,
Any now blest expansion, but at first
A pang, remorse-like, shot to the inmost seats
Of moral being ? To do anything,
Distinct on any one thing to decide,
To leave the habitual and the old, and quit
The easy-chair of use and wont, seems crime
To the weak soul, forgetful how at first
Sitting down seemed so too. And, oh ! this woman's
      heart,
Fain to be forced, incredulous of choice,
And waiting a necessity for God.
   Yet I could think, indeed, the perfect call
Should force the perfect answer. If the voice
Ought to receive its echo from the soul,
Wherefore this silence ? If it *should* rouse my being,
Why this reluctance ? Have I not thought o'ermuch
Of other men, and of the ways of the world ?
But what they are, or have been, matters not.

To thine own self be true, the wise man says.
Are then my fears myself? O double self!
And I untrue to both! Oh, there are hours,
When love, and faith, and dear domestic ties,
And converse with old friends, and pleasant walks,
Familiar faces, and familiar books,
Study, and art, upliftings unto prayer,
And admiration of the noblest things,
Seem all ignoble only; all is mean,
And nought as I would have it. Then at others,
My mind is in her rest; my heart at home
In all around; my soul secure in place,
And the vext needle perfect to her poles.
Aimless and hopeless in my life I seem
To thread the winding byways of the town,
Bewildered, baffled, hurried hence and thence,
All at cross-purpose even with myself,
Unknowing whence or whither. Then at once,
At a step, I crown the Campanile's top,
And view all mapped below; islands, lagoon,
A hundred steeples and a million roofs,
The fruitful champaign, and the cloud-capt Alps,
And the broad Adriatic. Be it enough;
If I lose this, how terrible! No, no,
I am contented, and will not complain.
To the old paths, my soul! Oh, be it so!
I bear the workday burden of dull life
About these footsore flags of a weary world,
Heaven knows how long it has not been; at once,
Lo! I am in the spirit on the Lord's day
With John in Patmos. Is it not enough,
One day in seven? and if this should go,
If this pure solace should desert my mind,
What were all else? I dare not risk this loss.
To the old paths, my soul!

[From *Poems on Life and Duty.*]

THE STREAM OF LIFE.

O stream descending to the sea,
  Thy mossy banks between,
The flowerets blow, the grasses grow,
  The leafy trees are green.

In garden plots the children play,
  The fields the labourers till,
And houses stand on either hand,
  And thou descendest still.

O life descending into death,
  Our waking eyes behold,
Parent and friend thy lapse attend,
  Companions young and old.

Strong purposes our mind possess,
  Our hearts affections fill,
We toil and earn, we seek and learn,
  And thou descendest still.

O end to which our currents tend,
  Inevitable sea,
To which we flow, what do we know,
  What shall we guess of thee?

A roar we hear upon thy shore,
  As we our course fulfil ;
Scarce we divine a sun will shine
  And be above us still.

[From *The Bothie of Tober-na-Vuolich.*]

THE HIGHLAND STREAM.

There is a stream (I name not its name, lest inquisitive tourist
Hunt it, and make it a lion, and get it at last into guide-books),
Springing far off from a loch unexplored in the folds of great
  mountains,

Falling two miles through rowan and stunted alder, enveloped
Then for four more in a forest of pine, where broad and ample
Spreads, to convey it, the glen with heathery slopes on both
    sides :
Broad and fair the stream, with occasional falls and narrows ;
But, where the glen of its course approaches the vale of the
    river,
Met and blocked by a huge interposing mass of granite,
Scarce by a channel deep-cut, raging up, and raging onward,
Forces its flood through a passage so narrow a lady would
    step it.
There, across the great rocky wharves, a wooden bridge goes,
Carrying a path to the forest ; below, three hundred yards, say,
Lower in level some twenty-five feet, through flats of shingle,
Stepping-stones and a cart-track cross in the open valley.
    But in the interval here the boiling pent-up water
Frees itself by a final descent, attaining a basin,
Ten feet wide and eighteen long, with whiteness and fury
Occupied partly, but mostly pellucid, pure, a mirror ;
Beautiful there for the colour derived from green rocks under ;
Beautiful, most of all, where beads of foam uprising
Mingle their clouds of white with the delicate hue of the stillness,
Cliff over cliff for its sides, with rowan and pendent birch boughs,
Here it lies, unthought of above at the bridge and pathway,
Still more enclosed from below by wood and rocky projection.
You are shut in, left alone with yourself and perfection of water,
Hid on all sides, left alone with yourself and the goddess of
    bathing.
    Here, the pride of the plunger, you stride the fall and clear it ;
Here, the delight of the bather, you roll in beaded sparklings,
Here into pure green depth drop down from lofty ledges.

ELSPIE AND PHILIP

But a revulsion wrought in the brain and bosom of Elspie ;
And the passion she just had compared to the vehement ocean,
Urging in high spring-tide its masterful way through the moun-
    tains,

Forcing and flooding the silvery stream, as it runs from the
    inland ;
That great power withdrawn, receding here and passive,
Felt she in myriad springs, her sources far in the mountains,
Stirring, collecting, rising, upheaving, forth-outflowing,
Taking and joining, right welcome, that delicate rill in the valley,
Filling it, making it strong, and still descending, seeking,
With a blind forefeeling descending ever, and seeking,
With a delicious forefeeling, the great still sea before it ;
There deep into it, far, to carry, and lose in its bosom,
Waters that still from their sources exhaustless are fain to be
    added.

    As he was kissing her fingers, and knelt on the ground before
        her,
Yielding backward she sank to her seat, and of what she was
        doing
Ignorant, bewildered, in sweet multitudinous vague emotion,
Stooping, knowing not what, put her lips to the hair on his
        forehead :
And Philip, raising himself, gently, for the first time round her
Passing his arms, close, close, enfolded her, close to his bosom.
As they went home by the moon, Forgive me, Philip, she
        whispered ;
I have so many things to think of, all of a sudden ;
I who had never once thought a thing,—in my ignorant High-
        lands.

PHILIP TO ADAM.

These are fragments again without date addressed to Adam.
As at return of tide the total weight of ocean,
Drawn by moon and sun from Labrador and Greenland,
Sets-in amain, in the open space betwixt Mull and Scarba,
Heaving, swelling, spreading, the might of the mighty Atlantic ;
There into cranny and slit of the rocky, cavernous bottom
Settles down, and with dimples huge the smooth sea-surface
Eddies, coils, and whirls ; by dangerous Corryvreckan :
So in my soul of souls, through its cells and secret recesses,
Comes back, swelling and spreading, the old democratic fervour

But as the light of day enters some populous city,
Shaming away, ere it come, by the chilly day-streak signal,
High and low, the misusers of night, shaming out the gaslamps—
All the great empty streets are flooded with broadening clearness,
Which, withal, by inscrutable simultaneous access
Permeates far and pierces to the very cellars lying in
Narrow high back-lane, and court, and alley of alleys :—
He that goes forth to his walks, while speeding to the suburb,
Sees sights only peaceful and pure ; as labourers settling
Slowly to work, in their limbs the lingering sweetness of slumber ;
Humble market-carts, coming in, bringing in, not only
Flower, fruit, farm-store, but sounds and sights of the country
Dwelling yet on the sense of the dreamy drivers ; soon after
Half-awake servant-maids unfastening drowsy shutters
Up at the windows, or down, letting in the air by the doorway,
School-boys, school-girls soon, with slate, portfolio, satchel,
Hampered as they haste, those running, these others maidenly
    tripping ;
Early clerk anon turning out to stroll, or it may be
Meet his sweetheart—waiting behind the garden gate there ;
Merchant on his grass-plat haply bare-headed ; and now by this
    time
Little child bringing breakfast to 'father' that sits on the timber
There by the scaffolding ; see, she waits for the can beside him ;
Meantime above purer air untarnished of new-lit fires :
So that the whole great wicked artificial civilised fabric—
All its unfinished houses, lots for sale, and railway out-works—
Seems reaccepted, resumed to Primal Nature and Beauty :—
—Such—in me, and to me, and on me the love of Elspie !

[*From Songs in Absence.*]

COME BACK !

Come back, come back, behold with straining mast,
And swelling sail, behold her steaming fast ;
With one new sun to see her voyage o'er,
With morning light to touch her native shore.
    Come back, come back.

Come back, come back, while westward labouring by,
With sailless yards, a bare black hulk we fly.
See how the gale we fight with sweeps her back,
To our lost home, on our forsaken track.
    Come back, come back.

Come back, come back, across the flying foam,
We hear faint far-off voices call us home,
Come back, ye seem to say; ye seek in vain;
We went, we sought, and homeward turned again.
    Come back, come back.

Come back, come back; and whither back or why?
To fan quenched hopes, forsaken schemes to try;
Walk the old fields; pace the familiar street;
Dream with the idlers, with the bards compete.
    Come back, come back.

Come back, come back; and whither and for what?
To finger idly some old Gordian knot,
Unskilled to sunder, and too weak to cleave,
And with much toil attain to half-believe.
    Come back, come back.

Come back, come back; yea back, indeed, do go
Sighs panting thick, and tears that want to flow;
Fond fluttering hopes upraise their useless wings,
And wishes idly struggle in the strings;
    Come back, come back.

Come back, come back, more eager than the breeze,
The flying fancies sweep across the seas,
And lighter far than ocean's flying foam,
The heart's fond message hurries to its home.
    Come back, come back!

Come back, come back!
Back flies the foam; the hoisted flag streams back;
The long smoke wavers on the homeward track,
Back fly with winds things which the winds obey,
The strong ship follows its appointed way.

WHERE LIES THE LAND?

Where lies the land to which the ship would go?
Far, far ahead, is all her seamen know.
And where the land she travels from? Away,
Far, far behind, is all that they can say.

On sunny noons upon the deck's smooth face,
Linked arm in arm, how pleasant here to pace;
Or, o'er the stern reclining, watch below
The foaming wake far widening as we go.

On stormy nights when wild north-westers rave,
How proud a thing to fight with wind and wave!
The dripping sailor on the reeling mast
Exults to bear, and scorns to wish it past.

Where lies the land to which the ship would go?
Far, far ahead, is all her seamen know.
And where the land she travels from? Away,
Far, far behind, is all that they can say.

[From *Miscellaneous Poems.*]

SAY NOT THE STRUGGLE NOUGHT AVAILETH.

Say not, the struggle nought availeth,
    The labour and the wounds are vain,
The enemy faints not, nor faileth,
    And as things have been they remain.

If hopes were dupes, fears may be liars;
    It may be, in yon smoke concealed,
Your comrades chase e'en now the fliers,
    And, but for you, possess the field.

For while the tired waves, vainly breaking,
    Seem here no painful inch to gain,
Far back, through creeks and inlets making,
    Comes silent, flooding in, the main,

And not by eastern windows only,
    When daylight comes, comes in the light,
In front, the sun climbs slow, how slowly,
    But westward, look, the land is bright.

CHARLES KINGSLEY.

[B RN at Holne Vicarage, Devonshire, in 1819, and educated, partly at Helston Grammar School, and partly at King's College, London, and at Magdalene College, Cambridge. He was Rector of Eversley in Hampshire; Professor of Modern History at his old university from 1860 to 1869; and Canon of Westminster in 1872. Chief among his thirty-five publications are *The Saint's Tragedy* (1848), *Alton Locke* and *Yeast* (1849), *Hypatia* (1853), *The Heroes* (1855), *Andromeda* (1858), *The Water-Babies* (1863) and *Prose-Idylls* (1873). He died in 1875.]

Charles Kingsley, author on the one hand of *Cheap Clothes and Nasty*, and of *The Water-Babies* on the other, was the type of a certain order of modern man : the man of whom much is expected, who is trained up to the fulfilment of many purposes, who is subject to many influences, open to many sorts of impressions, and possessed of many active holds upon life. He came of choice and generous stock ; and from the first it was determined for him that he should do something and be somebody. It seems natural that he should have developed into one of the busiest men of his time. His, indeed, was a sane and active mind in a sane and active body, and he made noble use of the endowment. He died after a lifetime of such steady, earnest, and varied endeavour as is within the compass of but few.

As a writer, he is seen to greatest advantage in his prose, which is clear, nervous, full of vivacity and significance, and often very powerful and expressive. His verse, however, has a great deal of merit, and may be read with some true pleasure. He had a capacity for poetry, as he had capacities for many things beside, and he cultivated it as he cultivated all the others. His sense of rhythm seems to have been imperfect. His ear was correct, and he often hit on a right and beautiful cadence ; but his music grows monotonous, his rhythmical ideas are seldom well sustained or happily developed. His work abounds in charming phrases and in those verbal inspirations that catch the ear and linger long about the memory :—as witness the notes that are audible in the opening verses of *The Sands of Dee*, the 'pleasant Isle of Avès' of

The Last Buccanier, and the whole first stanza of the song of the Old Schoolmistress in *The Water-Babies*. But, as it is with his music, so is it with his craftsmanship as well. He would begin brilliantly and suggestively and end feebly and ill, so that of perfect work he has left little or none. It is also to be noted of him that his originality was decidedly eclectic—an originality informed with many memories and showing sign of many influences; and that his work, even when its purpose is most dramatic, is always very personal, and has always a strong dash in it of the sentimental manliness, the combination of muscularity and morality, peculiar to its author. For the rest, Kingsley had imagination, feeling, some insight, a great affection for man and nature, a true interest in things as they were and are and ought to be—above all, as they ought to be!—and a genuine vein of lyric song. His work is singularly varied in quality and tone as in purpose and style. Now it is hot and crude and violent—violent without power—as in *Alton Locke's Song* and *The Bad Squire*; now, mannered and affected, as in *The Red King* and the *Weird Lady*; now, human and pathetic, as in *The Last Buccanier* and *Airly Beacon*; now, fierce and random and turbid, as in *Santa Maura* and *The Saint's Tragedy*; now, aesthetic, experimental, even imitative, as in *The Longbeards' Saga, Earl Haldane's Daughter*, and *Andromeda*; now rhetorical and vague and insincere, and now natural, simple, direct, large in handling and earnest in expression, as only true poetry can be. There are fine passages everywhere in Kingsley, and of spirit and point he has an abundance. But it is as a writer of songs that the public have chosen to remember him, and they, as it seems to me, are right. The best of his songs will take rank with the second best in the language.

On the whole, Charles Kingsley was not so much a man of genius as a man of many instincts, many accomplishments, and many capacities. He will always be remembered with respect and admiration; for he was, in John Mill's phrase, 'one of the good influences of his time,' and an excellent writer beside.

W E. HENLEY.

PALLAS IN OLYMPUS.

[From *Andromeda.*]

Blissful, they turned them to go : but the fair-tressed Pallas
    Athené
Rose, like a pillar of tall white cloud, toward silver Olympus ;
Far above ocean and shore, and the peaks of the isles and the
    mainland ;
Where no frost nor storm is, in clear blue windless abysses,
High in the home of the summer, the seats of the happy Im-
    mortals,
Shrouded in keen deep blaze, unapproachable ; there ever youthful
Hebé, Harmonié, and the daughter of Jove, Aphrodité,
Whirled in the white-linked dance with the gold-crowned Hours
    and the Graces,
Hand within hand, while clear piped Phoebe, queen of the wood-
    lands.
All day long they rejoiced : but Athené still in her chamber
Bent herself over her loom, as the stars rang loud to her singing,
Chanting of order and right, and of foresight, warden of nations ;
Chanting of labour and craft, and of wealth in the port and the
    garner ;
Chanting of valour and fame, and the man who can fall with
    the foremost,
Fighting for children and wife, and the field which his father
    bequeathed him.
Sweetly and solemnly sang she, and planned new lessons for
    mortals ;
Happy who, hearing, obey her, the wise unsullied Athené.

THE LAST BUCCANIER.

O England is a pleasant place for them that's rich and high,
But England is a cruel place for such poor folks as I ;
And such a port for mariners I ne'er shall see again
As the pleasant Isle of Avès, beside the Spanish Main.

There were forty craft in Avès that were both swift and stout,
All furnished well with small arms and cannons round about;
And a thousand men in Avès made laws so fair and free
To choose their valiant captains and obey them loyally.

Thence we sailed against the Spaniard with his hoards of plate
    and gold,
Which he wrung with cruel torture from Indian folk of old;
Likewise the merchant captains, with hearts as hard as stone,
Who flog men and keelhaul them, and starve them to the bone.

O the palms grew high in Avès, and fruits that shone like gold
And the colibris and parrots they were gorgeous to behold;
And the negro maids to Avès from bondage fast did flee,
To welcome gallant sailors, a-sweeping in from sea.

O sweet it was in Avès to hear the landward breeze,
A-swing with good tobacco in a net between the trees,
With a negro lass to fan you, while you listened to the roar
Of the breakers on the reef outside, that never touched the shore,

But Scripture saith, an ending to all fine things must be;
So the King's ships sailed on Avès, and quite put down were we.
All day we fought like bull-dogs, but they burst the booms at
    night;
And I fled in a piragua, sore wounded, from the fight.

Nine days I floated starving, and a negro lass beside,
Till, for all I tried to cheer her, the poor young thing she died;
But as I lay a-gasping, a Bristol sail came by,
And brought me home to England here, to beg until I die.

And now I'm old and going—I'm sure I can't tell where;
One comfort is, this world's so hard, I can't be worse off there:
If I might but be a sea-dove, I'd fly across the main,
To the pleasant Isle of Avès, to look at it once again.

THE SANDS OF DEE.

[From *Al on Locke.*]

'O Mary, go and call the cattle home,
　　And call the cattle home,
　　And call the cattle home,
　　　Across the sands o' Dee;'
The western wind was wild and dank wi' foam,
　And all alone went she.

The creeping tide came up along the sand,
　　And o'er and o'er the sand,
　　And round and round the sand,
　　　As far as eye could see;
The blinding mist came down and hid the land—
　And never home came she.

'Oh, is it weed, or fish, or floating hair—
　　A tress o' golden hair,
　　O' drownèd maiden's hair,
　　　Above the nets at sea?
Was never salmon yet that shone so fair,
　Among the stakes on Dee.'

They rowed her in across the rolling foam,
　　The cruel, crawling foam,
　　The cruel, hungry foam,
　　　To her grave beside the sea;
But still the boatmen hear her call the cattle home,
　Across the sands o' Dee.

A FAREWELL.

My fairest child, I have no song to give you;
　No lark could pipe to skies so dull and gray:
Yet, ere we part, one lesson I can leave you
　　For every day.

Be good, sweet maid, and let who will be clever;
　Do noble things, not dream them, all day long.
And so make life, death, and that vast for ever
　　One grand, sweet song.

Dolcino to Margaret.

The world goes up and the world goes down,
  And the sunshine follows the rain ;
And yesterday's sneer and yesterday's frown
  Can never come over again,
      Sweet wife ;
  No, never come over again.

For woman is warm though man be cold,
  And the night will hallow the day !
Till the heart which at even was weary and cold
  Can rise in the morning gay,
      Sweet wife ;
  To its work in the morning gay.

Airly Beacon.

Airly Beacon, Airly Beacon ;
  O the pleasant sight to see
Shires and towns from Airly Beacon,
  While my love climbed up to me !

Airly Beacon, Airly Beacon ;
  O the happy hours we lay
Deep in fern on Airly Beacon,
  Courting through the summer's day !

Airly Beacon, Airly Beacon ;
  O the weary haunt for me,
All alone on Airly Beacon
  With his baby on my knee !

A Boat-Song.

[From *Hypatia.*]

Loose the sail, rest the oar, float away down,
Fleeting and gliding by tower and town.
Life is so short at best ! snatch, while thou canst, thy rest,
  Sleeping by me.

[From *The Water-Babies.*]

THE SONG OF MADAME DO-AS-YOU-WOULD-BE-DONE-BY.

I once had a sweet little doll, dears,
    The prettiest doll in the world;
Her cheeks were so red and so white, dears,
    And her hair was so charmingly curled.
But I lost my poor little doll, dears,
    As I played in the heath one day;
And I cried for her more than a week, dears,
    But I never could find where she lay.

I found my poor little doll, dears,
    As I played in the heath one day:
Folks say she is terribly changed, dears,
    For her paint is all washed away,
And her arm trodden off by the cows, dears,
    And her hair not the least bit curled:
Yet, for old sake's sake, she is still, dears,
    The prettiest doll in the world.

THE 'OLD, OLD SONG.'

When all the world is young, lad,
    And all the trees are green;
And every goose a swan, lad,
    And every lass a queen;
Then hey for boot and horse, lad,
    And round the world away;
Young blood must have its course, lad,
    And every dog his day.

When all the world is old, lad,
    And all the trees are brown;
And all the sport is stale, lad,
    And all the wheels run down:
Creep home, and take your place there,
    The spent and maimed among:
God grant you find one face there
    You loved when all was young.

SYDNEY DOBELL.

[SYDNEY DOBELL was born at Cranbrook in Kent in 1824, was educated at home, and for the greater part of his life was engaged in business in Gloucestershire. His first published poem *The Roman*, inspired by his life-long enthusiasm for the Italian cause, appeared in 1850; his next, *Balder*, was finished in 1853. In 1855 he wrote in conjunction with Alexander Smith a series of sonnets, suggested by the Crimean struggle. This volume was followed by another, of descriptive and lyrical verses, on the same theme, *England in Time of War*. Subsequently his health gave way, and after living for several years, the winters of which he passed abroad, more or less in the condition of an invalid, he died at Barton End House near Nailsworth, in 1874. A complete edition of his poems was published in 1875.]

The above outline in great measure accounts for the fact that most of Dobell's poetry was the product of his earlier years— the last eighteen of his life having been spent in forced abstinence from literary labour. The success of his first considerable work, *The Roman*, was rapid and unmistakable. The theme and its treatment, in accord with popular sentiment, in no less degree the flow of the lyrics, the strong sweep of the graver verse, the frequent richness of the imagery, enlisted the favour alike of the general public and of discerning critics. With defects readily condoned to the writer's youth, and many minor merits, its main charm lay in the novelty of its aim. It was hailed as the product of a man of refined culture, whose sympathies went beyond the mere love of ' harmony in tones and numbers' lisp,' and crossed the ' silver streak' to welcome the wider movements of his age. *The Roman* was continental in a sense that the work of none of our poets, since Byron, had been. *Balder*, the embodiment of the author's deepest though still somewhat chaotic thought, was less fortunate. The incomplete and painful plot was felt to be unnatural, and many of the details were disagreeable. The luxuriance of its imagery was like cloth of gold thrown over the limbs of a Frank-enstein. But few contemporary English poets had scaled the heights of its finest passages. Every chapter bore witness to the author's analytic subtlety and passionate power. Few descriptions of external nature surpass the master sketches of *Balder*: they are drawn by the eye and pencil of one who, from a watch-tower on the hills, outgazed the stars and paid homage, like the Persian, to a hundred dawns, and

> 'hung his room with thought
> Morning and noon, and eve, and night, and all
> The changing seasons.'

Dobell's *Chamouni* almost rivals that of Coleridge. His springs are redolent of Shelley. The pastoral of the summer day on the hills (Scene 24) recalls the Bohemia of *The Winter's Tale*. The music of Amy's songs ripples by the terror and tumult of the tragedy with 'a dying fall like the sweet south.' *Balder* is not likely to become popular in our generation : but, for all its flagrant defects, it will keep its place as a mine for poets.

In spite of manifest faults, on the side of violence or of occasional obscurity, Dobell seems to us to claim a permanent place among the English poets of this century. He belonged to the so-called Spasmodic school, with which he was especially during his residence in Edinburgh often associated, in virtue of defects shared with men otherwise indefinitely his inferiors. Of these the chief were involutions of style, recalling the conceits of Donne and others of the absurdly named 'Metaphysical' school of the seventeenth century, a provoking excess of metaphor, and a weakness, latterly outgrown, for outré 'fine things.' But from the graver intellectual offences of the galvanic and merely sentimental schools he was wholly free. Though unequal, his verse at its best is both strong and delicate ; his imagery, though redundant, original and incisive. But the great merit of his work is that it is steeped in that higher atmosphere in which all enduring literature breathes and moves. In our age his most distinctive quality is the intensity of thought, the freshness, depth and width of sympathy only possible to 'the breed of noble bloods,' and which endeared him to all who were privileged to enjoy the 'liberal education of his society.'

JOHN NICHOL.

MONK'S SONG.

[From *The Roman.*]

There went an incense through the land one night,
Through the hushed holy land, when tired men slept.
                    [*Interlude of music.*
The haughty sun of June had walked, long days,
Through the tall pastures which, like mendicants,
Hung their sere heads and sued for rain: and he
Had thrown them none. And now it was high hay-time,
Through the sweet valley all the flowery wealth
At once lay low, at once ambrosial blood
Cried to the moonlight from a thousand fields.
And through the land the incense went that night,
Through the hushed holy land when tired men slept.
It fell upon the sage; who with his lamp
Put out the light of heaven. He felt it come
Sweetening the musty tomes, like the fair shape
Of that one blighted love, which from the past
Steals oft among his mouldering thoughts of wisdom.
And SHE came with it, borne on airs of youth;
Old days sang round her, old memorial days;
She crowned with tears, they dressed in flowers, all faded—
And the night-fragrance is a harmony
All through the old man's soul. Voices of eld,
The home, the church upon the village green,
Old thoughts that circle like the birds of Even
Round the grey spire. Soft sweet regrets, like sunset
Lighting old windows with gleams day had not.
Ghosts of dead years, whispering old silent names
Through grass-grown pathways, by halls mouldering now.
Childhood—the fragrance of forgotten fields;
Manhood—the unforgotten fields whose fragrance
Passed like a breath; the time of buttercups,
The fluttering time of sweet forget-me-nots;
The time of passion and the rose—the hay-time
Of that last summer of hope! The old man weeps,

The old man weeps.
His aimless hands the joyless books put by;
As one that dreams and fears to wake, the sage
With vacant eye stifles the trembling taper,
Lets in the moonlight—and for once is wise.

SONNETS.

AMERICA.

Men say, Columbia, we shall hear thy guns.
But in what tongue shall be thy battle-cry?
Not that our sires did love in years gone by,
When all the Pilgrim Fathers were little sons
In merrie homes of Englaunde? Back, and see
Thy satchelled ancestor! Behold, he runs
To mine, and, clasped, they tread the equal lea
To the same village-school, where side by side
They spell 'Our Father.' Hard by, the twin pride
Of that grey hall whose ancient oriel gleams
Thro' yon baronial pines, with looks of light
Our sister-mothers sit beneath one tree.
Meanwhile our Shakespeare wanders past and dreams
His Helena and Hermia. Shall we fight?

Nor force nor fraud shall sunder us? Oh ye
Who north or south, on east or western land,
Native to noble sounds, say truth for truth,
Freedom for freedom, love for love, and God
For God; oh ye who in eternal youth
Speak with a living and creative flood
This universal English, and do stand
Its breathing book; live worthy of that grand
Heroic utterance—parted, yet a whole,
Far, yet unsevered,—children brave and free
Of the great Mother-tongue, and ye shall be
Lords of an Empire wide as Shakespeare's soul,
Sublime as Milton's immemorial theme,
And rich as Chaucer's speech, and fair as Spenser's dream.

THE COMMON GRAVE.

Last night beneath the foreign stars I stood,
And saw the thoughts of those at home go by
To the great grave upon the hill of blood.
Upon the darkness they went visibly,
Each in the vesture of its own distress.
Among them there came One, frail as a sigh,
And like a creature of the wilderness
Dug with her bleeding hands. She neither cried
Nor wept ; nor did she see the many stark
And dead that lay unburied at her side.
All night she toiled ; and at that time of dawn,
When Day and Night do change their More and Less,
And Day is More, I saw the melting Dark
Stir to the last, and knew she laboured on.

ENGLAND.

[From *Balder*.]

This dear English land !
This happy England, loud with brooks and birds,
Shining with harvests, cool with dewy trees
And bloomed from hill to dell ; but whose best flowers
Are daughters, and Ophelia still more fair
Than any rose she weaves ; whose noblest floods
The pulsing torrent of a nation's heart ;
Whose forests stronger than her native oaks
Are living men ; and whose unfathomed lakes
For ever calm the unforgotten dead
In quiet graveyards willowed seemly round,
O'er which To-day bends sad, and sees his face.
Whose rocks are rights, consolidate of old
Through unremembered years, around whose base
The ever-surging peoples roll and roar
Perpetual, as around her cliffs the seas
That only wash them whiter ; and whose mountains

Souls that from this mere footing of the earth
Lift their great virtues thro' all clouds of Fate
Up to the very heavens, and make them rise
To keep the gods above us !

CHAMOUNI.

If

Thou hast known anywhere amid a storm
Of thunder, when the Heavens and Earth were moved,
A gleam of quiet sunshine that hath saved
Thine heart ; or where the earthquake hath made wreck,
Knowest a stream, that wandereth fair and sweet
As brooks go singing thro' the fields of home ;
Or on a sudden when the sea, distent
With windy pride, upriseth thro' the clouds
To set his great head equal with the stars,
Hast sunk Hell-deep, thy noble ship a straw
Betwixt two billows ; or in any wild
Barbaric, hast, with half-drawn breath, passed by
The sleeping savage, dreadful still in sleep,
Scarred by a thousand combats, by his side
His rugged spouse—in aught but sex a chief—
Their babe between ; or where the stark roof-tree
Of a burnt home blackened and sear lies dark,
Betwixt the gaunt-ribbed ruin, hast thou seen
The rose of peace ; or in some donjon deep,
Rent by a giant in the blasted rock
And proof against his peers,—hast thou beheld
Prone in the gloom, naked and shining sad
In her own light of loveliness, a fair
Daughter of Eve : Then as thou seest God
In some material likeness, less and more,
Thou hast seen Chamouni, 'mid sternest Alps
The gentlest valley ; bright meandering track
Of summer when she winds among the snows
From Land to Land.

JAMES THOMSON.

[JAMES THOMSON, whose father was a seafaring man, was born at Port Glasgow on the 23rd November, 1834. His early career had many vicissitudes. Educated at the Royal Caledonian Asylum, he subsequently entered the Training School, Chelsea, for the purpose of eventually becoming an army schoolmaster. We next find him in a solicitor's office in London; then in America as secretary to a silver mine company; then in Spain as correspondent of the *New York World*. His first volume, *The City of Dreadful Night, and other Poems*, some parts of which had previously appeared in *The National Reformer*, was published in 1880. This was succeeded, in 1881, by *Vane's Story, and other Poems*. In the same year a volume of prose essays proceeded from his pen; and besides these he has left behind him many posthumous poems and translations. He died June 3rd, 1882.]

James Thomson, though his works were few and his death comparatively early, was still one of the remarkable poets of this century. Most of the poets of our time have flirted with pessimism, but through their beautifully expressed sorrow we cannot help seeing that on the whole they are less sad than they seem, or that, like Mr. Matthew Arnold, they have laid hold of a stern kind of philosophic consolation. It was reserved for Thomson to write the real poem of despair; it was for him to say the ultimate word about melancholia: for, of course, it is the result of that disorder which is depicted in *The City of Dreadful Night*. It was for him to gauge its horrible shapes, to understand its revelations of darkness, as Shelley and others have understood revelations of light. As soon as we have read the opening pages of *The City of Dreadful Night*, we feel transported to a land of infinite tragedy. It has been contended that because life itself is so tragic, such poems as Thomson's are worse than needless; but the true reason for the existence of this particular poem is given by its author in the following lines :—

> 'Yes, here and there some weary wanderer
>   In that same city of tremendous night,
> Will understand the speech, and feel a stir
>   Of fellowship in all-disastrous fight;

> "I suffer mute and lonely, yet another
> Uplifts his voice to let me know a brother
> Travels the same wild paths though out of sight."'

Happily all men have not walked in Thomson's City of Despair, but too many have done so, and they must feel a bitter kind of comfort, such comfort as comes of tears, in having all its horrors so faithfully and sympathetically recorded.

In the gloomy delineation of life Thomson has had of course many predecessors, but perhaps none of them have equalled him in the intense spirit of desolation revealed in *The City of Dreadful Night*, not only in direct utterance, but in imagery large and terribly majestic, and in the thorough keeping of the illustrations of the poem with its general sentiment. The colossal imagination of both idea and symbol show the influence of no other writer. Equally graphic and equally earnest, though in a distinctly different vein, are two poems in the same volume called *Sunday at Hampstead*, and *Sunday up the River*. They are genuine idyls of the people, yet without any trace of vulgarity. They are charged with brightness and healthy joy in living, as fully as the leading poem of the book is fraught with darkness and despair.

In these days of poetic schools, to some one of which a man must generally be relegated, if his work is to be considered at all, there is something remarkable in the solitariness of this poet, who can be classed in no poetic fraternity. It is not likely that *The City of Dreadful Night*, through the awful blackness of which no ray of light penetrates, will ever be a popular poem, but amid the uncertainties of modern speculation, the hesitating lights which still too often discover no sure track, the poem will stand out as a monument of solemn and uncompromising gloom. Intense sincerity, joined to a vivid imagination, constitute Thomson's claims to be remembered. Whether he speaks to us from the fastnesses of his Dreadful City, or in a happier mood breaks into snatches of song as he drifts down stream in his boat, one feels brought in contact with a strong personal individuality. This strong individuality, whether expressing itself in life or poetry, is not welcome to all persons, but those on whom it seizes find in it a fascination which it *is* difficult for any other quality to substitute.

PHILIP BOURKE MARSTON.

THE CITY OF DREADFUL NIGHT.

I.

The City is of Night ; perchance of Death,
   But certainly of Night ; for never there
Can come the lucid morning's fragrant breath
   After the dewy dawning's cold grey air ;
The moon and stars may shine with scorn or pity ;
The sun has never visited that city,
   For it dissolveth in the daylight fair.

Dissolveth like a dream of night away ;
   Though present in distempered gloom of thought
And deadly weariness of heart all day.
   But when a dream night after night is brought
Throughout a week, and such weeks few or many
Recur each year for several years, can any
   Discern that dream from real life in aught?

For life is but a dream whose shapes return,
   Some frequently, some seldom, some by night
And some by day, some night and day: we learn,
   The while all change and many vanish quite,
In their recurrence with recurrent changes
A certain seeming order ; where this ranges
   We count things real ; such is memory's might.

A river girds the city west and south,
   The main north channel of a broad lagoon,
Regurging with the salt tides from the mouth ;
   Waste marshes shine and glister to the moon
For leagues, then moorland black, then stony ridges ;
Great piers and causeways, many noble bridges,
   Connect the town and is'et suburbs strewn.

Upon an easy slope it lies at large,
　And scarcely overlaps the long curved crest
Which swells out two leagues from the river marge.
　A trackless wilderness rolls north and west,
Savannahs, savage woods, enormous mountains,
Bleak uplands, black ravines with torrent fountains;
　And eastward rolls the shipless sea's unrest.

The city is not ruinous, although
　Great ruins of an unremembered past,
With others of a few short years ago
　More sad, are found within its precincts vast.
The street-lamps always burn; but scarce a casement
In house or palace front from roof to basement
　Doth glow or gleam athwart the mirk air cast.

The street-lamps burn amidst the baleful glooms,
　Amidst the soundless solitudes immense
Of rangèd mansions dark and still as tombs.
　The silence which benumbs or strains the sense
Fulfils with awe the soul's despair unweeping:
Myriads of habitants are ever sleeping,
　Or dead, or fled from nameless pestilence!

Yet as in some necropolis you find
　Perchance one mourner to a thousand dead,
So there; worn faces that look deaf and blind
　Like tragic masks of stone. With weary tread,
Each wrapt in his own doom, they wander, wander,
Or sit foredone and desolately ponder
　Through sleepless hours with heavy drooping head.

Mature men chiefly, few in age or youth,
　A woman rarely, now and then a child:
A child! If here the heart turns sick with ruth
　To see a little one from birth defiled,
Or lame or blind, as preordained to languish
Through youthless life, think how it bleeds with anguish
　To meet one erring in that homeless wild.

They often murmur to themselves, they speak
  To one another seldom, for their woe
Broods maddening inwardly and scorns to wreak
  Itself abroad ; and if at whiles it grow
To frenzy which must rave, none heeds the clamour,
Unless there waits some victim of like glamour,
  To rave in turn, who lends attentive show.

The City is of Night, but not of Sleep ;
  There sweet sleep is not for the weary brain ;
The pitiless hours like years and ages creep,
  A night seems termless hell. This dreadful strain
Of thought and consciousness which never ceases,
Or which some moments' stupor but increases,
  This, worse than woe, makes wretches there insane.

They leave all hope behind who enter there :
  One certitude while sane they cannot leave,
One anodyne for torture and despair ;
  The certitude of Death, which no reprieve
Can put off long ; and which, divinely tender,
But waits the outstretched hand to promptly render
  That draught whose slumber nothing can bereave.

*　　*　　*　　*　　*　　*

XVII.

How the moon triumphs through the endless nights!
  How the stars throb and glitter as they wheel
Their thick processions of supernal lights
  Around the blue vault obdurate as steel
And men regard with passionate awe and yearning
The mighty marching and the golden burning,
  And think the heavens respond to what they feel.

Boats gliding like dark shadows of a dream,
  Are glorified from vision as they pass
The quivering moonbridge on the deep black stream ;
  Cold windows kindle their dead glooms of glass

To restless crystals ; cornice, dome, and column
Emerge from chaos in the splendoui solemn ;
　　Like faëry lakes gleam lawns of dewy grass.

With such a living light these dead eyes shine,
　　These eyes of sightless heaven, that as we gaze
We read a pity, tremulous, divine,
　　Or cold majestic scorn in their pure rays :
Fond man! they are not haughty, are not tender ;
There is no heart or mind in all their splendour,
　　They thread mere puppets all their marvellous maze

If we could near them with the flight unflown,
　　We should but find them worlds as sad as this,
Or suns all self-consuming like our own
　　Enringed by planet worlds as much amiss :
They wax and wane through fusion and confusion ;
The spheres eternal are a grand illusion,
　　The empyrean is a void abyss.

＊　　＊　　＊　　＊　　＊　　＊

XXI.

Anear the centre of that northern crest
　　Stands out a level upland bleak and bare,
From which the city east and south and west
　　Sinks gently in long waves ; and thronèd there
An Image sits, stupendous, superhuman,
The bronze colossus of a wingèd Woman,
　　Upon a graded granite base foursquare[1].

Low-seated she leans forward massively,
　　With cheek on clenched left hand, the forearm's might
Erect, its elbow on her rounded knee ;
　　Across a clasped book in her lap the right
Upholds a pair of compasses ; she gazes
With full set eyes, but wandering in thick mazes
　　Of sombre thought beholds no outward sight.

[1] The description refers to Albert Dürer's 'Melencolia.'

Words cannot picture her; but all men know
   That solemn sketch the pure sad artist wrought
Three centuries and threescore years ago,
   With phantasies of his peculiar thought:
The instruments of carpentry and science
Scattered about her feet, in strange alliance
   With the keen wolf-hound sleeping undistraught;

Scales, hour-glass, bell, and magic-square above
   The grave and solid infant perched beside,
With open winglets that might bear a dove,
   Intent upon its tablets, heavy-eyed;
Her folded wings as of a mighty eagle,
But all too impotent to lift the regal
   Robustness of her earth-born strength and pride;

And with those wings, and that light wreath which seems
   To mock her grand head and the knotted frown
Of forehead charged with baleful thoughts and dreams,
   The household bunch of keys, the housewife's gown
Voluminous, indented, and yet rigid
As if a shell of burnished metal frigid,
   The feet thick-shod to tread all weakness down;

The comet hanging o'er the waste dark seas,
   The massy rainbow curved in front of it
Beyond the village with the masts and trees;
   The snaky imp, dog-headed, from the Pit,
Bearing upon its batlike leathern pinions
Her name unfolded in the sun's dominions,
   The 'MELENCOLIA' that transcends all wit.

Thus has the artist copied her, and thus
   Surrounded to expound her form sublime,
Her fate heroic and calamitous;
   Fronting the dreadful mysteries of Time,
Unvanquished in defeat and desolation,
Undaunted in the hopeless conflagration
   Of the day setting on her baffled prime.

Baffled and beaten back she works on still,
   Weary and sick of soul she works the more,
Sustained by her indomitable will:
   The hands shall fashion and the brain shall pore,
And all her sorrow shall be turned to labour,
Till Death the friend-foe piercing with his sabre
   That mighty heart of hearts ends bitter war.

But as if blacker night could dawn on night,
   With tenfold gloom on moonless night unstarred,
A sense more tragic than defeat and blight,
   More desperate than strife with hope debarred,
More fatal than the adamantine Never
Encompassing her passionate endeavour,
   Dawns glooming in her tenebrous regard:

The sense that every struggle brings defeat
   Because Fate holds no prize to crown success;
That all the oracles are dumb or cheat
   Because they have no secret to express;
That none can pierce the vast black veil uncertain
Because there is no light beyond the curtain;
   That all is vanity and nothingness.

Titanic from her high throne in the north,
   That City's sombre Patroness and Queen,
In bronze sublimity she gazes forth
   Over her Capital of teen and threne,
Over the river with its isles and bridges,
The marsh and moorland, to the stern rock-ridges,
   Confronting them with a coëval mien.

The moving moon and stars from east to west
   Circle before her in the sea of air;
Shadows and gleams glide round her solemn rest.
   Her subjects often gaze up to her there:
The strong to drink new strength of iron endurance,
The weak new terrors; all, renewed assurance
   And confirmation of the old despair.

ARTHUR O'SHAUGHNESSY.

[ARTHUR WILLIAM EDGAR O'SHAUGHNESSY was born on the 14th of March, 1844. He was an ichthyologist by profession, and his entire life, from boyhood to the day of his death, was passed in the service of the British Museum. He died, after a very short illness, from the effects of a neglected cold, on the 30th of January, 1881. He published during his lifetime three volumes of verse, *An Epic of Women*, 1870; *Lays of France*, 1872; *Music and Moonlight*, 1874. His posthumous volume, *Songs of a Worker*, appeared in 1881.]

The same month that saw O'Shaughnessy's death deprived English literature of one of its most vigorous representatives, a woman who had no less ambition than he had to excel in verse. In the chorus of praise and regret which followed George Eliot to the grave, O'Shaughnessy passed away almost unperceived. As far as intellect is concerned he had no claim to be mentioned near her. But in poetry the battle is not always to the strong, and he seems to have possessed, what we all confess that she lacked, the indescribable quality which gives the smallest warbler admission to that forkèd hill from which Bacon and Hobbes are excluded. In O'Shaughnessy this quality was thin, and soon exhausted. His earliest book had most of it ; his posthumous book, which ought never to have been published, had none of it. It was volatile, and evaporated with the passage of youth. But when his work has been thoroughly sifted, there will be found to remain a small residuum of exquisite poetry, full of odour and melody, all in one key, and essentially unlike the verse of anyone else. I have ventured to indicate as the central feature of this poetry its habit of etherealising human feeling, and of looking upon mundane emotion as the broken echo of a subtle and supernatural passion. This is what seems to make O'Shaughnessy's best pieces, such as *The Fountain of Tears, Barcarolle, There is an Earthly Glimmer in the Tomb, Song of Betrothal, Outcry*, and even, as the reverse of the medal, the were-wolf ballad of *Bisclaveret*, so delicate and unique. We have nothing else quite like them in English ; the Germans had a kindred product in the songs of Novalis.

EDMUND W. GOSSE.

From 'Bisclaveret.'

[Epic of Women.]

Now over intervening waste
　　Of lowland drear, and barren wold,
I scour, and ne'er assuage my haste,
　　Inflamed with yearnings manifold;

Drinking a distant sound that seems
　　To come around me like a flood;
While all the track of moonlight gleams
　　Before me like a streak of blood;

And bitter stifling scents are past
　　A-dying on the night behind,
And sudden piercing stings are cast
　　Against me in the tainted wind.

And lo, afar, the gradual stir,
　　And rising of the stray wild leaves;
The swaying pine, and shivering fir,
　　And windy sound that moans and heaves

In first fits, till with utter throes
　　The whole wild forest lolls about;
And all the fiercer clamour grows,
　　And all the moan becomes a shout;

And mountains near and mountains far
　　Breathe freely; and the mingled roar
Is as of floods beneath some star
　　Of storms, when shore cries unto shore.

But soon, from every hidden lair
　　Beyond the forest tracks, in thick
Wild coverts, or in deserts bare,
　　Behold they come,—renewed and quick—

The splendid fearful herds that stray
  By midnight, when tempestuous moons
Light them to many a shadowy prey,
  And earth beneath the thunder swoons.

Song.

[From *Lays of France*.]

Has summer come without the rose,
  Or left the bird behind?
Is the blue changed above thee,
  O world? or am I blind?
Will you change every flower that grows,
  Or only change this spot—
Where she who said, I love thee,
  Now says, I love thee not?

The skies seemed true above thee;
  The rose true on the tree;
The bird seemed true the summer through;
  But all proved false to me:
World, is there one good thing in you—
  Life, love, or death—or what?
Since lips that sang I love thee
  Have said, I love thee not?

I think the sun's kiss will scarce fall
  Into one flower's gold cup;
I think the bird will miss me,
  And give the summer up:
O sweet place, desolate in tall
  Wild grass, have you forgot
How her lips loved to kiss me,
  Now that they kiss me not?

Be false or fair above me;
  Come back with any face,
Summer! do I care what you do?
  You cannot change one place—

The grass, the leaves, the earth, the dew,—
  The grave I make the spot,
Here where she used to love me,
  Here where she loves me not.

Song.

[From *Music and Moonlight.*]

I made another garden, yea,
    For my new love;
I left the dead rose where it lay,
    And set the new above.
Why did the summer not begin?
    Why did my heart not haste?
My old love came and walked therein,
    And laid the garden waste.

She entered with her weary smile,
    Just as of old;
She looked around a little while,
    And shivered at the cold.
Her passing touch was death to all,
    Her passing look a blight;
She made the white rose-petals fall,
    And turned the red rose white.

Her pale robe, clinging to the grass
    Seemed like a snake
That bit the grass and ground, alas!
    And a sad trail did make.
She went up slowly to the gate;
    And then, just as of yore,
She turned back at the last to wait,
    And say farewell once more.

DANTE GABRIEL ROSSETTI.

[DANTE GABRIEL ROSSETTI. poet and painter, was born in London, in the year 1828; his father, by birth and education an Italian, being distinguished as a curious commentator upon Dante. He became in early youth a student of painting, in which art, though never a public exhibitor, he grew steadily to fame as an imaginative designer and a colourist of the highest rank. With two years of wedded life (1860–1862) and with some intimate friendships, he passed his days in much seclusion; residing from the year 1863 chiefly at an old and picturesque house in Cheyne Walk, Chelsea. In 1861 he published *Translations from the Early Italian Poets*; in 1870 *Poems*; and in 1881 *Ballads and Sonnets*. After a period of failing health he died at Birchington-on Sea, on Easter Day, 1882. The student of his life and work should consult *Recollections of Dante Gabriel Rossetti*, by T. Hall Caine; *Dante Gabriel Rossetti, a Record and a Study*, by William Sharp; and, in the *Nineteenth Century*, March 1883, *The Truth about Rossetti*, by Theodore Watts.]

It was characteristic of a poet who had ever something about him of mystic isolation, and will still appeal perhaps, though with a name it may seem now established in English literature, to a special and limited audience, that some of his poems had won a kind of exquisite fame before they were in the full sense published. *The Blessed Damozel*, although actually printed twice before the year 1870, was eagerly circulated in manuscript; and the volume which it now opens came at last to satisfy a long-standing curiosity as to the poet, whose pictures also had become an object of the same peculiar kind of interest. For those poems were the work of a painter, understood to belong to, and to be indeed the leader, of a new school then rising into note; and the reader of to-day may observe already, in *The Blessed Damozel*, written at the age of eighteen, a prefigurement of the chief characteristics of that school, as he will recognise in it also, in proportion as he really knows Rossetti, many of the characteristics which are most markedly personal and his own. Common to that school and to him, and in both alike of primary significance, was the quality of sincerity, already felt as one of the charms of that earliest poem—a perfect sincerity, taking effect in the delibera. use of the most direct and unconventicnal expression, for the conveyance of a poetic sense which recognised no conventional standard of what poetry was called upon to be. At a time when poetic originality in England might seem to have had its utmost play, here was certainly one new poet more, with a structure and music of verse, a vocabulary, an accent, unmistakeably novel, yet felt to be no mere tricks of manner adopted with a view to forcing attention—an accent which might rather count as the very seal of reality on one man's own proper speech ; as that speech itself was the wholly natural expression of certain wonderful things he really felt and saw. Here was one, who had a matter to present to his readers, to himself at least, in the first instance, so valuable, so real and definite, that his primary aim, as regards form or expression in his verse, would be but its exact equivalence to those *data* within. That he had this gift of transparency in language—the control of a style which did but obediently shift and shape itself to the mental motion, as a welltrained hand can follow on the tracing paper the outline of an original drawing below it, was proved afterwards by a volume of typically perfect translations from the delightful but difficult 'early Italian poets' : such transparency being indeed the secret of all genuine style, of all such style as can truly belong to one man and not to another. His own meaning was always personal and even recondite, in a certain sense learned and casuistical, sometimes complex or obscure ; but the term was always, one could see, deliberately chosen from many competitors, as the just transcript of that peculiar phase of soul which he alone knew, precisely as he knew it.

One of the peculiarities of *The Blessed Damozel* was a definiteness of sensible imagery, which seemed almost grotesque to some, and was strange, above all, in a theme so profoundly visionary. The gold bar of heaven from which she leaned, her hair yellow like ripe corn, are but examples of a general treatment, as naively detailed as the pictures of those early painters contemporary with Dante, who has shown a similar care for minute and definite imagery in his verse ; there, too, in the very midst of profoundly mystic vision. Such definition of outline is indeed one among many points ir. which Rossetti resembles the great Italian poet, of whom, led to him at first by family circumstances, he was ever a lover—'a servant and singer,' as faithful, as Dante 'of Florence and of Beatrice'—with some close inward conformities of genius, independent of any mere circumstances of education. It was said by a critic of the last century, not wisely though agreeably to the practice of his time, that poetry rejoices in abstractions. For Rossetti, as for Dante, without question on his part, the first condition of the poetic way of seeing and presenting things is particularisation. 'Tell me now,' he writes, for Villon's

> 'Di tes-moy où, n'en quel pays,
> Est Flora, la belle Romaine'—

> 'Tell me now, in what hidden way is
> Lady Flora the lovely Roman:'

—'way,' in which one might actually chance to meet her; the unmistakeably poetic effect of the couplet in English being dependent on the definiteness of that single word (though actually lighted on in the search after a difficult double rhyme) for which every one else would have written, like Villon himself, a more general one, just equivalent to place or region.

And this delight in concrete definition is allied with another of his conformities to Dante, the really imaginative vividness, namely, of his personifications—his hold upon them, or rather their hold upon him, with the force of a Frankenstein, when once they have taken life from him. Not Death only and Sleep, for instance, and the winged spirit of Love, but certain particular aspects of them, a whole 'populace' of special hours and places, 'the hour' even ' which might have been, yet might not be,' are living creatures, with hands and eyes and articulate voices.

> 'Stands it not by the door—
> Love's Hour—till she and I shall meet;
> With bodiless form and unapparent feet
> That cast no shadow yet before,
> Though round its head the dawn begins to pour
> The breath that makes day sweet?'—

> 'Nay, why
> Name the dead hours? I mind them well:
> Their ghosts in many darkened doorways dwell
> With desolate eyes to know them by.'

Poetry as a *mania*—one of Plato's two higher forms of 'divine' mania—has, in all its species, a mere insanity incidental to it, the 'defect of its quality,' into which it may lapse in its moment of weakness : and the insanity which follows a vivid poetic anthropomorphism like that of Rossetti may be noted here and there in his work, in a forced and almost grotesque materialising of abstractions, as Dante also became at times a mere subject of the scholastic realism of the Middle Age.

In *Love's Nocturn* and *The Stream's Secret*, congruously perhaps with a certain feverishness of soul in the moods they present, there is in places a near approach (may it be said ?) to such insanity of realism—

> ' Pity and love shall burn
> In her pressed cheek and cherishing hands ;
> And from the living spirit of love that stands
> Between her lips to soothe and yearn,
> Each separate breath shall clasp me round in turn
> And loose my spirit's bands.'

But even if we concede this,—if we allow, in the very plan of those two compositions, something of the literary conceit—what exquisite, what novel flowers of poetry, we must admit them to be, as they stand ! In the one, what a delight in all the natural beauty of water, all its details for the eye of a painter ; in the other, how subtle and fine the imaginative hold upon all the secret ways of sleep and dreams ! In both of them, with much the same attitude and tone, Love—sick and doubtful Love—would fain inquire of what lies below the surface of sleep, and below the water ; stream or dream being forced to speak by Love's powerful 'control'; and the poet would have it foretell the fortune, issue, and event of his wasting passion. Such artifices were not unknown in the old Provençal poetry of which Dante had learned something. Only, in Rossetti at least, they are redeemed by a serious purpose, by that sincerity of his, which allies itself readily to a serious beauty, a sort of grandeur of literary workmanship—to a great style. One seems to hear there a really new kind of poetic utterance, with effects which have nothing else like them ; as there is nothing else, for instance, like the narrative of Jacob's Dream, or Blake's design of the Singing of the Morning Stars, or Addison's Nineteenth Psalm.

With him indeed, as in some revival of the old mythopœic age, common things—dawn, noon, night—are full of human or personal expression, full of sentiment. The lovely little sceneries scattered up and down his poems, glimpses of a landscape, not indeed of broad open-air effects, but rather that of a painter concentrated upon the picturesque effect of one or two selected objects at a time— the 'hollow brimmed with mist,' or the 'ruined weir,' as he sees it from one of the windows, or reflected in one of the mirrors of his 'house of life' (the vignettes for instance seen by Rose Mary ‌ㅼ. the magic beryl) attest, by their very freshness and simplicity, to a pictorial or descriptive power in dealing with the inanimate world, which is certainly still one half of the charm, in that other, more remote and mystic, use of it. For with Rossetti this sense of, after all lifeless, nature, is translated to a higher service, in which it does but incorporate itself with some phase of strong emotion. Every one understands how this may happen at critical moments of life ; what a weirdly expressive soul may have crept, even in full noonday, into 'the white-flower'd elder-thicket,' when Godiva saw it 'gleam through the Gothic archways in the wall,' at the end of her ride. To Rossetti it is so always, because to him life is a crisis at every moment. A sustained impressibility towards the mysterious conditions of man's every-day life, towards the very mystery itself in it, gives a singular gravity to all his work : those matters never became trite to him. But throughout, it is the ideal intensity of love—of love based upon a perfect yet peculiar type of physical or material beauty, which is enthroned in the midst of those mysterious powers ; Youth and Death, Destiny and Fortune, Fame —Poetic Fame, Memory, Oblivion, and the like. Rossetti is one of those who, in the words of Mérimée, *se passionnent pour la passion*, one of Love's lovers.

And yet, again as with Dante, to speak of his ideal type of beauty as material, is partly misleading. Spirit and matter indeed have been for the most part opposed, with a false contrast or antagonism, by schoolmen, whose artificial creation those abstractions really are. In our actual concrete experience, the two trains of phenomena which they do but roughly distinguish, play inextricably into each other. Practically, the church of the Middle Age by its æsthetic worship, its sacramentalism, its real faith in the resurrection of the flesh, had set itself against that Manichean opposition of spirit and matter, and its results in men's way of taking life ; and in this, Dante is the central representative of its spirit. To him, in the vehement and impassioned heat of his conceptions, the material and the spiritual are fused and blent : if the spiritual attains the definite character of a crystal, what is material loses its earthiness and impurity. And here again by force of instinct, Rossetti is one with him. His chosen type of beauty is one,

> 'Whose speech Truth knows not from her thought,
> Nor Love her body from her soul.'

Like Dante, he knows no region of spirit which shall not be sensuous also, or material. The shadowy world, which he realises so powerfully, has still the ways and houses, the land and water, the light and darkness, the fire and flowers, that had so much to do in the moulding of those bodily powers and aspects which counted for so large a part of the soul, here.

For Rossetti, then, the great affections of persons to each other, swayed and determined, in the case of his highly pictorial genius, mainly by that so-called material loveliness, formed the great undeniable reality in things, the solid resisting substance, in a world where all beside might be but shadow. The fortunes of those affections—of the great love so determined ; its casuistries, its languor sometimes ; above all, its sorrows ; its fortunate or unfortunate collisions with those other great matters ; how it looks, as the long day of life goes round, in the light and shadow of them —that, conceived with an abundant imagination, and a deep, a philosophic reflectiveness, is the matter of his verse, and especially of what he designed as his chief poetic work, 'a work to be called *The House of Life*,' towards which the majority of his sonnets and songs were contributions.

The dwelling-place in which one finds oneself by chance or destiny, yet can partly fashion for oneself ; never properly one's own at all, if it be changed too lightly ; in which every object has its associations—the dim mirrors, the portraits, the lamps, the books, the hair-tresses of the dead and visionary magic crystals in the secret drawers, the names and words scratched on the windows— windows open upon prospects the saddest or the sweetest—the house which one must quit, yet taking perhaps how much of its quietly active light and colour along with us !—grown now to be a kind of raiment to one's body, as the body, according to Swedenborg, is but the raiment of the soul—under that image, the whole of Rossetti's work might count as a *House of Life*, of which he is but the 'Interpreter.' And it is a 'haunted' house. A sense of power in love, defying distance, and those barriers which are so much more than physical distance—of unutterable desire penetrating into the world of sleep, however lead-bound, was one of those anticipative notes obscurely struck in *The B.essed Damozel*, and, in his later work, makes him speak sometimes almost like a believer in mesmerism. Dream-land, as we said, with its 'phantoms of the body,' deftly coming and going on love's service, is to him, in no mere fancy or figure of speech, a real country, a veritable expansion of, or addition to, our waking life ; and he did well perhaps to wait carefully upon sleep, the lack of which became mortal disease with him. One may recognise even a sort of over-hasty and morbid making ready for death itself, which increases on him ; the thoughts and imageries of it coming with a frequency and importunity, in excess, one might think, of even the very saddest, quite wholesome wisdom.

And indeed the publication of his second volume of *Ballads and Sonnets* preceded his death by scarcely a twelvemonth. That volume bears witness to the reverse of any failure of power or falling-off from his early standard of literary perfection, in every one of his then accustomed forms of poetry—the song, the sonnet, and the ballad. The newly printed sonnets, now completing the *House of Life*, certainly advanced beyond those earlier ones, in clearness ; his dramatic power in the ballad, was here at its height ; while one monumental lyrical piece, *Soothsay*, testifies, more clearly even than the *Nineveh* of his first volume, to the reflective force, the dry reason, always at work behind his imaginative creations, which at no time dispensed with a genuine intellectual structure. For in matters of pure reflection also, Rossetti maintained the painter's sensuous clearness of conception ; and this has something to do with the capacity, largely illustrated by his ballads, of telling some red-hearted story of impassioned action with effect.

Were there indeed ages, in which the external conditions of poetry such as Rossetti's were of more spontaneous growth than in our own ? The archaic side of Rossetti's work, his preferences in regard to earlier poetry, connect him with those who have certainly thought so, who fancied they could have breathed more largely in the age of Chaucer, or of Ronsard, in one of those ages, in the words of Stendhal—*ces siècles de passions ou les âmes pouvaient se livrer franchement à la plus haute exaltation, quand les passions qui font la possibilité comme les sujets des beaux arts existaient.* We may think, perhaps, that such old time as that has never really existed except in the fancy of poets ; but it was to find it, that Rossetti turned so often from modern life to the chronicle of the past. Old Scotch history, perhaps beyond any other, is strong in the matter of heroic and vehement hatreds and love, the tragic Mary herself being but the perfect blossom of them ; and it is from that history that Rossetti has taken the subjects of the two longer ballads of his second volume : of the three admirable ballads in it, *The King's Tragedy* (in which Rossetti has dexterously interwoven some relics of James's own exquisite early verse) reaching the highest level of dramatic success, and marking per-fection, perhaps, in this kind of poetry ; which, in the earlier volume, gave us, among other pieces, *Troy Town, Sister Helen*, and *Eden Bower.*

Like those earlier pieces, the ballads of the second volume bring with them the question of the poetic value of the 'refrain'—

> 'Eden bower's in flower:
> And O the bower and the hour !'

—and the like. Two of those ballads—*Troy Town* and *Eden Bower*, are terrible in theme ; and the refrain serves, perhaps, to relieve their bold aim at the sentiment of terror. In *Sister Helen* again, it has a real, sustained purpose (being here duly varied also) and performs the part of a chorus, as the story proceeds. Yet even in these cases, whatever its effect may be in actual recitation, it may indeed be questioned, whether, to the mere reader their actual effect is not that of a positive interruption and drawback, at least in pieces so lengthy; and Rossetti himself, it would seem, came to think so, for in the shortest of his later ballads, *The White Ship*--that old true history of the generosity with which a youth, worthless in life, flung himself upon death—he has contented himself with a single utterance of the refrain, 'given out' like the key-note or tune of a chant.

In *The King's Tragedy*, Rossetti has worked upon a motive, broadly human, in the phrase of popular criticism, such as one and all may realise. Rossetti, indeed, with all his self-concentration upon his own circle of work, by no means ignored those general interests which are external to poetry as he conceived it; as he has shown here and there, in this poetic, as also in pictorial, work. It was but that, in a life to be shorter even than the average, he found enough to occupy him in the fulfilment of a task, plainly 'given him to do.' Perhaps, if one had to name a single composition of his to a reader who desired to make acquaintance with him for the first time, it is *The King's Tragedy* one would select—that poem so moving, so popularly dramatic and lifelike. Not withstanding this, his work, it must be conceded, certainly through no narrowness or egotism, but in the faithfulness of a true workman to a vocation so emphatic, was mainly of the esoteric order. But poetry, at all times, exercises two distinct functions : it may reveal, it may unveil to every eye, the ideal aspects of common things, after Gray's way (though Gray too, it is well to remember, seemed in his own day, seemed even to Johnson, obscure) or it may actually add to the number of motives poetic and uncommon in themselves, by the imaginative creation of things, ideal from their very birth. Rossetti did something, something excellent, of the former kind ; but his characteristic, his really revealing work, lay in the adding to poetry of fresh poetic material, of a new order of phenomena, in the creation of a new ideal.

WALTER H. PATER.

The Blessed Damozel.

The blessed damozel leaned out
   From the gold bar of Heaven;
Her eyes were deeper than the depth
   Of waters stilled at even;
She had three lilies in her hand,
   And the stars in her hair were seven.

Her robe, ungirt from clasp to hem,
   No wrought flowers did adorn,
But a white rose of Mary's gift
   For service meetly worn;
Her hair that lay along her back
   Was yellow like ripe corn.

Herseemed she scarce had been a day
   One of God's choristers;
The wonder was not yet quite gone
   From that still look of hers;
Albeit, to them she left, her day
   Had counted as ten years.

(To one, it is ten years of years,
  . . .   Yet now, and in this place,
Surely she leaned o'er me—her hair
   Fell all about my face.   .   .   .
Nothing: the autumn fall of leaves.
   The whole year sets apace.)

It was the rampart of God's house
   That she was standing on;
By God built over the sheer depth
   The which is Space begun;
So high, that looking downward thence
   She scarce could see the sun.

It lies in Heaven, across the flood
  Of ether, as a bridge.
Beneath, the tides of day and night
  With flame and darkness ridge
The void, as low as where this earth
  Spins like a fretful midge.

Heard hardly, some of her new friends
  Amid their loving games
Spake evermore among themselves
  Their virginal chaste names;
And the souls mounting up to God
  Went by her like thin flames.

And still she bowed herself and stooped
  Out of the circling charm;
Until her bosom must have made
  The bar she leaned on warm,
And the lilies lay as if asleep
  Along her bended arm.

From the fixed place of Heaven she saw
  Time like a pulse shake fierce
Through all the worlds. Her gaze still strove
  Within the gulf to pierce
Its path; and now she spoke as when
  The stars sang in their spheres.

The sun was gone now; the curled moon
  Was like a little feather
Fluttering far down the gulf; and now
  She spoke through the still weather.
Her voice was like the voice the stars
  Had when they sang together.

(Ah sweet! Even now, in that bird's song,
  Strove not her accents there,
Fain to be hearkened? When those bells
  Possessed the mid-day air,
Strove not her steps to reach my side
  Down all the echoing stair?)

'I wish that he were come to me,
  For he will come,' she said.
'Have I not prayed in heaven?—on earth,
  Lord, Lord, has he not pray'd?
Are not two prayers a perfect strength?
  And shall I feel afraid?

'When round his head the aureole clings,
  And he is clothed in white,
I'll take his hand and go with him
  To the deep wells of light;
We will step down as to a stream,
  And bathe there in God's sight.

'We two will stand beside the shrine,
  Occult, withheld, untrod,
Whose lamps are stirred continually
  With prayer sent up to God;
And see our old prayers, granted, melt
  Each like a little cloud.

'We two will lie i' the shadow of
  That living mystic tree
Within whose secret growth the Dove
  Is sometimes felt to be,
While every leaf that His plumes touch
  Saith His Name audibly.

'And I myself will teach to him,
  I myself, lying so,
The songs I sing here; which his voice
  Shall pause in, hushed and slow,
And find some knowledge at each pause,
  Or some new thing to know.'

(Alas! We two, we two, thou say'st!
  Yea, one wast thou with me
That once of old. But shall God lift
  To endless unity
The soul whose likeness with thy soul
  Was but its love for thee?)

'We two,' she said, 'will seek the groves
   Where the lady Mary is,
With her five handmaidens, whose names
   Are five sweet symphonies,
Cecily, Gertrude, Magdalen,
   Margaret and Rosalys.

'Circlewise sit they, with bound locks
   And foreheads garlanded ;
Into the fine cloth white like flame
   Weaving the golden thread,
To fashion the birth-robes for them
   Who are just born, being dead.

'He shall fear, haply, and be dumb :
   Then will I lay my cheek
To his, and tell about our love,
   Not once abashed or weak :
And the dear Mother will approve
   My pride, and let me speak.

'Herself shall bring us, hand in hand,
   To Him round whom all souls
Kneel, the clear-ranged unnumbered heads
   Bowed with their aureoles :
And angels meeting us shall sing
   To their citherns and citoles.

'There will I ask of Christ the Lord
   Thus much for him and me :—
Only to live as once on earth
   With Love,— only to be,
As then awhile, for ever now
   Together, I and he.'

She gazed and listened and then said,
   Less sad of speech than mild,—
'All this is when he comes.' She ceased.
   The light thrilled towards her, fill'd
With angels in strong level flight.
   Her eyes prayed, and she smil'd.

(I saw her smile.) But soon their path
  Was vague in distant spheres :
And then she cast her arms along
  The golden barriers,
And laid her face between her hands
  And wept. (I heard her tears.)

LOVE ENTHRONED.

I marked all kindred Powers the heart finds fair :—
  Truth, with awed lips ; and Hope, with eyes upcast ;
  And Fame, whose loud wings fan the ashen Past
To signal-fires, Oblivion's flight to scare ;
And Youth, with still some single golden hair
  Unto his shoulder clinging, since the last
  Embrace wherein two sweet arms held him fast ;
And Life, still wreathing flowers for Death to wear.

Love's throne was not with these ; but far above
  All passionate wind of welcome and farewell
He sat in breathless bowers they dream not of ;
  Though Truth foreknow Love's heart, and Hope foretell,
  And Fame be for Love's sake desirable,
And Youth be dear, and Life be sweet to love.

LOVE'S NOCTURN.

Master of the murmuring courts
  Where the shapes of sleep convene !—
Lo ! my spirit here exhorts
  All the powers of thy demesne
  For their aid to woo my queen.
    What reports
  Yield thy jealous courts unseen?

Vaporous unaccountable,
  Dreamland lies forlorn of light,
Hollow like a breathing shell.
  Ah! that from all dreams I might
  Choose one dream and guide its flight!
    I know well
  What her sleep should tell to-night.

There the dreams are multitudes :
  Some whose buoyance waits not sleep,
Deep within the August woods ;
  Some that hum while rest may steep
  Weary labour laid a-heap ;
    Interludes,
  Some, of grievous moods that weep.

Poets' fancies all are there :
  There the elf-girls flood with wings
Valleys full of plaintive air ;
  There breathe perfumes ; there in rings
  Whirl the foam-bewildered springs ;
    Siren there
  Winds her dizzy hair and sings.

Thence the one dream mutually
  Dreamed in bridal unison,
Less than waking ecstasy ;
  Half-formed visions that make moan
  In the house of birth alone ;
    And what we
  At death's wicket see, unknown.

But for mine own sleep, it lies
  In one gracious form's control,
Fair with honourable eyes,
  Lamps of an auspicious soul :
  O their glance is loftiest dole,
    Sweet and wise,
  Wherein Love descries his goal.

Reft of her, my dreams are all
   Clammy trance that fears the sky:
Changing footpaths shift and fall;
   From polluted coverts nigh,
   Miserable phantoms sigh;
         Quakes the pall,
   And the funeral goes by.

Master, is it soothly said
   That, as echoes of man's speech
Far in secret clefts are made,
   So do all men's bodies reach
   Shadows o'er thy sunken beach,—
         Shape or shade
   In those halls pourtrayed of each?

Ah! might I, by thy good grace
   Groping in the windy stair,
(Darkness and the breath of space
   Like loud waters everywhere,)
   Meeting mine own image there
         Face to face,
   Send it from that place to her!

Nay, not I; but oh! do thou,
   Master, from thy shadowkind
Call my body's phantom now:
   Bid it bear its face declin'd
   Till its flight her slumbers find,
         And her brow
   Feel its presence bow like wind.

Where in groves the gracile Spring
   Trembles, with mute orison
Confidently strengthening,
   Water's voice and wind's as one
   Shed an echo in the sun.
         Soft as Spring
   Master, bid it sing and moan.

Song shall tell how glad and strong
  Is the night she soothes alway ;
Moan shall grieve with that parched tongue
  Of the brazen hours of day :
  Sounds as of the springtide they,
        Moan and song,
  While the chill months long for May.

Not the prayers which with all leave
  The world's fluent woes prefer,—
Not the praise the world doth give,
  Dulcet fulsome whisperer ;—
  Let it yield my love to her,
        And achieve
  Strength that shall not grieve or err.

Wheresoe'er my dreams befall,
  Both at night-watch (let it say,)
And where round the sundial
  The reluctant hours of day,
  Heartless, hopeless of their way,
        Rest and call ; —
  There her glance doth fall and stay.

Suddenly her face is there :
  So do mounting vapours wreathe
Subtle-scented transports where
  The black firwood sets its teeth.
  Part the boughs and look beneath,—
        Lilies share
  Secret waters there, and breathe.

Master, bid my shadow bend
  Whispering thus till birth of light,
Lest new shapes that sleep may send
  Scatter all its work to flight ;—
  Master, master of the night,
        Bid it spend
  Speech, song, prayer, and end aright.

Yet, ah me! if at her head
  There another phantom lean
Murmuring o'er the fragrant bed,—
  Ah! and if my spirit's queen
  Smile those alien words between,—
        Ah! poor shade!
  Shall it strive, or fade unseen?

How should love's own messenger
  Strive with love and be love's foe?
Master, nay! If thus, in her,
  Sleep a wedded heart should show,—
  Silent let mine image go,
        Its old share
Of thy sunken air to know.

Like a vapour wan and mute,
  Like a flame, so let it pass;
One low sigh across her lute,
  One dull breath against her glass;
  And to my sad soul, alas!
        One salute
Cold as when death's foot shall pass.

Then, too, let all hopes of mine,
  All vain hopes by night and day,
Slowly at thy summoning sign
  Rise up pallid and obey.
  Dreams, if this is thus, were they:—
        Be they thine,
And to dreamland pine away.

Yet from old time, life, not death,
  Master, in thy rule is rife:
Lo! through thee, with mingling breath,
  Adam woke beside his wife.
  O Love bring me so, for strife,
        Force and faith,
Bring me so not death but life!

Yea, to Love himself is pour'd
 This frail song of hope and fear.
Thou art Love, of one accord
 With kind Sleep to bring her near,
Still-eyed, deep-eyed, ah how dear!
  Master, Lord,
In her name implor'd, O hear!

LOVE'S LOVERS.

Some ladies love the jewels in Love's zone
 And gold-tipped darts he hath for painless play
 In idle scornful hours he flings away;
And some that listen to his Lute's soft tone
Do love to vaunt the silver praise their own;
 Some prize his blindfold sight; and there be they
 Who kissed his wings which brought him yesterday
And thank his wings to-day that he is flown.

My lady only loves the heart of Love:
 Therefore Love's heart, my lady, hath for thee
 His bower of unimagined flower and tree:
There kneels he now, and all-anhungered of
Thine eyes grey-lit in shadowing hair above,
 Seals with thy mouth his immortality.

LOVE-LILY.

Between the hands, between the brows,
 Between the lips of Love-Lily,
A spirit is born whose birth endows
 My blood with fire to burn through me;
Who breathes upon my gazing eyes,
 Who laughs and murmurs in mine ear,
At whose least touch my colour flies,
 And whom my life grows faint to hear.

Within the voice, within the heart,
  Within the mind of Love-Lily,
A spirit is born who lifts apart
  His tremulous wings and looks at me ;
Who on my mouth his finger lays,
  And shows, while whispering lutes confer,
That Eden of Love's watered ways
  Whose winds and spirits worship her.

Brows, hands, and lips, heart, mind, and voice,
  Kisses and words of Love-Lily,—
Oh ! bid me with your joy rejoice
  Till riotous longing rest in me !
Ah ! let not hope be still distraught,
  But find in her its gracious goal,
Whose speech Truth knows not from her thought
  Nor Love her body from her soul.

PARTED LOVE.

What shall be said of this embattled day
  And armed occupation of this night
  By all thy foes beleaguered,—now when sight
Nor sound denotes the loved one far away?
Of these thy vanquished hours what shalt thou say,—
  As every sense to which she dealt delight
  Now labours lonely o'er the stark noon-height
To reach the sunset's desolate disarray?

Stand still, fond fettered wretch ! while Memory's art
  Parades the Past before thy face, and lures
  Thy spirit to her passionate portraitures :
Till the tempestuous tide-gates flung apart
Flood with wild will the hollows of thy heart,
  And thy heart rends thee, and thy body endures.

The Portrait.

This is her picture as she was:
  It seems a thing to wonder on,
As though mine image in the glass
  Should tarry when myself am gone.
I gaze until she seems to stir,—
Until mine eyes almost aver
    That now, even now, the sweet lips part
    To breathe the words of the sweet heart:—
And yet the earth is over her.

Alas! even such the thin-drawn ray
  That makes the prison-depths more rude,—
The drip of water night and day
  Giving a tongue to solitude.
Yet this, of all love's perfect prize,
Remains; save what in mournful guise
    Takes counsel with my soul alone,—
    Save what is secret and unknown,
Below the earth, above the skies.

In painting her I shrined her face
  Mid mystic trees, where light falls in
Hardly at all; a covert place
  Where you may think to find a din
Of doubtful talk, and a live flame
Wandering, and many a shape whose name
    Not itself knoweth, and old dew,
    And your own footsteps meeting you,
And all things going as they came.

A deep dim wood; and there she stands
  As in that wood that day: for so
Was the still movement of her hands
  And such the pure line's gracious flow.

And passing fair the type must seem,
Unknown the presence and the dream.
   'Tis she : though of herself, alas !
   Less than her shadow on the grass
Or than her image in the stream.

That day we met there, I and she
   One with the other all alone ;
And we were blithe ; yet memory
   Saddens those hours, as when the moon
Looks upon daylight. And with her
I stooped to drink the spring-water,
   Athirst where other waters sprang ;
   And where the echo is, she sang,—
My soul another echo there.

But when that hour my soul won strength
   For words whose silence wastes and kills,
Dull raindrops smote us, and at length
   Thundered the heat within the hills.
That eve I spoke those words again
Beside the pelted window-pane ;
   And there she hearkened what I said,
   With under-glances that surveyed
The empty pastures blind with rain.

Next day the memories of these things,
   Like leaves through which a bird has flown,
Still vibrated with Love's warm wings ;
   Till I must make them all my own
And paint this picture. So, 'twixt ease
Of talk and sweet long silences,
   She stood among the plants in bloom
   At windows of a summer room,
To feign the shadow of the trees.

And as I wrought, while all above
   And all around was fragrant air,
In the sick burthen of my love
   It seemed each sun-thrilled blossom there

Beat like a heart among the leaves.
O heart that never beats nor heaves,
 In that one darkness lying still,
 What now to thee my love's great will
Or the fine web the sunshine weaves?

For now doth daylight disavow
 Those days,—nought left to see or hear.
Only in solemn whispers now
 At night-time these things reach mine ear,
When the leaf-shadows at a breath
Shrink in the road, and all the heath,
 Forest and water, far and wide,
 In limpid starlight glorified,
Lie like the mystery of death.

Last night at last I could have slept,
 And yet delayed my sleep till dawn,
Still wandering. Then it was I wept:
 For unawares I came upon
Those glades where once she walked with me:
And as I stood there suddenly,
 All wan with traversing the night,
 Upon the desolate verge of light
Yearned loud the iron-bosomed sea.

Even so, where Heaven holds breath and hears
 The beating heart of Love's own breast,—
Where round the secret of all spheres
 All angels lay their wings to rest,—
How shall my soul stand rapt and awed,
When, by the new birth borne abroad
 Throughout the music of the suns,
 It enters in her soul at once
And knows the silence there for God!

Here with her face doth memory sit
 Meanwhile, and wait the day's decline,
Till other eyes shall look from it,
 Eyes of the spirit's Palestine,

Even than the old gaze tenderer :
While hopes and aims long lost with **her**
  Stand round her image side by side,
  Like tombs of pilgrims that have died
About the Holy Sepulchre.

Sibylla Palmifera.

(*For a Picture.*)

Under the arch of Life, where love and death,
  Terror and mystery, guard her shrine, I saw
  Beauty enthroned ; and though her gaze struck awe,
I drew it in as simply as my breath.
Hers are the eyes which, over and beneath,
  The sky and sea bend on thee,—which can draw,
  By sea or sky or woman, to one law,
The allotted bondman of her palm and wreath.

This is that Lady Beauty, in whose praise
  Thy voice and hand shake still,—long known to thee
  By flying hair and fluttering hem,—the beat
  Following her daily of thy heart and feet,
  How passionately and irretrievably,
In what fond flight, how many ways and days !

Newborn Death.

I.

To-day Death seems to me an infant child
  Which her worn mother Life upon my knee
  Has set to grow my friend and play with me ;
If haply so my heart might be beguil'd
To find no terrors in a face so mild,—
  If haply so my weary heart might be
  Unto the newborn milky eyes of thee,
O Death, before resentment reconcil'd.

How long, O Death? And shall thy feet depart
  Still a young child's with mine, or wilt thou stand
Fullgrown the helpful daughter of my heart,
  What time with thee indeed I reach the strand
Of the pale wave which knows thee what thou art,
  And drink it in the hollow of thy hand?

II.

And thou, O Life, the lady of all bliss,
  With whom, when our first heart beat full and fast,
  I wandered till the haunts of men were pass'd,
And in fair places found all bowers amiss
Till only woods and waves might hear our kiss,
  While to the winds all thought of Death we cast :—
  Ah, Life! and must I have from thee at last
No smile to greet me and no babe but this?

Lo! Love, the child once ours; and Song, whose hair
  Blew like a flame and blossomed like a wreath;
And Art, whose eyes were worlds by God found fair;
  These o'er the book of Nature mixed their breath
With neck-twined arms, as oft we watched them there:
  And did these die that thou might'st bear me Death?

SOOTHSAY.

Let no man ask thee of anything
Not yearborn between Spring and Spring.
More of all worlds than he can know,
Each day the single sun doth show.
A trustier gloss than thou canst give
From all wise scrolls demonstrative,
The sea doth sigh and the wind sing.

Let no man awe thee on any height
Of earthly kingship's mouldering might.
The dust his heel holds meet for thy brow
Hath all of it been what both are now;
And thou and he may plague together
A beggar's eyes in some dusty weather
When none that is now knows sound or sight.

Crave thou no dower of earthly things
Unworthy Hope's imaginings.
To have brought true birth of Song to be
And to have won hearts to Poesy,
Or anywhere in the sun or rain
To have loved and been beloved again,
Is loftiest reach of Hope's bright wings.

The wild waifs cast up by the sea
Are diverse ever seasonably.
Even so the soul-tides still may land
A different drift upon the sand.
But one the sea is evermore :
And one be still, 'twixt shore and shore,
As the sea's life, thy soul in thee.

Say, hast thou pride?   How then may fit
Thy mood with flatterer's silk-spun wit?
Haply the sweet voice lifts thy crest,
A breeze of fame made manifest.
Nay, but then chaf'st at flattery?   Pause :
Be sure thy wrath is not because
It makes thee feel thou lovest it.

Let thy soul strive that still the same
Be early friendship's sacred flame.
The affinities have strongest part
In youth, and draw men heart to heart :
As life wears on and finds no rest,
The individual in each breast
Is tyrannous to sunder them.

In the life-drama's stern cue-call,
A friend's a part well-prized by all :
And if thou meet an enemy,
What art thou that none such should be?
Even so : but if the two parts run
Into each other and grow one,
Then comes the curtain's cue to fall.

Whate'er by other's need is claimed
More than by thine,—to him unblamed
Resign it : and if he should hold
What more than he thou lack'st, bread, gold
Or any good whereby we live,—
To thee such substance let him give
Freely : nor he nor thou be shamed.

Strive that thy works prove equal : lest
That work which thou hast done the best
Should come to be to thee at length
(Even as to envy seems the strength
Of others) hateful and abhorr'd,—
Thine own above thyself made lord,—
Of self-rebuke the bitterest.

Unto the man of yearning thought
And aspiration, to do nought
Is in itself almost an act,—
Being chasm-fire and cataract
Of the soul's utter depths unseal'd.
Yet woe to thee if once thou yield
Unto the act of doing nought !

How callous seems beyond revoke
The clock with its last listless stroke !
How much too late at length !—to trace
The hour on its forewarning face,
The thing thou hast not dared to do !....
Behold, this *may* be thus ! Ere true
It prove, arise and bear thy yoke.

Let lore of all Theology
Be to thy soul what it *can* be :
But know,—the Power that fashions man
Measured not out thy little span
For thee to take the meting-rod
In turn, and so approve on God
Thy science of Theometry.

To God at best, to Chance at worst,
Give thanks for good things, last as first.
But wind-strown blossom is that good
Whose apple is not gratitude.
Even if no prayer uplift thy face,
Let the sweet right to render grace
As thy soul's cherished child be nurs'd.

Didst ever say, ' Lo, I forget ' ?
Such thought was to remember yet.
As in a gravegarth, count to see
The monuments of memory.
Be this thy soul's appointed scope :—
Gaze onward without claim to hope,
Nor, gazing backward, court regret.

HOPE OVERTAKEN.

I deemed thy garments, O my Hope, were grey,
　　So far I viewed thee.　Now the space between
　　Is passed at length ; and garmented in green
Even as in days of yore thou stand'st to-day.
Ah God ! and but for lingering dull dismay,
　　On all that road our footsteps erst had been
　　Even thus commingled, and our shadows seen
Blent on the hedgerows and the water-way.

O Hope of mine whose eyes are living love,
　　No eyes but hers,—O Love and Hope the same !—
　　Lean close to me, for now the sinking sun
That warmed our feet scarce gilds our hair above.
　　O hers thy voice and very hers thy name !
　　Alas, cling round me, for the day is done !

THE MONOCHORD.

(*Written during music.*)

Is it this sky's vast vault or ocean's sound
　　That is Life's self and draws my life from me,
　　And by instinct ineffable decree
Holds my breath quailing on the bitter bound ?

Nay, is it Life or Death, thus thunder-crown'd,
  That 'mid the tide of all emergency
  Now notes my separate wave, and to what sea
Its difficult eddies labour in the ground?

Oh! what is this that knows the road I came,
The flame turned cloud, the cloud returned to flame,
  The lifted shifted steeps and all the way?—
That draws round me at last this wind-warm space,
And in regenerate rapture turns my face
  Upon the devious coverts of dismay?

AVE.

Mother of the Fair Delight,
Thou handmaid perfect in God's sight,
Now sitting fourth beside the Three,
Thyself a woman-Trinity,—
Being a daughter borne to God,
Mother of Christ from stall to rood,
And wife unto the Holy Ghost:—
Oh when our need is uttermost,
Think that to such as death may strike
Thou once wert sister sisterlike!
Thou headstone of humanity,
Groundstone of the great Mystery,
Fashioned like us, yet more than we!

Mind'st thou not (when June's heavy breath
Warmed the long days in Nazareth,)
That eve thou didst go forth to give
Thy flowers some drink that they might live
One faint night more amid the sands?
Far off the trees were as pale wands
Against the fervid sky: the sea
Sighed further off eternally
As human sorrow sighs in sleep.
Then suddenly the awe grew deep,

As of a day to which all days
Were footsteps in God's secret ways:
Until a folding sense, like prayer,
Which is, as God is, everywhere,
Gathered about thee; and a voice
Spake to thee without any noise,
Being of the silence:—'Hail,' it said,
'Thou that art highly favourèd;
The Lord is with thee here and now;
Blessed among all women thou.'

Ah! knew'st thou of the end, when first
That Babe was on thy bosom nurs'd?—
Or when He tottered round thy knee
Did thy great sorrow dawn on thee?—
And through His boyhood, year by year
Eating with Him the Passover,
Didst thou discern confusedly
That holier sacrament, when He,
The bitter cup about to quaff,
Should break the bread and eat thereof?—
Or came not yet the knowledge, even
Till on some day forecast in Heaven
His feet passed through thy door to press
Upon His Father's business?—
Or still was God's high secret kept?

Nay, but I think the whisper crept
Like growth through childhood. Work and play,
Things common to the course of day,
Awed thee with meanings unfulfill'd;
And all through girlhood, something still'd
Thy senses like the birth of light,
When thou hast trimmed thy lamp at night
Or washed thy garments in the stream;
To whose white bed had come the dream
That He was thine and thou wast His
Who feeds among the field-lilies.

O solemn shadow of the end
In that wise spirit long contain'd!
O awful end! and those unsaid
Long years when It was Finishèd!

Mind'st thou not (when the twilight gone
Left darkness in the house of John)
Between the naked window-bars
That spacious vigil of the stars?
For thou, a watcher even as they,
Wouldst rise from where throughout the day
Thou wroughtest raiment for His poor;
And, finding the fixed terms endure
Of day and night which never brought
Sounds of His coming chariot,
Wouldst lift through cloud-waste unexplor'd
Those eyes which said, 'How long, O Lord?'
Then that disciple whom He loved,
Well heeding, haply would be moved
To ask thy blessing in His name;
And that one thought in both, the same
Though silent, then would clasp ye round
To weep together,—tears long bound,
Sick tears of patience, dumb and slow.
Yet, 'Surely I come quickly,'—so
He said, from life and death gone home.
Amen: even so, Lord Jesus, come!

But oh! what human tongue can speak
That day when death was sent to break
From the tir'd spirit, like a veil,
Its covenant with Gabriel
Endured at length unto the end?
What human thought can apprehend
That mystery of motherhood
When thy Beloved at length renew'd
The sweet communion severèd,—
His left hand underneath thine head

And His right hand embracing thee?—
Lo! He was thine, and this is He!

Soul, is it Faith, or Love, or Hope,
That lets me see her standing up
Where the light of the Throne is bright?
Unto the left, unto the right,
The cherubim, arrayed, conjoint,
Float inward to a golden point,
And from between the seraphim
The glory issues for a hymn.
O Mary Mother, be not loth
To listen,—thou whom the stars clothe,
Who seëst and mayst not be seen!
Hear us at last, O Mary Queen!
Into our shadow bend thy face,
Bowing thee from the secret place,
O Mary Virgin, full of grace!

ROBERT BROWNING.

[ROBERT BROWNING was born in 1812. His father was an official in the Bank of England, his mother of Scotch and German origin. In 1833 he published *Pauline ;* in 1835 *Paracelsus.* In 1837 his tragedy of *Strafford* was produced by Macready, and in 1841, *A Blot on the Scutcheon.* *Sordello* appeared in 1840. From 1841 to 1846 he produced a series of poems under the name of *Bells and Pomegranates :* it comprised most of his plays and some of his finest Dramatic Romances and Lyrics, but it had not a large sale. In 1846 he married Elizabeth Barrett, the poetess, and they lived in Italy till her death in 1861. During these years he published *Christmas Eve and Easter Day*, *In a Balcony*, and *Men and Women.* He returned to England in 1861 and lived chiefly in London. In 1864 he published *Dramatis Personæ ;* in 1868-9 *The Ring and the Book.* During the last twenty years of his life his literary activity was great. He published *Balaustion's Adventure, Prince Hohenstiel-Schwangau, Fifine at the Fair, Aristophanes' Apology, The Agamemnon of Æschylus, The Inn Album, Pachiarotto, La Saisiaz, The Two Poets of Croisic, Dramatic Idyls, Jocoseria, Ferishtah's Fancies, Parleyings with certain People of Importance in their Day.* He died at Venice on Dec. 12, 1889, and almost on the same day was published his latest volume of poems, *Asolando.* He was buried in Westminster Abbey.]

Seventy years ago the critics and the public alike were bowing Tom Moore into the House of Fame and letting down the latch upon Shelley and Keats outside. This and other shocking examples of the vanity of contemporary criticism might impose eternal silence on the critic, did they not also make it plain that his mistakes are of no earthly consequence. For such door-keepers are but mortals, and the immortals have plenty of time ; they keep on knocking. The door was obdurately shut against Browning for many years, but when it opened, it opened wide ; and he is surely not of those whom another age shows out by the back way. But his exact position in England's House of Fame that other age must determine. Mere versatility does not there count for much ; since in the scales of time one thing right well done is sure to outweigh many pretty well done. But that variousness of genius which springs from a wide-sweeping imagination and sympathies that range with it counts for very much. In his comprehension of the varied aspects of human nature, in his power of dramatically presenting them, Browning stands alone among the poets of a great poetic age. Will these things loom larger in the distance, or when Prince Posterity comes to be King, will his royal eye be caught first by uncouth forms, by obscurities and weary prolixities ? We cannot tell whether our poet will be freshly crowned or coldly honoured, for he beyond all others is the intellectual representative of his own generation, and his voice is still confused, and it may be magnified by its echoes in the minds of his hearers.

His own generation indeed meant more than one. He represented in some respects the generation into which he was born, but yet more a later one which he ante-dated. This being so, he could not expect an eager welcome from his earlier contemporaries. Phantoms of the past are recognisable, and respectable, but phantoms of the future are rarely popular. Yet it was fortunate that he stood just where he did in time, rather than nearer to those who were coming to meet him and call him Master. For he was born while the divine breath of Poetry, that comes we know not whence and goes we know not whither, was streaming over England. He grew up through years when she stood elate, with victory behind her, and looking forward with all manner of sanguine beliefs in the future. So he brought into a later age not only the fuller poetic inspiration, the sincere Romance of the earlier, but its sanguine confident temperament. This temperament alone would not have recommended him to a generation which had been promised Canaan and landed in a quagmire, had it not been combined with others which made him one of themselves. But this being so, his cheerful courage, his belief in God and the ultimate triumph of good were as a tower of strength to his weaker brethren. It was not only as a poet, but as a prophet or philosopher, that he won his disciples. He himself once said that " the right order of things " is " Phi-

losophy first, and Poetry, which is its highest outcome, afterwards." Yet this union of Philosophy and Poetry is dangerous,
especially if Philosophy be allowed to take precedence. For
Philosophy is commonly more perishable than Poetry, or at any
rate it is apt sooner to require resetting to rid it of an antiquated
air. Whatever is worth having in the philosophy of a Rousseau
soon passes into the common stock. *Emile* is dead, but Rousseau lives by his pictures of beautiful Nature and singular human
nature.

Browning's philosophy is mainly religious. It has been said
of him with truth : ' His processes of thought are often scientific
in their precision of analysis ; the sudden conclusion which he
imposes upon them is transcendental and inept.' This was not
so much due to a defect in his own mind as to the circumstances
of the world of thought about him. An interest in theological
questions had been quickened and spread by more than one
religious revival, and then scientific and historical criticism
began to make its voice heard. Intelligent religious people
could not close their ears to it, but they were as yet unprepared
either to accept or to effectually combat its conclusions. Hence
there arose in very many minds a confusion between two opposing strains of thought, similar to that which has been remarked
in Browning's poetry, and something like a religious system in
which what was called Doubt and Faith had each its allotted
part. Here was plainly a transition state of thought, and it is
one from which men's minds have already moved away in opposite directions ; but it has left deep traces on the literature of
the middle Victorian period. Browning's philosophy does not
fundamentally differ from that of other poets and writers of the
time. It was by his superior powers of analysis, by the swiftness
and ingenuity of his mind, that he was in advance of them and
retained his influence over a generation that had ceased to look
to them for guidance. Besides, his philosophy does not all bear
the stamp of the temporary. He has some less transient religious thoughts, and many varied and fertile views of human life,
breathing energy, courage, benignant wisdom ; and those who
like can make a system of them.

But it is not by Philosophy, it is by Imagination and Form,
that a poet lives. In a century that has been wonderfully

enriched with song, a time when we have all grown epicures in our taste for exquisite verse, too much has been said about Browning's want of form. It would be an absurdity to call a man a poet who had no sense of poetic form, who could not sing. Browning was a poet but not always a singer ; song was not to him the inevitable language, the supreme instinct. When he strains his metre by attempting to pack more meaning into a line than it will bear with grace, when he juggles with far-fetched and hideous rhymes, he really ceases to be a poet and puts his laurels in jeopardy. But oftener his form, more especially his blank verse form, is justified by the fact that he is essentially a dramatic poet ; his verse must fit the character and the mood in which he speaks. The Elizabethans, who were no fumblers in the matter of metre, had their reasons for choosing a form for dramatic verse which should be not severe, but loose and flexible—a form which might alternately approach the classical iambus, a lyric measure and plain prose, yet remain more forcible than prose by the retention of a certain beat. It resembles not a mask and cothurn, but a fine and flowing garment, following the movements of the actor's limbs. Great is the liberty of English unrhymed verse, and nobly it has been used ; it has given us the most various treasures, from the ordered magnificence of *Paradise Lost* to the lyric cry of Romeo at Juliet's grave. Browning has often misused his liberty, but by no means so often as his hasty critics suppose. Try to think of *Caliban on Setebos*, and even *Dominus Hyacinthus* in prose, and you see at once by the loss involved that they are really poems ; that is, that the verse form, and their own special form, is an essential part of their excellence. His unrhymed verse is seldom or never rich and stately, it is sometimes harsh and huddled ; but it is constantly vigorous and appropriate ; it can flow with a clear idyllic grace, as in *Cleon* and *Andrea del Sarto*, or spring up in simple lyric beauty, as in *One Word more* and the dedication to *The Ring and the Book*. He had that great gift of singing straight from the heart which some great poets have lacked. Such songs have always an incommunicable charm, a piercing sweetness of their own. A strong emotion, whether personal or dramatic, has a magical effect in smoothing what is rugged and clearing what is turbid in Browning's style.

For the rest, he wrote *Pippa passes*, the gallant marching *Cavalier Songs*, the galloping ballad of *How we brought the Good News*, the serene harmonies of *Love among the Ruins*. These, and many other outbursts of beautiful song, make it doubly ridiculous to speak of him as a poet who could not sing. Yet it is true that he frequently sacrificed sound to sense. This the plain person thinks right, but the poet knows or should know it to be wrong. And it did not even save him from obscurity. Such are his deficiencies—the more noticeable because the whole tendency of the century has been and is toward the perfecting of lyric and narrative forms of verse. In dramatic poetry this age of poets has been strangely poor. Let Shelley's lurid drama of *The Cenci* be set aside in the high place that it deserves : after that the first seventy years of this century produced nothing of importance as dramatic poetry except Browning's work. For what makes work dramatic ? Not special fitness for the stage, but the author's impersonality and power of characterisation ; the clash of human passions and interests on each other, the event, or even the accident, that as in a lightning-flash reveals the dim hearts of men. In his dramatic power Browning stands alone among the poets of the nineteenth century.

In another aspect he stands alone. While they have remained curiously untouched by the most important literary movement of the last fifty years, he has been in it, and even, for a time, in advance of it. In his measure as a poet he is a realist. His aim, like that of contemporary writers of prose fiction, is to see and represent human life and character as it is. The history of literature during the entire century has been a history of revolts. Daumier represents the eloquent M. Prudhomme telling his son, with a noble sweep of the arm, how on the place where they now stand once stood a tyrannous barrier, but he, M. Prudhomme, and his friends right bravely knocked it down. 'Yes, dear papa,' returns the child, looking a few yards ahead, 'and then I see you built it up again a little further on.' The barrier of the conventional has been constantly moved on, here quickly, there slowly ; but in English poetry, since the great move that separated the eighteenth from the nineteenth century, it has been stationary. Browning climbed over it. He climbed over

other barriers too, which have since been moved on. He was
not afraid of passion when mild sentiment was the literary
thing. Some one when he died made a sonnet commemorating
him as the Poet of Love. For a moment it seemed strange that
the philosopher, the psychologist, the man, the ruggedness of
whose genius had challenged so much criticism, should be
lamented as the Poet of Love. Yet such he emphatically was.
He was so not only because he had that power of singing
straight from the heart to which I have before referred, but
because he was fearlessly truthful in his presentation of human
nature, and also because he was drawn by his dramatic bent to
the strong situations which cannot be evolved out of mild sentiments. In the fearlessness as well as the subtlety of his psychology, he is from the first with Balzac rather than with his
contemporaries in England, where the barriers were many and
moved reluctantly. The play of light and shadow in the world,
of good and evil in complex characters, has an endless attraction
for him. The clear sweet song of his Pippa runs sparkling
through dark scenes of crime and treachery ; Chiappino is at
the height of heroism when the Nuncio comes to him, and like
a wise, benevolent kind of devil, shows him the stupidity of
heroism and all that sort of thing, and how much better he
can serve the world by serving his own interests first. Twice,
in *Paracelsus* and in *The Return of the Druses*, he has taken
impostors for his heroes, and shown them to have been so largely
because they were men of finer mould than the most honest
of their dupes. From first to last he feels a passionate interest
in 'the story of a soul.' Now the simple soul, like the knife-
grinder, has got no story. The simple heart, however, may
have story enough, and it is the Pippa of all his work. It is,
above all, truth of which he is in search, whether he paints the
sixteenth-century Bishop ordering his tomb, or the nineteenth-
century Bishop chatting over his wine. His aim is to keep
poetry in touch not merely with the life of the imagination,
but with life in general. It is of course where it touches this
modern life of ours that the real poetic *crux* occurs. There
will always be the stuff of poetry in the world, so long as there
are hearts and souls in it, and so long as the earth moves on
through starry space, clothed in her beautiful vesture of air.

But either the surface of our life has really grown prosaic, or we think it has, which comes to the same thing. It requires tact as well as boldness and power to harmonise it with the imaginative atmosphere that we expect in poetry. Browning sometimes failed in tact; at other times, as in *Waring* and the brief poem called *Confessions*, his touch was sure. But this realism of his, at its best as well as its worst, inevitably repelled readers who were only just beginning to relish realism in prose. Besides, he had a language of his own, with a strange new flavour about it, which made him seem much more obscure than he really was. So here a little ahead of his contemporaries and there a great way, most of Robert Browning's road was something solitary. The pleasanter for him when one fine day he found a troop of followers marching behind him; young folk, full of sympathy and enthusiasm.

He had other things in common with them, besides realistic and psychological tendencies. His poems from *Sordello* onwards bear witness to his love and knowledge of Italian Art. This he had gained for himself as he travelled through Italy, looking round him with a painter's eye. But Ruskin taught a younger generation to share it with him. Then, though from first to last a sturdy lover of England, he was something of a cosmopolitan in his sympathies; and cosmopolitanism is strongly characteristic of the literature of to-day, and even mildly characteristic of the literary man. It used not to be so. The novelists of Browning's date can never quite repress their chuckles at the idea of any one being ridiculous enough to be born a Frenchman or a German. The other poets travelled and even made their homes in Italy, but they were interested only in its scenery and romance. Browning not only travelled much, but formed intimate friendships outside his own country, and when he and his wife lived in Florence it was not as strangers and sojourners. Their poems reflect their sympathy with the national life about them. For this freedom from provincialism, as well as for some other kindred qualities, he doubtless owed much thanks to his education, which was remarkable for its appropriateness to his genius. He was not machine made.

In yet another and a more important characteristic he was in

harmony with the most modern developments. His dramatic
bent was unseasonable in the middle years of this century.
English literature had turned its back on the theatre, in spite of
Macreadys and Kembles. Not only so, but its tendencies were
non-dramatic. Scenes may of course be found in the works of
the great novelists of the period which stand in contradiction
to this. But all the same the tendency was towards a gentle
development of plot and character, an absence of central situations, of crucial moments in the affairs and minds of men ; that
is, towards the non-dramatic. Browning instinctively turned
towards the stage. He did not succeed there, yet one cannot
but think that had circumstances encouraged the clever young
man to go on writing stage-plays, he would eventually have
learned the business. There is nothing to regret in the fact
that he did not. His genius found for itself the most full and
fitting expression. Through the plays, the Dramatic Romances
and Lyrics, it swept on to that Dramatic Epic of *The Ring and
the Book*, which perhaps most perfectly embodied it. The plan
of *The Ring and the Book* grew so naturally out of the docu-
ments on which it was founded and his own habitual manner of
writing, that probably he himself was hardly conscious of its
originality, of its excellence as a device for breaking the
monotony of a long poem. The brilliant Introduction tells the
facts of the story with a lucidity to which he did not always
attain. By thus on the threshold revealing his whole plot, he
at once asserts and vindicates his old belief in the interest of the
story of souls ; for no one would wish it otherwise. Then at
the touch of the magician's wand arise out of their dust the
' hearts that beat hard,' the brains that ' ticked two centuries
since.' All Rome is there, Arezzo too, yet the plan of the poem
permits the principal figures to stand out clear against that
crowded background. They re-act dramatically upon each
other, yet they are more complete than they could be in a play,
where much must be left to conjecture. Long as it is, it is
seldom long-winded. When it is, the remedy is plainly in the
reader's own hands ; another virtue of the plan. General practice has long suppressed Doctor Bottinius, and many persons
think they can do without Tertium Quid ; but this is not universal. At any rate it is possible without these to realize the

rest; the pathetic figure of Pompilia, the wise great Pope, the philoprogenitive Dominus Hyacinthus, and Guido couched in his dungeon like a wolf at bay.

This great poem, which touches the high-water mark of Browning's genius, received at once its meed of praise. He had been ignored, he had been ridiculed, and now a reaction set in. The little band of Browning enthusiasts rapidly increased to a multitude, till at length he became a fashion. His very faults were glorified, and too much attention bestowed on such tentative and immature work as *Sordello*. There were many people to whom an obscure passage in Browning gave the amusement of an acrostic, *plus* the pleasures of intellectuality. Thus his obscurity was as much exaggerated by his admirers as by his opponents. Sometimes that obscurity may be justified by his own belief—a belief on which he did not always act—that poetry should suggest trains of thought rather than carry them out. At others it results from a real failure to crystallize a thought, or again from a kind of overwhelming of his powers of expression by the hurrying crowd of his ideas. But modern life is crowded and hurrying too. Already what may be called the acrostic interest in Browning is on the wane. As a fashion it needs must go. But besides the literary modists, there are in every generation the lovers of literature. To these we may leave in all confidence the works of Robert Browning, sure that they cannot miss seeing the treasure of true if alloyed gold that lies there; sure too that they will understand, as we cannot understand, how to send

a spirt

> O' the proper fiery acid o'er its face;
> And forth the alloy unfastened flies in fume,
> While, self sufficient now, the shape remains,
> The rondure brave, the lilied loveliness,
> Gold as it was, is, shall be evermore.

MARGARET L. WOODS.

How they brought the Good News from Ghent to Aix.

I.

I sprang to the stirrup, and Joris, and he;
I galloped, Dirck galloped, we galloped all three;
' Good speed!' cried the watch, as the gate-bolts undrew;
' Speed!' echoed the wall to us galloping through;
Behind shut the postern, the lights sank to rest,
And into the midnight we galloped abreast.

II.

Not a word to each other; we kept the great pace
Neck by neck, stride by stride, never changing our place:
I turned in my saddle and made its girths tight.
Then shortened each stirrup, and set the pique right,
Rebuckled the cheek-strap, chained slacker the bit,
Nor galloped less steadily Roland a whit.

III.

'Twas moonset at starting; but while we drew near
Lokeren, the cocks crew, and twilight dawned clear;
At Boom, a great yellow star came out to see;
At Düffeld, 'twas morning as plain as could be;
And from Mecheln church-steeple we heard the half chime,
So, Joris broke silence with, ' Yet there is time!'

IV.

At Aershot, up leaped of a sudden the sun,
And against him the cattle stood black every one,
To stare thro' the mist at us galloping past,
And I saw my stout galloper Roland at last,
With resolute shoulders, each butting away
The haze, as some bluff river headland its spray;

V.

And his low head and crest, just one sharp ear bent back
For my voice, and the other pricked out on his track;
And one eye's black intelligence,—ever that glance
O'er its white edge at me, his own master, askance !
And the thick heavy spume-flakes which aye and anon
His fierce lips shook upwards in galloping on.

VI.

By Hasselt, Dirck groaned ; and cried Joris, ' Stay spur !
Your Roos galloped bravely, the fault's not in her,
We'll remember at Aix '—for one heard the quick wheeze
Of her chest, saw the stretched neck and staggering knees,
And sunk tail, and horrible heave of the flank,
As down on her haunches she shuddered and sank.

VII.

So, we were left galloping, Joris and I,
Past Looz and past Tongres, no cloud in the sky;
The broad sun above laughed a pitiless laugh,
'Neath our feet broke the brittle bright stubble like chaff;
Till over by Dalhem a dome-spire sprang white,
And 'Gallop,' gasped Joris, 'for Aix is in sight ! '

VIII.

' How they'll greet us !'—and all in a moment his roan
Rolled neck and croup over, lay dead as a stone;
And there was my Roland to bear the whole weight
Of the news which alone could save Aix from her fate,
With his nostrils like pits full of blood to the brim,
And with circles of red for his eye-sockets' rim.

IX.

Then I cast loose my buff coat, each holster let fall,
Shook off both my jack-boots, let go belt and all,
Stood up in the stirrup, leaned, patted his ear,
Called my Roland his pet-name, my horse without peer ;
Clapped my hands, laughed and sang, any noise, bad or good,
Till at length into Aix Roland galloped and stood.

X.

And all I remember is, friends flocking round
As I sat with his head 'twixt my knees on the ground ;
And no voice but was praising this Roland of mine,
As I poured down his throat our last measure of wine,
Which (the burgesses voted by common consent)
Was no more than his due who brought good news from Ghent.

(1838.)

PIPPA'S SONG.

The year's at the spring,
And day's at the morn ;
Morning's at seven ;
The hill-side's dew-pearled ;
The lark's on the wing ;
The snail's on the thorn :
God's in his heaven—
All's right with the world !

(1841.)

THE BISHOP ORDERS HIS TOMB AT SAINT PRAXED'S CHURCH.

ROME, 15—.

Vanity, saith the preacher, vanity !
Draw round my bed : is Anselm keeping back ?
Nephews—sons mine . . . ah God, I know not ! Well—
She, men would have to be your mother once,
Old Gandolf envied me, so fair she was !
What's done is done, and she is dead beside,
Dead long ago, and I am Bishop since,
And as she died so must we die ourselves,
And thence ye may perceive the world's a dream.
Life, how and what is it ? As here I lie
In this state-chamber, dying by degrees,
Hours and long hours in the dead night, I ask
'Do I live, am I dead ?' Peace, peace seems all.
Saint Praxed's ever was the church for peace ;

And so, about this tomb of mine. I fought
With tooth and nail to save my niche, ye know:
—Old Gandolf cozened me, despite my care;
Shrewd was that snatch from out the corner South
He graced his carrion with, God curse the same!
Yet still my niche is not so cramped but thence
One sees the pulpit on the epistle-side,
And somewhat of the choir, those silent seats,
And up into the aery dome where live
The angels, and a sunbeam's sure to lurk.
And I shall fill my slab of basalt there,
And 'neath my tabernacle take my rest,
With those nine columns round me, two and two,
The odd one at my feet where Anselm stands:
Peach-blossom marble all, the rare, the ripe
As fresh-poured red wine of a mighty pulse.
—Old Gandolf with his paltry onion-stone,
Put me where I may look at him! True peach,
Rosy and flawless: how I earned the prize!
Draw close: that conflagration of my church
—What then? So much was saved if aught were missed!
My sons, ye would not be my death! Go dig
The white-grape vineyard where the oil-press stood,
Drop water gently till the surface sink,
And if ye find . . . Ah God, I know not, I! . .
Bedded in store of rotten figleaves soft,
And corded up in a tight olive-frail,
Some lump, ah God, of *lapis lazuli*.
Big as a Jew's head cut off at the nape,
Blue as a vein o'er the Madonna's breast . . .
Sons, all have I bequeathed you, villas, all,
That brave Frascati villa with its bath,
So, let the blue lump poise between my knees,
Like God the Father's globe on both his hands
Ye worship in the Jesu Church so gay,
For Gandolf shall not choose but see and burst!
Swift as a weaver's shuttle fleet our years:
Man goeth to the grave, and where is he?
Did I say basalt for my slab, sons? Black—

'Twas ever antique-black I meant! How else
Shall ye contrast my frieze to come beneath?
The bas-relief in bronze ye promised me,
Those Pans and Nymphs ye wot of, and perchance
Some tripod, thyrsus, with a vase or so,
The Saviour at his sermon on the mount,
Saint Praxed in a glory, and one Pan
Ready to twitch the Nymph's last garment off,
And Moses with the tables . . . but I know
Ye mark me not! What do they whisper thee,
Child of my bowels, Anselm? Ah, ye hope
To revel down my villas while I gasp
Bricked o'er with beggar's mouldy travertine
Which Gandolf from his tomb-top chuckles at!
Nay, boys, ye love me—all of jasper, then!
'Tis jasper ye stand pledged to, lest I grieve
My bath must needs be left behind, alas!
One block, pure green as a pistachio-nut,
There's plenty jasper somewhere in the world—
And have I not Saint Praxed's ear to pray
Horses for ye, and brown Greek manuscripts,
And mistresses with great smooth marbly limbs?
—That's if ye carve my epitaph aright,
Choice Latin, picked phrase, Tully's every word,
No gaudy ware like Gandolf's second line—
Tully, my masters? Ulpian serves his need!
And then how I shall lie through centuries,
And hear the blessed mutter of the mass,
And see God made and eaten all day long,
And feel the steady candle-flame, and taste
Good strong thick stupefying incense-smoke!
For as I lie here, hours of the dead night,
Dying in state and by such slow degrees,
I fold my arms as if they clasped a crook,
And stretch my feet forth straight as stone can point,
And let the bedclothes, for a mortcloth, drop
Into great laps and folds of sculptor's work:
And as yon tapers dwindle, and strange thoughts
Grow, with a certain humming in my ears,

About the life before I lived this life,
And this life too, popes, cardinals, and priests,
Saint Praxed at his sermon on the mount,
Your tall pale mother with her talking eyes,
And new-found agate urns as fresh as day,
And marble's language, Latin pure, discreet,
—Aha, ELUCESCEBAT quoth our friend?
No Tully, said I, Ulpian at the best!
Evil and brief hath been my pilgrimage.
All *lapis*, all, sons! Else I give the Pope
My villas! Will ye ever eat my heart?
Ever your eyes were as a lizard's quick,
They glitter like your mother's for my soul,
Or ye would heighten my impoverished frieze,
Piece out its starved design, and fill my vase
With grapes, and add a vizor and a Term,
And to the tripod ye would tie a lynx
That in his struggle throws the thyrsus down,
To comfort me on my entablature
Whereon I am to lie till I must ask
'Do I live, am I dead?' There, leave me, there!
For ye have stabbed me with ingratitude
To death: ye wish it—God, ye wish it! Stone—
Gritstone, a-crumble! Clammy squares which sweat
As if the corpse they keep were oozing through—
And no more *lapis* to delight the world!
Well go! I bless ye. Fewer tapers there,
But in a row: and, going, turn your backs
—Ay, like departing altar-ministrants,
And leave me in my church, the church for peace,
That I may watch at leisure if he leers—
Old Gandolf, at me, from his onion-stone
As still he envied me, so fair she was!

(1845.)

The Lost Leader.

I.

Just for a handful of silver he left us,
　Just for a riband to stick in his coat—
Found the one gift of which fortune bereft us,
　Lost all the others she lets us devote;
They, with the gold to give, doled him out silver,
　So much was theirs who so little allowed:
How all our copper had gone for his service!
　Rags—were they purple, his heart had been proud!
We that had loved him so, followed him, honoured him,
　Lived in his mild and magnificent eye,
Learned his great language, caught his clear accents,
　Made him our pattern to live and to die!
Shakespeare was of us, Milton was for us,
　Burns, Shelley, were with us,—they watch from their graves!
He alone breaks from the van and the freemen,
　—He alone sinks to the rear and the slaves!

II.

We shall march prospering,—not thro' his presence;
　Songs may inspirit us,—not from his lyre;
Deeds will be done,—while he boasts his quiescence,
　Still bidding crouch whom the rest bade aspire.
Blot out his name, then, record one lost soul more,
　One task more declined, one more footpath untrod,
One more devil's-triumph and sorrow for angels,
　One wrong more to man, one more insult to God!
Life's night begins: let him never come back to us!
　There will be doubt, hesitation and pain,
Forced praise on our part—the glimmer of twilight,
　Never glad confident morning again!
Best fight on well, for we taught him—strike gallantly,
　Menace our heart ere we master his own;
Then let him receive the new knowledge and wait us,
　Pardoned in heaven, the first by the throne!

(1845.)

DAVID SINGING BEFORE SAUL.

(From *Saul.*)

VIII.

And I paused, held my breath in such silence, and listened apart;
And the tent shook, for mighty Saul shuddered : and sparkles 'gan
    dart
From the jewels that woke in his turban, at once with a start,
All its lordly male-sapphires, and rubies courageous at heart.
So the head : but the body still moved not, still hung there erect.
And I bent once again to my playing, pursued it unchecked,
As I sang,—

IX.

    ' Oh, our manhood's prime vigour ! No spirit feels waste,
Not a muscle is stopped in its playing nor sinew unbraced.
Oh, the wild joys of living ! the leaping from rock up to rock,
The strong rending of boughs from the fir-tree, the cool silver shock
Of the plunge in a pool's living water, the hunt of the bear,
And ·the sultriness showing the lion is couched in his lair.
And the meal, the rich dates yellowed over with gold dust divine,
And the locust-flesh steeped in the pitcher, the full draught of wine,
And the sleep in the dried river-channel where bulrushes tell
That the water was wont to go warbling so softly and well.
How good is man's life, the mere living ! how fit to employy
All the heart and the soul and the senses for ever in joy !
Hast thou loved the white locks of thy father, whose sword thou
    didst guard
When he trusted thee forth with the armies, for glorious reward?
Didst thou kiss the thin hands of thy mother, held up as men sung
The low song of the nearly departed, and hear her faint tongue
Joining in while it could to the witness, " Let one more attest,
I have lived, seen God's hand thro' a lifetime, and all was for
    best " ?
Then they sung thro' their tears in strong triumph, not much,
    but the rest.
And thy brothers, the help and the contest, the working whence
    grew
Such result as, from seething grape-bundles, the spirit strained true :

And the friends of thy boyhood—that boyhood of wonder and hope,
Present promise and wealth of the future beyond the eye's scope,—
Till lo, thou art grown to a monarch; a people is thine;
And all gifts, which the world offers singly, on one head combine!
On one head, all the beauty and strength, love and rage (like
  the throe
That, a-work in the rock, helps its labour and lets the gold go)
High ambition and deeds which surpass it, fame crowning
  them,—all
Brought to blaze on the head of one creature—King Saul!'

X.

And lo, with that leap of my spirit,—heart, hand, harp and voice,
Each lifting Saul's name out of sorrow, each bidding rejoice
Saul's fame in the light it was made for—as when, dare I say,
The Lord's army, in rapture of service, strains through its array,
And upsoareth the cherubim-chariot—'Saul!' cried I, and stopped,
And waited the thing that should follow. Then Saul, who hung
  propped
By the tent's cross-support in the centre, was struck by his name.
Have ye seen when Spring's arrowy summons goes right to the aim,
And some mountain, the last to withstand her, that held (he alone,
While the vale laughed in freedom and flowers) on a broad bust
  of stone
A year's snow bound about for a breastplate,—leaves grasp of
  the sheet?
Fold on fold all at once it crowds thunderously down to his feet,
And there fronts you, stark, black, but alive yet, your mountain
  of old,
With his rents, the successive bequeathings of ages untold:
Yea, each harm got in fighting your battles, each furrow and scar
Of his head thrust 'twixt you and the tempest—all hail, there
  they are!
—Now again to be softened with verdure, again hold the nest
Of the dove, tempt the goat and its young to the green on his crest
For their food in the ardours of summer. One long shudder thrilled
All the tent till the very air tingled, then sank and was stilled
At the King's self left standing before me, released and aware.

            (1845.)

HOME THOUGHTS, FROM ABROAD.

I.

Oh, to be in England
Now that April's there,
And whoever wakes in England
Sees, some morning, unaware,
That the lowest boughs and the brushwood sheaf
Round the elm-tree bole are in tiny leaf,
While the chaffinch sings on the orchard bough
In England—now!

II.

And after April, when May follows,
And the whitethroat builds, and all the swallows !
Hark, where my blossomed pear-tree in the hedge
Leans to the field and scatters on the clover
Blossoms and dewdrops—at the bent spray's edge—
That's the wise thrush; he sings each song twice over,
Lest you should think he never could recapture
The first fine careless rapture !
And, though the fields look rough with hoary dew,
All will be gay when noontide wakes anew
The buttercups, the little children's dower
—Far brighter than this gaudy melon-flower!

(1845.)

LOVE AMONG THE RUINS.

I.

Where the quiet-coloured end of evening smiles,
          Miles and miles,
On the solitary pastures where our sheep
          Half-asleep
Tinkle homeward thro' the twilight, stray or stop
          As they crop—
Was the site once of a city great and gay,
          (So they say)
Of our country's very capital, its prince,
          Ages since,
Held his court in, gathered councils, wielding far
          Peace or war.

II.

Now,—the country does not even boast a tree,
    As you see,
To distinguish slopes of verdure, certain rills
    From the hills
Intersect and give a name to, (else they run
    Into one)
Where the domed and daring palace shot its spires
    Up like fires
O'er the hundred-gated circuit of a wall
    Bounding all,
Made of marble, men might march on nor be pressed
    Twelve abreast.

III.

And such plenty and perfection, see, of grass
    Never was !
Such a carpet as, this summer-time, o'erspreads
    And embeds
Every vestige of the city, guessed alone,
    Stock or stone—
Where a multitude of men breathed joy and woe
    Long ago ;
Lust of glory pricked their hearts up, dread of shame
    Struck them tame ;
And that glory and that shame alike, the gold
    Bought and sold.

IV.

Now,—the single little turret that remains
    On the plains,
By the caper overrooted, by the gourd
    Overscored,
While the patching houseleek's head of blossom winks
    Through the chinks—
Marks the basement whence a tower in ancient time
    Sprang sublime,
And a burning ring, all round, the chariots traced
    As they raced,
And the monarch and his minions and his dames
    Viewed the games.

V.

And I know, while thus the quiet-coloured eve
    Smiles to leave
To their folding, all our many tinkling fleece
    In such peace,
And the slopes and rills in undistinguished grey
    Melt away—
That a girl with eager eyes and yellow hair
    Waits me there
In the turret whence the charioteers caught soul
    For the goal,
When the king looked, where she looks now, breathless, dumb
    Till I come.

VI.

But he looked upon the city, every side,
    Far and wide,
All the mountains topped with temples, all the glades,
    Colonnades,
All the causeys, bridges, aqueducts,—and then,
    All the men!
When I do come, she will speak not, she will stand,
    Either hand
On my shoulder, give her eyes the first embrace
    Of my face,
Ere we rush, ere we extinguish sight and speech
    Each on each.

VII.

In one year they sent a million fighters forth
    South and North,
And they built their gods a brazen pillar high
    As the sky,
Yet reserved a thousand chariots in full force—
    Gold, of course.
Oh heart! oh blood that freezes, blood that burns!
    Earth's returns
For whole centuries of folly, noise, and sin!
    Shut them in,
With their triumphs and their glories and the rest!
    Love is best.

(1855.)

INCIDENT OF THE FRENCH CAMP.

I.

You know, we French stormed Ratisbon:
    A mile or so away,
On a little mound, Napoleon
    Stood on our storming-day;
With neck out-thrust, you fancy how,
    Legs wide, arms locked behind,
As if to balance the prone brow
    Oppressive with its mind.

II.

Just as perhaps he mused 'My plans
    That soar, to earth may fall,
Let once my army-leader Lannes
    Waver at yonder wall,—'
Out 'twixt the battery-smokes there flew
    A rider, bound on bound
Full-galloping; nor bridle drew
    Until he reached the mound.

III.

Then off there flung in smiling joy,
    And held himself erect
By just his horse's mane, a boy:
    You hardly could suspect—
(So tight he kept his lips compressed,
    Scarce any blood came through)
You looked twice ere you saw his breast
    Was all but shot in two.

IV.

'Well,' cried he, 'Emperor, by God's grace
    We've got you Ratisbon!
The Marshal's in the market-place,
    And you'll be there anon
To see your flag-bird flap his vans
    Where I, to heart's desire,
Perched him!' The chief's eye flashed; his plans
    Soared up again like fire.

V.

The chief's eye flashed ; but presently
    Softened itself, as sheathes
A film the mother-eagle's eye
    When her bruised eaglet breathes.
'You 're wounded !' 'Nay,' the soldier's pride
    Touched to the quick, he said :
'I 'm killed, Sire !' And his chief beside,
    Smiling the boy fell dead.

TWO IN THE CAMPAGNA.

I.

I wonder do you feel to-day
    As I have felt since, hand in hand,
We sat down on the grass, to stray
    In spirit better through the land,
This morn of Rome and May?

II.

For me, I touched a thought, I know,
    Has tantalized me many times,
(Like turns of thread the spiders throw
    Mocking across our path) for rhymes
To catch at and let go.

III.

Help me to hold it ! First it left
    The yellowing fennel, run to seed
There, branching from the brickwork's cleft,
    Some old tomb's ruin : yonder weed
Took up the floating weft,

IV.

Where one small orange cup amassed
    Five beetles,—blind and green they grope,
Among the honey-meal : and last,
    Everywhere on the grassy slope,
I traced it. Hold it fast !

V.

The champaign with its endless fleece
    Of feathery grasses everywhere!
Silence and passion, joy and peace,
    An everlasting wash of air—
Rome's ghost since her decease.

VI.

Such life here, through such lengths of hours,
    Such miracles performed in play,
Such primal naked forms of flowers,
    Such letting nature have her way
While heaven looks from its towers!

VII.

How say you? Let us, O my dove,
    Let us be unashamed of soul,
As earth lies bare to heaven above!
    How is it under our control
To love or not to love?

VIII.

I would that you were all to me,
    You that are just so much, no more.
Nor yours nor mine, nor slave nor free!
    Where does the fault lie? What the core
O' the wound, since wound must be?

IX.

I would I could adopt your will,
    See with your eyes, and set my heart
Beating by yours, and drink my fill
    At your soul's springs,—your part my part
In life, for good and ill.

X.

No. I yearn upward, touch you close,
    Then stand away. I kiss your cheek,
Catch your soul's warmth,—I pluck the rose
    And love it more than tongue can speak—
Then the good minute goes.

XI.

Already how am I so far
　Out of that minute? Must I go
Still like the thistle-ball, no bar,
　Onward, whenever light winds blow,
Fixed by no friendly star?

XII.

Just when I seemed about to learn!
　Where is the thread now? Off again.
The old trick! Only I discern—
　Infinite passion, and the pain
Of finite hearts that yearn.

(1855.)

UP AT A VILLA—DOWN IN THE CITY.

(As distinguished by an Italian Person of quality.)

I.

Had I but plenty of money, money enough and to spare,
The house for me, no doubt, were a house in the city-square;
Ah, such a life, such a life, as one leads at the window there!

II.

Something to see, by Bacchus, something to hear, at least!
There, the whole day long, one's life is a perfect feast;
While up at a villa one lives, I maintain it, no more than a beast.

III.

Well now, look at our villa! stuck like the horn of a bull
Just on a mountain edge as bare as the creature's skull,
Save a mere shag of a bush with hardly a leaf to pull!
—I scratch my own, sometimes, to see if the hair's turned wool.

IV.

But the city, oh the city—the square with the houses! Why?
They are stone-faced, white as a curd, there's something to take
　　the eye!
Houses in four straight lines, not a single front awry;

You watch who crosses and gossips, who saunters, who hurries by ;
Green blinds, as a matter of course, to draw when the sun gets
    high ;
And the shops with fanciful signs which are painted properly.

V.

What of a villa? though winter be over in March by rights,
'Tis May perhaps ere the snow shall have withered well off the
    heights :
You've the brown ploughed land before, where the oxen steam
    and wheeze,
And the hills over-smoked behind by the faint grey olive-trees.

VI.

Is it better in May, I ask you? You've summer all at once ;
In a day he leaps complete with a few strong April suns.
'Mid the sharp short emerald wheat, scarce arisen three fingers well,
The wild tulip, at end of its tube, blows out its great red bell
Like a thin clear bubble of blood, for the children to pick and sell.

VII.

Is it ever hot in the square? There's a fountain to spout and
    splash !
In the shade it sings and springs ; in the shine such foam-bows
    flash
On the horses with curling fish-tails, that prance and paddle
    and pash
Round the lady atop in her conch—fifty gazers do not abash,
Though all that she wears is some weeds round her waist in a
    sort of sash.

VIII.

All the year long at the villa, nothing to see though you linger,
Except yon cypress that points like death's lean lifted forefinger.
Some think fireflies pretty, when they mix i' the corn and mingle,
Or thrid the stinking hemp till the stalks of it seem a-tingle.
Late August or early September, the stunning cicala is shrill,
And the bees keep their tiresome whine round the resinous firs
    on the hill.
Enough of the seasons,—I spare you the months of the fever
    and chill.

IX.

Ere you open your eyes in the city, the blessed church-bells
    begin :
No sooner the bells leave off than the diligence rattles in :
You get the pick of the news, and it costs you never a pin.
By and by there's the travelling doctor gives pills, lets blood,
    draws teeth ;
Or the Pulcinello-trumpet breaks up the market beneath.
At the post-office such a scene-picture—the new play, piping hot!
And a notice how, only this morning, three liberal thieves were
    shot.
Above it, behold the Archbishop's most fatherly of rebukes,
And beneath, with his crown and his lion, some little new law
    of the Duke's !
Or a sonnet with flowery marge, to the reverend Don So-and-so
Who is Dante, Boccaccio, Petrarca, Saint Jerome and Cicero,
'And moreover,' (the sonnet goes rhyming,) 'the skirts of Saint
    Paul has reached,
Having preached us those six Lent-lectures more unctuous than
    ever he preached.'
Noon strikes,—here sweeps the procession! our Lady borne
    smiling and smart,
With a pink gauze gown all spangles, and seven swords stuck
    in her heart !
Bang-whang-whang goes the drum, *tootle-te-tootle* the fife ;
No keeping one's haunches still : it's the greatest pleasure in life.

X.

But bless you, it's dear—it's dear ! fowls, wine, at double the rate.
They have clapped a new tax upon salt, and what oil pays
    passing the gate
It's a horror to think of. And so, the villa for me, not the city !
Beggars can scarcely be choosers : but still—ah, the pity, the pity
Look, two and two go the priests, then the monks with cowls
    and sandals,
And the penitents dressed in white shirts, a-holding the yellow
    candles ;

One, he carries a flag up straight, and another a cross with
    handles,
And the Duke's guard brings up the rear, for the better prevention
    of scandals:
Bang-whang-whang goes the drum, *tootle-te-tootle* the fife.
Oh, a day in the city-square, there is no such pleasure in life!

                        (1855.)

MAY AND DEATH.

I.

I wish that when you died last May,
    Charles, there had died along with you
Three parts of spring's delightful things;
    Ay, and, for me, the fourth part too.

II.

A foolish thought, and worse, perhaps!
    There must be many a pair of friends
Who, arm in arm, deserve the warm
    Moon-births and the long evening-ends.

III.

So, for their sake, be May still May!
    Let their new time, as mine of old,
Do all it did for me: I bid
    Sweet sights and songs throng manifold.

IV.

Only, one little sight, one plant,
    Woods have in May, that starts up green
Save a sole streak which, so to speak,
    Is spring's blood, spilt its leaves between,—

V.

That, they might spare; a certain wood
    Might miss the plant; their loss were small:
But I,—whene'er the leaf grows there,
    Its drop comes from my heart, that's all.

                        (1857.)

PROSPICE.

Fear death?—to feel the fog in my throat,
    The mist in my face,
When the snows begin, and the blasts denote
    I am nearing the place,
The power of the night, the press of the storm,
    The post of the foe;
Where he stands, the Arch Fear in a visible form,
    Yet the strong man must go:
For the journey is done and the summit attained,
    And the barriers fall,
Though a battle's to fight ere the guerdon be gained,
    The reward of it all.
I was ever a fighter, so—one fight more,
    The best and the last!
I would hate that death bandaged my eyes, and forbore,
    And bade me creep past.
No! let me taste the whole of it, fare like my peers
    The heroes of old,
Bear the brunt, in a minute pay glad life's arrears
    Of pain, darkness and cold.
For sudden the worst turns the best to the brave,
    The black minute's at end,
And the elements' rage, the fiend-voices that rave,
    Shall dwindle, shall blend,
Shall change, shall become first a peace out of pain,
    Then a light, then thy breast,
O thou soul of my soul! I shall clasp thee again,
    And with God be the rest!

                (1861.)

Rabbi Ben Ezra.

I.

Grow old along with me!
The best is yet to be,
The last of life, for which the first was made:
Our times are in His hand
Who saith 'A whole I planned,
Youth shows but half; trust God: see all nor be afraid!'

II.

Not that, amassing flowers,
Youth sighed 'Which rose make ours
Which lily leave and then as best recall?'
Not that, admiring stars,
It yearned 'Nor Jove, nor Mars;
Mine be some figured flame which blends, transcends them all!'

III.

Not for such hopes and fears
Annulling youth's brief years,
Do I remonstrate: folly wide the mark!
Rather I prize the doubt
Low kinds exist without,
Finished and finite clods, untroubled by a spark.

IV.

Poor vaunt of life indeed,
Were man but formed to feed
On joy, to solely seek and find and feast:
Such feasting ended, then
As sure an end to men;
Irks care the crop-full bird? Frets doubt the maw-crammed beast?

V.

Rejoice we are allied
To That which doth provide
And not partake, effect and not receive!
A spark disturbs our clod;
Nearer we hold of God
Who gives, than of His tribes that take, I must believe.

VI.

Then, welcome each rebuff
That turns earth's smoothness rough,
Each sting that bids nor sit nor stand but go!
Be our joys three-parts pain!
Strive, and hold cheap the strain;
Learn, nor account the pang; dare, never grudge the throe!

VII.

For thence,—a paradox
Which comforts while it mocks,—
Shall life succeed in that it seems to fail:
What I aspired to be,
And was not, comforts me:
A brute I might have been, but would not sink i' the scale.

VIII.

What is he but a brute
Whose flesh has soul to suit,
Whose spirit works lest arms and legs want play?
To man, propose this test—
Thy body at its best,
How far can that project thy soul on its lone way?

IX.

Yet gifts should prove their use:
I own the Past profuse
Of power each side, perfection every turn:
Eyes, ears took in their dole,
Brain treasured up the whole;
Should not the heart beat once 'How good to live and
learn?'

X.

Not once beat 'Praise be Thine!
I see the whole design,
I, who saw power, see now love perfect too:
Perfect I call Thy plan:
Thanks that I was a man!
Maker, remake, complete,—I trust what Thou shalt do!'

XI.

For pleasant is this flesh;
 Our soul, in its rose-mesh
Pulled ever to the earth, still yearns for rest:
 Would we some prize might hold
 To match those manifold
Possessions of the brute,—gain most, as we did best!

XII.

Let us not always say
 'Spite of this flesh to-day
I strove, made head, gained ground upon the whole!'
 As the bird wings and sings,
 Let us cry 'All good things
Are ours, nor soul helps flesh more, now, than flesh helps
  soul!'

XIII.

Therefore I summon age
 To grant youth's heritage,
Life's struggle having so far reached its term:
 Thence shall I pass, approved
 A man, for aye removed
From the developed brute; a god though in the germ.

XIV.

And I shall thereupon
 Take rest, ere I be gone
Once more on my adventure brave and new:
 Fearless and unperplexed,
 When I wage battle next,
What weapons to select, what armour to indue.

XV.

Youth ended, I shall try
 My gain or loss thereby:
Leave the fire ashes, what survives is gold:
 And I shall weigh the same,
 Give life its praise or blame:
Young, all lay in dispute; I shall know, being old.

XVI.

For, note when evening shuts,
A certain moment cuts
The deed off, calls the glory from the grey :
A whisper from the west
Shoots—' Add this to the rest,
Take it and try its worth : here dies another day.'

XVII.

So, still within this life,
Though lifted o'er its strife,
Let me discern, compare, pronounce at last,
' This rage was right i' the main,
That acquiescence vain :
The Future I may face now I have proved the Past.'

XVIII.

For more is not reserved
To man, with soul just nerved
To act to-morrow what he learns to-day :
Here, work enough to watch
The Master work, and catch
Hints of the proper craft, tricks of the tool's true play.

XIX.

As it was better, youth
Should strive, through acts uncouth,
Toward making, than repose on aught found made :
So, better, age, exempt
From strife, shou'd know, than tempt
Further.   Thou waitedest age : wait death nor be afraid !

XX.

Enough now, if the Right
And Good and Infinite
Be named here, as thou call'st thy hand thine own,
With knowledge absolute,
Subject to no dispute
From fools that crowded youth, nor let thee feel alone.

XXI.

Be there, for once and all,
Severed great minds from small,
Announced to each his station in the Past!
Was I, the world arraigned,
Were they, my soul disdained,
Right? Let age speak the truth and give us peace at last!

XXII.

Now, who shall arbitrate?
Ten men love what I hate,
Shun what I follow, slight what I receive;
Ten, who in ears and eyes
Match me: we all surmise,
They this thing, and I that: whom shall my soul believe?

XXIII.

Not on the vulgar mass
Called 'work,' must sentence pass,
Things done, that took the eye and had the price;
O'er which, from level stand,
The low world laid its hand,
Found straightway to its mind, could value in a trice:

XXIV.

But all, the world's coarse thumb
And finger failed to plumb,
So passed in making up the main account:
All instincts immature
All purposes unsure,
That weighed not as his work, yet swelled the man's amount:

XXV.

Thoughts hardly to be packed
Into a narrow act,
Fancies that broke through language and escaped:
All I could never be,
All, men ignored in me,
This, I was worth to God, whose wheel the pitcher shaped.

XXVI.

Ay, note that Potter's wheel,
That metaphor! and feel
Why time spins fast, why passive lies our clay,—
Thou, to whom fools propound
When the wine makes its round,
'Since life fleets, all is change; the Past gone, seize to-day!'

XXVII.

Fool! All that is, at all,
Lasts ever, past recall;
Earth changes, but thy soul and God stand sure:
What entered into thee,
That was, is, and shall be:
Time's wheel runs back or stops: Potter and clay endure.

XXVIII.

He fixed thee mid this dance
Of plastic circumstance,
This Present, thou, forsooth, wouldst fain arrest:
Machinery just meant
To give thy soul its bent,
Try thee and turn thee forth, sufficiently impressed.

XXIX.

What though the earlier grooves
Which ran the laughing loves
Around thy base, no longer pause and press?
What though, about thy rim,
Scull-things in order grim
Grow out, in graver mood, obey the sterner stress?

XXX.

Look not thou down but up!
To uses of a cup,
The festal board, lamp's flash and trumpet's peal,
The new wine's foaming flow,
The Master's lips a-glow!
Thou, heaven's consummate cup, what need'st thou with
earth's wheel?

XXXI.

But I need, now as then,
Thee, God, who mouldest men!
And since, not even while the whirl was worst,
Did I,—to the wheel of life
With shapes and colours rife,
Bound dizzily,—mistake my end, to slake Thy thirst:

XXXII.

So, take and use Thy work,
Amend what flaws may lurk,
What strain o' the stuff, what warpings past the aim!
My times be in Thy hand!
Perfect the cup as planned!
Let age approve of youth, and death complete the same!
(1864.)

CONFESSIONS.

I.

What is he buzzing in my ears?
'Now that I come to die,
Do I view the world as a vale of tears?'
Ah, reverend sir, not I!

II.

What I viewed there once, what I view again
Where the physic bottles stand
On the table's edge,—is a suburb lane,
With a wall to my bedside hand.

III.

That lane sloped, much as the bottles do,
From a house you could descry
O'er the garden-wall: is the curtain blue
Or green to a healthy eye?

IV.

To mine, it serves for the old June weather
Blue above lane and wall;
And that farthest bottle labelled 'Ether'
Is the house o'ertopping all.

V.

At a terrace, somewhere near the stopper,
    They watched for me, one June,
A girl: I know, sir, it's improper,
    My poor mind's out of tune.

VI.

Only, there was a way . . . you crept
    Close by the side, to dodge
Eyes in the house, two eyes except:
    They styled their house 'The Lodge.'

VII.

What right had a lounger up their lane?
    But, by creeping very close,
With the good wall's help,—their eyes might strain
    And stretch themselves to Oes,

VIII.

Yet never catch her and me together,
    As she left the attic, there,
By the rim of the bottle labelled 'Ether,'
    And stole from stair to stair,

IX.

And stood by the rose-wreathed gate. Alas,
    We loved, sir—used to meet:
How sad and bad and mad it was—
    But then, how it was sweet!

(1864.)

THE RING AND THE BOOK.

(Dedication.)

O lyric love, half angel and half bird
And all a wonder and a wild desire,—
Boldest of hearts that ever braved the sun,
Took sanctuary within the holier blue,
And sang a kindred soul out to his face,—
Yet human at the red-ripe of the heart—
When the first summons from the darkling earth
Reached thee amid thy chambers, blanched their blue,
And bared them of the glory—to drop down,
To toil for man, to suffer or to die,—
This is the same voice: can thy soul know change?
Hail then, and harken from the realms of help!
Never may I commence my song, my due
To God who best taught song by gift of thee,
Except with bent head and beseeching hand—
That still, despite the distance and the dark,
What was, again may be; some interchange
Of grace, some splendour once thy very thought,
Some benediction anciently thy smile:
—Never conclude, but raising hand and head
Thither where eyes, that cannot reach, yet yearn
For all hope, all sustainment, all reward,
Their utmost up and on,—so blessing back
In those thy realms of help, that heaven thy home,
Some whiteness which, I judge, thy face makes proud,
Some wanness where, I think, thy foot may fall!

(1868.)

The Householder.

(Epilogue to *Fifine at the Fair.*)

I.

Savage I was sitting in my house, late, lone:
  Dreary, weary with the long day's work:
Head of me, heart of me, stupid as a stone:
  Tongue-tied now, now blaspheming like a Turk;
When, in a moment, just a knock, call, cry,
  Half a pang and all a rapture, there again were we!—
'What, and is it really you again?' quoth I:
  'I again, what else did you expect?' quoth She.

II.

'Never mind, hie away from this old house—
  Every crumbling brick embrowned with sin and shame!
Quick, in its corners ere certain shapes arouse!
  Let them—every devil of the night—lay claim,
Make and mend, or rap and rend, for me! Goodbye!
  God be their guard from disturbance at their glee,
Till, crash, down comes the carcass in a heap!' quoth I:
  'Nay, but there's a decency required!' quoth She.

III.

'Ah, but if you knew how time has dragged, days, nights!
  All the neighbour-talk with man and maid—such men!
All the fuss and trouble of street-sounds, window-sights:
  All the worry of flapping door and echoing roof; and then
All the fancies . . . Who were they had leave, dared try
  Darker arts that almost struck despair in me?
If you knew but how I dwelt down here!' quoth I:
  'And was I so better off up there?' quoth She.

IV.

'Help and get it over! *Reunited to his wife*
　(How draw up the paper lets the parish-people know?)
Lies M., or N., departed from this life,
　Day the this or that, month and year the so and so.
What i' the way of final flourish? Prose, verse? Try!
　Affliction sore long time he bore, or, what is it to be?
Till God did please to grant him ease. Do end!' quoth I:
　'I end with—Love is all and Death is nought!' quoth She.

(1872.)

EPILOGUE TO ASOLANDO.

At the midnight in the silence of the sleep-time,
　When you set your fancies free,
Will they pass to where—by death, fools think, imprisoned—
Low he lies who once so loved you, whom you loved so,
　　　　—Pity me?

Oh to love so, be so loved, yet so mistaken!
　What had I on earth to do
With the slothful, with the mawkish, the unmanly?
Like the aimless, helpless, hopeless did I drivel
　　　　—Being—who?

One who never turned his back but marched breast forward,
　Never doubted clouds would break,
Never dreamed, though right were worsted, wrong would triumph,
Held we fall to rise, are baffled to fight better,
　　　　Sleep to wake.

No, at noonday in the bustle of man's work-time
　Greet the unseen with a cheer!
Bid him forward, breast and back as either should be,
'Strive and thrive!' cry 'Speed,—fight on, fare ever
　　　　There as here!'

(1889.)

MATTHEW ARNOLD.

[ELDEST son of Dr. Arnold, of Rugby; born Dec. 24, 1822, at Laleham, near Staines; educated at Winchester, Rugby, and Balliol College, Oxford. Won the Newdigate Prize, 1843, with a poem on 'Cromwell.' Published *The Strayed Reveller, and other Poems.* By A., 1849; *Empedocles on Etna, and other Poems* (same signature), 1852; *Poems, First Series,* 1853; *Poems, Second Series,* 1855. Elected Professor of Poetry at Oxford, 1857; re-elected, 1862 till 1867. It was as professorial lectures that his chief critical essays were first given to the world. He published *Merope, a Tragedy,* 1858; *New Poems,* 1867; and issued his collected poems in 1877, 1881, and 1885. His numerous prose writings were published between 1853 and 1888. He died suddenly, at Liverpool, on April 15, 1888.]

It is with a sad appropriateness that we include in the 'definitive' edition of *The English Poets* the poems of the eminent writer to whom we owe the General Introduction to the volumes. The fourteen years which have elapsed since their first publication have brought to a close the life of many a great Englishman, and to the poets they have been especially fatal. Rossetti went first, then Arnold, then his seniors, Browning and Tennyson. Sharing as Arnold did the greatness of the last two, there is a first and great distinction to be noticed between them and him. They were poets by profession, so to speak; they lived for poetry, and went on producing it regularly till the end of their long lives. He, on the other hand, was a busy public official, and from the year 1851 till his retirement from the Education Department in 1885, all the time that he could give to literature was saved from an exhausting daily round of work. Again, his literary vocation was not all poetical, as theirs was. It was as a critic that he was, in his life-time, most widely known, and that he had the most immediate effect upon his generation. But if the stream of his verse is scanty; if his three volumes look slight beside the sixteen volumes of Browning ; if, during a wide space of his middle life he almost ceased to write poetry—on the other hand, how little there is that one could wish away ! A certain largeness of production is undoubtedly necessary before one can admit the claim of an artist to the highest place ; but at the same time, excess of production is a commoner fault with poets than its contrary is. Instances of an over-chastened muse like Gray's, or in a less degree, like Arnold's, are comparatively rare among true poets. While of Dryden, of Wordsworth, of Byron, more than half might well be spared, there is scarcely anything in Arnold's volumes—except perhaps *Balder Dead*—that has not a distinct value of its own, scarcely anything that ought not to be preserved. Of no poet is it more difficult to make a satisfying selection ; and we may echo in serious earnest the answer that he used laughingly to make to the friends who complained that this or that favourite was excluded from the poems chosen by him for the Golden Treasury volume—' If I had had my own way I should have included everything ! '

Matthew Arnold's writings, in poetry and in prose, are their own commentary ; at least, even those who knew him best can say little about their genesis or their sources beyond what they themselves convey. No man of letters was ever more genial, or more affectionate to his friends, and yet none ever told less, even in intimate private letters, about his literary work or about those inmost thoughts of his which from time to time found expression in poetry. As a rule, he composed "in his head," like Wordsworth, and wrote down his verse on any scraps of paper that came handy ; whereas, his prose was always written methodically, in the early morning hours. He had the habit, almost the passion, of destroying whatever manuscripts had served their purpose ; and at his death scarcely any scraps of his writings were found, and scarcely any of the multitudes of letters that he had received. Yet his letters to his family and friends remain, of course ; and it is to be hoped that before long we shall have Mr. George Russell's selections from them. This, though it will contain but few actual references to the poems, will naturally throw light upon them, and will show, as they do, how early his mind reached its maturity. The first little volume of poems, it will be remembered, was published in 1849, when Arnold was twenty-seven ; but five or six years before that he had written letters containing judgments which he would have felt and expressed in just the same way twenty years later. From the beginning, in verse as in his intimate prose, Arnold gave evidence of a singularly clear, open mind, " playing freely " upon all the aspects and all the problems of life as they presented themselves to him in turn. That was his natural endowment; but from the beginning, also, he set himself to enrich it by the persistent study of " the best that is known and thought in the world," as taught by the great writers of all times. Among these writers, the Greeks came first, and their influence penetrated deepest. Quite early in his poetical history he wrote his memorable sonnet ' To a Friend,' in answer to his question, ' Who prop, in these bad days, my mind ?"; and the answer that he gave was to name two Greek poets and a Greek moralist, Homer, Sophocles, Epictetus. Companions of his youth, these influences remained with him to the end. One of the most surprising qualities of Arnold's mind was his power, in spite of the complexity of his own culture—in spite of the Hebraistic elements in it, and of the cross-influences of his multifarious reading—his power of assimilating the Greek spirit in its simplicity, and of presenting ideas, characters, images, with the clearness of Phidian sculpture or of Sophoclean verse. None was more conscious than he of ' that disease of modern life, with its sick hurry, its divided aims '—but none was less personally infected by it. Lucidity, the subject of one of the latest and most brilliant of his public addresses, was his characteristic from the first ; a ' sad lucidity ' perhaps, if we are to trust the bulk of his poems, but one that was never clouded by confusion. This ' critic clearness ' was doubtless a gift of nature to him, but it was developed by a study of Greek literature which, with him, did not end when he left the University. Why, especially after the great success of his Oxford lecture on Theocritus ('Pagan and Mediæval Religious Sentiment')—why he never carried out his scheme of a volume on the Greek poets, his friends never quite understood. He was not, indeed, a professed scholar, in the school and college sense of the word, but no writer of his day could have written so adequately of the poetical qualities of Sophocles and Pindar, just as none has written so suggestively of translating Homer.

Like Goethe, Arnold assimilated Greek forms in many of his writings. 'Even after his master,' wrote Mr. Swinburne in 1867, 'this disciple of Sophocles holds his high place; he has matched against the Attic of the gods this Hyperborean dialect of ours, and has not earned the doom of Marsyas.' Such fragments as those from a *Deianira* and an *Antigone* are close imitations, while the lovely poem of *The Strayed Reveller* is as reminiscent of Greek form as of Greek matter. The special and characteristic Arnold metre, the unrhymed, lilting, quasi-anapaestic measure of *Heine's Grave* and *Rugby Chapel*, is a sort of adaptation, too, from Greek choric metres. It must not indeed be supposed, wrote Arnold in the preface to *Merope*, "that these last [he is speaking of the choruses there, but the words have a wider application] are the reproduction of any Greek choric measures. So to adapt Greek measures to English verse is impossible : what I have done is to try to follow rhythms which produced on my own feeling a similar impression to that produced on it by the rhythms of Greek choric poetry." The result is the metre of which we have spoken—Greek and yet not Greek ; like the Attic chorus, but very different.

But just as there is a difference between the Attic and the Hyperborean in form, so there is in matter. Strongly as Arnold's view of the world, his "criticism of life," was influenced by Greek poetry and philosophy, there is a great, an essential distinction between him and his models. How comes it, people often ask, that he, over whose conversation, and over most of whose prose work, there played a delightful and a perpetual humour, should in his verse be so uniformly grave, so far removed from humour ? How comes it that in his poetry he brings, not once nor twice, but perpetually, "the eternal note of sadness in"? The truth is, that verse was for him, except in two or three of the poems with which he amused some of his latest days, the expression of his gravest self, and his most abiding thought. And here there was, as it were, a permanent *nostalgie* of a simpler and earlier age ; a pained sense that the modern mind, delight as it may in the forms that ancient art has left us, can never re-create for itself the moral atmosphere in which that art had its origin. Hence the almost tragic note that sounds through so much of Arnold's poetry ; the sad reflexion that he, whom nature and training had endowed with Hellenic clearness of vision and utterance, should have to express the thoughts of an age in which all is confusion and perplexity.

Hence, again, his fondness for certain types, repeating one another to a certain extent : Empedocles, who in his inability to live either for himself or in the world, plunges into the crater of Etna ; the Scholar Gypsy, who seeks refuge among a primitive race from the torment of civilization ; Obermann, retreating to the Swiss mountains to contemplate life and his own soul. That so much of Arnold's poetry is given up to this class of subjects and of thoughts is largely due to the fact that his early man-hood, the time when his poetic production was most active, lay in those years of "storm and stress," 1840 to 1850—the years of Chartism, of the "Oxford Movement," of continental revolution, of railway expansion, the years of Carlyle's greatest activity, and of George Sand's greatest effectiveness.

We have said that in counting up the literary influences that worked upon Arnold, the chief place must be given to the Greeks. He cared much less for the Latin than for the Greek writers, and was less touched by the charm of Virgil than Tennyson was ; the lines to "The Mantovano," indeed, would have found as little response in him as would the alcaics "To Milton." In an Oxford lecture, famous at the time, but never printed, he called Lucretius "morbid" ; another lecture, on Propertius, he often announced but never delivered. Of the author of *Literature and Dogma* it need hardly be said that the Bible, considered both as literature and as a storehouse of profound reflexions upon human life, had a strong and perma-nent influence upon him. Some of the Fathers touched him a good deal ; he studied St. Augustine's *Confessions* and the *Imitation*, and felt their power and charm ; and the Introduc-tion to these volumes of ours has put on record his view of Dante, that crown and flower of the mediaeval Italian mind. But none of these were so much to him as the moderns— Shakespeare and Montaigne in their degree, Wordsworth and Byron of course, but most of all Goethe and some French

writers of his own generation. One of his most treasured
books was a fine copy of the thirty-volume edition of Goethe,
which he had read through and assimilated as he assimilated
the Greek classics in his boyhood. The " wide and luminous
view " of the writer whom Arnold called " the greatest poet of
his time, the greatest critic of all times," had an extraordinary
attraction for him. Sanity, the absence of caprice—these were
to him the essential things ; he found them in the Greeks, in
Goethe, and the great French tradition from Molière to Leconte
de Lisle, from Montaigne to Sainte-Beuve. It was because he
did not find them in Victor Hugo that he could never bring
himself to join the body of that poet's votaries, and that he once
said to the present writer, " There is more in the one little volume
of André Chénier than in the whole forty volumes of Hugo."

It is hoped that the following selections, though far too brief
to represent fully the work of a poet so rich in thought as Arnold
was, will be found to contain the most perfect, and many of the
most suggestive and stimulating, of his poems. Many old
favourites, indeed, will be missed altogether, and in two or three
instances—not more—extracts have been given where the complete poems might have been expected or wished for. From a
long narrative poem such as *Sohrab and Rustum*, this choice
of a mere fragment was of course inevitable ; and the Editor,
after much consideration, has decided to exclude the whole of
the beautiful early poem *Resignation*, except the famous page
about the Poet. Arnold himself, though he never moved away
from the conclusions of a poem which taught that the secret of
life was "not joy but peace," came to regard it as faulty in
workmanship, diffuse, and immature. One of the most interesting of his poems, speaking biographically, the *Stanzas from the
Grande Chartreuse*, has also been shut out, on the ground of a
certain monotony in its composition ; and the same fate, merely
for reasons of space, has befallen that vivid summary, as it may
be called, of the mental history of Europe, *Obermann Once
More*. We have printed *Thyrsis*, but have been forced to omit
the poem which is, as it were, the introduction to it, *The
Scholar Gypsy*, though it is one of the most characteristic of
all, and though the long simile with which it concludes is as
famous as anything the author ever wrote. Again, we have

been forced to limit ourselves to one small fragment of *Empedo-cles on Etna*, the Song of Callicles, and have had to exclude the splendid monologue of the philosopher. Arnold for many years condemned it himself, and withdrew from publication the whole poem for the reasons which he gave in the celebrated Preface of 1853; but reflexion and the persuasions of his friends led him to cancel the sentence of banishment, and *Empedocles* reappeared in the "New Poems" of 1867. Since that time it has held its place in every edition, and the opinion of all readers of poetry has confirmed the inclusion of it, however true may have been the poet's feeling that it was wanting in dramatic action, and was, for enjoyment, too monotonously grave.

EDITOR.

To a Friend.

Who prop, thou ask'st, in these bad days, my mind?—
He much, the old man, who, clearest-soul'd of men,
Saw The Wide Prospect, and the Asian Fen [1],
And Tmolus hill, and Smyrna bay, though blind.

Much he, whose friendship I not long since won
That halting slave, who in Nicopolis
Taught Arrian, when Vespasian's brutal son
Clear'd Rome of what most shamed him. But be his

My special thanks, whose even-balanced soul,
From first youth tested up to extreme old age,
Business could not make dull, nor passion wild;

Who saw life steadily, and saw it whole;
The mellow glory of the Attic stage,
Singer of sweet Colonus, and its child.

Shakespeare.

Others abide our question. Thou art free.
We ask and ask—Thou smilest and art still,
Out-topping knowledge. For the loftiest hill,
Who to the stars uncrowns his majesty,

Planting his steadfast footsteps in the sea,
Making the heaven of heavens his dwelling-place,
Spares but the cloudy border of his base
To the foil'd searching of mortality;

---

[1] The name Europe (Εὐρώπη, *the wide prospect*) probably describes the appearance of the European coast to the Greeks on the coast of Asia Minor opposite. The name Asia, again, comes, it has been thought, from the muddy fens of the rivers of Asia Minor, such as the Cayster or Maeander, which struck the imagination of the Greeks living near them. (*Author's Note.*)

And thou, who didst the stars and sunbeams know,
Self-school'd, self-scann'd, self-honour'd, self-secure,
Didst tread on earth unguess'd at.—Better so!

All pains the immortal spirit must endure,
All weakness which impairs, all griefs which bow,
Find their sole speech in that victorious brow.

REQUIESCAT.

Strew on her roses, roses,
    And never a spray of yew!
In quiet she reposes;
    Ah, would that I did too!

Her mirth the world required;
    She bathed it in smiles of glee.
But her heart was tired, tired,
    And now they let her be.

Her life was turning, turning,
    In mazes of heat and sound.
But for peace her soul was yearning,
    And now peace laps her round.

Her cabin'd, ample spirit,
    It flutter'd and fail'd for breath.
To-night it doth inherit
    The vasty hall of death.

HUMAN LIFE.

What mortal, when he saw,
Life's voyage done, his heavenly Friend,
Could ever yet dare tell him fearlessly:
'I have kept uninfringed my nature's law;
The inly-written chart thou gavest me,
To guide me, I have steer'd by to the end'?

Ah! let us make no claim,
On life's incognisable sea,
To too exact a steering of our way;
Let us not fret and fear to miss our aim,
If some fair coast have lured us to make stay,
Or some friend hail'd us to keep company.

Ay! we would each fain drive
At random, and not steer by rule.
Weakness! and worse, weakness bestow'd in vain.
Winds from our side the unsuiting consort rive,
We rush by coasts where we had lief remain;
Man cannot, though he would, live chance's fool.

No! as the foaming swath
Of torn-up water, on the main,
Falls heavily away with long-drawn roar
On either side the black deep-furrow'd path
Cut by an onward-labouring vessel's prore,
And never touches the ship-side again;

Even so we leave behind,
As, charter'd by some unknown Powers,
We stem across the sea of life by night,
The joys which were not for our use design'd;—
The friends to whom we had no natural right,
The homes that were not destined to be ours.

[From *Resignation.*]

The poet, to whose mighty heart
Heaven doth a quicker pulse impart,
Subdues that energy to scan
Not his own course, but that of man.
Though he move mountains, though his day
Be pass'd on the proud heights of sway,
Though he hath loosed a thousand chains,
Though he hath borne immortal pains,
Action and suffering though he know—
He hath not lived, if he lives so.

He sees, in some great-historied land,
A ruler of the people stand,
Sees his strong thought in fiery flood
Roll through the heaving multitude,
Exults—yet for no moment's space
Envies the all-regarded place.
Beautiful eyes meet his—and he
Bears to admire uncravingly;
They pass—he, mingled with the crowd,
Is in their far-off triumphs proud.
From some high station he looks down,
At sunset, on a populous town;
Surveys each happy group, which fleets,
Toil ended, through the shining streets,
Each with some errand of its own—
And does not say: *I am alone.*
He sees the gentle stir of birth
When morning purifies the earth;
He leans upon a gate and sees
The pastures, and the quiet trees.
Low, woody hill, with gracious bound,
Folds the still valley almost round;
The cuckoo, loud on some high lawn,
Is answer'd from the depth of dawn;
In the hedge straggling to the stream,
Pale, dew-drench'd, half-shut roses gleam;
But, where the farther side slopes down,
He sees the drowsy new-waked clown
In his white quaint-embroider'd frock
Make, whistling, tow'rd his mist-wreathed flock—
Slowly, behind his heavy tread,
The wet, flower'd grass heaves up its head.
Lean'd on his gate, he gazes—tears
Are in his eyes, and in his ears
The murmur of a thousand years.
Before him he sees life unroll,
A placid and continuous whole—
That general life, which does not cease,
Whose secret is not joy, but peace;

That life, whose dumb wish is not miss'd
If birth proceeds, if things subsist;
The life of plants, and stones, and rain,
The life he craves—if not in vain
Fate gave, what chance shall not control,
His sad lucidity of soul.

[From *Sohrab and Rustum.*]

He spoke; and as he ceased, he wept aloud,
Thinking of her he left, and his own death.
He spoke; but Rustum listen'd, plunged in thought.
Nor did he yet believe it was his son
Who spoke, although he call'd back names he knew;
For he had had sure tidings that the babe,
Which was in Ader-baijan born to him,
Had been a puny girl, no boy at all—
So that sad mother sent him word, for fear
Rustum should seek the boy, to train in arms—
And so he deem'd that either Sohrab took,
By a false boast, the style of Rustum's son;
Or that men gave it him, to swell his fame.
So deem'd he; yet he listen'd, plunged in thought
And his soul set to grief, as the vast tide
Of the bright rocking Ocean sets to shore
At the full moon; tears gather'd in his eyes;
For he remember'd his own early youth,
And all its bounding rapture; as, at dawn,
The shepherd from his mountain-lodge descries
A far, bright city, smitten by the sun,
Through many rolling clouds—so Rustum saw
His youth; saw Sohrab's mother, in her bloom;
And that old king, her father, who loved well
His wandering guest, and gave him his fair child
With joy; and all the pleasant life they led,
They three, in that long-distant summer-time—
The castle, and the dewy woods, and hunt
And hound, and morn on those delightful hills

In Ader-baijan. And he saw that Youth,
Of age and looks to be his own dear son,
Piteous and lovely, lying on the sand,
Like some rich hyacinth which by the scythe
Of an unskilful gardener has been cut,
Mowing the garden grass-plots near its bed,
And lies, a fragrant tower of purple bloom,
On the mown, dying grass—so Sohrab lay,
Lovely in death, upon the common sand.
And Rustum gazed on him with grief, and said :—

'O Sohrab, thou indeed art such a son
Whom Rustum, wert thou his, might well have loved.
Yet here thou errest, Sohrab, or else men
Have told thee false—thou art not Rustum's son.
For Rustum had no son ; one child he had—
But one—a girl ; who with her mother now
Plies some light female task, nor dreams of us—
Of us she dreams not, nor of wounds, nor war.'

But Sohrab answer'd him in wrath ; for now
The anguish of the deep-fix'd spear grew fierce,
And he desired to draw forth the steel,
And let the blood flow free, and so to die—
But first he would convince his stubborn foe ;
And, rising sternly on one arm, he said :—

'Man, who art thou who dost deny my words?
Truth sits upon the lips of dying men,
And falsehood, while I lived, was far from mine.
I tell thee, prick'd upon this arm I bear
That seal which Rustum to my mother gave,
That she might prick it on the babe she bore.'

He spoke ; and all the blood left Rustum's cheeks,
And his knees totter'd, and he smote his hand
Against his breast, his heavy mailed hand,
That the hard iron corslet clank'd aloud ;
And to his heart he press'd the other hand,
And in a hollow voice he spake, and said :—

'Sohrab, that were a proof which could not lie!
If thou show this, then art thou Rustum's son.'

Then, with weak hasty fingers, Sohrab loosed

His belt, and near the shoulder bared his arm,
And show'd a sign in faint vermilion points
Prick'd ; as a cunning workman, in Pekin,
Pricks with vermilion some clear porcelain vase,
An emperor's gift—at early morn he paints,
And all day long, and, when night comes, the lamp
Lights up his studious forehead and thin hands—
So delicately prick'd the sign appear'd
On Sohrab's arm, the sign of Rustum's seal.
It was that griffin, which of old rear'd Zal,
Rustum's great father, whom they left to die,
A helpless babe, among the mountain-rocks ;
Him that kind creature found, and rear'd, and loved—
Then Rustum took it for his g'orious sign.
And Sohrab bared that image on his arm,
And himself scann'd it long with mournful eyes,
And then he touch'd it with his hand and said :—

'How say'st thou? Is that sign the proper sign
Of Rustum's son, or of some other man's ?'

He spoke; but Rustum gazed, and gazed, and stood
Speechless ; and then he utter'd one sharp cry :
O boy—thy father !— and his voice choked there.
And then a dark cloud pass'd before his eyes,
And his head swam, and he sank down to earth.
But Sohrab crawl'd to where he lay, and cast
His arms about his neck, and kiss'd his lips,
And with fond faltering fingers stroked his cheeks,
Trying to call him back to life ; and life
Came back to Rustum, and he oped his eyes,
And they stood wide with horror ; and he seized
In both his hands the dust which lay around,
And threw it on his head, and smirch'd his hair,—
His hair, and face, and beard, and glittering arms ;
And strong convulsive groanings shook his breast,
And his sobs choked him ; and he clutch'd his sword,
To draw it, and for ever let life out.
But Sohrab saw his thought, and held his hands,
And with a soothing voice he spake, and said :—

'Father, forbear ! for I but meet to-day

The doom which at my birth was written down
In Heaven, and thou art Heaven's unconscious hand.
Surely my heart cried out that it was thou,
When first I saw thee ; and thy heart spoke too,
I know it ! but fate trod those promptings down
Under its iron heel ; fate, fate engaged
The strife, and hurl'd me on my father's spear.
But let us speak no more of this ! I find
My father ; let me feel that I have found !
Come, sit beside me on this sand, and take
My head betwixt thy hands, and kiss my cheeks,
And wash them with thy tears, and say: *My son!*
Quick ! quick ! for number'd are my sands of life,
And swift ; for like the lightning to this field
I came, and like the wind I go away—
Sudden, and swift, and like a passing wind.
But it was writ in Heaven that this should be.'

So said he, and his voice released the heart
Of Rustum, and his tears broke forth ; he cast
His arms round his son's neck, and wept aloud,
And kiss'd him. And awe fell on both the hosts,
When they saw Rustum's grief; and Ruksh, the horse,
With his head bowing to the ground and mane
Sweeping the dust, came near, and in mute woe
First to the one then to the other moved
His head, as if inquiring what their grief
Might mean ; and from his dark, compassionate eyes,
The big warm tears roll'd down, and caked the sand.
But Rustum chid him with stern voice, and said:—

'Ruksh, now thou grievest ; but, O Ruksh, thy feet
Should first have rotted on their nimble joints,
Or ere they brought thy master to this field !'

But Sohrab look'd upon the horse and said:—
'Is this, then, Ruksh ? How often, in past days,
My mother told me of thee, thou brave steed,
My terrible father's terrible horse ! and said,
That I should one day find thy lord and thee.
Come, let me lay my hand upon thy mane !
O Ruksh, thou art more fortunate than I ;

For thou hast gone where I shall never go,
And snuff'd the breezes of my father's home.
And thou hast trod the sands of Seistan,
And seen the River of Helmund, and the Lake ·
Of Zirrah ; and the aged Zal himself
Has often stroked thy neck, and given thee food,
Corn in a golden platter soak'd with wine,
And said : *O Ruksh ! bear Rustum well !*—but I
Have never known my grandsire's furrow'd face,
Nor seen his lofty house in Seistan,
Nor slaked my thirst at the clear Helmund stream ;
But lodged among my father's foes, and seen
Afrasiab's cities only, Samarcand,
Bokhara, and lone Khiva in the waste,
And the black Toorkmun tents ; and only drunk
The desert rivers, Moorghab and Tejend,
Kohik, and where the Kalmuks feed their sheep,
The northern Sir ; and this great Oxus stream,
The yellow Oxus, by whose brink I die.'

  Then, with a heavy groan, Rustum bewail'd :—
'Oh, that its waves were flowing over me!
Oh, that I saw its grains of yellow silt
Roll tumbling in the current o'er my head !'

  But, with a grave mild voice, Sohrab replied :—
'Desire not that, my father ! thou must live.
For some are born to do great deeds, and live,
As some are born to be obscured, and die.
Do thou the deeds I die too young to do,
And reap a second glory in thine age ;
Thou art my father, and thy gain is mine.
But come ! thou seest this great host of men
Which follow me ; I pray thee, slay not these !
Let me entreat for them ; what have they done ?
They follow'd me, my hope, my fame, my star.
Let them all cross the Oxus back in peace.
But me thou must bear hence, not send with them,
But carry me with thee to Seistan,
And place me on a bed, and mourn for me,
Thou and the snow-hair'd Zal, and all thy friends.

And thou must lay me in that lovely earth,
And heap a stately mound above my bones,
And plant a far-seen pillar over all.
That so the passing horseman on the waste
May see my tomb a great way off, and cry:
Sohrab, the mighty Rustum's son, lies there,
Whom his great father did in ignorance kill!
And I be not forgotten in my grave.'
    And, with a mournful voice, Rustum replied:—
'Fear not! as thou hast said, Sohrab, my son,
So shall it be; for I will burn my tents,
And quit the host, and bear thee hence with me,
And carry thee away to Seistan,
And place thee on a bed, and mourn for thee,
With the snow-headed Zal, and all my friends.
And I will lay thee in that lovely earth,
And heap a stately mound above thy bones,
And plant a far-seen pillar over all,
And men shall not forget thee in thy grave.
And I will spare thy host; yea, let them go!
Let them all cross the Oxus back in peace!
What should I do with slaying any more?
For would that all that I have ever slain
Might be once more alive; my bitterest foes,
And they who were call'd champions in their time,
And through whose death I won that fame I have—
And I were nothing but a common man,
A poor, mean soldier, and without renown,
So thou mightest live too, my son, my son!
Or rather would that I, even I myself,
Might now be lying on this bloody sand,
Near death, and by an ignorant stroke of thine,
Not thou of mine! and I might die, not thou;
And I, not thou, be borne to Seistan;
And Zal might weep above my grave, not thine;
And say: *O son, I weep thee not too sore,*
For willingly, I know, thou met'st thine end!
But now in blood and battles was my youth,
And full of blood and battles is my age,

And I shall never end this life of blood.'
   Then, at the point of death, Sohrab replied:—
'A life of blood indeed, thou dreadful man!
But thou shalt yet have peace; only not now,
Not yet! but thou shalt have it on that day,
When thou shalt sail in a high-masted ship,
Thou and the other peers of Kai Khosroo,
Returning home over the salt blue sea,
From laying thy dear master in his grave.'
   And Rustum gazed in Sohrab's face, and said:—
'Soon be that day, my son, and deep that sea!
Till then, if fate so wills, let me endure.'
   He spoke; and Sohrab smiled on him, and took
The spear, and drew it from his side, and eased
His wound's imperious anguish; but the blood
Came welling from the open gash, and life
Flow'd with the stream;—all down his cold white side
The crimson torrent ran, dim now and soil'd,
Like the soil'd tissue of white violets
Left, freshly gather'd, on their native bank,
By children whom their nurses call with haste
Indoors from the sun's eye; his head droop'd low,
His limbs grew slack; motionless, white, he lay—
White, with eyes closed; only when heavy gasps,
Deep heavy gasps quivering through all his frame,
Convulsed him back to life, he open'd them,
And fix'd them feebly on his father's face;
Till now all strength was ebb'd, and from his limbs
Unwillingly the spirit fled away,
Regretting the warm mansion which it left,
And youth, and bloom, and this delightful world.
   So, on the bloody sand, Sohrab lay dead;
And the great Rustum drew his horseman's cloak
Down o'er his face, and sate by his dead son.
As those black granite pillars, once high-rear'd
By Jemshid in Persepolis, to bear
His house, now 'mid their broken flights of steps
Lie prone, enormous, down the mountain side—
So in the sand lay Rustum by his son.

And night came down over the solemn waste,
And the two gazing hosts, and that sole pair,
And darken'd all; and a cold fog, with night,
Crept from the Oxus. Soon a hum arose,
As of a great assembly loosed, and fires
Began to twinkle through the fog; for now
Both armies moved to camp, and took their meal;
The Persians took it on the open sands
Southward, the Tartars by the river marge;
And Rustum and his son were left alone.

But the majestic river floated on,
Out of the mist and hum of that low land,
Into the frosty starlight, and there moved,
Rejoicing, through the hush'd Chorasmian waste,
Under the solitary moon;—he flow'd
Right for the polar star, past Orgunjè,
Brimming, and bright, and large; then sands begin
To hem his watery march, and dam his streams,
And split his currents; that for many a league
The shorn and parcell'd Oxus strains along
Through beds of sand and matted rushy isles—
Oxus, forgetting the bright speed he had
In his high mountain-cradle in Pamere,
A foil'd circuitous wanderer—till at last
The long'd-for dash of waves is heard, and wide
His luminous home of waters opens, bright
And tranquil, from whose floor the new-bathed stars
Emerge, and shine upon the Aral Sea.

THE FORSAKEN MERMAN.

Come, dear children, let us away;
Down and away below!
Now my brothers call from the bay,
Now the great winds shoreward blow,
Now the salt tides seaward flow;
Now the wild white horses play,

Champ and chafe and toss in the spray.
Children dear, let us away!
This way, this way!

Call her once before you go—
Call once yet!
In a voice that she will know:
' Margaret! Margaret!'
Children's voices should be dear
(Call once more) to a mother's ear;
Children's voices, wild with pain—
Surely she will come again!
Call her once and come away;
This way, this way!
' Mother dear, we cannot stay!
The wild white horses foam and fret.'
Margaret! Margaret!

Come, dear children, come away down;
Call no more!
One last look at the white-wall'd town,
And the little grey church on the windy shore;
Then come down!
She will not come though you call all day;
Come away, come away!

Children dear, was it yesterday
We heard the sweet bells over the bay?
In the caverns where we lay,
Through the surf and through the swell,
The far-off sound of a silver bell?
Sand-strewn caverns, cool and deep,
Where the winds are all asleep;
Where the spent lights quiver and gleam,
Where the salt weed sways in the stream,
Where the sea-beasts, ranged all round,
Feed in the ooze of their pasture-ground;
Where the sea-snakes coil and twine,
Dry their mail and bask in the brine;
Where great whales come sailing by,

Sail and sail, with unshut eye,
Round the world for ever and aye?
When did music come this way?
Children dear, was it yesterday?

Children dear, was it yesterday
(Call yet once) that she went away?
Once she sate with you and me,
On a red gold throne in the heart of the sea,
And the youngest sate, on her knee.
She comb'd its bright hair, and she tended it well,
When down swung the sound of a far-off bell.
She sigh'd, she look'd up through the clear green sea;
She said: 'I must go, for my kinsfolk pray
In the little grey church on the shore to-day.
'Twill be Easter-time in the world--ah me!
And I lose my poor soul, Merman! here with thee.'
I said: 'Go up, dear heart, through the waves;
Say thy prayer, and come back to the kind sea-caves!'
She smiled, she went up through the surf in the bay.
Children dear, was it yesterday?

    Children dear, were we long alone?
'The sea grows stormy, the little ones moan;
Long prayers,' I said, 'in the world they say;
Come!' I said; and we rose through the surf in the bay.
We went up the beach, by the sandy down
Where the sea stocks bloom, to the white-wall'd town;
Through the narrow paved streets, where all was still,
To the little grey church on the windy hill.
From the church came a murmur of folk at their prayers,
But we stood without in the cold blowing airs.
We climb'd on the graves, on the stones worn with rains,
And we gazed up the aisle through the small leaded panes.
She sate by the pillar; we saw her clear:
'Margaret, hist! come quick, we are here!
Dear heart,' I said, 'we are long alone;
The sea grows stormy, the little ones moan.'
But, ah, she gave me never a look,
For her eyes were seal'd to the holy book!

Loud prays the priest; shut stands the door.
Come away, children, call no more!
Come away, come down, call no more!

Down, down, down!
Down to the depths of the sea!
She sits at her wheel in the humming town,
Singing most joyfully.
Hark what she sings: 'O joy, O joy,
For the humming street, and the child with its toy!
For the priest, and the bell, and the holy well;
For the wheel where I spun,
And the blessed light of the sun!'
And so she sings her fill,
Singing most joyfully,
Till the spindle drops from her hand,
And the whizzing wheel stands still.
She steals to the window, and looks at the sand,
And over the sand at the sea;
And her eyes are set in a stare;
And anon there breaks a sigh,
And anon there drops a tear,
From a sorrow-clouded eye,
And a heart sorrow-laden,
A long, long sigh;
For the cold strange eyes of a little Mermaiden
And the gleam of her golden hair.

Come away, away children;
Come children, come down!
The hoarse wind blows coldly;
Lights shine in the town.
She will start from her slumber
When gusts shake the door;
She will hear the winds howling,
Will hear the waves roar.
We shall see, while above us
The waves roar and whirl,
A ceiling of amber,
A pavement of pearl.

Singing : ' Here came a mortal,
But faithless was she!
And alone dwell for ever
The kings of the sea.'

But, children, at midnight,
When soft the winds blow,
When clear falls the moonlight,
When spring-tides are low ;
When sweet airs come seaward
From heaths starr'd with broom,
And high rocks throw mildly
On the blanch'd sands a gloom ;
Up the still, glistening beaches,
Up the creeks we will hie,
Over banks of bright seaweed
The ebb-tide leaves dry.
We will gaze from the sand-hills,
At the white, sleeping town ;
At the church on the hill side —
And then come back down.
Singing : ' There dwells a loved one,
But cruel is she !
She left lonely for ever
The kings of the sea.'

AUSTERITY OF POETRY.

That son of Italy who tried to blow [1],
Ere Dante came, the trump of sacred song,
In his light youth amid a festal throng
Sate with his bride to see a public show.

Fair was the bride, and on her front did glow
Youth like a star ; and what to youth belong—
Gay raiment, sparkling gauds, elation strong.
A prop gave way! crash fell a platform ! lo,

---

[1] Giacopone di Todi.

'Mid struggling sufferers, hurt to death, she lay!
Shuddering, they drew her garments off—and found
A robe of sackcloth next the smooth, white skin.

Such, poets, is your bride, the Muse! young, gay,
Radiant, adorn'd outside; a hidden ground
Of thought and of austerity within.

TO MARGUERITE.

Yes! in the sea of life enisled,
With echoing straits between us thrown,
Dotting the shoreless watery wild,
We mortal millions live *alone*.
The islands feel the enclasping flow,
And then their endless bounds they know.

But when the moon their hollows lights,
And they are swept by balms of spring,
And in their glens, on starry nights,
The nightingales divinely sing;
And lovely notes, from shore to shore,
Across the sounds and channels pour—

Oh! then a longing like despair
Is to their farthest caverns sent;
For surely once, they feel, we were
Parts of a single continent!
Now round us spreads the watery plain—
Oh might our marges meet again!

Who order'd, that their longing's fire
Should be, as soon as kindled, cool'd?
Who renders vain their deep desire?—
A God, a God their severance ruled!
And bade betwixt their shores to be
The unplumb'd, salt, estranging sea.

THE STRAYED REVELLER.

THE PORTICO OF CIRCE'S PALACE. EVENING.

A Youth. Circe.

The Youth.

Faster, faster,
O Circe, Goddess,
Let the wild, thronging train,
The bright procession
Of eddying forms,
Sweep through my soul!

Thou standest, smiling
Down on me! thy right arm,
Lean'd up against the column there,
Props thy soft cheek;
Thy left holds, hanging loosely,
The deep cup, ivy-cinctured,
I held but now.

Is it, then, evening
So soon? I see the night-dews,
Cluster'd in thick beads, dim
The agate brooch-stones
On thy white shoulder;
The cool night-wind, too,
Blows through the portico,
Stirs thy hair, Goddess,
Waves thy white robe!

Circe.

Whence art thou, sleeper?

The Youth.

When the white dawn first
Through the rough fir-planks
Of my hut, by the chestnuts,

Up at the valley-head,
Came breaking, Goddess!
I sprang up, I threw round me
My dappled fawn-skin;
Passing out, from the wet turf,
Where they lay, by the hut door,
I snatch'd up my vine-crown, my fir-staff,
All drench'd in dew—
Came swift down to join
The rout early gather'd
In the town, round the temple,
Iacchus' white fane
On yonder hill.

Quick I pass'd, following
The wood-cutters' cart-track
Down the dark valley;—I saw
On my left, through the beeches,
Thy palace, Goddess,
Smokeless, empty!
Trembling, I enter'd; beheld
The court all silent,
The lions sleeping,
On the altar this bowl.
I drank, Goddess!
And sank down here, sleeping,
On the steps of thy portico.

Circe.

Foolish boy! Why tremblest thou?
Thou lovest it, then, my wine?
Wouldst more of it? See, how glows,
Through the delicate, flush'd marble,
The red, creaming liquor,
Strown with dark seeds!
Drink, then! I chide thee not,
Deny thee not my bowl.
Come, stretch forth thy hand, then—so!
Drink—drink again!

The Youth.

Thanks, gracious one !
Ah, the sweet fumes again !
More soft, ah me,
More subtle-winding
Than Pan's flute-music !
Faint—faint ! Ah me,
Again the sweet sleep !

Circe.

Hist ! Thou—within there !
Come forth, Ulysses !
Art tired with hunting ?
While we range the woodland,
See what the day brings.

Ulysses.

Ever new magic !
Hast thou then lured hither,
Wonderful Goddess, by thy art,
The young, languid-eyed Ampelus,
Iacchus' darling
Or some youth beloved of Pan,
Of Pan and the Nymphs ?
That he sits, bending downward
His white, delicate neck
To the ivy-wreathed marge
Of thy cup ; the bright, glancing vine-leaves
That crown his hair,
Falling forward, mingling
With the dark ivy-plants—
His fawn-skin, half untied,
Smear'd with red wine-stains ? Who is he,
That he sits, overweigh'd
By fumes of wine and sleep,
So late, in thy portico ?
What youth, Goddess,—what guest
Of Gods or mortals ?

Circe.

Hist ! he wakes !
I lured him not hither, Ulysses.
Nay, ask him !

The Youth.

Who speaks ? Ah, who comes forth
To thy side, Goddess, from within ?
How shall I name him ?
This spare, dark-featured,
Quick-eyed stranger ?
Ah, and I see too
His sailor's bonnet,
His short coat, travel-tarnish'd,
With one arm bare !—
Art thou not he, whom fame
This long time rumours
The favour'd guest of Circe, brought by the waves ?
Art thou he, stranger ?
The wise Ulysses,
Laertes' son ?

Ulysses.

I am Ulysses.
And thou, too, sleeper ?
Thy voice is sweet.
It may be thou hast follow'd
Through the islands some divine bard,
By age taught many things,
Age and the Muses ;
And heard him delighting
The chiefs and people
In the banquet, and learn'd his songs,
Of Gods and Heroes,
Of war and arts,
And peopled cities,
Inland, or built
By the grey sea.—If so, then hail !
I honour and welcome thee.

The Youth.

The Gods are happy.
They turn on all sides
Their shining eyes,
And see below them
The earth and men.

They see Tiresias
Sitting, staff in hand,
On the warm, grassy
Asopus bank,
His robe drawn over
His old, sightless head,
Revolving inly
The doom of Thebes.

They see the Centaurs
In the upper glens
Of Pelion, in the streams,
Where red-berried ashes fringe
The clear-brown shallow pools,
With streaming flanks, and heads
Rear'd proudly, snuffing
The mountain wind.

They see the Indian
Drifting, knife in hand,
His frail boat moor'd to
A floating isle thick-matted
With large-leaved, low-creeping melon-plants,
And the dark cucumber.
He reaps, and stows them,
Drifting—drifting;—round him,
Round his green harvest-plot,
Flow the cool lake-waves,
The mountains ring them.

They see the Scythian
On the wide stepp, unharnessing

His wheel'd house at noon.
He tethers his beast down, and makes his meal—
Mares' milk, and bread
Baked on the embers ;—all around
The boundless, waving grass-plains stretch, thick-starr'd
With saffron and the yellow hollyhock
And flag-leaved iris-flowers.
Sitting in his cart
He makes his meal ; before him, for long miles,
Alive with bright green lizards,
And the springing bustard-fowl,
The track, a straight black line,
Furrows the rich soil ; here and there
Clusters of lonely mounds
Topp'd with rough-hewn,
Grey, rain-blear'd statues, overpeer
The sunny waste.

They see the ferry
On the broad, clay-laden
Lone Chorasmian stream ;—thereon,
With snort and strain,
Two horses, strongly swimming, tow
The ferry-boat, with woven ropes
To either bow
Firm harness'd by the mane ; a chief,
With shout and shaken spear,
Stands at the prow, and guides them ; but astern
The cowering merchants, in long robes,
Sit pale beside their wealth
Of silk-bales and of balsam-drops,
Of gold and ivory,
Of turquoise-earth and amethyst,
Jasper and chalcedony,
And milk-barr'd onyx-stones.
The loaded boat swings groaning
In the yellow eddies ;
The Gods behold them.
They see the Heroes

Sitting in the dark ship
On the foamless, long-heaving
Violet sea,
At sunset nearing
The Happy Islands.

These things, Ulysses,
The wise bards also
Behold and sing.
But oh, what labour !
O prince, what pain !

They too can see
Tiresias ;—but the Gods,
Who give them vision,
Added this law :
That they should bear too
His groping blindness,
His dark foreboding,
His scorn'd white hairs ;
Bear Hera's anger
Through a life lengthen'd
To seven ages.

They see the Centaurs
On Pelion ;—then they feel,
They too, the maddening wine
Swell their large veins to bursting ; in wild pain
They feel the biting spears
Of the grim Lapithae, and Theseus, drive,
Drive crashing through their bones ; they feel
High on a jutting rock in the red stream
Alcmena's dreadful son
Ply his bow ;—such a price
The Gods exact for song :
To become what we sing.

They see the Indian
On his mountain lake ; but squalls
Make their skiff reel, and worms

In the unkind spring have gnawn
Their melon-harvest to the heart.—They see
The Scythian; but long frosts
Parch them in winter-time on the bare stepp,
Till they too fade like grass; they crawl
Like shadows forth in spring.

They see the merchants
On the Oxus stream;—but care
Must visit first them too, and make them pale.
Whether, through whirling sand,
A cloud of desert robber-horse have burst
Upon their caravan; or greedy kings,
In the wall'd cities the way passes through,
Crush'd them with tolls; or fever-airs,
On some great river's marge,
Mown them down, far from home.

They see the Heroes
Near harbour;—but they share
Their lives, and former violent toil in Thebes,
Seven-gated Thebes, or Troy;
Or where the echoing oars
Of Argo first
Startled the unknown sea.

The old Silenus
Came, lolling in the sunshine,
From the dewy forest-coverts,
This way, at noon.
Sitting by me, while his Fauns
Down at the water-side
Sprinkled and smoothed
His drooping garland,
He told me these things.

But I, Ulysses,
Sitting on the warm steps,
Looking over the valley,
All day long, have seen,

Without pain, without labour,
Sometimes a wild-hair'd Maenad—
Sometimes a Faun with torches—
And sometimes, for a moment,
Passing through the dark stems
Flowing-robed, the beloved,
The desired, the divine,
Beloved Iacchus.

Ah, cool night-wind, tremulous stars!
Ah, glimmering water,
Fitful earth-murmur,
Dreaming woods!
Ah, golden-hair'd, strangely smiling Goddess,
And thou, proved, much enduring,
Wave-toss'd Wanderer!
Who can stand still?
Ye fade, ye swim, ye waver before me—
The cup again!

Faster, faster,
O Circe, Goddess,
Let the wild, thronging train,
The bright procession
Of eddying forms,
Sweep through my soul!

CALLICLES' SONG.

[From *Empedocles on Etna*.]

Through the black, rushing smoke-bursts
Thick breaks the red flame,
All Etna heaves fiercely
Her forest-clothed frame.

Not here, O Apollo!
Are haunts meet for thee.
But, where Helicon breaks down
In cliff to the sea,

Where the moon-silver'd inlets
Send far their light voice
Up the still vale of Thisbe,
O speed, and rejoice!

On the sward at the cliff-top
Lie strewn the white flocks,
On the cliff-side the pigeons
Roost deep in the rocks.

In the moonlight the shepherds,
Soft lull'd by the rills,
Lie wrapt in their blankets
Asleep on the hills.

—What forms are these coming
So white through the gloom?
What garments out-glistening
The gold-flower'd broom?

What sweet-breathing presence
Out-perfumes the thyme?
What voices enrapture
The night's balmy prime?—

'Tis Apollo comes leading
His choir, the Nine.
—The leader is fairest,
But all are divine.

They are lost in the hollows!
They stream up again!
What seeks on this mountain
The glorified train?—

They bathe on this mountain,
In the spring by their road;
Then on to Olympus,
Their endless abode.

—Whose praise do they mention?
Of what is it told?—
What will be for ever;
What was from of old.

First hymn they the Father
Of all things; and then,
The rest of immortals,
The action of men.

The day in his hotness
The strife with the palm;
The night in her silence,
The stars in their calm.

DOVER BEACH.

The sea is calm to-night.
The tide is full, the moon lies fair
Upon the straits;—on the French coast the light
Gleams and is gone; the cliffs of England stand,
Glimmering and vast, out in the tranquil bay.
Come to the window, sweet is the night-air!
Only, from the long line of spray
Where the sea meets the moon-blanch'd land,
Listen! you hear the grating roar
Of pebbles which the waves draw back, and fling,
At their return, up the high strand,
Begin, and cease, and then again begin,
With tremulous cadence slow, and bring
The eternal note of sadness in.

Sophocles long ago
Heard it on the Aegaean, and it brought
Into his mind the turbid ebb and flow
Of human misery; we
Find also in the sound a thought,
Hearing it by this distant northern sea.

The Sea of Faith
Was once, too, at the full, and round earth's shore
Lay like the folds of a bright girdle furl'd!
But now I only hear

Its melancholy, long, withdrawing roar,
Retreating, to the breath
Of the night-wind, down the vast edges drear
And naked shingles of the world.

Ah, love, let us be true
To one another! for the world, which seems
To lie before us like a land of dreams,
So various, so beautiful, so new,
Hath really neither joy, nor love, nor light,
Nor certitude, nor peace, nor help for pain;
And we are here as on a darkling plain
Swept with confused alarms of struggle and flight,
Where ignorant armies clash by night.

PALLADIUM.

Set where the upper streams of Simois flow
Was the Palladium, high 'mid rock and wood;
And Hector was in Ilium, far below,
And fought, and saw it not—but there it stood!

It stood, and sun and moonshine rain'd their light
On the pure columns of its glen-built hall.
Backward and forward roll'd the waves of fight
Round Troy—but while this stood, Troy could not fall.

So, in its lovely moonlight, lives the soul.
Mountains surround it, and sweet virgin air;
Cold plashing, past it, crystal waters roll;
We visit it by moments, ah, too rare!

We shall renew the battle in the plain
To-morrow;—red with blood will Xanthus be;
Hector and Ajax will be there again,
Helen will come upon the wall to see.

Then we shall rust in shade, or shine in strife,
And fluctuate 'twixt blind hopes and blind despairs,
And fancy that we put forth all our life,
And never know how with the soul it fares.

Still doth the soul, from its lone fastness high
Upon our life a ruling effluence send.
And when it fails, fight as we will, we die;
And while it lasts, we cannot wholly end.

MORALITY.

We cannot kindle when we will
The fire which in the heart resides;
The spirit bloweth and is still,
In mystery our soul abides.
    But tasks in hours of insight wil''d
    Can be through hours of gloom fulfill'd.

With aching hands and bleeding feet
We dig and heap, lay stone on stone;
We bear the burden and the heat
Of the long day, and wish 'twere done.
    Not till the hours of light return
    All we have built do we discern.

Then, when the clouds are off the soul,
When thou dost bask in Nature's eye,
Ask, how *she* view'd thy self-control,
Thy struggling, task'd morality—
    Nature, whose free, light, cheerful air,
    Oft made thee, in thy gloom, despair.

And she, whose censure thou dost dread,
Whose eye thou wast afraid to seek,
See, on her face a glow is spread,
A strong emotion on her cheek!
    'Ah child!' she cries, 'that strife divine,
    Whence was it, for it is not mine?

' There is no effort on *my* brow—
I do not strive, I do not weep;
I rush with the swift spheres and glow
In joy, and when I will, I sleep.
    Yet that severe, that earnest air,
    I saw, I felt it once—but where?

‘ I knew not yet the gauge of time,
Nor wore the manacles of space ;
I felt it in some other clime,
I saw it in some other place.
  ’Twas when the heavenly house I trod,
  And lay upon the breast of God.’

Memorial Verses.

April, 1850.

Goethe in Weimar sleeps, and Greece,
Long since, saw Byron’s struggle cease.
But one such death remain’d to come ;
The last poetic voice is dumb —
We stand to-day by Wordsworth’s tomb.

When Byron’s eyes were shut in death,
We bow’d our head and held our breath.
He taught us little ; but our soul
Had *felt* him like the thunder’s roll.
With shivering heart the strife we saw
Of passion with eternal law ;
And yet with reverential awe
We watch’d the fount of fiery life
Which served for that Titanic strife.

When Goethe’s death was told, we said :
Sunk, then, is Europe’s sagest head.
Physician of the iron age,
Goethe has done his pilgrimage.
He took the suffering human race,
He read each wound, each weakness clear ;
And struck his finger on the place,
And said : *Thou ailest here, and here !*
He look’d on Europe’s dying hour
Of fitful dream and feverish power ;
His eye plunged down the weltering strife,
The turmoil of expiring life—

He said : *The end is everywhere,*
Art still has truth, take refuge there!
And he was happy, if to know
Causes of things, and far below
His feet to see the lurid flow
Of terror, and insane distress,
And headlong fate, be happiness.

And Wordsworth !—Ah, pale ghosts, rejoice !
For never has such soothing voice
Been to your shadowy world convey'd,
Since erst, at morn, some wandering shade
Heard the clear song of Orpheus come
Through Hades, and the mournful gloom.
Wordsworth has gone from us—and ye,
Ah, may ye feel his voice as we !
He too upon a wintry clime
Had fallen—on this iron time
Of doubts, disputes, distractions, fears.
He found us when the age had bound
Our souls in its benumbing round ;
He spoke, and loosed our heart in tears.
He laid us as we lay at birth
On the cool flowery lap of earth,
Smiles broke from us and we had ease ;
The hills were round us, and the breeze
Went o'er the sun-lit fields again ;
Our foreheads felt the wind and rain.
Our youth return'd ; for there was shed
On spirits that had long been dead,
Spirits dried up and closely furl'd,
The freshness of the early world.

Ah! since dark days still bring to light
Man's prudence and man's fiery might,
Time may restore us in his course
Goethe's sage mind and Byron's force ;
But where will Europe's latter hour
Again find Wordsworth's healing power?

Others will teach us how to dare,
And against fear our breast to steel;
Others will strengthen us to bear—
But who, ah! who, will make us feel?
The cloud of mortal destiny,
Others will front it fearlessly—
But who, like him, will put it by?

Keep fresh the grass upon his grave,
O Rotha, with thy living wave!
Sing him thy best! for few or none
Hears thy voice right, now he is gone.

RUGBY CHAPEL.

NOVEMBER, 1857.

Coldly, sadly descends
The autumn-evening. The field
Strewn with its dank yellow drifts
Of wither'd leaves, and the elms,
Fade into dimness apace,
Silent;—hardly a shout
From a few boys late at their play!
The lights come out in the street,
In the school-room windows—but cold,
Solemn, unlighted, austere,
Through the gathering darkness, arise
The chapel-walls, in whose bound
Thou, my father! art laid.

There thou dost lie, in the gloom
Of the autumn evening. But ah!
That word, *gloom*, to my mind
Brings thee back, in the light
Of thy radiant vigour, again;
In the gloom of November we pass'd
Days not dark at thy side;

Seasons impair'd not the ray
Of thy buoyant cheerfulness clear.
Such thou wast ! and I stand
In the autumn evening, and think
Of bygone autumns with thee.

Fifteen years have gone round
Since thou arosest to tread,
In the summer-morning, the road
Of death, at a call unforeseen,
Sudden. For fifteen years,
We who till then in thy shade
Rested as under the boughs
Of a mighty oak, have endured
Sunshine and rain as we might,
Bare, unshaded, alone,
Lacking the shelter of thee.

O strong soul, by what shore
Tarriest thou now ? For that force,
Surely, has not been left vain !
Somewhere, surely, afar,
In the sounding labour-house vast
Of being, is practised that strength,
Zealous, beneficent, firm !

Yes, in some far-shining sphere,
Conscious or not of the past,
Still thou performest the word
Of the Spirit in whom thou dost live—
Prompt, unwearied, as here !
Still thou upraisest with zeal
The humble good from the ground,
Sternly repressest the bad !
Still, like a trumpet, dost rouse
Those who with half-open eyes
Tread the border-land dim
'Twixt vice and virtue ; reviv'st,
Succourest !—this was thy work,
This was thy life upon earth.

What is the course of the life
Of mortal men on the earth?—
Most men eddy about
Here and there—eat and drink,
Chatter and love and hate,
Gather and squander, are raised
Aloft, are hurl'd in the dust,
Striving blindly, achieving
Nothing; and then they die—
Perish;—and no one asks
Who or what they have been,
More than he asks what waves,
In the moonlit solitudes mild
Of the midmost Ocean, have swell'd,
Foam'd for a moment, and gone.

And there are some, whom a thirst
Ardent, unquenchable, fires,
Not with the crowd to be spent,
Not without aim to go round
In an eddy of purposeless dust,
Effort unmeaning and vain.
Ah, yes! some of us strive
Not without action to die
Fruitless, but something to snatch
From dull oblivion, nor all
Glut the devouring grave!
We, we have chosen our path—
Path to a clear-purposed goal,
Path of advance!—but it leads
A long, steep journey, through sunk
Gorges, o'er mountains in snow.
Cheerful, with friends, we set forth—
Then, on the height, comes the storm.
Thunder crashes from rock
To rock, the cataracts reply,
Lightnings dazzle our eyes.
Roaring torrents have breach'd
The track, the stream-bed descends

In the place where the wayfarer once
Planted his footstep—the spray
Boils o'er its borders ! aloft
The unseen snow-beds dislodge
Their hanging ruin ; alas,
Havoc is made in our train !
Friends, who set forth at our side,
Falter, are lost in the storm.
We, we only are left !
With frowning foreheads, with lips
Sternly compress'd, we strain on,
On—and at nightfall at last
Come to the end of our way,
To the lonely inn 'mid the rocks ;
Where the gaunt and taciturn host
Stands on the threshold, the wind
Shaking his thin white hairs—
Holds his lantern to scan
Our storm-beat figures, and asks:
Whom in our party we bring?
Whom we have left in the snow?

Sadly we answer : We bring
Only ourselves ! we lost
Sight of the rest in the storm.
Hardly ourselves we fought through,
Stripp'd, without friends, as we are.
Friends, companions, and train,
The avalanche swept from our side.

But thou would'st not *alone*
Be saved, my father ! *alone*
Conquer and come to thy goal,
Leaving the rest in the wild.
We were weary, and we
Fearful, and we in our march
Fain to drop down and to die.
Still thou turnedst, and still
Beckonedst the trembler, and still
Gavest the weary thy hand.

If, in the paths of the world,
Stones might have wounded thy feet,
Toil or dejection have tried
Thy spirit, of that we saw
Nothing—to us thou wast still
Cheerful, and helpful, and firm!
Therefore to thee it was given
Many to save with thyself;
And, at the end of thy day,
O faithful shepherd! to come,
Bringing thy sheep in thy hand.

And through thee I believe
In the noble and great who are gone;
Pure souls honour'd and blest
By former ages. who else—
Such, so soulless, so poor,
Is the race of men whom I see—
Seem'd but a dream of the heart,
Seem'd but a cry of desire.
Yes! I believe that there lived
Others like thee in the past,
Not like the men of the crowd
Who all round me to-day
Bluster or cringe, and make life
Hideous, and arid, and vile;
But souls temper'd with fire,
Fervent, heroic, and good,
Helpers and friends of mankind.

Servants of God!—or sons
Shall I not call you? because
Not as servants ye knew ·
Your Father's innermost mind,
His, who unwillingly sees
One of his little ones lost—
Yours is the praise, if mankind
Hath not as yet in its march
Fainted, and fallen, and died!

See! In the rocks of the world
Marches the host of mankind,
A feeble, wavering line.
Where are they tending?—A God
Marshall'd them, gave them their goal.
Ah, but the way is so long!
Years they have been in the wild!
Sore thirst plagues them, the rocks,
Rising all round, overawe;
Factions divide them, their host
Threatens to break, to dissolve.
—Ah, keep, keep them combined!
Else, of the myriads who fill
That army, not one shall arrive;
Sole they shall stray; in the rocks
Stagger for ever in vain,
Die one by one in the waste.

Then, in such hour of need
Of your fainting, dispirited race,
Ye, like angels, appear,
Radiant with ardour divine!
Beacons of hope, ye appear!
Languor is not in your heart,
Weakness is not in your word,
Weariness not on your brow.
Ye alight in our van! at your voice,
Panic, despair, flee away.
Ye move through the ranks, recall
The stragglers, refresh the outworn,
Praise, re-inspire the brave!
Order, courage, return.
Eyes rekindling, and prayers,
Follow your steps as ye go.
Ye fill up the gaps in our files,
Strengthen the wavering line,
Stablish, continue our march,
On, to the bound of the waste,
On, to the City of God.

THYRSIS.

A MONODY, *to commemorate the author's friend,*
ARTHUR HUGH CLOUGH, *who died at Florence,* 1861.

How changed is here each spot man makes or fills!
  In the two Hinkseys nothing keeps the same;
    The village-street its haunted mansion lacks,
  And from the sign is gone Sibylla's name,
    And from the roofs the twisted chimney-stacks—
      Are ye too changed, ye hills?
  See, 'tis no foot of unfamiliar men
    To-night from Oxford up your pathway strays!
  Here came I often, often, in old days—
Thyrsis and I; we still had Thyrsis then.

Runs it not here, the track by Childsworth Farm,
  Past the high wood, to where the elm-tree crowns
    The hill behind whose ridge the sunset flames?
  The signal-elm, that looks on Ilsley Downs,
    The Vale, the three lone weirs, the youthful Thames?—
      This winter-eve is warm,
  Humid the air! leafless, yet soft as spring,
    The tender purple spray on copse and briers!
    And that sweet city with her dreaming spires,
  She needs not June for beauty's heightening,

Lovely all times she lies, lovely to-night!—
  Only, methinks, some loss of habit's power
    Befalls me wandering through this upland dim.
  Once pass'd I blindfold here, at any hour;
    Now seldom come I, since I came with him.
      That single elm-tree bright
  Against the west—I miss it! is it gone?
    We prized it dearly; while it stood, we said,
    Our friend, the Gipsy-Scholar, was not dead;
  While the tree lived, he in these fields lived on.

Too rare, too rare, grow now my visits here,
  But once I knew each field, each flower, each stick;
    And with the country-folk acquaintance made
  By barn in threshing-time, by new-built rick.
    Here, too, our shepherd-pipes we first assay'd.
      Ah me! this many a year
  My pipe is lost, my shepherd's holiday!
    Needs must I lose them, needs with heavy heart
    Into the world and wave of men depart;
  But Thyrsis of his own will went away.

It irk'd him to be here, he could not rest.
  He loved each simple joy the country yields,
    He loved his mates; but yet he could not keep,
  For that a shadow lour'd on the fields,
    Here with the shepherds and the silly sheep.
      Some life of men unblest
  He knew, which made him droop, and fill'd his head.
    He went; his piping took a troubled sound
    Of storms that rage outside our happy ground;
  He could not wait their passing, he is dead.

So, some tempestuous morn in early June,
  When the year's primal burst of bloom is o'er,
    Before the roses and the longest day—
  When garden-walks and all the grassy floor
    With blossoms red and white of fallen May
      And chestnut-flowers are strewn—
  So have I heard the cuckoo's parting cry,
    From the wet field, through the vext garden-trees,
    Come with the volleying rain and tossing breeze:
  The bloom is gone, and with the bloom go I!

Too quick despairer, wherefore wilt thou go?
  Soon will the high Midsummer pomps come on,
    Soon will the musk carnations break and swell,
  Soon shall we have gold-dusted snapdragon,
    Sweet-William with his homely cottage-smell,
      And stocks in fragrant blow;

Roses that down the alleys shine afar,
   And open, jasmine-muffled lattices,
   And groups under the dreaming garden-trees,
And the full moon, and the white evening-star.

He hearkens not! light comer, he is flown!
   What matters it? next year he will return,
      And we shall have him in the sweet spring-days,
   With whitening hedges, and uncrumpling fern,
      And blue-bells trembling by the forest-ways,
         And scent of hay new-mown.
   But Thyrsis never more we swains shall see;
      See him come back, and cut a smoother reed,
      And blow a strain the world at last shall heed—
   For Time, not Corydon, hath conquer'd thee!

Alack, for Corydon no rival now!—
   But when Sicilian shepherds lost a mate,
      Some good survivor with his flute would go,
   Piping a ditty sad for Bion's fate;
      And cross the unpermitted ferry's flow,
         And relax Pluto's brow,
   And make leap up with joy the beauteous head
      Of Proserpine, among whose crowned hair
      Are flowers first open'd on Sicilian air,
   And flute his friend, like Orpheus, from the dead.

O easy access to the hearer's grace
   When Dorian shepherds sang to Proserpine!
      For she herself had trod Sicilian fields,
   She knew the Dorian water's gush divine,
      She knew each lily white which Enna yields,
         Each rose with blushing face;
   She loved the Dorian pipe, the Dorian strain.
      But ah, of our poor Thames she never heard!
      Her foot the Cumner cowslips never stirr'd;
   And we should tease her with our plaint in vain!

Well! wind-dispersed and vain the words will be,
   Yet, Thyrsis, let me give my grief its hour
      In the old haunt, and find our tree-topp'd hill!

Who, if not I, for questing here hath power?
  I know the wood which hides the daffodil,
    I know the Fyfield tree,
I know what white, what purple fritillaries
  The grassy harvest of the river-fields,
  Above by Ensham, down by Sandford, yields,
And what sedged brooks are Thames's tributaries;

I know these slopes; who knows them if not I?—
  But many a dingle on the loved hill-side,
    With thorns once studded, old, white-blossom'd trees,
  Where thick the cowslips grew, and far descried
    High tower'd the spikes of purple orchises,
      Hath since our day put by
  The coronals of that forgotten time;
  Down each green bank hath gone the ploughboy's team,
    And only in the hidden brookside gleam
Primroses, orphans of the flowery prime.

Where is the girl, who by the boatman's door,
  Above the locks, above the boating throng,
    Unmoor'd our skiff when through the Wytham flats,
  Red loosestrife and blond meadow-sweet among
    And darting swallows and light water-gnats,
      We track'd the shy Thames shore?
  Where are the mowers, who, as the tiny swell
  Of our boat passing heaved the river-grass,
    Stood with suspended scythe to see us pass?—
They all are gone, and thou art gone as well!

Yes, thou art gone! and round me too the night
  In ever-nearing circle weaves her shade.
    I see her veil draw soft across the day,
  I feel her slowly chilling breath invade
    The cheek grown thin, the brown hair sprent with grey;
      I feel her finger light
  Laid pausefully upon life's headlong train;—
    The foot less prompt to meet the morning dew,
    The heart less bounding at emotion new,
  And hope, once crush'd, less quick to spring again.

And long the way appears, which seem'd so short
  To the less practised eye of sanguine youth;
    And high the mountain-tops, in cloudy air,
  The mountain-tops where is the throne of Truth,
    Tops in life's morning-sun so bright and bare!
        Unbreachable the fort
  Of the long-batter'd world uplifts its wall;
    And strange and vain the earthly turmoil grows,
    And near and real the charm of thy repose,
  And night as welcome as a friend would fall.

But hush! the upland hath a sudden loss
  Of quiet!—Look, adown the dusk hill-side,
    A troop of Oxford hunters going home,
  As in old days, jovial and talking, ride!
    From hunting with the Berkshire hounds they come.
        Quick! let me fly, and cross
  Into yon farther field!—'Tis done; and see,
    Back'd by the sunset, which doth glorify
    The orange and pale violet evening-sky,
  Bare on its lonely ridge, the Tree! the Tree!

I take the omen! Eve lets down her veil,
  The white fog creeps from bush to bush about,
    The west unflushes, the high stars grow bright,
  And in the scatter'd farms the lights come out.
    I cannot reach the signal-tree to-night,
        Yet, happy omen, hail!
  Hear it from thy broad lucent Arno-vale
    (For there thine earth-forgetting eyelids keep
    The morningless and unawakening sleep
  Under the flowery oleanders pale),

Hear it, O Thyrsis, still our tree is there!—
  Ah, vain! These English fields, this upland dim,
    These brambles pale with mist engarlanded,
  That lone, sky-pointing tree, are not for him;
    To a boon southern country he is fled,
        And now in happier air,

Wandering with the great Mother's train divine
(And purer or more subtle soul than thee,
I trow, the mighty Mother doth not see)
Within a folding of the Apennine,

Thou hearest the immortal chants of old !—
Putting his sickle to the perilous grain
In the hot cornfield of the Phrygian king,
For thee the Lityerses-song again
Young Daphnis with his silver voice doth sing;
Sings his Sicilian fold,
His sheep, his hapless love, his blinded eyes —
And how a call celestial round him rang,
And heavenward from the fountain-brink he sprang,
And all the marvel of the golden skies.

There thou art gone, and me thou leavest here
Sole in these fields ! yet will I not despair.
Despair I will not, while I yet descry
Neath the mild canopy of English air
That lonely tree against the western sky.
Still, still these slopes, 'tis clear,
Our Gipsy-Scholar haunts, outliving thee !
Fields where soft sheep from cages pull the hay,
Woods with anemones in flower till May,
Know him a wanderer still ; then why not me?

A fugitive and gracious light he seeks,
Shy to illumine; and I seek it too.
This does not come with houses or with gold,
With place, with honour, and a flattering crew;
'Tis not in the world's market bought and sold—
But the smooth-slipping weeks
Drop by, and leave its seeker still untired ;
Out of the heed of mortals he is gone,
He wends unfollow'd, he must house alone;
Yet on he fares, by his own heart inspired.

Thou too, O Thyrsis, on like quest wast bound ;
Thou wanderedst with me for a little hour !

3 C 2

Men gave thee nothing; but this happy quest,
If men esteem'd thee feeble, gave thee power,
  If men procured thee trouble, gave thee rest.
    And this rude Cumner ground,
Its fir-topped Hurst, its farms, its quiet fields,
  Here cam'st thou in thy jocund youthful time,
  Here was thine height of strength, thy golden prime!
And still the haunt beloved a virtue yields.

What though the music of thy rustic flute
  Kept not for long its happy, country tone;
  Lost it too soon, and learnt a stormy note
Of men contention-tost, of men who groan,
    Which task'd thy pipe too sore, and tired thy throat—
    It fail'd, and thou wast mute!
Yet hadst thou alway visions of our light,
  And long with men of care thou couldst not stay,
  And soon thy foot resumed its wandering way,
Left human haunt, and on alone till night.

Too rare, too rare, grow now my visits here!
  'Mid city-noise, not, as with thee of yore,
  Thyrsis! in reach of sheep-bells is my home.
—Then through the great town's harsh, heart-wearying roar,
  Let in thy voice a whisper often come,
    To chase fatigue and fear;
Why faintest thou? I wander'd till I died.
  Roam on! The light we sought is shining still.
  Dost thou ask proof? Our tree yet crowns the hill,
Our Scholar travels yet the loved hill-side.

ALFRED, LORD TENNYSON.

[ALFRED TENNYSON was born on Aug. 6, 1809, at Somersby Rectory, Lincolnshire. He was the third son of the Rev. George Clayton Tennyson, LL.D., Rector of Somersby; his mother was a daughter of the Rev. Stephen Fytche. After education at Louth Grammar School, and at home, he went in 1828 to Trinity College, Cambridge. His ' Poems, chiefly Lyrical,' appeared in 1830. In 1850, having meanwhile won the foremost place among living English poets, he succeeded Wordsworth as Poet Laureate (Nov. 19). In June of the same year he married Miss Emily Sellwood. His first home after marriage was at Twickenham, where his eldest son, Hallam, was born in 1852. In 1853 he removed to Farringford, near Freshwater, in the Isle of Wight, where his second son, Lionel, was born in 1854. From the year 1869 onwards he had also a second home, Aldworth, near Haslemere, in Surrey, where he usually passed the summer and early autumn. In January, 1884, he was created a peer, by the title of Baron Tennyson, of Aldworth and Farringford. He died at Aldworth on Oct. 6, 1892, aged eighty-three years and two months; and on Oct. 12 was buried in Westminster Abbey.]

The gifts by which Tennyson has won, and will keep, his place among the great poets of England are pre-eminently those of an artist. His genius for vivid and musical expression was joined to severe self-restraint, and to a patience which allowed nothing to go forth from him until it had been refined to the utmost perfection that he was capable of giving to it. And his ' law of pure and flawless workmanship ' (as Matthew Arnold defines the artistic quality in poetry) embraced far more than language : the same instinct controlled his composition in the larger sense ; it is seen in the symmetry of each work as a whole, in the due subordination of detail, in the distribution of light and shade, in the happy and discreet use of ornament. His versatility is not less remarkable : no English poet has left masterpieces in so many different kinds of verse. On another side the spiritual subtlety of the artist is seen in the power of finding words for dim and fugitive traits of consciousness; as the artist's vision, at once minute and imaginative, is seen in his pictures of nature. By this varied and consummate excellence Tennyson ranks with the great artists of all time.

This is the dominant aspect of his poetry. But there is another which presents itself as soon as we take the historical point of view, and inquire into the nature of his influence upon his age. Tennyson was not primarily, like Wordsworth, a philosophical thinker, who felt called upon to be a teacher. But from the middle of the century onwards he was the accepted poet, in respect to thought on religion and on many social questions, of that large public which might be described as the world of cultivated and moderately liberal orthodoxy. Multitudes of these readers were imperfectly capable of appreciating him as an artist : have not some of them been discussing who is 'the Pilot' in *Crossing the Bar* ? But at any rate they heard a voice which they could generally understand ; they felt that it was beautiful and noble ; and they loved it because it soothed and elevated them. They cherished a poet who placed the centre of religion in a simple reliance on the divine love ; who taught that, through all struggles and perplexities, the time was being guided towards some final good ; who saw the results of science not as dangers but as reinforcements to faith ; who welcomed material progress and industrial vigour, but always sought to maintain the best traditions of English history and character. Now, this popular element in Tennyson's fame—as it may be called relatively to those elements which sprang from a full appreciation of his art—was not due to any conscious self-adaptation on his part to prevailing currents of thought and feeling. It arose from the peculiar relation of his genius to the period in which he grew up to manhood. His early youth was in England a day of bright dreams and confident auguries ; for democracy and steam, all things were to be possible. Then came the reaction ; doubts and difficulties thickened ; questions started up in every field, bringing with them unrest, discouragement, or even despair. At such a season the poet who is preeminently an artist has a twofold opportunity ; by creating beauty he can comfort the weary ; but a yet higher task is to exercise, through his art, an ennobling and harmonizing influence on those more strenuous yet half-desponding spirits who bear the stress of the transition, while new and crude energies are threatening an abrupt breach with the past. It is a great work to do for a people, to win the popular ear at such a time for counsels of reverence and chivalry ; to make them feel that these things are beautiful, and are bonds of the national life, while the forces that tend to disintegration are also tending to make the people sordid and cynical. This is the work that Sophocles, in his later years, did for Athens, and this is what Tennyson did for the England of his prime.

His reputation was established with comparative ease. The volume, 'Poems by Two Brothers' (1827), which he and his brother Charles published before they went to Cambridge, showed chiefly a love of poetry, and (in *Persia*) an exceptional ear for sound : but the Cambridge prize-poem on 'Timbuctoo' (1829) was really notable, both in style and in the command of blank verse ; it was a presage, however faint and immature, of the future, and was hailed with a natural delight by the author's friends. In 1830 he brought out 'Poems, chiefly Lyrical'—a thin volume, comprising many poems that have held their place, such as *Claribel, Mariana,* and *The Dying Swan.* Writing in the *Englishman's Magazine,* Arthur Hallam said, 'The features of original genius are clearly and strongly marked. The author imitates nobody.' Tennyson's style was, indeed, from the first wholly distinct from that of any poet who had preceded him. Two years later (1832) he published another volume, entitled simply ' Poems,' and including, among other, *Œnone, The Palace of Art, The Lotus-Eaters, A Dream of Fair Women,* and *The Lady of Shalott.* There was riper art here than in the former book—larger range of themes, greater depth of feeling, and more human interest ; but, though the new work was cordially received by many, the full day of Tennyson's fame was not yet. In that charming poem of his latest years, *Merlin and the Gleam*—an allegorical retrospect of the poet's own career—a certain moment in one of its earlier stages is indicated by ' the croak of a raven,' a bird which, indeed, seldom fails to cross a new singer's path at one point or another. The world at large was still (to quote *Merlin* again), 'blind to the magic, and deaf to the melody.' Then it was that Tennyson showed his reserved strength. He was silent for ten years, during which he subjected his old work to unsparing revision, and disciplined himself for work yet better by unwearying self-criticism. In 1842 'Poems by Alfred Tennyson' appeared in two volumes. The first volume contained chiefly old poems, revised or re-cast. The pieces in the second volume were almost all new ; among them were *The Gardener's Daughter, Locksley Hall, Break, break, break, The Two Voices, Ulysses,* and *Morte d'Arthur.* The success was rapid and great. Wordsworth, in a letter to a friend, generously described the author as ' decidedly the first of our living poets.' Tennyson was then only thirty-three. In the popular estimate his reputation was perhaps not much enhanced by *The Princess* (1847), many as are its beauties, especially lyrical. But when *In Memoriam* appeared, in 1850, it soon won for him a fame as wide as the English-speaking world.

In Memoriam is a typical product of his art, but it is even more representative of his attitude towards the problems and mysteries of human life ; it is the poem which best reveals the secret of his largest popularity. It might have seemed hopeless to expect general favour for an elegy of such unprecedented length on a youth who had ' miss'd the earthly wreath,' leaving a memory cherished by a few friends, who alone could measure the unfulfilled promise. Never, perhaps, has mastery of poetical resource won a more remarkable triumph than in Tennyson's treatment of this theme. The stanza selected, with its twofold capacity for pathos and for resonance, is exactly suited to a flow of self-communing thought, prevailingly pensive, but passing at moments into a loftier or more jubilant note. The rhythm of this stanza also suits the division of the poem into sections ; since the cadence of the fourth line—where the rhyme has less emphasis than in the central couplet—can introduce a pause without giving a sense of abruptness. Hence the music of the poem as a whole is continuous, while at the same time each section is an artistic unit. But this felicity is not merely technical ; it is closely related to the treatment of the subject-matter. Two strains are interwoven throughout ; one is personal—the memory and the sorrow, as they affect the poet ; the other is broadly human and general—the experience of the

soul as it contemplates life and death, as it finds or misses comfort in the face of nature, as it struggles through doubt to faith,
or through anguish to peace. The blending of these two strains
—which are constantly passing into each other—serves to ideal-
ize the theme, and so to justify the large scale of the treatment ;
it has also this effect, that the poem becomes a record of successive spiritual moods, varied as the range of thought and emotion
into which the personal grief broadens out. The composition of
In Memoriam was, indeed, spread over seventeen years. The
form has thus an inner correspondence with the material ; each
lyric section is a spiritual mood—not sharply separated from
that which precedes or from that which follows it, yet with a
completeness of its own. Among particular traits, one which
deserves especial notice is the wonderful adumbration of the
lost friend's power and charm. Neither quite definite nor yet
mystic, the presence made sacred by death flits, with a strange
light around it, through the poem ; it never comes or goes without making us feel that this great sorrow is no fantasy, but has
its root in a great loss. The religious thought of *In Memoriam*
bears the stamp of the time at which it was produced, in so far
as doubts, frankly treated, are met with a sober optimism of a
purely subjective and emotional kind. But the poem has also an
abiding and universal significance as the journal of a mind slowly
passing through a bitter ordeal, and as an expression of reliance
on the 'Strong Son of God, immortal Love.'

The *Idylls of the King*, in their complete form, include work
of various periods. Tennyson's interest in the legends of the
Arthurian cycle was shown at an early date, and was fruitful at
intervals during half a century. *The Lady of Shalott* (1832)
was his lyric prelude to the theme ; two kindred lyrics—*Sir
Galahad* and *Sir Lancelot and Queen Guinevere*—found place
in the volumes of 1842, which contained also the epic *Morte
d'Arthur*, now incorporated in *The Passing of Arthur*. A
half-playful prologue introduces the *Morte d'Arthur* as the
only surviving canto of an epic which had been consigned to
the flames : perhaps the poet felt, in 1842, that the taste for ' romance ' had so far waned as to render this ' fragment ' somewhat
of an experiment. It is one of his finest pieces of blank verse,
and the reception given to it was an invitation to continue the

strain. But it was not till 1859 that he published the first set of Idylls—*Enid, Vivien, Elaine,* and *Guinevere.* In 1870 appeared *The Coming of Arthur, The Holy Grail, Pelleas and Ettarre,* and *The Passing of Arthur ;* followed in 1872 by *Gareth and Lynette* and *The Last Tournament,* and in 1885 by *Balin and Balan.* The twelve books (two being given to Enid) are now arranged in the order of events ; but in the order of composition, as we have seen, the last portion of the story came first, the beginning next, and the middle last. Such a process of growth is in itself a warning that the series, though it had been planned from the outset as a whole, should not be tried by the ordinary tests of an epic : the unity is here less strict ; the main current of narrative is less continuous. 'Idyll' is, indeed, exactly the right word ; each is a separate picture, rich in passages of brilliant power, but distinguished especially by finish of detail. Arthur's ideal purpose is rather a golden thread, common to the several pieces but not equally vital to all, than an organic bond among them ; and the pervading allegory of 'sense at war with soul' is at most a link of another kind. But instead of epic concentration these *Idylls* have a charm of their own. From tracing the destiny of the king, they lead us aside, now and again, into those by-ways of romance where a light tinged with modern thought and fancy is thrown on mediaeval forest and castle, on tournament and bower, on the chivalry, the tenderness, the violence, the enchantments, and the faith. Arthur's fortunes are illustrated by his age. No other single work shows so comprehensively the range of Tennyson's power ; the variety of the theme demands a corresponding wealth of resource ; there is scarcely any mood of the mind, any phase of action, any aspect of nature, which does not find expression somewhere or other in the *Idylls.*

But a poet who is everywhere an exquisite artist, and who is also remarkably versatile, cannot be adequately judged except by the sum total of his work ; there are notes which he may strike only once or twice in the whole of it. Thus in *Maud*— never a popular poem, in spite of the marvellous lyrics—he touches his highest point in the utterance of passion ; its dramatic power is undisputed. The general verdict upon his plays has been that they are more distinguished by excellence of literary execution than by qualities properly dramatic ; though few critics, perhaps, would deny the dramatic effectiveness of particular scenes or passages, in *Harold*, for example, or *Becket*, or *The Cup*. But whatever may be the final judgment upon the plays, *Maud* remains to prove that, among Tennyson's gifts, the dramatic gift was at least not originally absent ; though its manifestation in that poem is necessarily limited to a particular phase. Turning next to a different region of his work, we see in *The Northern Farmer* ('old style') a quality which hardly any imaginative writer of this century has better exemplified— the power of faithfully conceiving a very narrow mental horizon, without allowing a single disturbing ray to steal in from the artist's own mind. Again : in the interpretation of feeling, this poet can seize impressions so transient, so difficult of analysis, that they might seem to defy the grasp of language ; one recognizes them almost with a start, as if some voice, once familiar, were unexpectedly heard ;

> 'Moreover something is or seems,
> That touches me with mystic gleams,
> Like glimpses of forgotten dreams.'

Or :

> 'The glory of the sum of things
> Will flash along the chords and go.'

Akin to this faculty is Tennyson's subtle expression of *desiderium*, the indefinable yearning towards 'the days that are no more,' as in *Break, break, break*, or in *Tears, idle tears*.

His descriptions of nature exhibit two qualities, distinct in essence, though sometimes combined. One appears in his landscape-painting : it is the gift of selecting salient features and composing them into an artistic picture—such as that of the 'vale in Ida,' where

> 'The swimming vapour floats athwart the glen,
> Puts forth an arm, and creeps from pine to pine
> And loiters, slowly drawn';

or of that coral island where Enoch Arden heard

> 'The league-long roller thundering on the reef,
> The moving whisper of huge trees that branch'd
> And blossom'd in the zenith . . .'

The distinction of his imaginary landscapes is not merely vividness or truth, but the union of these with a certain dreamy and
aërial charm. His other great quality as a nature-poet is seen
in the treatment of detail—in vignettes where the result or
minute and keen insight is made to live before us in some magical phrase ; such as ‘The shining levels of the lake’; ‘The
twinkling laurel scatters silver lights’; the shoal of fish that
‘came slipping o’er their shadows on the sand.’ His accuracy
in this province is said to be unerring : thus a critic who twitted
him with having made a ‘crow’ lead a ‘rookery’ had to learn
that in Lincolnshire, as in some other parts of Britain, ‘crow’ is
the generic term. In this context we must not forget *Owd Roä*
—as pathetic a tribute as any in English poetry to the heroism
of a dog. In regard to the vegetation of England, and, generally, to the peculiar charm of English scenery, Tennyson is the
foremost of English poets ; no one else has painted them with
such accurate felicity. Among the English poets of the sea,
too, he has a high place ; he can describe, as in *Elaine*, the wind
in strife with the billow of the North Sea, ‘green-glimmering
toward the summit’; but especially his verse can give back all
the tones of the sea upon the shore, and can interpret their sympathy with the varying moods of the human spirit.

Seven of his poems are on subjects from Greek mythology—
*The Lotus-Eaters, Ulysses, Œnone, The Death of Œnone,
Tithonus, Tiresias, Demeter and Persephone*. In each case he
has chosen a theme which left scope for artistic originality—the
ancient material being either meagre or second-rate. Each
poem presents, in small or moderate compass, the picture of a
moment, or of an episode ; ‘brief idyll’ is the phrase by which
he describes his *Tiresias* (in the lines on the death of Edward
Fitzgerald). The common characteristic of these seven poems
is the consummate art which has caught the spirit of the antique,
without a trace of pedantry in form or in language. The blank
verse (used for all except *The Lotus-Eaters*) has a restrained
power, and a flexible yet majestic grace, which produces an
effect analogous to that of Greek sculpture. Tennyson’s instinct
for classical literary art appears in his epitome of Virgil’s style—

‘ All the charm of all the Muses often flowering in a lonely word ’;

as, again, his sympathy with the temper of the old world's sorrow is seen in the verses written at 'olive-silvery Sirmio,' and suggested by the lines of Catullus, *Frater ave atque vale.* In *Lucretius* Tennyson shows an intimate knowledge of that poet's work, and a curious skill in reproducing his tone ; but the highest interest of this masterpiece is psychological and dramatic. It translates the sober earnestness of Lucretius into a morbid phase. The *De Rerum Natura* is silent on the difficulty of reconciling the gods with the cosmology of Epicurus. But now, when the whole inner life of Lucretius is unhinged by the workings of the poison, the doubt, so long repressed by reverence for the Greek master, starts up—

> ' The Gods ! the Gods !
> If all be atoms, how then should the Gods
> Being atomic, not be dissoluble,
> Not follow the great law ? '

Tennyson's English is always pure and idiomatic, avoiding foreign words, though without pedantic rigour ; and he commands many different shades of diction, finely graduated according to the subject. One of his aims was to recall expressive words which had fallen out of common use ; in the *Idylls*, more especially, he found scope for this. His melody, in its finer secrets, eludes analysis ; but one element of it, the delicate management of vowel-sounds, can be seen in such lines as ' The mellow ouzel fluted in the elm '; or, ' Katie walks by the long wash of Australasian seas.' The latter verse illustrates also another trait of his melody—the restrained use of alliteration, which he scarcely allows, as a rule, to strike the ear, unless he has some artistic motive for making it prominent, as in parts of *Maud,* and in some of the songs in *The Princess.* As a metrist, he is the creator of a new blank verse, different both from the Elizabethan and from the Miltonic. He has known how to modulate it to every theme, and to elicit a music appropriate to each ; attuning it in turn to a tender and homely grace, as in *The Gardener's Daughter ;* to the severe and ideal majesty of the antique, as in *Tithonus ;* to meditative thought, as in *The Ancient Sage,* or *Akbar's Dream ;* to pathetic or tragic tales of contemporary life, as in *Aylmer's Field,* or *Enoch Arden ;* or to

sustained romantic narrative, as in the *Idylls*.   No English poet
has used blank verse with such flexible variety, or drawn from
it so large a compass of tones ; nor has any maintained it so
equably on a high level of excellence.   In lyric metres Tennyson
has invented much, and has also shown a rare power of adaptation.   Many of his lyric measures are wholly his own ; while
others have been so treated by him as to make them virtually
new.   The *In Memoriam* stanza had been used before him,
though he was unaware of this when he adopted it ; but no predecessor had shown its full capabilities.   In the first part of *The
Lotus-Eaters* he employs the Spenserian stanza, but gives it a
peculiar tone, suited to the theme ; the melody is so contrived
that languor seems to weigh upon every verse.   To illustrate his
lyric harmonies of form and matter would be to enumerate his
lyrics ; two or three instances must suffice.   The close-locked
three-line stanza of *The Two Voices* suits the series of compact
sentiments or points :

> ' Then to the still small voice I said,
>   Let me not cast in endless shade
>   What is so wonderfully made.'

In *The Palace of Art*, the shortened fourth line of the quatrain
gives a restful pause, inviting to the contemplation of pictures :—

> Or in a clear-walled city on the sea,
>   Near gilded organ-pipes, her hair
> Wound with white roses, slept St. Cecily ;
>   An angel look'd at her.

The stanza of *The Daisy*, again, suits the light grace which plays
around those memories of travel :—

> O Love, what hours were thine and mine,
>   In lands of palm and southern pine ;
>   In lands of palm, of orange-blossom,
> Of olive, aloe, and maize and vine.

These are, however, only a few lyric examples of a quality
which belongs to all his work.   Throughout its wide range, he
has everywhere accomplished the harmony of form and matter :
the charm of the utterance is indivisible from the charm of the

thought. Poetical art which has done this is raised above changes of tendency or fashion ; it is as permanent as beauty. Tennyson, in wielding the English language, has been a great and original artist ; he has enriched English literature with manifold and imperishable models of excellence. He has expressed, with absolute felicity, numberless phases in the great primary emotions of human nature—love, joy, grief, hope, despondency, the moods of youth and of age, the response in the soul to the various aspects of nature, the sense of awful mystery in human life, the instincts, vague yet persistent, which aspire to immortality, and seem to promise it, the yearning faith in divine goodness and guidance—feelings common to humanity, no doubt, but not therefore commonplace, unless that epithet is applicable to sunrise and starlight. His teaching has been pure, high-hearted, and manly ; full of love for his country, and true to the things which have made England great. Among all the masters of English song, there is none who can give more exquisite delight to those who feel his inmost charm ; and there is probably none who has brought a larger gift of noble pleasure and of comfort to people of all sorts, especially to those in perplexity or sorrow.

R. C. JEBB.

CLARIBEL.

A MELODY.

I.

Where Claribel low-lieth
 The breezes pause and die,
  Letting the rose-leaves fall:
But the solemn oak-tree sigheth,
 Thick-leaved, ambrosial,
 With an ancient melody
 Of an inward agony,
Where Claribel low-lieth.

II.

At eve the beetle boometh
 Athwart the thicket lone:
At noon the wild bee hummeth
 About the moss'd headstone:
At midnight the moon cometh,
 And looketh down alone.
Her song the lintwhite swelleth,
The clear-voiced mavis dwelleth,
 The callow throstle lispeth,
The slumbrous wave outwelleth,
 The babbling runnel crispeth,
The hollow grot replieth
 Where Claribel low-lieth.

A DIRGE.

I.

Now is done thy long day's work;
Fold thy palms across thy breast,
Fold thine arms, turn to thy rest.
  Let them rave.
Shadows of the silver birk
Sweep the green that folds thy grave.
  Let them rave.

II.

Thee nor carketh care nor slander;
Nothing but the small cold worm
Fretteth thine enshrouded form.
    Let them rave.
Light and shadow ever wander
O'er the green that folds thy grave.
    Let them rave.

III.

Thou wilt not turn upon thy bed;
Chaunteth not the brooding bee
Sweeter tones than calumny?
    Let them rave.
Thou wilt never raise thine head
From the green that folds thy grave.
    Let them rave.

IV.

Crocodiles wept tears for thee;
The woodbine and eglatere
Drip sweeter dews than traitor's tear.
    Let them rave.
Rain makes music in the tree
O'er the green that folds thy grave.
    Let them rave.

V.

Round thee blow, self-pleached deep,
Bramble roses. faint and pale,
And long purples of the dale.
    Let them rave.
These in every shower creep
Thro' the green that folds thy grave.
    Let them rave.

VI.

The gold-eyed kingcups fine ;
The frail bluebell peereth over
Rare broidry of the purple clover.
          Let them rave.
Kings have no such couch as thine,
As the green that folds thy grave.
          Let them rave.

VII.

Wild words wander here and there :
God's great gift of speech abused
Makes thy memory confused :
          But let them rave.
The balm-cricket carols clear
In the green that folds thy grave.
          Let them rave.

The Lady of Shalott.

Part I.

On either side the river lie
Long fields of barley and of rye,
That clothe the wold and meet the sky ;
And thro' the field the road runs by
          To many-tower'd Camelot ;
And up and down the people go,
Gazing where the lilies blow
Round an island there below,
          The island of Shalott.

Willows whiten, aspens quiver.
Little breezes dusk and shiver
Thro' the wave that runs for ever
By the island in the river
          Flowing down to Camelot,

Four gray walls, and four gray towers,
Overlook a space of flowers,
And the silent isle embowers
    The Lady of Shalott.

By the margin, willow-veil'd,
Slide the heavy barges trail'd
By slow horses; and unhail'd
The shallop flitteth silken-sail'd
    Skimming down to Camelot:
But who hath seen her wave her hand?
Or at the casement seen her stand?
Or is she known in all the land,
    The Lady of Shalott?

Only reapers, reaping early
In among the bearded barley,
Hear a song that echoes cheerly
From the river winding clearly,
    Down to tower'd Camelot:
And by the moon the reaper weary,
Piling sheaves in uplands airy,
Listening, whispers ''Tis the fairy
    Lady of Shalott.'

PART II.

There she weaves by night and day
A magic web with colours gay.
She has heard a whisper say,
A curse is on her if she stay
    To look down to Camelot.
She knows not what the curse may be,
And so she weaveth steadily,
And little other care hath she,
    The Lady of Shalott.

And moving thro' a mirror clear
That hangs before her all the year,
Shadows of the world appear.
There she sees the highway near
    Winding down to Camelot:

There the river eddy whirls,
And there the surly village-churls,
And the red cloaks of market girls,
    Pass onward from Shalott.

Sometimes a troop of damsels glad,
An abbot on an ambling pad,
Sometimes a curly shepherd-lad,
Or long-hair'd page in crimson clad,
    Goes by to tower'd Camelot;
And sometimes thro' the mirror blue
The knights come riding two and two:
She hath no loyal knight and true,
    The Lady of Shalott.

But in her web she still delights
To weave the mirror's magic sights,
For often thro' the silent nights
A funeral, with plumes and lights
    And music, went to Camelot:
Or when the moon was overhead,
Came two young lovers lately wed;
'I am half sick of shadows,' said
    The Lady of Shalott.

Part III.

A bow-shot from her bower-eaves,
He rode between the barley-sheaves,
The sun came dazzling thro' the leaves,
And flamed upon the brazen greaves
    Of bold Sir Lancelot.
A red-cross knight for ever kneel'd
To a lady in his shield,
That sparkled on the yellow field,
    Beside remote Shalott.

The gemmy bridle glitter'd free,
Like to some branch of stars we see
Hung in the golden Galaxy.
The bridle bells rang merrily
    As he rode down to Camelot:

And from his blazon'd baldric slung
A mighty silver bugle hung,
And as he rode his armour rung,
    Beside remote Shalott.

All in the blue unclouded weather
Thick-jewell'd shone the saddle-leather,
The helmet and the helmet-feather
Burn'd like one burning flame together,
    As he rode down to Camelot.
As often thro' the purple night,
Below the starry clusters bright,
Some bearded meteor, trailing light,
    Moves over still Shalott.

His broad clear brow in sunlight glow'd;
On burnish'd hooves his war-horse trode;
From underneath his helmet flow'd
His coal-black curls as on he rode,
    As he rode down to Camelot.
From the bank and from the river
He flash'd into the crystal mirror,
'Tirra lirra,' by the river
    Sang Sir Lancelot.

She left the web, she left the loom,
She made three paces thro' the room,
She saw the water-lily bloom,
She saw the helmet and the plume,
    She look'd down to Camelot.
Out flew the web and floated wide;
The mirror crack'd from side to side;
'The curse is come upon me,' cried
    The Lady of Shalott.

PART IV.

In the stormy east-wind straining,
The pale yellow woods were waning,
The broad stream in his banks complaining,
Heavily the low sky raining
    Over tower'd Camelot;

Down she came and found a boat
Beneath a willow left afloat,
And round about the prow she wrote
    The Lady of Shalott.

And down the river's dim expanse
Like some bold seër in a trance,
Seeing all his own mischance—
With a glassy countenance
    Did she look to Camelot.
And at the closing of the day
She loosed the chain, and down she lay;
The broad stream bore her far away,
    The Lady of Shalott.

Lying, robed in snowy white
That loosely flew to left and right—
The leaves upon her falling light—
Thro' the noises of the night
    She floated down to Camelot:
And as the boat-head wound along
The willowy hills and fields among,
They heard her singing her last song,
    The Lady of Shalott.

Heard a carol, mournful, holy,
Chanted loudly, chanted lowly,
Till her blood was frozen slowly,
And her eyes were darken'd wholly,
    Turn'd to tower'd Camelot.
For ere she reach'd upon the tide
The first house by the water-side,
Singing in her song she died,
    The Lady of Shalott.

Under tower and balcony,
By garden-wall and gallery,
A gleaming shape she floated by,
Dead-pale between the houses high,
    Silent into Camelot.

Out upon the wharfs they came,
Knight and burgher, lord and dame,
And round the prow they read her name,
    The Lady of Shalott.

Who is this? and what is here?
And in the lighted palace near
Died the sound of royal cheer;
And they cross'd themselves for fear,
    All the knights at Camelot:
But Lancelot mused a little space;
He said, 'She has a lovely face;
God in his mercy lend her grace,
    The Lady of Shalott.'

ELEÄNORE.

I.

Thy dark eyes open'd not,
    Nor first reveal'd themselves to English air,
        For there is nothing here,
Which, from the outward to the inward brought,
Moulded thy baby thought.
Far off from human neighbourhood,
    Thou wert born, on a summer morn,
A mile beneath the cedar-wood.
Thy bounteous forehead was not fann'd
    With breezes from our oaken glades,
But thou wert nursed in some delicious land
    Of lavish lights, and floating shades:
And flattering thy childish thought
    The oriental fairy brought,
        At the moment of thy birth,
From old well-heads of haunted rils,
And the hearts of purple hills,
    And shadow'd coves on a sunny shore,
        The choicest wealth of all the earth,
    Jewel or shell, or starry ore,
    To deck thy cradle, Eleänore.

II.

Or the yellow-banded bees,
Thro' half-open lattices
Coming in the scented breeze,
　　Fed thee, a child, lying alone,
　　　With whitest honey in fairy gardens cull'd—
　　A glorious child, dreaming alone,
　　In silk-soft folds, upon yielding down,
With the hum of swarming bees
　　Into dreamful slumber lull'd.

III.

Who may minister to thee?
Summer herself should minister
　　To thee, with fruitage golden-rinded
　　On golden salvers, or it may be,
Youngest Autumn, in a bower
Grape-thicken'd from the light, and blinded
　　With many a deep-hued bell-like flower
Of fragrant trailers, when the air
　　Sleepeth over all the heaven,
　　And the crag that fronts the Even,
　　All along the shadowing shore,
Crimsons over an inland mere,
　　Eleänore!

IV.

How may full-sail'd verse express,
　　How may measured words adore
　　The full-flowing harmony
Of thy swan-like stateliness,
　　　Eleänore?
　　The luxuriant symmetry
Of thy floating gracefulness,
　　　Eleänore?
　　Every turn and glance of thine,
　　Every lineament divine,
　　　Eleänore,

And the steady sunset glow,
   That stays upon thee? For in thee
   Is nothing sudden, nothing single;
Like two streams of incense free
   From one censer in one shrine,
   Thought and motion mingle,
Mingle ever. Motions flow
To one another, even as tho'
They were modulated so
      To an unheard melody,
Which lives about thee, and a sweep
   Of richest pauses, evermore
Drawn from each other mellow-deep;
   Who may express thee, Eleänore?

v.

I stand before thee, Eleänore;
   I see thy beauty gradually unfold,
Daily and hourly, more and more.
I muse, as in a trance, the while
   Slowly, as from a cloud of gold,
Comes out thy deep ambrosial smile.
I muse, as in a trance, whene'er
   The languors of thy love-deep eyes
Float on to me. I would I were
   So tranced, so rapt in ecstasies,
To stand apart, and to adore,
Gazing on thee for evermore,
Serene, imperial Eleänore!

VI.

Sometimes, with most intensity
Gazing, I seem to see
Thought folded over thought, smiling asleep,
Slowly awaken'd, grow so full and deep
In thy large eyes, that, overpower'd quite,
I cannot veil, or droop my sight,
But am as nothing in its light:
As tho' a star, in inmost heaven set,
Ev'n while we gaze on it,

Should slowly round his orb, and slowly grow
To a full face, there like a sun remain
Fix'd—then as slowly fade again,
    And draw itself to what it was before;
      So full, so deep, so slow,
       Thought seems to come and go
    In thy large eyes, imperial Eleänore.

VII.

As thunder-clouds that, hung on high,
    Roof'd the world with doubt and fear,
Floating thro' an evening atmosphere,
Grow golden all about the sky;
In thee all passion becomes passionless,
Touch'd by thy spirit's mellowness,
Losing his fire and active might
    In a silent meditation,
Falling into a still delight,
    And luxury of contemplation:
As waves that up a quiet cove
    Rolling slide, and lying still
    Shadow forth the banks at will:
Or sometimes they swell and move,
   Pressing up against the land,
   With motions of the outer sea:
    And the self-same influence
    Controlleth all the soul and sense
Of Passion gazing upon thee.
His bow-string slacken'd, languid Love,
   Leaning his cheek upon his hand,
   Droops both his wings, regarding thee,
    And so would languish evermore,
    Serene, imperial Eleänore.

VIII.

But when I see thee roam, with tresses unconfined,
While the amorous, odorous wind
   Breathes low between the sunset and the moon;
    Or, in a shadowy saloon,
On silken cushions half reclined;

I watch thy grace ; and in its place
My heart a charmed slumber keeps,
    While I muse upon thy face ;
    And a languid fire creeps
        Thro' my veins to all my frame,
    Dissolvingly and slowly : soon
        From thy rose-red lips MY name
    Floweth ; and then, as in a swoon,
        With dinning sound my ears are rife,
            My tremulous tongue faltereth,
    I lose my colour, I lose my breath,
    I drink the cup of a costly death,
Brimm'd with delirious draughts of warmest life.
    I die with my delight, before
        I hear what I would hear from thee ;
    Yet tell my name again to me,
    I *would* be dying evermore,
    So dying ever, Eleänore.

Of old sat Freedom on the Heights.

Of old sat Freedom on the heights,
    The thunders breaking at her feet :
Above her shook the starry lights :
    She heard the torrents meet.

There in her place she did rejoice,
    Self-gather'd in her prophet-mind,
But fragments of her mighty voice
    Came rolling on the wind.

Then stept she down thro' town and field
    To mingle with the human race,
And part by part to men reveal'd
    The fullness of her face—

Grave mother of majestic works,
    From her isle-altar gazing down,
Who, God-like, grasps the triple forks,
    And, King-like, wears the crown :

Her open eyes desire the truth.
  The wisdom of a thousand years
Is in them. May perpetual youth
  Keep dry their light from tears ;

That her fair form may stand and shine,
  Make bright our days and light our dreams,
Turning to scorn with lips divine
  The falsehood of extremes !

LOVE THOU THY LAND.

Love thou thy land, with love far-brought
    From out the storied Past, and used
    Within the Present, but transfused
Thro' future time by power of thought.

True love turn'd round on fixed poles,
    Love, that endures not sordid ends,
    For English natures, freemen, friends,
Thy brothers and immortal souls.

But pamper not a hasty time,
    Nor feed with crude imaginings
    The herd, wild hearts and feeble wings
That every sophister can lime.

Deliver not the tasks of might
    To weakness, neither hide the ray
    From those, not blind, who wait for day,
Tho' sitting girt with doubtful light.

Make knowledge circle with the winds ;
    But let her herald, Reverence, fly
    Before her to whatever sky
Bear seed of men and growth of minds.

Watch what main-currents draw the years :
    Cut Prejudice against the grain :
    But gentle words are always gain :
Regard the weakness of thy peers :

Nor toil for title, place, or touch
    Of pensions, neither count on praise :
    It grows to guerdon after-days :
Nor deal in watch-words overmuch :

Not clinging to some ancient saw ;
    Not master'd by some modern term ;
    Not swift nor slow to change, but firm :
And in its season bring the law ;

That from Discussion's lip may fall
    With Life, that, working strongly, binds—
    Set in all lights by many minds,
To close the interests of all.

For Nature also, cold and warm,
    And moist and dry, devising long,
    Thro' many agents making strong,
Matures the individual form.

Meet is it changes should control
    Our being, lest we rust in ease.
    We all are changed by still degrees,
All but the basis of the soul.

So let the change which comes be free
    To ingroove itself with that which flies,
    And work, a joint of state, that plies
Its office, moved with sympathy.

A saying, hard to shape in act ;
    For all the past of Time reveals
    A bridal dawn of thunder-peals,
Wherever Thought hath wedded Fact.

Ev'n now we hear with inward strife
    A motion toiling in the gloom—
    The Spirit of the years to come
Yearning to mix himself with Life.

A slow develop'd strength awaits
    Completion in a painful school ;
    Phantoms of other forms of rule,
New Majesties of mighty States—

The warders of the growing hour,
    But vague in vapour, hard to mark ;
    And round them sea and air are dark
With great contrivances of Power.

Of many changes, aptly join'd,
    Is bodied forth the second whole.
    Regard gradation, lest the soul
Of Discord race the rising wind ;

A wind to puff your idol-fires,
    And heap their ashes on the head ;
    To shame the boast so often made,
That we are wiser than our sires.

Oh yet, if Nature's evil star
    Drive men in manhood, as in youth,
    To follow flying steps of Truth
Across the brazen bridge of war—

If New and Old, disastrous feud,
    Must ever shock, like armed foes,
    And this be true, till Time shall close,
That Principles are rain'd in blood ;

Not yet the wise of heart would cease
    To hold his hope thro' shame and guilt,
    But with his hand against the hilt,
Wou'd pace the troubled land, like Peace ;

Not less, tho' dogs of Faction bay,
    Would serve his kind in deed and word,
    Certain, if knowledge bring the sword,
That knowledge takes the sword away—

Would love the gleams of good that broke
    From either side, nor veil his eyes :
    And if some dreadful need should rise
Would strike, and firmly, and one stroke :

To-morrow yet would reap to-day,
    As we bear blossom of the dead ;
    Earn well the thrifty months, nor wed
Raw Haste, half-sister to Delay.

You ask me, why, tho' ill at ease.

You ask me, why, tho' ill at ease,
    Within this region I subsist,
    Whose spirits falter in the mist,
And languish for the purple seas.

It is the land that freemen till,
    That sober-suited Freedom chose,
    The land, where girt with friends or foes
A man may speak the thing he will;

A land of settled government,
    A land of just and old renown,
    Where Freedom slowly broadens down
From precedent to precedent:

Where faction seldom gathers head,
    But by degrees to fullness wrought,
    The strength of some diffusive thought
Hath time and space to work and spread.

Should banded unions persecute
    Opinion, and induce a time
    When single thought is civil crime,
And individual freedom mute;

Tho' Power should make from land to land
    The name of Britain trebly great—
    Tho' every channel of the State
Should fill and choke with golden sand—

Yet waft me from the harbour-mouth,
    Wild wind! I seek a warmer sky,
    And I will see before I die
The palms and temples of the South.

MORTE D'ARTHUR.

So all day long the noise of battle roll'd
Among the mountains by the winter sea;
Until King Arthur's table, man by man,
Had fallen in Lyonness about their Lord,
King Arthur: then, because his wound was deep,
The bold Sir Bedivere uplifted him,
Sir Bedivere, the last of all his knights,
And bore him to a chapel nigh the field,
A broken chancel with a broken cross,
That stood on a dark strait of barren land.
On one side lay the Ocean, and on one
Lay a great water, and the moon was full.
  Then spake King Arthur to Sir Bedivere:
'The sequel of to-day unsolders all
The goodliest fellowship of famous knights
Whereof this world holds record. Such a sleep
They sleep—the men I loved. I think that we
Shall never more, at any future time,
Delight our souls with talk of knightly deeds,
Walking about the gardens and the halls
Of Camelot, as in the days that were.
I perish by this people which I made,—
Tho' Merlin sware that I should come again
To rule once more—but let what will be, be,
I am so deeply smitten thro' the helm
That without help I cannot last till morn.
Thou therefore take my brand Excalibur,
Which was my pride: for thou rememberest how
In those old days, one summer noon, an arm
Rose up from out the bosom of the lake,
Clothed in white samite, mystic, wonderful,
Holding the sword—and how I row'd across
And took it, and have worn it, like a king:
And, wheresoever I am sung or told
In aftertime, this also shall be known:
But now delay not: take Excalibur,

And fling him far into the middle mere:
Watch what thou seëst, and lightly bring me word.'

To him replied the bold Sir Bedivere:
'It is not meet, Sir King, to leave thee thus,
Aidless, alone, and smitten thro' the helm.
A little thing may harm a wounded man.
Yet I thy hest will all perform at full,
Watch what I see, and lightly bring thee word.'

So saying, from the ruin'd shrine he stept
And in the moon athwart the place of tombs,
Where lay the mighty bones of ancient men,
Old knights, and over them the sea-wind sang
Shrill, chill, with flakes of foam. He, stepping down
By zig-zag paths, and juts of pointed rock,
Came on the shining levels of the lake.

There drew he forth the brand Excalibur,
And o'er him, drawing it, the winter moon,
Brightening the skirts of a long cloud, ran forth
And sparkled keen with frost against the hilt:
For all the haft twinkled with diamond sparks,
Myriads of topaz-lights, and jacinth-work
Of subtlest jewellery. He gazed so long
That both his eyes were dazzled, as he stood,
This way and that dividing the swift mind,
In act to throw: but at the last it seem'd
Better to leave Excalibur conceal'd
There in the many-knotted waterflags,
That whistled stiff and dry about the marge.
So strode he back slow to the wounded King.

Then spake King Arthur to Sir Bedivere:
'Hast thou perform'd my mission which I gave?
What is it thou hast seen? or what hast heard?'

And answer made the bold Sir Bedivere:
'I heard the ripple washing in the reeds,
And the wild water lapping on the crag.'

To whom replied King Arthur, faint and pale:
'Thou hast betray'd thy nature and thy name,
Not rendering true answer, as beseem'd
Thy fëalty, nor like a noble knight:

For surer sign had follow'd, either hand,
Or voice, or else a motion of the mere.
This is a shameful thing for men to lie.
Yet now, I charge thee, quickly go again
As thou art lief and dear, and do the thing
I bad thee, watch, and lightly bring me word.'

Then went Sir Bedivere the second time
Across the ridge, and paced beside the mere,
Counting the dewy pebbles, fix'd in thought;
But when he saw the wonder of the hilt,
How curiously and strangely chased, he smote
His palms together, and he cried aloud,

'And if indeed I cast the brand away,
Surely a precious thing, one worthy note,
Should thus be lost for ever from the earth,
Which might have pleased the eyes of many men.
What good should follow this, if this were done?
What harm, undone? deep harm to disobey,
Seeing obedience is the bond of rule.
Were it well to obey then, if a king demand
An act unprofitable, against himself?
The King is sick, and knows not what he does.
What record, or what relic of my lord
Should be to aftertime, but empty breath
And rumours of a doubt? but were this kept,
Stored in some treasure-house of mighty kings,
Some one might show it at a joust of arms,
Saying, "King Arthur's sword, Excalibur,
Wrought by the lonely maiden of the Lake.
Nine years she wrought it, sitting in the deeps
Upon the hidden bases of the hills."
So might some old man speak in the aftertime
To all the people, winning reverence.
But now much honour and much fame were lost.'

So spake he, clouded with his own conceit,
And hid Excalibur the second time,
And so strode back slow to the wounded King.

Then spoke King Arthur, breathing heavily:
'What is it thou hast seen? or what hast heard?'

And answer made the bold Sir Bedivere :
' I heard the water lapping on the crag,
And the long ripple washing in the reeds.'
  To whom replied King Arthur, much in wrath :
' Ah, miserable and unkind, untrue,
Unknightly, traitor-hearted ! Woe is me !
Authority forgets a dying king,
Laid widow'd of the power in his eye
That bow'd the wi.l. I see thee what thou **art,**
For thou, the latest-left of all my knights,
In whom should meet the offices of all,
Thou wouldst betray me for the precious hilt ;
Either from lust of gold, or like a girl
Valuing the giddy pleasure of the eyes.
Yet, for a man may fail in duty twice,
And the third time may prosper, get thee **hence :**
But, if thou spare to fling Excalibur,
I will arise and slay thee with my hands.'
  Then quickly rose Sir Bedivere, and ran,
And, leaping down the ridges lightly, plunged
Among the bulrush-beds, and clutch'd the sword,
And strongly wheel'd and threw it. The great brand
Made lightnings in the splendour of the moon,
And flashing round and round, and whirl'd in an arch,
Shot like a streamer of the northern morn,
Seen where the moving isles of winter shock
By night, with noises of the northern sea.
So flash'd and fell the brand Excalibur :
But ere he dipt the surface, rose an arm
Clothed in white samite, mystic, wonderful,
And caught him by the hilt, and brandish'd him
Three times, and drew him under in the mere.
And lightly went the other to the King.
  Then spoke King Arthur, drawing thicker breath
' Now see I by thine eyes that this is done.
Speak out: what is it thou hast heard, or seen ? '
  And answer made the bold Sir Bedivere :
' Sir King, I closed mine eyelids, lest the gems
Should blind my purpose, for I never saw,

Nor shall see, here or elsewhere, till I die,
Not tho' I live three lives of mortal men,
So great a miracle as yonder hilt.
Then with both hands I flung him, wheeling him;
But when I look'd again, behold an arm,
Clothed in white samite, mystic, wonderful,
That caught him by the hilt, and brandish'd him
Three times, and drew him under in the mere.'

And answer made King Arthur, breathing hard:
' My end draws nigh; 'tis time that I were gone.
Make broad thy shoulders to receive my weight,
And bear me to the margin; yet I fear
My wound hath taken cold, and I shall die.'

So saying, from the pavement he half rose,
Slowly, with pain, reclining on his arm,
And looking wistfully with wide blue eyes
As in a picture. Him Sir Bedivere
Remorsefully regarded thro' his tears,
And would have spoken, but he found not words,
Then took with care, and kneeling on one knee,
O'er both his shoulders drew the languid hands,
And rising bore him thro' the place of tombs.

ULYSSES.

It little profits that an idle king,
By this still hearth, among these barren crags,
Match'd with an aged wife, I mete and dole
Unequal laws unto a savage race,
That hoard, and sleep, and feed, and know not me.
I cannot rest from travel: I will drink
Life to the lees: all times I have enjoy'd
Greatly, have suffer'd greatly, both with those
That loved me, and alone; on shore, and when
Thro' scudding drifts the rainy Hyades
Vext the dim sea: I am become a name;
For always roaming with a hungry heart
Much have I seen and known; cities of men
And manners, climates, councils, governments,

Myself not least, but honour'd of them all;
And drunk delight of battle with my peers,
Far on the ringing plains of windy Troy.
I am a part of all that I have met ;
Yet all experience is an arch wherethro'
Gleams that untravell'd world, whose margin fades
For ever and for ever when I move.
How dull it is to pause, to make an end,
To rust unburnish'd, not to shine in use!
As tho' to breathe were life. Life piled on life
Were all too little, and of one to me
Little remains : but every hour is saved
From that eternal silence, something more,
A bringer of new things ; and vile it were
For some three suns to store and hoard myself,
And this gray spirit yearning in desire
To follow knowledge like a sinking star,
Beyond the utmost bound of human thought.

This is my son, mine own Telemachus,
To whom I leave the sceptre and the Isle—
Well-loved of me, discerning to fulfil
This labour, by slow prudence to make mild
A rugged people, and thro' soft degrees
Subdue them to the useful and the good.
Most blameless is he, centred in the sphere
Of common duties, decent not to fail
In offices of tenderness, and pay
Meet adoration to my household gods,
When I am gone. He works his work, I mine.

There lies the port; the vessel puffs her sail :
There gloom the dark broad seas. My mariners,
Souls that have toil'd, and wrought, and thought with me—
That ever with a frolic welcome took
The thunder and the sunshine, and opposed.
Free hearts, free foreheads—you and I are old ;
Old age hath yet his honour and his toil ;
Death closes all : but something ere the end,
Some work of noble note, may yet be done,
Not unbecoming men that strove with Gods.

The lights begin to twinkle from the rocks :
The long day wanes : the slow moon climbs : the deep
Moans round with many voices. Come, my friends,
'Tis not too late to seek a newer world.
Push off, and sitting well in order smite
The sounding furrows ; for my purpose holds
To sail beyond the sunset, and the baths
Of all the western stars, until I die.
It may be that the gulfs will wash us down :
It may be we shall touch the Happy Isles,
And see the great Achilles, whom we knew.
Tho' much is taken, much abides ; and tho'
We are not now that strength which in old days
Moved earth and heaven ; that which we are, we are;
One equal temper of heroic hearts,
Made weak by time and fate, but strong in will
To strive, to seek, to find, and not to yield.

St. Agnes' Eve.

Deep on the convent-roof the snows
    Are sparkling to the moon :
My breath to heaven like vapour goes :
    May my soul follow soon !
The shadows of the convent-towers
    Slant down the snowy sward,
Still creeping with the creeping hours
    That lead me to my Lord :
Make Thou my spirit pure and clear
    As are the frosty skies,
Or this first snowdrop of the year
    That in my bosom lies.

As these white robes are soil'd and dark,
    To yonder shining ground ;
As this pale taper's earthly spark,
    To yonder argent round ;
So shows my soul before the Lamb,
    My spirit before Thee ;

So in mine earthly house I am,
  To that I hope to be.
Break up the heavens, O Lord! and far,
  Thro' all yon starlight keen,
Draw me, thy bride, a glittering star,
  In raiment white and clean.

He lifts me to the golden doors;
  The flashes come and go;
All heaven bursts her starry floors,
  And strows her lights below,
And deepens on and up! the gates
  Roll back, and far within
For me the Heavenly Bridegroom waits,
  To make me pure of sin.
The sabbaths of Eternity,
  One sabbath deep and wide—
A light upon the shining sea—
  The Bridegroom with his bride!

BREAK, BREAK, BREAK.

Break, break, break,
  On thy cold gray stones, O Sea!
And I would that my tongue could utter
  The thoughts that arise in me.

O well for the fisherman's boy,
  That he shouts with his sister at play!
O well for the sailor lad,
  That he sings in his boat on the bay!

And the stately ships go on
  To their haven under the hill;
But O for the touch of a vanish'd hand,
  And the sound of a voice that is still!

Break, break, break,
  At the foot of thy crags, O Sea!
But the tender grace of a day that is dead
  Will never come back to me.

[From *The Princess.*]

I.

THE SPLENDOUR FALLS ON CASTLE WALLS.

The splendour falls on castle walls
    And snowy summits old in story:
The long light shakes across the lakes,
    And the wild cataract leaps in glory.
Blow, bugle, blow, set the wild echoes flying,
Blow, bugle; answer, echoes, dying, dying, dying.

    O hark, O hear! how thin and clear,
        And thinner, clearer, farther going!
    O sweet and far from cliff and scar
        The horns of Elfland faintly blowing!
Blow, let us hear the purple glens replying:
Blow, bugle; answer, echoes, dying, dying, dying.

    O love, they die in yon rich sky,
        They faint on hill or field or river:
    Our echoes roll from soul to soul,
        And grow for ever and for ever.
Blow, bugle, blow, set the wild echoes flying,
And answer, echoes, answer, dying, dying, dying.

II.

TEARS, IDLE TEARS.

Tears, idle tears, I know not what they mean,
Tears from the depth of some divine despair
Rise in the heart, and gather to the eyes,
In looking on the happy Autumn-fields,
And thinking of the days that are no more.

Fresh as the first beam glittering on a sail,
That brings our friends up from the underworld,
Sad as the last which reddens over one
That sinks with all we love below the verge;
So sad, so fresh, the days that are no more.

Ah, sad and strange as in dark summer dawns
The earliest pipe of half-awaken'd birds
To dying ears, when unto dying eyes
The casement slowly grows a glimmering square;
So sad, so strange, the days that are no more.

Dear as remember'd kisses after death,
And sweet as those by hopeless fancy feign'd
On lips that are for others; deep as love,
Deep as first love, and wild with all regret;
O Death in Life, the days that are no more.

[From *In Memoriam.*]

XIX.

The Danube to the Severn gave
    The darken'd heart that beat no more;
    They laid him by the pleasant shore,
And in the hearing of the wave.

There twice a day the Severn fills;
    The salt sea-water passes by,
    And hushes half the babbling Wye,
And makes a silence in the hills.

The Wye is hush'd nor moved along,
    And hush'd my deepest grief of all,
    When fill'd with tears that cannot fall,
I brim with sorrow drowning song.

The tide flows down, the wave again
    Is vocal in its wooded walls;
    My deeper anguish also falls,
And I can speak a little then.

XXXV.

Yet if some voice that man could trust
    Should murmur from the narrow house,
    'The cheeks drop in; the body bows;
Man dies: nor is there hope in dust:'

Might I not say? 'Yet even here,
    But for one hour, O Love, I strive
    To keep so sweet a thing alive:'
But I should turn mine ears and hear

The moanings of the homeless sea,
    The sound of streams that swift or slow
    Draw down Æonian hills, and sow
The dust of continents to be;

And Love would answer with a sigh,
    'The sound of that forgetful shore
    Will change my sweetness more and more,
Half-dead to know that I shall die.'

O me, what profits it to put
    An idle case? If Death were seen
    At first as Death, Love had not been,
Or been in narrowest working shut,

Mere fellowship of sluggish moods,
    Or in his coarsest Satyr-shape
    Had bruised the herb and crush'd the grape,
And bask'd and batten'd in the woods.

LIV.

Oh yet we trust that somehow good
    Will be the final goal of ill,
    To pangs of nature, sins of will,
Defects of doubt, and taints of blood;

That nothing walks with aimless feet;
    That not one life shall be destroy'd,
    Or cast as rubbish to the void,
When God hath made the pile complete;

That not a worm is cloven in vain;
    That not a moth with vain desire
    Is shrivell'd in a fruitless fire,
Or but subserves another's gain.

Behold, we know not anything;
    I can but trust that good shall fall
    At last—far off—at last, to all,
And every winter change to spring.

So runs my dream: but what am I?
    An infant crying in the night:
    An infant crying for the light:
And with no language but a cry.

CIX.

Heart-affluence in discursive talk
    From household fountains never dry;
    The critic clearness of an eye,
That saw thro' all the Muses' walk;

Seraphic intellect and force
    To seize and throw the doubts of man;
    Impassion'd logic, which outran
The hearer in its fiery course;

High nature amorous of the good,
    But touch'd with no ascetic gloom;
    And passion pure in snowy bloom
Thro' all the years of April blood;

A love of freedom rarely felt,
    Of freedom in her regal seat
    Of England; not the schoolboy heat,
The blind hysterics of the Celt;

And manhood fused with female grace
    In such a sort, the child would twine
    A trustful hand, unask'd, in thine,
And find his comfort in thy face;

All these have been, and thee mine eyes
    Have look'd on: if they look'd in vain,
    My shame is greater who remain,
Nor let thy wisdom make me wise.

CXXIII.

There rolls the deep where grew the tree.
 O earth, what changes hast thou seen!
 There where the long street roars, hath been
The stillness of the central sea.

The hills are shadows, and they flow
 From form to form, and nothing stands;
 They melt like mist, the solid lands,
Like clouds they shape themselves and go.

But in my spirit will I dwell,
 And dream my dream, and hold it true;
 For tho' my lips may breathe adieu,
I cannot think the thing farewell.

[From *Maud*, Part I. xviii.]

I.

I have led her home, my love, my only friend.
There is none like her, none.
And never yet so warmly ran my blood
And sweetly, on and on
Calming itself to the long-wish'd-for end,
Full to the banks, close on the promised good.

II.

None like her, none.
Just now the dry-tongued laurels' pattering talk
Seem'd her light foot along the garden walk,
And shook my heart to think she comes once more;
But even then I heard her close the door,
The gates of Heaven are closed, and she is gone.

III.

There is none like her, none.
Nor will be when our summers have deceased.
O, art thou sighing for Lebanon
In the long breeze that streams to thy delicious East,
Sighing for Lebanon,
Dark cedar, tho' thy limbs have here increased,

Upon a pastoral slope as fair,
And looking to the South, and fed
With honey'd rain and delicate air,
And haunted by the starry head
Of her whose gentle will has changed my fate,
And made my life a perfumed altar-flame ;
And over whom thy darkness must have spread
With such delight as theirs of old, thy great
Forefathers of the thornless garden, there
Shadowing the snow-limb'd Eve from whom she came.

IV.

Here will I lie, while these long branches sway,
And you fair stars that crown a happy day
Go in and out as if at merry play,
Who am no more so all forlorn,
As when it seem'd far better to be born
To labour and the mattock-harden'd hand,
Than nursed at ease and brought to understand
A sad astrology, the boundless plan
That makes you tyrants in your iron skies,
Innumerable, pitiless, passionless eyes,
Cold fires, yet with power to burn and brand
His nothingness into man.

V.

But now shine on, and what care I,
Who in this stormy gulf have found a pearl
The countercharm of space and hollow sky,
And do accept my madness, and would die
To save from some slight shame one simple girl.

VI.

Would die ; for sullen-seeming Death may give
More life to Love than is or ever was
In our low world, where yet 'tis sweet to live.
Let no one ask me how it came to pass ;
It seems that I am happy, that to me
A livelier emerald twinkles in the grass,
A purer sapphire melts into the sea.

VII.

Not die ; but live a life of truest breath,
And teach true life to fight with mortal wrongs.
O, why should Love, like men in drinking-songs,
Spice his fair banquet with the dust of death?
Make answer, Maud my bliss,
Maud made my Maud by that long loving kiss,
Life of my life, wilt thou not answer this?
'The dusky strand of Death inwoven here
With dear Love's tie, makes Love himself more dear.'

VIII.

Is that enchanted moan only the swell
Of the long waves that roll in yonder bay?
And hark the clock within, the silver knell
Of twelve sweet hours that past in bridal white,
And died to live, long as my pulses play ;
But now by this my love has closed her sight
And given false death her hand, and stol'n away
To dreamful wastes where footless fancies dwell
Among the fragments of the golden day.
May nothing there her maiden grace affright!
Dear heart, I feel with thee the drowsy spell.
My bride to be, my evermore delight,
My own heart's heart, my ownest own, farewell;
It is but for a little space I go :
And ye meanwhile far over moor and fell
Beat to the noiseless music of the night!
Has our whole earth gone nearer to the glow
Of your soft splendours that you look so bright?
I have climb'd nearer out of lonely Hell.
Beat, happy stars, timing with things below,
Beat with my heart more blest than heart can tell,
Blest, but for some dark undercurrent woe
That seems to draw—but it shall not be so:
Let all be well, be well.

THE BROOK.

I come from haunts of coot and hern,
    I make a sudden sally,
And sparkle out among the fern,
    To bicker down a valley.

By thirty hills I hurry down,
    Or slip between the ridges,
By twenty thorps, a little town,
    And half a hundred bridges.

Till last by Philip's farm I flow
    To join the brimming river,
For men may come and men may go,
    But I go on for ever.

I chatter over stony ways,
    In little sharps and trebles,
I bubble into eddying bays,
    I babble on the pebbles.

With many a curve my banks I fret
    By many a field and fallow,
And many a fairy foreland set
    With willow-weed and mallow.

I chatter, chatter, as I flow
    To join the brimming river,
For men may come and men may go,
    But I go on for ever.

I wind about, and in and out,
    With here a blossom sailing,
And here and there a lusty trout,
    And here and there a grayling,

And here and there a foamy flake
    Upon me, as I travel
With many a silvery waterbreak
    Above the golden gravel,

And draw them all along, and flow
  To join the brimming river,
For men may come and men may go,
  But I go on for ever.

I steal by lawns and grassy plots,
  I slide by hazel covers;
I move the sweet forget-me-nots
  That grow for happy lovers.

I slip, I slide, I gloom, I glance,
  Among my skimming swallows;
I make the netted sunbeam dance
  Against my sandy shallows.

I murmur under moon and stars
  In brambly wildernesses;
I linger by my shingly bars;
  I loiter round my cresses;

And out again I curve and flow
  To join the brimming river,
For men may come and men may go,
  But I go on for ever.

ODE ON THE DEATH OF THE DUKE OF WELLINGTON.

[Published in 1852.]

I.

Bury the Great Duke
  With an empire's lamentation,
Let us bury the Great Duke
  To the noise of the mourning of a mighty nation,
Mourning when their leaders fall,
Warriors carry the warrior's pall,
And sorrow darkens hamlet and hall.

II.

Where shall we lay the man whom we deplore?
Here, in streaming London's central roar.
Let the sound of those he wrought for,
And the feet of those he fought for,
Echo round his bones for evermore.

III.

Lead out the pageant: sad and slow,
As fits an universal woe,
Let the long long procession go,
And let the sorrowing crowd about it grow,
And let the mournful martial music blow;
The last great Englishman is low.

IV.

Mourn, for to us he seems the last,
Remembering all his greatness in the Past.
No more in soldier fashion will he greet
With lifted hand the gazer in the street.
O friends, our chief state-oracle is mute:
Mourn for the man of long-enduring blood,
The statesman-warrior, moderate, resolute,
Whole in himself, a common good.
Mourn for the man of amplest influence,
Yet clearest of ambitious crime,
Our greatest yet with least pretence,
Great in council and great in war,
Foremost captain of his time,
Rich in saving common-sense,
And, as the greatest only are,
In his simplicity sublime.
O good gray head which all men knew,
O voice from which their omens all men drew,
O iron nerve to true occasion true,
O fall'n at length that tower of strength
Which stood four-square to all the winds that blew!

Such was he whom we deplore.
The long self-sacrifice of life is o'er.
The great World-victor's victor will be seen no more.

V.

All is over and done:
Render thanks to the Giver,
England, for thy son.
Let the bell be toll'd.
Render thanks to the Giver,
And render him to the mould.
Under the cross of gold
That shines over city and river,
There he shall rest for ever
Among the wise and the bold.
Let the bell be toll'd:
And a reverent people behold
The towering car, the sable steeds:
Bright let it be with its blazon'd deeds,
Dark in its funeral fold.
Let the bell be toll'd:
And a deeper knell in the heart be knoll'd;
And the sound of the sorrowing anthem roll'd
Thro' the dome of the golden cross;
And the volleying cannon thunder his loss;
He knew their voices of old.
For many a time in many a clime
His captain's-ear has heard them boom
Bellowing victory, bellowing doom:
When he with those deep voices wrought,
Guarding realms and kings from shame;
With those deep voices our dead captain taught
The tyrant, and asserts his claim
In that dread sound to the great name,
Which he has worn so pure of blame,
In praise and in dispraise the same,
A man of well-attemper'd frame.
O civic muse, to such a name,

To such a name for ages long,
To such a name,
Preserve a broad approach of fame,
And ever-echoing avenues of song.

VI.

Who is he that cometh, like an honour'd guest,
With banner and with music, with soldier and with priest,
With a nation weeping, and breaking on my rest?
Mighty Seaman, this is he
Was great by land as thou by sea.
Thine island loves thee well, thou famous man,
The greatest sailor since our world began.
Now, to the roll of muffled drums,
To thee the greatest soldier comes;
For this is he
Was great by land as thou by sea;
His foes were thine; he kept us free;
O give him welcome, this is he
Worthy of our gorgeous rites,
And worthy to be laid by thee;
For this is England's greatest son,
He that gain'd a hundred fights,
Nor ever lost an English gun;
This is he that far away
Against the myriads of Assaye
Clash'd with his fiery few and won;
And underneath another sun,
Warring on a later day,
Round affrighted Lisbon drew
The treble works, the vast designs
Of his labour'd rampart-lines,
Where he greatly stood at bay,
Whence he issued forth anew,
And ever great and greater grew,
Beating from the wasted vines
Back to France her banded swarms,
Back to France with countless blows,

Till o'er the hills her eagles flew
Beyond the Pyrenean pines,
Follow'd up in valley and glen
With blare of bugle, clamour of men,
Roll of cannon and clash of arms,
And England pouring on her foes.
Such a war had such a close.
Again their ravening eagle rose
In anger, wheel'd on Europe-shadowing wings,
And barking for the thrones of kings;
Till one that sought but Duty's iron crown
On that loud sabbath shook the spoiler down;
A day of onsets of despair!
Dash'd on every rocky square
Their surging charges foam'd themselves away;
Last, the Prussian trumpet blew;
Thro' the long-tormented air
Heaven flash'd a sudden jubilant ray,
And down we swept and charged and overthrew.
So great a soldier taught us there,
What long-enduring hearts could do
In that world-earthquake, Waterloo!
Mighty Seaman, tender and true,
And pure as he from taint of craven guile,
O saviour of the silver-coasted isle,
O shaker of the Baltic and the Nile,
If aught of things that here befall
Touch a spirit among things divine,
If love of country move thee there at all,
Be glad, because his bones are laid by thine!
And thro' the centuries let a people's voice
In full acclaim,
A people's voice,
The proof and echo of all human fame,
A people's voice, when they rejoice
At civic revel and pomp and game,
Attest their great commander's claim
With honour, honour, honour, honour to **him**,
Eternal honour to his name.

VII.

A people's voice! we are a people yet.
Tho' all men else their nobler dreams forget,
Confused by brainless mobs and lawless Powers;
Thank Him who isled us here, and roughly set
His Briton in blown seas and storming showers,
We have a voice, with which to pay the debt
Of boundless love and reverence and regret
To those great men who fought, and kept it ours.
And keep it ours, O God, from brute control;
O Statesmen, guard us, guard the eye, the soul
Of Europe, keep our noble England whole,
And save the one true seed of freedom sown
Betwixt a people and their ancient throne,
That sober freedom out of which there springs
Our loyal passion for our temperate kings;
For, saving that, ye help to save mankind
Till public wrong be crumbled into dust,
And drill the raw world for the march of mind,
Till crowds at length be sane and crowns be just.
But wink no more in slothful overtrust.
Remember him who led your hosts;
He bad you guard the sacred coasts.
Your cannons moulder on the seaward wall;
His voice is silent in your council-hall
For ever; and whatever tempests lour
For ever silent; even if they broke
In thunder, silent; yet remember all
He spoke among you, and the Man who spoke;
Who never sold the truth to serve the hour,
Nor palter'd with Eternal God for power;
Who let the turbid streams of rumour flow
Thro' either babbling world of high and low;
Whose life was work, whose language rife
With rugged maxims hewn from life;
Who never spoke against a foe;
Whose eighty winters freeze with one rebuke
All great self-seekers trampling on the right:

Truth-teller was our England's Alfred named;
Truth-lover was our English Duke;
Whatever record leap to light
He never shall be shamed.

VIII.

Lo, the leader in these glorious wars
Now to glorious burial slowly borne,
Follow'd by the brave of other lands,
He, on whom from both her open hands
Lavish Honour shower'd all her stars,
And affluent Fortune emptied all her horn.
Yea, let all good things await
Him who cares not to be great,
But as he saves or serves the state.
Not once or twice in our rough island-story,
The path of duty was the way to glory:
He that walks it, only thirsting
For the right, and learns to deaden
Love of self, before his journey closes,
He shall find the stubborn thistle bursting
Into glossy purples, which outredden
All voluptuous garden-roses.
Not once or twice in our fair island-story,
The path of duty was the way to glory:
He, that ever following her commands,
On with toil of heart and knees and hands,
Thro' the long gorge to the far light has won
His path upward, and prevail'd,
Shall find the toppling crags of Duty scaled
Are close upon the shining table-lands
To which our God Himself is moon and sun.
Such was he: his work is done.
But while the races of mankind endure,
Let his great example stand
Colossal, seen of every land,
And keep the soldier firm, the statesman pure:
Till in all lands and thro' all human story
The path of duty be the way to glory:

And let the land whose hearths he saved from shame
For many and many an age proclaim
At civic revel and pomp and game,
And when the long-illumined cities flame,
Their ever-loyal iron leader's fame,
With honour, honour, honour, honour to him,
Eternal honour to his name.

IX.

Peace, his triumph will be sung
By some yet unmoulded tongue
Far on in summers that we shall not see:
Peace, it is a day of pain
For one about whose patriarchal knee
Late the little children clung:
O peace, it is a day of pain
For one, upon whose hand and heart and brain
Once the weight and fate of Europe hung.
Ours the pain, be his the gain!
More than is of man's degree
Must be with us, watching here
At this, our great solemnity.
Whom we see not we revere;
We revere, and we refrain
From talk of battles loud and vain,
And brawling memories all too free
For such a wise humility
As befits a solemn fane:
We revere, and while we hear
The tides of Music's golden sea
Setting toward eternity,
Uplifted high in heart and hope are we,
Until we doubt not that for one so true
There must be other nobler work to do
Than when he fought at Waterloo,
And Victor he must ever be.
For tho' the Giant Ages heave the hill
And break the shore, and evermore
Make and break, and work their will;

Tho' world on world in myriad myriads roll
Round us, each with different powers,
And other forms of life than ours,
What know we greater than the soul?
On God and Godlike men we build our trust.
Hush, the Dead March wails in the people's ears:
The dark crowd moves, and there are sobs and tears:
The black earth yawns: the mortal disappears;
Ashes to ashes, dust to dust;
He is gone who seem'd so great.—
Gone; but nothing can bereave him
Of the force he made his own
Being here, and we believe him
Something far advanced in State,
And that he wears a truer crown
Than any wreath that man can weave him.
Speak no more of his renown,
Lay your earthly fancies down,
And in the vast cathedral leave him.
God accept him, Christ receive him.

THE CHARGE OF THE LIGHT BRIGADE.

I.

Half a league, half a league,
    Half a league onward,
All in the valley of Death
    Rode the six hundred.
'Forward, the Light Brigade!
Charge for the guns!' he said:
Into the valley of Death
    Rode the six hundred.

II.

'Forward, the Light Brigade!'
Was there a man dismay'd?
Not tho' the soldier knew
    Some one had blunder'd:—

Their's not to make reply,
Their's not to reason why,
Their's but to do and die:
Into the valley of Death
   Rode the six hundred.

III.

Cannon to right of them,
Cannon to left of them,
Cannon in front of them
   Volley'd and thunder'd;
Storm'd at with shot and shell,
Boldly they rode and well,
Into the jaws of Death,
Into the mouth of Hell
   Rode the six hundred.

IV.

Flash'd all their sabres bare,
Flash'd as they turn'd in air
Sabring the gunners there,
Charging an army, while
   All the world wonder'd:
Plunged in the battery-smoke
Right thro' the line they broke;
Cossack and Russian
Reel'd from the sabre-stroke
   Shatter'd and sunder'd.
Then they rode back, but not
   Not the six hundred.

V.

Cannon to right of them,
Cannon to left of them,
Cannon behind them
   Volley'd and thunder'd;
Storm'd at with shot and shell,
While horse and hero fell,
They that had fought so well

Came thro' the jaws of Death,
Back from the mouth of Hell,
All that was left of them,
Left of six hundred.

VI.

When can their glory fade?
O the wild charge they made!
All the world wonder'd.
Honour the charge they made!
Honour the Light Brigade,
Noble six hundred!

NORTHERN FARMER.

OLD STYLE.

I.

Wheer 'asta beän saw long and meä liggin' 'ere aloän?
Noorse? thourt nowt o' a noorse: whoy, Doctor's abeän an' agoän:
Says that I moänt 'a naw moor aäle: but I beänt a fool:
Git ma my aäle, fur I beänt a-gawin' to breäk my rule.

II.

Doctors, they knaws nowt, fur a says what's nawways true:
Naw soort o' koind o' use to saäy the things that a do.
I've 'ed my point o' aäle ivry noight sin' I beän 'ere,
An' I've 'ed my quart ivry market-noight for foorty year.

III.

Parson's a beän loikewoise, an' a sittin' 'ere o' my bed.
'The amoighty's a taäkin o' you[1] to 'issén, my friend,' a said,
An' a towd ma my sins, an's toithe were due, an' I gied it in hond;
I done moy duty boy 'um, as I 'a done boy the lond.

IV.

Larn'd a ma' beä. I reckons I 'annot sa mooch to larn.
But a cast oop, thot a did, 'bout Bessy Marris's barne.
Thaw a knaws I hallus voäted wi' Squoire an' choorch and staäte,
An' i' the woost o' toimes I wur niver agin the raäte.

---

[1] ou as in hour.

V.

An' I hallus coom'd to 's choorch afoor moy Sally wur deäd,
An' 'eärd 'um a bummin' awaäy loike a buzzard-clock[1] ower my
  'eäd,
An' I niver knaw'd whot a meän'd, but I thowt a 'ad summut to
  saäy,
An' I thowt a said whot a owt to 'a said an' I coom'd awaäy.

VI.

Bessy Marris's barne! tha knaws she laäid it to meä.
Mowt a beän, mayhap, for she wur a bad un, sheä.
'Siver, I kep 'um, I kep 'um, my lass, tha mun understond;
I done moy duty boy 'um as I 'a done boy the lond.

VII.

But Parson a cooms an' a goäs, an' a says it eäsy an' freeä
'The amoighty's a taäkin o' you to 'issén, my friend,' says 'eä
I weänt saäy men be loiars, thaw summun said it in 'aäste:
But 'e reäds wonn sarmin a weeäk, an' I 'a stubb'd Thurnaby waäste.

VIII.

D'ya moind the waäste, my lass? naw, naw, tha was not born then,
Theer wur a boggle in it, I often 'eärd 'um mysen;
Moäst loike a butter-bump[2], fur I 'eärd 'um about an' about,
But I stubb'd 'um oop wi' the lot, an' raäved an' rembled 'um out.

IX.

Keäper's it wur; fo' they tun 'um theer a-laäid of 'is faäce
Down i' the woild 'enemies[3] afoor I coom'd to the plaäce.
Noäks or Thimbleby—toäner[4] 'ed shot 'um as deäd as a naäil.
Noäks wur 'ang'd for it oop at 'soize—but git ma my aäle.

X.

Dubbut looök at the waäste: theer warn't not feeäd for a cow;
Nowt at all but bracken an' fuzz, an' looök at it now
Warnt worth nowt a haäcre, an' now theer's lots of feeäd,
Fourscoor[5] yows upon it an' some on it down i' seeäd.

---

[1] Cockchafer.   [2] Bittern.   [3] Anemones.   [4] One or other.
                  [5] ou as in hour.

XI.

Nobbut a bit on it's left, an' I meän'd to 'a stubb'd it at fall,
Done it ta-year I meän'd, an' runn'd plow thruff it an' all,
If godamoighty an' parson 'ud nobbut let ma aloän,
Meä, wi' haäte hoonderd haäcre o' Squoire's, an' lond o' my oän.

XII.

Do godamoighty knaw what a's doing a-taäkin' o' meä?
I beänt wonn as saws 'ere a beän an' yonder a peä;
An' Squoire 'ull be sa mad an' all—a' dear a' dear!
And I 'a managed for Squoire coom Michaelmas thutty year.

XIII.

A mowt 'a taäen owd Joänes, as 'ant nor a 'aäpoth o' sense,
Or a mowt 'a taäen young Robins—a niver mended a fence:
But godamoighty a moost taäke meä an' taäke ma now
Wi' aäf the cows to cauve an' Thurnaby hoälms to plow!

XIV.

Looök 'ow quoloty smiles when they seeäs ma a passin' boy,
Says to thessén naw doubt 'what a man a beä sewer-loy!'
Fur they knaws what I beän to Squoire sin fust a coom'd to
    the 'All;
I done moy duty by Squoire an' I done moy duty boy hall.

XV.

Squoire's i' Lunnon, an' summun I reckons 'ull 'a to wroite,
For whoä's to howd the lond ater meä thot muddles ma quoit;
Sartin-sewer I beä, thot a weänt niver give it to Joänes,
Naw, nor a moänt to Robins—a niver rembles the stoäns.

XVI.

But summun 'ull come ater meä mayhap wi' 'is kittle o' steäm
Huzzin' an' maäzin' the blessed feälds wi' the Divil's oän teäm.
Sin' I mun doy I mun doy, thaw loife they says is sweet,
But sin' I mun doy I mun doy, for I couldn abeär to see it.

XVII.

What atta stannin' theer fur, an' doesn bring ma the aäle?
Doctor's a 'toättler, lass, an a's hallus i' the owd taäle;
I weänt breäk rules fur Doctor, a knaws naw moor nor a floy;
Git ma my aäle I tell tha, an' if I mun doy I mun doy.

TITHONUS.

The woods decay, the woods decay and fall,
The vapours weep their burthen to the ground,
Man comes and tills the field and lies beneath,
And after many a summer dies the swan.
Me only cruel immortality
Consumes : I wither slowly in thine arms,
Here at the quiet limit of the world,
A white-hair'd shadow roaming like a dream
The ever-silent spaces of the East,
Far-folded mists, and gleaming halls of morn.

Alas ! for this gray shadow, once a man—
So glorious in his beauty and thy choice,
Who madest him thy chosen, that he seem'd
To his great heart none other than a God !
I ask'd thee, 'Give me immortality.'
Then didst thou grant mine asking with a smile,
Like wealthy men who care not how they give.
But thy strong Hours indignant work'd their wills,
And beat me down and marr'd and wasted me,
And tho' they could not end me, left me maim'd
To dwell in presence of immortal youth,
Immortal age beside immortal youth,
And all I was, in ashes. Can thy love,
Thy beauty, make amends, tho' even now,
Close over us, the silver star, thy guide,
Shines in those tremulous eyes that fill with tears
To hear me ? Let me go : take back thy gift :
Why should a man desire in any way
To vary from the kindly race of men,
Or pass beyond the goal of ordinance
Where all should pause, as is most meet for all ?

A soft air fans the cloud apart; there comes
A glimpse of that dark world where I was born.
Once more the old mysterious glimmer steals
From thy pure brows, and from thy shoulders pure,
And bosom beating with a heart renew'd.
Thy cheek begins to redden thro' the gloom,
Thy sweet eyes brighten slowly close to mine,
Ere yet they blind the stars, and the wild team
Which love thee, yearning for thy yoke, arise,
And shake the darkness from their loosen'd manes,
And beat the twilight into flakes of fire.

Lo! ever thus thou growest beautiful
In silence, then before thine answer given
Departest, and thy tears are on my cheek.

Why wilt thou ever scare me with thy tears,
And make me tremble lest a saying learnt,
In days far-off, on that dark earth, be true?
'The Gods themselves cannot recall their gifts.'

Ay me! ay me! with what another heart
In days far-off, and with what other eyes
I used to watch—if I be he that watch'd—
The lucid outline forming round thee; saw
The dim curls kindle into sunny rings;
Changed with thy mystic change, and felt my blood
Glow with the glow that slowly crimson'd all
Thy presence and thy portals, while I lay,
Mouth, forehead, eyelids, growing dewy-warm
With kisses balmier than half-opening buds
Of April, and could hear the lips that kiss'd
Whispering I knew not what of wild and sweet,
Like that strange song I heard Apollo sing,
While Ilion like a mist rose into towers.

Yet hold me not for ever in thine East:
How can my nature longer mix with thine?
Coldly thy rosy shadows bathe me, cold
Are all thy lights, and cold my wrinkled feet
Upon thy glimmering thresholds, when the steam

Floats up from those dim fields about the homes
Of happy men that have the power to die,
And grassy barrows of the happier dead.
Release me, and restore me to the ground;
Thou seëst all things, thou wilt see my grave:
Thou wi t renew thy beauty morn by morn;
I earth in earth forget these empty courts,
And thee returning on thy silver wheels.

MILTON.

(Alcaics.)

O mighty-mouth'd inventor of harmonies,
O skill'd to sing of Time or Eternity,
   God-gifted organ-voice of England,
     Milton, a name to resound for ages;
Whose Titan angels, Gabriel, Abdiel,
Starr'd from Jehovah's gorgeous armouries,
   Tower, as the deep-domed empyrëan
     Rings to the roar of an angel onset—
Me rather all that bowery loneliness,
The brooks of Eden mazily murmuring,
   And bloom profuse and cedar arches
     Charm, as a wanderer out in ocean,
Where some refulgent sunset of India
Streams o'er a rich ambrosial ocean isle,
   And crimson-hued the stately palm-woods
     Whisper in odorous heights of even.

THE SAILOR BOY.

He rose at dawn and, fired with hope,
   Shot o'er the seething harbour-bar,
And reach'd the ship and caught the rope
   And whistled to the morning star.

And while he whistled long and loud
   He heard a fierce mermaiden cry,
'O boy, tho' thou art young and proud,
   I see the place where thou wilt lie.

'The sands and yeasty surges mix
    In caves about the dreary bay,
And on thy ribs the limpet sticks,
    And in thy heart the scrawl shall play.'

'Fool,' he answer'd, 'death is sure
    To those that stay and those that roam,
But I will nevermore endure
    To sit with empty hands at home.

'My mother clings about my neck,
    My sisters crying, "Stay for shame;"
My father raves of death and wreck,
    They are all to blame, they are all to blame.

'God help me! save I take my part
    Of danger on the roaring sea,
A devil rises in my heart,
    Far worse than any death to me.'

[From *Idylls of the King: Guinevere.*]

ARTHUR'S FAREWELL.

He paused, and in the pause she crept an inch
Nearer, and laid her hands about his feet.
Far off a solitary trumpet blew.
Then waiting by the doors the warhorse neigh'd
As at a friend's voice, and he spake again :

'Yet think not that I come to urge thy crimes,
I did not come to curse thee, Guinevere,
I, whose vast pity almost makes me die
To see thee, laying there thy golden head,
My pride in happier summers, at my feet.
The wrath which forced my thoughts on that fierce law,
The doom of treason and the flaming death,
(When first I learnt thee hidden here) is past.
The pang—which while I weigh'd thy heart with one
Too wholly true to dream untruth in thee,
Made my tears burn—is also past—in part.
And all is past, the sin is sinn'd, and I,
Lo! I forgive thee, as Eternal God
Forgives : do thou for thine own soul the rest.

But how to take last leave of all I loved?
O golden hair, with which I used to play
Not knowing! O imperial-moulded form,
And beauty such as never woman wore,
Until it came a kingdom's curse with thee—
I cannot touch thy lips, they are not mine,
But Lancelot's: nay, they never were the King's.
I cannot take thy hand; that too is flesh,
And in the flesh thou hast sinn'd; and mine own flesh,
Here looking down on thine polluted, cries
"I loathe thee:" yet not less, O Guinevere,
For I was ever virgin save for thee,
My love thro' flesh hath wrought into my life
So far, that my doom is, I love thee still.
Let no man dream but that I love thee still.
Perchance, and so thou purify thy soul,
And so thou lean on our fair father Christ,
Hereafter in that world where all are pure
We two may meet before high God, and thou
Wilt spring to me, and claim me thine, and know
I am thine husband—not a smaller soul,
Nor Lancelot, nor another. Leave me that,
I charge thee, my last hope. Now must I hence.
Thro' the thick night I hear the trumpet blow:
They summon me their King to lead mine hosts
Far down to that great battle in the west,
Where I must strike against the man they call
My sister's son—no kin of mine, who leagues
With Lords of the White Horse, heathen, and knights,
Traitors—and strike him dead, and meet myself
Death, or I know not what mysterious doom.
And thou remaining here wilt learn the event;
But hither shall I never come again,
Never lie by thy side; see thee no more—
Farewell!'

       And while she grovell'd at his feet,
She felt the King's breath wander o'er her neck,
And in the darkness o'er her fallen head,
Perceived the waving of his hands that blest.

The Revenge.

A Ballad of the Fleet.

I.

At Flores in the Azores Sir Richard Grenville lay,
And a pinnace, like a flutter'd bird, came flying from far away:
'Spanish ships of war at sea! we have sighted fifty-three!'
Then sware Lord Thomas Howard: ''Fore God I am no coward;
But I cannot meet them here, for my ships are out of gear,
And the half my men are sick. I must fly, but follow quick.
We are six ships of the line; can we fight with fifty-three?'

II.

Then spake Sir Richard Grenville: 'I know you are no coward;
You fly them for a moment to fight with them again.
But I've ninety men and more that are lying sick ashore.
I should count myself the coward if I left them, my Lord Howard,
To these Inquisition dogs and the devildoms of Spain.'

III.

So Lord Howard past away with five ships of war that day,
Till he melted like a cloud in the silent summer heaven;
But Sir Richard bore in hand all his sick men from the land
Very carefully and slow,
Men of Bideford in Devon,
And we laid them on the ballast down below;
For we brought them all aboard,
And they blest him in their pain, that they were not left to
    Spain,
To the thumbscrew and the stake, for the glory of the Lord.

IV.

He had only a hundred seamen to work the ship and to fight,
And he sailed away from Flores till the Spaniard came in sight,
With his huge sea-castles heaving upon the weather bow.
'Shall we fight or shall we fly?
Good Sir Richard, tell us now,
For to fight is but to die!

There 'll be little of us left by the time this sun be set.'
And Sir Richard said again : ' We be all good English men.
Let us bang these dogs of Seville, the children of the devil,
For I never turn'd my back upon Don or devil yet.'

V.

Sir Richard spoke and he laugh'd, and we roar'd a hurrah, and so
The little Revenge ran on sheer into the heart of the foe,
With her hundred fighters on deck, and her ninety sick below;
For half of their fleet to the right and half to the left were seen,
And the little Revenge ran on thro' the long sea-lane between.

VI.

Thousands of their soldiers look'd down from their decks and
     laugh'd,
Thousands of their seamen made mock at the mad little craft
Running on and on, till delay'd
By their mountain-like San Philip that, of fifteen hundred tons,
And up-shadowing high above us with her yawning tiers of guns,
Took the breath from our sails, and we stay'd.

VII.

And while now the great San Philip hung above us like a cloud
Whence the thunderbolt will fall
Long and loud,
Four galleons drew away
From the Spanish fleet that day,
And two upon the larboard and two upon the starboard lay,
And the battle-thunder broke from them all.

VIII.

But anon the great San Philip, she bethought herself and went
Having that within her womb that had left her ill content ;
And the rest they came aboard us, and they fought us hand to
     hand,
For a dozen times they came with their pikes and musqueteers,
And a dozen times we shook 'em off as a dog that shakes his ears
When he leaps from the water to the land.

IX.

And the sun went down, and the stars came out far over the
    summer sea,
But never a moment ceased the fight of the one and the fifty-
    three.
Ship after ship, the whole night long, their high-built galleons
    came,
Ship after ship, the whole night long, with her battle-thunder
    and flame ;
Ship after ship, the whole night long, drew back with her dead
    and her shame.
For some were sunk and many were shatter'd, and so could
    fight us no more—
God of battles, was ever a battle like this in the world before ?

X.

For he said ' Fight on ! fight on !'
Tho' his vessel was all but a wreck ;
And it chanced that, when half of the short summer night was
    gone,
With a grisly wound to be drest he had left the deck,
But a bullet struck him that was dressing it suddenly dead,
And himself he was wounded again in the side and the head,
And he said ' Fight on ! fight on !'

XI.

And the night went down, and the sun smiled out far over the
    summer sea,
And the Spanish fleet with broken sides lay round us all in a
    ring ;
But they dared not touch us again, for they fear'd that we still
    could sting,
So they watch'd what the end would be.
And we had not fought them in vain,
But in perilous plight were we,
Seeing forty of our poor hundred were slain,
And half of the rest of us maim'd for life
In the crash of the cannonades and the desperate strife ;

And the sick men down in the hold were most of them stark
    and cold,
And the pikes were all broken or bent, and the powder was all
    of it spent;
And the masts and the rigging were lying over the side;
But Sir Richard cried in his English pride,
'We have fought such a fight for a day and a night
As may never be fought again!
We have won great glory, my men!
And a day less or more
At sea or ashore,
We die—does it matter when?
Sink me the ship, Master Gunner—sink her, split her in twain!
Fall into the hands of God, not into the hands of Spain!'

XII.

And the gunner said 'Ay, ay,' but the seamen made reply:
'We have children, we have wives,
And the Lord hath spared our lives.
We will make the Spaniard promise, if we yield, to let us go;
We shall live to fight again and to strike another blow.'
And the lion there lay dying, and they yielded to the foe.

XIII.

And the stately Spanish men to their flagship bore him then,
Where they laid him by the mast, old Sir Richard caught at last,
And they praised him to his face with their courtly foreign grace;
But he rose upon their decks, and he cried:
'I have fought for Queen and Faith like a valiant man and true;
I have only done my duty as a man is bound to do:
With a joyful spirit I Sir Richard Grenville die!'
And he fell upon their decks, and he died.

XIV.

And they stared at the dead that had been so valiant and true,
And had holden the power and glory of Spain so cheap
That he dared her with one little ship and his English few;
Was he devil or man? He was devil for aught they knew,
But they sank his body with honour down into the deep,

And they mann'd the Revenge with a swarthier alien crew,
And away she sail'd with her loss and long'd for her own;
When a wind from the lands they had ruin'd awoke from sleep,
And the water began to heave and the weather to moan,
And or ever that evening ended a great gale blew,
And a wave like the wave that is raised by an earthquake grew,
Till it smote on their hulls and their sails and their masts and
  their flags,
And the whole sea plunged and fell on the shot-shatter'd navy
  of Spain,
And the little Revenge herself went down by the island crags
To be lost evermore in the main.

To Virgil.

*Written at the request of the Mantuans for the nineteenth centenary of
Virgil's death.*

I.

Roman Virgil, thou that singest
      Ilion's lofty temples robed in fire,
Ilion falling, Rome arising,
      wars, and filial faith, and Dido's pyre;

II.

Landscape-lover, lord of language
      more than he that sang the Works and Days,
All the chosen coin of fancy
      flashing out from many a golden phrase;

III.

Thou that singest wheat and woodland,
      tilth and vineyard, hive and horse and herd;
All the charm of all the Muses
      often flowering in a lonely word;

IV.

Poet of the happy Tityrus
      piping underneath his beechen bowers;
Poet of the poet-satyr
      whom the laughing shepherd bound with flowers;

V.

Chanter of the Pollio, glorying
 in the blissful years again to be,
Summers of the snakeless meadow,
 unlaborious earth and oarless sea;

VI.

Thou that seëst Universal
 Nature moved by Universal Mind;
Thou majestic in thy sadness
 at the doubtful doom of human kind;

VII.

Light among the vanish'd ages;
 star that gildest yet this phantom shore;
Golden branch amid the shadows,
 kings and realms that pass to rise no more;

VIII.

Now thy Forum roars no longer,
 fallen every purple Cæsar's dome—
Tho' thine ocean-roll of rhythm
 sound for ever of Imperial Rome—

IX.

Now the Rome of slaves hath perish'd,
 and the Rome of freemen holds her place,
I, from out the Northern Island
 sunder'd once from all the human race,

X.

I salute thee, Mantovano,
 I that loved thee since my day began,
Wielder of the stateliest measure
 ever moulded by the lips of man.

HYMN.*

[From *Akbar's Dream.*]

I.

Once again thou flamest heavenward, once again we see thee rise.
Every morning is thy birthday gladdening human hearts and eyes.
    Every morning here we greet it, bowing lowly down before
      thee,
Thee the Godlike, thee the changeless, in thine ever-changing
    skies.

II.

Shadow-maker, shadow-slayer, arrowing light from clime to clime,
Hear thy myriad laureates hail thee monarch in their woodland
    rhyme.
    Warble bird, and open flower, and, men, below the dome of
      azure
Kneel adoring Him the Timeless in the flame that measures
    Time !

GOD AND THE UNIVERSE.

I.

Will my tiny spark of being wholly vanish in your deeps and
    heights ?
Must my day be dark by reason, O ye Heavens, of your bound-
    less nights,
Rush of Suns, and roll of systems, and your fiery clash of
    meteorites ?

II.

'Spirit, nearing yon dark portal at the limit of thy human state,
Fear not thou the hidden purpose of that Power which alone is
    great,
Nor the myriad world, His shadow, nor the silent Opener of the
    Gate.'

* Copyright, 1892, by MACMILLAN & Co.

CROSSING THE BAR.

Sunset and evening star,
  And one clear call for me!
And may there be no moaning of the bar,
  When I put out to sea,

But such a tide as moving seems asleep,
  Too full for sound and foam,
When that which drew from out the boundless deep
  Turns again home.

Twilight and evening bell,
  And after that the dark!
And may there be no sadness of farewell,
  When I embark;

For tho' from out our bourne of Time and Place
  The flood may bear me far,
I hope to see my Pilot face to face
  When I have crost the bar.

INDEX I. AUTHORS AND EDITORS.

———◆———

INDEX II. EDITORS, WITH THE NAMES OF THE AUTHORS TREATED.

MATTHEW ARNOLD'S WORKS.

PUBLISHED BY

THE MACMILLAN COMPANY.

PROSE WRITINGS.

LIBRARY EDITION.

In Nine Volumes. Globe 8vo, each, $1.50.

(Uniform with the Eversley Edition of Charles Kingsley's Novels.)

CONTENTS OF THE VOLUMES:

Vol. 1. Essays in Criticism.
Vol. 2. On the Study of Celtic Literature — On Translating Homer.
Vol. 3. Culture and Anarchy—Friendship's Garland.
Vol. 4. Mixed Essays—Irish Essays.
Vol. 5. Literature and Dogma.
Vol. 6. God and the Bible.
Vol. 7. St. Paul and Protestantism—Last Essays on Church and Religion.
Vol. 8. Discourses in America.
Vol. 9. Essays in Criticism, Second Series.

The Set of Nine Volumes, in paper box, $13.50.

POEMS.

LIBRARY EDITION.

In Three Volumes. Globe 8vo, $5.00.

The Prose and Poetical Works, Library Edition, complete in Twelve Volumes, in paper box, $18.00.

American Edition of the Poems, complete in One Volume, 12mo, $1.50.

"It is to him and Clough that the men of the future will come who desire to find the clearest poetic expression of the sentiment and reflection of the most cultivated and thoughtful men of our generation."—*The Nation.*

"Yet I know numbers of young men—and some, alas! no longer young—who have found in Matthew Arnold's poetry a more exact answer to their intellectual and emotional wants than in any poetry of Tennyson's, or even of Emerson's."—*Henry A. Beers, in the Century Magazine.*

"Contains some of the wisest and most melodious verse that this age has produced."—*London Athenæum.*

SELECTED POEMS.

Golden Treasury Series. 18mo, $1.25.

"A volume which is a thing of beauty in itself."—*Pall Mall Gazette.*

PASSAGES FROM THE
PROSE WRITINGS.

12mo, $1.

"Mr. Arnold's writings so abound in impressive and suggestive passages, which bear separation from the text in which they appear, and are worthy of frequent re-reading, that his works may be said to lend themselves in a peculiar and unusual degree to this sort of anthological treatment."
—*Evening Post.*

THE MACMILLAN COMPANY, NEW YORK.

MATTHEW ARNOLD'S WORKS

PUBLISHED BY

THE MACMILLAN COMPANY.

PROSE WRITINGS.

LIBRARY EDITION.

In Nine Volumes. Globe 8vo, each $1.50.

(*Volumes sold separately, except Vols. V. and VI. which are together.*)

CONTENTS OF THE VOLUMES:

Vol. I. Essays in Criticism.
Vol. II. Mixed Essays, Irish Essays, and the Future.
Vol. III. Discourses in America.

Vol. V. God and the Bible.
Vol. VI. St. Paul and Protestantism, Last Essays on Church and Religion.
Vol. VII. Democracy in America.
Vol. VIII. Essays in Criticism, Second Series.

The Set of Nine Volumes, in paper box, $13.50.

POEMS.

LIBRARY EDITION.

In Three Volumes. Globe 8vo, $4.50.

The Verse and Dramatic Works. Library Edition, complete in Twelve Volumes, in royal 8vo, $18.00.

American Edition, of the Poems, complete in One Volume, 12mo, $2.00.

"It is to him and Clough that the mass of thinking culture who desire to find the scattered poetic expression of the spiritual and religious life of the most cultivated and thoughtful men of our generation."—*The Nation.*

"To ... the higher class of young men, and especially to college young men who have lived in Matthew Arnold's poetry a most potent power to lead the intellectual and moral movement, standard of the present, of the nation, to wean of literature."—*Andrew D. White, in the Century Magazine.*

"Upon my copy of the whole and most published verse, that this age has produced."—*Edward Dowden.*

SELECTED POEMS.

Golden Treasury Series. 18mo, $1.25.

"A volume which is a mine of beauty to each."—*Pall Mall Gazette.*

PASSAGES FROM THE

PROSE WRITINGS.

12mo, $1.50.

"Mr. Arnold's writings so abound in memorable and suggestive passages which lose separation from the text in which they are set, and are worthy of frequent reading, that his works have a worth in such themselves and a peculiar and personal degree to the aid of ... throughout its career."—*Morning Post.*

THE MACMILLAN COMPANY, NEW YORK.

RANDALL LIBRARY-UNCW

3 0490 0072248 $